Roger LeRoy Miller
University of Miami

David VanHoose
Department of Economics
University of Alabama

MACROECONOMICS

Theories, Policies,
and International Applications

SOUTH-WESTERN

SOUTH-WESTERN COLLEGE PUBLISHING
An International Thomson Publishing Company

Publisher/Team Director: Jack Calhoun
Acquisitions Editor: John Alessi
Development Editor: Jan Lamar
Production Editor: Ann Rudrud
Marketing Manager: Lisa Lysne
Cover Design: Doug Abbott
Internal Design: Ann Rudrud
Index: Bob Marsh

Images and logos used throughout this text and on the
cover: © 1998 Photodisc, Inc.

Library of Congress Cataloging-in-Publication Data
Miller, Roger LeRoy.
    Macroeconomics : theory, policy & international applications /
      Roger LeRoy Miller, David Van Hoose.
          p.   cm.
    Includes bibliographical references and index.
    ISBN 0–538–88994-2 (alk. paper)
    1. Macroeconomics.   I. Van Hoose, David, 1957–   .   II. Title.
HB172.5.M544   1998
339–dc21   98–28402
                                                              CIP

23456789 WCBS 654321098

Printed in the United States of America

I(T)P®   .

International Thomson Publishing
South-Western College Publishing is an ITP Company.
The ITP trademark is used under license.

CONTENTS

UNIT II: CLASSICAL AND TRADITIONAL
MACROECONOMIC THEORY   52

Chapter 4: Utopia Just Beyond the Horizon or Future Shock?— The Theory of Economic Growth   94

Chapter 8: Is There a Trade-off between Unemployment and Inflation?—The Keynesian and Monetarist Views on Price and Output Determination   253

UNIT III: RATIONAL EXPECTATIONS AND MODERN MACROECONOMIC THEORY   291

UNIT IV: MACROECONOMIC POLICY 389

PREFACE

TO THE INSTRUCTOR

Any course in intermediate macroeconomics presents a challenge to most students. Our goal in writing *Macroeconomics: Theories, Policies, and International Applications* was to take the student reader past that challenge into a sophisticated, yet accessible understanding of the subject matter. We have done so in a variety of ways:

- All macroeconomics basics are clearly presented.
- The various competing theories are compared and contrasted with each other.
- Current issues of high interest are presented throughout.
- The global economy is fully integrated throughout.
- Frequent directions for use with the Internet are included.
- Access to a special set of CD-ROM applications is provided.

Presentation of Intermediate Macro Theory

We feel that we have covered all of the essential elements of intermediate macroeconomics in the pages that follow. These include:

- Gross domestic product, price indexes, and the balance of payments.
- The classical theory of output, employment, price-level, and interest-rate determination.
- The essential determinants of economic growth.
- The Keynesian income-expenditure theory, the *IS-LM* model, and trade-balance determination.
- Short-run and long-run Phillips curves, monetarism, and the theory of political monetary cycles.
- Rational expectations, new classical macroeconomics, modern Keynesian contracting theory, and recent developments in new Keynesian and real-business-cycle models.
- Rules versus discretion in monetary, fiscal, and exchange-rate policies.
- Macroeconomic policymaking with fixed versus floating exchange rates.

Features that Teach and Reinforce

Interspersed throughout all chapters students will find important features that motivate learning. Two general categories are included.

Policy Notebooks Because policy is so frequently in the news, we felt it appropriate to include a special feature concerned only with policy issues. These features are appropriately placed, referred to in the text itself, and cover a wide variety of topics including:

- Can the amount of money in circulation be controlled when there are electronic cash cards?
- Can policymakers predict interest rates?
- Do new technologies signal the end of work?
- Is there a relationship between the natural rate of unemployment and inflation?
- Can the Fed improve its reputation by using the opportunistic disinflation approach to monetary policy?
- Should we care whether we have a private payments deficit?

Global Notebooks Macroeconomics can no longer be considered only a domestic subject. Events in the United States affect economies all over the world and vice versa. Not only are global issues exciting to read about, but they are also important to understanding macroeconomics. We have included the following, among others:

- Does it matter that Germany and Japan invest more than the United States?
- Using government infrastructure spending to boost Malaysia's rate of growth.
- Islam and the Laffer curve.
- Can European policymakers exploit the Phillips curve?
- Will Europe ever have a single currency?
- Trading foreign currencies on the Internet.
- Underground economies around the world.

Critical-Thinking Exercises

Critical thinking is an important aspect of every college student's education. We make sure that students are introduced to critical-thinking activities by ending each Policy and Global Notebook with critical-thinking questions called "For Critical Analysis." Suggested answers to these questions are included in the *Instructor's Manual.*

Full Global Integration Throughout

Macroeconomics: Theories, Policies, and International Applications is the first text in this field to fully integrate global economics, starting with Chapter 1. The student is introduced to world macroeconomic facts at the outset in Chapter 1 and is then presented with a straightforward explanation of how international transactions are measured in Chapter 2. Chapter 3 presents the international dimensions of classical theory, including exchange-rate determination and the purchasing power parity doctrine. By Chapter 5, full integration of the balance of trade in a macroeconomic model is presented. Every chapter that follows continues this integration within each model that is discussed. Of course, the text ends with a chapter on "Policymaking in the World Economy—International Dimensions of Macroeconomic Policy."

The Importance of Growth

We have developed a modern chapter on the theory of economic growth, which we present early in the text. In addition to standard growth models, we look at labor force participation, population growth, freedom, immigration, and protection as these topics relate to economic growth.

Additionally, we examine new growth theory, specifically knowledge, innovation, and the importance of education. We ask the question "Does growth feed on itself?"

Accessing the Internet: The World Wide Web

Most students, particularly those taking intermediate-level economics courses, are familiar with how to use the Internet. We provide three important features for them:

1. **Margin URLs:** Throughout the text, a feature entitled "On the Web" appears in appropriate places. Each presents a relevant URL.
2. **In-Text On-Line Sources:** Throughout all chapters, students will find a feature entitled "Internet Source." Each Internet Source not only specifies a particular topic and URL, but it also explains to the student a navigation system that will guarantee arrival at the chosen Web site.
3. **Chapter-Ending On-Line Applications:** At the end of every chapter is an extensive Internet exercise that takes the students to a particular URL and then asks them to engage in an application.

Those who post Web sites change the content and addresses of their sites from time to time. Thus, it is likely that a few sites will change after this book is printed. Therefore, our Chapter 1 On-Line Application shows students how to use a popular Internet search engine, which could come in handy for locating any sites whose addresses change before publication of the next edition of *Macroeconomics: Theories, Policies, and International Applications.*

More on the Web for Your Students

This text has its own Web home page, http://macro.swcollege.com, developed and maintained by Professor Tim Yeager of Humboldt State University. Your students will find an "Updates" link that contains the latest macroeconomic news and events. For example, did the Federal Reserve raise interest rates? What was the growth rate in the previous quarter?

There is also a separate Web page corresponding to each chapter in the text. Each chapter Web page contains

- links to relevant sites on the Web, including the Web sites referred to in the text
- an on-line quiz that tests and grades the student's knowledge of the course material
- some chapters also contain other interactive tools to better the student's understanding of concepts presented in the text.

A Special Note on the Graphs

We have spent considerable effort in developing more than 150 graphs for this textbook. All of the lines and curves are color coded in a consistent manner to help students understand the relationships between the various curves. In addition, we have provided full explanations underneath or alongside each graph or set of graphs.

Finally, you will notice that certain graphs have a special logo (see left margin). This indicates that that graph is further developed in the accompanying CD-ROM for this text (described in more detail below).

Key Pedagogy

Learning cannot occur in a vacuum. We have made sure that students using this text have an ample number of pedagogical devices to help them master the material.

Fundamental Issues and Answers within the Text of Each Chapter   A unique feature of *Macroeconomics: Theories, Policies, and International Applications* is the simultaneous inclusion of four to seven fundamental issues at the beginning of each chapter. Within the text itself, the fundamental issues are repeated with the appropriate answers. While reading the chapter, the student immediately sees the relationship between the text materials and the fundamental issues.

Vocabulary Is Stressed   Because vocabulary is often a stumbling block, we have **boldfaced** all important vocabulary terms within the text. Definitions of these terms appear immediately in the adjoining margin. The terms are further defined in the end-of-text glossary.

Chapter Summary   The Chapter Summary follows a numbered point-by-point format that corresponds to the chapter-opening fundamental issues. This format further reinforces the circular nature of the learning process for each chapter.

Questions and Problems   Each chapter ends with 10 questions and problems. Suggested answers are provided in the *Instructor's Manual*.

Selected References and Further Reading   Appropriate references for materials in the chapter are given in the Selected References and Further Reading section at the end of each chapter.

CD-ROM Exercises and Applications

Unique to *Macroeconomics: Theories, Policies, and International Applications* is a supplemental CD-ROM. By using the latest pedagogical and computer technology, the student is able to explore key graphs from each chapter on this CD-ROM. The interactivities are extensive. In order to add to these interactivities, we have included a special section at the end of each chapter called "CyberTutor Exercises." These consist of:

- Theoretical applications: Questions designed to assist the student in reasoning out how changes in household or firm behavior or in government policies affect macroeconomic variables according to alternative theories.
- Empirical applications: Questions that give the student the opportunity to use real-world data to evaluate the relevance of the theories.

The Supplements

Macroeconomics: Theories, Policies, and International Applications is supported by the strongest set of supplements currently available.

CD-ROM The CyberTutor *CD-ROM*, which was developed by Jonathan Lave, Mikhail Lokshin, and Benny Balak, is an innovative feature of *Macroeconomics: Theories, Policies, and International Applications*. It has a user-friendly "Internet feel" and includes detailed chapter summaries, "click-on" features with definitions of key terms, brilliantly illustrated theoretical exercises using diagrams based on the chapter's coverage, and empirical applications and data-plotting capabilities unmatched by software accompanying other macroeconomics texts.

Study Guide The *Study Guide*, which was written by text author David VanHoose, is designed to facilitate active learning by students. It provides a summary of each chapter's contents, along with reference to a key diagram from each chapter and a list of the key terms for students to look for and define in their own words as they read the text. To assist students in testing their understanding of the material, the *Study Guide* also includes 20 multiple-choice and 10 short-answer questions per chapter.

Instructor's Manual The *Instructor's Manual*, written by David Findlay of Colby College, is intended to simplify the teaching tasks that instructors face. For each chapter it offers an overview of key concepts and objectives, a detailed outline built upon chapter headings in the text, and a special "teaching tips" section. Also included are suggested answers to the critical-thinking questions in the Policy Notebooks and Global Notebooks and answers to chapter questions and problems.

Test Bank One of the most challenging aspects of teaching is evaluating student performance. To assist instructors in this endeavor, a *Test Bank* that includes between

30 and 70 multiple-choice questions per chapter, along with correct answers, is available to all adopters of *Macroeconomics: Theories, Policies, and International Applications*.

ACKNOWLEDGMENTS

We benefited from an extremely active and conscientious group of reviewers of the manuscript for this first edition of *Macroeconomics: Theories, Policies, and International Applications*. At times they were harsh and without pity, but the rewrites of the manuscript improved accordingly. To the following reviewers, we extend our sincere appreciation for the critical nature of your comments that helped make this a better text.

Audrey B. Davidson
University of Louisville

John W. Graham
Rutgers University

Clinton Greene
University of Missouri at St. Louis

Robert G. James
California State University at Chico

Elia Kacapyer
Ithaca College

Stephen Mathis
Shippensburg University

Michael A. McPherson
University of North Texas

Christine Meyer
Bentley College

Mark Prus
SUNY College at Cortland

Bryan Taylor
California State Polytechnic University at Pomona

James R. Wible
University of New Hampshire

Tim Yeager
Humboldt State University

Of course, no textbook project is done by the authors alone. We wish to thank our editor, John Alessi, for his continued guidance. Our production team of Bill Stryker and Ann Rudrud came up with what we believe to be the best design ever as well as providing consistent guidance throughout the project. The copyeditor, Patricia Lewis, masterfully rearranged our manuscript to make the book read more smoothly. Sue Jasin of K&M Consulting helped with the manuscript preparation and formatting, and for that we extend our sincere thanks. The authors of the CD-ROM, Jonathan Lave, Mikhail Lokshin, and Benny Balak, provided a great service to this project, and we thank them profusely. David Findlay, the author of the *Instructor's Manual* and *Test Bank,* essentially served as an additional manuscript reviewer, and we are especially grateful for his comments and suggestions.

We anticipate revising this text for years to come and therefore welcome all comments and criticism from students and professors alike.

R.L.M.
D.D.V.

Unit I

INTRODUCTION

THE MACROECONOMY

FUNDAMENTAL ISSUES

1. What is macroeconomics, and what are its distinguishing features?

2. What are key macroeconomic variables?

3. What are the key issues in macroeconomics?

4. Why is macroeconomics a controversial subject?

Once a month a London-based betting house called City Index obtains what the head of its financial desk calls "the most important number in the world." That number is how many U.S. residents found or lost jobs in the previous month. Each month the head of the financial desk at City Index takes the average of analysts' predictions about the increase or decrease in U.S. nonfarm employment, hopes for a bit of luck, and sets a figure, say, an increase of somewhere between 170,000 and 190,000 jobs.

Punters, as bettors who bet against "the bank" are called in England, take it from there. They can bet as little as £5 per 10,000 jobs. So, if U.S. nonfarm employment goes up, say, 150,000 above the City Index's top estimate, a £50 bet per point will earn £750 (15 × £50) or about $1,200.

What City Index likes about the monthly U.S. nonfarm employment data is that no one has the slightest idea what the number is going to be. It could be up 300,000 or down 200,000, no matter what hundreds of expert economists around the world predict.

Changes in U.S. employment data are not just for bettors in London to wager on. Increases or decreases in U.S. employment may have serious consequences for the outcome of presidential elections, influence the actions of the head of this country's monetary system, and affect congressional policies involving taxes and government spending. How well the overall economy is doing has become a critical piece of information for literally millions of Americans as well as millions of policymakers, businesspersons, and bettors around the world.

OBJECTIVES OF THIS BOOK
AND HOW THEY RELATE TO YOU

Not surprisingly, the key objective of this text is to help you understand how the macroeconomy works and, more specifically, how monetary and fiscal policy might be able to reduce the frequency and severity of nationwide business fluctuations. In this chapter, you will learn some macroeconomic facts for the United States and for the world, as well as why macroeconomics continues to be a controversial subject. In Chapter 2, you will learn how we measure macroeconomic variables, including those associated with international transactions. Indeed, sections dealing with international trade and finance appear in virtually every chapter in this text.

Chapters 12, 13, and 14 discuss what policymakers should be doing, but to participate in that discussion, you need a foundation in macroeconomic theory. Thus, you first will learn about classical and traditional macroeconomic theory and also about the most modern macroeconomic theories that economists use today.

This foundation in macroeconomics will be of value whatever your plans for the future. If you continue your studies in economics, an in-depth knowledge of macroeconomics is critical to understanding monetary theory, international trade and finance, as well as economic growth and development. If you choose a career in business economics, a knowledge of macroeconomics is also essential. If you are going to study business and management in general, you will face a variety of problems, dilemmas, and issues throughout your studies and your business career, all of which will relate in some way to what you are going to learn in this text.

Finally, even students who go into other fields can benefit from a course in intermediate macroeconomics. Virtually every day, you will read about macroeconomic issues in the print press as well as hear about them on radio and television.

THE SUBJECT OF MACROECONOMICS

Macroeconomics is the branch of economics concerned with the study of a nation's total economic activity. In contrast to **microeconomics,** which focuses on studying

MACROECONOMICS The branch of economics that focuses on the study of the total economic activity of a nation.

MICROECONOMICS The branch of economics that focuses on the study of the allocation of resources and the determination of prices and quantities in individual markets.

resource allocation and price determination in *individual* markets for goods and services, macroeconomics seeks to understand the *overall* structure and performance of a nation's economy.

The Relationship between Macroeconomics and Microeconomics

In 1964 one observer defined macroeconomics as "a laudable attempt to explain how large parts (or the whole) of an economy work, without pretending to know how the component parts work." At that time, there may have been something to this observation. Many economists who specialized in macroeconomics, known as *macroeconomists,* regarded their field as very distinct from microeconomics.

Now, however, as we enter the twenty-first century, most macroeconomists view their field of study as inseparable from microeconomics. Even though macroeconomists still do *not* try to understand every aspect of the economy's components—this remains the domain of microeconomists—today macroeconomics is much more closely related to microeconomics than it was in the 1960s. Indeed, many macroeconomists insist that their theories of how the economy works possess **microeconomic foundations.** In other words, they believe that useful theories in macroeconomics should have a basis in a microeconomic understanding of the behavior of the economy's *key* components.

MICROECONOMIC FOUNDATIONS A basic understanding of the behavior of individual components of the economy that underlies many macroeconomic theories.

AGGREGATION The act of summing up the individual parts of the economy to obtain total measures of economy-wide performance.

The Distinguishing Features of Macroeconomics

Nevertheless, macroeconomics differs from microeconomics in two important ways. First, **aggregation,** the summing of individual economic components to obtain totals for the economy as a whole, is central to macroeconomics. A microeconomist studies individual consumers, workers, and business firms, which by themselves are too small relative to the economy for their individual decisions to affect a nation's overall economic performance. In contrast, a macroeconomist cares about the *aggregate* effects of the sum total of all the individual decisions by these consumers, workers, and firms. Although understanding how individual decisions are reached is often useful to a macroeconomist, the real issue in macroeconomics is the big picture, or how the economy as a whole performs.

For instance, health-care expenses constitute a much larger portion of total spending in the U.S. economy than they did half a century ago. Furthermore, health care is of considerable importance to each of us. Yet a macroeconomist typically does not believe that a detailed analysis of the market for health care is needed to understand the overall determinants of U.S. economic performance. The market for health care is just one of many among which U.S. residents allocate their expenditures. There also are markets for entertainment services, the provision of electricity, and so on. What matters to a macroeconomist is the aggregate spending of U.S. residents, not how they allocate their spending among consumption of health care, entertainment, and electricity.

Can the Amount of Money in Circulation Be Controlled When There Are Electronic Cash Cards?

Not too long ago, AT&T and Wells Fargo & Company formed the U.S. affiliate of Mondex, a growing global electronic cash program. Mondex was originally developed by the National Westminster Bank of Britain. The goal was to replace bills and coins with electronic cash cards. With the advent of the Internet, though, AT&T and Wells Fargo saw greater possibilities for an electronic cash card—it could be used to make purchases over the Internet as well as to provide a type of identification.

To get a global electronic cash program moving, more than fifteen banks from around the world along with AT&T invested more than $100 million to buy shares in Mondex International, the parent of the U.S. affiliate. Already, competitors to Mondex have emerged. Both Visa International and MasterCard International, Inc., originally offered competing smart cards. Sun Microsystems offer SwapSmart, which allows you to refill your cash card using your personal computer. Initially, though, these competing cards could not be used on the Internet.

As electronic cards proliferate, little by little people are finding that electronic cash is better than credit cards for making small purchases on the Internet. Embedded in an electronic cash card is a computer chip, which is more difficult for hackers to "break" than software that just uses passwords. Users pay about $20 to buy a device that allows their computer to read and write information from the chip. With this device customers can load electronic cash from their bank accounts onto their Mondex cards. They can spend that cash both on the Internet and in stores. In addition, anyone with a Mondex card can transfer electronic cash to anybody else with a card.

Electronic cash cards raise numerous policy concerns, not the least of which are the possibilities of counterfeiting the cards and money laundering. The cards also raise a major macroeconomic issue: Can central banks around the world control the amount of money in circulation when it can be created "out of thin air" by the purveyors of electronic cash cards? No one knows the answer yet because the electronic cash card systems are too new.

FOR CRITICAL ANALYSIS:
Explain how electronic cash programs allow for money laundering.

Nevertheless, one item does stand out as important to understanding the overall performance of the economy. This is *money,* or the item that we typically use to facilitate the exchange of goods and services (see Policy Notebook: *Can the Amount of Money in Circulation Be Controlled When There Are Electronic Cash Cards?*). As you will discover as you progress through this text, most macroeconomists believe that understanding the role of this particular good is a key aspect of developing a full theory of how the economy functions. After all, people use money in the bulk of their exchanges for goods and services in *all* markets in the economy. Money, therefore, ought to matter for everyone. As we shall discuss, the key issue for many macroeconomists is *how* money matters. While some macroeconomists believe that changes in the total amount of money in circulation exert significant short-run effects on aggregate production of goods and services, others contend that such changes mainly affect the prices of goods and services without influencing actual production.

In sum, aggregation and a consideration of the role that money plays are the two distinguishing features of macroeconomics. As you will see, these key themes will surface throughout this text:

> **Any theory of overall economic activity must seek to explain how aggregate economic variables are determined and what role money plays in this process.**

FUNDAMENTAL ISSUE #1

What is macroeconomics, and what are its distinguishing features? Macroeconomics is the study of the economy as a whole. Its two distinguishing features are its focus on the determination of aggregate variables and its need to consider the role of the quantity of money in circulation.

MACROECONOMIC FACTS: THE UNITED STATES

MACROECONOMIC VARIABLES
Aggregate measures of total economic activity.

Before we consider the various issues that macroeconomists seek to address, we need to think about some important **macroeconomic variables,** or aggregate measures that summarize various aspects of overall economic activity. There are three broad groupings of macroeconomic variables: (1) aggregate output and employment, (2) money growth and inflation, and (3) measures of international trade and of the U.S. dollar's exchange value relative to other nations' currencies.

Output and Employment

Figure 1–1 displays measures of aggregate output and employment in the U.S. economy for every year since 1959. The output measure is *real gross domestic product,* or *real GDP.* As we shall discuss in detail in Chapter 2, real gross domestic product is a measure of the total amount of production of final goods and services. The employment measure is the annual average of monthly totals of the number of people over the age of sixteen employed in income-generating jobs.

Changes in U.S. Productivity and Living Standards   Figure 1–1 shows that the U.S. economy experienced significant growth during the latter half of the twentieth century. The total number of people employed doubled between 1959 and 1997, and the total output of goods and services more than tripled. Because the production of goods and services grew faster than employment, the per worker production of goods and services clearly increased during this interval. This means that a

FIGURE 1–1 OUTPUT AND EMPLOYMENT IN THE UNITED STATES, 1959–PRESENT

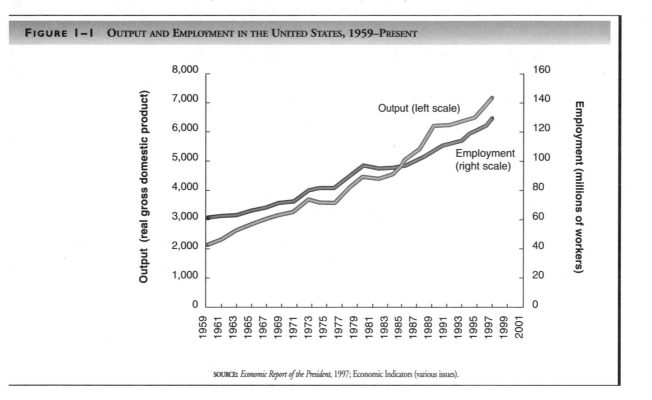

SOURCE: *Economic Report of the President,* 1997; Economic Indicators (various issues).

typical worker became *more productive*. Indeed, in 1959 the average output of an employed individual was equal to $34,230 (in 1992 prices) worth of real output of goods and services. By 1997, this amount had increased to nearly $55,000 (in 1992 prices), so a typical U.S. worker was over 50 percent more productive in 1997 as compared with 1959.

An implication of this productivity improvement has been that a typical U.S. resident can consume more goods and services as compared with years past. This means that the overall U.S. **standard of living,** or overall capability of an average employed resident to consume goods and services, has increased considerably.

STANDARD OF LIVING The capability of an average resident of a nation to consume goods and services.

The Unemployment Record   Of course, not all people who might like to have a job are actually employed. Such people are among the ranks of the unemployed, and the total number of these individuals constitutes the economy's **unemployment,** which is simply the number of people who currently are interested in gainful employment but do not have a job. Figure 1–2 displays unemployment in the United States since 1959. As you can see, unemployment can vary considerably from year to year.

UNEMPLOYMENT The number of people who are interested in finding a job but currently do not have one.

As we shall discuss, these data on output and employment and unemployment raise a host of questions for macroeconomists. Two questions in particular are obvious: What determines the long-run output and employment performance of an economy such as that of the United States? What causes year-to-year changes in this performance that result in the unemployment variations that we observe?

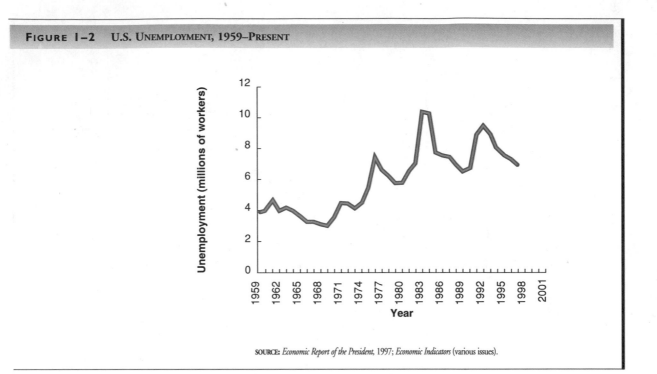

FIGURE 1–2   U.S. UNEMPLOYMENT, 1959–PRESENT

SOURCE: *Economic Report of the President,* 1997; *Economic Indicators* (various issues).

Money Growth and Inflation

Figure 1–3 shows annual growth rates for measures of the quantity of money in circulation and of the overall level of prices in the United States. Money growth is the annual rate of change in a Federal Reserve measure of money called *M2,* which includes currency, checking accounts, savings accounts, and small-denomination savings deposits. The price measure is the *consumer price index (CPI),* which is a weighted average of the prices of goods and services purchased by a typical U.S. resident.

As you can see, money growth rates and inflation rates can exhibit considerable year-to-year variability. These two macroeconomic variables appear to be closely related during some intervals but not during others.

As noted earlier, macroeconomists have good reason to think that, in the long run, the amount of money in circulation affects the overall level of prices that consumers pay for goods and services. Therefore, understanding the changing relationship between money growth and inflation is an important issue in macroeconomics.

International Trade and the Value of the Dollar

The sets of macroeconomic variables we have just considered are known as **domestic variables.** They are aggregate measures of economic activity relating primarily to the U.S. economy in isolation from the rest of the world. Like many other nations today,

ON THE WEB
Visit the White House's Economic Statistics Briefing Room at:
http://www.whitehouse.gov/fsbr/esbr.html

DOMESTIC VARIABLES
Macroeconomic variables that provide information about a nation's economic activity in isolation from the rest of the world.

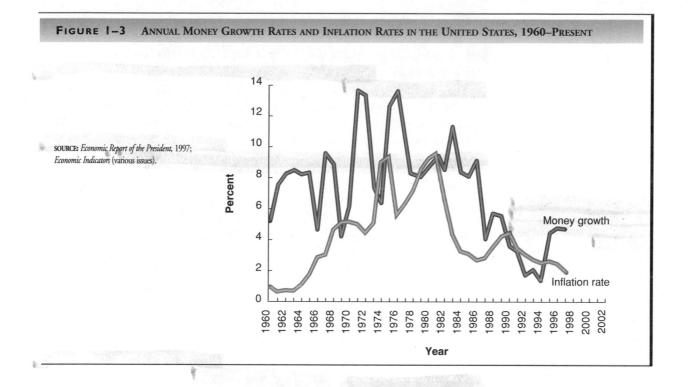

FIGURE 1–3 ANNUAL MONEY GROWTH RATES AND INFLATION RATES IN THE UNITED STATES, 1960–PRESENT

SOURCE: *Economic Report of the President,* 1997; *Economic Indicators* (various issues).

however, the United States engages in a considerable amount of international exchange of goods, services, and financial assets such as stocks, bonds, and currencies.

International Trade and the Trade Deficit Although nations exchange more services across their borders than in years past, a sizable portion of international exchange still entails transfers of physical goods. *International trade* refers primarily to exchanges of goods. Domestic purchases of goods manufactured and sold by business firms located abroad are **merchandise imports.** Sales of goods manufactured and sold by domestic firms to residents of other nations are **merchandise exports.** The difference between merchandise exports and merchandise imports is a nation's **merchandise balance of trade,** or the *trade balance.* A country with a positive trade balance—merchandise exports exceed merchandise imports—experiences a *trade surplus.* In contrast, a country with a negative trade balance, meaning that its residents import more goods than they export, runs a *trade deficit.*

In Chapter 2 we shall discuss the pros and cons of using the merchandise balance of trade as an indicator of a nation's performance in the world economy. Despite some important shortcomings with this interpretation, many observers use the trade balance as a bellwether for a country's relative standing in the world economy. A common interpretation, particularly in the media and political circles, is that a country that consistently experiences a trade surplus is more "competitive" in the world economy than a nation that consistently runs a trade deficit.

MERCHANDISE IMPORTS Domestic residents' purchases of physical goods manufactured and sold by business firms located abroad.

MERCHANDISE EXPORTS Domestic firms' sales of physical goods to residents of other nations.

MERCHANDISE BALANCE OF TRADE Merchandise exports minus merchandise imports.

Figure 1–4 shows that *if* one accepts this interpretation, then since at least the late 1970s the U.S. position in the world economy has been on the decline. For the first three decades after the end of World War II, the United States consistently operated with a trade surplus. Since 1976, however, the United States has experienced a trade deficit every single year.

Why the U.S. trade balance was consistently positive before the late 1970s but has been negative each year thereafter is another question that is relevant to the field of macroeconomics. As you will learn in Chapter 5, most macroeconomists believe that U.S. government deficits have a lot to do with the U.S. balance of trade.

Exchange Rates   Another macroeconomic variable that relates to a nation's performance in the world economy is the **exchange rate,** or the value of a nation's currency in terms of the currencies of other nations. There are different rates of exchange among all the currencies of the world (see the Global Notebook on page 12: *Trading Foreign Currencies on the Internet*). For instance, on a given day one dollar might trade at a market exchange rate of 100 Japanese yen per dollar or 0.65 British pounds per dollar. Nevertheless, Figure 1–5 displays an overall index measure of the U.S. dollar's value relative to the currencies of its major trading partners around the globe.

As you can see, the dollar's value relative to other currencies rose considerably in the early 1980s. The dollar's value then declined very quickly through the early 1990s before leveling off and rising again in recent years. Why such movements in exchange rates occur is another important macroeconomic issue.

EXCHANGE RATE The value of a nation's currency measured in terms of the currency of another nation.

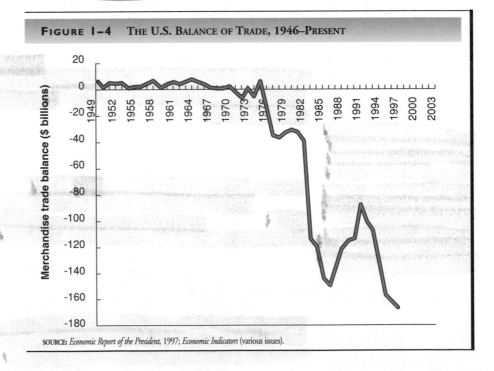

FIGURE 1–4   **THE U.S. BALANCE OF TRADE, 1946–PRESENT**

SOURCE: *Economic Report of the President*, 1997; *Economic Indicators* (various issues).

FIGURE 1–5   THE CHANGING VALUE OF THE DOLLAR

Aside from a significant increase during the mid-1980s, in general the value of the dollar has been steady or slightly falling since the 1970s.

SOURCE: *Economic Report of the President,* 1997; *Federal Reserve Bulletin* (various issues).

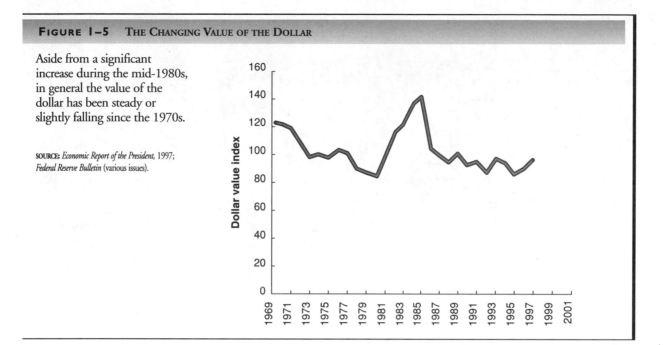

FUNDAMENTAL ISSUE #2

What are key macroeconomic variables? The field of macroeconomics seeks to explain movements in several macroeconomic variables, or aggregate measures of economic activity. These include domestic variables, such as a nation's total output, employment, and unemployment and its money growth rate and inflation rate, or measure of price changes. Macroeconomics also addresses international variables such as a nation's trade balance and the rate of exchange between its currency and the currencies of other nations.

MACROECONOMIC FACTS: THE WORLD

Levels of economic activity often differ markedly across nations of the world. Standards of living are often higher in small nations than in large nations. Output and employment sometimes grow at very high rates in some countries even as other nations experience little or no growth in output and employment. Likewise, inflation rates may decline in some nations even as they rise in others.

GLOBAL NOTEBOOK
Trading Foreign Currencies on the Internet

Every day about $1.2 trillion in foreign currencies are traded throughout the world. Until recently, most corporations and banks that trade currencies had to use real-time quotes over private networks connected to costly desktop terminals supplied by an information system, such as those offered by Reuters Holdings PLC, Knight-Ridder, Inc., and Dow Jones Telerate, Inc.

Now anyone wanting information on the price of foreign currencies can use much cheaper services offered over the Internet. Currency Management Corporation of London, First Money Garden Corporation of New York, and NY Quotes, Inc., offer real-time pricing information on foreign currencies on the Internet. Anyone with a personal computer and standardized inexpensive software can instantly learn the current price of a foreign currency and in many cases can trade in a foreign currency. Now smaller investors who don't have expensive proprietary computer terminals or who don't

want to depend on foreign exchange brokers can make such transactions themselves. Because Internet foreign exchange trading is handled entirely by computer, no time lag occurs between the investor's decision to buy or sell a foreign currency and the actual transaction.

Some problems still have to be solved, however, particularly with respect to security about payments for foreign exchange transactions. Also, some Internet access hardware and software are still too slow for many foreign exchange traders. Nevertheless, the founder of Currency Management Corporation, Peter Cruddas, believes that "the Internet is the future of foreign exchange trading—we're on the edge of a revolution in the financial markets."

FOR CRITICAL ANALYSIS:
Even with on-line financial trading, some people will still want to use brokers. Why?

Output and Inflation: International Comparisons

Because nations' populations vary, direct comparisons of total output levels can be misleading. For instance, the population of China is much larger than the population of the United Kingdom, and China's total output of goods and services is also larger. Nevertheless, the standard of living of a typical British resident is much higher than that of a resident of China.

Consequently, economists typically compare nations' output performances by calculating and comparing measures of output per person, called *output per capita.* Figure 1–6 displays estimates of per capita output for selected nations. Also shown is the estimated average output per capita for the world. As the figure indicates, a few nations such as Japan and the United States, with per capita output levels at six to seven times the world average, have very high living standards as compared with the rest of the world. In contrast, nations such as China, Nigeria, and Bolivia have per capita output levels well below the world average. Using output per capita as a benchmark, relatively "average" nations of the world at present include Gabon in sub-Saharan Africa and Oman in the Middle East, although both of these nations have experienced declines in per capita output.

ON THE WEB
Visit the United Nations at:
http://www.un.org/

FIGURE 1–6   PER CAPITA OUTPUT COMPARISONS FOR SELECTED NATIONS

Although some nations have per capita output levels very close to the world average, there also are considerable disparities in per capita output levels.

SOURCE: *World Bank, World Tables,* 1996.

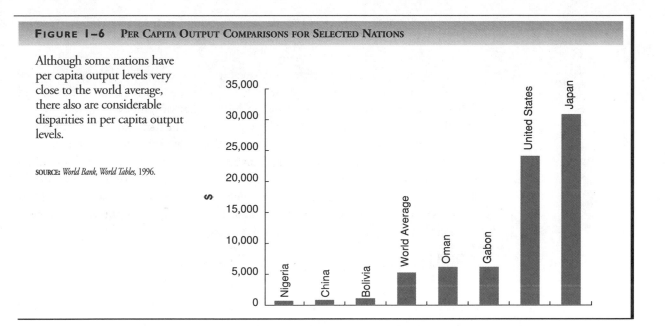

Some parts of the world currently are growing quickly, while others are experiencing relatively low output growth. This can be seen in Figure 1–7, which compares estimated 1997 output growth rates of three industrialized nations—the United States, Japan, and Germany—with estimated 1997 output growth rates of four less-

FIGURE 1–7   OUTPUT GROWTH COMPARISONS

With the exception of developing nations of the Western Hemisphere, developing regions have been experiencing output growth rates at least as great as those of the United States, Japan, and Germany.

SOURCE: International Monetary Fund, *World Economic Outlook,* May 1997.

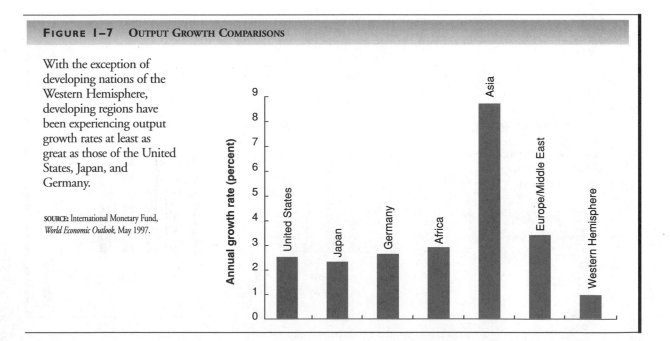

developed regions of the world. With the exception of nations of the Western Hemisphere, the less-developed regions currently are growing at a more rapid pace than the United States, Japan, and Germany.

Inflation rates can also differ considerably across countries and regions of the world. Panel (a) of Figure 1–8 shows the recent inflation experiences of the United States, nations of the European Union (including Germany, the Netherlands, and the United Kingdom), Japan, and developing countries of Asia (including China, the Philippines, and Vietnam). Although panel (a) indicates that developing nations in Asia have experienced higher inflation than the United States, the European Union nations, and Japan, panel (b) shows that inflation rates have been even higher in developing countries in Africa (such as Angola, Kenya, and the Sudan), in the Middle East and Europe (including Iran, Jordan, and Turkey), and in the Western Hemisphere (including Argentina, Brazil, and Nicaragua).

World Output and Its Changing Distribution

The world is a collection of distinct, though interrelated, national economies. Nevertheless, it is possible to use market exchange rates to measure the total output of all nations of the world in U.S. dollar terms. Panel (a) of Figure 1–9 shows how this measure of total world output has changed over time.

Panel (b) shows how the distribution of world output between the United States and other nations of the world has changed during the latter years of the twentieth century. The large share of world output accounted for by the U.S. economy in each

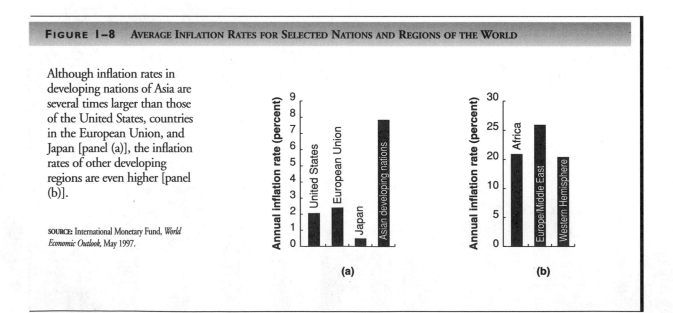

FIGURE 1–8   AVERAGE INFLATION RATES FOR SELECTED NATIONS AND REGIONS OF THE WORLD

Although inflation rates in developing nations of Asia are several times larger than those of the United States, countries in the European Union, and Japan [panel (a)], the inflation rates of other developing regions are even higher [panel (b)].

SOURCE: International Monetary Fund, *World Economic Outlook*, May 1997.

FIGURE 1-9   WORLD OUTPUT AND THE DECLINING PREDOMINANCE OF THE UNITED STATES

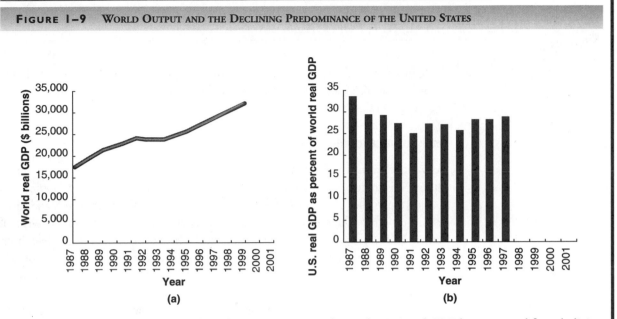

Panel (a) shows how an aggregate world real GDP measure has changed since the late 1980s. Panel (b) displays the ratio of U.S. real GDP to this world real GDP measure: it indicates that U.S. real GDP has accounted for a declining share of world real GDP.

SOURCE: International Monetary Fund, *World Economic Outlook,* May 1997, *Economic Report of the President,* 1997, and Economic Indicators (various issues).

selected year is striking. Nevertheless, as this panel indicates, the share of total world output produced in the United States is declining as other nations grow and develop. The United States still has the preeminent economy of the world, but other countries gradually are catching up.

INTERNET SOURCE

Economic Growth and Inequality across Nations

The World Bank—Inequality, Poverty, and Growth
Internet URL: **http://www.worldbank.org/html/dec/annual/docs/growth1.htm**

Navigation: Start at the World Bank homepage (**http://www.worldbank.org**). Key in "Inequality" in the search dialog box. Click on INEQUALITY, POVERTY, AND (SUMMARY).

THE KEY ISSUES OF MACROECONOMICS

In light of the evidence on macroeconomic variables that we have presented, let's now identify the issues that stand out as important to consider in the study of macroeconomics.

Long-Run Economic Growth

As we have seen, the United States has possessed the world's preeminent economy during this century. Before the eighteenth century, however, the U.S. economy was among the smaller economies of the world. During most of the eighteenth and nineteenth centuries, the economies of Britain, France, Germany, and Austria were all larger. In the sixteenth and seventeenth centuries, Spain and Portugal had been among the economic powerhouses of the world. In earlier centuries, civilizations located in what are now Italy, Greece, Turkey, Egypt, and China had contended for economic preeminence.

What has accounted for the changes in the relative positions of world economies? The answer must be that during certain periods some economies have grown faster than others, which has allowed them ultimately to bypass economies that previously had been predominant in output, income, and wealth.

Thus, if we are to sort out the reasons why nations' prospects for world economic leadership rise or fall, we must understand the determinants of economic growth. This is an important subject of macroeconomics. Although the topic of economic growth surfaces at various points throughout this text, Chapter 4 is devoted solely to this subject.

Short-Run Variations in Output and Employment

The determinants of economic growth ultimately explain the performances of national economies over periods of many years. Factors that influence a nation's long-run growth rarely attract bold media headlines, however. For better or worse, most of us find ourselves captivated by news of near-term variations in nationwide economic activity, which, after all, can have an immediate impact on our lives.

Traditionally, therefore, a key objective of macroeconomics is to try to understand why an economy's near-term performance can depart considerably from levels consistent with its long-term potential. For instance, what accounted for the significant economic slowdowns in the United States in the mid-1970s and early 1980s? Why did a brief but sharp slowdown in economic activity occur in the early 1990s? Looking into the past, what factors caused the great economic contraction of the 1930s? How do international trade and foreign exchange markets influence short-run economic performance? These questions matter, because even short-run variations in

GLOBAL NOTEBOOK

The European Union Faces Increasing Unemployment

While the United States has suffered several slowdowns in the last two decades, so too has Europe. The difference between the United States and Europe, though, is that unemployment in the United States has never remained at the high levels it attained during recessions. Rather, it has always fallen back to a more or less long-run level. As Figure 1–10 shows, only in Germany (and only in the part that used to be West Germany) have unemployment rates in recent years matched those in the United States. (Taken as a whole, Germany today has an unemployment rate above 12 percent, or more than double the U.S. rate.) The average unem-

ployment rate in the fifteen countries of the European Union is over 11 percent. The United States has both a growing labor force and growing employment. Between 1993 and 1997, for example, the number of jobs in the United States increased by about 10 million, whereas zero net new jobs were created in the European Union.

FOR CRITICAL ANALYSIS:

Does it matter to you as a citizen of the United States what unemployment rates are elsewhere in the world? Why or why not?

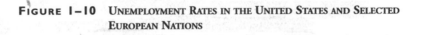

FIGURE 1–10 UNEMPLOYMENT RATES IN THE UNITED STATES AND SELECTED EUROPEAN NATIONS

With only a few exceptions, such as the United Kingdom, unemployment rates in major European Union nations have risen in recent years. During the same period, U.S. unemployment rates have remained relatively level or, in the most recent period, declined.

SOURCE: International Monetary Fund, *World Economic Outlook*, May 1997, and *Economic Report of the President*, 1997.

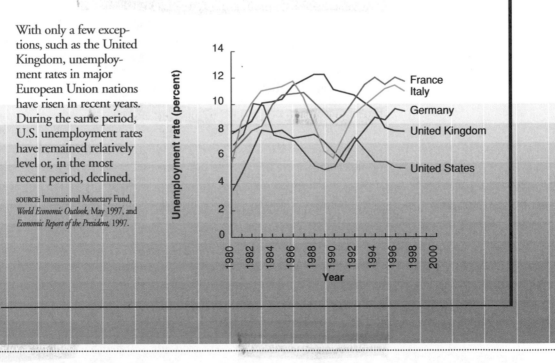

economic activity can entail significant social costs in the form of lost jobs and temporarily or even permanently derailed careers (see Global Notebook: *The European Union Faces Increasing Unemployment*).

Our basis for thinking about both long-run growth and short-run economic fluctuations is the *classical macroeconomic model* discussed in Chapter 3. This model of the determination of employment, output, prices, and the exchange rate provides a foundation for Chapter 4's discussion of economic growth as well as for the traditional views of short-run economic performance that are the subject of Chapters 5 through 8.

Money, Expectations, and Inflation

As noted earlier, a key element of any macroeconomic theory is the role of the quantity of money in circulation. You will learn in the chapters that follow that a key division among alternative theories of economic activity relates to this issue. Some theories propose an important role for money as a factor influencing output and employment. In contrast, competing macroeconomic theories hold that the only macroeconomic variables that the quantity of money can affect are prices and exchange rates.

Chapters 9, 10, and 11 discuss modern perspectives on this issue. You will learn that *expectations* are a key element of current macroeconomic theories. According to these theories, the extent to which people anticipate future events and policies is a crucial determinant of current and future economic activity. Although the proponents of expectation-based macroeconomic theories agree on this fundamental point, they reach different conclusions about how the quantity of money affects the economy and how macroeconomic policymaking should be conducted.

Macroeconomic Policy

By its nature, macroeconomics is a policy-oriented subject. What, if anything, should policymakers do to try to influence aggregate economic activity? How should they formulate policies? These questions depend in part upon which macroeconomic theory one adopts, which is why the first twelve chapters of this text focus on theoretical issues in macroeconomics.

Nevertheless, certain questions are specific to *policy* issues alone. Among these are the following: What are appropriate goals for macroeconomic policy? Should policymakers follow explicit rules in policymaking, or should they simply do what seems best at the time? These issues are addressed in Chapters 12 and 13.

International Trade, Exchange Rates, and Macroeconomic Performance and Policy

The extent of international trade increased sharply during the 1970s and has grown gradually since that decade. Many economists argue that nations' economies have become more interdependent as a result of this increase in trade. Since World War II, variations in U.S. economic performance have affected the economies of Europe and Japan. Now, however, a sharp downturn in economic activity in Japan can have broader effects than in years past, when only a few U.S. export and import industries might have felt the aftershocks.

The structure of this text reflects this changed world environment. Although Chapter 14 focuses solely on issues relating to international macroeconomic policy, such topics as the balance of payments, exchange-rate determination, the role of international trade as a factor in economic growth, and potential conflicts between domestic and international policy objectives surface in nearly every chapter. Today, students of macroeconomics cannot ignore international issues, no matter where they live.

INTERNET SOURCE

ACNielsen—Economic Overview

International Trade and the Value of the Dollar
Internet URL: http://www.nielsen.com/home/trends/econ0495.htm

Navigation: Start at the ACNielsen Market Trends homepage (http://www.nielsen.com/home/trends/). Click on "Chicken Little," and read the latest report on U.S. trade partners and the dollar's value in world markets.

FUNDAMENTAL ISSUE #3

What are the key issues in macroeconomics? One key issue is determining the factors that influence a nation's long-term growth in output and employment. Another is isolating the reasons that output and employment can vary so much from their long-run levels as a result of short-run fluctuations in economic activity. A third important issue is resolving the role that the quantity of money plays in affecting a nation's output, employment, and prices. Fourth, determining the proper goals and implementation of policies is a centerpiece issue of macroeconomics. Finally, macroeconomists recognize that greater interdependence among the world's nations means that it is important to understand how factors such as exchange rates and international trade affect a country's economic performance.

WHY MACROECONOMICS IS A CONTROVERSIAL SUBJECT

Historically, one of the hallmarks of macroeconomics has been that people can disagree sharply about how the economy works and how macroeconomic policies should be conducted. To a student taking an intermediate macroeconomics course, these disagreements can make the study of macroeconomics somewhat frustrating at times. After all, shouldn't macroeconomists be able to develop one single, *correct* theory to explain macroeconomic performance and to guide policymakers?

Unfortunately for macroeconomics students, there is no one macroeconomic theory that economists regard as "truth." Although all macroeconomists work with the same data and use the same basic economics tools to try to understand the functioning of the economy, many of them have reached different conclusions. From a student's perspective, the negative aspect of this state of affairs is that the student must learn more than one approach to macroeconomic theory. The positive aspect, however, is that the current disagreements make macroeconomics an interesting area to study.

The Problem of Aggregation

Traditionally, one of the main sources of contention about macroeconomics has been the issue of aggregation. Just how much can we aggregate before developing a theory of how the economy works?

An Example of the Aggregation Problem   Consider an example of a property-casualty insurance company with three lines of business: auto insurance, liability insurance, and workers' compensation insurance. All three types of insurance share the common characteristics that the company earns income from selling policies and experiences losses arising from claims of policyholders. Because the company knows that it will experience some losses, it, like other insurers, maintains cash reserves from which it makes payments when losses occur. Hence, a key issue for the company is estimating its policyholders' losses in auto, liability, and workers' compensation insurance so that it can hold the appropriate amount of reserves.

There are at least two basic approaches that the company might use to estimate the losses that its policyholders will experience. One approach is to carefully examine how losses evolve over time in each *separate* line of business. In auto insurance, losses will depend on how safely insured policyholders drive, how safe the roads are in the areas where they live, and so on. In liability insurance, such factors as the legal treatment of claims against policyholders will affect potential losses. Finally, in workers' compensation insurance, the care that employers and employees take in the workplace will determine the magnitude of losses resulting from injuries or deaths on the job. The insurance company's *actuaries,* professionals who specialize in the analysis of statistical data, could analyze past losses in each line of business individually to determine appropriate cash reserves for each type of policy. Then, the company could total these amounts to determine the total cash reserve that it should maintain.

An alternative approach is for the company's actuaries to add up the past losses of all three lines of business *before* doing their statistical analysis and estimating future losses. With this purely aggregative approach, the actuaries could then calculate the company's total cash reserve needs directly. Most insurance company actuaries do not use this alternative approach, however, because the three lines of business are very different. Auto loss experiences of policyholders typically depend on factors that are very different from workers' compensation losses. The same is true of liability losses. Consequently, insurance actuaries rarely use such a purely aggregative approach to calculate a company's needed cash reserves.

How Much Should Macroeconomists Aggregate? This example illustrates a problem that some have with macroeconomics as a field of study and research. Critics of macroeconomics commonly argue that trying to understand the behavior of aggregate variables of concern to macroeconomists is not unlike summing up three insurance business lines to estimate a company's loss reserves. Just as aggregation is misleading to an insurance company, they argue, it can lead to the wrong answers for economists.

If macroeconomists fully accepted this argument, they would have to give up macroeconomics. If they did, we would be left in a quandary. Economic policymakers would have no guidance when trying to determine how their policies might affect the economy. Business firms would have no theory to guide their efforts to understand the overall business climate that they face. When choosing among potential leaders, individual citizens would have no understanding of the broad macroeconomic issues their nation faces. In short, we would live in a world where people would no longer try to understand aggregate macroeconomic variables, even though those variables are crucial to their welfare.

Another possible reaction would be to decide that the answer might lie in **general equilibrium analysis.** In this approach to economics, the economy is regarded as a collection of many consumers, workers, and firms. Each makes its own choices, and then all these choices interact to determine wages, prices, quantities of output, and incomes in many *individual* markets. A general equilibrium theorist could *then* develop aggregate measures of wages, prices, output, and income to contemplate how these aggregates change when all people in the economy respond to some external event, such as a new policy action.

Returning to our insurance example, this approach would be analogous to insurance actuaries computing a company's cash reserves by estimating losses for *each individual policyholder.* An insurance company would face two problems in such a task. First, if it is a large company, then it might have to analyze thousands and thou-

GENERAL EQUILIBRIUM ANALYSIS An approach to analyzing the economy by examining the multiple interactions of all individual consumers, workers, and firms.

sands of policyholders. Second, not all policyholders experience losses from auto accidents, liability claims, or workers' compensation losses. Indeed, some policyholders might be loss-free for years before filing a claim. Others by chance might experience a number of losses. The issue for the insurance company, of course, is predicting the *average* losses across all policyholders. In this case, insurance actuaries can actually *benefit* from some aggregation. This is why they study the loss experiences of full *lines of business* instead of individual policyholders.

Analogously, economists potentially can *gain* from aggregating, as long as they do not overdo it. As you will see in future chapters, complete macroeconomic models can never really be boiled down to a single diagram or equation. Just as actuaries aggregate the loss experiences of policies in similar lines of business, economists aggregate across similar markets. They consider aggregations of labor markets, financial markets, and markets for goods and services under the assumption that individual behavior in markets for labor, financial assets, and goods and services is essentially the same. Then macroeconomists develop theories about how these various aggregated components of the economy function and interact. Ultimately, these theories permit macroeconomists to develop a theory of how fully aggregate variables such as total output and income are determined. In the same way, an actuary works out cash reserves for broad lines of business before determining the insurance company's total cash needs.

The key issue, naturally, is how much aggregation is appropriate. Not surprisingly, economists disagree on this point. As you will see in future chapters, this issue is a source of division between alternative approaches to macroeconomics.

Data Problems

Another potential source of division among macroeconomists involves the data that they are able to observe. We shall discuss measures of key macroeconomic variables, such as aggregate output, aggregate income, and the price level, in Chapter 2. All these measures have two important characteristics in common. First, they are artificially constructed measures. As you will learn, for instance, measures of the overall price level are index numbers. In contrast to a market price, which is the actual price at which buyers and sellers agree to exchange a good or service, a measure of the aggregate price level is an index number that economists construct after the fact. This can lead to disagreement about how to interpret changes in the price level or in other macroeconomic variables.

Second, macroeconomic data can rarely be regarded as the result of a *controlled experiment*. Chemists and physicists, for example, can control background conditions to test their theories. Some microeconomists also have developed experimental methods to test various theories of market interactions. Macroeconomists, however, are limited to the aggregate data they observe. Conducting a controlled experiment for the entire economy is not feasible. In this regard, macroeconomics is somewhat like astronomy: Astronomical researchers can observe the planets, stars, quasars, galaxies, and so on but cannot act upon them. Like an astronomer, all a macroeconomist can do is interpret the data as well as possible. Naturally, the end result can be further differences in interpretation among macroeconomists.

As you will learn in this text, there have indeed been wide differences in the ways that macroeconomists have perceived the world that they observe, as revealed to them by data on macroeconomic variables. Although all macroeconomic theories share a number of basic elements, they also differ in many respects. Before we can discuss these issues further, however, it is important that you understand the data with which macroeconomists work. We turn to this issue in the next chapter.

FUNDAMENTAL ISSUE #4

Why is macroeconomics a controversial subject? Two aspects of macroeconomics in particular lead to disagreements among economists. One is that economists may diverge in their views about how much aggregation is appropriate. Another is that macroeconomists work with artificially constructed aggregate measures of economic activity that cannot be manipulated through controlled experiments. These two features of macroeconomics lead to differences in opinion and divergent interpretations, thereby leading to theoretical controversies.

 CHAPTER SUMMARY

1. **Macroeconomics and Its Distinguishing Features:** Macroeconomics is the study of the entire economy. One distinguishing feature of macroeconomics is its focus on the aggregate, economy-wide variables. The other is the requirement to explain the role of the quantity of money in circulation, given money's use in all markets in the economy.

2. **Key Macroeconomic Variables:** The primary measures of overall economic activity include domestic variables, such as the total output, employment, and unemployment of a nation and its money growth and inflation rates, and international variables, including the trade balance and exchange rates of a nation.

3. **Key Issues in Macroeconomics:** One primary issue is determining the factors that influence a nation's long-term growth in output and employment. Another is identifying the reasons that output and employment fluctuate in the short run. A third key issue is determining what influence the quantity of money has on a nation's output, employment, and prices. A fourth important issue is identifying the appropriate goals of macroeconomic policies and determining how they should be implemented. Finally, macroeconomics seeks to understand how factors such as exchange rates and international trade affect a country's economic performance.

4. **Why Macroeconomics Is a Controversial Subject:** Two features of macroeconomics in particular engender conflicting views. One is that macroeconomists may disagree about how much aggregation is optimal. Another is that macroeconomists observe and analyze artificially constructed data on economic activity, which they cannot manipulate via controlled experiments. These features of macroeconomics naturally produce different interpretations and foster controversies.

QUESTIONS AND PROBLEMS

1. Explain in your own words the difference between microeconomics and macroeconomics.

2. Why does the quantity of money in circulation occupy a central role in macroeconomics?

3. Why does it make sense to compare nations' output performances on a per capita basis?

4. As an example of the aggregation problem that macroeconomists face, suppose that you were asked to predict the overall grade point average at your college or university. Discuss the pros and cons of making such a prediction based on an analysis using data at the level of (a) all individual students and professors, (b) departments, and (c) the college or university.

CYBERTUTOR EXERCISES

1. Use CyberTutor to compare employment over time. Observe the periods of decline in employment. What do you think causes these declines?

2. Create a new variable called Output Per Worker by dividing the real GDP (called GDP Real) by employment and plot Output per Worker over time. Does this plot confirm that U.S. productivity has generally been increasing over time?

3. Examine U.S. unemployment from 1959 to the present. Does unemployment seem to be cyclical or constant over time? Relate historical events to unemployment levels, paying particular attention to the years 1974–75, 1980–82, and 1990–91. Are the levels of unemployment experienced in the United States over the past three years unusual?

4. Economists are interested not only in how variables change over time, but also in what influences these variables. One way of exploring this is by plotting one variable against another. From reading newspapers, one might suspect that when the economy is growing quickly, the unemployment rate should be falling. Conversely, when the growth rate is negative, unemployment rates should be rising. Let's find out. Plot the unemployment rate against the real GDP growth rate. Does the plot support our hypothesis? If so why?

ON-LINE APPLICATION

An excellent resource for information about the economic performances of different regions of the United States is the Federal Reserve's "Beige Book." This publication is compiled by the Federal Reserve's Board of Governors in Washington, D.C., based on contributions from the twelve Federal Reserve Banks.

Internet URL: http://www.bog.frb.fed.us/fomc/bb/current

Title: The Beige Book

Navigation: Begin with the **Yahoo** Internet search engine (http://www.yahoo.com).
Click on *Social Sciences* (http://www.yahoo.com/Business).
Then click on *Economics@* (http://www.yahoo.com/Social_Science/Economic/).
Scan down the page to economics sites, and then click on *Beige Book.* Then click on *Summary.*

Application: Read the Beige Book Summary and answer the following questions:

1. What measures of overall business activity does the Beige Book's analysis consider? According to these measures, do regional variations in business activity exist at present? What is the outlook for overall U.S. business activity?

2. What measures of inflation does the Beige Book's analysis focus on? Are there currently any regional differences in inflation pressures? What is the outlook for overall U.S. inflation?

SELECTED REFERENCES AND FURTHER READING

Economic Report of the President. Washington, D.C.: U.S. Government Printing Office. Published annually.

International Monetary Fund. *World Economic Outlook.* Published biannually in May and October.

President's Council of Economic Advisers. *Economic Indicators.* Washington, D.C.: U.S. Government Printing Office. Published monthly.

How Do We Know How We're Doing? —

MEASURING MACROECONOMIC VARIABLES

FUNDAMENTAL ISSUES

1. What is gross domestic product, and how is it calculated?

2. How do economists measure international transactions?

3. What is the difference between nominal GDP and real GDP?

4. What are the consumer price index and the producer price index?

Approximately 50 days after the end of every quarter, the federal government releases its estimates of our economy's rate of growth for the previous quarter, measured on an annualized basis. If, for example, total national real output was estimated to increase by 0.5 percent during the previous quarter, the government would announce a first-quarter growth rate of 2 percent per year. Once these statistics are announced, journalists have a field day analyzing whether the economy is growing, not growing, slowing down, headed for a soft landing, overheating, and so on. Indeed, economists and government officials throughout the rest of the world often make predictions about what will happen in their own economies based on those annualized quarterly statistics from the United States.

These initial quarterly statistics have a problem, though—they are often wrong. On occasion, quarterly annualized economic growth rates in the United States have been corrected a month later by as much as 75 percent! Consequently, it is usually a good idea to wait a few months and to examine only revised statistics from the U.S. Department of Commerce.

How does the federal government come up with its quarterly statistics about the health of the U.S. economy? That is the subject matter of this chapter. National economic statistics may sometimes be revised, and are certainly sometimes biased, but they constitute an important part of studying the macroeconomy nevertheless.

The Circular Flow of Income and Product

To have any idea how the economy as a whole is doing, economists must have a measure of aggregate performance. Economists have developed several such measures. The most important is the measure of the economy's output. As we noted in Chapter 1, this can give us some idea about how a nation's overall standard of living is changing.

Gross Domestic Product

GROSS DOMESTIC PRODUCT (GDP) The value of all final goods and services produced during a given period; tabulated using market prices. GDP includes foreign residents' earnings from home production but excludes home residents' earnings abroad.

The key measure of the aggregate output of an economy is **gross domestic product (GDP)**, which is the total of all *final* goods and services produced within the nation's borders during a given interval (such as a year) and valued at market prices. GDP is a measure of the flow of aggregate output produced in an economy. To avoid having to add together very different items such as annual fish harvests, the production of diamond rings, and the provision of travel services, economists add up the dollar values of the final goods and services. To construct these dollar values, market prices are multiplied by the quantities produced and sold. To have market prices, however, the final goods and services must be traded in markets. This means that GDP excludes nonmarket transactions such as child-care services provided by husbands or wives who stay at home to care for their young children instead of working outside the home and sending their children to a day-care center. In addition, only the values of final goods and services are part of GDP. Hence, GDP does not include the values of exchanges of stocks, bonds, or other financial assets.

Furthermore, we cannot emphasize too much that GDP counts only the production of goods and services in their *final form* during a given period of time. If an automobile company purchases auto parts from various manufacturers and assembles them into a sport-utility vehicle during 1999 and sells the assembled vehicle that year, then only the sale price of the *vehicle* counts in GDP. The market values of the auto parts that the company purchased before assembling the sport-utility vehicle are not included in GDP separately. Doing so would result in double-counting the production and sale of these parts, because their value is already included in the sale price of the final vehicle.

Suppose, however, that when we compute 1999 GDP at the end of that year, the company still has a stock of unassembled parts and several partially assembled vehicles. Then we would count the market value of the unassembled or partially assembled parts as *inventory investment* in materials used in the production process. What if the auto company also has some fully assembled vehicles that are still unsold at the time of our GDP calculation? Any produced but unsold goods are also included in the inventory investment. GDP includes all inventory investment that takes place during the year to ensure that we total up all production that occurred during that year.

Another item counted in GDP is **depreciation,** which is the value of productive equipment that is used up or worn out as part of the production process and must be replaced if the existing amount of equipment is to be maintained. Economists refer to the total stock of productive equipment as **capital goods,** or goods that may be used to produce other goods and services in the future. Depreciation expense, therefore, is the allocation of new production to maintaining the current amount of capital. Because depreciation is a part of a year's production of goods, it is counted in GDP.

DEPRECIATION The total market value of capital goods that are expended during the process of production.

CAPITAL GOOD A good that may be used in the production of other goods and services in the future.

Income Equals the Value of Product

When thinking about the GDP measure of aggregate economic performance, Figure 2–1 can be helpful. This figure depicts a basic **circular flow diagram,** which is a chart illustrating the aggregate flows of income and product in the economy. Business firms use the total factor services—labor services, the service flow from capital goods, the flow of services from land, and entrepreneurship or business know-how—to produce goods and services. Firms sell these goods and services in *product markets.* In turn, households, which are individuals or families, purchase these goods and services with the income that they earn by providing factor services to firms. The households receive this income in the form of wages and salaries, interest, rents, and profits. The values of these services, in turn, are determined in the *factor markets,* which are the markets for labor, capital, land, and entrepreneurship.

CIRCULAR FLOW DIAGRAM A chart that depicts the economy's flows of income and product.

It is easy to see how the circular flow diagram gets its name. The diagram indicates that households purchase the product of firms—their output, or GDP—using the income that they earn from providing the factor services that go into producing GDP. Thus the value of the circular flow in Figure 2–1 *is* the amount of GDP. This means that:

> **GDP serves both as a measure of the economy's total output *and* as a measure of the total income of all individuals in that economy.**

GDP measures both total output and total income because it is the production of output that generates the income of households.

Throughout this text, therefore, we shall think of GDP as both an overall measure of output and as an overall measure of income. As we shall see later, in a purely accounting sense there are slight distinctions between GDP and "national income." In a broader conceptual sense, however, the two are equivalent.

MEASURING DOMESTIC VARIABLES: THE NATIONAL INCOME ACCOUNTS

A look at the circular flow diagram suggests that there ought to be two ways to calculate GDP. Totaling up the value of all spending on goods and services produced and sold or counted as inventory investment should give us GDP, as should adding

---

FIGURE 2–1   THE CIRCULAR FLOW OF INCOME AND PRODUCT

Business firms make factor payments to households in return for the use of households' factor services. The total value of these factor payments constitutes total household income, which households spend on the goods and services that firms produce. The aggregate value of these goods and services is gross domestic product (GDP).

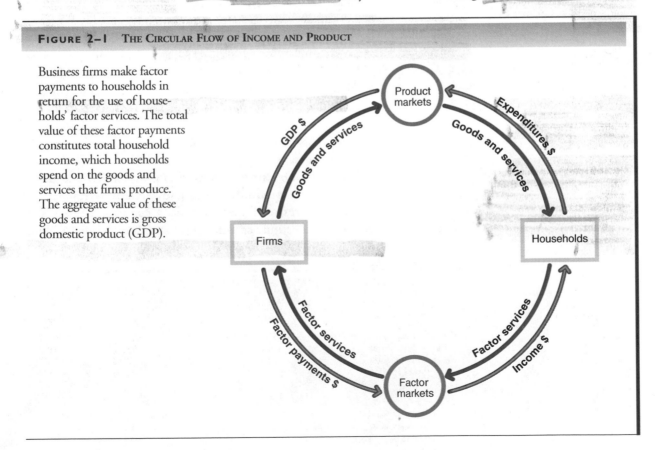

NATIONAL INCOME ACCOUNTS
Tabulations of the values of a nation's flows of income and product.

together all the income earnings. Indeed, the **national income accounts,** which are the formal tabulations of the nation's income and product, take into consideration both of these approaches to computing GDP.

The Product Approach to GDP

Because our basic definition of GDP is a measure of output, it makes sense to begin with the *product approach* to accounting for a nation's income and product. This approach entails summing up the aggregate expenditures on final goods and services produced during a given year. You can think of it as determining the size of the upper flow—the flow through the product markets—in the circular flow diagram.

CONSUMPTION SPENDING Total purchases of goods and services by households.

INVESTMENT SPENDING The sum of purchases of new capital goods, spending on new residential construction, and inventory investment.

Table 2–1 illustrates this way of computing GDP. There are four basic types of spending on final goods and services during the year. The first is **consumption spending** by households. The second is **investment spending.** This includes business spending on new capital goods, net accumulations of inventories of newly produced goods, and expenditures on residential construction—houses and apartment buildings—by households as well as business firms. *Gross investment* includes all investment spending during the course of a year. A portion of this spending, however, is directed to replacement of worn-out capital, or depreciation. Hence, *net investment* is equal to gross investment less depreciation. Economists regard net investment as the best indicator of the addition to the economy's stock of capital goods during a year. Nevertheless, gross investment measures total spending on such goods. For this reason, the full amount of gross investment is included in GDP.

GOVERNMENT SPENDING Total state, local, and federal government expenditures on goods and services.

NET EXPORT SPENDING The difference between spending on domestically produced goods and services by residents of other countries and spending on foreign-produced goods and services by residents of the home country.

The third form of spending on final goods and services produced in an economy is **government spending.** This is the total expenditures on goods and services by state, local, and federal governments.

The final component of GDP is **net export spending,** which is equal to total spending on domestically produced goods and services by residents of other nations, less expenditures on foreign-produced goods and services by home residents that do not constitute spending on home production. As Table 2–1 indicates, since the early 1980s net export spending has been negative,

TABLE 2–1   THE PRODUCT APPROACH TO CALCULATING GROSS DOMESTIC PRODUCT

	1981	1986	1991	1997*
Consumption Spending	1,941.3	2,892.7	3,975.1	5,154.4
Investment spending	556.2	722.5	736.2	1,117.0
Government spending	633.4	938.5	1,225.9	1,406.4
Net export spending	−15.0	−131.5	−20.5	−98.7
Gross domestic product	3,115.9	4,422.2	5,916.7	7,576.1

SOURCE: 1997 *Economic Report of the President* and *Economic Indicators* (various issues).
NOTE: Amounts are in billions of dollars.
*Authors' estimates.

TABLE 2-2 THE INCOME APPROACH TO CALCULATING GROSS DOMESTIC PRODUCT

	1981	1986	1991	1996*
Wages and salaries	1,827.8	2,572.4	3,457.9	4,448.5
Interest income	234.5	363.1	448.0	403.3
Rental income	45.7	42.3	68.4	126.8
Business profits	362.2	538.7	745.4	1,172.3
National income	2,470.2	3,516.5	4,719.7	6,150.9
Indirect taxes and transfers	260.5	365.7	489.6	526.2
Net national product	2,730.7	3,882.2	5,209.3	6,677.1
Depreciation	419.9	552.9	723.1	890.0
Gross national product	3,150.6	4,435.1	5,932.4	7,567.1
Net Income payments abroad	−34.7	−12.9	−15.7	+9.0
Gross domestic product	3,115.9	4,422.2	5,916.7	7,576.1

SOURCE: 1997 *Economic Report of the President; Economic Indicators.*
NOTE: Amounts are in billions of dollars.
*Authors' estimates.

reflecting the fact that spending by U.S. residents on foreign goods and services has exceeded foreign spending on U.S.-produced goods and services. The total of all four types of spending on domestically produced final goods and services during a year is that year's GDP.

The Income Approach to GDP

Table 2–2 shows the alternative approach to calculating GDP—the *income approach.* This approach attempts to measure the lower flow, through the factor markets, in the circular flow diagram in Figure 2–1. The income approach involves three steps: First, economists add together wages and salaries, interest income, rental income, and business profits. In the national income accounts, this total is called **national income,** or simply the total of all factor earnings in the economy. Second, economists add indirect taxes and transfer payments to businesses, which are sales and excise taxes and government subsidies that artificially reduce reported income flows. The sum of national income and indirect taxes is **net national product.** Next, economists add depreciation to obtain **gross national product (GNP).** Finally, they add net income earned by foreign residents from U.S.-based production to gross national product, and the result is GDP. Hence, GNP and GDP are different measures of a nation's output:

> **GNP includes earnings of home residents abroad but excludes foreign residents' earnings from home production. In contrast, GDP excludes earnings of home residents abroad but includes foreign residents' earnings from home production. For this reason, GDP measures the value of all goods and services produced within a nation's borders.**

NATIONAL INCOME The sum of all factor earnings, or net domestic product minus indirect business taxes.

NET NATIONAL PRODUCT GNP minus depreciation, or national income plus indirect business taxes.

GROSS NATIONAL PRODUCT A measure of a nation's total production that includes home residents' earnings abroad but excludes foreign residents' earnings from home production.

INTERNET • SOURCE

Tracking U.S. Gross Domestic Product

The Federal Reserve Bank of St. Louis's FRED (Federal Reserve Economic Data)—
Quarterly Gross Domestic Product and Components
Internet URL: http://www.stls.frb.org/fred/

Navigation: Start at the Federal Reserve Bank of St. Louis homepage
(http://www.stls.frb.org). Click on *FRED* (http://www.stls.frb.org/fred/). Select
Data files and then click on *Quarterly Gross Domestic Product and Components*. Then
scan down to *Gross Domestic Product* options and click your choice.

What GDP Is and Is Not

Like any statistical measure, gross domestic product is a concept that can be both well
used and misused. As already noted, economists find it invaluable as an overall indicator of a nation's economic performance. As discussed in Chapter 1, and as we shall
reemphasize in Chapter 4, the ratio of GDP to the number of people in a country,
or per capita GDP, is a useful benchmark measure of the standard of living of a typical resident of a nation.

Nevertheless, it is important to realize that GDP has weaknesses. Because it
includes only the value of goods and services traded in markets, it excludes *nonmarket
production*, such as the household services of homemakers discussed earlier. This
omission can cause problems when comparing the GDP of an industrialized country with the GDP of a highly agrarian nation where nonmarket production typically
is relatively more important. It also causes problems if nations have different definitions of legal versus illegal activities. For instance, a nation where gambling is legal will
count the value of gambling services, which have a reported market value. In a country where gambling is illegal, however, those who provide such services naturally will
not report their market value, and they will not be counted in that country's GDP
(see Global Notebook: *Underground Economies around the World*).

Although GDP is often used as a benchmark measure for standard-of-living calculations, it is not necessarily a good measure of the well-being of a nation. As the
now-defunct Soviet Union illustrated to the world, the large-scale production of such
goods as minerals, electricity, and irrigation for farming can have negative effects on
the environment: deforestation from strip mining, air and soil pollution from partic-
ulate emissions or accidents at nuclear power plants, and erosion of the natural balance between water and salt in bodies of water such as the Aral Sea. Hence, it is
important to recognize the following point:

**GDP is a measure of production and an indicator of economic activity.
It is not a measure of a nation's overall welfare.**

GLOBAL NOTEBOOK:
Underground Economies around the World

An obvious part of the unmeasured underground economy consists of illegal activities—drug trafficking, prostitution, gambling, and the like. When government statisticians in the United States or elsewhere calculate the GDP, they typically do not even guess at the value of these activities. The largest part of the underground economy, however, consists of unmeasured *legal* activities, not *illegal* activities. Everywhere in the world most of the underground economy involves income derived from legal activities that is earned but not reported. The provision of services is a good example. Lawn maintenance and gardening, baby-sitting, house cleaning, and the like are often paid for in cash. No records are kept and no taxes are paid on the income earned. Consequently, such unreported income does not work its way into official GDP statistics.

Typically, the size of a country's underground economy is positively correlated with the maximum marginal personal income tax rate. After all, the higher the marginal income tax rate, the greater the incentive to hide income earned. In the United States, when federal marginal income tax rates were 70 percent and higher, tax evasion was certainly more prevalent and hence so was the size of the underground economy relative to published GDP statistics. Figure 2–2 shows the estimated size of the underground economy in selected countries.

FOR CRITICAL ANALYSIS:
What else might determine the relative size of a nation's underground economy?

FIGURE 2–2   THE RELATIVE SIZE OF THE UNDERGROUND ECONOMY IN SELECTED NATIONS

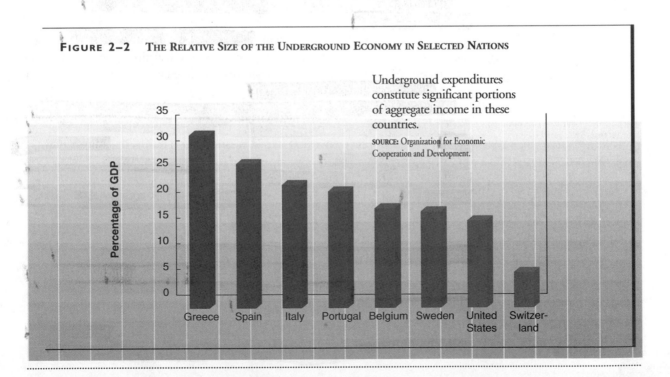

Underground expenditures constitute significant portions of aggregate income in these countries.

SOURCE: Organization for Economic Cooperation and Development.

FUNDAMENTAL ISSUE #1

What is gross domestic product, and how is it calculated? Gross domestic product (GDP) is the market value of all final goods and services produced during a given period. Using the product approach, GDP is equal to the sum of consumption spending, investment spending, government expenditures, and net export spending. Under the income approach, GDP is equal to the sum of wages and salaries, net interest, rental income, profits, indirect taxes, and depreciation.

MEASURING INTERNATIONAL TRANSACTIONS: THE BALANCE OF PAYMENTS

BALANCE OF PAYMENTS ACCOUNTS
A tabulation of all transactions between the residents of a nation and the residents of all other nations in the world.

CURRENT ACCOUNT The balance of payments account that tabulates international trade and transfers of goods and services and flows of income.

CAPITAL ACCOUNT The balance of payments account that records all nongovernmental international asset transactions.

OFFICIAL SETTLEMENTS BALANCE A balance of payments account that records international asset transactions involving agencies of home and foreign governments.

In addition to keeping track of large domestic flows of income and product, economists must account for sizable flows of payments across nations' borders. To do this, they use a system of accounting known as the **balance of payments accounts.** The U.S. balance of payments accounts consist of a complete tabulation of the exchanges between U.S. residents and residents of all other nations. The accounts include all transactions in goods, services, income earnings and payments, and assets by individuals, businesses, and governments across U.S. borders.

The balance of payments accounts consist of three separate accounts. The first is the **current account.** This account tabulates international trade and transfers of goods and services and flows of income. The second is the **capital account,** which tabulates all nongovernmental international asset transactions. Finally, international asset transactions involving governmental agencies appear in an account called the **official settlements balance.**

In all three accounts, any cross-border exchange entailing a *payment* by a U.S. individual, business, or government agency is a deficit item that appears as a *negative* entry. This accounting convention is used because such a transaction causes funds to flow out of the United States. By way of contrast, any international transaction that leads to a *receipt* by a U.S. resident, company, or government agency appears as a *positive* entry. Such a receipt indicates that funds have flowed into the United States.

Exports, Imports, and the Current Account

The most straightforward balance of payments account is the *current account.* This account also commonly receives the most public notice, because it includes U.S. trade of goods and services. A subtotal of this account is the *merchandise balance of trade,* which tends to be the focus of media attention, as Chapter 1 noted.

The Merchandise Trade Balance Recall from Chapter 1 that the merchandise balance of trade refers only to cross-border purchases and sales of *physical goods.* Sales

TABLE 2–3 THE U.S. MERCHANDISE TRADE BALANCE ($ MILLIONS)

	1986	1991	1996
Merchandise exports	+223,344	+416,913	+611,669
Merchandise imports	−368,425	−490,981	−799,343
Merchandise trade balance	−135,081	−74,068	−187,674

SOURCES: *Economic Report of the President* and *Economic Indicators.*

of goods by U.S. firms to residents of other nations are *merchandise exports,* while the value of goods that U.S. residents purchase from abroad are *merchandise imports.* Table 2–3 gives dollar values of U.S. merchandise exports and imports for recent years. Note that exports generate receipts by U.S. residents and appear as positive entries in the table. Imports, in contrast, entail payments abroad by U.S. residents. Consequently, these appear in the table as negative entries.

The final row in Table 2–3 displays the *merchandise trade balance* for each year. As we noted in Chapter 1, when the merchandise trade balance is positive, a *trade surplus* exists. In that case, U.S. residents would be exporting more goods than they import. As the table indicates, however, the reverse situation has arisen in recent years. Typically, U.S. merchandise imports have exceeded merchandise exports, so the U.S. merchandise trade balance has been negative, and by wide margins. The United States has experienced significant *trade deficits.*

The Current Account Balance   Although the media pay considerable attention to the merchandise balance of trade, a number of economists contend that this balance can be a misleading indicator. Since the 1970s, they point out, the share of total U.S. output by service industries has increased, while the output share of industries that produce physical goods has declined. Travel, transportation, and financial services have become conspicuously more important among U.S. producers.

As Table 2–4 indicates, net international exchanges of services are part of the current account in the U.S. balance of payments accounts. In recent years U.S. residents have sold more services to residents of other nations than they have purchased from abroad. Consequently, service transactions on net have generated receipts for U.S. residents. This is reflected by the positive entries for this category in the second row of Table 2–4.

If we add together the first and second rows of Table 2–4, we obtain the *balance on goods and services,* which appears in the third row of the table. This balance includes *both* goods *and* services. For this reason, most economists believe that this statistic is a more useful indicator of U.S. trade performance than the merchandise trade balance, even though the latter receives more media attention. Nevertheless, as you can

TABLE 2–4   THE U.S. CURRENT ACCOUNT ($ MILLIONS)

	1986	1991	1996
Merchandise trade balance	−145,081	−74,068	−187,674
Net service transactions	+4,945	+44,196	+73,467
Balance on goods and services	−140,136	−29,872	−114,207
Net Income flow	+12,881	+15,844	−8,416
Unilateral transfers	−24,833	+4,510	−42,472
Current account balance	−152,088	−9,518	−165,095

SOURCES: *Economic Report of the President* and *Economic Indicators*.

see, the U.S. balance on goods and services has run a deficit for some time. The growth of U.S. service industries that typically generate net receipts of funds has not made up for the net payments that U.S. residents have made on cross-border transactions in physical goods.

The U.S. current account also tabulates international flows of income receipts to U.S. residents and payments abroad by U.S. residents. Individuals and firms that reside in the United States earn income on assets that they hold in other nations. Such income earnings appear as positive entries in the U.S. current account. At the same time, foreign individuals and firms earn income on assets that they own in the United States. These flows of income to foreigners from the United States appear as negative entries in the U.S. current account. The fourth line of Table 2–4 shows the *net income flow* for each period.

The final component of the current account is a tabulation of all *unilateral transfers.* These are gifts that U.S. residents give to residents or governments of other nations or that foreign residents or governments give to U.S. residents. Transfers from foreigners to U.S. residents are receipts by U.S. residents and are positive entries, while transfers from U.S. residents to foreigners are payments by U.S. residents and are negative entries. The fifth line of Table 2–4 shows total *net* unilateral transfers. The U.S. government has provided sizable amounts of foreign aid and military transfers to other countries, so net unilateral transfers typically have been negative.

The final line of Table 2–4 gives the sum of lines 3 through 5. This total is the *current account balance,* which is the sum of all net international flows of goods, services, income, and transfers. The U.S. current account balance has been negative for all recent intervals, so the United States has experienced *current account deficits*. In fact, the U.S. current account balance has consistently been in deficit since 1981. Since that year, U.S. residents have persistently paid out more to the rest of the world than they have received in international transactions of goods and services, income flows, and transfers (see Policy Notebook: *Are We Putting Too Much Emphasis on Our Trade Statistics?*).

Are We Putting Too Much Emphasis on Our Trade Statistics?

Some policy critics in the United States argue that policymakers are putting too much emphasis on the international trade statistics that are released on a monthly, quarterly, and yearly basis. Indeed, virtually every month a slew of articles and TV soundbites about the U.S. trade deficit appear. The official numbers may be in error, however, for they ignore the multinational nature of many modern firms. U.S. international trade figures exclude sales in other countries by subsidiaries of U.S. companies. For this reason and others, some critics of these statistics—including government economists—believe that they are underestimating the value of U.S. exports by as much as 10 percent.

Economist Paul Krugman of Stanford University agrees. When he added up the value of world exports and compared it with the value of world imports, he found that the planet earth had a trade deficit of $100 billion! He suggests that maybe we are trading with aliens and don't know it.

FOR CRITICAL ANALYSIS:
Why do accurate figures on international trade matter?

U.S. Exports and Imports

The Federal Reserve Bank of St. Louis's FRED (Federal Reserve Economic Data)—Quarterly Gross Domestic Product and Components.
Internet URL: http://www.stls.frb.org/fred/

Navigation: Start at the Federal Reserve Bank of St. Louis homepage (http://www.stls.frb.org). Click on *FRED* (http://www.stls.frb.org/fred/). Select *Data files* and then click on *Gross Domestic Product and Components*. Scan down to *Real Exports of Goods and Services in Billions of Chained 1992 Dollars* or to *Real Imports of Goods and Services in Billions of Chained 1992 Dollars*.

The Capital Account, the Private Payments Balance, and the Overall Balance of Payments

Changes in asset holdings by U.S. residents and residents of other nations take place in international financial markets and are recorded outside the current account. The private *capital account* tabulates asset transactions involving private individuals or companies. Asset transactions involving official governmental entities such as the U.S. Treasury or the Federal Reserve enter a third account called the *official settlements balance*. Economists sometimes combine these two tabulations of asset transactions into a single, overall "capital account." We shall refer to them as separate accounts, however, because this approach can be helpful in understanding the operation of government policies concerning international financial transactions.

The Capital Account and the Private Payments Balance   All changes in private asset holdings by U.S. residents abroad and by foreigners in the United States appear in the capital account. U.S. acquisitions of foreign assets, such as purchases of shares of ownership of plants or equipment, or purchases of securities such as bonds are negative entries in the U.S. capital account. Foreign acquisitions of such assets within U.S. borders are positive entries.

The total of all these asset changes for individuals and businesses is the *capital account balance.* U.S. capital account balances for recent years are shown in the second line of Table 2–5. Since 1981, this balance has been positive, indicating that on net U.S. residents have been acquiring less foreign assets relative to acquisitions of U.S. assets by foreigners.

The first line of Table 2–5 shows the current account balances from Table 2–4. The sum of the first and second lines of Table 2–5—that is, the sum of the current account balance and the private capital account balance—is the **private payments balance.** The private payments balance gives the net total of all private exchanges between U.S. individuals and businesses and the rest of the world. Commonly, the private payments balance is referred to as the "balance of payments." Unfortunately, as we shall discuss shortly, this term is misleading. Therefore, we shall be careful to refer to it mainly by its proper name: the *private payments balance.*

Since the early 1980s, private U.S. individuals and businesses have made more payments to foreigners relative to their receipts from foreigners, so the U.S. private payments balance has persistently been negative. This means that the United States has experienced *private payments deficits,* commonly called "balance of payments deficits."

The Official Settlements Balance and the Overall Balance of Payments   As we noted earlier, governments also make cross-border asset exchanges. Purchases of foreign assets or overseas deposits of funds by the U.S. Treasury, the Federal Reserve, or other agencies of the U.S. government are receipts that appear as negative entries in the *official settlements balance,* the last account of the balance of payments accounts.

PRIVATE PAYMENTS BALANCE The sum of the current account balance and the private capital account balance, or the net total of all private exchanges between U.S. individuals and businesses and the rest of the world.

Table 2–5 The U.S. Private Payments Balance ($ Millions)			
	1986	**1991**	**1996**
Current account balance	−152,088	−9,518	−165,095
Capital Account balance	+85,419	+10,518	+89,435
Private payments balance	−66,669	+1,000	−75,660

SOURCES: *Economic Report of the President* and *Economic Indicators.*

ON THE WEB
Visit the Federal Reserve at:
http://www.bog.frb.fed.us

Acquisitions of U.S. assets or deposits by foreign central banks or governments are recorded as inflows and appear as positive entries in this account.

Governments and central banks of various nations also keep deposit accounts with other countries' central banks. If the U.S. Treasury or the Federal Reserve deposits additional funds with another nation's central bank, then this outflow of funds from the United States appears as a negative entry in the U.S. official settlements balance. In contrast, if a foreign government or central bank deposits more funds at the Federal Reserve, then the inflow of funds appears as a positive entry in the U.S. official settlements balance.

The total net amount of all governmental and central bank transactions is the final amount of the official settlements balance. The second line of Table 2–6 gives recent values for the U.S. official settlements balance, which typically has been positive.

The first line of Table 2–6 carries down the private payments balance figures from Table 2–5. If all this international accounting goes well, then the sum of the first two lines of Table 2–6 should be the *overall balance of payments,* or the net of *all* transactions of U.S. individuals, businesses, and governmental agencies with all other nations of the world. In the end, however, the accounting rarely works out exactly, and a significant *statistical discrepancy* occurs in each period. The statistical discrepancy for each year appears in the third line of Table 2–6. One reason for this discrepancy is that errors naturally occur during the collection of the large volume of data on international transactions. Another reason is the significant number of illegal international exchanges, relating to such activities as illicit drug trade or armaments shipments, that cannot be recorded because those who engage in the transactions go to great lengths to keep them secret.

The final line of Table 2–6 is the overall balance of payments, which *must always equal zero.* The reason is that every transaction between a U.S. resident and a foreign resident involves both a payment and a receipt. As a result, across all the accounts the payments and receipts *must* cancel out. This means that the overall balance of payments must equal zero.

We noted earlier that using the term "balance of payments" to describe the private payments balance is misleading. The reason, as you now can see, is that the *overall balance of payments always is equal to zero.* The private payments balance, in contrast, may be positive (a private payments surplus) or negative (a private payments deficit).

TABLE 2–6 THE OVERALL U.S. BALANCE OF PAYMENTS ($ MILLIONS)			
	1986	**1991**	**1996**
Private payments balance	−66,669	+1,000	−75,660
Official settlements balance	+33,940	+25,843	+128,781
Statistical discrepancy	+32,729	−26,843	−53,121
Overall balance of payments	0	0	0

SOURCES: *Economic Report of the President* and *Economic Indicators.*

The traditional, though misleading, term for a private payments surplus is "balance of payments surplus," and the traditional term for a private payments deficit is "balance of payments deficit." Because these terms are used so widely by the media, many economists use them as well, while keeping in mind that the *true* balance of payments is the overall figure that must equal zero.

An important point follows from the zero value for the overall balance of payments:

> **After allowing for the statistical discrepancy, the private payments balance must always be offset by the official settlements balance.**

For example, if there is a private payments deficit, then the official settlements balance must be positive. If a private payments deficit occurs, then U.S. residents pay more to residents of other countries than they receive from foreigners. Eventually, however, other countries' governments and central banks accumulate dollars that the U.S. residents have paid, on net, to those countries. Foreign governments and central banks hold many of these dollars in deposit accounts in the United States. The result is an increase in the U.S. official settlements balance that tends to make its value positive. In the end, in the absence of statistical discrepancies, the two balances offset each other. This leads to a zero value for the overall balance of payments.

FUNDAMENTAL ISSUE #2

How do economists measure international transactions? They use the balance of payments accounts. The balance of payments is composed of three accounts that tabulate exchanges between U.S. residents and residents of other nations. The current account tabulates cross-border exchanges of goods and services, unilateral transfers, and income flows. The capital account records private asset transactions, and the official settlements balance tabulates governmental asset transactions.

 ## ACCOUNTING FOR INFLATION: PRICE DEFLATORS AND REAL GDP

Figure 2–3 shows that U.S. GDP has risen each year for the past forty years. Does this mean that the U.S. economy has grown without letup? The answer is no. Annual GDP has increased for two reasons. One, of course, is that in many years the economy really *has* grown. Over the past forty years, U.S. businesses have expanded their resources and developed innovative ways to increase their production and sale of goods and services.

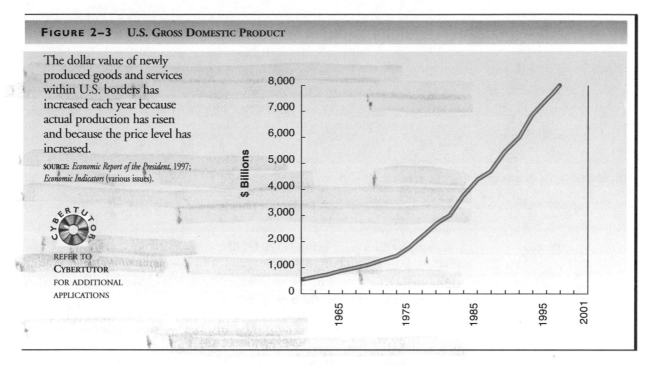

FIGURE 2-3   U.S. GROSS DOMESTIC PRODUCT

The dollar value of newly produced goods and services within U.S. borders has increased each year because actual production has risen and because the price level has increased.

SOURCE: *Economic Report of the President*, 1997; *Economic Indicators* (various issues).

REFER TO
CYBERTUTOR
FOR ADDITIONAL
APPLICATIONS

During some years, however, business production has actually declined, even though GDP increased. Statistically, this happened because of inflation. Recall that economists calculate GDP each year using market prices to value the production of firms. Economy-wide price increases, therefore, increase the *measured value* of output.

Thus, we cannot conclude from Figure 2–3 that the true production of goods and services has risen persistently in the United States. The United States has experienced inflation almost every year since World War II, so at least some portion of the general rise in the annual GDP data in the figure occurred simply because of rising prices.

Nominal GDP, Real GDP, and the GDP Price Deflator

If we were to use unadjusted calculations of GDP in an inflationary environment, the result would be persistent *overstatements* of the actual volume of economic activity. Therefore, if we are to make year-to-year comparisons of an economy's productive performance, we must somehow adjust GDP data to correct for the bias that inflation creates.

Real versus Nominal GDP   To see clearly why we need to adjust GDP for price changes, suppose that your employer told you that she intended to increase your hourly wage by 100 percent. Ignoring any taxes or other deductions from your pay, this raise would double your hourly income. Suppose, however, that the inflation rate also happened to equal 100 percent, which would imply that the prices you would have to pay to purchase goods and services would also double. In that case, your 100 percent pay raise would merely maintain the purchasing power of your wage. You would be no better off than you were before your wage increase.

Similarly, if measured GDP were to double solely as a result of a 100 percent increase in the overall price level, the total volume of economic activity would not really have changed. Annual GDP changes thus would be vastly distorted measures of the *real* growth in economic activity.

To deal with this potential problem with making year-to-year comparisons of inflation-distorted GDP figures, economists have developed an inflation-adjusted measure of GDP. This is **real gross domestic product,** or *real GDP.* This measure of aggregate output accounts for price changes and thereby more accurately reflects the economy's true volume of productive activity, net of any artificial increases resulting from inflation.

Economists distinguish between real GDP and the unadjusted GDP measure by calling the latter **nominal gross domestic product,** or *nominal GDP.* This means "GDP in name only." In other words, nominal GDP is calculated in current dollars with no adjustment for the effects of price changes.

The GDP Price Deflator If properly calculated, real GDP should measure the economy's actual volume of production of goods and services. This implies that multiplying real GDP by a measure of the overall level of prices should yield the value of real GDP measured in current prices, which in turn is our definition of nominal GDP. If we let y denote real GDP and let P denote a measure of the overall price level, then nominal GDP, denoted Y, must be

$$Y = y \times P.$$

In words, nominal GDP equals real GDP times a measure of the overall price level.

Indeed, the factor P is a standard measure of the price level, which economists call the **GDP price deflator,** or simply the "GDP deflator." P is called a "deflator" because if we solve our expression for nominal GDP, $Y = y \times P$, for y, we get

$$y = Y/P.$$

Thus, real GDP, y, is equal to nominal GDP, Y, adjusted by dividing, or "deflating," by the factor P. For example, suppose that nominal GDP measured in current prices, Y, is equal to $8.9 trillion and the value of the GDP deflator, P, is equal to 3. Then calculating real GDP would entail deflating the $8.9 trillion nominal GDP by a factor of one-third. To do this, we divide $8.9 trillion by 3 to arrive at $2.97 trillion for real GDP.

Denoting a Base Year Knowing that the GDP deflator P is equal to 3 tells us little, however, unless we have a reference point for interpreting this value. To provide a reference point, economists define a **base year** for the GDP deflator, which is a year in which nominal GDP is equal to real GDP ($Y = y$), so that the GDP deflator's value is one ($P = 1$). Consequently, if the base year were, say, 1965, and the value of

---

REAL GROSS DOMESTIC PRODUCT (REAL GDP) A price-adjusted measure of aggregate output, or nominal GDP divided by the GDP price deflator.

NOMINAL GROSS DOMESTIC PRODUCT (NOMINAL GDP) The value of final production of goods and services calculated in current dollars with no adjustment for the effects of price changes.

GDP PRICE DEFLATOR A flexible-weight measure of the overall price level; equal to nominal GDP divided by real GDP.

BASE YEAR A reference year for price-level comparisons, which is a year in which nominal GDP is equal to real GDP, so that the GDP deflator's value is equal to one.

P in 1999 were equal to 3, then this would indicate that between 1965 and 1999 the overall level of prices tripled.

At present, the U.S. government uses 1992 as the base year in its real GDP calculations. Panel (a) of Figure 2–4 shows the values of the GDP deflator since 1959. The overall level of prices increased by almost a factor of 5, from 0.26 to about 1.3, between 1959 and 1997. This means that an item that required \$1 to purchase in 1959 would have cost nearly \$5 in 1997. Alternatively stated, \$5 in 1997 would have purchased only the equivalent amount of goods and services that \$1 purchased in 1959.

Panel (b) of Figure 2–4 plots real and nominal GDP figures since 1959. Note that in 1992 nominal and real GDP are equal because 1992 is the base year in which *P* = 1 so that *Y = y*. Clearly, adjusting for price changes has a significant effect on our interpretation of GDP data. This is why it is so important to convert nominal GDP into real GDP using the GDP price deflator. Thus:

> **Only real GDP data can provide useful information about true year-to-year changes in the economy's productive performance.**

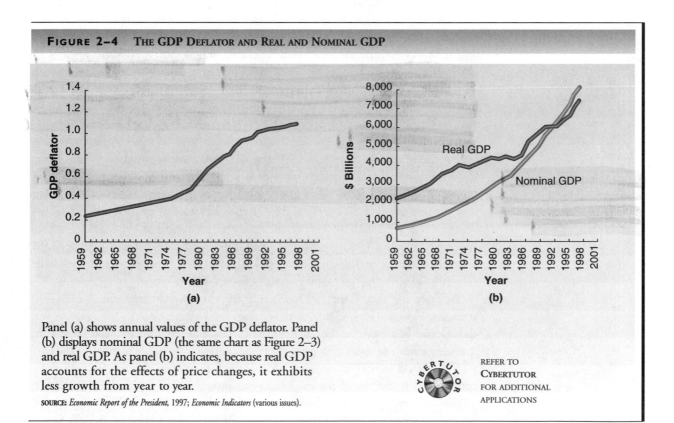

FIGURE 2–4   THE GDP DEFLATOR AND REAL AND NOMINAL GDP

Panel (a) shows annual values of the GDP deflator. Panel (b) displays nominal GDP (the same chart as Figure 2–3) and real GDP. As panel (b) indicates, because real GDP accounts for the effects of price changes, it exhibits less growth from year to year.

SOURCE: *Economic Report of the President,* 1997; *Economic Indicators* (various issues).

REFER TO
CYBERTUTOR
FOR ADDITIONAL
APPLICATIONS

FUNDAMENTAL ISSUE #3

What is the difference between nominal GDP and real GDP?
Nominal GDP is the total value of newly produced goods and services
computed using the prices at which they sold during the year they were
produced. In contrast, real GDP is the value of final goods and services
after adjusting for the effects of year-to-year price changes. The basic
approach to calculating real GDP is to divide nominal GDP by the
GDP deflator, which is a measure of the level of prices relative to prices
for a base year.

Chain-Weight Real GDP   In actuality, the real GDP data plotted in panel (b) of
Figure 2–4 were not calculated using the simple computation method described
above. That method computes real GDP for each year using the prices from the base
year only. The government used this simple fixed-base-year approach for nearly fifty
years before switching to a new approach at the end of 1995.

The problem with using a fixed base year to calculate real GDP is that as prices
change, households and businesses change how they allocate their purchases. They
buy fewer of the goods and services whose prices rise the most and more of the goods
and services whose prices rise the least. As a result, output increases most for those
goods and services whose prices rise the least. Using fixed-base-year GDP, which
ignores such changes in the pattern of purchases, tends to produce slightly biased
measurements of growth in real output. In an inflationary environment, real output
growth tends to be overstated in years after the base year and slightly understated in
years before the base year.

For this reason, at the end of 1995 the U.S. government switched to calculating
chain-weight real GDP. Under this approach, the government computes real GDP
using prices for both the year in question and the preceding year as weights. For
instance, the calculation of 1995 real GDP that is plotted in panel (b) of Figure 2–4
uses prices in 1994 and 1995 as weights, and the calculation of 1996 real GDP uses
prices in 1995 and 1996 as weights. Real GDP for all other years is calculated the
same way. Hence, as the calculation procedure moves through time it forms the
"chain" of weights that gives this measure of real GDP its name.

As Table 2–7 shows, the 1995 switch to the chain-weight measure of real GDP
increased measured real GDP growth for years before those close to 1987, which was
the relevant base year for the calculations at that time. In addition, the increase in
average growth rates was greater for the earlier period, 1961–1975, than for the later
period, 1975–1986. This happened because the further from the base year, the more
pronounced is the bias of the fixed-base-year procedure. In contrast, for years after
1987, the new approach *reduced* measured growth in real GDP. This occurred
because, as we noted earlier, people purchased fewer of the goods and services whose

CHAIN-WEIGHT REAL GDP A
method of calculating real GDP
for a given year that uses prices for
both the year in question and the
preceding year as weights.

	CHAIN WEIGHT	FIXED WEIGHT (1987 DOLLARS)	CHANGE IN GROWTH RATE
TABLE 2–7	**AVERAGE ANNUAL REAL GDP GROWTH RATES WITH FIXED-WEIGHT AND CHAIN-WEIGHT CALCULATIONS OF REAL GDP**		
PERIOD			
1961–1975	3.75	3.38	+0.37
1975–1986	3.18	2.88	+0.30
1986–1991	2.02	2.02	0
1991–1994	2.72	3.16	−0.44

SOURCE: Patricia Pollard, "Introducing Chain-Weight GDP Data in *National Economic Trends*," Federal Reserve Bank of St. Louis, *National Economic Trends*, October 1995.

prices increased the most, so the fixed-weight measure of real GDP overestimated increases in real output.

The big drawback of the chain-weight real GDP measure is that it is much more complicated to calculate. Fortunately for students in intermediate macroeconomics, however, inflation rates in the United States typically have been relatively low. Consequently, the differences in U.S. real GDP calculations under the alternative procedures are small enough for us to abstract from in this text. The fixed-base-year approach is much simpler to use, so we shall rely on it to illustrate basic points about nominal versus real GDP.

Fixed-Weight Price Indexes

Even though the basic GDP calculation, $y = Y/P$, produces a slight bias in measured output growth, the GDP price deflator that real GDP calculations imply nevertheless is a **flexible-weight price index.** With this price index, the weights of various goods and services change automatically as the output of goods and services varies over time. Alternative measures of the overall price level are **fixed-weight price indexes,** which are calculated by selecting a fixed set of goods and services and then tracking the prices of these specific goods and services from year to year.

As a simple example of a fixed-weight price index, let's devise the "college consumer price index." Suppose that the "typical" college student spends one-fourth of his available resources on tuition, one-fourth on housing, one-fourth on food and clothing, and one-fourth on supplies and other expenses. To create the index, we would collect information on the average prices of each of these components of the typical student's expenses. Then we could multiply each price by one-fourth and sum the results to obtain a numerical value for our college consumer price index.

The Consumer and Producer Price Indexes   The government computes the actual, overall **consumer price index (CPI)** in the same basic manner as in our fictitious example, although the CPI is a weighted sum of prices of a full set of goods and services that the government determines a typical U.S. consumer purchases each year. Among the categories of expenditures that the government incorporates into its

FLEXIBLE-WEIGHT PRICE INDEX An overall measure of the price level that automatically gives variable weights to the output of goods and services across time.

FIXED-WEIGHT PRICE INDEX An overall measure of the price level that is computed using a weighted average of the prices of a fixed set of goods and services.

CONSUMER PRICE INDEX (CPI) A weighted average of the prices of a large group of goods and services that the government determines a representative U.S. consumer buys each year.

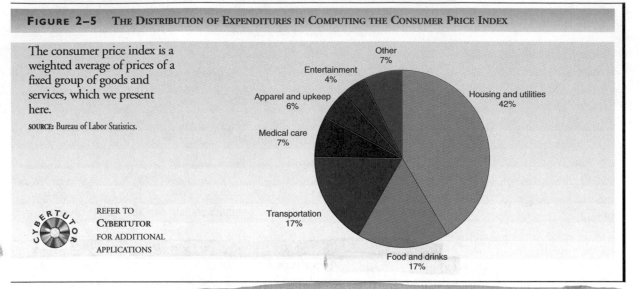

FIGURE 2–5 **THE DISTRIBUTION OF EXPENDITURES IN COMPUTING THE CONSUMER PRICE INDEX**

The consumer price index is a weighted average of prices of a fixed group of goods and services, which we present here.

SOURCE: Bureau of Labor Statistics.

REFER TO **CYBERTUTOR** FOR ADDITIONAL APPLICATIONS

Other 7%
Entertainment 4%
Apparel and upkeep 6%
Medical care 7%
Housing and utilities 42%
Transportation 17%
Food and drinks 17%

weighting scheme for the CPI are a typical consumer's annual purchases of housing and utilities, food and beverages, transportation, medical care, apparel, and entertainment. Figure 2–5 shows the current distribution of these expenditures in the computation of the CPI. All told, the Bureau of Labor Statistics (BLS), the government agency that collects the price data to compute the CPI, samples prices on about 95,000 different items. In addition, the government calculates a number of alternative consumer price indexes, such as CPIs for urban consumers, for rural consumers, and so on.

Another fixed-weight price index that the government calculates is the **producer price index (PPI).** This is a weighted average of prices of goods that a typical business firm purchases from other businesses and then uses in its own production process. As for the CPI, the government computes several versions of the PPI. The basic categories that the government uses in its various PPI weighting schemes are finished goods; intermediate materials, supplies, and components; crude materials that require extensive additional processing by a business firm; and food materials.

For reasons discussed below, economists often prefer to use the GDP deflator as a basic measure of the overall price level. Certainly, the GDP deflator is an easier price measure to use in an intermediate macroeconomics course. Nevertheless, the U.S. government uses the CPI to adjust certain government benefits, such as Social Security payments, to account for price changes. In addition, as you know from your own experience, the media commonly report inflation rates calculated using annual percentage changes in the CPI.

Problems with Fixed-Weight Price Indexes   Although the CPI and PPI are popular measures of the overall price level, they suffer from some important drawbacks related to the fact that they are fixed-weight indexes. The most glaring problem is that

PRODUCER PRICE INDEX (PPI) A weighted average of the prices of goods that the government determines a representative business buys from other businesses.

relative prices of goods change over time, and people change their spending allocations accordingly by substituting among goods. This means that the fixed weights that the BLS assigns to a "typical" consumer are *artificially* fixed. For any truly representative consumer, the weights surely must change somewhat from year to year. Indeed, an extreme example of this problem occurs when new goods that previously had not existed arrive on the scene. Unless the CPI is reformulated, the prices of such goods will not even be included in this measure of the overall price level.

Furthermore, using fixed weights for price indexes ignores the potential for *quality* changes in the goods and services that consumers buy. For example, one year a typical consumer might purchase a personal computer with a PentiumPro-based processing unit, but the next year yet another speed enhancement may be available in a typical personal computer that sells for the same price. To the consumer, the quality enhancement available in the next year at the same price effectively amounts to a lower price per constant quality unit. To the CPI, however, a personal computer is a personal computer, and no price change would be factored into the calculation of the CPI in the year of the quality improvement.

Another problem is the way data are collected. The BLS collects data on *list* prices, which are the prices that businesses formally print in catalogs, price lists, and so on. In fact, though, during times when competition for business is most pressing, consumers often can get bargain prices below those in the formal price lists available to the BLS. The proliferation of discount retailers in the 1980s and 1990s may have worsened this problem.

Indeed, during the past several years Congress has contemplated a restructuring of the CPI. In 1995 Congress asked five prominent economists (Michael Boskin of Stanford University, Ellen Dulberger of IBM Corporation, Robert Gordon of Northwestern University, and Zvi Giliches and Dale Jorgenson of Harvard University) to evaluate the various problems with the CPI. The economists estimated that the failure of the CPI to account for quality improvements added about 0.2 percent to annual CPI inflation and that the failure to incorporate new products quickly added another 0.3 percent. In addition, they concluded that the CPI's lack of recognition of consumers' ability to substitute among goods added another 0.3 percent to annual CPI inflation rates and that the failure to account for the growth of discount retail outlets added yet another 0.2 percent. All told, therefore, the economists concluded that these inherent problems with the CPI made annual inflation rates computed using this price index about 1 percent higher than they would have been otherwise. Thus, if the CPI inflation rate for a given year was 3 percent, the *true* inflation rate may actually have been only 2 percent (see Policy Notebook: *How Important Is a Small Bias in the Consumer Price Index?*)

We should note, nevertheless, that the GDP price deflator and the CPI generally give us the same basic indications about the overall price level. Figure 2–6 shows annual values of the GDP price deflator and the CPI from 1959 until 1997. As you can see, both follow roughly the same path. From a broad perspective, therefore, both price measures provide similar information.

POLICY NOTEBOOK

How Important Is a Small Bias in the Consumer Price Index?

This discussion may have given you the impression that a 1 percentage point bias in the CPI isn't very important. Realize, though, that the CPI is the official price index used to adjust numerous government-provided transfer payments as well as many components of the tax system. As soon as the economists announced their estimate that the CPI was biased by 1 percentage point a year, Senator Daniel Patrick Moynihan (D., New York) wrote an op-ed piece for the *Washington Post* in which he stated that "If we were to do no more than declare that henceforth the cost of living adjustment will be CPI minus 1 percentage point, we would save $634 billion over the next 10 years." He was talking about the resultant decrease in Social Security, supplemental security income, veterans pensions, federal retirement payments, and the earned income tax credits.

Other, more carefully developed estimates do not predict such large savings. Nevertheless, even the Federal Reserve estimated that by the year 2000, a significant part of the budget deficit would be reduced were the CPI to be revised downward. The Fed studies took into account increased taxes because of the lower CPI. Taxes would be affected, because standard deductions, personal exemptions, and marginal tax brackets are all automatically increased each year according to the official rate of inflation. A lower CPI would therefore result in everybody paying a bit more in taxes each year.

FOR CRITICAL ANALYSIS:
What groups of individuals would be made worse off by a reduction in the officially measured CPI?

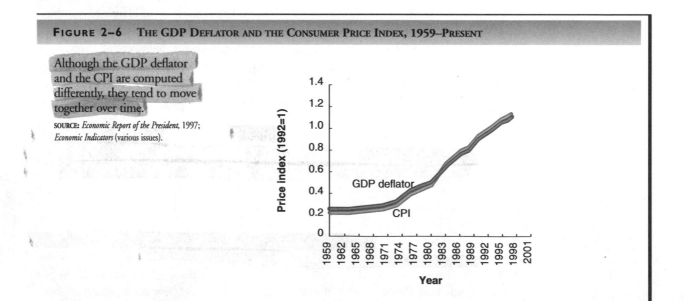

FIGURE 2–6 THE GDP DEFLATOR AND THE CONSUMER PRICE INDEX, 1959–PRESENT

Although the GDP deflator and the CPI are computed differently, they tend to move together over time.

SOURCE: *Economic Report of the President*, 1997; *Economic Indicators* (various issues).

What are the consumer price index and the producer price index?
They are the most important examples of fixed-weight price indexes. In
these weighted-average measures of the overall price level, the weights
of different goods in the average are invariant over time. The consumer
price index is a weighted average of the prices of goods and services
purchased by a representative U.S. consumer, and the producer price
index is a weighted average of the prices that businesses pay for goods
that they buy from other firms.

CHAPTER SUMMARY

1. **Gross Domestic Product and Its Computation:** By definition, gross domestic product
   (GDP) is the total of all final goods and services produced during a given period, evaluated at market prices. The product approach totals consumption spending, investment
   spending, government expenditures, and net export spending to obtain GDP. The income
   approach yields GDP as the sum of wages and salaries, net interest, rental income, profits,
   indirect taxes, and depreciation.

2. **How Economists Measure International Transactions:** The balance of payments
   accounts measure the values of cross-border exchanges. There are three balance of payments accounts. The current account tracks international exchanges of goods and services,
   unilateral transfers, and income flows. The capital account tabulates private asset transactions. Finally, the official settlements balance accounts for governmental asset transactions.

3. **The Difference between Nominal GDP and Real GDP:** Nominal GDP is the market
   value of final goods and services evaluated in terms of the prices at which the goods and
   services traded during the year they were produced. Real GDP, in contrast, is the value of
   final goods and services after taking into account the effects of price variations. We compute real GDP by dividing nominal GDP by the GDP deflator, which measures the price
   level relative to the price level of goods and services in a base year.

4. **The Consumer Price Index and the Producer Price Index:** Both of these measures of
   the overall price level are fixed-weight price indexes. Such indexes are weighted averages of
   various prices, in which the weights assigned to the prices do not change with the passage
   of time. The consumer price index is a weighted average of the prices of goods and services bought by a typical U.S. consumer. The producer price index is a weighted average of
   the prices of goods that a representative business purchases from other firms.

QUESTIONS AND PROBLEMS

1. In your own words, define GDP. Carefully distinguish between GDP and GNP.
2. Using the following data ($ billions) for a given year and assuming that GDP equals

GNP, calculate (a) gross domestic product, (b) national income, (c) net national product, (d) indirect business taxes:

Consumption spending:	$3,500	Wages and salaries:	$4,500
Net interest:	500	Depreciation:	50
Rental income	150	Government spending:	1,500
Investment spending	1,250	Net export spending:	−150
Profits:	750		

3. Why should the income approach and the product approach to computing GDP both yield the same value? Explain.

4. Explain, in your own words, the distinction between nominal GDP and real GDP.

5. What does the merchandise trade balance measure? Why is it not necessarily a good indicator of a nation's trade position vis-à-vis other countries if the nation has relatively large service-oriented industries?

6. Explain, in your own words, why a nation's overall balance of payments must equal zero.

7. Consider a two-good economy. In 1998, firms in this economy produced 25 units of good X, which sold at a market price of $4 per unit, and 15 units of good Y, which sold at a market price of $3 per unit. In 1999, the economy produced the same amounts of both X and Y, but the price of good X rose to $5 per unit, and the price of good Y increased to $4 per unit. What were the values of nominal GDP in 1998 and 1999? If 1998 is the base year, what were the values of real GDP in 1998 and 1999?

8. Using your answers from question 7 and assuming again that 1998 is the base year, what is the value of the GDP price deflator for 1998? What is the approximate value (rounded to the nearest hundredth) of the GDP price deflator for 1999? What is the approximate value (rounded to the nearest percentage point) of inflation between 1998 and 1999?

9. Suppose that the GDP deflator for the year considered in question 2 has a value of 1.25. Based on your answer to part (a) in question 2, what is real GDP for this year?

10. In your own words, explain why the consumer price index may overstate the average annual inflation rate for the United States.

 CYBERTUTOR EXERCISES

1. Figure 2–3 in the text indicates that U.S. nominal GDP has grown rapidly over the past five years. Compare the U.S. experience with that of Japan and France. Are they similar? Does this rapid growth in nominal GDP necessarily mean that Europeans and Americans are wealthier?

2. Figure 2–4 in the text shows the GDP deflator. Create a new variable called Real GDP-1 by using the GDP deflator and nominal GDP. Plot Real GDP-1 and nominal GDP over time. Why do the curves cross? What does this graph tell us about the relationship between

In the top-left margin, handwritten calculations:

NI
4500
500
150
750
5900   50
5950
5950

real and nominal GDP? Does a sharp increase in nominal GDP necessarily mean that people have become much wealthier?

3. Consider Figure 2–5 in the text. Inflation is the percentage change in the price index, but the inflation rate is sensitive to the price index that is used. Two common price indices are the GDP Deflator and the CPI. Use CyberTutor to determine which price index results in higher average inflation rates. Why do you think this is so?

ON-LINE APPLICATION

To view the most current information concerning the consumer price index (CPI), take a look at the homepage of the Bureau of Labor Statistics. As noted in this chapter, the CPI is a fixed-weight index measure of the U.S. price level.

Internet URL: http://stats.bls.gov:80/eag/table/html

Title: **Bureau of Labor Statistics: Economy at a Glance**

Navigation: Begin at the homepage of the Bureau of Labor Statistics (http://stats.bls.gov).

Application: Perform the indicated operations, and answer the following questions:

1. On the Bureau of Labor Statistics homepage, click on *Keyword Search of BLS Web Pages* and key in "CPI" (within the dialog box). Then click on *Consumer Price Indexes Home Page*. Under the heading "CPI Fact Sheets," click on *How to Use the Consumer Price Index for Escalation*. Read the material at this location. Based on this discussion, what exactly does the CPI measure?

2. Return to the BLS homepage, and click on *Economy at a Glance*. Then scan down to "Prices," and click on the graph box for *Consumer Price Index*. Take a look at both the graph box and the tabular summary. How much does the CPI appear to vary from year to year? Has it varied much in the most recent year?

SELECTED REFERENCES AND FURTHER READING

Clayton, Gary E., and Martin Gerhard Giesbrecht. *A Guide to Everyday Economic Statistics.* New York: McGraw-Hill, 1995.

Council of Economic Advisers. *Economic Report of the President.* Washington, D.C.: U.S. Government Printing Office, February 1997.

Council of Economic Advisers, *Economic Indicators.* Washington, D.C.: U.S. Government Printing Office, various issues.

International Monetary Fund. *World Economic Outlook.* Washington, D.C.: October 1996.

U.S. Department of Commerce. *Survey of Current Business.* Washington, D.C.: various issues.

CLASSICAL AND TRADITIONAL MACROECONOMIC THEORY

The Self-Adjusting Economy—

CLASSICAL MACROECONOMIC THEORY

FUNDAMENTAL ISSUES

1. What are the key assumptions of classical macroeconomic theory?

2. How are the aggregate levels of labor employment and real output of goods and services determined in the classical model?

3. What factors determine the price level in the classical framework, and how does the classical model explain persistent inflation?

4. How are interest rates determined in the classical theory?

5. How is the value of a nation's currency determined in the classical model?

As a manager of a small group in your company, you are expected to recommend salary increases for your subordinates at a specific time each year. In keeping with company guidelines, you are using a software program that rates each employee according to a set of criteria involving twenty-two separate factors. With the help of the software program, you recommend salary increases ranging from 1 percent to more than 10 percent for each of your subordinates.

Upper management agrees with all of your recommendations. You therefore pass out notices to everyone in your group. Those who received the highest per-

centage of increases are, of course, the happiest. But what if your employees anticipate a 5 percent rate of inflation for the coming twelve-month period? Won't those who received raises of less than 5 percent realize that their real compensation is falling? Won't those who received, say, a 6 percent raise realize that their real standard of living may go up by only 1 percent (barring any extra taxes they might have to pay)?

If the answer is yes, then your employees cannot be fooled by nominal salary increases that do not fully reflect inflation. If the answer is no, then your employees can be fooled, and they are suffering from what is known as money illusion.

The concept of money illusion is key to understanding the classical model of how our macroeconomy works. The classical model was the first systematic and rigorous attempt to explain the determinants of macroeconomic variables such as aggregate employment, real GDP, and the price level. Classical macroeconomics was the predominant school of thought from the 1770s until the 1930s, and contributors to this framework of analysis included such intellectual giants as Adam Smith (1723–1790), David Hume (1711–1776), and David Ricardo (1772–1823).

In this chapter you will find out that the classical economists generally assumed that the workers in the above situation could not be fooled—that they would understand the relationship between the rate of inflation and their real salary increases. You will also learn that the classical economists made several other important assumptions about the economy. Perhaps most important, they assumed that prices of goods and services and factors of production are sufficiently flexible to help the economy "self-adjust" in response to changing circumstances.

KEY CLASSICAL ASSUMPTIONS

Three fundamental assumptions provide a foundation for the classical macroeconomic theory:

1. Workers, consumers, and entrepreneurs are motivated by rational self-interest.
2. People do not experience *money illusion.*
3. Pure competition prevails in the markets for goods and services and for factors of production.

Let's consider each of these assumptions in turn.

Rational Self-Interest

A key tenet of the classical theory is that both households and businesspersons desire to maximize their total satisfaction. This means that in their everyday roles as workers and consumers, members of each household seek to attain the highest possible overall well-being, or utility. Thus, in the classical system, households are *utility maximizers.*

Businesses operate to produce the highest net income for the household entrepreneurs who own them. The net income of any business is its profit flow. Consequently, in the classical theory, businesses are *profit maximizers.*

Absence of Money Illusion

Consider the following example. A college student has a part-time job at a local fast-food establishment. The manager offers to increase her hourly wage rate from $5.00 per hour to $5.50 per hour, or by 10 percent. At the same time, however, prices of the goods and services that the student purchases have also risen by 10 percent, largely because of hefty increases in college tuition and fees. Thus, given the 10 percent rise in her living costs, the student is no better off in real terms than she was before her wage increase.

Suppose, though, that the student nevertheless feels so good about the 10 percent increase in her nominal wages that she offers to work more hours. If she does, she is exhibiting **money illusion.** This is the inclination for a household or business to alter desired trades of goods, services, or factors of production simply because of *nominal* price changes.

MONEY ILLUSION A situation that exists when economic agents change their behavior in response to changes in nominal values, even though real (adjusted for the price level) values have not changed.

A central hypothesis of classical theory is that people do not experience such money illusion. Instead, when they make decisions about how much to produce, sell, or purchase, they pay attention only to *real* variables, which have been adjusted for the price level. In the absence of changes in real quantities, individuals and businesses will not change their market transactions.

Pure Competition

Classical economists recognize that monopoly businesses, such as electric utilities, exist. Nevertheless, they contend that the predominant mode of interaction among business firms in the aggregate economy is **pure competition.** Under pure competition, there are sufficiently large numbers of buyers and sellers of a typical good, service, or factor of production that no single buyer or seller can affect the market price of the good, service, or factor of production.

PURE COMPETITION A situation in which there are large numbers of buyers and sellers in a market for a good, service, or factor of production and in which no single buyer or seller can affect the market price.

As a result, each buyer and seller is a *price taker.* The buyer or seller takes market prices as "given" and incapable of change by means of purchases or sales initiated by the buyer or seller in isolation. Nonetheless, collective—though typically uncoordinated—purchases or sales of a good, service, or factor of production can change market prices. In other words, the forces of demand and supply determine market prices. These prices, in turn, adjust flexibly to variations in demand or supply.

FUNDAMENTAL ISSUE #1

What are the key assumptions of classical macroeconomic theory?
The classical macroeconomic model is based on the idea that people pursue their own self-interest. It also presumes that people do not experience money illusion, meaning that people recognize that they are no better off with higher nominal wages if prices also are higher. The third key assumption of the classical model is that there is pure competition throughout the economy, meaning that there are a large number of buyers and sellers of goods and services who individually cannot influence market prices.

THE CLASSICAL THEORY OF
PRODUCTION AND EMPLOYMENT

Any macroeconomic theory must provide an explanation of how many goods and services businesses produce and how many units of factors of production, such as labor, they utilize. The classical theory is no exception. Indeed, as you will discover in later chapters, the classical theory of production and employment is the benchmark, or starting point of comparison, for all other macroeconomic theories. Consequently, understanding this topic is crucial to comprehending the subject as a whole.

The Production Function

PRODUCTION FUNCTION A relationship between possible quantities of factors of production, such as labor services, and the amount of output of goods and services that firms can produce with current technology.

The aggregate **production function** is a relationship between the quantities of factors of production—labor, capital, land, and entrepreneurship—employed by all firms in the economy and the total production of real output by those firms, given the technology currently available. In this chapter we shall focus on the *short run,* which is a time horizon short enough that firms cannot vary all factors of production. We shall consider the *long run,* in which firms can adjust the amounts of all factors of production, in our discussion of economic growth in Chapter 4.

ON THE WEB
Visit the U.S. Department of Commerce at:
http://www.doc.gov

Short-Run Production   In the short run firms cannot adjust the amounts of capital, land, and entrepreneurship. The only variable factor of production for firms is the quantity of labor that they employ on an hourly and weekly basis, which we denote N.

There are three measures of the amount of labor that firms employ. One measure is simply the number of people employed during a given time interval. An alternative measure is the total time worked by all people employed by firms, which is just the total hours of work by all employees during a period. Finally, we can measure employment via a combination of these first two measures, known as *person-hours*.

In the short run firms use labor together with their fixed quantities of other productive factors to produce output. Some firms, such as fast-food restaurants, may use very simple production processes. Others, such as microcomputer manufacturers, may assemble components manufactured at remote points around the world. The aggregate production function sums up the result of these processes as the total quantity of real output of goods and services, y, that results from the use of the total quantity of labor, N, by firms:

$$y = F(N).$$

This expression says that the aggregate amount of real output is a *function* of the amount of labor employed by all firms in the economy.

Panel (a) of Figure 3–1 displays a sample aggregate production function, $F(N)$. Any point along this function tells us how much real output firms can produce for a given quantity of labor employed. For instance, if firms employ an amount of labor equal to N_1, their total output of goods and services, or real GDP, is equal to y_1. If firms employ a larger quantity of labor, N_2, then naturally they are able to produce a larger amount of real output. Real GDP then would be at a higher level, y_2.

The production function in panel (a) of Figure 3–1 is *concave*, meaning that it is bowed downward. This means that the production function's *slope*—the change in output resulting from a change in employment, or "rise" divided by "run"—varies along the function. To see this, note that the slope of the function at the employment level N_1 is given by the slope of the line tangent to the function at this point, or $\Delta y_1/\Delta N$, where the symbol Δ denotes a change in a quantity. But at the higher employment level N_2, the same change in employment, ΔN, yields a smaller change in output, Δy_2. This means that the slope of the production function at the employment level N_2, which is equal to $\Delta y_2/\Delta N$, must be smaller than the slope of the production function at the employment level N_1.

The Marginal Product of Labor   The decline in the slope of the production function as the amount of labor employed by firms rises is consistent with the **law of diminishing marginal returns.** This law states that eventually the additional output produced by an additional unit of labor declines as more units of labor are employed by firms. By definition, the slope of the production function, $\Delta y/\Delta N$, is the additional amount of output that firms can produce by employing an additional unit of labor. This is the **marginal product of labor,** or MP_N. In other words, $MP_N \equiv \Delta y/\Delta N$, or the slope of the production function at a given quantity of labor. (The three-barred equals sign $\equiv$ means that a relationship is true by definition; it is an identity.)

Panel (b) of Figure 3–1 graphs the marginal product of labor. At the employment level N_1, the marginal product of labor is equal to $\Delta y_1/\Delta N$, or the slope of the production function at this employment level. The value of this slope is assumed to equal

LAW OF DIMINISHING MARGINAL RETURNS The law that states that each successive addition of a unit of a factor of production, such as labor, eventually produces a smaller gain in real output produced, other factors holding constant.

MARGINAL PRODUCT OF LABOR The change in total output resulting from a one-unit increase in the quantity of labor employed in production.

FIGURE 3–1 | **THE AGGREGATE PRODUCTION FUNCTION AND THE MARGINAL-PRODUCT-OF-LABOR (MP_N) SCHEDULE**

Given a fixed stock of capital and a current state of technology, higher levels of labor employment are necessary to achieve increased production of real output. The bowed, or concave, shape of the production function in panel (a) reflects the law of diminishing marginal returns, which states that total output increases at a decreasing rate for each additional one-unit rise in employment of labor. Consequently, as shown in panel (b), the marginal product of labor declines as employment rises.

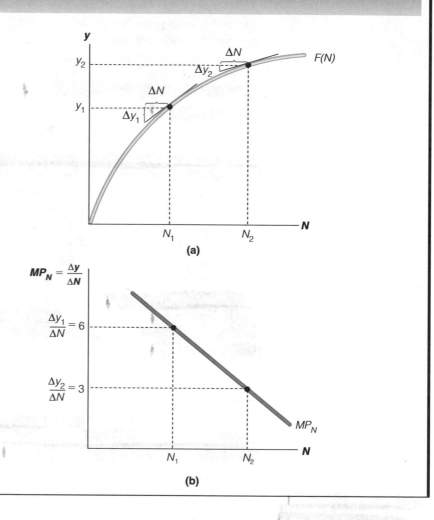

(a)

(b)

6. If total employment rises to N_2, then the slope of the production function declines to $\Delta y_2/\Delta N$, which is assumed to equal 3; thus the marginal product of labor is lower at this higher employment level.

The employment levels N_1 and N_2 are just two examples, of course. At employment levels less than N_1, the marginal product of labor would be larger than $\Delta y_1/\Delta N$. At employment levels greater than N_2, the marginal product of labor would be smaller than $\Delta y_2/\Delta N$. At successively greater employment levels between N_1 and N_2, the marginal product of labor would decline. Consequently, there is a downward-sloping set of values for the marginal product of labor that corresponds to the production function shown in panel (a) of Figure 3–1. This is the *marginal-product-of-labor schedule*, or MP_N *schedule,* displayed in panel (b). The MP_N schedule shows the marginal product of labor, or slope of the production function, at any given quantity of labor. Its downward slope reflects the law of diminishing marginal returns.

The Demand for Labor

Because the marginal product of labor measures how much more output an additional unit of labor produces, it is crucial to any firm's decision about how much labor to employ. Another key factor that a firm must consider, of course, is the expense that it must incur by employing a unit of labor. To maximize its profits, a firm must balance the revenue gain from the sale of the additional production generated by another unit of labor against the cost of hiring that labor unit.

A Firm's Demand for Labor   A profit-maximizing firm produces output to the point at which its marginal revenue (MR), or additional revenue stemming from production and sale of an additional unit of output, equals its marginal cost (MC), or additional production cost that it incurs in this endeavor. If MR exceeds MC at a given level of production, then the firm would earn a positive net profit from the last unit of production. This would encourage the firm to produce more units. If MC exceeds MR, however, then the firm's net profit on the last unit produced would be negative, which would induce the firm to cut back on its production. Consequently, when $MR = MC$, the firm has produced the output level that ensures positive net profits for every unit of production up to the last unit produced. Thus, the firm has maximized its profit on its total output production.

Recall that a central hypothesis of the classical theory is that pure competition prevails, so prices are market determined. Because no single firm can affect the market price, each unit of output that the firm produces by definition yields the same marginal revenue, which is the market price. Therefore, each purely competitive, profit-maximizing firm produces output up to the point at which

$$MR \equiv P = MC.$$

In words, a purely competitive firm produces output to the point at which price equals marginal cost.

In the short run, however, a firm's marginal cost depends on the expense that it incurs by employing its single variable factor of production, labor. The firm's labor expense is the money wage rate that it pays a unit of labor, denoted by W and measured in dollars per labor unit. For instance, suppose that the current market wage rate is $W_1 = \$30$ per unit of labor. A firm's marginal cost is measured in dollars spent per unit of output produced. Suppose that the marginal product of labor at the firm's current output level is $MP_N = \Delta y/\Delta N = 3$ units of output per unit of labor. Then, to calculate the firm's marginal cost of producing output at the money wage $W_1 = \$30$ per unit of labor, we divide W_1 by MP_N, which gives $MC = (\$30$ per unit of labor)/(3 units of output per unit of labor) $= \$10$ per unit of output. Consequently, marginal cost by definition is equal to W/MP_N.

This means that we can rewrite a purely competitive firm's profit-maximizing condition, $P = MC$, as

$$P = W/MP_N.$$

Now, if we multiply both sides of this equation by MP_N, we get

$$P \times MP_N = (W/MP_N) \times MP_N = W.$$

This tells us that another way to express the firm's profit-maximizing condition is

$$W = P \times MP_N.$$

This is the firm's profit-maximizing rule for employing labor. It says that a purely competitive firm that seeks to maximize its profit should employ labor to the point at which the money wage that the firm pays each unit of labor is equal to the price it receives for each unit of output that labor produces times the marginal product of labor. The price per unit of output times the marginal product of labor is called the **value of the marginal product of labor,** or $VMP_N = P \times MP_N$. For instance, if the market price of a firm's output is $5 per unit of output and the marginal product of labor is 6 units of output per unit of labor, then the value of labor's marginal product is equal to the product of these two figures, or $30 per unit of labor.

Panel (a) of Figure 3–2 shows how the value of the marginal product of labor typically varies with the amount of labor employed by a firm. We obtain this schedule by multiplying the firm's output price, P, times the MP_N schedule in panel (b) of Figure 3–1. The result is another downward-sloping schedule, called the *value-of-marginal-product-of-labor schedule,* or VMP_N schedule.

As panel (a) of Figure 3–2 indicates, if the market wage that the firm must pay each unit of labor it employs is $W_1 = \$30$, then the firm employs labor to the point at which the value of labor's marginal product is equal to $30 per unit of labor, which in the figure implies employment level N_1. At a lower wage rate of $W_2 = \$15$ per unit of labor, however, the firm requires a smaller value of marginal product to maximize its profit, so it *increases* the amount of labor it employs, to the quantity of labor N_2. A fall in the market wage rate causes the firm to increase the quantity of labor it demands. Hence, the firm decides how many units of labor it desires to employ by moving along its VMP_N schedule. This leads to the following important conclusion:

> The VMP_N schedule for a purely competitive firm is that firm's labor demand schedule showing how many units of labor, N, the firm demands at any given money wage, W.

Note that we can rearrange the firm's profit-maximizing condition, $W = P \times MP_N$, by dividing both sides of the condition by P, which yields the expression

$$W/P = MP_N.$$

This expression says that another way of stating the firm's profit-maximizing condition is that the firm should hire labor to the point at which W/P, the *real* wage

VALUE OF THE MARGINAL PRODUCT OF LABOR The marginal product of labor times the price of output.

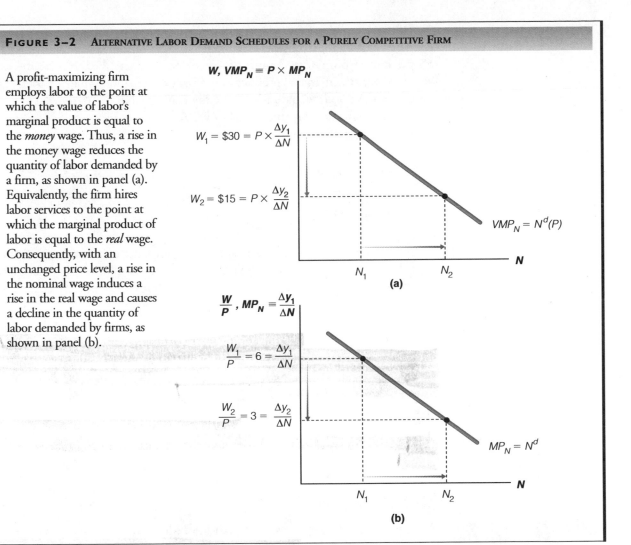

FIGURE 3–2   ALTERNATIVE LABOR DEMAND SCHEDULES FOR A PURELY COMPETITIVE FIRM

A profit-maximizing firm employs labor to the point at which the value of labor's marginal product is equal to the *money* wage. Thus, a rise in the money wage reduces the quantity of labor demanded by a firm, as shown in panel (a). Equivalently, the firm hires labor services to the point at which the marginal product of labor is equal to the *real* wage. Consequently, with an unchanged price level, a rise in the nominal wage induces a rise in the real wage and causes a decline in the quantity of labor demanded by firms, as shown in panel (b).

that the firm pays, is equal to the marginal product of labor. Panel (b) of Figure 3–2 illustrates this condition for two examples. One example is for the money wage W_1 = $30 per unit of labor. Because the price of the firm's output, P, is $5 per unit, the real value of this money wage is $30 per unit of labor divided by $5 per unit of output, or 6 units of output per unit of labor. In other words, the $30 wage that the firm pays each unit of labor is equivalent to a payment of 6 units of the firm's output. This is the real wage that the firm pays. To maximize its profit, the firm therefore employs labor to the point at which the marginal product of labor is equal to 6 units of output per unit of labor and employs a total of N_1 units of labor. Thus the firm pays the worker an amount equal to the real value of the labor that the worker provides the firm.

If the market wage rate were to fall to $W_2 = \$15$ per unit of labor, then the real wage paid by the firm would decline to $15 per unit of labor divided by $P = \$5$ per unit of output, or 3 units of output per unit of labor. Hence, the firm would require the marginal product of the last unit of labor employed to equal 3 units of output, so it would raise its employment of labor to N_2 units. Thus, the firm would demand more units of labor when the real market wage declines. We have come to another important conclusion:

> The MP_N schedule for a purely competitive firm is that firm's labor demand schedule. This schedule shows how many units of labor, N, the firm demands at any given real wage, W/P.

In both panels of Figure 3–2, the same money wage decline, from $W_1 = \$30$ per unit of labor to $W_2 = \$15$ per unit of labor, leads to the same increase in desired labor employment by the firm. We may conclude that both schedules depict the same choices by the firm. This makes sense, because in constructing both labor demand schedules, we have worked with the same, single profit-maximizing condition for a purely competitive firm. The only distinction is that the VMP_N schedule in panel (a) is the labor demand schedule if we measure the nominal wage as the factor price of labor, whereas the MP_N schedule in panel (b) is the labor demand schedule if we measure the real wage as the factor price of labor. The labor demand schedule graphed against the money wage, W, in panel (a) depends on the output price P, so we label it $N^d(P)$ to recognize this dependence. The labor demand schedule graphed against the real wage W/P in panel (b) does not depend on the value of P, and so we simply label it N^d.

The Supply of Labor

ON THE WEB
Visit the U.S. Department of Labor at:
http://www.dol.gov

All of us strive to find employment in a field in which we can do work that gives us satisfaction. Nevertheless, the time that we devote to work is time that we could otherwise have devoted to leisure activities that we would enjoy. The value we place on leisure time thereby represents an *opportunity cost* that we incur when we devote our time to work. This is why firms must pay us wages to induce us to devote large chunks of our days to work-related activities.

Measuring Labor Compensation: The Real Wage   Classical theorists focus on the *real wage* as the relevant measure of the compensation that laborers receive for time that they spend at work. The reason is that the real wage gives the purchasing power of a worker's earnings.

To see why this is true, consider a simple example. During a full year, an individual works 40 hours per week and earns a weekly money wage of $500. Over the course of the year, however, the level of prices of goods and services that the person consumes *doubles*. By the end of the year, therefore, the $500 weekly wage is worth

POLICY NOTEBOOK
Are Real Wages in America Truly Stagnant?

A major policy debate over real wages has occurred throughout the 1990s. Specifically, officially measured real wages appear to have stagnated since about 1973 or, at best, to have risen very little on a compounded growth basis. Numerous studies have appeared purporting to show that the gap between the "haves" and the "have-nots" in the United States has widened during the 1990s. Additionally, some researchers and politicians have argued that increasing foreign competition has kept real wages in the United States from rising.

Some recent research into total worker compensation, per capita personal income, and per capita real personal consumption expenditures reveals a different story. Look at Figure 3–3. One of the reasons that total compensation is so much higher than average hourly wages is that the latter do not include employee benefits such as retirement contributions, vacations, sick leave, family leave, and health care.

When rents, interest, profits, and net government transfers (transfers minus taxes paid) per person are considered, growth is even more impressive. The highest curve in Figure 3–3 shows that per capita personal income has increased at about 1.4 percent annually since 1973.

Finally, what probably matters most for people's well-being is their per capita real personal consumption expenditures. For the two decades starting in 1973, that variable increased by 1.7 percent per year. While officially measured hourly real wages have fallen slightly since 1973, real total compensation and per capita real personal income have grown steadily.

FOR CRITICAL ANALYSIS:
What is the difference between real total compensation and per capita real personal income?

FIGURE 3–3   REAL WAGES AND INCOMES

Real wages appear to have stagnated since the early 1970s. Total labor compensation, however, also includes the value of additional employee benefits. In addition, personal income includes rents, interest, profits, and net governmental transfers. These measures of per capita incomes indicate continued growth since the 1970s.

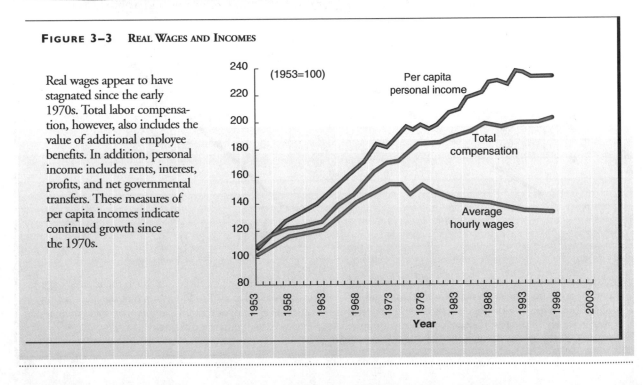

half as much to the worker as it was at the beginning of the year. Consequently, it is not the money wage alone that matters to a worker. What matters is how many goods and services that money wage can be used to buy. This is why the real wage is the appropriate measure of a worker's compensation for labor time (see on page 63 Policy Notebook: *Are Real Wages in America Truly Stagnant?*).

The Labor Supply Schedule   Holding all other factors unchanged, the only way that an individual may be induced to give up some leisure time and work more hours is if the real wage increases. Because the real wage is equal to the money wage divided by the price level, W/P, there are two ways that the real wage can rise. One is if the money wage rises relative to the price level; the other is if the price level falls relative to the money wage.

Figure 3–4 illustrates the effect on an individual's labor supply of a rise in the money wage from an initial value W_1 to a higher value W_2, with the price level unchanged at P_1. As panel (a) shows, this causes the real wage to increase, and the quantity of labor supplied also increases from N_1 to N_2 as workers respond to the higher real wage by giving up leisure time to work. Economists call this the *substitution effect* stemming from a rise in the real wage, because workers substitute labor for leisure. Note that at sufficiently high real wages, theoretically an *income effect* could arise: workers' incomes could be high enough that they would prefer to work

---

FIGURE 3–4   THE LABOR-SUPPLY EFFECTS OF A RISE IN THE MONEY WAGE (NOMINAL)

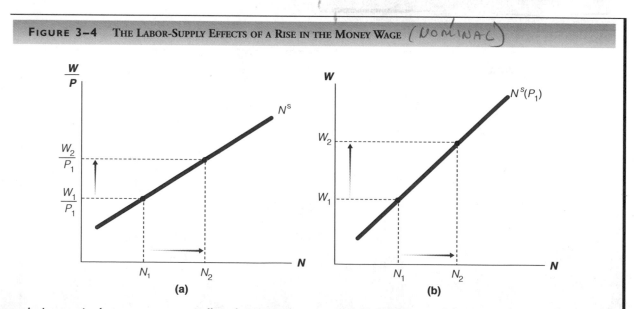

An increase in the money wage typically induces a worker to give up leisure time to work. Hence, workers supply more labor as the money wage rises relative to the price level, as shown in panel (a). Therefore the labor supply schedule slopes upward against the real wage. Alternatively, panel (b) displays this effect of a rise in the money wage for a given price level and indicates that the labor supply schedule also slopes upward if the money wage alone is measured along the vertical axis.

less so that they could enjoy more leisure time. Most evidence indicates, however, that the substitution effect predominates in the aggregate. Consequently, the labor supply schedule, N^s, typically slopes upward, as in the figure.

Panel (b) of Figure 3–4 shows another depiction of the labor supply schedule. Here, only the money wage appears on the vertical axis. Again, a rise in the money wage from W_1 to W_2 causes the amount of labor that workers supply to rise from N_1 to N_2. As panel (b) shows, however, this occurs only because the price level has remained unchanged at P_1, so we label this version of labor supply $N^s(P_1)$. In both panels, a rise in the money wage with unchanged prices causes a rightward *movement along* the labor supply schedule.

Figure 3–5 examines the labor supply effect of a decline in the price level. Panel (a) shows that a fall in the price level, from an initial value P_1 to a lower level P_2, increases the real wage that an individual earns. The effect is the same as if the money wage had risen with prices unchanged: Individuals work more hours, so the quantity of labor supplied increases from N_1 to N_2.

Panel (b) illustrates the effect of a price-level decrease when we measure only the money wage on the vertical axis of a labor supply diagram. Again the money wage remains unchanged. Nevertheless, the fall in the price level causes the real wage to increase, inducing individuals to work more hours and increase the quantity of labor

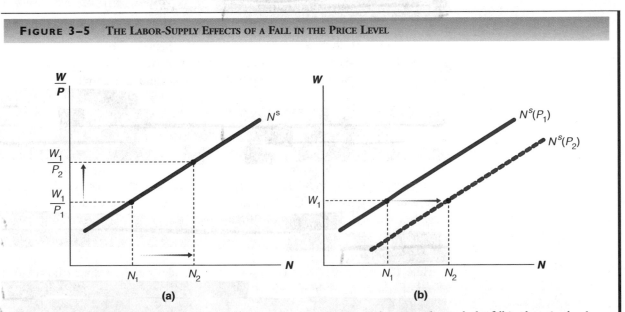

FIGURE 3–5   THE LABOR-SUPPLY EFFECTS OF A FALL IN THE PRICE LEVEL

A reduction in the price level, from P_1 to P_2, with the money wage unchanged, causes the real wage to rise. As a result, workers choose to supply more labor services, as shown in panel (a). Equivalently, panel (b) shows that with the nominal wage unchanged, the fall in the price level induces workers to increase their supply of labor services, so the labor supply schedule graphed against the money wage alone must shift rightward.

supplied from N_1 to N_2. Consequently, the labor supply schedule in panel (b) *shifts to the right* as a result of the decline in the price level.

Labor-Market Equilibrium and Aggregate Supply

The total demand for labor is the sum of the labor demand schedules for all the firms in the economy. Likewise, the total supply of labor is the sum of the labor supply schedules of all people in the economy who participate in the labor force. In the classical system, the interactions among firms and workers through the forces of demand and supply in the labor market determine the equilibrium money wage and the equilibrium level of employment. In addition, the aggregate production function then yields the aggregate level of real output produced in the economy.

The Price Level, Employment, and Real Output   Figure 3–6 (see next page) depicts the determination of wages, employment, and output in the classical theory. Panels (a) and (b) are alternative illustrations of equilibrium in the labor market. In both panels, an initial equilibrium *money* wage, W_1, arises at which the quantity of labor demanded by firms is equal to the quantity of labor supplied by workers, *given* the prevailing price level, P_1. This equilibrium quantity of labor demanded and supplied is the equilibrium employment level, N_1. The aggregate production function in panel (c) then indicates the equilibrium level of real output, y_1, that is produced with this aggregate amount of labor employed. Finally, panel (d) shows that this yields a price level and real output combination of P_1 and y_1.

The price level ultimately is determined in the aggregate market for goods and services. Nonetheless, we can consider the effects of changes in the price level on money wages, employment, and output via a simple, and rather extreme, example in which the price level doubles from P_1 to $2P_1$. In panel (a), this doubling of the price level causes the real wage, which is measured along the vertical axis, to decline by a factor of two, or to half its original value. The result is an excess quantity of labor demanded, because firms would like to hire more workers at the reduced real wage, but individuals are less willing to supply labor to firms. Firms begin to bid up the money wage to induce individuals to supply more labor, and ultimately the real wage returns to its original level. This happens, however, only after the equilibrium money wage has doubled. Consequently, the end result in response to the doubling of the price level is a doubling of the money wage and no change in the equilibrium employment level.

Panel (b) of Figure 3–6 provides an alternative illustration of these labor-market effects of a doubling of the price level. When the price level doubles, so does the value of marginal product at all firms in the economy. Therefore, labor demand increases, as shown by the rightward shift of the labor demand schedule. At the same time, however, workers perceive that the purchasing power of the money wage is half its previous level, inducing them to reduce their supply of labor. Hence, the labor supply schedule shifts leftward. The result, as in panel (a), is a doubling of the equilib-

FIGURE 3–6 THE EFFECTS OF A DOUBLING OF THE PRICE LEVEL ON THE EQUILIBRIUM MONEY WAGE, EMPLOYMENT, AND REAL OUTPUT

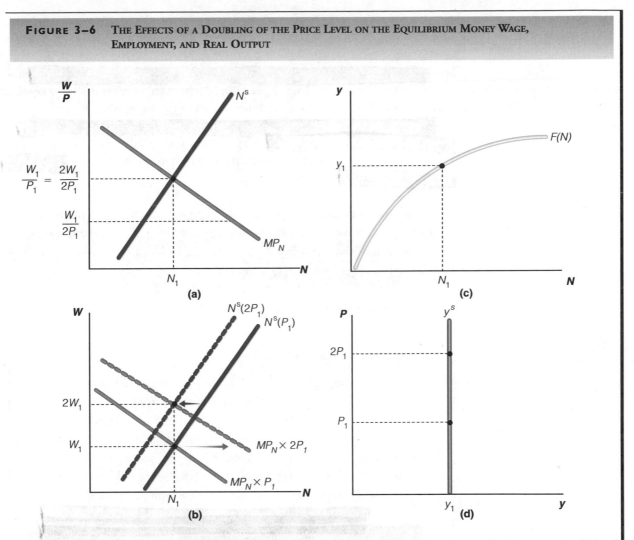

If the price level doubles, then the real wage falls to half its original level in panel (a). At the lower real wage, there is an excess quantity of labor demanded. The money wage is bid upward until labor market equilibrium is reattained. Equivalently, in panel (b) the doubling of the price level doubles the value of the marginal product of labor, and so the demand for labor rises. Workers, however, realize that the real wage has declined and reduce their supply of labor. On net, in both panels (a) and (b), equilibrium employment is unchanged. Thus equilibrium output also is unchanged, as shown in panel (c). As a result, the increase in the price level has no effect on the production of real output, implying that the aggregate supply schedule in panel (d) is vertical.

rium money wage. Again, equilibrium employment is unaffected by the rise in the price level.

The Classical Aggregate Supply Schedule   Equilibrium employment does not change when the price level doubles, so panel (c) in Figure 3–6 indicates no change

AGGREGATE SUPPLY SCHEDULE (y^s)
Combinations of various price levels and levels of real output that maintain equilibrium in the market for labor services.

in real output. In panel (d), however, there is a new price level-real output combination, $2P_1$ and y_1. This combination, along with the original combination P_1 and y_1, lies along a schedule of price level-real output combinations that is vertical, meaning that any given change in the price level would leave real output unchanged. This vertical schedule is the classical **aggregate supply schedule,** which is the set of combinations of prices and real output at which the labor market is in equilibrium.

Because the aggregate supply schedule is vertical, we can say that the level of real output is "supply determined." Most economists credit Jean Baptiste Say (1767–1832) with first emphasizing this point, which led to the dictum, "Supply creates its own demand." That is:

> **No matter what shape the economy's demand schedule might take, the classical theory of aggregate supply implies that equilibrium real output is determined solely by factors that influence the position of the vertical aggregate supply schedule.**

These factors are discussed in detail in Chapter 4.

FUNDAMENTAL ISSUE #2

How are the aggregate levels of labor employment and real output of goods and services determined in the classical model? The demand for labor stems from the marginal product of labor, which is the slope of the aggregate production function. Equilibrium employment occurs at the real wage at which the quantity of labor demanded by firms equals the quantity of labor supplied by households. Equilibrium output then is determined by the aggregate production function. In the classical model, a change in the price level has no effect on equilibrium employment or output, so the classical aggregate supply schedule is vertical.

MONEY, AGGREGATE DEMAND, AND INFLATION

As we have seen, in the classical system the quantity of real output is determined by the position of the aggregate supply schedule. This feature led to the central classical idea of supply-determined output. Nevertheless, the concept of the aggregate demand for output is crucial to understanding how the price level is determined in the classical theory.

The Demand for Money

As you will learn, the classical economists concluded that the primary factor explaining changes in the price level is variability in the amount of money in circulation, which, in turn, induces variations in aggregate demand. Consequently, a prerequisite to understanding the classical theory of aggregate demand for output is ascertaining how households and businesses decide how much money they desire to hold. Therefore, the classical theory of aggregate demand and price-level determination is developed from a theory of the *demand for money.*

The Functions of Money Although we tend to think of money as coins or dollar bills, the classical economists realized that any item that people are willing to accept in exchange for goods and services is **money.** Modern definitions of money, for instance, include funds that households and businesses hold in accounts in financial institutions such as banks, savings and loan associations, and credit unions.

Money performs four important functions:

1. *Medium of exchange* The fundamental role of money is as a **medium of exchange.** When people trade goods and services, they are willing to accept money in exchange. This saves people from having to engage in **barter,** or the act of exchanging goods and services directly. Barter is a costly process, because it requires locating others willing to exchange items directly. Using money saves on such costs.

2. *Store of value* A second function of money is as a **store of value.** An individual can set money aside for later use in purchasing goods, services, or financial assets. While the funds sit idle, they retain value that the individual can draw upon to make the future purchases. For instance, the individual can hold funds in a checking account for several days and then use the funds to buy groceries as needed.

3. *Unit of account* Money's third function is as a **unit of account.** Households and businesses can value goods and services in terms of money. In addition, people can quote prices of goods and services in money terms. For example, when an individual shops at a U.S. grocery store, the prices of goods are expressed in dollar terms.

4. *Standard of deferred payment* Finally, money also serves as a **standard of deferred payment.** When people reach contractual agreements that require future payments, they specify that the payments will be made with money. Bank loans, for example, specify future dollar repayments.

INTERNET ● SOURCE

What's New with U.S. Money

The U.S. Department of the Treasury—What's New about Your Money
Internet URL: http://www. ustreas.gov/treasury/whatsnew/newcur

Navigation: Start at the U.S. Treasury Department homepage (**http://www. ustreas.gov**). Click on *Search* and key in "currency" within the dialog box. Then click on the subject of your choice to learn about security features of U.S. currency.

MONEY An item that people are willing to accept in exchange for goods and services.

MEDIUM OF EXCHANGE Money's role as a means of payment for goods and services.

BARTER The direct exchange of goods and services.

STORE OF VALUE A function of money in which it is held for future use without loss of value.

UNIT OF ACCOUNT A function of money in which it is used as a measure of the value of goods, services, and financial assets.

STANDARD OF DEFERRED PAYMENT Money's role as a means of valuing future receipts in loan contracts.

The Quantity Theory of Money Although the original classical theorists recognized that money performs these four functions, they viewed money's property as a medium of exchange as the key to explaining why money exists. After all, they reasoned, if money did not function as a medium of exchange, then people could barter goods, services, and financial assets directly. People would not even use money if it did not perform this key function.

For this reason, the classical theory of the demand for money focuses on money's role as a medium of exchange. To understand how much money people desire to hold, the classical economists concentrated on explaining the demand for money for purchases of newly produced goods and services. The transactions-based theory of money demand that they developed is now known as the **quantity theory of money.**

The starting point for the quantity theory of money is the **equation of exchange:**

$$M \times V \equiv P \times y.$$

In the equation of exchange, M is the nominal quantity of money, or the current-dollar value of currency and checking deposits held by the nonbank public. The term V represents the **income velocity of money,** or the average number of times people spend each unit of money on final goods and services per unit of time. Consequently, the left side of the equation of exchange is the value of current-dollar monetary payments for final goods and services. On the right side of the equation, the price level for final goods and services is multiplied by the quantity of output of goods and services. Note, however, that this quantity is also the current-dollar value of monetary payments for final goods and services. Hence both sides of the equation of exchange must be identical. The equation of exchange is thus an accounting definition, or identity. It states that the product of the nominal quantity of money times the average number of times that people use money to buy goods and services ($M \times V$) must equal the market value of the goods and services that people use the money to purchase ($P \times y$).

An economic identity is a truism. It is not a theory of how people behave. The basis of the quantity *theory* of money is the **Cambridge equation,** so named because it was first proposed by Alfred Marshall (1842–1924) and other economists at Cambridge University in England. According to the Cambridge equation:

$$M^d = k \times Y,$$

where M^d denotes the total quantity of money all people in the economy wish to hold and k is a fraction ($0 < k < 1$). The Cambridge equation, therefore, says that people desire to hold some fraction of their nominal income as money. Recall from Chapter 2 that the nominal value of real output, $P \times y$, corresponds to the total level of nominal income, Y. This means that the Cambridge equation may also be written as

$$M^d = k \times P \times y.$$

The idea behind this equation is simple. The fraction k represents the public's desired holdings of nominal money balances relative to total nominal income. For instance, if $k = 0.2$, then people wish to hold 20 percent, or one-fifth, of their nom-

QUANTITY THEORY OF MONEY The theory that people hold money for transactions purposes.

EQUATION OF EXCHANGE An accounting identity that states that the nominal value of all monetary transactions for final goods and services is equal to the nominal value of the output of goods and services purchased.

INCOME VELOCITY OF MONEY The average number of times that each unit of money is used to purchase final goods and services in a given interval.

CAMBRIDGE EQUATION An equation developed by economists at Cambridge University, England, which indicates that individuals desire to hold money in proportion to their nominal income.

inal income as money. They hold this money in anticipation of exchanges they will make during the coming days and weeks. They allocate the rest of their income to immediate consumption of goods and services. It is for this reason that the theory of money demand is directly related to the classical theory of the aggregate demand for real output.

Aggregate Demand and the Price Level

We now have the essential building blocks that we need to see how aggregate demand and the price level are determined in the classical theory.

The Aggregate Demand Schedule   Suppose that the quantity of nominal money balances supplied through the actions of a central bank is equal to an amount M_1. In equilibrium, all individuals in the economy desire to hold this quantity of money balances, so that

$$M^d = M_1.$$

The Cambridge equation then indicates that

$$M_1 = k \times P \times y.$$

If we divide both sides of this equation by $k \times P$, we obtain

$$M_1/(k \times P) = y.$$

Reversing the two sides of this equation leaves us with

$$y^d = M_1/(k \times P).$$

AGGREGATE DEMAND SCHEDULE **(y^d)** Combinations of various price levels and levels of real output for which individuals are satisfied with their consumption of output and their holdings of money.

This is an equation for the economy's **aggregate demand schedule.** The aggregate demand schedule is all combinations of real output and prices for which households are satisfied holding the available quantity of nominal money balances (M_1 in this example), given their average desired ratio of money holdings, k.

Figure 3–7 (on page 72) depicts the aggregate demand schedule. As the equation for the aggregate demand schedule indicates, the quantity of real output of goods and services that people wish to purchase declines as the price level rises. This is so because as the price level increases, so do nominal income earnings. According to the Cambridge equation $M^d = k \times Y = k \times P \times y$, individuals will, as a result, desire to hold more money balances, leaving them with less of their income to purchase real goods and services. As a result, the amount of real output demanded falls from y_1 to y_2 when the price level rises from P_1 to P_2. This is a leftward *movement along* the aggregate demand schedule.

Shifts in the Aggregate Demand Schedule   Two factors can cause the aggregate demand schedule's *position* to change. One is a change in the quantity of money supplied by the government or by a central bank. As we can see by referring to the equation for the schedule, $y^d = M_1/(k \times P)$, a rise in the quantity of money to an

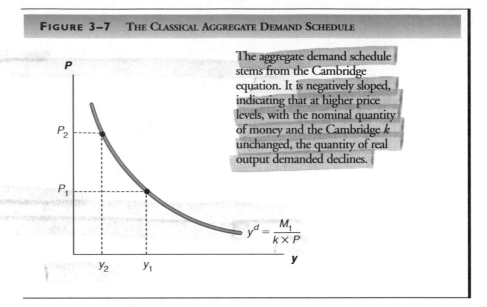

FIGURE 3–7   THE CLASSICAL AGGREGATE DEMAND SCHEDULE

The aggregate demand schedule stems from the Cambridge equation. It is negatively sloped, indicating that at higher price levels, with the nominal quantity of money and the Cambridge k unchanged, the quantity of real output demanded declines.

$$y^d = \frac{M_1}{k \times P}$$

amount larger than M_1 would increase the right side of the equation. This means that nominal purchasing power available to all individuals in the economy would be higher at any given price level, so people would desire to purchase more real goods and services at any given price level. The aggregate demand schedule would shift to the right, and aggregate demand would *rise*. In contrast, a decline in the quantity of money would shift the aggregate demand schedule to the left, and aggregate demand would *fall*.

The other factor that can alter the position of the aggregate demand schedule is a change in k in the Cambridge equation. For example, a technological change might reduce people's desire to demand as much money—for instance, both debit cards and automated teller machines at banks reduce the desire to keep ready cash on hand. In that case, the value of k would decline. People would hold fewer money balances relative to their nominal income, $Y = P \times y$. This would free up income for purchasing goods and services. Referring once more to the equation for the aggregate demand schedule, $y^d = M_1/(k \times P)$, we can see that a decline in k, because it reduces the denominator of the right-hand side of the equation, increases the total purchasing power available to individuals in the economy. Just as an increase in the quantity of money supplied causes a rise, or rightward shift outward, in aggregate demand, so does a decline in the demand for money by individuals. In contrast, a rise in money demand induces a reduction, or leftward shift inward, in aggregate demand.

Price Level Determination   Figure 3–8 displays the aggregate demand and aggregate supply schedules together on the same diagram. This is a diagram of the *market for real output*, as visualized in the classical theory. Equilibrium in this market occurs at the point at which the aggregate demand schedule crosses the aggregate supply

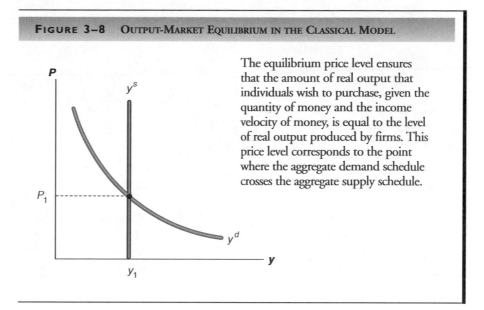

FIGURE 3–8   OUTPUT-MARKET EQUILIBRIUM IN THE CLASSICAL MODEL

The equilibrium price level ensures that the amount of real output that individuals wish to purchase, given the quantity of money and the income velocity of money, is equal to the level of real output produced by firms. This price level corresponds to the point where the aggregate demand schedule crosses the aggregate supply schedule.

schedule. At this point on the aggregate demand schedule, the quantity of output demanded equals the amount of output supplied, y_1. The *equilibrium price level* is P_1. At this price level, individuals are satisfied with their current money holdings and with their current purchases of real goods and services.

Velocity in the Classical Theory   In the output-market equilibrium shown in Figure 3–8, the equation of exchange identity tells us that $M_1 \times V \equiv P_1 \times y_1$. We also know that in equilibrium, the aggregate demand equation is satisfied, so $y_1 = M_1/(k \times P_1)$. If we substitute this value for real output into the equation of exhange identity, we obtain

$$M_1 \times V \equiv P_1 \times M_1/(k \times P_1) = M_1/k.$$

Now, if we divide both sides of this equation by M_1, we obtain

$$V = 1/k.$$

This says that a key assumption of the classical theory is that the income velocity of money, or the average number of times that the quantity of money is used in exchange for real goods and services, is equal to the reciprocal of the k factor of proportionality in the Cambridge equation.

The Cambridge equation assumes that k is constant, so the classical theory of aggregate demand and price-level determination must also implicitly assume that the income velocity of money is constant. Is this a reasonable assumption? Figure 3–9 (on page 74) shows the behavior of the U.S. income velocity of money through 1997. As you can see, it has not been constant over time. The original classical theorists recognized that velocity does change, but they argued that the key factor affecting the ability of their

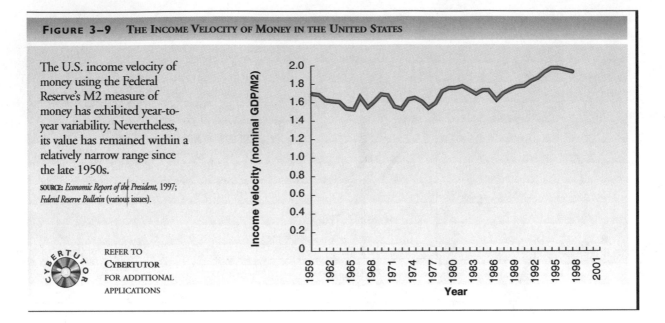

FIGURE 3–9 **THE INCOME VELOCITY OF MONEY IN THE UNITED STATES**

The U.S. income velocity of money using the Federal Reserve's M2 measure of money has exhibited year-to-year variability. Nevertheless, its value has remained within a relatively narrow range since the late 1950s.

SOURCE: *Economic Report of the President*, 1997; *Federal Reserve Bulletin* (various issues).

REFER TO **CYBERTUTOR** FOR ADDITIONAL APPLICATIONS

model to explain current and future price-level movements was the *predictability* of velocity. As long as velocity could be predicted fairly accurately, they argued, their theory would provide a reasonable explanation of price-level movements.

Causes of Inflation

Figure 3–10 shows annual U.S. inflation rates for the past few decades. Clearly, inflation rates have been variable. Just as obvious, however, is that inflation rates have consistently been *positive*. The price level in the United States has *risen* in almost every year (see also Figure 2–6 in Chapter 2).

Supply-Side Inflation?   What causes such persistent inflation? The classical model provides two possible explanations for inflation. One potential rationale is depicted in panel (a) of Figure 3–11. This panel shows a rise in the price level caused by a *decline in aggregate supply.* Hence, one possible reason for persistent inflation would be continual reductions in the production of real output.

The overall rise in real GDP that has taken place during the past few decades, however, tells us that the aggregate supply schedule has actually shifted *rightward,* not leftward, over time. Consequently, the classical model indicates that a *supply-side* explanation for persistent inflation *cannot* be the *true* explanation.

Demand-Side Inflation   According to the classical theory, this leaves only one other explanation for the observation of persistent inflation. This explanation is depicted in panel (b) of Figure 3–11. If aggregate demand increases for a given level of aggregate supply, then the price level must increase. The reason is that, at an initial

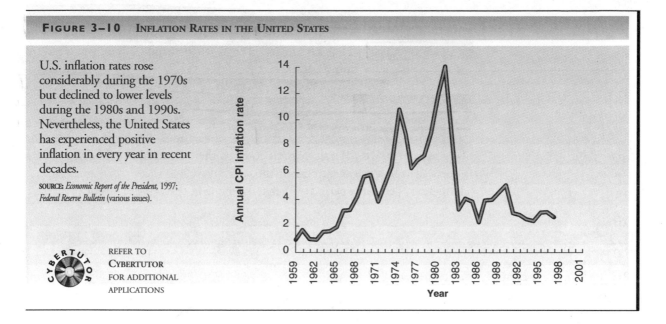

FIGURE 3–10   INFLATION RATES IN THE UNITED STATES

U.S. inflation rates rose considerably during the 1970s but declined to lower levels during the 1980s and 1990s. Nevertheless, the United States has experienced positive inflation in every year in recent decades.

SOURCE: *Economic Report of the President,* 1997; *Federal Reserve Bulletin* (various issues).

REFER TO CYBERTUTOR FOR ADDITIONAL APPLICATIONS

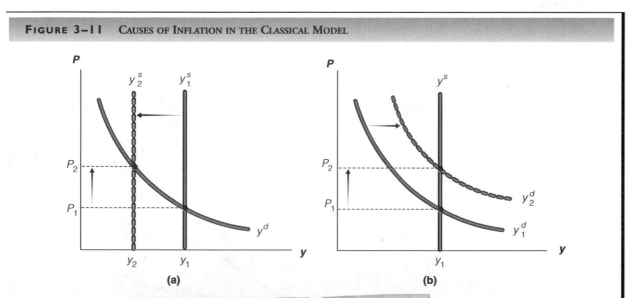

FIGURE 3–11   CAUSES OF INFLATION IN THE CLASSICAL MODEL

As panel (a) indicates, one possible cause of a rise in the price levels is a reduction in aggregate supply, which could result from such factors as a population decline, a fall in labor productivity, or higher wage taxes or government benefits that induce individuals to reduce their supply of labor services to firms. Panel (b) shows another possible cause of inflation in the classical model, which is an increase in aggregate demand owing to a rise in the quantity of money in circulation or a reduction in the value of the Cambridge k.

price level such as P_1, people desire to purchase more real goods and services (y_2) than firms are willing and able to produce (y_1) given the currently available technology and present labor supply. As a result, the rise in aggregate demand leads only to a general rise in the price level, from P_1 to P_2.

Recall that there are two possible reasons why aggregate demand might shift rightward over time. One reason is persistent reductions in the demand for money, which would imply year-to-year declines in the factor of proportionality k in the Cambridge equation. Panel (a) of Figure 3–12 shows the behavior of k since the 1950s. [Recall that k is equal to the reciprocal of velocity, so panel (a) actually plots the reciprocal of the velocity values shown in Figure 3–11.] There have been some periods of general decline in the value of k, but there have

---

FIGURE 3–12 **THE CLASSICAL VIEW OF FACTORS INFLUENCING AGGREGATE DEMAND IN THE UNITED STATES**

In the classical model, aggregate demand increases if either the value of the Cambridge k declines or the quantity of money in circulation rises. Panel (a) shows that the value of the Cambridge k, which is computed using the Federal Reserve's M2 measure of the quantity of money, has trended downward slightly in recent years but otherwise has been relatively stable. In contrast, panel (b) shows that the Federal Reserve's M1 and M2 measures of the quantity of money in circulation have both grown considerably. Thus, classical theory tends to indicate that U.S. inflation may result from excessive growth in the quantity of money.

SOURCE: *Economic Report of the President*, 1997; *Federal Reserve Bulletin* (various issues).

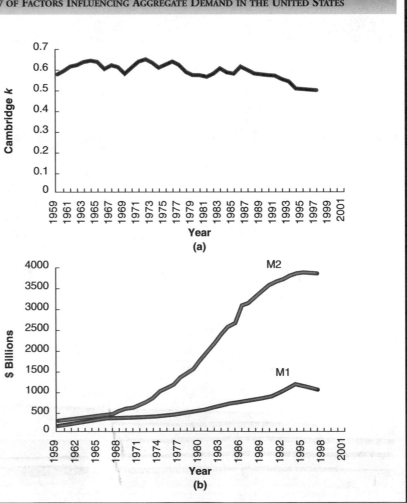

Tells us causes of inflation — Destroys

D continuous increase of money supply (we have no control over money supply)

also been some periods of increase as well. Hence, while changes in *k* undoubtedly have influenced the price level, from a classical perspective this cannot be the main factor explaining U.S. inflation.

The other factor that classical theory indicates could cause persistent increases in aggregate demand is consistent growth of the quantity of money. Panel (b) of Figure 3–12 shows how the Federal Reserve's M1 and M2 measures of the quantity of money have changed since the 1950s. Aside from recent dips in M1, both measures of the amount of money in circulation have shown considerable growth. *This,* most classical theorists argue, is the key explanation for the persistence of inflation. Persistent money growth, they contend, has produced persistent inflation (see Global Notebook on page 78: *Is There a Relationship between Money Supply Growth Rates and Inflation Worldwide?*).

Classical economists emphasize that sustained money growth is inflationary. By itself, money growth can do nothing to influence real output of goods and services. The classical economists call this concept the **neutrality of money.** Changes in money growth are neutral, meaning that such monetary changes have no effects on employment and real output. Variations in money growth can influence only the price level and inflation rates.

NEUTRALITY OF MONEY A key classical conclusion that states that variations in money growth can influence only the price level and year-to-year inflation rates but have no effects on labor employment or the level of real output of goods and services.

FUNDAMENTAL ISSUE #3

What factors determine the price level in the classical framework, and how does the classical model explain persistent inflation? In the classical theory, the equilibrium price level adjusts to equate the quantity of real output demanded with the supply-determined quantity of real output produced. Although leftward shifts in the position of the vertical classical aggregate supply schedule could account for short-term periods of inflation, the classical model indicates that the best explanation for persistent long-term inflation is persistently high growth of the quantity of money.

INTEREST RATES IN THE CLASSICAL MODEL

Every day, publications such as the *Wall Street Journal* and *The Financial Times* keep their readers abreast of interest rates. Such newspapers list interest rates on Treasury securities issued by the U.S. government, corporate bonds and commercial paper issued by firms, certificates of deposit issued by banks, and money, bond, and equity fund shares issued by mutual funds. In addition, these publications commonly run stories speculating about what effects changes in interest rates may have on economic activity.

GLOBAL NOTEBOOK

Is There a Relationship between Money Supply Growth Rates and Inflation Worldwide?

How much evidence is there that the rate of inflation is closely linked to the rate of monetary growth? The answer seems to be quite clear-cut in the long run—there is a correlation between these two variables. Figure 3–13 shows the rate of growth of the money supply (consisting of cash and checking-type account balances) on the horizontal axis (in ratio form). On the vertical axis is the annual rate of inflation (also on a ratio scale). Note that a line drawn through the average of the points would slope upward: Faster monetary growth seems to lead to a higher rate of inflation across different countries.

The relationship between the money supply growth rates and inflation rates is most obvious in countries that are experiencing hyperinflation and try so-called currency reform. In Brazil, for example, prices sometimes have changed at a rate

of over 1000 percent a year. Government authorities in that country have apparently believed that changing the name and the denominations of its currency would make a difference. Since the mid-1980s, Brazilians have had to get used to five different currencies, each with a different name. The latest change in the mid-1990s was a new *real* that was swapped for old *reales* at the rate of 1 to 2,750! But even a crude understanding of the classical theory of the relationship between money and prices tells you that changing the name of the currency will not affect the *rate* of inflation.

FOR CRITICAL ANALYSIS:

Do the data in Figure 3–13 "prove" the classical theory of the relationship between money and prices?

FIGURE 3–13 **MONEY GROWTH AND INFLATION**

This figure shows that there has been a positive relationship between the growth rate of the quantity of money in circulation and inflation. Across various nations, higher money growth rates appear to lead to higher inflation rates.

SOURCE: *Economic Report of the President,* 1997; *Federal Reserve Bulletin* (various issues).

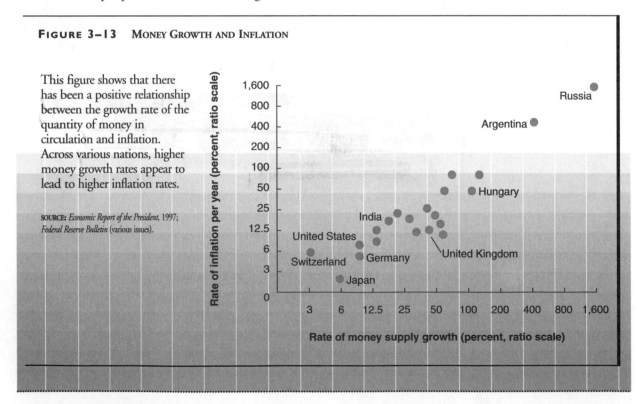

As you will learn in later chapters, theories of short-run variations in economic activity do indicate that interest-rate variations can lead to changes in prices and output. In the basic classical framework, however, interest rates do not perform such a "causal" role. Instead, they adjust to equate quantities demanded and supplied in markets for credit.

The Loanable Funds Market and the Classical Theory of Interest Rates

Not everyone spends all income that he or she earns. Many people save a portion of their earnings. This means that somewhere along the multiple chains of expenditures that take place in the economy, there is a *leakage* from the total flow of expenditures when people save. To achieve equilibrium in the market for real output, however, all goods and services produced ultimately must be purchased. Hence, all saving ultimately must find its way back into the aggregate flow of spending on goods and services. In the classical model, the role of interest rates is to ensure that this occurs in equilibrium.

Real versus Nominal Interest Rates   Before we discuss how interest rates matter, it is important to understand the distinction between *nominal interest rates* and *real interest rates*. Nominal interest rates are easy to understand. These are the interest rates that appear in the daily and weekly financial periodicals. They also are the loan and deposit interest rates that your bank, savings institution, or credit union posts on its walls. A nominal interest rate is simply the current market rate of interest expressed as the nominal value of a flow of interest relative to a nominal base, or principal amount of funds. For example, a quoted annual auto loan rate of 9 percent means that for every $100 borrowed to finance an auto purchase, the borrower must pay $9 per year in interest to the lender.

Suppose, though, that when the auto loan was negotiated, both the lender and the borrower anticipated an annual inflation rate of 3 percent during the term of the loan. In this case, the real value of the principal amount of the loan would decline by $3 each year. As a result, the *real* interest payment that the borrower anticipates making and the lender anticipates receiving would be reduced by this $3 amount each year. Consequently, the real interest paid each year on the initial $100 principal would be $9 − $3, or $6 per year. The *real interest rate*, therefore, would be 6 percent, or the nominal interest rate of 9 percent minus the expected inflation rate of 3 percent. Thus, we can define the **real interest rate** as the difference between the nominal interest rate and the expected rate of inflation. If we denote the nominal interest rate as r, the expected inflation rate as π^e (the Greek letter pi denotes the inflation rate, and the *e* superscript indicates an expectation of that rate), then the real interest rate, ρ (the Greek letter rho), is equal to

$$\rho = r - \pi^e.$$

REAL INTEREST RATE The nominal interest rate minus the expected rate of inflation

Saving and the Supply of Loanable Funds   In the classical theory, the main determinant of real saving per unit of time is the real interest rate, ρ. People care about the real interest rate because this is the correct measure of their real return on saving. The key hypothesis is that there is a direct relationship between the real interest rate and the amount that households save out of a given level of real income, holding all other factors unchanged. If the real interest rate rises, the real return on saving rises, and households will save more of a given level of income and thereby choose to consume a smaller portion of that income. If the real interest rate falls, households will save less and consume more of a given level of income. Figure 3–14 illustrates this direct relationship between real saving, *s*, and the real interest rate, ρ.

The saving of households represents claims on real goods and services, so the original classical economists called these financial claims **loanable funds.** Therefore, the saving schedule *s* in Figure 3–14 is a supply schedule in the market for these loanable funds, and the real interest rate is the price of loanable funds.

LOANABLE FUNDS The term used by classical economists to refer to the amount of real income that households save, representing claims on real output.

Investment and the Demand for Loanable Funds   Not everyone saves. At any given time many people desire to spend more than their incomes would otherwise permit them to spend. This is especially true for owners of businesses. To be able to produce goods and services, owners of business firms often need to purchase or build expensive capital goods such as machines and factories. The required capital expenditures commonly exceed the real incomes of the individuals who own these firms. For this reason, firm owners often desire to borrow funds from those who save; that

---

FIGURE 3–14   THE CLASSICAL MARKET FOR LOANABLE FUNDS

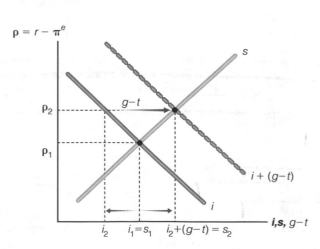

For a given level of real income, individuals save more and consume less as the real interest rate rises. Therefore the saving schedule, which is the supply of loanable funds, slopes upward. In contrast, desired real investment spending by firms declines as the real interest rate increases. As a result, the investment schedule slopes downward. In the absence of a government budget deficit, the equilibrium real interest rate equilibrates investment and saving. In the presence of a government deficit, however, investment and the government budget deficit together constitute the downward-sloping demand for loanable funds. The result is a rise in the equilibrium real interest rate that induces greater saving and lower consumption. The increase in the real interest rate also causes investment to decline. The total decline in private consumption and investment is equal to the rise in the government budget deficit, so deficit spending "crowds out" an equal amount of private spending in the classical model.

is, those who *invest* in new capital equipment *demand loanable funds.* Then they use these funds to purchase capital goods. In this way, a large portion of the saving leakage from the economy's flow of spending is *reinjected* into that flow.

In the classical framework, the amount of desired investment spending depends negatively upon the real interest rate. As the real interest rate rises, the price of loanable funds for firm investment increases, and business owners respond by reducing the quantity of loanable funds demanded. As the real interest rate declines, the quantity of loanable funds demanded by firms rises. This inverse relationship between desired investment spending and the interest rate is shown as the *investment schedule,* labeled i in Figure 3–14.

The saving schedule and investment schedule cross at the real interest rate ρ_1. At this real rate of interest, the quantity of loanable funds supplied by household savers, s_1, is equal to the quantity of loanable funds demanded by business owners to fund private investment, i_1.

If businesses were the only source of demand for loanable funds in the economy, then ρ_1 would be the *equilibrium* real rate of interest. It also would be the real interest rate at which the market for real output is in equilibrium. This would be so because at this real interest rate the equality of desired saving and desired investment would imply that all leakages from the flow of real expenditures in the form of savings would be reinjected into that flow as investment expenditures.

Government Deficits and the Demand for Loanable Funds   In fact, however, business firms are not the only source of demand for loanable funds. Another key borrower of such funds is the government. The government often borrows loanable funds because it typically spends more on goods and services than it receives in tax revenues. We denote the quantity of real government spending on goods and services as g and the amount of real government tax revenues less transfer payments as t. Then, if government spending exceeds taxes, it needs to fund a deficit equal to $g - t$. This is known as the *primary deficit,* which is the most basic measure of the government's deficit. It ignores other potentially important government expenditures, such as interest payments on outstanding government debt issued in earlier periods.

Figure 3–14 shows the effect of including the government's budget deficit as a component of the total demand for loanable funds. If we assume that the government simply desires to fund a lump-sum deficit of amount $g - t$ at any given real interest rate, then we can add this quantity of loanable funds demanded by the government horizontally to the private loanable funds demanded by business firms. We do this by adding the amount $g - t$ to the amount of desired investment by business firms at each possible interest rate. This produces the total demand schedule for loanable funds in Figure 3–14.

At the intersection of the saving, or loanable funds supply, schedule with the schedule for combined demand for loanable funds by both businesses and the government, the equilibrium real interest rate is ρ_2. At this real interest rate, households save the amount s_2, which is the equilibrium quantity of loanable funds supplied.

This amount is equal to the equilibrium quantity of loanable funds demanded, which is the sum of the amount of desired investment by firms at the equilibrium real interest rate, i_2, plus the amount of the government's deficit, $g - t$.

Fiscal Policy in the Classical Model   Figure 3–14 also illustrates the classical view of the effects of **fiscal policy,** or variations in government spending or taxes. The effect of increasing the government's deficit from a value of zero to the amount $g - t$ results in a rightward shift in the demand schedule for loanable funds that is equal to $g - t$. This causes the equilibrium real interest rate to rise from ρ_1 to ρ_2. This increase in the real interest rate induces households to raise the amount of saving from s_1 to s_2. Because real income in the classical model is determined by the position of the aggregate supply schedule, which is fixed in the short run, a rise in household saving corresponds to a decline in household consumption spending on real goods and services. Therefore, one effect of an increase in government spending or reduction in taxes that widens the deficit is a *fall in private consumption.*

There is also another effect, however: the rise in the real interest rate from ρ_1 to ρ_2 raises the price of loanable funds for business firms. This causes firm owners to reduce their desired investment expenditures from i_1 to i_2. Consequently, another outcome induced by a rise in government spending or tax cut that increase the government's deficit is a *fall in private investment.*

Consequently, the classical theory of the loanable funds market indicates that a fiscal policy action that increases the government's deficit causes an increase in the real rate of interest that induces reductions in private consumption and investment. The total decline in private spending—the sum of the amount by which private saving rises and private investment falls—exactly equals the amount by which the deficit rose, which is the distance $g - t$ in Figure 3–14.

This reduction in private spending caused by an increase in the government deficit is known as the **crowding-out effect.** Figure 3–14 shows that expansions of government deficits through fiscal policies that raise government spending and/or reduce government tax revenues "crowd out" an equal amount of private spending. In the classical model, therefore:

> **If the government consumes a larger share of the total output of goods and services via deficit finance, an equally smaller amount of output is available for private use.**

Money and Interest Rates   It is important to recognize that in the classical theory, monetary policy plays no role in determining the real interest rate. The equilibrium real interest rate is determined solely by the real income allocations of savers and borrowers of loanable funds.

In the classical model, monetary policy actions determine the *nominal* rate of interest. Because the real interest rate is equal to the nominal interest rate minus

---

FISCAL POLICY Actions by the government to vary its spending or taxes

CROWDING-OUT EFFECT The situation when private spending is reduced due to a rise in the real interest rate induced by an increase in the government's deficit.

the expected inflation rate, or $\rho = r - \pi^e$, we can express the nominal interest rate as the real interest rate plus the expected inflation rate, or $r = \rho + \pi^e$. As we discussed earlier, changes in the quantity of money cause the price level to rise, holding all other factors unchanged. Thus, in the classical model, an increase of 3 percent in the rate of money growth will cause the price level to rise by 3 percent, assuming real GDP and velocity are unchanged. Lenders and borrowers expect a sustained 3 percent inflation rate, so the nominal rate of interest that they negotiate in bond or loan contracts accounts for this anticipated rate of inflation. Ultimately, then the growth rate of the quantity of money determines the nominal interest rate. Higher money growth raises expected inflation and causes an increase in the nominal interest rate. Lower money growth reduces expected inflation and causes a decrease in the nominal interest rate (see Global Notebook on page 84: *Predicting the Rate of Inflation with Bond Rates in England*).

FUNDAMENTAL ISSUE #4

How are interest rates determined in the classical theory? The real interest rate, which is equal to the nominal interest rate minus the expected rate of inflation, adjusts to equate the quantity of loanable funds supplied (saving) with the quantity of loanable funds demanded (desired investment plus the government deficit). Higher government deficits induce a rise in the demand for loanable funds that increases the equilibrium real interest rate and thereby induces a fall in private investment and a rise in private saving, which corresponds to a fall in private consumption. Hence, higher government deficits crowd out private expenditures on goods and services. By changing the expected rate of inflation, growth of the quantity of money determines the nominal interest rate in the classical model.

INTERNATIONAL DIMENSIONS OF CLASSICAL THEORY

CLOSED ECONOMY An economy that operates in isolation from the rest of the world

OPEN ECONOMY An economy that is linked by trade with other economies of the world.

To this point, we have considered the classical theory of a **closed economy.** This is an economy that functions in isolation from the rest of the world. In a closed economy, either no international trade occurs, or the government prohibits such trade.

Few economies are truly closed. Like most other nations of the world, the United States is increasingly becoming an **open economy,** in which international trade accounts for a significant portion of a nation's total income. In 1997, exports and imports accounted for about 11 and 13 percent, respectively, of U.S. GDP, as compared with 1960 figures of 5 and 4 percent.

GLOBAL NOTEBOOK

Predicting the Rate of Inflation with Bond Rates in England

In principle, the nominal interest rate is equal to the real interest rate plus the anticipated rate of inflation. Is it possible, therefore, to use nominal bond interest rates to predict the rate of inflation? Usually, it is not, unless a country has a long history of issuing *indexed* bonds. Indexed-linked bonds pay investors a specific *real* rate of interest independent of the inflation rate. The payment each year on the bond, as well as the redemption value of the bond, is revalued according to the actual rate of inflation. Britain, along with Australia, Canada, and Sweden (and now the United States), is one of the few countries that issues such bonds. They now account for more than 15 percent of outstanding British government debt.

The Bank of England uses the yields on such bonds to measure inflation expectations. Economists there subtract the real yield on a 10-year indexed-linked bond from the nominal yield on nonindexed 10-year bonds to obtain the markets' expectations of average inflation over the next 10 years. While there are certainly complications with this method, Figure 3–15 shows that expected and actual rates of inflation measured in this way move relatively close together. Although the expected level does not always fit the actual level of inflation, the expected change in estimated inflation seems to be a good indicator of the actual change of inflation in the future.

FOR CRITICAL ANALYSIS:

Why couldn't our government simply conduct interview surveys to determine the average of people's expectations of future rates of inflation?

FIGURE 3–15   **ACTUAL AND EXPECTED INFLATION IN THE UNITED KINGDOM**

Actual British inflation rates and expected inflation rates inferred from inflation-indexed bonds tend to move together.

SOURCE: *Bank of England.*

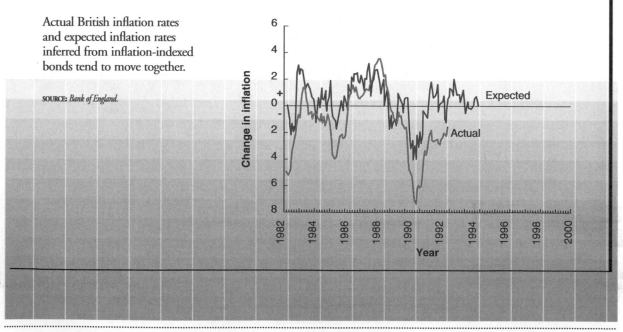

Greater openness engenders greater interest in determinants of the exchange value of a nation's currency relative to other world currencies. As Figure 3–16 indicates, the U.S. dollar's relative value has varied considerably since the 1970s. How would a classical theorist explain these movements in the dollar's value? Before answering this question, let's consider some important facts about the exchange rate.

The Exchange Rate, Depreciation, and Appreciation

First, recall from Chapter 1 that the *exchange rate* is the value of one nation's currency in terms of the currency of another nation. In the case of the U.S. dollar ($) and the German deutschemark (DM), for instance, the dollar-deutschemark exchange rate may be calculated as the price of the deutschemark, measured in dollars per DM. Figure 3–17 shows exchange rate data from the *Wall Street Journal* for January 9, 1997. Reading across the row labeled "U.S." to the column labeled "D-mark," the figure indicates that on this date, a U.S. resident would have to pay $0.63387 to obtain one German deutschemark and so the exchange rate could be expressed as $E = \$0.63387/1$ DM, or 0.63387 dollars per deutschemark. Another way to express the same rate of exchange, however, is to calculate the exchange rate as the price of the German deutschemark measured in dollars. This is the reciprocal of the dollar price of the deutschemark, or $1/E = 1/(\$0.63387/1 \text{ DM}) = 1.5776$ DM/$1, or 1.5776 deutschemarks per dollar. This can be seen by reading down the "Dollar" column to "Germany" in Figure 3–17.

Suppose that the dollar-deutschemark exchange rate were to *rise* to $E' = \$0.75/1$ DM, or 75 cents per deutschemark. Now an individual would have to pay more dol-

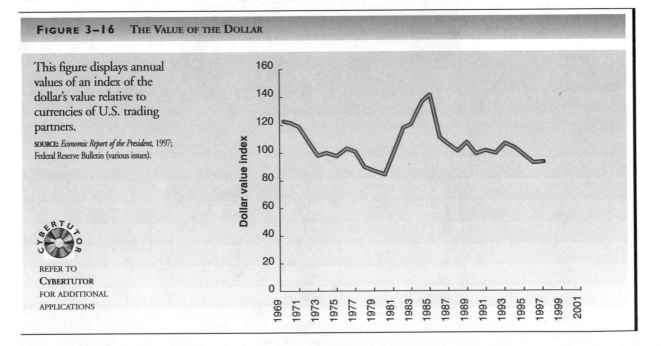

FIGURE 3–16 THE VALUE OF THE DOLLAR

This figure displays annual values of an index of the dollar's value relative to currencies of U.S. trading partners.

SOURCE: *Economic Report of the President*, 1997; Federal Reserve Bulletin (various issues).

REFER TO
CYBERTUTOR
FOR ADDITIONAL
APPLICATIONS

FIGURE 3–17 **EXCHANGE RATES FOR SELECTED CURRENCIES**

Key Currency Cross Rates Late New York Trading Jan 9, 1997

	Dollar	Pound	SFranc	Guilder	Peso	Yen	Lira	D-Mark	FFranc	CdnDlr
Canada	1.3518	2.2928	.98708	.76360	.17245	.01161	.00088	.85687	.25400	
France	5.3220	9.0266	3.8861	3.0063	.67891	.04572	.00346	3.3735		3.9370
Germany	1.5776	2.6758	1.1520	.89115	.20125	.01355	.00103		.29643	1.1670
Italy	1538.5	2609.4	1123.4	869.06	196.26	13.217		975.22	289.08	1138.1
Japan	116.4	197.43	84.995	65.752	14.849		.07566	73.783	21.871	86.107
Mexico	7.8390	13.296	5.7240	4.4281		.06735	.00510	4.9689	1.4729	5.7989
Netherlands ..	1.7703	3.0026	1.2927		.22583	.01521	.00115	1.1221	.33264	1.3096
Switzerland ...	1.3695	2.3228		.77360	.17470	.01177	.00089	.86809	.25733	1.0131
U.K.	.58959		.43051	.33304	.07521	.00507	.00038	.37372	.11078	.43615
U.S.		1.6961	.73019	.56488	.12757	.00859	.00065	.63387	.18790	.73975

Each day *The Wall Street Journal* lists exchange rates for the currencies of ten nations.
SOURCE: *Dow Jones Telerate Inc.*

DEPRECIATION A decline in the relative value of a nation's currency.

APPRECIATION A rise in the relative value of a nation's currency.

lars to obtain one German deutschemark. Consequently, the dollar would lose some of its value relative to the deutschemark. A currency that loses value relative to the currency of another country has experienced a **depreciation.** Hence, a *rise* in the value of E implies a *depreciation* of the value of the dollar relative to the deutschemark. At the same time that the dollar depreciates relative to the deutschemark, the deutschemark experiences an **appreciation** relative to the dollar. Looking at the reciprocal, $1/E' = 1/(\$0.75/1 \text{ DM}) = 1.33 \text{ DM}/\$1$, we can see that now fewer deutschemarks are needed to obtain a dollar. The deutschemark's dollar value increases with a rise in the exchange rate E.

INTERNET SOURCE

Tracking Exchange Rates

The Federal Reserve Bank of New York—Exchange Rates
Internet URL: **http://www.ny.frb.org/pihome/mktrates/forex10.html**

Navigation: Start at the Federal Reserve Bank of New York's homepage
(**http://www.ny.frb.org**). Select *Statistics*
(**http://www.ny.frb.org/pihome/mktrates**). Click on *FX 10 A.M.*

Exchange-Rate Determination in the Classical System

What might cause such a dollar depreciation? According to the classical theory, the key to the answer is found in a concept known as **purchasing power parity.** Under purchasing power parity, the price of a good in one nation should be the same as the price of the same good in another nation, adjusted for the exchange rate. For instance, suppose that an economics textbook sells for a deutschemark price of $P^* = 50$ DM in Germany, where P^* is the price in the foreign currency. If the rate of exchange of deutschemarks for dollars is equal to $E = \$0.63387/1$ DM, then according to purchasing power parity the price of the same book in the United States should be $P = P^* \times E = (50 \text{ DM}) \times (\$0.63387/1 \text{ DM}) = \$31.69$.

According to the purchasing power parity idea, the only factor causing the prices of the textbooks in the two nations to differ is that they are measured in different currency units. If not for the fact that the textbook is priced in different currencies, its price would be the same in both countries. If E were equal to one, so that dollars and deutschemarks could be traded one for one, the U.S. price would be $P = P^* \times E = (50 \text{ DM}) \times (\$1/1 \text{ DM}) = \$50$. In other words, the only reason that the currency prices of the same textbook differs in the two countries is that the currencies *cannot* be exchanged on a one-for-one basis. Otherwise, the textbook would have the same price in both nations.

The Rationale for Purchasing Power Parity　　The main motivation for purchasing power parity is the classical hypothesis of pure competition. If the exchange rate is $E = \$0.63387/1$ DM and the 50 DM textbook were to sell for, say, \$25 in the United States, then a smart college student could buy, say, 1,000 copies of the textbook at \$25 each, box them up, and ship them to Germany for a shipping cost of \$1,000. Thus, the student's total expenditures would be \$26,000. In Germany the textbooks could be sold at 50 DM each to yield revenues of 50,000 DM. Converted to dollars at the exchange rate of \$0.63387/1 DM, these revenues would amount to ($\$0.63387/1$ DM) $\times$ 50,000 DM = \$31,694. Thus the profit from this enterprise would be \$31,694 − \$26,000 = \$5,694. This might pay part of the student's tuition for the next year.

In our example, the college student engaged in **international arbitrage,** which is the act of buying a good in one nation and selling it in another nation. The student profited from a *deviation* from purchasing power parity. What would happen if enough students (and others) engaged in international arbitrage? Eventually, enough textbooks would make their way from the United States to Germany that the German textbook price would begin to fall toward the U.S. textbook price. This process would continue until the textbook price was approximately the same in both countries, adjusting for the exchange rate, or until $P = P^* \times E$.

Purchasing Power Parity and the Exchange Rate　　Not all goods and services can be bought and sold internationally. As an extreme example, it is impossible for a Canadian mother to hire an Italian baby-sitter for an evening, so international arbi-

PURCHASING POWER PARITY A condition that states that if international arbitrage is possible, then the price of a good in one nation should be the same as the price of the same good in another nation, adjusted for the exchange rate.

INTERNATIONAL ARBITRAGE The act of buying a good in one nation and selling it in another.

trage in short-run baby-sitting services is not feasible. This is true of many services, although some types of services, such as those that banks provide in financial markets, can be provided by computer connections that extend beyond national borders.

The original classical economists recognized that there are limits on international arbitrage for some goods and services, but they regarded purchasing power parity as a *benchmark* for understanding how a nation's exchange rate is determined. Figure 3–18 shows how purchasing power parity can be combined with the theory of price-level determination to provide an explanation of why a nation's currency might depreciate over time. The diagram in panel (a) of Figure 3–18 displays an initial equilibrium price level, denoted P_1, at the intersection of the classical aggregate demand and aggregate supply schedules. Panel (b) is a diagram of the purchasing power parity condition, $P = P^* \times E$. Recall that the intercept-slope equation for a straight line says that a variable measured along the y-axis of a diagram is equal to an intercept plus the slope times a variable measured on the x-axis. Hence, the condition $P = P^* \times E$ is just the equation of a straight line in which the domestic price level, P, is measured along the y-axis in panel (b), and the exchange rate, E, is measured along the x-axis. The intercept of this equation is equal to zero, and the foreign price

FIGURE 3–18 **EXCHANGE-RATE DETERMINATION IN THE CLASSICAL MODEL**

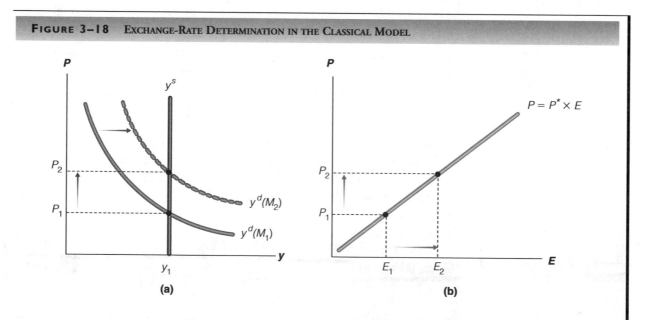

In the classical model, a nation's price level is determined in the market for real output, as in panel (a). A rise in aggregate demand caused by an increase in the nation's money stock causes an increase in the price level. According to the purchasing power parity relationship, the price level can be expressed as $P = P^* \times E$, where P^* is the foreign price level and E is the exchange rate in units of home currency per unit of foreign currency. The graph of this relationship is a straight line, as shown in panel (b). There you can see that a rise in the price level results in an increase in the exchange rate, so more units of the home currency must be given up in exchange for units of the foreign currency. Consequently, the home currency depreciates relative to the foreign currency.

GLOBAL NOTEBOOK

Do Changes in Foreign Currency Values Reflect Changes in the Rate of Inflation Worldwide?

Under the theory of purchasing power parity, the prices of tradable goods, correcting for transportation and so on, should be the same in any two countries when expressed in a common currency. There are many problems with the purchasing power parity theory, of course. One of them has to do with the fact that not all goods are traded. The other has to do with the fact that resources are not instantly mobile, particularly labor resources. Nonetheless, some fairly strong empirical evidence indicates that in the long run inflation rates do determine relative foreign currency values. Figure 3–19 shows the changes in the dollar exchange rate of foreign currencies measured against national inflation rates relative to U.S. inflation. We have drawn a line that shows the general correlation between these two variables in the period since 1973. Countries with inflation rates that are relatively low compared with the rate in the United States tend to have experienced relatively small changes in their exchanges rates compared to the dollar. In contrast, countries such as Italy and Spain with relatively high inflation rates have witnessed relatively large changes in their foreign exchange rates relative to the dollar.

The purchasing power parity doctrine can never be fully accurate, of course. After all, it assumes that there are no barriers to trade, even though tariffs and other barriers exist throughout the world. Also, prices tend to be distorted by taxes.

FOR CRITICAL ANALYSIS:
Why are barriers to trade important for understanding the accuracy of the purchasing power parity doctrine?

FIGURE 3–19   THE RELATIONSHIP BETWEEN CHANGES IN FOREIGN EXCHANGE RATES AND INFLATION

This figure plots the changes in dollar exchange rates of selected nations and those nations' inflation rates relative to U.S. inflation for years since 1973. As predicted by the purchasing power parity relationship, there is a positive relationship between these two variables. Source: International Monetary Fund.

SOURCE: International Monetary Fund

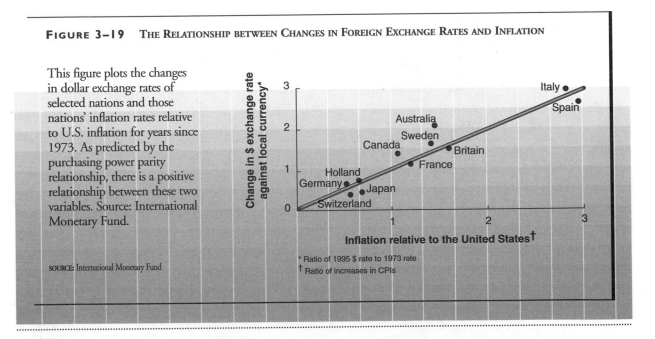

level, P^*, is the *slope* of the line. At the current price level in our home nation, P_1, the purchasing power parity condition yields an equilibrium exchange rate equal to E_1.

As we discussed earlier, the classical model indicates that a likely reason for persistent inflation is consistently high growth in the quantity of money that shifts the aggregate demand schedule to the right over time. Panel (a) in Figure 3–18 shows such a rightward shift in aggregate demand that causes the home price level to rise to P_2. According to the purchasing power parity condition, if foreign prices remain unchanged at P^*, our nation's exchange rate must rise to E_2. If the "home nation" is the United States, then the exchange rate E would be measured in dollars per unit of foreign currency (for instance, deutschemarks). Hence, when the exchange rate rises from E_1 to E_2, more dollars will be needed to purchase foreign currency. The value of the dollar will have *depreciated*. In other words, the classical model predicts that persistent growth in the quantity of money in the United States will cause a fall in the value of the dollar as well as persistent U.S. inflation (see on the previous page the Global Notebook: *Do Changes in Foreign Currency Values Reflect Changes in the Rate of Inflation Worldwide?*).

FUNDAMENTAL ISSUE #5

How is the value of a nation's currency determined in the classical model? The value of a country's currency is its exchange rate. In the classical model, a key benchmark for understanding how the exchange rate is determined is the purchasing power parity condition, which states that the home price level is equal to the foreign price level times the exchange rate. Given the foreign price level and the determination of the home price level in the market for real output, the exchange rate adjusts to maintain purchasing power parity.

CHAPTER SUMMARY

1. **Key Assumptions of Classical Macroeconomic Theory:** One key assumption is that people rationally pursue their own self-interest. A second assumption is that people do not experience money illusion, so they are not fooled by current-dollar changes that make no difference to their real incomes. The final key assumption is that markets for goods, services, and factors of production are purely competitive, meaning that there are large numbers of buyers and sellers, none of whom individually can affect market prices.

2. **The Determination of Employment and Output in the Classical Model:** According to the classical framework, the amount of labor employed in the economy is determined by labor-market equilibrium. The real and money wages adjust to keep the quantity of labor supplied by workers equal to the quantity of labor demanded by firms. The equilibrium amount of real aggregate output then is the amount that firms can produce with this

quantity of labor, given their use of other factors of production and the technology available to them. Because the equilibrium money wage adjusts in equal proportion to changes in prices, employment and output are unchanged in response to price-level variations. Consequently, the classical aggregate supply schedule is vertical.

3. **The Classical Theory of Prices and Inflation:** The equilibrium price level is the level that ensures that the quantity of real output demanded is equal to the amount supplied by firms. This occurs at the point where the aggregate demand schedule, whose position is determined by the quantity of money in circulation and the income velocity of money, crosses the vertical classical aggregate supply schedule.

4. **Interest-Rate Determination in the Classical Framework:** In the classical model, the real interest rate adjusts to equalize the quantity of loanable funds supplied, or aggregate private saving, with the quantity of loanable funds demanded, or the sum of total desired private investment and the government deficit. A rise in the government's deficit increases the demand for loanable funds, thereby causing a crowding-out effect as the resulting rise in the real interest rate induces a decrease in private spending. An increase in anticipated growth of the quantity of money causes expected inflation to rise, thereby increasing the nominal interest rate, which is equal to the real interest rate plus the expected inflation rate.

5. **The Value of a Nation's Currency:** The exchange rate is the value, or price, of one nation's currency in terms of that of another nation. The classical theory's benchmark for understanding how exchange rates are determined is purchasing power parity, which states that if international arbitrage can occur, then the price level in one nation should equal the foreign price level times the exchange rate. Once a home nation's price level is determined in its market for real output, and given the foreign price level, the home nation's exchange rate adjusts to maintain purchasing power parity. Persistent inflation in the home nation caused by excessive money growth thereby will be accompanied by persistent depreciation in, or decline in the value of, the home nation's currency.

QUESTIONS AND PROBLEMS

1. As we shall discuss in Chapter 4, economists typically measure economic growth using the growth of real GDP as a starting point. Therefore, according to the classical framework, what factors should influence the rate of economic growth? Explain.

2. During the 1970s and 1980s, women entered the U.S. labor force in increasing numbers. Use the classical model to predict the effects that this would have on the equilibrium real wage, equilibrium employment, and equilibrium real GDP.

3. Based on your answer to question 2, determine the effect that a rise in female labor-force participation would have on the price level in the classical model, holding all other factors constant. Explain your answer.

4. Suppose that a nation becomes involved in a war that results in the destruction of a significant fraction of its capital stock. Use the classical model to predict the effects that this would have on the equilibrium real wage, equilibrium employment, and equilibrium real GDP.

5. Based on your answer to question 4, determine the effect that destruction of part of the nation's capital stock would have on the country's price level in the classical model, holding all other factors constant. Explain your answer.

6. Suppose that the increasing use of the Internet to make transactions without reliance on money causes the income velocity of money to decline substantially. Use the classical model to predict what, if any, effects this would have on the price level, real GDP, the real interest rate, and the nominal interest rate.

7. Suppose that the Cambridge *k* is equal to 0.25, real GDP is equal to 6 trillion base-year dollars, and the price level is equal to 1.2 current-year dollars per base-year dollar. What is the current-dollar value of the quantity of money in circulation?

8. Explain how, according to the classical theory, a nation's nominal interest rate could decline without a change in the real rate of interest. Would it be possible for the real interest rate to rise even as the nominal rate of interest declined? Explain your reasoning.

9. Suppose that the central bank of a small European nation keeps the quantity of money in circulation stable. Its government's budget is balanced. In addition, its income velocity of money is stable, as are conditions in its labor market. Its technology and other factors of production also have not changed. Nevertheless, the value of the nation's currency is persistently depreciating relative to that of its major trading partner. Given the conditions the small country faces, what *single* factor would the classical model indicate must account for this steady depreciation of its currency?

10. During recent decades, several governments in South America have experienced significant deficits that they funded in large measure by purchasing government bonds with new money printed by central banks. Apply the classical model to explain the effects that such government actions would likely have on prices, real GDP, the real interest rate, the nominal interest rate, and the exchange rate of a nation that finds itself in this situation.

 CYBERTUTOR EXERCISES

1. Suppose that people become more myopic—they consume more and save less. What effect will this have on prices, output and wages?

2. Suppose the Federal Reserve feels that the dollar is overvalued. Should the Federal Reserve increase or decrease the money stock? What will be the effect on the exchange rate?

3. What will happen to the exchange rate if the level of output falls?

4. Suppose that foreign aggregate demand rises. What will happen to the exchange rate, domestic prices, and domestic output?

5. Classical theory predicts that the income velocity of money should be relatively stable. Figure 3–9 in the text, which looks at the velocity of money using the Federal Reserve's M2 measure of money, suggests that this is not always the case. Is the U.S. experience similar to that of France and Japan?

6. Figure 3–10 in the text shows that in the 1970's, inflation rose considerably. Extend the graph to include the entire data set. Is the experience in the 1970's usual? Can you explain what historical events coincided with periods of high inflation?

7. Consider Figure 3–16 in the text. Some economic theories suggest that there should be a relationship between the exchange value of the dollar and the balance of trade. Create a scatter plot of the dollar's value against the balance of trade. Does a relationship exist? If so what is the relationship? Does the relationship change over time?

ON-LINE APPLICATION

The Federal Reserve's Beige Book (see Chapter 1's *On-Line Application*) provides a wealth of information about the current status of U.S. labor markets. You can access this Internet locale to keep track of developments in wages, employment, and unemployment in the United States.

Internet URL: http://www.bog.frb.fed.us/fomc/bb/current/summary.htm

Title: The Beige Book—Summary

Navigation: Begin with the Federal Reserve Board's homepage (**http://www.bog.frb.fed.us**).
Scan down to Federal Open Market Committee (FOMC). Then click on *Beige Book* to access the Beige Book homepage
(**http://www.bog.frb.fed.us/fomc/bb/current/**).
Scan down to "Current Report," and then click on *Summary.*

Application: Read the sections entitled "Labor Markets" and "Prices," and answer the following questions.

1. Has overall employment been rising or falling during the most recent year? According to the classical model, what factors might account for this pattern? Does the Beige Book summary bear out any of these theoretical explanations for changes in aggregate U.S. employment?

2. Have nominal wages been rising or falling during the most recent year? Does the Beige Book provide any information that permits you to deduce the implications for aggregate real wages?

SELECTED REFERENCES AND FURTHER READING

Fisher, Irving. *The Theory of Interest*. New York: Macmillan, 1930.

Hicks, John R. *Theory of Wages*. London: Macmillan, 1932.

Marshall, Alfred. *Principles of Economics*. New York: Macmillan, 1925.

Mill, John S. *Principles of Economics*. New York: Macmillan, 1848.

Say, Jean B. *A Treatise on Political Economy*. London: Longmans, 1821.

Wicksell, J. G. K. *Interest and Prices*, trans. R. F. Kahn. London: Macmillan, 1936.

Utopia Just Beyond the Horizon or Future Shock?—

THE THEORY OF ECONOMIC GROWTH

At the beginning of the twentieth century, Argentina had the sixth highest per capita income in the world. Today, Argentina's per capita income ranks about fortieth, on a par with that of Iran. Less than a hundred years ago, Hong Kong was basically a barren rock. When the People's Republic of China took it over *in 1997, Hong Kong's per capita income exceeded that of France and Great Britain.*

Can we explain such dramatic changes in relative living standards? Certainly, from an arithmetic point of view, we can: Argentina experienced little and in some cases negative economic growth over the past century, whereas Hong Kong had significant economic growth. This answer, though, does not tell us why economic growth rates differed in these two countries.

Small annual differences in rates of economic growth over a long enough period can have dramatic effects. Consider that the average rate of economic growth in the United States since 1870 has been about 1.75 percent per year. If it had been just 1 percentage point higher, or 2.75 percent per year, today's per capita real GDP would be more than three times its actual value, or over $90,000.

The task of this chapter is to help you understand why economic growth rates differ across nations. Economic growth and the reasons behind it are also important to your future standard of living and that of your children and grandchildren.

MEASURING ECONOMIC GROWTH

Most people have a general idea of what economic growth means. When the economy of a nation grows, its residents must be better off in terms of their material well-being. Nevertheless, we do not measure the well-being of any nation solely in terms of its total output of real goods and services, or real GDP, without making some adjustments. After all, GDP in India typically is roughly triple the size of GDP in Switzerland, yet the Indian population is about 125 times larger than the Swiss population. Clearly, measuring a country's growth in terms of annual increases in real GDP requires adjusting for population growth. This leads to the following measure of a nation's overall **economic growth:**

ECONOMIC GROWTH The annual rate of change in per capita real GDP.

> **A nation's economy grows when it experiences increases in per capita real GDP. We measure economic growth as *the rate of change in per capita real GDP (income) per year.***

Table 4–1 (on page 96) displays average annual rates of growth of per capita real GDP for several industrialized nations. Notice that for the period since 1970, the economic growth rate of the United States was above the growth rates of some

TABLE 4–1 PER CAPITA GROWTH RATES IN VARIOUS COUNTRIES, 1970–PRESENT (%)

COUNTRY		COUNTRY	
Switzerland	1.8	Italy	2.8
Sweden	1.9	Canada	3.0
Netherlands	2.2	Spain	3.1
United Kingdom	2.3	Japan	4.8
Germany	2.4	Turkey	5.3
France	2.7	China	6.1
United States	2.8		

SOURCES: World Bank; International Monetary Fund.

nations but below that of others. This illustrates an important point: Current wealth and productive capacity are not necessarily indicators of current or future economic growth. A nation with considerable wealth at a point in time, such as the United States at the beginning of the twenty-first century, will not necessarily enjoy an expanding economy in the future.

Some Problems with the Per Capita GDP Growth Measure

Defining growth as the rate of change in per capita income should, in principle, make economic growth relatively straightforward to measure. Nevertheless, this growth measure suffers from some problems.

Data Problems Per capita income growth can be computed easily provided that economists can obtain dependable data about a nation's real GDP and its population. In many developing nations, however, governments do not have the resources to collect accurate real income data. Furthermore, a number of nations do not conduct careful censuses of their populations. Even the United States, which devotes considerable resources to census taking, conducts a complete census only once each decade. All media reports of world population depend on population *estimates* of varying quality for a large fraction of the countries of the world. Likewise, annual figures on per capita GDP growth necessarily are economists' best estimates.

Growth for Whom? In addition to data problems, some conceptual problems can arise when using per capita income as a measure of economic growth. One is that this measure tells us nothing about how output is *distributed* among the residents of a nation. During a period when a country's measured per capita output grew very rapidly, its poorest residents might have become even poorer. Therefore, when using the rate of increase in GDP per capita as a growth measure, we must recognize that it tells us nothing about relative incomes of various groups within a country.

Growth in Living Standards? Furthermore, the rate of increase in real GDP per capita is at best an indicator of improvements in the average living standard of a nation's residents. Real standards of living can advance without per capita income growth. This can happen if people, on average, enjoy more leisure time while producing as much as they did before. For example, if a country's per capita real income remained unchanged for ten years while the average hours of work per week declined, we could not automatically conclude that its residents were, on average, no better off. In fact, their average standard of living would definitely be higher at the end of the ten-year period, because they would be working fewer hours per week to produce and consume the same real output. In the United States, for instance, average hours worked per week fell steadily until the 1960s before leveling off. Hence, before the 1970s, measured U.S. economic growth, in terms of increased real income per capita, tended to understate the true growth in living standards that had actually taken place.

The Quality Problem Finally, measured per capita GDP growth does not fully account for *quality* changes that take place over time. In the 1960s, for instance, athletic shoes were known as tennis shoes or, in some locales, "sneakers." Though there was some variety in athletic shoes, typically they were relatively flat-soled and shaded a single-toned white. Now there are athletic shoes specifically designed for walking, jogging, running, or heavy-duty jumping on basketball courts. Athletic shoes also come in every imaginable color. Yet official measures of output lump athletic shoes together into the same basic category of the "sneakers" of old. The official statistics on athletic shoe production tabulate the large growth in the number of athletic shoes produced between the 1960s and the 1990s without accounting for the simultaneous improvement in the quality and variety of the shoes.

Why Economic Growth Matters

Table 4–1 indicates that the growth rates in real per capita income for most countries typically differ by just a few percentage points or even by just tenths of percentage points. Nevertheless, a small difference in growth rates between any two nations can translate into considerable differences in future per capita output levels.

Compound Growth The reason for these differences is that growth has a cumulative, or *compound*, effect over the years. Suppose, for example, that Country A's per capita real GDP was $10,000 at the end of 1996. Then suppose that this economy grew at a sizable rate of 20 percent per year in 1997 and 1998. At the end of 1997, Country A's per capita GDP would equal the sum of the initial $10,000 and an additional GDP growth during the year of $10,000 × 0.2 = $2,000, for a total of $12,000. During 1998, the economy would grow by another 20 percent. By the end of 1998, then, its real income per capita would equal the initial 1996 per capita GDP of $10,000 plus the $2,000 in growth that occurred in 1997, *plus* 20 percent of the initial 1996 per capita GDP of $10,000 *plus* 20 percent of the $2,000 growth in per capita GDP that took place in 1997. Thus, Country A's per capita real GDP for 1998 would be $10,000 + ($10,000 × 0.2) + ($12,000 × 0.2) = $14,400. Note that this 1998 per capita GDP figure would reflect accumulated growth that occurred

COMPOUNDED GROWTH
Accumulated growth in per capita real GDP over a given interval.

COMPOUND GROWTH RATE The annual rate at which per capita real GDP accumulates over a given interval.

during both 1997 and 1998. Such accumulated growth in per capita income is called an economy's **compounded growth.** The 20 percent annual rate of growth that accumulates across years is the economy's **compound growth rate.**

To see why an economy's compound growth rate makes such a difference over time, consider Table 4–2. It shows how a dollar in per capita real GDP compounds across years with different growth rates. For instance, in our example of Country A, each dollar of 1996 per capita income grew at 20 percent for two years. Referring to Table 4–2, we see that this rate would yield $1.44 in accumulated income after two years of growth. Applying this figure to Country A's $10,000 in per capita income in 1996 again yields the $14,400 we computed for 1998.

We can use Table 4–2 to determine how much difference a nation's compound growth rate can make. Consider Country B, where the per capita 1996 income was $20,000, or double that of Country A. If Country B's compound growth rate is 3 percent for the next ten years, then Table 4–2 indicates that its real income per capita in 2006 would be $20,000 × 1.34 = $26,800. Suppose, though, that Country A—which was much poorer in 1996 with a per capita income of only $10,000—could maintain its 20 percent compound growth rate for ten years. By the year 2006, its per capita income would have grown to $10,000 × 6.19 = $61,900. Thus, by 2006 the nation that was much poorer initially would have well over twice the per capita income of the nation with the higher 1996 income.

TABLE 4–2   ONE DOLLAR IN REAL INCOME PER CAPITA COMPOUNDED ANNUALLY AT DIFFERENT GROWTH RATES

This table displays the value of a dollar in income at the end of a given period during which it has compounded annually at a specified growth rate. For instance, suppose $1 in income today grows at 6 percent per year. At the end of one year, it will have grown to $1.06. At the end of 10 years, $1.79, and at the end of 50 years, it will be $18.40.

NUMBER OF YEARS	GROWTH RATE						
	3%	4%	5%	6%	8%	10%	20%
1	1.03	1.04	1.05	1.06	1.08	1.10	1.20
2	1.06	1.08	1.10	1.12	1.17	1.21	1.44
3	1.09	1.12	1.16	1.19	1.26	1.33	1.73
4	1.13	1.17	1.22	1.26	1.36	1.46	2.07
5	1.16	1.22	1.28	1.34	1.47	1.61	2.49
6	1.19	1.27	1.34	1.41	1.59	1.77	2.99
7	1.23	1.32	1.41	1.50	1.71	1.94	3.58
8	1.27	1.37	1.48	1.59	1.85	2.14	4.30
9	1.30	1.42	1.55	1.68	2.00	2.35	5.16
10	1.34	1.48	1.63	1.79	2.16	2.59	6.19
20	1.81	2.19	2.65	3.20	4.66	6.72	38.30
30	2.43	3.24	4.32	5.74	10.00	17.40	237.00
40	3.26	4.80	7.04	10.30	21.70	45.30	1,470.00
50	4.38	7.11	11.50	18.40	46.90	117.00	9,100.00

Catching Up Takes Time Few nations ever achieve a compound growth rate as high as 20 percent, however. Even countries that are able to achieve such growth rates typically cannot maintain them. Although differences in compound growth rates explain why nations' relative per capita incomes have changed so much over the course of history, these changes typically occur over a number of years. The reason is that nations' growth rates typically differ only by small amounts over long spans of time.

As an example, consider the United Kingdom and Sweden. In 1870, the United Kingdom's GDP per capita was nearly twice that of Sweden, meaning that the typical British resident had a real income two times the income of a Swede. During the next 120 years, the United Kingdom's average annual rate of per capita income growth was 1.4 percent, whereas Sweden's rate was slightly higher at 2.1 percent. By 1920, British per capita income was still about one and a half times that of Sweden. By 1950, however, per capita real GDP was only 6 percent higher in the United Kingdom than in Sweden. By the 1990s, Sweden's slightly higher compound growth rate had allowed it to pass the United Kingdom in per capita income. The typical resident of Sweden then earned about 10 percent more than a resident of the United Kingdom.

How quickly a nation's relative position in per capita income changes clearly depends on how fast it can grow. Before examining the factors that determine the speed of a nation's economic growth, though, let's first consider whether economic growth is always *desirable.*

Is High Economic Growth Always a Good Thing?

A number of modern commentators maintain that defining economic growth in terms of real GDP per capita ignores potential ill effects of income growth. Some even contend that per capita growth can make people worse off in some respects. Economic growth, they argue, also creates new "needs" that can make human beings feel worse off as they grow richer. Psychologists, for instance, sometimes find that people's expectations for "success" increase as their real incomes rise. As a result, individuals may be disappointed with their economic achievements even though their real incomes have grown considerably.

Negative Spillovers from Growth Critics of "too much" economic growth also point to the potential for other negative spillover effects arising from growth. Economists call such a spillover effect an *externality.* Economic growth can create **intergenerational externalities,** or spillover effects that span decades and thereby affect the well-being of people born in different periods. For instance, when oil drilling led to significant economic growth in Pennsylvania during the 1890s, gasoline was regarded as a useless by-product of the oil refining process. (Remember that gasoline-driven automobiles did not appear on the scene until a couple of decades later.) Refiners dumped gasoline into rivers and streams, creating an ecological mess that was not fully cleaned up for more than a decade. Discarding the gasoline not only saddled

INTERGENERATIONAL EXTERNALITIES Spillover effects of economic growth that take years to influence human welfare and therefore have different effects across generations.

future residents of Pennsylvania with polluted streams but also deprived them of higher incomes that they could have earned when future uses of gasoline were developed.

Costs and Benefits of Growth   Any economic activity has costs and benefits. Economic growth is widely credited with significantly improving health care and extending life expectancies. It permits greater expenditures on education, which has led to higher literacy rates. Economic growth also can contribute to political stability, particularly if it is shared to some extent by all residents of a nation. At the same time, economic growth can lead to intergenerational externalities such as the pollution caused by the dumping of gasoline in Pennsylvania in the 1890s. Critics of economic growth also cite urban congestion and the psychological problems it can create as significant externality effects. Some commentators also blame economic growth for perceived deteriorations in traditional social structures, such as the widely documented breakdown of family units for many people. Others blame economic growth for the increase in crime rates in the late twentieth century.

Economists and other social scientists continue to try to understand all the costs and benefits that stem from economic growth. Placing value judgments on these costs and benefits, however, is up to each individual. Our goal for the rest of this chapter is to try to explain recent patterns in economic growth around the world, how economic growth occurs, and what factors contribute to or detract from economic growth.

FUNDAMENTAL ISSUE #1

How do economists measure economic growth? The key measure of a nation's overall economic growth is the annual rate of growth in per capita real GDP. This measure tells how much the real income of an average resident of a country grows from year to year. Economists recognize that this is an imperfect measure, because it does not tell us how total income is distributed within a country, does not account for changes in product quality, and fails to consider possible intergenerational externalities. Nevertheless, per capita real GDP is the best available measure of the growth of a nation's economy.

THE GREAT GROWTH SLOWDOWN

As we enter the twenty-first century, economists are asking a very fundamental question: Has economic growth all but ended for a number of nations? While several nations, such as China and Malaysia, have experienced rapid growth during the 1990s, the same has not been true for much of Europe and the United States.

Documenting the Slowdown

ON THE WEB

Visit China's Homepage at:
http://www.ihep.ac.cn/china.html

Table 4–3 shows average annual growth rates in per capita incomes for selected industrialized countries over three intervals: 1970–1979, 1980–1989, and 1990–1996. As you can see, growth rates in these nations had peaked by the 1980s. Since then all these high-income nations have experienced declines in their rates of economic growth.

Note that the figures in Tables 4–1 and 4–3 show growth rates for *intervals* of years. When assessing trends in economic growth, it is important not to get caught up in *annual* growth rates. To see why, consider Figure 4–1 (on page 102). Panel (a) shows actual per capita real GDP for the United States since 1959. As you can see, aside from a few dips U.S. per capita income has experienced steady growth. Panel (b) shows the year-to-year growth rates that correspond to the data displayed in panel (a). As panel (b) makes clear, year-to-year growth rates in per capita real GDP can be extremely volatile.

Looking at ranges of years smooths out such annual variations and helps us identify longer-term trends in economic growth rates. Table 4–4 on page 102 shows two ways that we can do this. One is to look at averages of year-to-year rates of growth in per capita income for ranges of years. Another is to look at compound rates of growth for such ranges. Either way we look at the data, however, it is clear that the experience of the United States has paralleled that of the other developed nations of the world, as summarized in Table 4–3. U.S. economic growth has slowed considerably since the 1970s.

Is Slowed Growth a Cause for Concern?

Recall that growth rates are compounded over time. For any nation, relatively low economic growth this year ultimately means relatively lower real GDP per capita

TABLE 4–3	**SLOWED ECONOMIC GROWTH RATES IN SELECTED INDUSTRIALIZED NATIONS (%)**		
	1970–1979	**1980–1989**	**1990–1997**
Canada	3.4	2.1	0.4
France	3.4	1.8	1.1
Germany	2.9	1.9	1.9
Italy	2.7	2.3	1.3
Japan	4.0	3.6	1.9
United Kingdom	2.2	2.5	1.1

SOURCE: International Monetary Fund, *World Economic Outlook*, various issues.
NOTE: Figures are average annual percentage changes in per capita real GDP.

FIGURE 4–1   REAL GDP PER CAPITA AND YEAR-TO-YEAR CHANGES IN REAL GDP PER CAPITA
IN THE UNITED STATES

As panel (a) indicates, U.S. real
GDP per capita has trended
upward in recent decades.
Nevertheless, panel (b) shows
that annual rates of change in
per capita real GDP have been
highly variable from year to
year.

SOURCE: *Economic Report of the President,* 1997;
Economic Indicators (various issues).

REFER TO
CYBERTUTOR
FOR ADDITIONAL
APPLICATIONS

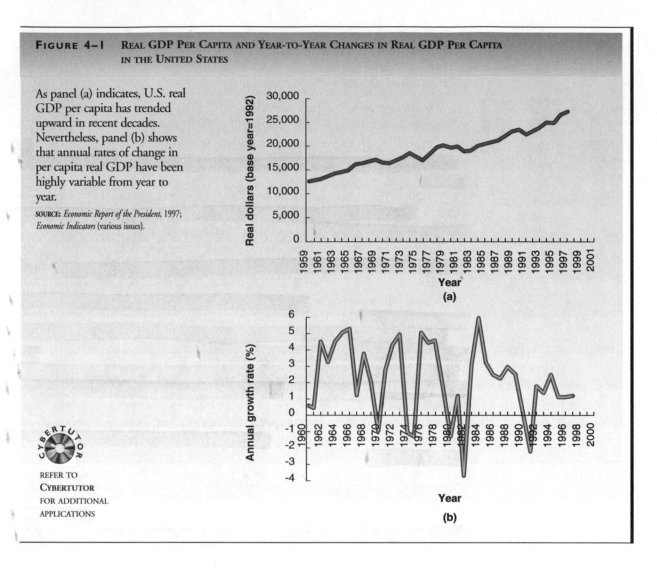

TABLE 4–4   SLOWED ECONOMIC GROWTH RATES IN THE UNITED STATES

	AVERAGE GROWTH RATE (%)	COMPOUND GROWTH RATE (%)
1960–1969	3.0	3.0
1970–1979	2.1	2.1
1980–1989	1.8	1.8
1990–1997	0.9	0.8

SOURCE: *Economic Report of the President,* 1997; *Economic Indicators* (various issues).
NOTE: Figures are percentage changes in per capita real GDP.

in all future years. For the United States and other developed nations, reduced growth rates during the past two decades ultimately will lead to significantly smaller per capita incomes than these nations otherwise might have attained.

As discussed earlier, lower economic growth is not necessarily bad. Indeed, critics of the negative intergenerational spillovers that growth can cause would regard reduced growth as a good thing. Nevertheless, the United States and other low-growth nations have reasons to be concerned. One is that to the extent that economic growth *does* reflect living standards, the consistently lower growth rates of recent years indicate a poor outlook for improvement in overall living standards. Another is that some government programs, such as social security programs that transfer incomes from young people to members of older generations, can come under significant pressures when economic growth fades.

THE DETERMINANTS OF ECONOMIC GROWTH

Why do economic growth rates differ so much across nations? Why do growth rates for any given nation differ over time? Finally, why has average worldwide economic growth slowed in recent decades?

These are tough questions. Although economists still argue about which answers are "right," they generally agree about how to try to find those answers. This, you will see, is because the per capita real GDP measure of economic growth implies that there are three important factors that determine growth.

The Key Factors that Determine Economic Growth

Recall from our analysis of the classical macroeconomic model in Chapter 3 that the *short-run* aggregate production function is $y = F(N)$, where y is real GDP and N is the amount of labor employed. We called this the *short-run* production function because we only considered a period short enough that labor was the only factor of production whose quantity firms could vary. But the economy has another crucial factor of production. This is **capital,** or goods that may be used to produce other goods and services in the future, such as tools, machinery, and factories. Although there are other factors of production, such as land and entrepreneurship, let's focus our attention on labor and capital, because these are the most important productive factors.

CAPITAL Goods that people can use to produce other goods and services in the future.

The Long-Run Aggregate Production Function
In the long run, real output of goods and services depends on the nature of the production function that applies to a period lengthy enough that firms can adjust the amount of capital that they employ. Consequently, any consideration of economic growth must include capital in the production function. In addition, over a number of years the technology that firms can use also can change. The long-run production function must therefore account

for technological change as well. These considerations indicate that a long-run aggregate production function for the economy is

$$y = F(N, K) \times A,$$

where capital, K, is a factor of production along with labor and where A is a measure of the degree to which technical progress permits firms to increase the amount of goods and services that they produce using labor and capital. This factor A commonly is referred to as a measure of *long-run overall productivity of capital and labor*. As we shall explain shortly, this factor captures the potential for economic growth through technological change rather than through growth in labor and capital.

In the short-run classical model in Chapter 3, we assumed that technology was fixed, which allowed us to abstract from long-run productivity changes. In addition, we assumed that capital was fixed in the short run, which allowed us to ignore it. When thinking about the long run, however, both must be considered.

The Components of GDP Growth   Our measure of economic growth is the rate at which real GDP per capita increases each year. In terms of our notation, a proportionate increase in real GDP, which is how we measure real GDP growth, is $\Delta y/y$. We can see from the expression for the aggregate production function that a proportionate increase in y could arise for any one of three reasons. One possibility is a proportionate rise in productivity, which is a change in productivity relative to total productivity, or $\Delta A/A$. If the amounts of labor and capital are unchanged, but both become more productive, then more output can be produced.

Another reason that output might grow is a proportionate rise in output caused by growth in labor employment. Suppose that β_N is the proportionate increase in output induced by a proportionate increase in employment. Then the contribution of employment growth to output growth would be $\beta_N \times \Delta N/N$, where $\Delta N/N$ is the proportionate growth in the labor input.

Finally, output could grow because of a proportionate increase in output induced by growth in the amount of capital. If β_K is the proportionate increase in output induced by a proportionate increase in capital, then the contribution of capital growth to output growth would be $\beta_K \times \Delta K/K$, where $\Delta K/K$ is the proportionate growth in capital.

Consequently, we can write a nation's overall output growth over a year's time as the sum of these three components, or

$$\Delta y/y = (\beta_N \times \Delta N/N) + (\beta_K \times \Delta K/K) + (\Delta A/A).$$

We could then divide by the nation's population (which typically would be larger than N, because not all people are in the labor force or employed) to calculate per capita output growth. The above expression tells us that economic growth is equal to the contribution of employment growth to output growth plus the contribution of capital growth to output growth plus the rate of growth in the productivity of capital and labor. Hence, an understanding of the determinants of economic growth must focus on these three factors.

FUNDAMENTAL ISSUE #2

What key factors determine the rate of economic growth? The growth of real GDP has three components. One is the growth in labor's contribution to real GDP, and another is the growth in capital's contribution to real GDP. The third is the growth in productivity of labor and capital. Any attempt to understand why cross-country differences in economic growth exist or why countries grow at different rates over time must focus on these three factors.

Labor-Force Participation and Growth

Economists have estimated that the proportionate response of output to a proportionate rise in labor employment, β_N, is approximately equal to 0.7. This means that a 10 percent increase in employment would, holding other determinants of growth unchanged, cause output to grow by about 7 percent. Consequently, we might expect that employment growth would have a lot to do with output growth.

Labor Force Participation, Employment, and Aggregate Supply   To understand how employment growth affects output growth, let's return to the classical model that we developed in Chapter 3. There you learned that a key determinant of the amount of labor services that people supply to firms is the real wage.

Nevertheless, the real wage is not the only factor that influences a person's decision to enter the labor force and work for a wage. A number of other factors also play important roles in this decision. For instance, consider the choices that a married couple may make during their years together. Early on, they may both choose to enter the labor force to earn the highest possible combined income so that they can make major investments in education, housing, and so on that will have long-term benefits for their household. Then, if the couple has a child, one of the parents may leave the work force for a time until the child is old enough for day care or school. To pay for the child's college education, one or both parents may take on extra work, such as moonlighting or consulting. All of these decisions naturally depend in part on the real wages that both parents can earn in the labor market. Clearly, though, the decisions are also influenced by other factors, including actions and policies of local, state, and federal governments.

For instance, the extent of labor-force participation depends in part on the taxes that governments impose on wage income. Suppose that the federal government significantly reduces taxes on wage income. The couple in our example may decide that after-tax earnings from work are now high enough that they can afford to hire outside child care. Consequently, such a tax cut could induce the parent who stayed home to reenter the labor force. Likewise, reductions in government benefits, such as unemployment insurance or other governmentally supported supplemental income benefits, could induce more individuals to enter the labor force.

Figure 4–2 illustrates the effects of a rise in overall labor-force participation, caused perhaps by a cut in taxes on wage income. At any given real wage [panel (a)] or money wage [panel (b)], people supply more labor services, so the labor supply schedule shifts rightward. As a result, the equilibrium money wage declines, and equilibrium employment rises. This causes a rightward movement along the aggregate production function [panel (c)] and an increase in real output. Consequently, the aggregate supply schedule shifts rightward [panel (d)]. The result is short-run growth in real output. Whether or not this growth will be sustained over a long horizon will depend upon the duration of the tax cut.

Figure 4–2 illustrates a key argument proposed by adherents of the school of thought known as **supply-side economics.** According to this view, the primary way for governmental policy actions to have real effects is by influencing the position of the aggregate supply schedule. Policies that encourage labor-force participation, such as low tax rates on wage income, are central supply-side policy prescriptions.

Population Growth, Freedom, and Economic Growth   As the twenty-first century begins, the world's population will reach 6 billion people, and it will continue to grow by about 100 million people per year. Population growth does not occur evenly over the earth's surface, however. Women in the relatively wealthy nations of Europe bear an average of 1.6 children during their life spans. In the United States, a typical woman has 2 children. Meanwhile, in the generally poorer nations of Africa, women bear an average of 6 children.

Does a large population contribute to or detract from economic growth? On the one hand, population growth naturally tends to induce a rise in a nation's labor-force participation. As we have discussed, this expands equilibrium employment and spurs economic growth. On the other hand, a larger population directly reduces growth in *per capita* real GDP.

Which of these effects dominates? The answer seems to depend on which nation one considers. In some nations with high population densities, such as Japan, Singapore, and Hong Kong, population growth historically has been positively related to economic growth. In nations such as Bangladesh, Kenya, and Nigeria, however, so far there has been a negative relationship between population growth and per capita real GDP growth.

One crucial factor affecting the relationship between population growth and economic growth appears to be the extent of economic freedom—the rights to own private property and to exchange goods, services, and financial assets with minimal government interference—available to the residents of a nation. According to a survey of 82 nations conducted by Freedom House, two-thirds of the world's population live in 33 nations whose people have no economic freedom. Even though the bulk of the world's population lives in these nations, their economies produce only

---

SUPPLY-SIDE ECONOMICS A school of economic thought that promotes government policies intended to influence real GDP by affecting the position of the economy's aggregate supply schedule.

ON THE WEB
Visit Singapore's Homepage at: http://www.ait.ac. th/Asia/infosg.html

FIGURE 4–2 **THE EFFECTS OF A RISE IN LABOR-FORCE PARTICIPATION ON THE EQUILIBRIUM MONEY WAGE, EMPLOYMENT, AND AGGREGATE SUPPLY EMPLOYMENT, AND REAL OUTPUT**

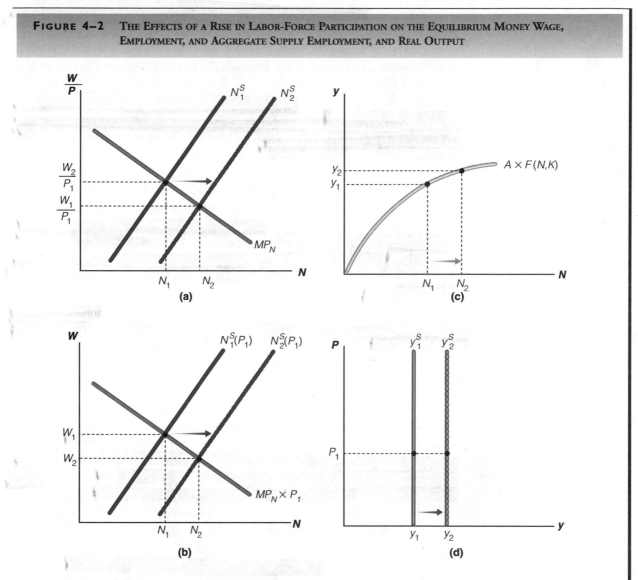

As panels (a) and (b) show, increased labor-force participation results in a rightward shift in the labor supply schedule. The equilibrium money wage declines, and equilibrium employment rises. As a result, as panel (c) indicates, aggregate output increases. Thus, as panel (d) shows, the economy's aggregate supply schedule shifts to the right. At a given price level, real output rises. If population is unchanged, the result is an increase in per capita real output.

13 percent of the world's total output. The survey determined that only 17 nations, with 17 percent of the world's people, granted their residents complete economic freedom. These nations, some of which are very populous relative to their geographic size, together account for 81 percent of total world output.

Interestingly, political freedom seems to have less to do with the interaction between population and economic growth than does economic freedom. Some nations that grant considerable economic freedom to their citizens impose relatively strong restrictions on their residents' freedoms of speech and the press. In fact, Robert Barro of Harvard University studied more than a hundred countries over the past three decades and found that greater democracy in a nation tends to moderately *reduce* economic growth. Political freedom in the form of democracy gives special interest groups the chance to gain at the expense of society as a whole by finding ways to pass laws that inhibit competition. For instance, business interests in democratic societies can band together to convince a legislature to prevent lower-priced goods from entering the country to compete with existing businesses. This reduction in competition stifles growth by reducing the incentive for home businesses to innovate.

Barro's research also indicates that nondemocratic countries that achieve high standards of living through consistent economic growth tend to become more democratic over time. Overall this evidence indicates that economic freedom together with population growth tends to stimulate economic growth, which then leads to more political freedom. At the same time, nations with high population growth rates that fail to grant significant economic freedom can fall into a terrible trap. The population growth reduces per capita incomes, and the restrictions on economic freedom inhibit real GDP growth. The lack of economic growth then perpetuates nondemocratic institutions. As a result, many people of the world continue to suffer from meager output growth as well as from the absence of political and economic freedom.

Immigration and Economic Growth   In centuries past, people in nations that had fallen into this trap often could escape their predicament by emigrating to other lands with fewer restrictions on economic and political freedom. Today, however, believing that continued immigration will harm their interests, the citizens of many democratic nations have erected significant barriers to immigrants. Indeed, many social commentators argue that immigration slows economic growth. This view has recently gained broader currency in the United States, which previously was one of the most open nations to immigration. Indeed, with the exception of Native Americans, every citizen of the United States is descended from immigrants.

From one perspective, immigration is just a form of population growth. According to this perspective, the answer to whether immigration spurs or inhibits economic growth is the same as the answer to the question of whether population growth speeds or slows economic growth. In nations with significant economic freedom, immigration should stimulate growth, but in nations lacking economic freedom, immigration likely will stunt the economy's growth. Consequently, a nation such as the United States should gain from immigration over the long term. This has been the rationale for relative openness to immigration in the United States, and it has paid off handsomely during the first two centuries of the nation's existence.

INTERNET SOURCE

Evaluating the Potential Contributions of Immigrants to U.S. Growth

The U.S. Immigration and Naturalization Service—Characteristics of Legal Immigrants
Internet URL: http://www.usdoj.gov/ins/index.html

Navigation: Begin at the homepage of the U.S. Department of Justice (http://www.usdoj.gov). Click on *Justice Department Organizations—Alphabetically by Organization Name.* Then click on *Immigration and Naturalization Services.* Next, click on *Public Information.* Then click on *Statistical Information* and click on *Immigration to the United States in Fiscal Year 1998* (or most recent report). Finally, click on *Characteristics of Legal Immigrants.*

So why are many U.S. citizens less open to immigration than they were in the past? One possible answer is provided by Barro's research discussed above. In a democracy, special interests may sway the electorate to vote for short-term protections from competition even though these barriers may slow the long-run growth of the economy as a whole. Another possible answer is provided by the research of George Borjas, also of Harvard University. Borjas, himself an emigrant to the United States from Cuba, argues that today's immigrants to the United States are less educated than immigrants of the past. He and other observers also contend that many current immigrants come to the United States for different reasons than the immigrants in years past. In previous periods, he says, immigrants sought to use their skills or to develop new skills in an economically unhindered environment. As a result, they contributed to U.S. economic growth. Today, goes this argument, many immigrants seek social benefits offered by government programs. They tend to become unproductive residents who add nothing to growth calculations except that they expand the nation's population and thereby reduce per capita GDP. Essentially, this view is that well-meaning social programs created by U.S. democracy may have undercut the past benefits of permitting relatively unrestricted immigration.

The net effect of immigration on economic growth remains an unresolved issue for economists. Certainly, it is likely to be a contentious issue in the twenty-first century as the world becomes a more populous place with fewer open spaces to fill.

INTERNET SOURCE

Immigration and Its Effects on U.S. Employment

The Cato Institute—Immigration: The Demographic and Economic Facts
Internet URL: http://www.cato.org/pubs/policy_report/pr-imnative.html

continued

Navigation: Begin at the homepage of the Cato Institute (http://www.cato.org). Select "Publications Library." At the bottom of the page, key "Immigration" into the search dialog box. Then click on *Immigration: The Demographic and Economic Facts.* Finally, click on *Effects of Immigration on Native Employment.*

FUNDAMENTAL ISSUE #3

How does labor-force participation affect economic growth? Do population growth and immigration increase or reduce economic growth? A rise in labor-force participation causes an increase in labor supply, which spurs employment and causes a rise in real GDP. Hence, if more members of the current population enter the labor force, per capita income definitely rises. A larger population has two effects on per capita income. One is the positive effect from a rise in the labor force, but another is the negative effect of reducing the average share of GDP available to each person in a nation. Whether population growth leads to economic growth seems to be related to the extent of the nation's economic freedom. Immigration is a form of population growth, so its effects on economic growth also depend on how the positive and negative effects net out.

Labor Productivity and Economic Growth

As we have seen, labor-force participation affects growth. So does the productivity of labor that firms employ. We can also use the classical model of Chapter 3 to understand why labor productivity can be an important determinant of a nation's growth.

Labor Productivity, Employment, and Aggregate Supply   Business and financial publications such as the *Wall Street Journal* often feature articles on recent developments in labor productivity. Improvements in labor productivity are treated as "good news" for businesses because of the cost savings—and potentially higher short-run profits—that productivity improvements yield.

Nevertheless, a key effect of a productivity improvement arises in the labor market, and a general rise in labor productivity can have important economy-wide effects. We can see this in Figure 4–3. A rise in labor productivity means that each unit of labor is capable of producing a larger amount of output. Another way of saying this is that the marginal product of labor increases at any given quantity of labor, so the MP_N schedule shifts upward, as shown in panel (a). Because the value of marginal product is equal to the marginal product of labor times the price of output, the

FIGURE 4–3   **THE EFFECTS OF A RISE IN THE MARGINAL PRODUCT OF LABOR EMPLOYMENT, AND REAL OUTPUT**

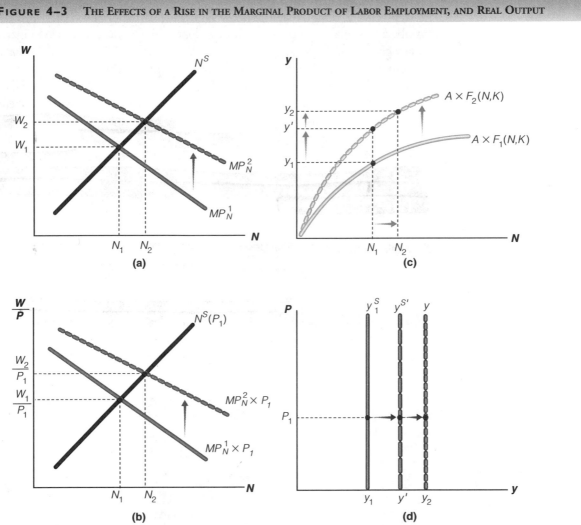

A rise in the marginal product of labor leads to an increase in the demand for labor, as shown in panels (a) and (b). As a result, the equilibrium money wage and employment level increase. Thus, if the economy's productive capabilities were to remain the same, real output would increase as a result of the rise in employment, and the aggregate supply schedule would shift rightward as in panel (d). Nevertheless, the marginal-product-of-labor schedule shows the slope of the production function at each level of employment. Hence, an increase in the marginal product of labor rotates the production function upward, as in panel (c). For this reason, an additional increase in real output occurs as a result of the greater productive capabilities owing to the rise in labor's marginal product, and the aggregate supply schedule shifts farther to the right in panel (d).

VMP_N schedule also shifts rightward, as shown in panel (b). Consequently, a rise in labor productivity results in an increase in the demand for labor, which induces a rise in the money wage and an increase in employment.

This is not the only effect of the rise in productivity, however. Recall that the marginal product of labor is the slope of the aggregate production function. Hence, a rise in labor's marginal product means that the slope of the production function increases at any given quantity of labor. As panel (c) shows, the result is an *upward rotation* in the production function. A rise in labor productivity thereby leads to a rise in equilibrium real output that has two causes. First, with any given quantity of labor, firms can produce more output. As shown in panel (c), even if employment were to remain at N_1, real output would increase to y'. Second, the rise in equilibrium employment, from N_1 to N_2, that is induced by the increase in labor's marginal product leads to a further increase in the production of output. Panel (d) shows that as a result of these combined increases in production of output, the aggregate supply schedule shifts rightward. A rise in labor productivity, like an increase in labor-force participation, leads to growth in real output.

Labor Productivity Growth and Employment Growth Move Together   Note that employment and productivity very naturally often move in the same direction. Figure 4–4 verifies this essential relationship between employment growth and output growth, which can make it difficult for economists to separate the effects of productivity improvements from those arising solely from employment growth.

This relationship also tends to confuse journalists who write about economic growth. Sometimes their writings seem to suggest that improvements in labor pro-

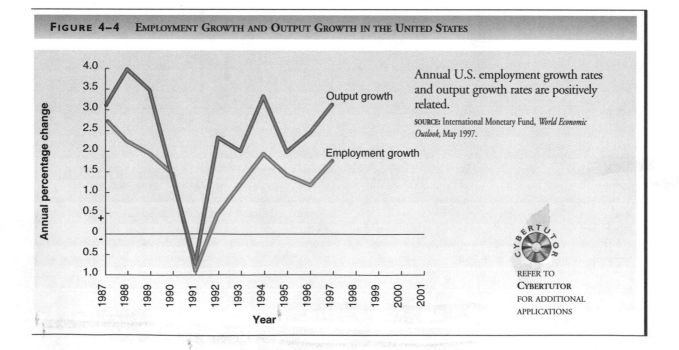

FIGURE 4–4   EMPLOYMENT GROWTH AND OUTPUT GROWTH IN THE UNITED STATES

Annual U.S. employment growth rates and output growth rates are positively related.

SOURCE: International Monetary Fund, *World Economic Outlook,* May 1997.

REFER TO
CYBERTUTOR
FOR ADDITIONAL
APPLICATIONS

ductivity necessarily lead to fewer people being employed by firms. As you can see, however, economic theory indicates that this is not necessarily true. If people generally become more productive, perhaps by making personal investments in education and training that improve their ability to produce goods and services, then the result is increased per capita incomes. The big issue, as we shall discuss shortly, is the extent to which people can make themselves sufficiently productive to avoid being replaced by machines.

FUNDAMENTAL ISSUE #4

How do changes in labor productivity influence economic growth?
A rise in the marginal product of labor enables firms to produce more output with any given amount of employment. A rise in labor's marginal product also leads to an increase in the demand for labor by firms, which stimulates employment. These two effects together yield growth in real GDP per capita.

Capital Investment, Saving, and Growth

GROSS INVESTMENT Total spending on capital goods during a year, including depreciation expenditures.

DEPRECIATION Spending to repair or replace existing capital goods.

NET INVESTMENT Gross investment minus depreciation; the result is equal to total expenditures on new capital goods.

As you learned in Chapter 2, when economists use the term *investment,* they have in mind the accumulation of capital goods. **Gross investment** is the term for total spending on capital goods during a year. Such expenditures typically include spending to repair existing capital. For instance, a part on a machine in a factory may wear out, or *depreciate,* during the year and need to be replaced. Spending to repair or replace existing capital goods is called the *depreciation allowance* or, more simply, **depreciation.**

The difference between gross investment and depreciation is **net investment.** This is the amount of spending during the year that adds to the existing stock of capital goods. Hence, by engaging in net investment expenditures during a year, a society creates new capital that can help fuel future economic growth.

Capital and Economic Growth   To see why capital accumulation via net investment induces economic growth, recall first that the long-run aggregate production function indicates that the amount of real output produced depends on capital as well as labor. To this point, we have graphed the production function with output (y) and employment (N) on the axes, nevertheless, but we can also draw a diagram of the production function in which we relate output to the amount of capital (K), as in Figure 4–5 (on page 114). Holding employment of labor unchanged, an increase in the amount of capital causes real output to increase.

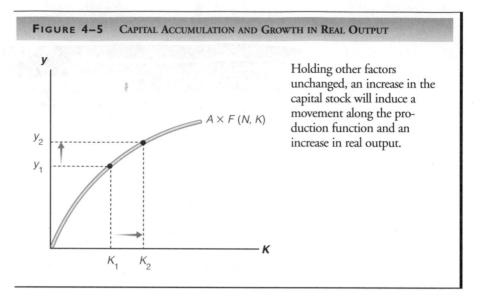

FIGURE 4–5   CAPITAL ACCUMULATION AND GROWTH IN REAL OUTPUT

Holding other factors unchanged, an increase in the capital stock will induce a movement along the production function and an increase in real output.

It follows that greater capital accumulation leads to higher economic growth. Capital accumulation, in turn, requires people and businesses to undertake net investment. Therefore, to understand the factors that can influence capital formation and its contribution to economic growth, we must consider the determinants of net investment.

Investment and the Marginal Product of Capital   Recall from Chapter 3 that desired investment is a component of the demand for loanable funds. According to the classical theory, the desired investment schedule is downward sloping in a diagram in which the real interest rate appears on the vertical axis. *Equilibrium* investment then is determined by the interplay between saving by households, investment spending that is done mainly by firms, and the demand for loanable funds by the government to finance its deficit.

How do we come up with the desired investment schedule used in the diagram of the loanable funds market? Let's begin by assuming that depreciation is a small enough component of gross investment that the difference between gross and net investment is negligible. (In fact, depreciation typically *is* just a fraction of gross investment.) Now consider Figure 4–6. Panel (a) shows the diagram of the aggregate production function from Figure 4–5. As in Figure 4–5, panel (a) of Figure 4–6 shows that a rise in the amount of capital, from K_1 to K_2, causes real output to increase from y_1 to y_2. In addition, however, panel (a) shows that the slope of lines tangent to the production function declines as the amount of capital increases. The slope of each of these tangent lines is the rise divided by the run, or a change in output divided by a change in the capital stock. In words, the slope of each line tangent to the production function is the additional output resulting from an additional unit of capital, which is the **marginal product of capital,** denoted MP_K.

MARGINAL PRODUCT OF CAPITAL (MP_K) The additional output that can be produced following the addition of another unit of capital.

Panel (b) of Figure 4–6 displays a marginal-product-of-capital schedule, or MP_K schedule, corresponding to the production function. Because the production function is concave, the law of diminishing marginal returns holds, and the MP_K schedule slopes downward. The rise in the amount of capital displayed in panel (a) causes a movement downward and rightward along the MP_K schedule.

Why would a firm choose to increase its capital stock? Recall from Chapter 3 that the real interest rate is the real rate of return from an investment in capital. The real interest rate, ρ, is the additional output that a firm receives from making an investment expenditure on new capital. These are the same units of measurement used to calculate the marginal product of capital. Consequently, there must be a relationship between the marginal product of capital, the real interest rate, and investment.

Figure 4–7 (see page 116) explains this relationship. Suppose that the current amount of capital is equal to K_1, so that the marginal product of capital is equal to MP_K^1, as shown in panel (a). The real interest rate, however, is equal to ρ'. Because the real interest rate is the market return on saving, it is the price of new capital to owners of the firm. By using the amount of capital K_1, the firm would be using too little capital relative to the amount consistent with the price of capital, ρ'. The firm would earn fewer profits than it otherwise could by increasing its capital to K_2, thereby reducing the marginal product of capital to MP_K^2, which is equal to the real interest rate ρ'. This capital increase would be the firm's investment, $i' = K_2 - K_1$.

FIGURE 4–6   THE MARGINAL-PRODUCT-OF-CAPITAL (MP_K) SCHEDULE

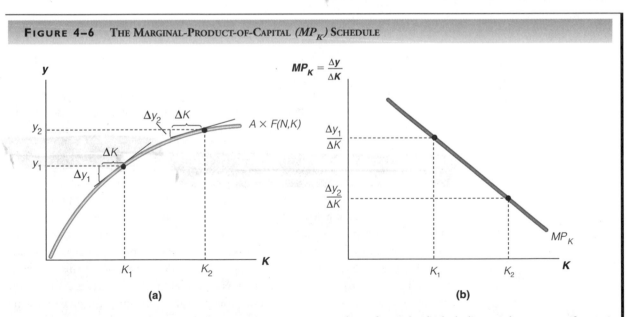

(a) (b)

As shown in panel (a), we can graph the aggregate production function with the amount of capital measured along the horizontal axis. The slope of the production function at any given quantity of capital is the marginal product of capital, which declines as the amount of capital increases. Hence, the marginal-product-of-capital schedule slopes downward, as in panel (b).

FIGURE 4–7 **THE REAL INTEREST RATE AND THE INVESTMENT SCHEDULE**

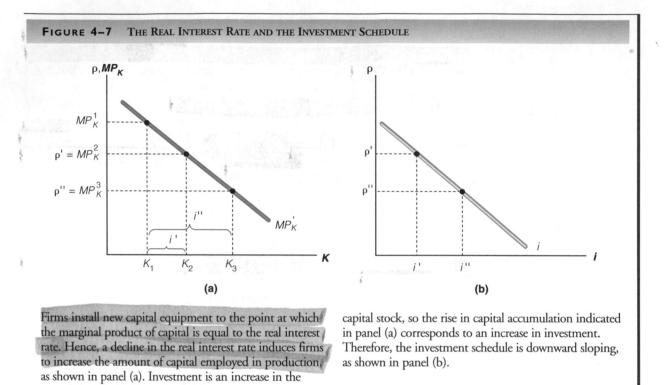

(a)

(b)

Firms install new capital equipment to the point at which the marginal product of capital is equal to the real interest rate. Hence, a decline in the real interest rate induces firms to increase the amount of capital employed in production, as shown in panel (a). Investment is an increase in the capital stock, so the rise in capital accumulation indicated in panel (a) corresponds to an increase in investment. Therefore, the investment schedule is downward sloping, as shown in panel (b).

Hence, as panel (b) shows, at the real interest rate ρ', the firm's desired investment would equal i'.

Now consider how a firm currently using the amount of capital K_1 would respond to a fall in the current real interest rate to ρ''. As panel (a) indicates, the firm would increase its use of capital goods further, to K_3. Consequently, it would undertake a larger amount of capital investment of $i'' = K_3 - K_1$. A reduction in the real interest rate would stimulate more capital investment by the firm. As a result, the firm's desired investment schedule would slope downward, as shown in panel (b).

What happens if capital becomes more productive? For example, suppose part of a firm's capital consists of computer equipment, and a software breakthrough improves the computers' functioning, so that the firm can produce more output with the same amount of computers. How does this improvement in productivity influence the firm's investment decision? Figure 4–8 provides the answer to this question. If capital becomes more productive, then its marginal product increases at any given amount of capital. As panel (a) shows, the marginal-product-of-capital schedule would shift upward and to the right. Consequently, at any given market real interest rate, the firm would desire to make a greater capital investment. This means that the investment schedule would shift to the right, following a rise in the marginal product of capital, as shown in panel (b).

FIGURE 4-8   DESIRED INVESTMENT AND A RISE IN THE MARGINAL PRODUCT OF CAPITAL

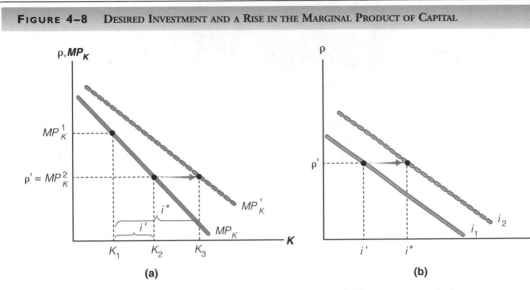

At a given real interest rate, an increase in the marginal product induces firms to employ additional capital in production, as shown in panel (a). The result, displayed in panel (b), is an increase in investment spending. Thus, a rise in the marginal product of capital shifts the investment schedule rightward.

A rise in investment, or increased capital formation, leads to an increase in the capital stock. A rise in the capital stock, in turn, yields an increase in real output. Therefore:

An increase in the productivity of capital leads to a rise in output growth. Thus, nations that are successful in developing ways to make their capital more productive generally grow faster than other nations.

(See on page 118 the Global Notebook: *Germany and Japan Invest More Than the United States, but Does It Matter?*)

Investment, Saving, and Economic Growth   The productivity of capital is only one factor influencing capital formation and economic growth. Any factor that affects the equilibrium amount of investment by all firms affects how much the capital stock and output will expand.

Figure 4–9 on page 118 illustrates one factor that affects equilibrium aggregate investment. This factor is total desired saving. The figure shows the market for loanable funds, where for the moment we ignore the existence of a government deficit. As we discussed in Chapter 3, the supply of loanable funds is the saving schedule, and in the absence of a government deficit the demand for loanable funds is the investment schedule. At the equilibrium real interest rate ρ_1, the amount of loanable funds supplied, saving, is equal to the amount of loanable funds demanded, investment, or $s_1 = i_1$.

ON THE WEB

Visit Germany's Homepage at:
http://www.chemie.fu-berlin.
de/adressen/brd.html

GLOBAL NOTEBOOK

Germany and Japan Invest More Than the United States, But Does It Matter?

According to researchers at the McKinsey Global Institute, on a per capita basis Germany has 13 percent more invested capital than the United States and Japan has more than 22 percent more. This is not surprising, given that, on average, German and Japanese saving rates have been more than twice the U.S. rate. Nevertheless, the United States creates more wealth per capita than do Germany and Japan. According to the McKinsey researchers, over the last twenty years, the United States created $26,500 of new wealth per capita (in 1993 prices) compared with $21,900 for Germany and $20,900 for Japan.

The difference can be attributed at least in part to the ability of the United States to use its capital stock more efficiently than either Germany or Japan. For the business sector as a whole, a unit of capital input in Germany or Japan generates final output that is about one-third lower than that in the United States. In other words, if a factory that makes a million units of a product each year costs $1 million in Japan or Germany, a comparable factory would cost about $670,000 in the United States. Some argue that the open and efficient stock and bond markets in the United States relentlessly pressure managers to be more profitable. As a result, since 1974, U.S. industry has had an average return on capital of 9 percent per annum compared to just over 7 percent in Germany and Japan.

FOR CRITICAL ANALYSIS:

"The United States overconsumes, undersaves, and underinvests." How do the facts presented here counter such a statement?

If household saving were to increase at any given real interest rate, the saving schedule would shift to the right. This would cause the equilibrium real interest rate to decline to ρ_2, which would induce firms to increase their investment. Capital formation would increase, as would economic growth, at least in the near term.

FIGURE 4–9   THE EFFECT ON EQUILIBRIUM INVESTMENT OF A RISE IN SAVING

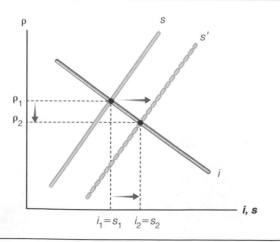

A rise in saving at any given real interest rate implies a rightward shift in the saving schedule. As a result, equilibrium saving and investment rise.

What might cause saving to rise? The answer is that saving would increase if households had incentives to save a larger portion of their earnings. For this reason, supply-side proponents often argue that income tax rates applied to households' returns from saving should be reduced or even eliminated. Such an action would cause the saving schedule to shift rightward, as in Figure 4–9, and induce greater capital investment.

Another factor that plays a role in determining equilibrium investment is the government deficit. As you learned in Chapter 3, an increase in the government's deficit *crowds out* private investment. To the extent that government spending financed by the deficit is purely consumption spending instead of investment in capital goods such as roads or bridges, the result is a decline in capital formation. For this reason supply-side enthusiasts also argue for reductions in government deficits as a way to stimulate greater capital formation and economic growth.

Does Capital Crowd Out Labor?   Classic science fiction stories of the 1940s and 1950s envisioned a future world where machines based on robotics technology could perform many of the mental and physical tasks previously performed only by human labor. In some of the darker stories, many human workers were unemployed as a result of the new technology, and only a few human beings reaped the rewards from the use of robots—a then futuristic type of capital good.

Although today's robots have not quite achieved the level of sophistication of the old science fiction stories, robot machines are commonplace in many of today's factories. Many factories also employ fewer workers than they did in the past. Does this mean that the science fiction stories were correct? Are capital and labor **substitutes in production**—meaning that greater use of capital leads to less use of labor in the production of goods and services? Or were the stories operating under a false premise? Could capital and labor be **complements in production,** so that greater use of capital goods actually stimulates employment of labor?

At the level of an individual firm or a specific industry, it turns out that some capital goods are substitutes for labor, while others are complements. In most cases, for instance, robot machines *do* substitute for human workers. Personal computers also can substitute for human beings. Accountants and actuaries who once needed human clerks to operate calculators by hand for hours on end now can program their personal computers to do the calculations for them in seconds.

At the same time, however, capital and labor can be complements in other environments. To the extent that there are **economies of scale** in a production process, meaning that savings in average production costs can be realized by increasing the size of a firm's operations by increasing its use of capital and other resources, it can pay for a business to grow larger. This can lead to a simultaneous increase in both capital and labor.

The development of new types of capital, such as robots or personal computers, can also create a need for human workers who can operate and repair the new capital equipment. For instance, even as the ranks of human clerks at accounting and actuarial firms have declined, the firms' staffs of human computer consultants have expanded.

SUBSTITUTES IN PRODUCTION The term for the situation in which increased use of capital leads to reduced use of labor in the production of real output.

COMPLEMENTS IN PRODUCTION The term for the situation in which an increased use of capital goods leads to greater use of labor in the production of goods and services.

ECONOMIES OF SCALE The realization of reduced average production costs via an increase in the size of a firm's operations through acquisition of new capital.

Do New Technologies Signal the End of Work?

Throughout the world, the media as well as numerous experts have painted a gloomy picture for the average working person. They point out that the newest technologies have led to a reduction in the percentage of workers who devote their time to manufacturing. Efficient production lines certainly do require fewer workers, and modern telecommunications have reduced the need for physical offices. During a recent talk show in England, the commentator stated that "The rich no longer need the poor. More and more goods can be produced with fewer and fewer workers. Therefore, permanent unemployment will grow."

Such commentaries have been popular since the invention of a weaving machine with a single operator that could produce as much cloth as ten people did previously. The fear was that the other nine workers would be unemployed forever.

Both theory and data render such analyses basically meaningless. In the United States, in spite of dramatic increases in technology, the number of new jobs created has averaged 2.5 million per year since 1975. Moreover, there has not been a dramatic increase in the trend in unemployment over the same period.

Theoretically, there are no limits to employment. Labor employment is a function of the supply and demand for labor. The demand for labor is not a fixed constant based on a mechanical relationship between the number of widgets produced and the number of workers needed to produce them. Workers released from industries that are more productive because of new technologies must—and do—find employment elsewhere, often in other industries that are expanding. As long as human wants are unlimited, there will always be new industries with new jobs. A key issue, as we discuss below, is whether people will have the knowledge and training to find good jobs in such industries.

FOR CRITICAL ANALYSIS:
Is it possible to predict the new types of jobs that will exist in fifty years? Why or why not?

The implication of these offsetting effects across firms and industries is that human beings will not be replaced by new and improved capital as long as they are willing and able to adapt to the new capital goods (see the Policy Notebook: *Do New Technologies Signal the End of Work?*). Humans who cannot adapt, or who choose not to do so, may find themselves substitute inputs in firms' production processes. Such humans may join the ranks of the unemployed. Those who do adapt, however, can find that the rewards are very high.

FUNDAMENTAL ISSUE #5

Why are saving and capital investment important for economic growth? A firm maximizes its profit when the marginal product of capital is equal to the real interest rate. A rise in the marginal product of capital or a decline in the real interest rate induces a firm to increase its investment in additional capital. Equilibrium total investment depends on the flow of saving. A rise in saving leads to greater investment, as does a decline in the government's deficit. Greater investment lays a foundation for higher economic growth.

KNOWLEDGE, INNOVATION, AND GROWTH

Humans adapt to new types of capital and ways of doing things by *learning*. That is, they acquire *knowledge* about new forms of capital and new ways to produce goods and services.

Innovation and Knowledge

Typically, we think of technological progress as, say, the invention of the electric motor, motion pictures and television, or the microchip. By themselves, however, inventions do not translate into greater economic growth. For instance, nearly a quarter of a century passed before the electric motor transformed the workplace and induced rapid growth in productive capabilities in the United States. The fact that a swift succession of moving images can trick the eye into perceiving motion was first understood in the 1830s, but more than fifty years passed before the first motion pictures were shown in theaters. The radio technology necessary for television was in wide use by the 1920s, but televisions did not become widespread in U.S. homes until the 1950s. Personal computers have been around since the 1970s, but only during the 1990s have they begun to change the way that the average U.S. worker works. Despite the significant growth in computer technology, computers amount to only 2 percent of the net investment by businesses and an even smaller percentage of all the machinery, equipment, and buildings owned by firms.

INNOVATION The process by which a new invention is integrated into the economy, where it reduces production costs or provides people with new types of goods and services.

Innovation   These examples illustrate that more than invention is needed to change the way that people produce goods and services. **Innovation,** or the transformation of something new, such as an invention, into something that benefits the economy either by lowering production costs or providing new types of goods and services, is required.

A natural question is how the process of innovation works (for an example, see the Global Notebook on page 122: *Innovation in the Japanese Automobile Industry*). For instance, have innovations in the United States been fueled by rising demand for new products in a rapidly expanding nation? Or does innovation itself spur a demand for goods and services that a new invention like the personal computer can make possible? Economists do not yet know the answer to this chicken-or-the-egg puzzle. What they do know, however, is the following:

ON THE WEB
Visit Japan's Web Sites at:
http://web.mit.edu/afs/
athena.mit.edu/user/r/o/
royk/www/JAPAN.html

GLOBAL NOTEBOOK

Innovation in the Japanese Automobile Industry

The automobile has been in production for more than a hundred years. By the 1950s, automobile manufacturers in the United States believed that by using time-and-motion studies they had developed the most efficient assembly-line operations in the world. Each worker on the assembly line had to adhere to a set of directions that enabled a given task to be performed in the least amount of time.

The Japanese decided to try to improve on the U.S. assembly lines. They used a process of experimentation and discovery—small innovations in the production process that were almost random. In Japanese automobile plants, workers were encouraged to experiment with minor changes in how they assembled a car. Should the door molding go on before or after the door is put on the car? Were one or two workers needed inside the car to attach the dashboard? Gradually, Japanese automobile workers became more efficient than their U.S. counterparts. The efficiency came about through small innovative changes, not one great invention.

FOR CRITICAL ANALYSIS:
Is it possible to calculate how many ways an automobile can be put together?

Innovation cannot occur without the capacity for human beings to *create*. People must have knowledge of their world and must have the ability to *apply* that knowledge if innovation is to occur.

HUMAN CAPITAL The knowledge and skills possessed by people in a nation's labor force.

Human Capital The knowledge and skills that people in the labor force possess constitute their **human capital.** People develop human capital through education, on-the-job training, and self-teaching. Just as physical capital cannot be accumulated without investment in capital goods, human capital accumulation requires investment in activities and experiences that add to people's knowledge and train their minds to apply that knowledge in new tasks.

Productivity, innovation, and human capital are all related. A poorly trained work force cannot be highly innovative and productive. As we have discussed, productivity is a key component of growth. Yet total productivity in the United States has not grown much in recent years. As Figure 4–10 shows, overall productivity grew slowly and steadily from 1870 until 1930. After the Great Depression of the 1930s, productivity grew at a rapid pace until the late 1970s. Since then, however, productivity has leveled off. Its recent performance is similar to that of the 1870s, a period that predated the development of mass electric power generation and distribution as well as other innovations, such as the adoption and use of automotive and air travel, radio and television, and computers.

Some economists argue that one explanation for the leveling off of U.S. productivity in the 1980s and 1990s has been a relative decline in human capital investment in the United States. This is one of the reasons why concerned citizens and political

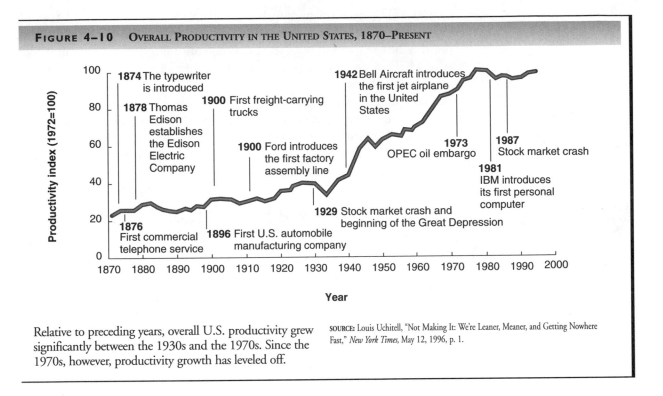

FIGURE 4–10 OVERALL PRODUCTIVITY IN THE UNITED STATES, 1870–PRESENT

Relative to preceding years, overall U.S. productivity grew significantly between the 1930s and the 1970s. Since the 1970s, however, productivity growth has leveled off.

SOURCE: Louis Uchitell, "Not Making It: We're Leaner, Meaner, and Getting Nowhere Fast," *New York Times*, May 12, 1996, p. 1.

leaders have been rethinking the structure of the nation's education system. As Figure 4–10 indicates, the highest productivity growth occurred between the mid-1930s and the late 1970s, which was also a period of rapid development of the nation's secondary schools and colleges and universities. These schools and colleges became the centers of human capital development. Most provided firm grounding in science and mathematics—precisely the areas that are required for developing better technology.

The Importance of Education

Many critics of U.S. secondary schools and colleges have pointed out that the slowing of U.S. productivity growth depicted in Figure 4–10 began after the bulk of these educational institutions sharply reduced the number of required courses in science and mathematics. These critics argue that one way to reattain the productivity growth of the 1940–1980 period would be to return to the educational standards of those years.

Other observers argue that simply requiring more courses is unlikely to turn around today's low productivity growth rates. So far, however, little progress has been made in determining exactly what measures *would* achieve this goal. On the one hand, some economists argue that increased government spending on education at local, state, and federal levels would improve education and provide the human capital base for future productivity growth. On the other hand, others contend that such gains can be achieved only if governments limit their role in the educational system. This, they believe, would force the nation's educational system to adapt to market forces, which in turn would place high value on productivity-enhancing gains in human capital accumulation.

Clearly, the question of how to lay the best foundation of human capital to spur future innovation and growth has no simple answer. Nevertheless, economists agree that education is crucial to economic growth. In the long run, nations that fail to invest—either individually or collectively—in human capital cannot expect to keep pace with those that do make such investments.

NEW GROWTH THEORY: DOES GROWTH FEED ON ITSELF?

Economists' interest in the determinants of productivity growth is a relatively recent phenomenon. Although economists have always recognized that growth in productivity is important to economic growth, traditionally they tended to focus their attention on the contributions that stemmed from the relatively more easily measured and understood growth of labor and capital. Typically, economists regarded productivity growth as an external factor and did not try very hard to explain it.

The New Growth Theory

NEW GROWTH THEORY A theory of economic growth that focuses on productivity growth as a key determinant of technological progress and the rate of growth of an economy.

In contrast, economists called *new growth theorists* now focus on productivity and technology as driving forces of economic growth. According to **new growth theory,** technological growth is crucial to economic growth, and technological growth in turn is fueled by improvements in productivity. This means that to understand what makes an economy grow, we must understand what factors determine productivity growth.

Two factors have helped to spur the development of new growth theory. One is the apparent relationship between the recent declines in economic growth and the leveling off of productivity growth. The other factor has been the recognition that technological change can play a significant role in explaining even the slow growth rates of recent years.

Consider some startling statistics about the growth in computer technology. Microprocessor speeds may increase from 350 megahertz to 1,000 megahertz by the year 2010. By that same year, the size of the thinnest circuit line in a transistor likely will decrease by over 75 percent. The typical memory capacity of computers may increase by a factor of one thousand. Even before these changes have occurred, microchip manufacturers should be able to produce a thousand transistors a week for every person on earth.

As noted earlier, investment in computer hardware accounts for only a small fraction of total capital investment. To new growth theorists, however, this is not the main contribution of computers. The key issue for growth, they contend, is the extent to which people can raise their productivity and the productivity of the other capital they use to produce goods and services by adapting technological improvements in computers. In other words, the relative importance of computers in the overall capital stock may be less important than how much the use of computers contributes to production and manufacturing knowledge and innovation.

Knowledge and Self-Perpetuating Growth

To new growth theorists, production and manufacturing knowledge is at least as important to determining economic growth as other factors. These adherents of new growth theory argue that as an aspect of human capital accumulation, knowledge is a factor of production that people accumulate by forgoing current consumption. Nations must therefore invest in knowledge just as they invest in machines.

New growth theorists view recent advances in computer technology as an example of how economic growth can be *self-perpetuating*. An investment in capital such as computer equipment can make it more profitable to acquire more knowledge. This newly acquired knowledge then creates a need for new and better computer equipment. As a result, an initial investment in computer technology can increase knowledge, but then the new knowledge can stimulate greater investment.

According to the traditional theory of economic growth, a onetime increase in the rates of saving and investment leads to a higher plateau for a nation's standard of living, but the standard of living does not continue to rise as a result. If knowledge itself stimulates economic growth, however, as suggested by the new growth theory, then a onetime increase in a country's rate of investment may permanently raise that country's growth rate. This means that economic growth can continue as long as people keep coming up with new ideas and developing greater knowledge.

The new growth theory, therefore, places greater emphasis on human capital and education. The process of acquiring and applying knowledge may be the key to continuous economic growth. For this process to work, however, people must be able to apply their minds effectively.

FUNDAMENTAL ISSUE #6

What role does human knowledge play in economic growth? Is growth self-perpetuating? According to the new growth theory, the acquisition and use of knowledge that people gain from investment can contribute to further investment. As a result, economic growth can be self-perpetuating, provided that people make human capital investments that enable them to engage in the process of acquiring and using knowledge.

INTERNATIONAL TRADE AND ECONOMIC GROWTH

Should a nation that desires greater growth encourage or discourage trade with other countries? On the one hand, promoting trade could permit a nation to specialize in production of goods and services that its industries can produce most efficiently. On the other hand, inhibiting trade might protect fledgling industries from foreign competition and permit them to grow more quickly.

The Case for Protectionism

PROTECTIONISM The adoption of policies that impose legal and economic barriers to international trade.

QUOTAS Quantity limitations on international trade of goods and services.

TARIFFS Taxes imposed on the values of goods and services that are traded internationally.

In years past, and even today, some economists have argued that **protectionism,** or the use of various legal and economic barriers to international trade, promoted economic growth. They advocated **quotas,** or numerical limits on cross-border shipments of goods and services, and **tariffs,** or taxes on the values of such shipments, as means of protecting home industries from foreign competition.

The basis of the argument for protectionism is the idea that pure competition may not be the best market structure to promote economic growth. Instead, proponents of protectionism favor the view that the centralization of resources among a few home businesses may permit them to grow more rapidly. In addition, they argue that protection from foreign competition can keep new home industries from failing prematurely in the face of short-term profit fluctuations that might occur if they were exposed to variations in world prices.

INTERNET • SOURCE

Opening Up Trade in the Search for Greater North American Economic Growth—NAFTA

The North American Free Trade Agreement
Internet URL: **http://www.iep.doc.gov/border/nafta.htm**

Navigation: Begin with Yahoo! (**http://yahoo.com**). Click on *Business and Economy.* Then click on *NAFTA.* Then click on *Nafta Border* and select desired topic.

The Open Economy and Economic Growth

Nevertheless, today most economists who study economic growth tend to believe that greater openness to trade is the best way to promote growth. For instance, new growth theorists emphasize the importance of ideas and knowledge, which can be diffused around the globe more rapidly if technologies can move freely across national borders.

Furthermore, more open economies may experience higher rates of economic growth because their own industries have access to a larger market. Home industries that are protected by trade barriers such as tariffs or quotas can become isolated from world technological progress. Former Communist countries and a number of developing nations in Latin America and elsewhere experienced this problem in years past.

Economists continue to debate this issue. At present, however, those who promote openness have some strong evidence favoring their view. As Figure 4–11 shows, there seems to be some evidence of an inverse relationship between economic growth and the level of protectionism in a nation. So far, experience indicates that greater openness may be more conducive to higher economic growth.

| FIGURE 4–11 | PROTECTIONISM VERSUS ECONOMIC GROWTH |

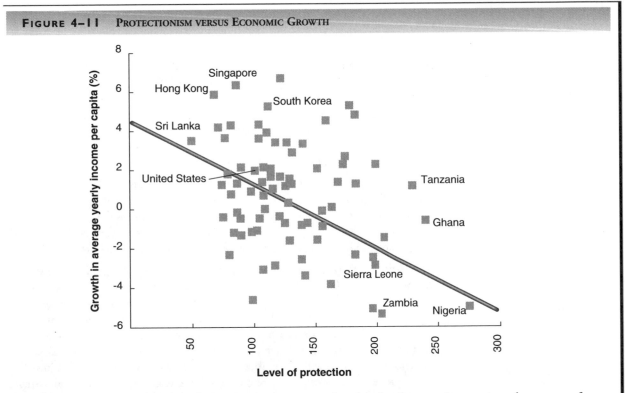

In nations with closed economies, the government prevents imports from entering the country and sometimes keeps exports from leaving the country. Such protectionism closes off the nation to new technologies and other sources of economic growth. The data appear to favor the view that closed economies experience lower rates of growth, all other things held constant.

SOURCE: David M. Gould, Roy J. Ruffin, and Graeme L. Woodbridge, "The Theory and Practice of Free Trade," Federal Reserve Bank of Dallas *Economic Review,* Fourth Quarter 1993, 1–16.

FUNDAMENTAL ISSUE #7

How does international trade affect economic growth? Arguably, prohibiting cross-border trade flows can promote the growth of the productive capabilities of home industries by protecting them from profit variability and enabling them to marshal home resources. At the same time, however, protectionist policies can inhibit economic growth by stifling the flow of new ideas and technologies. Many economists believe that the bulk of the evidence favors the view that, on net, protectionism slows growth.

CHAPTER SUMMARY

1. **Measuring Economic Growth:** The annual rate of change in per capita real GDP is the measure of economic growth. This measure is imperfect, because it fails to account for changes in the quality of goods and services, does not always reflect improvements in living standards, and does not tell us how many residents of a nation actually benefit from growth. This measure also cannot capture negative intergenerational externalities that growth may create. Nevertheless, it is the best available measure of how much the real income of a nation's average resident grows over time.

2. **The Key Factors Determining the Rate of Economic Growth:** Three crucial factors influence the growth of per capita GDP. One is the growth of labor's contribution to GDP resulting from a rise in the number of workers. A second factor is the growth in the contribution of capital to GDP as a nation accumulates a larger amount of capital. Finally, higher productivity of existing labor and capital can add to economic growth.

3. **The Growth Effects of Increased Labor-Force Participation, Larger Populations, and Immigration:** Holding a nation's population unchanged, greater labor-force participation leads to higher employment of labor and increased real GDP, which raises the rate of economic growth. Population growth tends to increase the number of workers, which adds to real GDP, but it also increases the number of people among whom real GDP is divided. As a result, the effect of population growth on economic growth is not obvious. Current evidence favors the view that population growth enhances economic growth in nations with a greater degree of economic freedom but depresses growth in nations with restraints on economic freedom. Traditionally, immigration has spurred economic growth, although the growth effects of immigration are hotly debated today.

4. **Labor Productivity and Economic Growth:** Greater productivity of labor enhances economic growth. In recent years, however, labor productivity in the United States and other developed countries has stagnated, as has economic growth.

5. **How Saving and Capital Investment Matter for Economic Growth:** Nations accumulate new capital by forgoing consumption and saving resources. This permits capital investment to occur. Firms add to their use of capital by investing to the point at which the marginal product of capital is equal to the real interest rate. Consequently, increased national saving, a fall in the real interest rate, or a rise in the productivity of capital leads to a rise in capital accumulation and greater long-run economic growth.

6. **Human Knowledge and the Idea of Self-Perpetuating Growth:** The new growth theory emphasizes the importance of productivity growth as a determinant of economic growth. According to this view, investments in human capital, or the ability of people to use their minds to acquire and use knowledge, and in knowledge-enhancing technologies are crucial for raising rates of long-term economic growth. Such investments lead to growth in knowledge, which then spurs further investment, which can make economic growth a self-perpetuating process.

7. **International Trade and Economic Growth:** A traditional argument is that protecting home industries from foreign competition and allowing a few firms in these industries to command most of a nation's resources can enhance the speed of economic growth. Most economists today, and especially new growth theorists, believe that such protectionism also slows the global flows of new ideas and technologies. The net effect of protectionism on economic growth can thereby be negative. Experience appears to offer some support for this latter view.

QUESTIONS AND PROBLEMS

1. The following table presents growth rate data for four countries (A, B, C, and D) between 1998 and 2008:

	Annual Growth Rate (%)			
	A	B	C	D
Nominal GDP	30	22	15	8
Price level	18	10	5	2
Population	10	8	2	1

   a. Which country has the largest rate of output growth per capita?

   b. Which country has the smallest rate of output growth per capita?

2. Use Table 4–2 to answer the following questions:

   a. Country X has a growth rate of 3 percent, and Country Y has a growth rate of 4 percent. Assume that they both start off with equal incomes. How much richer will Country Y be after twenty years? After fifty years?

   b. Assume that Country H has twice the income per capita of Country K. Country H is growing at 3 percent., and Country K is growing at 4 percent. Will Country K ever catch up? If so, when?

3. During a given interval, a nation's overall productivity grows at a compounded rate of 2 percent. Its population growth rate and degree of labor-force participation do not change over this time span. The nation accumulates new capital at a compounded rate

of growth of 1 percent, and the coefficient governing the proportionate increase in real GDP production in response to a proportionate rise in the amount of capital is equal to 0.3. What is the compound growth rate of real GDP during this interval?

4. A nation's rate of economic growth in 1997 was 5 percent. It accumulated capital at a rate of 5 percent and added to its employment of labor at a rate of 5 percent. The proportionate increase in real GDP in response to a proportionate increase in capital was 0.2, and the proportionate rise in real GDP following a proportionate increase in labor was 0.8. What was the growth in the overall productivity of labor and capital during 1997?

5. Explain in your own words why population growth has theoretically uncertain effects on economic growth.

6. Immigration has become a thorny political issue in the United States at the dawning of the new century, just as it was at the dawning of the twentieth century. In light of what you have learned in this chapter, discuss why this is not surprising.

7. Explain in your own words why nations with more productive capital grow faster.

8. A lower real rate of interest tends to spur investment spending, thereby stimulating expansion of the nation's capital stock. Based on this relationship, some observers argue that the Federal Reserve should "keep interest rates low" to encourage greater economic growth. Based on what you learned about real and nominal interest-rate determination in Chapter 3, does it appear that the Federal Reserve could actually play a central role in regulating a nation's real GDP growth? Explain your reasoning.

9. Explain in your own words why the new growth theory regards education as central to a nation's long-term growth prospects.

10. Theories of economic growth developed during the 1960s assumed that aggregate production exhibits "constant returns to scale," which means that a proportionate change in all factors of production leads to an equal proportionate increase in output produced. Is the new growth theory consistent with this assumption? Explain your reasoning.

CYBERTUTOR EXERCISES

1. Consider Figure 4–1 in the text. Using the real US GDP per-capita series, construct the growth rate in real GDP per-capita. Plot this against time. Is the growth of real US GDP per-capita volatile? Can you identify recessions? How does the American experience compare with the experience of Japan and France?

2. Figure 4–4 in the text suggests that there is a strong relationship between employment growth and output growth suggested by US data. See if this relationship continues to hold for France and Japan. Are the results what you expected? Why?

ON-LINE APPLICATION

As discussed in this chapter, growth in productivity is a key factor determining a nation's overall economic growth. This application helps you to perform your own evaluation of the factors contributing to U.S. growth.

Internet URL: http://stats.bls.gov/news.release/prod3.toc.htm

Title: **Bureau of Labor Statistics: Multifactor Productivity Trends**

Navigation: Begin at the homepage of the Bureau of Labor Statistics (http://stats.bls.gov). Select "Surveys and Programs," and then click on *Productivity and Technology*. Click on *Multifactor Productivity*. Then click on *Multifactor Productivity Trends*.

Application: Read the report and answer the following questions:

1. What does multifactor productivity measure? How do multifactor productivity and labor productivity differ?

2. Based on your reading of this chapter, how does multifactor productivity relate to the determination of economic growth?

SELECTED REFERENCES AND FURTHER READING

Federal Reserve Bank of Kansas City. *Policies for Long-Run Economic Growth.* 1992.

Filardo, Andrew. "Has the Productivity Trend Steepened in the 1990s?" Federal Reserve Bank of Kansas City *Economic Review,* Fourth Quarter 1995, pp. 41–59.

Gould, David, and Roy Ruffin. "What Determines Economic Growth?" Federal Reserve Bank of Dallas *Economic Review,* Second Quarter 1993, pp. 25–40.

Ireland, Peter. "Two Perspectives on Growth and Taxes." Federal Reserve Bank of Richmond *Economic Review,* Winter 1994, pp. 1–18.

Romer, Paul. "Increasing Returns and Economic Growth." *Journal of Political Economy,* 95 (October 1986): 1002–1037.

Solow, Robert. "A Contribution to the Theory of Economic Growth." *Quarterly Journal of Economics* 70 (February 1956): 65–94.

Business Cycles and Short-Run Macroeconomics—

ESSENTIALS OF THE KEYNESIAN SYSTEM

Every month the U.S. Department of Commerce issues a publication of about a hundred pages, most of which are filled with statistics on the economy. Now called the Survey of Current Business, *it was known as the* Business Cycle Digest *until the 1970s. Purportedly, the Department of Commerce changed the name of this publication because government economists in the 1960s thought that the "business cycle" was dead because the U.S. economy had experienced a relatively long period of expansion.*

Today, no one believes that national business fluctuations are obsolete. Since the Department of Commerce changed the name of its statistical publication, the economy has experienced four officially recognized recessions. Perhaps in recognition that fluctuations in overall national business activity are here to stay, a few years ago the Department of Commerce transferred a number of statistical responsibilities to the Conference Board—a private organization. Now the Conference Board publishes all of these statistics in a monthly magazine called Business Cycle Indicators.

Part of what you will learn in this chapter involves the different phases of a typical business cycle. The remainder of the chapter will introduce you to the traditional Keynesian explanation of changes in the equilibrium level of real GDP and the resulting changes in employment.

FROM THE LONG RUN TO THE SHORT RUN: BUSINESS CYCLES

A nation's rate of economic growth determines the future standard of living of its citizens. Typically, however, a nation's citizens care more about their living standards *today* than about their well-being down the road. To at least some extent, people typically *discount* the future, meaning that they place less weight on possible future outcomes relative to events that affect them in the present. As a result, although people recognize that economic choices they make today will affect their lives in future years, they tend to care more about how those choices influence their lives right now.

A single parent of two young children, for instance, certainly would be pleased if her real income prospects would grow at a compounded rate of 4 percent over the next twenty years instead of at the current U.S. average income growth rate of 0.9 percent. If business conditions this month have been so poor, however, that her employer has cut back on production and placed her on a long-term layoff from her full-time job, differences in long-term growth rates become purely academic issues. The issue in her mind this month is not her income prospects twenty years from now, but her ability to earn sufficient income to feed, clothe, and provide supervision for her children during the coming weeks and months.

Business Cycles

This natural human concern about current economic prospects is why people typically worry about fluctuations in their real incomes. Fluctuations in aggregate real

BUSINESS CYCLE Fluctuations in aggregate real income above or below its long-run growth path.

NATURAL GDP The level of real GDP that is consistent with the economy's natural rate of growth.

RECESSION A decline in real GDP lasting at least two consecutive quarters, which can cause real GDP to fall below its long-run, natural level.

TROUGH The point along a business cycle at which real GDP is at its lowest level relative to the long-run natural GDP level.

DEPRESSION An especially severe recession.

income relative to its long-run growth path are **business cycles.** Figure 5–1 illustrates some key concepts associated with a single complete business cycle. The dashed line in the figure shows a hypothetical growth path for **natural GDP,** or the level of real GDP along the long-run growth path that the economy would tend to follow in the absence of cyclical fluctuations. The solid curve is a hypothetical growth path for *actual* GDP, which fluctuates over time.

Recessions and Business Cycle Troughs When actual real GDP declines, the economy is said to be in a phase in the business cycle known as a **recession.** The National Bureau of Economic Research defines a recession as a period of at least two consecutive quarters in which real GDP falls.

At the low point of a recession, actual real GDP is at its lowest point relative to its natural path, meaning that the downward vertical distance between the natural GDP growth path and the actual growth path reaches its maximum size for the cycle. This point is called the **trough** of the business cycle. At the trough, actual real GDP may be well below the economy's natural level. If such a significant recession and trough are particularly long lasting, then economists say that the economy experiences a severe recession, or a **depression.** Although economists often disagree about when recessions are sufficiently severe for this term to apply, all agree that a depression occurred in the United States during the 1930s.

FIGURE 5–1   A HYPOTHETICAL BUSINESS CYCLE

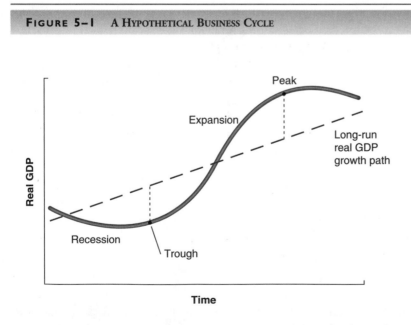

At a business cycle trough, actual real GDP is at its lowest point relative to the long-run growth path of real GDP, so the downward vertical distance between long-run and actual real GDP levels reaches its largest size over the cycle. The period in which real GDP declines toward this trough is a recession. Beyond the trough, actual real GDP rises back toward and beyond its long-run growth path until it reaches its peak for the cycle. This period is called a business cycle expansion. At the peak of the expansion, the upward vertical distance between the long-run real GDP growth path and the actual growth path reaches its maximum size.

EXPANSION The period during a business cycle when actual GDP begins to rise, perhaps even above its natural, long-run level.

PEAK The point along a business cycle at which real GDP is at its highest level relative to its long-run, natural level.

Expansions and Business Cycle Peaks When actual real GDP begins to rise again, the economy enters the **expansion** phase of the business cycle. At the point where actual real GDP rises to its highest level relative to natural GDP, the business cycle is at its **peak.** Then the cycle begins anew.

Actual business cycles are not as simple as the one illustrated in Figure 5–1. The actual path of real GDP typically is much less smooth than the hypothetical path shown in the figure, and the durations of expansions and recessions are rarely of equal length. Table 5–1 tabulates the durations between troughs and peaks of the twenty-one business cycles that the United States has experienced since 1899. As the table indicates, the lengths of expansion and recession phases of business cycles have varied considerably.

Unemployment and the Business Cycle

Business cycles entail movements in aggregate GDP that have implications for all of us. When business cycle recessions cause more people to lose their jobs, as in our ear-

---

TABLE 5–1 **BUSINESS CYCLE EXPANSIONS AND RECESSIONS IN THE UNITED STATES**

| | | | DURATION IN MONTHS* | | |
PEAK	TROUGH	PEAK	RECESSION	EXPANSION	CYCLE
June 1899	December 1900	September 1902	18	21	39
September 1902	August 1904	May 1907	23	33	56
May 1907	June 1908	January 1910	13	19	32
January 1910	January 1912	January 1913	24	12	36
January 1913	December 1914	August 1918	23	44	67
August 1918	March 1919	January 1920	7	10	17
January 1920	July 1921	May 1923	18	22	40
May 1923	July 1924	October 1926	14	27	41
October 1926	November 1927	August 1929	13	21	34
August 1929	March 1933	May 1937	43	50	93
May 1937	June 1938	February 1945	13	80	93
February 1945	October 1945	November 1948	8	37	45
November 1948	October 1949	July 1953	11	45	56
July 1953	May 1954	August 1957	10	39	49
August 1957	April 1958	April 1960	8	24	32
April 1960	February 1961	December 1969	10	106	116
December 1969	November 1970	November 1973	11	36	47
November 1973	March 1975	January 1980	16	58	74
January 1980	July 1980	July 1981	6	12	18
July 1981	November 1982	July 1990	16	92	108
July 1990	March 1991		8	†	†

SOURCES: National Bureau of Economic Research and the *Survey of Current Business.*
*Cycles are measured from peak to peak.
†As of 1998.

lier example, the effects can hit especially hard. In contrast, expansions can pave the way to brighter futures for many families as they bring about an overall reduction in unemployment.

The Unemployment Rate   To track the extent of aggregate unemployment in the U.S. economy, the government tabulates the **unemployment rate,** which is simply the percentage of the civilian labor force that is unemployed. Terminology is important here: The civilian labor force consists of all individuals 16 to 65 years of age who are not in the military or confined to an institution such as a hospital and who either have a job or are actively seeking a job. The number of people in the civilian labor force who are unemployed includes all who are not working yet are available for and actively seeking a job. People who are not employed but who also are not actively looking for work are not included in either the civilian labor force or in the ranks of the unemployed. Such *discouraged workers* are not counted in calculations of the unemployment rate.

It is important to understand that the official unemployment rate is an *estimate.* The government does not calculate the entire labor force. On behalf of the Bureau of Labor Statistics, the Bureau of the Census conducts a monthly *Current Population Survey* covering 60,000 households in about 2,000 counties and cities across the fifty states and the District of Columbia. The Bureau of Labor Statistics uses the information from this monthly survey to calculate its estimates of the size of the labor force and of the number of people in the labor force who are unemployed. It then uses these estimates to calculate the unemployment rate.

Business Cycles and the Unemployment Rate   The unemployment rate varies systematically across business cycles, as Figure 5–2 shows. Recessions, which are the shaded periods in the figure, always are accompanied by higher unemployment rates. During expansion phases of business cycles, in contrast, unemployment rates tend to decline.

Economists identify three components of the unemployed portion of the civilian labor force. One is **frictional unemployment,** which refers to the portion of the labor force consisting of people who are qualified for gainful employment but are temporarily out of work. They may be in this situation because they recently quit a job to accept another job that will begin in a few weeks.

Another component of unemployment is **structural unemployment.** This refers to the portion of the civilian labor force made up of people who would like to be gainfully employed but lack skills and other attributes necessary to obtain a job. The duration of unemployment for these individuals can stretch into months or perhaps even years.

As we shall discuss in more detail in Chapter 8, most economists consider the ratio of those who are frictionally and structurally unemployed to the civilian labor force to be the **natural rate of unemployment,** or the unemployment rate that would exist if the economy could stay on its long-run growth path. The variations in the overall

---

UNEMPLOYMENT RATE The percentage of the civilian labor force that is unemployed.

FRICTIONAL UNEMPLOYMENT The portion of total unemployment arising from the fact that a number of workers are between jobs at any given time.

STRUCTURAL UNEMPLOYMENT The portion of total unemployment resulting from a poor match of workers' abilities and skills with current needs of employers.

NATURAL RATE OF UNEMPLOYMENT The portion of the unemployment rate that is accounted for by frictional and structural unemployment.

FIGURE 5–2   UNEMPLOYMENT RATES AND PHASES OF THE BUSINESS CYCLE

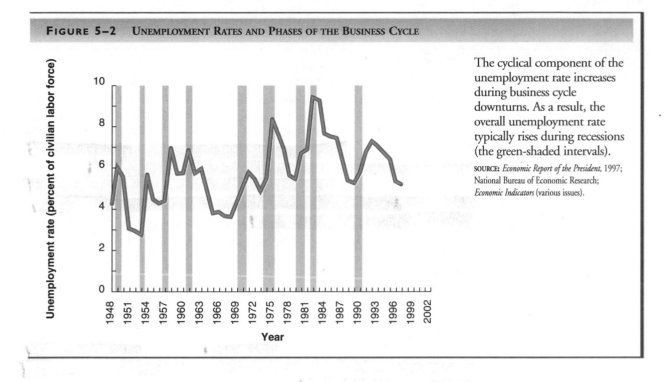

The cyclical component of the unemployment rate increases during business cycle downturns. As a result, the overall unemployment rate typically rises during recessions (the green-shaded intervals).

SOURCE: *Economic Report of the President*, 1997; National Bureau of Economic Research; *Economic Indicators* (various issues).

CYCLICAL UNEMPLOYMENT The portion of total unemployment resulting from business cycle fluctuations.

unemployment rate shown in Figure 5–2 arise from changes in the third category of unemployment, called **cyclical unemployment.** This is the portion of the civilian labor force composed of those who lose their jobs because of business cycle fluctuations.

FUNDAMENTAL ISSUE #1

What are business cycles, and what are their key features? Business cycles are fluctuations in real income above or below the level that is consistent with the economy's long-run growth. Recessions occur when real income falls below its long-run level, and expansions take place when real income rises back to or even above its long-run level. Although the existence of frictional and structural unemployment implies that there is a natural unemployment rate, the overall unemployment rate has a cyclical component that rises during recessions and falls during expansions.

Keynes's Critique of the Classical Theory

In a 1930 radio broadcast, the British economist John Maynard Keynes surveyed the severe recession the United Kingdom was experiencing and concluded, "If we just sit tight there will be still more than a million men unemployed six months or a year hence. That is why I feel that a radical policy of some kind is worth trying, even if there are risks about it." The "radical policy" that Keynes advocated entailed a departure from the policy prescriptions of the classical macroeconomic model that we presented in Chapter 3. Rather than keep government deficits low and maintain steady money growth, Keynes advocated active governmental policies to reduce the high cyclical unemployment rates of the 1930s. Indeed, Keynes proposed a broad abandonment of many aspects of classical theory and in its place offered a different way of looking at macroeconomics. This approach became known as "Keynesian macroeconomics."

The Alleged Shortsightedness of Long-Run Analysis

As a student, Keynes had learned all the elements of the classical theory. He did not advocate tossing aside all its features. The problem, he argued, was that the classical theory did not do a good job of explaining short-run movements in real GDP away from its long-run growth path. To Keynes, classical theory did not satisfactarily explain the business cycles that affected so many lives in the near term.

Short-Run Labor-Market Rigidities   Keynes felt that the classical theory of the labor market was especially defective. According to that theory, as you learned in Chapter 3, the labor supply schedule is upward sloping. Workers supply more labor services as the real wage rises and fewer labor services as the real wage falls. In either circumstance, the adjustment of the quantity of labor supplied to changes in real wages would bring about a new labor-market equilibrium in which both workers and firms were satisfied with the prevailing real wage.

According to Keynes, actual observations did not support this prediction of the classical labor-market model. Real wages in Britain, the United States, and elsewhere declined during the 1930s, yet millions of prospective workers could not find jobs. Furthermore, in Keynes' view the real wage did not fall as quickly or as much as classical theory predicted. Both of these observations of short-run labor-market adjustments induced Keynes to reject the classical theory of labor supply in favor of an alternative theory.

Money and Financial Markets   Keynes also questioned key aspects of the classical theory of money and financial markets. Recall from Chapter 3 that a change in the quantity of money by a government or central bank should, according to the quantity theory, have a direct effect on the aggregate demand for goods and services.

Keynes argued that the quantity theory overstated the extent to which monetary policy actions influence aggregate demand.

The problem, Keynes contended, was that classical theory ignored the fact that money is an asset that is part of a person's financial wealth along with bonds and stocks. Whenever people revise their bond or stock holdings based on speculations about interest-rate movements, the resulting reshuffling of financial assets entails short-run changes in desired money holdings. Consequently, a person's demand for money ought to depend on the interest rate. Classical theory did not give sufficient consideration to this relationship between desired money holdings and the interest rate, according to Keynes. This led him to develop a new theory of money demand.

Consumption, Saving, and Investment   Finally, Keynes questioned the classical model's view of the roles of consumption, saving, and investment. As you learned in Chapter 3, in the classical theory output is determined on the supply side, and then its division among households, firms, and the government is a distributional issue. The real interest rate adjusts in the loanable funds market to equate saving with the sum of investment and the government's deficit. The amount that households do not save (or pay in taxes) then is available for current consumption of goods and services.

To Keynes, this view reversed the proper order for understanding short-run fluctuations in real GDP. Key sources of such fluctuations, it seemed to him, were year-to-year variations in household consumption expenditures and investment spending by firms. For this reason, Keynes formulated a new theory of aggregate demand with consumption and investment as the centerpieces.

The Short-Run Focus: The Circular Flow of Income and Expenditures

As you will see in later chapters, not all economists today agree that the classical model was as seriously flawed as Keynes maintained. Nevertheless, Keynes's reformulation of macroeconomic theory has had dramatic effects on the way that economists think about macroeconomics today. For this reason, it is important to understand how Keynes' approach to macroeconomic analysis differed from the classical theory.

We will start where Keynes began—with the circular flow of income and expenditures, which we discussed in Chapter 2. Figure 5–3 on page 140 provides a more detailed version of the circular-flow diagram you saw there. This figure shows financial flows as well as flows of taxes and expenditures by the government. Despite the greater detail, one key point is the same:

> **The value of the flow of income to households must equal the value of the output produced by firms.**

Conceptually, if we abstract from depreciation and indirect business taxes and transfers that distinguish their definitions in the national income accounts, real income and real output are the same.

FIGURE 5–3 CIRCULAR FLOW OF INCOME AND EXPENDITURES

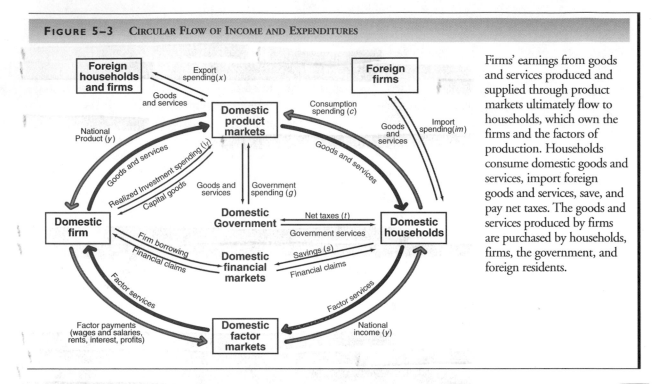

Firms' earnings from goods and services produced and supplied through product markets ultimately flow to households, which own the firms and the factors of production. Households consume domestic goods and services, import foreign goods and services, save, and pay net taxes. The goods and services produced by firms are purchased by households, firms, the government, and foreign residents.

REAL NET TAXES The amount of real taxes paid to the government by households, net of transfer payments.

TRANSFER PAYMENTS Governmentally managed income redistributions.

REAL CONSUMPTION The real amount of spending by households on domestically produced goods and services.

REAL IMPORTS The real flow of spending by households on goods and services produced by firms in other countries.

REAL SAVING The amount of income that households save through financial markets.

The Income Identity As Figure 5–3 indicates, households use their earnings of real income, denoted *y*, for four purposes. First, they use part of their real income to pay taxes to the government. **Real net taxes,** denoted *t*, are the total taxes that households pay net of any **transfer payments,** which are income redistributions that the government manages through programs such as Social Security, unemployment compensation, and so on. Hence, real net taxes are the funds that the government actually has available from total tax proceeds to purchase goods and services for its own use.

Second, households may spend some of their real income on goods and services produced in *domestic* markets, or markets for goods and services produced in their home country. Such domestic consumption spending is called **real consumption,** denoted *c*. Of course, households also may purchase goods and services produced in other nations. This is real import consumption or, more simply, **real imports,** denoted *im*.

Finally, households may allocate any untaxed or unspent portion of their real income earnings to **real saving,** denoted *s*. Households save by purchasing financial claims issued in the economy's financial markets.

Because households use their total real income in these four ways, real income must, by definition, equal the sum of real consumption, real saving, real net taxes, and real imports:

$$y \equiv c + s + t + im.$$

We use the three-bar equality symbol to indicate that this relation is a truism, or identity. Because it is a truism for how real income must be allocated in the circular flow, economists call it the **income identity.**

The Product Identity As the classical model emphasized, owners of business firms borrow a portion of real household saving by issuing financial claims, such as stocks and bonds, in the financial markets. The firms use these funds saved by households to finance purchases of capital goods, as well as other goods and services, from other firms. Firms may also use these funds to finance maintaining inventories of produced goods that they have not yet sold. Such actual real expenditures by firms constitute **real realized investment spending,** denoted i_r.

Any household saving that is not borrowed by firms is borrowed by the government, which issues bonds and other financial claims to households in exchange for the use of their saving. The government uses these funds to cover its deficit, which is the difference between real government spending, g, and real net taxes, t.

Note that there are three sources of spending on goods sold in domestic product markets: household consumption, realized investment by firms, and government spending. In addition, foreign residents may purchase goods and services produced by domestic firms. These purchases from abroad are exports by domestic firms, so they constitute the nation's **real exports,** denoted x. Adding this final type of spending on the output produced by domestic firms yields the **product identity** for the domestic economy:

$$y \equiv c + i_r + g + x.$$

Because this relationship is a truism, we again use the three-bar equality symbol.

Keynes was not the first to recognize the identities that the circular flow implies—the classical economists were well aware of them. Keynes, however, used the identities extensively in his effort to understand the nature of the short-run variations in real income that business cycles generate.

INCOME IDENTITY An identity that states that real national income equals the sum of real household consumption, real household saving, real net taxes, and real imports.

REAL REALIZED INVESTMENT SPENDING Actual real expenditures by firms in the product markets.

REAL EXPORTS Real value of goods and services produced by domestic firms and exported to other countries.

PRODUCT IDENTITY An identity that states that real national product is the sum of real household consumption, real realized investment, real government spending, and real export spending.

FUNDAMENTAL ISSUE #2

What are the key relationships implied by the circular flow of income and expenditures? We can infer two fundamental identities from the circular flow diagram. One is the income identity, which states that all real income is allocated to domestic consumption, saving, taxes, and import spending. The other is the product identity. This identity says that the real value of output of goods and services is equal to real expenditures on that output in the form of household consumption, business investment, government spending, and export spending by foreigners.

AGGREGATE INCOME AND EXPENDITURES FROM THE GROUND UP

Keynes viewed the flows among households, firms, and the government, and the national income and product identities that they imply, as the building blocks necessary to construct a foundation for macroeconomic theory. He analyzed each part of this foundation as a separate component.

Household Consumption and Saving

Because household consumption typically represents about two-thirds of total expenditures on goods and services, Keynesian theory emphasized its importance. The basic proposition of the Keynesian theory of household consumption is that the amount of such consumption depends positively upon **real disposable income,** or real income after taxes, denoted $y_d \equiv y - t$.

REAL DISPOSABLE INCOME A household's real after-tax income.

Note that we can rearrange the income identity, $y \equiv c + s + t + im$, by subtracting real net taxes, t, from both sides of the identity, which gives us $y - t \equiv c + s + im$. Thus, disposable income can be defined as $y_d \equiv c + s + im$. That is, households can allocate their after-tax income to consumption of domestic goods and services, saving, or purchases of imported goods and services.

Disposable Income Identities Because disposable income by definition is equal to $y_d \equiv c + s + im$, it follows that a *change in* disposable income must equal

$$\Delta y_d \equiv \Delta c + \Delta s + \Delta im.$$

Thus, households use any additional disposable income for additional consumption, additional saving, and additional spending on imports. If we divide both sides of this identity by Δy_d, we obtain the following relationship:

$$\frac{\Delta y_d}{\Delta y_d} = 1 \equiv \frac{\Delta c}{\Delta y_d} + \frac{\Delta s}{\Delta y_d} + \frac{\Delta im}{\Delta y_d}.$$

MARGINAL PROPENSITY TO CONSUME (*MPC*) The additional consumption caused by an increase in disposable income; the change in consumption spending divided by the corresponding change in disposable income; the slope of the consumption function.

This disposable income identity says that the sum of a change in consumption resulting from a change in disposable income ($\Delta c/\Delta y_d$), a change in saving resulting from a change in disposable income ($\Delta s/\Delta y_d$), and a change in real imports resulting from a change in disposable income ($\Delta im/\Delta y_d$) must be equal to 1.

Keynes called the first ratio on the right side of this identity, $\Delta c/\Delta y_d$, the **marginal propensity to consume** (*MPC*), or the change in real consumption that is induced by a change in real disposable income. For instance, a value of 0.85 for $\Delta c/\Delta y_d$ means that a one-dollar increase in real disposable income will induce households to increase their real consumption of domestically produced goods and services by 85 cents.

MARGINAL PROPENSITY TO SAVE (*MPS*) The additional saving caused by an increase in disposable income; the change in saving divided by the corresponding change in disposable income; the slope of the saving function.

Keynes referred to the second ratio, $\Delta s/\Delta y_d$, as the **marginal propensity to save (*MPS*)**, which is the change in real saving caused by a change in real disposable income. A value of 0.10 for $\Delta s/\Delta y_d$ means that a one-dollar rise in real disposable income will induce households to increase their real saving by 10 cents.

MARGINAL PROPENSITY TO IMPORT (*MPIM*) The additional import expenditures stimulated by an increase in disposable income; the change in import spending divided by the corresponding change in disposable income; the slope of the import function.

Finally, $\Delta im/\Delta y_d$ is the **marginal propensity to import** (*MPIM*), or the additional spending on imported goods and services by households. If $\Delta im/\Delta y_d$ is equal to 0.05, then each additional dollar of real disposable income to households will induce them to spend 5 cents on additional imported goods and services.

The identity says that all three marginal propensities must sum to 1, or $MPC + MPS + MPIM = 1$. Consequently, the 85 cents of each additional dollar of disposable real income used for domestic real consumption, the 10 cents of each additional dollar of disposable real income allocated to saving, and the 5 cents of each new dollar of real disposable real income spent on imports must sum to the total 1 dollar of additional disposable real income.

Because real disposable income is identically equal to $y_d \equiv c + s + im$, we can divide both sides by y_d to get another disposable income identity:

$$\frac{y_d}{y_d} = 1 \equiv \frac{c}{y_d} + \frac{s}{y_d} + \frac{im}{y_d}.$$

AVERAGE PROPENSITY TO CONSUME (*APC*) Real household consumption of domestically produced goods and services divided by real disposable income; the portion of disposable income allocated to consumption spending.

AVERAGE PROPENSITY TO SAVE (*APS*) Real household saving divided by real disposable income; the portion of disposable income allocated to saving.

AVERAGE PROPENSITY TO IMPORT (*APIM*) Real household spending on imports divided by real disposable income; the portion of disposable income allocated to spending on imported goods and services.

Keynes called the first ratio on the right side of this identity, c/y_d, or the ratio of real consumption to real disposable income, the **average propensity to consume (*APC*)**. He termed the second ratio, s/y_d, or the ratio of real saving to real disposable income, **the average propensity to save (*APS*)**. The third ratio, im/y_d, or imports divided by disposable income, is the **average propensity to import (*APIM*)**. Again, because households may only spend disposable income on domestic goods, allocate it to saving, or spend it on imports, these average propensities also must sum to 1, or $APC + APS + APIM = 1$.

The Saving Function In the Keynesian theory of household saving, a key determinant of households' annual saving flow is their disposable income. The basic idea is that as disposable income rises, households can increase their saving. This notion is captured by the function

$$s = -s_0 + (b \times y_d).$$

As panel (a) of Figure 5–4 shows, this is a straight-line function in its intercept-slope form, where $-s_0$ is the intercept and b is the slope. This *saving function* says that aggregate household saving is equal to a constant amount, $-s_0$, plus an amount that depends on disposable income, $b \times y_d$. The slope, b, is a fraction that tells us how much real saving rises with the receipt of additional real disposable income, y_d. Note that the constant intercept of the saving function, $-s_0$, is a negative number. The reason is that if disposable income were equal to zero, then households would need to draw down existing wealth to buy domestic and foreign goods. For instance, suppose that you had to make it through a semester of college with no disposable income and without any outside assistance from family members. Undoubtedly, you would have to withdraw funds from bank accounts and other accumulated wealth to buy books, food, and housing.

Hence, the basic Keynesian theory of household saving says that real domestic saving has two components. One is *induced saving*, $b \times y_d$, which is the saving

FIGURE 5–4 **THE SAVING, IMPORT, AND CONSUMPTION FUNCTIONS**

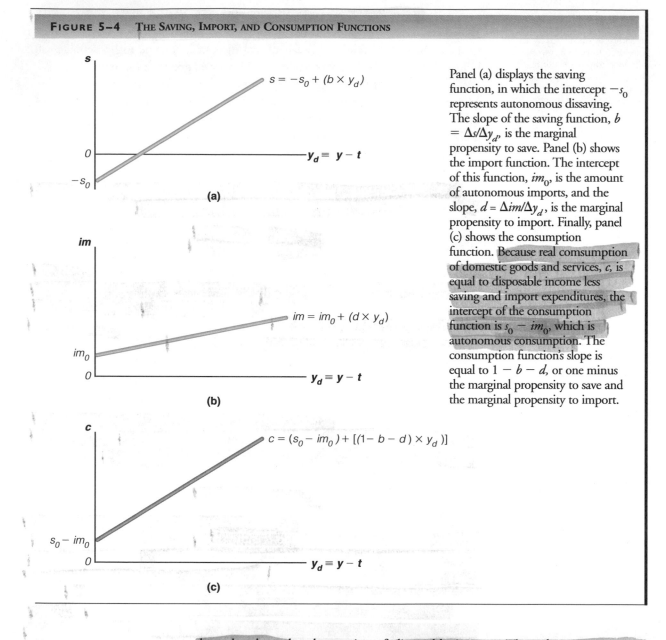

(a)

(b)

(c)

Panel (a) displays the saving function, in which the intercept $-s_0$ represents autonomous dissaving. The slope of the saving function, $b = \Delta s/\Delta y_d$, is the marginal propensity to save. Panel (b) shows the import function. The intercept of this function, im_0, is the amount of autonomous imports, and the slope, $d = \Delta im/\Delta y_d$, is the marginal propensity to import. Finally, panel (c) shows the consumption function. Because real comsumption of domestic goods and services, c, is equal to disposable income less saving and import expenditures, the intercept of the consumption function is $s_0 - im_0$, which is autonomous consumption. The consumption function's slope is equal to $1 - b - d$, or one minus the marginal propensity to save and the marginal propensity to import.

brought about by the receipt of disposable income. The other component is *autonomous dissaving*, $-s_0$, or the amount by which households wish to draw from their wealth to make purchases of domestic goods and services and foreign imports.

Because s_0 is constant, a change in s_0—Δs_0—is equal to zero. It follows that $\Delta s = -\Delta s_0 + b\Delta y_d = b\Delta y_d$, which tells us that $b = \Delta s/\Delta y_d$. In other words, *the saving function's slope, b, is the marginal propensity to save (MPS).*

ON THE WEB
*Learn About Trade Among
North American nations at*
http://www.nafta.net/it.htm

The Import Function   Import expenditures also consist of autonomous and induced components. This is captured by using the straight-line *import function:*

$$im = im_0 + (d \times y_d).$$

Here im_0 denotes *autonomous import spending,* which is the amount of spending on imports by households irrespective of their total disposable income, As panel (b) of Figure 5–4 shows, im_0 is the constant intercept of the import function. The amount $d \times y_d$ is *induced import spending.* This is the level of household spending on imports that is related directly to their earnings of disposable income. The fraction d is equal to $\Delta im/\Delta y_d$ and is the slope of the import function. Because $\Delta im/\Delta y_d$ by definition is the marginal propensity to import, *the slope of the import function is the marginal propensity to import (MPIM).*

The import function slopes upward. This means that growth in disposable income in the households' home country will induce a rise in imports. Recall from Chapter 2 that a nation's trade balance is exports minus imports. Consequently, if exports are unchanged, a rise in a nation's real disposable income causes its trade balance to decline. We shall return to this issue later in the chapter.

Note that in this chapter we shall abstract from another important determinant of desired import spending, which is the price of foreign goods relative to the price of domestic goods. A key factor influencing this relative price is the rate of exchange between foreign and domestic currency. To keep our basic Keynesian model as simple as possible for now, however, we shall postpone consideration of this issue until Chapter 7.

The Consumption Function   By definition, $y_d \equiv c + s + im$, so household disposable income is split among consumption expenditures on domestically produced output, saving, and import spending. This means that the saving and import functions automatically imply a domestic consumption function. To see this, let's substitute the saving function, $s = -s_0 + (b \times y_d)$, and the import function, $im = im_0 + (d \times y_d)$, into the disposable income identity to get

$$y_d = c + s + im,$$

or

$$y_d = c - s_0 + (b \times y_d) + im_0 + (d \times y_d).$$

Note that we now use an equals sign instead of a three-bar identity symbol because our saving and import functions are hypotheses that may or may not be true. If we rearrange the last equation and solve for c, we obtain

$$c = (s_0 - im_0) + [(1 - b - d) \times y_d],$$

AUTONOMOUS CONSUMPTION
Household consumption spending on domestically produced goods and services that is independent of the level of real income.

which is the consumption function implied by the Keynesian theories of saving and import spending. As panel (c) of Figure 5–4 shows, this is a straight-line function. Its intercept is equal to $s_0 - im_0$, which is **autonomous consumption** by households.

This is the amount of household domestic consumption expenditures that will take place irrespective of their disposable income. We shall assume that most of total household disposable income stays in the home country for domestic consumption and saving. This implies that autonomous consumption is a positive number, or that the consumption function's intercept, $s_0 - im_0$ is greater than zero, as in panel (c).

The slope of the consumption function is equal to $\Delta c/\Delta y_d = 1 - b - d$. Because $\Delta c/\Delta y_d$ is the marginal propensity to consume, *the slope of the consumption function is the marginal propensity to consume (MPC)*. Note that if we add the *MPC*, the *MPS*, and the *MPIM*, we have $MPC + MPS + MPIM = (1 - b - d) + b + d = 1$. Thus, as discussed earlier, the three marginal propensities sum to 1.

Investment Spending by Firms

The Keynesian theory of investment expenditures is based on the classical approach. As in the classical loanable funds theory, desired investment, which we shall assume takes place only domestically, depends negatively on the real interest rate, as shown in panel (a) of Figure 5–5. A decline in the real interest rate from ρ_0 to ρ_1 causes desired real investment spending to rise from i_0 to i_1. As you learned in Chapter 3, the real interest rate is equal to the nominal interest rate minus the expected inflation rate, so a fall in the real interest rate could take place because of a decline in the nominal interest rate or a rise in the expected inflation rate.

It is important to recognize the distinction between *desired* investment, i, and *realized* investment, i_r. The two can—and for short periods often do—deviate from one another. This occurs whenever firms experience unintended depletions or accumulations of inventories of finished goods, which are included in realized investment but were not desired by the firms. As we shall discuss shortly, such unplanned changes in inventories induce firms to vary their production and perform a key role in achieving an equilibrium flow of real income.

Panel (b) of Figure 5–5 shows another way that investment could rise from i_0 to i_1. Holding the real interest rate unchanged, the desired investment schedule itself could shift to the right, causing the same rise in desired investment. Keynes argued that such shifts in the desired investment schedule were commonplace and that they resulted from changes in firms' expectations of future profits. The rightward shift of the investment schedule in panel (b), for instance, could result from firms' general anticipation of higher profits in the future. This would induce the firms to increase both their total investment in capital goods, so as to expand future production, and their inventories of produced goods, which they would expect to sell in the near future.

Panel (c) of Figure 5–5 shows that, whether induced by a fall in the real interest rate or expectations of higher future profits, an increase in desired investment would cause investment to rise at any given level of aggregate income, y. Although some amount of investment is income induced, we shall assume for the sake of simplicity that investment is autonomous, or unrelated to income. Consequently, with invest-

FIGURE 5-5 FACTORS CAUSING CHANGES IN DESIRED INVESTMENT

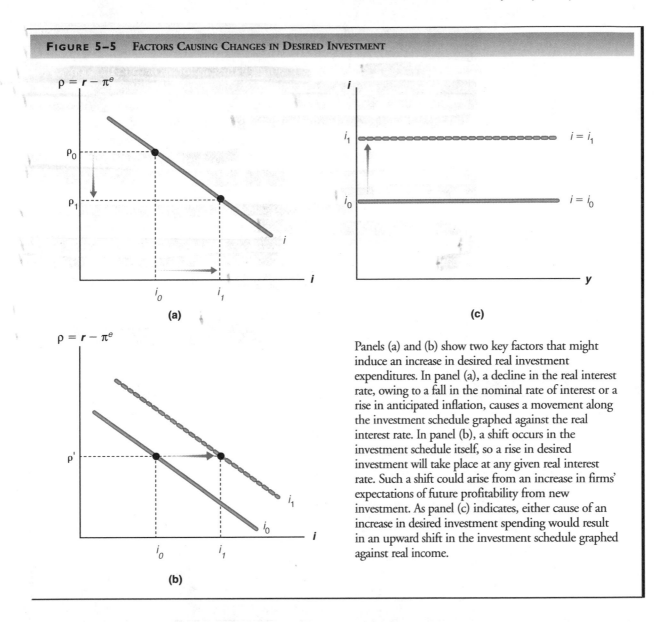

Panels (a) and (b) show two key factors that might induce an increase in desired real investment expenditures. In panel (a), a decline in the real interest rate, owing to a fall in the nominal rate of interest or a rise in anticipated inflation, causes a movement along the investment schedule graphed against the real interest rate. In panel (b), a shift occurs in the investment schedule itself, so a rise in desired investment will take place at any given real interest rate. Such a shift could arise from an increase in firms' expectations of future profitability from new investment. As panel (c) indicates, either cause of an increase in desired investment spending would result in an upward shift in the investment schedule graphed against real income.

ment measured along the vertical axis and real income measured along the horizontal axis, a rise in desired investment implies an upward shift in a horizontal desired investment schedule, from $i = i_0$ to $i = i_1$.

Government Spending and Taxation

A number of factors can influence the levels of government spending and taxation. How much a government spends may reflect as its concern about national defense and law enforcement; its wish to maintain national parks, monuments, and buildings; or even purely political factors such as the desire to satisfy certain constituencies. We shall simplify considerably by treating all these factors as beyond the scope of our theory and assuming that real government spending on domestic output is just equal to an autonomous amount, $g = g_0$. As panel (a) of Figure 5–6 shows, this means that the *government spending schedule* is horizontal. Suppose the government increases its spending on national defense or decides to build a new dam in West Virginia or an office building in Washington, D.C. Then the government spending schedule will shift upward by the rise in spending, to $g = g_1$, where g_1 is the new, higher level of government expenditures.

Governments have a number of possible sources of net taxes, including income taxes, sales taxes, excise taxes, and the like. Because a government's income tax revenues depend on the level of income, net taxes realistically depend on aggregate real income. Nevertheless, we again shall keep things simple by assuming that net taxes are equal to a lump-sum, autonomous amount. (We shall consider how income taxes change the nature of the basic Keynesian model in Chapter 7.) Under this simplification, the *net tax schedule* also is horizontal, as shown in panel (b) of Figure 5–6. If the government increases net taxes from an amount $t = t_0$ to a larger amount $t = t_1$,

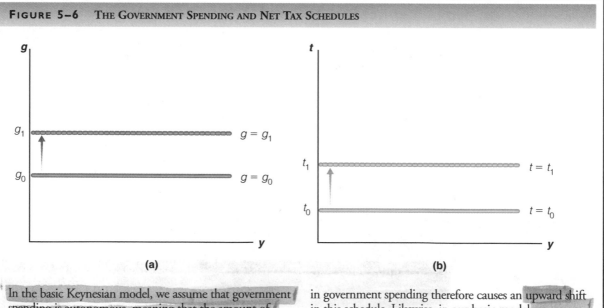

FIGURE 5–6   THE GOVERNMENT SPENDING AND NET TAX SCHEDULES

(a)

(b)

In the basic Keynesian model, we assume that government spending is autonomous, meaning that the amount of government spending does not vary with changes in the level of real income. Hence, the government spending schedule is horizontal, as shown in panel (a). An increase in government spending therefore causes an upward shift in this schedule. Likewise, in our basic model we assume that net taxes are autonomous, so the net tax schedule in panel (b) is also horizontal. An increase in net taxes results in an upward shift in this schedule.

then the net tax schedule will shift upward by the amount of the tax increase, as shown in Figure 5–6.

Spending on Exports

The final component of total spending in a nation's economy is the level of expenditures by foreign residents on the exports produced and sold by domestic firms. As we shall discuss briefly later in this chapter and in greater detail in Chapter 14, two key factors affect spending on a nation's exports. One is the real incomes of the nations whose residents purchase domestically produced goods. As other nations' incomes rise, their residents desire to purchase more domestic output. The other key factor influencing spending on a nation's exports is the rate of exchange between its domestic currency and the currencies of its trading partners. For instance, if the domestic currency *depreciates*, so that fewer units of foreign currency are required to obtain the domestic currency, then domestic exports become less expensive to foreigners, and they are likely to increase their spending on domestic exports.

Domestic income, y, has no effect on real exports, however. Consequently, the *export schedule* is horizontal, as shown in Figure 5–7. A rise in foreign nations' incomes or a depreciation of the domestic currency will cause exports to increase from an amount $x = x_0$ to a larger amount $x = x_1$. Thus, either type of change will cause the export schedule to shift upward, as shown in the figure.

Putting the Pieces Together: Aggregate Desired Expenditures

Total spending on domestically produced goods and services is the sum of household consumption spending, desired investment spending, government expenditures, and

ON THE WEB
Visit the World Trade Organization at
http://www.unicc.org/wto/

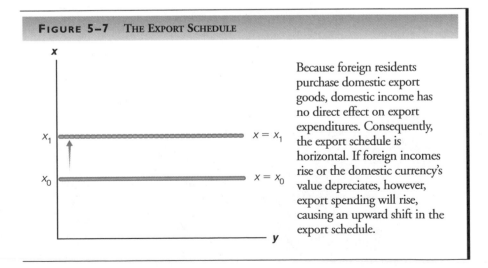

FIGURE 5–7   THE EXPORT SCHEDULE

Because foreign residents purchase domestic export goods, domestic income has no direct effect on export expenditures. Consequently, the export schedule is horizontal. If foreign incomes rise or the domestic currency's value depreciates, however, export spending will rise, causing an upward shift in the export schedule.

spending on domestic exports by residents of foreign nations. In terms of our notation, therefore, total expenditures on domestic output are equal to $c + i + g + x$.

Figure 5–8 shows how to add up these components of aggregate desired expenditures. Panel (a) sums up the purely autonomous components, which are desired investment spending, $i = i_0$, government spending, $g = g_0$, and spending on exports, $x = x_0$. This yields the horizontal schedule $i_0 + g_0 + x_0$ in panel (a).

Total spending on domestically produced goods and services also includes domestic consumption spending by households. In panel (b) of Figure 5–8, we again display the upward-sloping household consumption function, $c = (s_0 - im_0) + [(1 -$

FIGURE 5–8   DERIVING THE AGGREGATE EXPENDITURES SCHEDULE

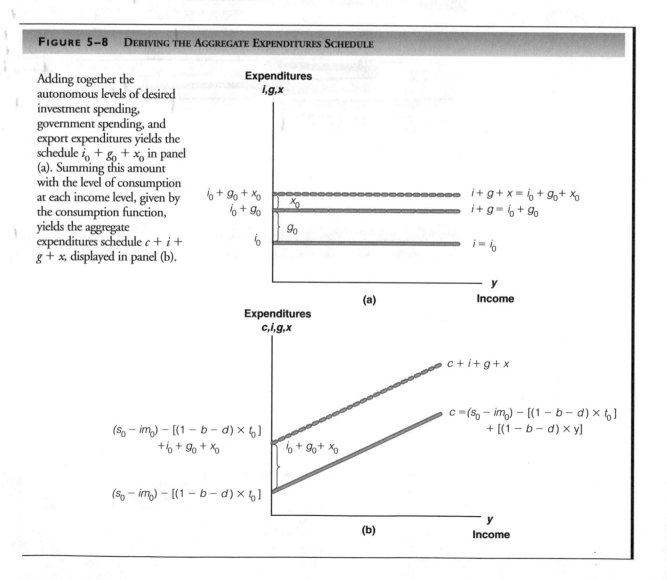

Adding together the autonomous levels of desired investment spending, government spending, and export expenditures yields the schedule $i_0 + g_0 + x_0$ in panel (a). Summing this amount with the level of consumption at each income level, given by the consumption function, yields the aggregate expenditures schedule $c + i + g + x$, displayed in panel (b).

$b - d) \times y_d]$. Note however, that we now recognize that disposable income, y_d, is equal to total real income, y, minus real net taxes, t. Hence, if t_0 is the current lump-sum amount of net taxes, we can substitute $y - t_0$ for y_d to get $c = (s_0 - im_0) + [(1 - b - d) \times (y - t_0)]$. This implies that the consumption function is

$$c = (s_0 - im_0) - [(1 - b - d) \times t_0] + [(1 - b - d) \times y].$$

With total real income measured on the horizontal axis, the consumption function's intercept, $(s_0 - im_0) - [(1 - b - d) \times t_0]$, takes into account the consumption-reducing effect of taxes. Its slope remains equal to the marginal propensity to consume, $MPC = 1 - b - d$.

At each level of income, we then add the vertical distance $i_0 + g_0 + x_0$ to the amount of consumption. This gives us the **aggregate expenditures schedule,** $c + i + g + x$. This schedule tells us how much households, firms, the government, and foreign residents combined will desire to spend on domestically produced output at any given level of domestic real income, y. Its intercept is **aggregate net autonomous expenditures,** or $(s_0 - im_0) - [(1 - b - d) \times t_0] + i_0 + g_0 + x_0$. This is the total net amount of spending on domestically produced output that is independent of the current level of total real income.

Because we have constructed the aggregate expenditures schedule by adding a fixed vertical distance all along the consumption function, the slope of the aggregate expenditures schedule is equal to the consumption function's slope. This slope is the marginal propensity to consume, which is equal to $MPC = 1 - b - d$. We shall assume that the sum of the marginal propensity to save and the marginal propensity to import, $b + d$, is a relatively small fraction, so that the MPC is a relatively large fraction. For example, if the marginal propensity to save is $b = 0.10$ and the marginal propensity to import is $d = 0.08$, then the marginal propensity to consume is equal to $1 - 0.10 - 0.08 = 0.82$.

AGGREGATE EXPENDITURES SCHEDULE A schedule that represents total desired expenditures by all the relevant sectors of the economy at any given level of real national income.

AGGREGATE NET AUTONOMOUS EXPENDITURES The sum of autonomous consumption, autonomous investment, autonomous government spending, and autonomous export spending, all of which are independent of the level of national income in the basic Keynesian model.

FUNDAMENTAL ISSUE #3

What are the components of aggregate desired expenditures in the basic Keynesian model? Aggregate desired expenditures are composed of household consumption on domestically produced goods and services, investment spending desired by firms, government spending, and export spending by foreigners. In the basic Keynesian model, we assume that desired investment, government spending and net taxes, and export spending are autonomous. Consumption spending, however, is positively related to disposable income. As a result, the aggregate expenditures schedule slopes upward.

EQUILIBRIUM NATIONAL INCOME

The detailed circular flow diagram in Figure 5–3 depicts the relationships that must exist among the various components of total income and aggregate expenditures. While it tells us the direction of the overall flow of income and spending, the circular flow diagram does not tell us anything about the total *magnitude* of the flow. The flow of water along a riverbed, for instance, might run from east to west, but it could be either a trickle or a torrent. Likewise, the size of the flow of income to households that ultimately flows to firms in the form of expenditures on goods and services could be meager, implying a weak economy, or it could be large, implying a robust economy.

The *equilibrium* flow of real income is the level at which households, firms, the government, and foreign residents desire to purchase all real output that is produced and sold by domestic firms. In other words, in equilibrium, households, firms, the government, and foreign residents are satisfied with the actual flow of income and expenditures through the domestic economy. If the actual flow were to differ from the desired level, then households, firms, the government, and foreign residents would have an incentive to change their expenditures, which in turn would affect the total flow of spending and income. Therefore, in equilibrium there is no tendency for the flow of real income and expenditures to change from its current level.

Determining the Equilibrium Flow of Income and Expenditures

EQUILIBRIUM REAL INCOME The real income level at which aggregate desired expenditures are equal to the real value of domestic output.

In light of this definition of equilibrium, we can define a nation's **equilibrium real income** as the real income level at which aggregate desired expenditures are equal to the real value of domestically produced output. The circular flow diagram tells us that the real value of output is equal to real income. Consequently, in equilibrium real income is equal to aggregate desired expenditures, or $y = c + i + g + x$.

45-DEGREE LINE A line that cuts in half the 90-degree angle of the coordinate axes on a diagram relating real income to aggregate desired expenditures; every point on the 45-degree line could, in principle, be a point of equilibrium at which real income equals aggregate desired expenditures.

The Income-Expenditure Equilibrium Figure 5–9 depicts a schedule of all the possible combinations of real income and aggregate desired expenditures that can satisfy our definition of equilibrium. This schedule is a **45-degree line,** because it cuts in half the 90-degree angle formed by the coordinate axes on the diagram. At any point along this 45-degree line, the level of real income along the horizontal axis is equal to the level of aggregate desired expenditures along the vertical axis. This means that every point on the 45-degree line could, in principle, satisfy our definition of equilibrium.

Panel (a) of Figure 5–10 on page 154 shows the determination of a single income-expenditure equilibrium. This figure combines Figures 5–8 and 5–9. The aggregate expenditures schedule, $c + i + g + x$, is taken from Figure 5–8. It displays all combinations of real income and desired expenditures by households, firms, the government, and foreign residents. As just discussed, the 45-degree line (Figure 5–9) displays all combinations of real income levels that could be equal to aggregate desired

---

FIGURE 5–9   THE 45-DEGREE LINE

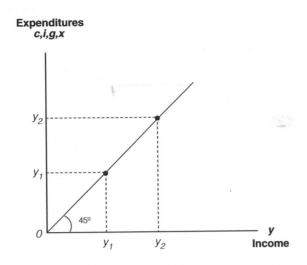

Expenditures
c,i,g,x

The economy is in equilibrium when aggregate desired expenditures equal aggregate real income. This will be true along the 45-degree line. If aggregate desired expenditures equal the amount y_1, then by reading over to the 45- degree line and downward to the horizontal axis, we find that this level of total spending is equal to the aggregate income level y_1. The same is true for the higher level of expenditures y_2. Consequently, any point along the 45-degree line is a potential equilibrium point.

---

expenditures. Hence, the point at which the two schedules intersect is the single point that satisfies the equilibrium condition $y = c + i + g + x$. The equilibrium level of real income at this point is denoted y_e.

The Leakages-Injections Approach to Determining Equilibrium Real Income   We can also think about equilibrium in another way. Substituting the real income identity, $y \equiv c + s + t + im$, for y in the equilibrium condition $y = c + i + g + x$ gives us

$$c + s + t + im = c + i + g + x.$$

If we subtract c from both sides of this equation, we get another expression for the equilibrium condition:

$$s + t + im = i + g + x.$$

If you look back at the circular flow diagram in Figure 5–3, you will see that the left side of this new condition is the sum of all *leakages* from the flow of spending on domestic output that take place because households save, pay taxes, and purchase imports from foreign firms. The right side consists of *injections* back into the flow of spending on domestically produced goods and services that take place when firms, the government, and foreign residents purchase domestically produced output. Hence, this equation says that in equilibrium, all leakages from the flow of spending ultimately are *reinjected* back into that flow.

Panel (b) of Figure 5–10 shows this alternative leakages-injections approach to determining equilibrium real income. The right side of the leakages-injections

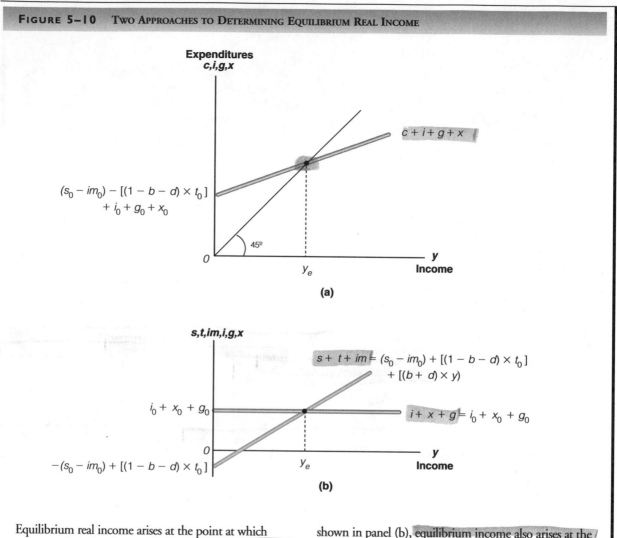

FIGURE 5–10   TWO APPROACHES TO DETERMINING EQUILIBRIUM REAL INCOME

(a)

(b)

Equilibrium real income arises at the point at which aggregate desired real expenditures, $c + i + g + x$, equal aggregate real income. This is true at the single real income level, y_e, where the aggregate expenditures schedule crosses the 45-degree line in panel (a). Alternatively, as shown in panel (b), equilibrium income also arises at the point at which leakages from the flow of spending on domestic output, given by $s + t + im$, equal total injections back into the spending flow, $i + g + x$.

equilibrium condition is described by the horizontal schedule $i_0 + g_0 + x_0$ from panel (a) of Figure 5–8. Using our saving and import functions discussed earlier, the left side of the equation, $s + t + im$, is equal to $-s_0 + (b \times y_d) + t_0 + im_0 + (d \times y_d)$. Remembering that $y_d \equiv y - t$, where $t = t_0$ is the current lump-sum level of taxes, we can rearrange this expression as

$$s + t + im = -(s_0 - im_0) + t_0 + [(b + d) \times (y - t_0)].$$

Finally, by factoring out the terms relating to t_0, we can rearrange a little more to obtain

$$s + t + im = -(s_0 - im_0) + [(1 - b - d) \times t_0] + [(b + d) \times y],$$

which is the equation of the upward-sloping "$s + t + im$" schedule displayed in panel (b) of Figure 5–10. The intersection of these two schedules then determines equilibrium real income, y_e. This is the same as the equilibrium real income level determined via the income-expenditures approach to equilibrium in panel (a) of Figure 5–10.

The Complete Depiction of Equilibrium Real Income   Figure 5–11 summarizes the graphical depiction of the determination of a nation's equilibrium real income flow. Households, firms, the government, and foreign residents purchase all the output produced domestically ($y = c + i + g + x$), and leakages from the spending flow ultimately are reinjected into that flow ($s + t + im = i + g + x$). From either perspective, equilibrium real income is equal to the same level, y_e.

Finally, remember that the national product identity is $y \equiv c + i_r + g + x$, where i_r is the amount of realized, or actual, investment spending by firms. In equilibrium, $y = c + i + g + x$. If we substitute the national product identity for y in this equi-

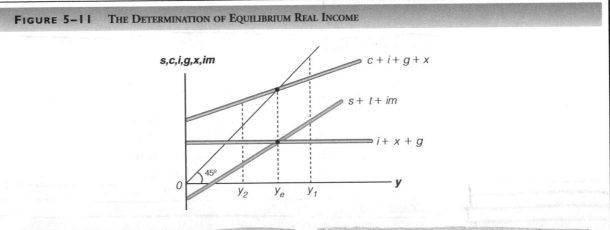

FIGURE 5–11   THE DETERMINATION OF EQUILIBRIUM REAL INCOME

Equilibrium real income is attained both when aggregate desired expenditures, $c + i + g + x$, equal real income and when spending-flow leakages, $s + t + im$, equal spending-flow injections, $i + g + x$. At an income level above the equilibrium level of real income, y_e, such as y_1, desired expenditures would be less than the value of real output, so firms would begin to accumulate inventories of unfinished goods. As a result, realized investment, i_r, would exceed desired investment at the income level y_1.

Firms would cut back on production, and real income would fall back toward the equilibrium level y_e. In contrast, at an income level below the equilibrium income level, such as y_2, desired expenditures would be greater than the value of real output, so firms would begin to experience unplanned inventory depletions. Realized investment i_r would be less than desired investment at the income level y_2. Firms would increase production, and real income would rise toward the equilibrium level y_e.

librium condition, we obtain $c + i_r + g + x = c + i + g + x$ in equilibrium. After subtracting $c + g + x$ from both sides of this equation, we find a third and final way to express equilibrium:

$$i_r = i.$$

This equation says that in equilibrium firms undertake the amount of investment spending that they *desire* to undertake. Thus, in equilibrium firms hold do not hold more inventories of finished goods than they desire to hold. Nor do firms hold fewer inventories of finished goods than they desire when the economy is in equilibrium.

In Figure 5–11, if real income somehow increased to y_1, above the equilibrium income level y_e, the increase could only be temporary. The reason is that at this higher income level y_1, real income—the real value of output—exceeds the level of desired spending on output, or $y > c + i + g + x$. Consequently, realized real investment would be greater than desired investment, or $i_r > i$. Firms would observe that their inventories of unsold goods had risen above desired levels and would cut their inventories. As a result, production of new output would decline, causing the value of real output, or real income, to decline toward the equilibrium level y_e.

In contrast, if real income declined to y_2, below the equilibrium income level y_e in Figure 5–11, real income would be less than the level of desired spending on output, or $y < c + i + g + x$. Realized real investment would therefore be lower than desired investment, or $i_r < i$. Firms would see their inventories of unsold goods fall below desired levels and would add to their inventories. As a result, production of new output would increase, causing the value of real output, or real income, to rise toward the equilibrium level y_e.

The Multiplier Effect and Short-Run Business Cycles

What factors could cause equilibrium real income to change, thereby generating cyclical changes in real income that we observe over business cycles? What factors account for the magnitudes of such cyclical income variations? To answer these questions, we need to understand one of the key implications of the basic Keynesian model of real income determination: the **multiplier effect.** This effect refers to the fact that a given 1-unit change in aggregate net autonomous expenditures—a 1-unit movement in the intercept of the aggregate desired expenditures schedule $c + i + g + x$ in panel (a) of Figure 5–10 and in Figure 5–11—causes a greater-than-1-unit change in equilibrium real income in the same direction.

MULTIPLIER EFFECT The ratio of a change in equilibrium real income to an increase in autonomous net aggregate expenditures. When the aggregate expenditure schedule shifts vertically, the equilibrium level of national income changes by a multiple of the amount of the shift.

The Autonomous Expenditures Multiplier   To see how the multiplier effect occurs, let's begin with a little algebra. The income-expenditure equilibrium condition is $y = c + i + g + x$. If we substitute from our consumption function, $c = (s_0 - im_0) - [(1 - b - d) \times t_0] + [(1 - b - d) \times y]$, and assume that net taxes and desired investment, government spending, and export spending are all autonomous, we can rewrite this condition as

$$y = (s_0 - im_0) - [(1 - b - d) \times t_0] + [(1 - b - d) \times y] + i_0 + g_0 + x_0.$$

Now, if we subtract $(1 - b - d) \times y$ from both sides of this equation, we obtain

$$y - [(1 - b - d) \times y] = (s_0 - im_0) - [(1 - b - d) \times t_0] + i_0 + g_0 + x_0,$$

or, since the left side is equal to $[1 - (1 - b - d)] \times y = (b + d) \times y$,

$$(b + d) \times y = (s_0 - im_0) - [(1 - b - d) \times t_0] + i_0 + g_0 + x_0.$$

Finally, if we divide both sides of the preceding equation by $(b + d)$, we get

$$y = 1/(b + d)\{(s_0 - im_0) - [(1 - b - d) \times t_0] + i_0 + g_0 + x_0\}.$$

This final expression is an equation for equilibrium real income. It tells us that equilibrium real income is equal to the ratio $1/(b + d)$ times aggregate net autonomous expenditures, $(s_0 - im_0) - [(1 - b - d) \times t_0] + i_0 + g_0 + x_0.$ The ratio $1/(b + d)$ is the Keynesian **autonomous expenditures multiplier,** which we shall simply call the "multiplier." This is a measure of the size of the multiplier effect on equilibrium real income caused by a change in the level of aggregate net autonomous expenditures. Because b is the marginal propensity to save (MPS) and d is the marginal propensity to import ($MPIM$), the multiplier is equal to $1/(MPS + MPIM)$. Of course, you learned earlier that $MPC + MPS + MPIM = 1$, so $MPS + MPIM$ is equal to $1 - MPC.$ So another way to express the multiplier is in the form $1/(1 - MPC).$ The MPC is between 0 and 1, so the multiplier is greater than 1. For example, if the marginal propensity to save is equal to 0.08 and the marginal propensity to import is equal to 0.12, the marginal propensity to consume is $MPC = 0.8.$ Then the multiplier is equal to $1/(1 - MPC) = 1/(1 - 0.8) = 1/0.2 = 5.$ Thus, a \$1 billion reduction in aggregate net autonomous expenditures per year would cause a \$5 billion decline in equilibrium real income per year.

The multiplier effect is illustrated in Figure 5–12 on page 158, where the initial equilibrium is point *A*, at the level of real income y_1. Now suppose that autonomous investment spending declines, perhaps because owners of business firms anticipate lower future profits. A decline in autonomous investment equal to Δi_0 causes the aggregate desired expenditures schedule to shift downward by that amount. As a result, equilibrium real income falls by a larger amount, from y_1 to y_2, or Δy, at point *B*. In fact, our final equation for equilibrium real income tells us that the exact amount of the decline in real income is equal to $\Delta y = [1/(1 - MPC)] \times \Delta i_0$. Real income would decline by the fall in autonomous investment times the autonomous spending multiplier, $1/(1 - MPC)$. (For an application of the multiplier effect, see on page 159 the Policy Notebook: *Can Spending on a Moon Shot Have a Multiplier Effect?*)

What accounts for the multiplier effect? Consider the following example in which $MPC = 0.80.$ This means that each dollar reduction in household disposable income induces a reduction in disposable income of 80 cents. If autonomous investment declines by an amount $\Delta i_0 = \$1$ billion, then firms now spend \$1 billion less than before on capital goods and inventories of finished goods. This spending reduction

AUTONOMOUS EXPENDITURES MULTIPLIER A measure of the size of the multiplier effect on equilibrium real income caused by a change in aggregate net autonomous expenditures; in the simple Keynesian model, the multiplier is equal to $1/(MPS + MPIM) = 1/(1 - MPC).$

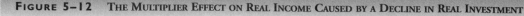

FIGURE 5–12   **THE MULTIPLIER EFFECT ON REAL INCOME CAUSED BY A DECLINE IN REAL INVESTMENT**

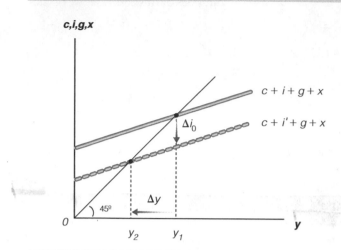

A decline in real autonomous investment expenditures equal to Δi_0 causes the aggregate expenditures schedule to shift downward by that amount and induces a movement from equilibrium point *A* to equilibrium point *B*. As a result, equilibrium real income declines by a larger amount than the fall in autonomous investment, given by $\Delta y = y_2 - y_1$. The amount of the fall in equilibrium real income is equal to $\Delta y = [1/(1 - MPC)] \times \Delta i_0$.

immediately reduces real income by $1 billion. The result is a $1 billion decline in disposable income, which in turn reduces household consumption spending by 80 percent of $1 billion, or $800,000. This in turn leads to an $800,000 reduction in the real income of the firms from which households would have purchased domestically produced goods and services. To this point, therefore, the $1 billion decline in autonomous investment has reduced total real income by $1.8 billion.

The process of spending reduction is not yet complete, however. The owners and workers at the firms that have lost $800,000 in sales and income earnings will reduce their consumption spending by 80 percent of this amount or 0.8 × $800,000 = $640,000. Furthermore, this spending reduction will generate a fall in real income of $640,000 for owners and workers at other firms, who then will reduce their consumption spending by 0.8 × $640,000 = $512,000.

Ultimately, the total reduction in real income will be the sum of all these declines ($1 billion + $800,000 + $640,000 + $512,000 + · · ·) in spending. As we determined earlier, if the *MPC* is equal to 0.8, the total decline in real income caused by a $1 billion fall in autonomous investment will be equal to $1 billion times 1/(1 − 0.8), or $1 billion times 5 or a real income reduction of $5 billion. (See on page 160 the Policy Notebook: *Did Changes in Investment Cause the Great Depression?* for a discussion of the role the multiplier effect played in the Great Depression.)

A Basic Keynesian Theory of Business Cycles   Note that a multiple decline in real income caused by a fall in autonomous investment would, if all other factors were unchanged, lead to a recession. Real income would fall relative to its long-run growth path, and equilibrium real income would not rise again until autonomous investment or some other component of aggregate net autonomous investment increased. The result would be a downturn in the business cycle.

Can Spending on a Moon Shot Have a Multiplier Effect?

More than a quarter of a century ago, the United States spent in excess of $100 billion in today's dollars to put a person on the moon. At one point, nearly 1 cent of every dollar of U.S. economic output went into Project Apollo. At that time, space research and work accounted for more than one-fifth of all private and government research expenditures. Even then, the president had serious doubts about spending so much to get to the moon. To calm the administration's fears, NASA commissioned elaborate reports about how its spending would affect the economy. The reports projected big multiplier effects as the government expenditures on the Apollo program poured into the economy. Additionally, the reports argued that enormous gains would result from civilian use of the newly developed space technology. In 1971, for example, the Midwest Research Institute concluded that every dollar that NASA spent on research and development would lead to a $7 increase in GDP. Chase Econometric Associates, Inc., predicted an eventual economic return of $14 for every dollar spent.

Did these multipliers actually exist? The answer to this question will never be known with certainty, but there seems to be great doubt that any long-term benefits materialized.

Much of the Apollo program's technical work was extremely specialized, and none of it created a useful infrastructure for the nation. Moreover, few technological transfers from the space program to the civilian sector seem to have occurred. Some lightweight metal materials were developed, but most of them are still too expensive for commercial use today. Some computerized techniques developed by the Apollo program formed the basis of medical imaging. The program also probably speeded up the development of electronic integrated circuits.

Today, however, most of the Apollo-specific technologies as well as hundreds of thousands of careers that went into the Apollo program have simply disappeared. Only one major theoretical breakthrough occurred: by examining moon rocks, astronomers were able to reformulate their understanding of the early history of the solar system. The question remains, was the program worth more than $100 billion of today's dollars?

FOR CRITICAL ANALYSIS:

Assuming the Midwest Research Institute's multipliers was correct, what was the implied marginal propensity to consume?

Our final equation for equilibrium real income indicates that a number of factors could cause such a downturn. Any change causing a reduction in aggregate net autonomous expenditures, $(s_0 - im_0) - [(1 - b - d) \times t_0] + i_0 + g_0 + x_0$, could induce a recession. For instance a fall in the value of s_0 equal to Δs_0 would cause real income to decline by $\Delta s_0 \times 1/(1 - MPC)$. Likewise, a rise in the value of im_0 equal to Δim_0 would cause real income to decline by $\Delta im_0 \times 1/(1 - MPC)$. Recall that autonomous consumption is equal to $s_0 - im_0$, so either of these changes would imply a decline in autonomous consumption of domestically produced goods and services, either because people decide to save more than they did before or because they choose to purchase more imports from abroad. The result would be a fall in equilibrium real income and a recession.

In addition, a significant fall in real export spending by foreign residents could induce an economic downturn. A decline in spending on real exports equal to Δx_0 would cause real income to decline by $\Delta x_0 \times 1/(1 - MPC)$.

POLICY NOTEBOOK

Did Changes in Investment Cause the Great Depression?

Changes in autonomous spending lead to shifts in total expenditures and cause a multiplier effect on the equilibrium level of real GDP per year. According to some researchers, a classical example occurred during the Great Depression. Indeed, some economists believe that an autonomous downward shift (collapse) in the real investment function provoked the Great Depression. Look at panel (a) of Figure 5–13. There you see net investment in the United States from 1929 to 1941 (expressed in 1992 dollars).

During business contractions, business decision makers may decide to postpone long-range investment plans for buildings and equipment. Unless those plans are revised, the business recovery may be weak. As panel (b) of Figure 5–13 shows, the contraction that started in 1929 reached its trough in 1933. During the next four years there was an expansion, but it was followed by another contraction from 1937 to 1938. Some researchers argue that the 1937–1938 contraction could have been even more severe than the one that started in 1929, but it was short-lived because long-range investment plans were revised upward in 1938.

FOR CRITICAL ANALYSIS:

How can net private domestic investment be negative, as it was during six years shown in panel (a) of Figure 5–13?

FIGURE 5–13   NET PRIVATE DOMESTIC INVESTMENT AND REAL GDP DURING THE GREAT DEPRESSION

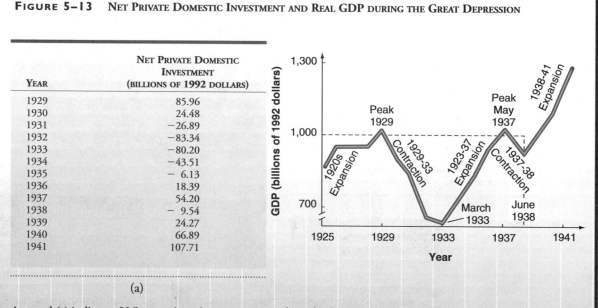

YEAR	NET PRIVATE DOMESTIC INVESTMENT (BILLIONS OF 1992 DOLLARS)
1929	85.96
1930	24.48
1931	−26.89
1932	−83.34
1933	−80.20
1934	−43.51
1935	− 6.13
1936	18.39
1937	54.20
1938	− 9.54
1939	24.27
1940	66.89
1941	107.71

(a)

As panel (a) indicates, U.S. net private investment turned negative in 1931 and remained negative until 1936 and 1937. It was negative once again in 1938. As panel (b) shows, changes in U.S. real GDP during this period closely mirrored these variations in net private investment.

SOURCE: U.S. Census Bureau.

Finally, changes in autonomous net taxes or government spending can also influence equilibrium real income. A rise in net taxes would reduce real income, as would a fall in government spending. The fact that the government can induce equilibrium real income to change via alterations in these *fiscal policy* variables led Keynes and his followers to propose a stabilization role for government.

FUNDAMENTAL ISSUE #4

How is equilibrium real income determined in the basic Keynesian model, and how does this theory explain short-run business cycles? In equilibrium, a nation's real income is equal to the aggregate desired expenditures on domestically produced goods and services by households, firms, the government, and foreign residents. Equilibrium real income changes are a multiple of any changes in aggregate net autonomous expenditures. Consequently, variations in autonomous spending can cause equilibrium real income to vary from a level consistent with the economy's long-run growth path.

FISCAL POLICY AND INCOME STABILIZATION

The basic Keynesian model provides a theory of the determination of equilibrium real income and of how changes in aggregate net autonomous expenditures can, through the multiplier effect, cause short-run cyclical variations in real income. Keynes argued that such variations in equilibrium real income from the economy's natural growth path were inefficient and, for the many people who lose their jobs during business downturns, even harmful. Because the government can affect the volume of aggregate net autonomous expenditures, Keynes felt that it was the government's obligation to offset business cycles.

INTERNET SOURCE
White House Economic Documents

The White House—Retrieving Economic Documents
Internet URL: **http://www.whitehouse.gov**

Navigation: Begin at the White House homepage above. Click on *Virtual Library.* Then click on *All White House Web Features Combined,* key in "Economics" in Term/Phrase dialog box, and, for, say, March 1998, set an earliest publication date of 3/1/98 and a most recent publication date of 3/31/98.

Recessionary and Inflationary Gaps

To understand the essence of Keynes's argument, consider Figure 5–14, which displays three possible levels of equilibrium real income resulting from three different positions of the aggregate desired expenditures schedule. The middle equilibrium point, *A*, is assumed to be an equilibrium real income level, y_{LR}, consistent with the economy's long-run growth path.

A fall in autonomous consumption, investment, or exports, however, would cause a decline in aggregate net autonomous expenditures and thereby shift the aggregate desired expenditures schedule downward by the distance *A–C*. The new short-run equilibrium point would be at *B*, which would yield a short-run equilibrium income level of y_1. The economy's real income would be lower than its long-run potential income level, y_{LR}. The result would be a recession and, as we discussed earlier, a higher unemployment rate. For this reason, economists call the distance *A–C* a **recessionary gap** in spending, or the amount by which aggregate desired expenditures would need to increase to move equilibrium real income back to its *natural level*, or the natural GDP level along its long-run growth path.

Recall that total *nominal* income is $Y \equiv y \times P$, where *P* is the GDP price deflator. In a recessionary gap situation at point *B*, real income is lower than its long-run level, which would imply lower nominal income as well. For this reason, there may

RECESSIONARY GAP The amount by which aggregate desired expenditures lie below the level that would cause equilibrium real income to equal its long-run, natural level.

FIGURE 5–14 **RECESSIONARY AND INFLATIONARY GAPS**

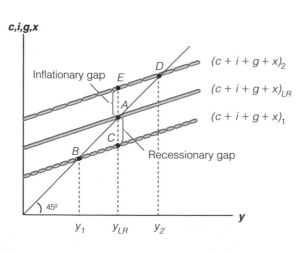

If the income-expenditure equilibrium is at point *A*, which is consistent with the economy's long-run path for real GDP at the amount y_{LR}, then there is no tendency for the economy to experience either a recession or a period of inflation. If the equilibrium point were at point *B*, however, then the income level y_1 would be below the economy's long-run growth path, and there would be a recession. The distance *A–C* would be the recessionary gap in aggregate expenditures, or the amount by which aggregate expenditures would need to increase to raise real income back to its long-run equilibrium level. In contrast, if the equilibrium point were at point *D*, then the income level y_2 would be above the economy's long-run growth path, and inflation would result. The distance *E–A* would be the inflationary gap in aggregate expenditures, or the amount by which aggregate expenditures would need to decline to reduce real income to its long-run equilibrium level.

be downward pressure on prices when the economy is in a recessionary gap. Indeed, during the Great Depression of the 1930s when Keynes was formulating his theory, there was significant deflation.

Now consider the situation that arises if the economy is at point *D* in Figure 5–14. At this point, aggregate desired expenditures are at a sufficiently high level that real income is equal to y_2, which is above the long-run potential income level, y_{LR}. Because the economy is operating above its long-run potential production level, there likely would be upward pressure on prices in this situation. Consequently, the amount by which the aggregate desired expenditures schedule lies above the long-run equilibrium point *A*, or the distance *E–A*, is called an **inflationary gap.** This is an excess amount of real aggregate desired expenditures relative to the amount necessary to keep the economy at its natural GDP.

INFLATIONARY GAP The amount by which aggregate desired expenditures exceed the level that would cause equilibrium real income to equal its long-run, natural level.

Countercyclical Fiscal Policy

Because autonomous consumption, investment, or exports could vary over time, Keynes and his followers viewed recessionary and inflationary gaps as events that were likely to make short-run business cycles commonplace occurrences. Furthermore, unexpectedly large variations in aggregate net autonomous expenditures could induce large gaps, causing equilibrium real income to diverge considerably from its natural level. In other words, severe recessions could not be ruled out.

In Keynes's view, however, the severity of the downturns could be reduced significantly by government action. For instance, suppose that the long-run real income level given by y_{LR} in Figure 5–14 is equal to $7,000 billion ($7,000,000,000,000), but the economy is in a recessionary gap with equilibrium real income y_1 equal to $6,500 billion. Thus, to reattain its long-run level of real income, the economy would need to witness a rise in real income equal to Δy = $7,000 billion − $6,500 billion = $500 billion.

Let's also continue to suppose that the marginal propensity to save is equal to 0.08 and the marginal propensity to import is equal to 0.12, so that the marginal propensity to consume is $MPC = 1 - MPS - MPIM = 1 - 0.08 - 0.12 = 0.8$. Then, as we calculated earlier, the autonomous spending multiplier is equal to $1/(MPS + MPIM) = 1/(1 - MPC) = 1/(1 - 0.8) = 1/0.2 = 5$. Then we can calculate the amount of the recessionary gap, *A–C*, by dividing Δy = $500 billion by the autonomous spending multiplier, $1/(1 - MPC) = 5$, which yields $100 billion. Aggregate desired expenditures need to rise by this amount to reattain the economy's long-run level of real GDP.

Recall that our final expression for equilibrium real income is

$$y = 1/(b + d)\ \{(s_0 - im_0) - [(1 - b - d) \times t_0] + i_0 + g_0 + x_0\},$$

where $1/(b + d) = 1/(MPS + MPIM) = 1/(1 - MPC)$, which in our example is equal to 5. This tells us that one way to induce a rise in equilibrium real income of Δy = $500 billion is to raise real government spending by $100 billion. In other words, the government could increase its autonomous spending level g_0 by exactly the amount of the recessionary gap A–C in Figure 5–14, which in this example is equal to $100 billion. This action would shift the aggregate desired expenditures schedule upward from $(c + i + g + x)_1$ to $(c + i + g + x)_{LR}$ and eliminate the recessionary gap. Equilibrium real income then would be at its long-run level, $y_{LR} = \$7,000$ billion. (For an application of this concept, see the Global Notebook: *Using Government Infrastructure Spending to Boost Malaysia's Rate of Growth.*)

The equation for equilibrium real income also indicates that a tax change could achieve the same outcome. A change in autonomous net taxes, Δt_0, would be multiplied by the factor $-(1 - b - d)$ and the factor $1/(b + d)$ to yield a change in equilibrium real income. Consequently, the multiplier effect of a change in autonomous taxes would equal $-(1 - b - d)/(b + d) = -(1 - MPS - MPIM)/(MPS + MPIM) = -MPC/(1 - MPC)$. This factor, $-MPC/(1 - MPC)$, is called the *autonomous tax multiplier*, because it indicates that a tax increase has a negative multiplier effect on real income. In our example, the value of this multiplier is equal to $-0.8/(1 - 0.8) = -0.8/0.2 = -4$, and the needed increase in real income is $\Delta y = \$500$ billion. Consequently, to achieve the long-run equilibrium level of income, the government could enact a *tax cut*, $\Delta t_0 = -\$125$ billion. Multiplying $-\$125$ billion times the autonomous tax multiplier of -4 yields the desired increase in real income of $500 billion.

Our example illustrates why Keynes concluded that a recessionary gap could be eliminated by government deficit spending. He likewise argued that inflationary gaps could be eliminated through government surpluses. The surpluses would be achieved either by reductions in government spending that were not balanced by tax cuts or by tax increases that were not balanced by hikes in government spending. Because short-run business cycles are relatively commonplace events, Keynes advocated **countercyclical fiscal policy,** in which the government runs deficits during times of recessions and surpluses during inflationary times. Such policies, he argued, would offset business cycle fluctuations.

COUNTERCYCLICAL FISCAL POLICY
A process for managing government spending and taxation so as to smooth out business cycles; the government runs deficits during times of recessions and surpluses during inflationary periods.

FUNDAMENTAL ISSUE #5

Why does the basic Keynesian model indicate that there may be a potential stabilizing role for fiscal policy? In the basic Keynesian theory, changes in government spending and taxation policies can influence aggregate net autonomous expenditures and the equilibrium level of real income. Because the theory indicates that short-run business cycle fluctuations result from variations in autonomous expenditures, fiscal policy potentially can play a role in smoothing out these variations, thereby stabilizing real income near its long-run, natural level.

GLOBAL NOTEBOOK

Using Government Infrastructure Spending to Boost Malaysia's Rate of Growth

Apparently, government economists in Malaysia believe in the positive effects of fiscal policy. A few years ago that country published a new five-year plan that called for public spending of 162.5 billion *ringit* (about $65 billion) through the year 2000. Most of the money will be spent on infrastructure. According to government officials, this additional government spending will keep Malaysia's real economic growth rate above 8 percent per year over the next five years.

According to Prime Minister Mahathir Mohamad, Malaysia can no longer rely heavily on private investment as

the engine for growth. Rather, it must increase productivity, and the government believes one way to do this is by improving the industrial infrastructure. Nowhere in the government's analysis of the increased spending was there a discussion of how it was to be financed, however.

FOR CRITICAL ANALYSIS:
In the traditional Keynesian model presented in this chapter, does it matter how expansionary fiscal policy is financed?

NATIONAL INCOME AND THE BALANCE OF TRADE

ON THE WEB
Visit Malaysia's Homepage at
http://www.jaring.my/

As we discussed in Chapter 2, the United States has run significant trade and current account deficits in recent years. What factors might explain these deficits? What policies might be enacted to address them? We can apply the Keynesian model that we have just developed to find some initial answers to these questions.

Exports, Imports, and National Income

Recall that the balance of trade is equal to exports minus imports. Using the model developed in this chapter, we can explore factors that influence the trade balance by looking at the quantity $x - im$. Our assumptions are that export spending is autonomous, so $x = x_0$, and that the import function is $im = im_0 + (d \times y_d)$. It follows that our measure of the trade balance is

$$x - im = x_0 - im_0 - (d \times y_d) = x_0 - im_0 + (d \times t_0) - (d \times y).$$

As panel (b) in Figure 5–15 on page 166 shows, this expression for the trade balance is a downward-sloping, straight-line function. We shall call this the *trade balance schedule*. The reason the trade balance schedule slopes downward is that a rise in aggregate real income raises household disposable income and stimulates higher import spending, which reduces the nation's balance of trade.

Note that a rise in autonomous exports or a fall in autonomous imports naturally would increase the trade balance at any given level of real income. Consequently, a

FIGURE 5–15 **DETERMINING THE EQUILIBRIUM TRADE BALANCE**

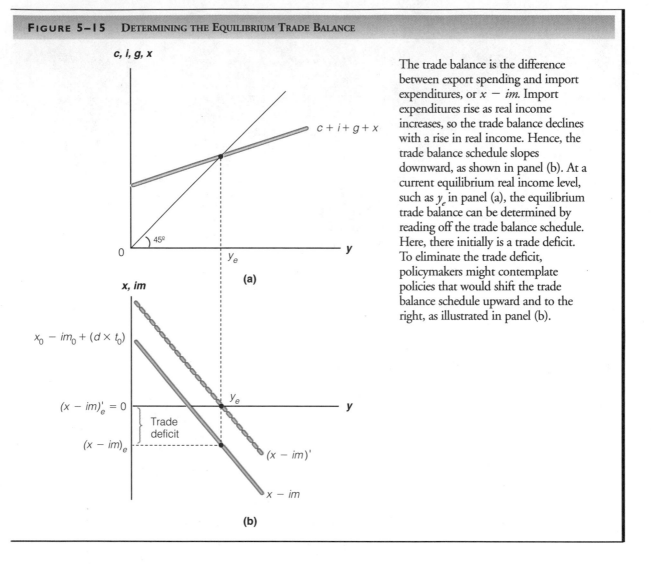

The trade balance is the difference between export spending and import expenditures, or $x - im$. Import expenditures rise as real income increases, so the trade balance declines with a rise in real income. Hence, the trade balance schedule slopes downward, as shown in panel (b). At a current equilibrium real income level, such as y_e in panel (a), the equilibrium trade balance can be determined by reading off the trade balance schedule. Here, there initially is a trade deficit. To eliminate the trade deficit, policymakers might contemplate policies that would shift the trade balance schedule upward and to the right, as illustrated in panel (b).

rise in x_0 or a fall in im_0 would raise the intercept of the trade balance schedule, thereby *shifting* the trade balance schedule upward. In addition, a tax increase would reduce household disposable income even if total real income is unchanged, thereby improving the trade balance. Therefore, a rise in autonomous net taxes, t_0, also raises the value of the intercept of the trade balance schedule and shifts the schedule upward.

The Equilibrium Balance of Trade   Figure 5–15 illustrates the determination of the equilibrium trade balance. Panel (a) shows the income-expenditure approach to the determination of the equilibrium level of real income, y_e. We can then read off the trade balance schedule $x - im$ in panel (b) to determine the equilibrium trade balance $(x - im)_e$. As drawn, these figures show a situation in which there is a trade deficit, so $(x - im)_e < 0$.

This theory of the equilibrium balance of trade can help to explain factors that cause a country to experience a trade deficit. Clearly, holding all other things constant, one factor that can induce a trade deficit is a high level of real income, which induces greater import spending, which, in turn, worsens the trade balance. Notice that any nation faces a potential trade-off: Holding other factors constant, higher growth of real output tends to improve the likelihood of running a trade deficit.

One way a trade deficit might be reduced is by inducing an upward shift of the trade balance schedule. For instance, if the trade balance schedule is shifted to the position shown by the dashed schedule $(x - im)'$ in panel (b) of Figure 5–15 while holding equilibrium real income constant, then exports would equal imports, and the nation's trade would be balanced at $(x - im)'_e = 0$. Such a shift might be accomplished by enacting policies intended to increase autonomous exports and reduce autonomous imports. One possibility is an exchange-rate depreciation, which would make foreign goods more expensive to domestic households and domestically produced goods less expensive to foreigners. Another approach is to provide subsidies to domestic industries to promote exports and to place tariffs on imports to discourage their consumption. Finally, higher net taxes at home would reduce household disposable income and thereby reduce import spending. Many nations have adopted such policies in the past in an effort to improve their trade balance.

It is important to recognize, however, that all the policies mentioned here would also affect panel (a) in Figure 5–15. For instance, a currency depreciation or subsidy policy that stimulated export spending would cause the aggregate desired expenditures schedule to shift upward, which would cause equilibrium real income to rise. This would tend to offset somewhat the trade balance improvement otherwise induced by the policy change. In addition, a tax increase would cause the aggregate desired expenditures schedule to shift downward, which would cause equilibrium real income to decline. This would reinforce the improvement in the trade balance induced by the tax increase, but at the cost of reduced real income for home residents.

The Twin Deficit Problem

During the 1980s and 1990s, the United States has not only experienced trade deficits, but has also seen its federal budget deficits expand significantly. The U.S. government consistently has spent more than it takes in through taxation, thereby running budget deficits. Although the U.S. government has experienced deficits nearly every year since World War II, in 1982 the scale of the deficits increased substantially. Figure 5–16 on page 168 plots both the private payments balance and the U.S. government budget deficit since the mid-1970s. Notice that until 1982 the government budget deficit ranged between about $-\$40$ billion and $-\$75$ billion, but since 1982 it has ranged between $-\$120$ billion and $-\$340$ billion.

FIGURE 5–16 U.S. GOVERNMENT BUDGET DEFICITS AND MERCHANDISE TRADE DEFICITS

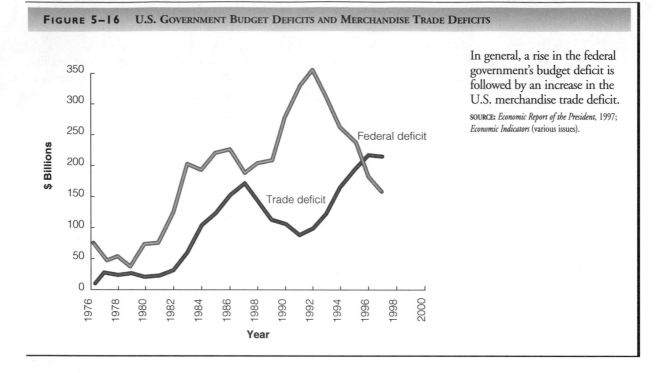

In general, a rise in the federal government's budget deficit is followed by an increase in the U.S. merchandise trade deficit.

SOURCE: *Economic Report of the President,* 1997; *Economic Indicators* (various issues).

As Figure 5–16 makes clear, the United States started to experience significant merchandise trade deficits at about the same time that the federal budget deficits mushroomed. Most economists believe that this is not a coincidence, and they refer to it as the *twin deficit problem.*

The relationship between the two deficits follows directly from combining the income identity, $y \equiv c + s + t + im$, with the product identity, $y \equiv c + i_r + g + x$. Setting the two equal, we get $c + s + t + im \equiv c + i_r + g + x$. After subtracting c from both sides, we can rearrange this identity in the form

$$s + (t - g) \equiv i_r + (x - im).$$

The left side of this identity is *net national saving,* or total private saving plus any saving by the government in the form of a budget surplus (if $t - g > 0$). The right side says that net national saving may be allocated either to greater realized investment or to a trade surplus.

In Japan, private saving rates are very high. In addition, for a number of years the Japanese government has run low deficits and even budget surpluses. This increases the net national saving rate, which permits Japan to undertake more investment and allows it to run consistent trade surpluses. In contrast, in the United States private saving rates are much lower, and government deficits exploded in the 1980s and early 1990s. Thus $t - g$ has been very negative during the past two decades, which has reduced the net national saving rate of the United States and made balanced trade infeasible.

Note that the identity above implies that Japan effectively exports some of its saving when it runs consistent trade surpluses, so that $x - im$ is positive in Japan. Where has this Japanese saving gone? The answer is that much of it has gone to the United States to fund U.S. government deficits. Because the U.S. government has run such sizable budget deficits, it has borrowed significant amounts from residents of nations that run trade surpluses. To purchase large volumes of U.S. government debt, however, Japanese residents must have dollars. They get them from the residents of the United States who purchase their products. By operating with significant negative merchandise trade balances, the United States effectively provides Japanese residents (and residents of other nations with trade surpluses) with the dollars that they use to help fund the U.S. government's budget deficit.

INTERNET SOURCE
Federal Taxes and Spending

The U.S. Department of Agriculture—Proposed Federal Budget
Internet URL: www.usda.gov

Navigation: Begin at the homepage of the U.S. Department of Agriculture. Click on *News and Information*. Then click on *1998 Budget Summary* (or proposed budget for most recent fiscal year).

FUNDAMENTAL ISSUE #6

How is the equilibrium trade balance determined, and what role may the government's budget play in affecting the size of the trade balance? Because import spending is positively related to disposable income, a nation's trade balance will, holding other factors unchanged, decline as its real income increases. Consequently, the equilibrium size of the trade balance varies with the equilibrium level of real income. Nevertheless, the identities implied by the circular flow of income and expenditures imply that nations with large budget deficits are more likely to experience trade deficits.

CHAPTER SUMMARY

1. **Business Cycles and Their Characteristics:** Business cycles are variations in real income around its long-run growth path. Recessions are periods of a decline in real income below

its long-run level, and expansions are increases in real income to levels that for a time can exceed its long-run level. Frictional and structural unemployment exist even without business cycles, but the overall unemployment rate has a cyclical component that tends to rise during recessions and decline during expansions.

2. **The Key Relationships Implied by the Circular Flow of Income and Expenditures:** One fundamental identity that can be inferred from the circular flow is the income identity. This identity says that all real income is allocated to domestic consumption, saving, taxes, and import spending. The other identity is the product identity, which states that the real value of output of goods and services is equal to real expenditures on that output in the form of household consumption, business investment, government spending, and export spending by foreigners.

3. **The Components of Aggregate Desired Expenditures in the Basic Keynesian Model:** Aggregate desired expenditures are equal to the sum of household consumption of domestically produced goods and services, investment spending desired by firms, government expenditures, and export spending by foreigners. In the most basic Keynesian theory, desired investment, government spending and net taxes, and export spending are autonomous, but consumption spending is positively related to disposable income. Therefore, the aggregate expenditures schedule is upward sloping.

4. **The Determination of Equilibrium Real Income and the Keynesian Explanation for Short-Run Business Cycles:** The fundamental equilibrium condition of the Keynesian model is that a nation's real income is equal to the aggregate desired expenditures on domestically produced goods and services by households, firms, the government, and foreign residents. Because equilibrium real income changes are a multiple of a change in aggregate net autonomous expenditures, such changes in autonomous spending can cause equilibrium real income to vary from its long-run level.

5. **The Potential Stabilizing Role of Fiscal Policy in the Basic Keynesian Model:** According to Keynesian theory, changes in government spending and taxation policies can affect the equilibrium level of real income by changing aggregate net autonomous expenditures. Consequently, fiscal policy potentially can play a role in smoothing out variations in autonomous expenditures, thereby stabilizing real income and smoothing business cycles.

6. **The Determination of the Equilibrium Trade Balance and the Relationship between the Government Budget and the Trade Balance:** Import spending is positively related to disposable income. Therefore, holding other factors unchanged, a nation's trade balance will tend to fall as its real income rises. The identities implied by the circular flow of income and expenditures imply, however, that nations with large budget deficits are more likely to experience merchandise trade deficits.

QUESTIONS AND PROBLEMS

1. In light of the definitions of business cycle peaks and troughs, explain why the trough of the idealized business cycle in Figure 5–1 does not correspond to the lowest level of real GDP over the cycle depicted and why the peak is not at the highest level of real GDP.

2. Suppose that the citizens of the United States decide to devote a portion of their tax dollars to reducing the natural rate of unemployment by increasing expenditures on one of the following: (a) primary and secondary education, (b) unemployment insurance programs, or (c) income transfer programs such as Aid to Families with Dependent Children. Which type of increased spending would be most effective in achieving the goal? Explain your reasoning.

3. In your own words, without relying on any algebraic equations, explain why the marginal propensities to save, import, and consume domestic goods must sum to 1.

4. In the simple Keynesian model, suppose that $MPS = 0.04$ and $MPC = 0.90$. What is the marginal propensity to import ($MPIM$)? Suppose disposable income increases from $900 billion to $1,000 billion. By how much would consumption rise? By how much would saving rise? By how much would imports rise? Is the sum of your answers equal to the change in income?

5. If the consumption function (in billions of dollars) for a closed economy is $c = \$20 + (0.8)y_d$, determine the level of consumption and the level of saving for $y_d = \$50$ billion, $150 billion, and $250 billion. Compute the associated values of the average propensity to consume (APC).

6. Explain, in your own words, the difference between desired investment and realized investment. Why are these two magnitudes equal at the equilibrium level of real income?

7. Suppose that the value of the autonomous spending multiplier is equal to 4, the marginal propensity to save is equal to 0.10, and the economy is open to international trade. What is the value of the marginal propensity to import? Show your work.

8. Suppose that the level of government spending is equal to $200 billion (in base-year dollars) and that the level of real net taxes is equal to $100 billion. This economy is closed to international trade. In equilibrium, will saving be equal to real desired investment? Why or why not?

9. A nation's government runs a deficit of $150 billion (in base-year dollars). Its total real saving is equal to $1,000 billion, and its realized investment is equal to $500 billion (in base-year dollars). What is this nation's trade balance? Does this nation experience a trade surplus or a trade deficit?

10. Suppose that equilibrium real income is $y = \$500$ billion (in base-year dollars). The consumption function is $c = \$50 + (0.75)y_d$. Real net taxes are equal to $100 billion, and real government spending is equal to $125 billion.

a. What is the equilibrium level of consumption?

b. If real desired investment is equal to $10 billion, what is the amount of autonomous real exports?

CyberTutor Exercises

1. Suppose that the government decides that it wants to reduce equilibrium income. What policies can be enacted to accomplish this? Using the two approaches to determining equilibrium real income, explain how these policies work.

2. What happens to the equilibrium level of income if firms decide to increase investment expenditures?

3. Will different multipliers result in a different equilibrium real income for a given rise in government spending? If so, how?

4. What impact will a decrease in autonomous export spending have on equilibrium income?

5. After many years of deficit the trade of the United States has at last reached balance! However, trade hawks in the U.S. congress have decided that the United States should run a surplus to punish those countries that had run trade surpluses vis-a-vis the United States. What might Congress do to accomplish this goal?

6. Plot the real GDP growth rate, the nominal GDP growth rate and the unemployment rate. Which growth rate (real or nominal) do you think is better to use? What relationship does the data suggest?

7. While times series plots can reveal some information about data, another useful tool is the scatter diagram. Develop a scatter plot of the nominal GDP growth rate and the unemployment rate and a scatter plot of the real GDP growth rate and the unemployment rate. What do these plots tell you about the relationship between economic growth and the unemployment rate? Does this relationship change over time?

8. Some economists believe that there ought to be a relationship between the unemployment rate and GDP growth. Does the data support this? Create a scatter plot of the nominal GDP growth rate and the unemployment rate and of the real GDP growth rate and the unemployment rate. What do these plots tell you about the relationship between economic growth and the unemployment rate? Does this relationship change over time?

ON-LINE APPLICATION

A quick way to keep up with the behavior of the components of GDP is via the "FRED" database made available on the Internet by the Federal Reserve Bank of St. Louis. You can use this information to understand which component of desired expenditures accounted for movements in equilibrium income.

Internet URL: http://www.stls.frb.org/fred/data/gdp/gdi

Title: **Quarterly Gross Domestic Product and Components**

Navigation: Begin at the homepage of the Federal Reserve Bank of St. Louis (http://www.stls.frb.org). Click on *FRED* (http://www.stls.frb.org/fred). Then click on *Gross Domestic Product and Components.*

Application:

1. Click on *Disposable Personal Income* and write down the amounts for 1994 to 1998. Then click on *Personal Consumption Expenditures.* Write down the amounts from 1994 to 1998. Use these data to calculate the average propensity to save for each of these quarters.

2. Back up to *Gross Domestic Product and Components.* Now click on *Gross Domestic Product in Chained (1992) Dollars.* Scan through the data since the mid-1960s. In which years did the largest downturns in real GDP take place?

SELECTED REFERENCES AND FURTHER READING

Branson, William. *Macroeconomic Theory and Policy.* New York: Macmillan, 1978.

Dillard, Dudley. *The Economics of John Maynard Keynes.* Englewood Cliffs, N.J.: Prentice Hall, 1948.

Hansen, Alvin. *A Guide to Keynes.* New York: Macmillan, 1953.

Keynes, John Maynard. *The General Theory of Employment, Interest, and Money.* New York: Harcourt Brace Jovanovich, 1964.

Klein, Lawrence. *The Keynesian Revolution.* 2d ed. New York: Macmillan, 1966.

LeKachman, Robert. *The Age of Keynes.* New York: Random House, 1966.

LeKachman, Robert, ed. *Keynes and the Classics,* Boston: Heath, 1965.

6

Do Central Banks Matter?— MONEY IN THE TRADITIONAL KEYNESIAN SYSTEM

After recovering from the recession, the U.S. economy seemingly faced the potential for another downturn because inventories of unsold goods were accumulat-

ing and the rate of unemployment was beginning to increase. Many wondered if the Federal Reserve might cut interest rates to stimulate the economy. At the same time the dollar's value with respect to some other currencies was under pressure. If the Fed cut interest rates, it might reduce the incentive for foreign investors to hold dollar-denominated assets. That might cause a decline in the dollar's international value.

Which way would the Fed go? To find out, reporters listened carefully to Alan Greenspan, chair of the Fed, as he gave a major speech. The day after the speech a New York Times *headline read "Greenspan sees chance of recession," but the* Wall Street Journal *headline said, "Fed chairman doesn't see recession on the horizon." A financial services firm then ran a full-page newspaper ad with both headlines followed by the comment, "Confused? Who wouldn't be?"*

During his next speech, aware of the attention his comments would receive, Greenspan remarked, "I spend a substantial amount of my time endeavoring to fend off questions and worry terribly that I might end up being too clear." In light of the confusion Greenspan generated, one New York economist suggested that a fitting inscription for the Fed chair's future tombstone might be "I am guardedly optimistic about the next world, but remain cognizant of the downside risk."

Because the chair of the Federal Reserve Board of Governors is the nation's foremost central banking official, financial analysts pick over every word that the chair utters for clues about the Federal Reserve's perceptions and future plans. Today, at least those in business and finance believe that central banks do matter. In this chapter you will learn about how monetary policy can affect the economy.

THE DEMAND FOR MONEY

The traditional Keynesian income-expenditure theory forms the heart of a simple theory of short-run business cycles and of the balance of trade. Missing from the basic framework discussed in Chapter 5, however, were any meaningful roles for money and other financial assets, interest rates, and monetary policy. You will learn in this chapter that the traditional Keynesian macroeconomic theory actually indicates that central banks potentially can assist in smoothing out business cycles via their ability to determine national monetary policies.

The reason for this conclusion is that the Keynesian theory proposes interactions among the interest rate, money, prices, and real income that are absent from the classical macroeconomic model that we discussed in Chapter 3. Part of the rationale for these interactions is provided by Keynes's theory of the demand for money, which emphasized the role of interest rates.

Recall that classical theorists emphasized the use of money as a medium of exchange. This led them to propose the Cambridge equation, $M^d = k \times Y$, where M^d denotes total desired money holdings, Y denotes total nominal income, and k represents the fraction of income that people wish to hold as money to use in planned exchanges for goods and services. As you will see later in the chapter, Keynes agreed that total income is an important determinant of desired money holdings. Nevertheless, he also argued that interest rates influence the prices of financial assets that people hold alongside the cash in their portfolios of financial wealth. This fact, Keynes contended, creates an important link between money demand and interest rates and, furthermore, implies mechanisms for interest-rate determination and monetary policy that operate very differently from those originally proposed by the classical economists.

The Transactions and Precautionary Motives for Holding Money

Keynes's theory of money demand starts by considering the specific *motives* that people have to hold money. It might seem obvious that people want to hold money, but consider that currency pays no interest and that checking deposits typically pay interest rates well below the rates that people can earn by holding other financial assets. Indeed, a key type of checking account, called a *demand deposit*, pays no interest at all. What Keynes tried to do was to identify the reasons why people hold coins, pieces of paper, and bank accounts that offer them little or no financial return. (For a discussion of new forms of money, see the Policy Notebook: *Does Technology in Banking Spell the End of Money?*)

The Transactions Motive   To Keynes, the classical theory of money demand, as summarized by the Cambridge equation, relied on two basic motives for holding money. One of these he called the **transactions motive**. This was the incentive to hold non-interest-bearing currency and non- (or low-) interest-bearing checking deposits for use as media of exchange in planned transactions. For instance, you need some cash on hand if you have a snack while you study between classes every afternoon. Money is also useful for buying groceries each week and for paying your rent and utility bills each month.

In turn, how lavishly you can afford to eat and live depends on your income. If you are a student with a relatively low income, your daily meals and apartment will likely be less elaborate than those of a student from a wealthy family who receives a monthly stipend from a trust fund. Consequently, Keynes agreed with the classical economists' argument that total income is a key determinant of total desired money

TRANSACTIONS MOTIVE The motive to hold money for use in planned exchanges.

In the last few years, many observers have suggested that technological innovations will "end the use of money." As examples, they point to the development of chip-enhanced ATM cards that are loaded with "smart money" and electronic cash (e-cash) that can be used on the Internet. Some observers also regard the more than $1 trillion of credit-card transactions made each year around the world as "non-money" transactions.

Another innovation has been the growing trend toward paying bills electronically rather than by check. An electronic payment process involves four steps: (1) the biller creates an electronic bill and sends it to the customer via computer; (2) using an Internet browser or banking software, the customer views the bill and fills out an electronic check authorizing payment; (3) the customer's bank transfers money from the customer's account to the biller's account via an electronic payment network; and (4) the customer receives a monthly statement itemizing the payments, with no paper checks.

Whether we are talking about smart cards, e-cash on the Internet, credit-card use, or electronic payment of bills, we are not seeing the elimination of money and checking account balances. Consider credit cards first. A credit card is not a substitute for money. At best, it constitutes a short-term loan from the issuer of the credit card to the user. At worst, if the user chooses not to pay off the balance, it constitutes a longer-term loan. In any event, the amount of credit-card balances that can be used for purchases is a small part of any measure of the U.S. money supply.

What about "smart" ATM cards and e-cash? These are simply another form of money rather than a way of eliminating money. Having a smart card in your wallet that has $100 embedded in its chip is not much different than having a $100 bill. The card is still money. If you have set up an account so that you can use e-cash over the Internet, the dollar balance in that account in e-cash is the same thing as currency or a checking account balance.

Finally, the use of paperless "checks" doesn't mean that checking account balances will disappear. Rather, it simply means the elimination of a paper trail.

FOR CRITICAL ANALYSIS:
If we truly eliminated money, what would happen?

---

holdings. As income rises, Keynes concluded, so does the total quantity of money demanded to satisfy the transactions motive for holding money.

PRECAUTIONARY MOTIVE The motive to hold money for use in unplanned exchanges.

The Precautionary Motive   Another related reason to hold money was what Keynes called the **precautionary motive**, or the desire to hold money in the event of a need to make unplanned transactions. For instance, your car might break down and require repair, or you might run across a great sale on an item that you had not previously planned to purchase. Most of us typically try to budget some extra cash to cover such unexpected transactions.

How much extra cash we include in our budgets as a precaution is likely to depend on our respective real incomes. Returning to our college student example, a low-income student with an eight-year-old automobile would probably experience lower repair bills in the event of a breakdown than would a high-income student with a late-model sports car with a high-performance engine. Likewise, the low-income student is likely to find an unexpectedly good buy while shopping at a discount store, while the high-income student is more likely to come across a sale at an upscale department store. Consequently, Keynes hypothesized that the amount of money held to satisfy the precautionary motive also should depend positively on total income.

The Portfolio Motive for Holding Money

Both the transactions and precautionary motives justify the classical theorists' emphasis on the importance of income as a key determinant of aggregate desired money holdings. What distinguishes Keynes's theory of the demand for money from the classical approach is the idea that interest rates affect desired money holdings. According to Keynes, there is also a *speculative motive* for holding money that arises from the interplay between interest rates and the prices of financial assets such as bonds. The modern term for this rationale for holding money is the **portfolio motive**. The idea behind the portfolio motive is that speculations about interest-rate changes and movements in bond prices induce people to adjust their desired holdings of bonds and money. As a result, interest-rate variations influence the quantity of money demanded.

PORTFOLIO MOTIVE The modern term for Keynes's basic idea of a speculative motive for holding money, in which people hold both money and bonds and adjust their holdings of both types of financial assets based on their speculations about interest-rate movements.

Money, Bonds, and Financial Wealth   People can hold accumulated wealth in a number of ways. One possibility is to hold nonfinancial assets, such as land, residential housing, or durable goods such as automobiles. Another is to hold financial assets, such as bonds, stocks, and savings accounts. Keynes also viewed money as a key part of a person's financial wealth.

To keep things simple, let's assume that an individual's financial wealth may be allocated only between money holdings, M, and another financial asset called "bonds," B. The factor that distinguishes money from bonds is that the nominal price of money is always equal to 1 unit of money (for instance, \$1, 1 franc, 1 yen, and the like). In contrast, the nominal price of a bond can change over time. As a result, an individual who holds a bond earns a *capital gain* if the nominal price of the bond increases over a given interval of time or a *capital loss* if the nominal price of the bond falls during some other period. A \$1 bill of U.S. currency or a \$1 portion of a checking account at a bank has the same \$1 *nominal* value over any given interval. Consequently, people cannot earn nominal capital gains or incur nominal capital losses if they hold all their financial wealth as currency or deposit forms of money.

To see how a person might decide to allocate financial wealth between money and bonds, let's suppose that at some given point in time, the person's nominal financial wealth is equal to some amount F. The individual can split this wealth between money holdings, M, which we shall assume are non-interest-bearing cash, and bond holdings, B, that earn a nominal interest rate of return r. Thus, at the point in time under consideration, the individual's financial wealth must be equal to holdings of money plus holdings of bonds:

$$F = M + B.$$

Because wealth is constant at a point in time, it must be true that the sum of changes in money and bond holdings must equal zero, or $\Delta M + \Delta B = 0$. That is, any change in bond holdings, ΔB, must be offset by an equal change in money holdings in the opposite direction, $-\Delta M$. For example, suppose that a person has $10,000 in financial wealth, with $5,000 in money and $5,000 in bonds. Suppose further that she wishes to increase her bond holdings by $2,000. Then, to maintain the same total financial wealth of $10,000, she must reduce her money holdings by $2,000, leaving her with $3,000 in cash and $7,000 in bonds.

This constraint that an individual faces in allocating a fixed amount of financial wealth provides the foundation for a relationship between the demand for money and the interest rate. Because bonds earn a nominal interest return, changes in the interest rate affect the market prices of bonds and an individual's desired bond holdings. Changing bond holdings, however, requires changes in money holdings. Consequently, interest-rate variations typically will induce changes in desired holdings of money.

Bond Prices and Interest Rates   How do interest-rate changes affect bond prices? To answer this question, let's consider the simplest kind of bonds, which are **perpetuities**. These are nonmaturing bonds, or bonds that have no final date of maturity. Over the years the governments of the United Kingdom and several nations of the British Commonwealth have issued such bonds, called *consols*. Perpetuities typically pay a fixed annual amount, or coupon return C, per year forever. If the nominal interest rate is r, then one important issue for anyone contemplating buying a perpetuity is how much to pay for this infinite-life bond.

To determine this, we must first think about the concept of **discounted present value**, or the value from today's perspective of funds to be received at a future date. If the annual interest rate is r, then the discounted present value of C dollars a year from now is equal to $C/(1 + r)$ dollars. This is true because if we had $C/(1 + r)$ dollars today, we could earn interest on this amount during the coming year, thereby obtaining $[C/(1 + r)] \times (1 + r) = C$ dollars a year from now. Likewise, the discounted present value of C dollars *two* years from now is equal to $C/(1 + r)^2$ dollars. If we had that sum today and saved it until next year, we would have $[C/(1 + r)^2] \times (1 + r) = C/(1 + r)$ dollars next year. Then, if we save that sum into the second year, we again would have $[C/(1 + r)] \times (1 + r) = C$ dollars. In general, therefore, we can reach an important conclusion:

> **The discounted present value of any amount C when the market interest rate is r is equal to $C/(1 + r)^n$, where n denotes the number of years into the future that we are considering.**

A perpetuity that we purchase today will pay C dollars next year, the year after that, and every other year into the future. That means that the discounted present value of this bond is the sum of the discounted present values of C dollars for all those years,

PERPETUITY Nonmaturing bond that pays an infinite stream of coupon returns.

DISCOUNTED PRESENT VALUE The value from today's perspective of funds to be received at a future date.

or the infinite sum $C/(1 + r) + C/(1 + r)^2 + C/(1 + r)^3 + C/(1 + r)^4 + \cdots$. In the absence of risk and exchange costs, this is the amount that we would be willing to pay for this bond, because it is today's value of the coupon returns the bond will yield. Consequently, the price of the perpetual bond, P_B, will equal

$$P_B = C/(1 + r) + C/(1 + r)^2 + C/(1 + r)^3 + C/(1 + r)^4 + \cdots.$$

When confronted with an infinite sum, it is tempting to throw up one's hands. Notice, though, that if we multiply both sides of the preceding equation by $(1 + r)$, we get

$$(1 + r) \times P_B = C + C/(1 + r) + C/(1 + r)^2 + C/(1 + r)^3 + C/(1 + r)^4 + \cdots.$$

From algebra, we know that we can always subtract one equation from another. So let's subtract the first equation from the second to get

$$[(1 + r) \times P_B] - P_B =$$

$$[C + C/(1 + r) + C/(1 + r)^2 + C/(1 + r)^3 + C/(1 + r)^4 + \cdots]$$

$$- [C/(1 + r) + C/(1 + r)^2 + C/(1 + r)^3 + C/(1 + r)^4 + \cdots]$$

Notice that $[(1 + r) \times P_B - P_B]$ is equal to $P_B + (r \times P_B) - P_B = r \times P_B$. In addition, we can see that all the terms on the right side of the last equation cancel out except for C. Consequently, this very messy equation involving differences between infinite sums reduces to

$$r \times P_B = C.$$

If we now divide both sides of this much simpler equation by r, we get a final expression for the price of a perpetuity, which is

$$P_B = C/r.$$

The price of a perpetual, nonmaturing bond is its annual coupon return divided by the market interest rate. Therefore, if the perpetuity pays $C = \$100$ per year forever and the market interest rate is 7 percent, then the price of the bond is equal to $P_B = C/r = \$100/(0.07) = \$1,428.57$.

Suppose that the market interest rate r increases. Then the ratio C/r would fall, and the price of the bond would decline. In our numerical example, if the market interest rate rises to 8 percent, then the price of the perpetuity with a $100 annual coupon return would be equal to $P_B = C/r = \$100/(0.08) = \$1,250.00$.

We can conclude that:

Holding the coupon return and all other factors unchanged, there is an inverse relationship between the price of existing bonds and the current nominal interest rate.

If the market nominal interest rate rises, then bond prices will fall, and people who hold bonds will incur a nominal capital loss. If the market nominal interest rate declines, then bond prices will rise, and people who hold bonds will earn a nominal capital gain.

INTERNET SOURCE

Tracking Interest Rates

The Federal Reserve Bank of New York—Selected Daily Rates
Internet URL: http://www.ny.frb.org/pihome/mktrates/dlyrates/

Navigation: Start at the Federal Reserve Bank of New York homepage (http://www.ny.frb.org). Click on *Statistics.* Click on *Selected Daily Rates.*

The Portfolio Motive   Now let's consider how a person might adjust her money and bond holdings as part of a speculative strategy involving expected changes in interest rates. This individual recognizes that her future capital gains or losses from bond holdings depend directly upon whether nominal market interest rates rise or fall in the future. Consequently, she will adjust the composition of her portfolio of money and bonds in light of her *anticipation* of future interest-rate movements.

Suppose that the market interest rate rises, in the present, to a level that our individual believes is rather high. As a result, she anticipates that the interest rate will decline in the future, causing bond prices to rise and providing her with a future capital gain on bonds that she holds as part of her financial wealth. To further increase her anticipated capital gains from bond holdings, she will allocate more of her financial wealth to bonds in the present. Her financial wealth is fixed in the present, however, so to do this, she will have to reduce her holdings of money. Consequently, for this individual a current rise in the market interest rate causes a present reduction in her desired money holdings. Her demand for money depends negatively on the market interest rate.

Suppose instead that the market interest rate falls, at present, to levels that our individual perceives to be rather low. Therefore, she anticipates that the market interest rate will rise in the future, causing bond prices to fall and causing her to incur capital losses on her existing bond holdings. To avoid some of these anticipated future losses, she will sell bonds in the present, thereby allocating more of her fixed current financial wealth to holdings of money. Hence, a current fall in the market interest rate induces her to increase the amount of money demanded. Again, the individual's demand for money is inversely related to the market interest rate.

Keynes concluded from this line of reasoning that the portfolio motive for holding money implies that a person's real income is not the only determinant of desired money holdings. The demand for money should also depend on the nominal interest rate. Furthermore, *there should be a negative relationship between the quantity of money demanded and the nominal interest rate.*

The Demand for Money

Our examination of the three motives for holding money indicates that two key variables should influence the total demand for money. One is real income. A rise in real income intensifies the transactions and precautionary motives for holding money, which we predict should lead to a rise in total desired money balances. The other key determinant of the quantity of money demanded is the nominal interest rate. The logic of the portfolio motive for holding money indicates that there should be an inverse relationship between the quantity of money demanded and the nominal interest rate, holding other factors unchanged.

The Money Demand Schedule   We can capture these relationships with a simple diagram of a *money demand schedule,* or a graphical depiction of the relationship between the quantity of money demanded and the nominal interest rate. A typical money demand schedule is shown in panel (a) of Figure 6–1. The downward slope of this schedule reflects the inverse relationship between the quantity of money demanded and the nominal interest rate that the portfolio motive indicates should exist. In addition, we label the money demand schedule $M^d(Y_1)$ to indicate that its *position* depends on the current level of nominal income, such as a nominal income level Y_1.

Panel (b) of Figure 6–1 illustrates the effect of an increase in nominal income, from Y_1 to a larger amount Y_2. Such a rise in income will increase the volume of planned transactions by all individuals in the economy. In addition, it will raise people's precautionary money holdings. Consequently, at any given nominal interest rate, people will demand more money. This means that the money demand schedule will shift rightward, from $M^d(Y_1)$ to $M^d(Y_2)$, as a result of the rise in total nominal income, as shown in panel (b).

The Demand for Real Money Balances   To simplify our notation, we have emphasized the demand for nominal, or current-dollar, money balances. When people decide how much cash to carry, however, what really matters is the purchasing power of the money that they hold. Suppose, for instance, that you decide one morning to carry $15 in cash to cover your intended purchases, say, lunch for $10 and an afternoon snack for $5. Imagine, however, that after you leave home the price level doubles. As a result, the price of lunch increases to $20, and the price of an afternoon snack rises to $10. Now your $15 will not even cover the cost of the lunch that you had planned to eat, and you will have to forgo your afternoon snack altogether. The problem is that the purchasing power of your $15 is now half its previous value. To purchase the same lunch and snack, you would have to double your nominal money balances to $30. A doubling of prices requires a doubling of nominal money balances to maintain the required purchasing power for the day's expenses.

The upshot of this example is that the real purchasing power of a person's nominal cash balances is the price-adjusted value of the money holdings, or $m = M/P$,

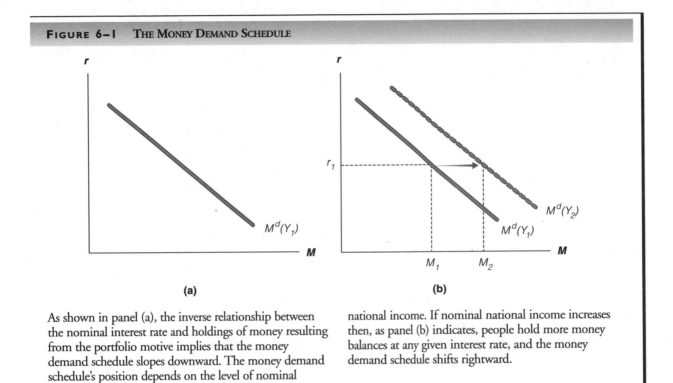

FIGURE 6–1   THE MONEY DEMAND SCHEDULE

As shown in panel (a), the inverse relationship between the nominal interest rate and holdings of money resulting from the portfolio motive implies that the money demand schedule slopes downward. The money demand schedule's position depends on the level of nominal national income. If nominal national income increases then, as panel (b) indicates, people hold more money balances at any given interest rate, and the money demand schedule shifts rightward.

REAL MONEY BALANCES The value of the nominal quantity of money adjusted for the price level; defined as the nominal money stock divided by the price level.

where m denotes **real money balances**. These are equal to nominal money holdings, M, divided by the price level, which we measure using the GDP deflator, P. Panel (a) of Figure 6–2 depicts a demand schedule for real money balances, $m^d = M^d/P$. The portfolio motive for holding money continues to apply to holdings of real money balances, so the demand schedule for real money balances also slopes downward.

The total real purchasing power that an individual desires to maintain will depend on the person's *real* income. As a person's real income rises, the real value of planned and unplanned transactions will increase, spurring the transactions and precautionary motives for holding real money balances. Therefore, a rise in real income, from an initial level y_1 to a larger amount y_2, causes an individual to increase desired holdings of real money balances at any given interest rate. This means that a rise in real income shifts the position of the demand schedule for real money balances to the right, $m^d(y_1)$ to $m^d(y_2)$, as shown in panel (b) of Figure 6–2 (next page).

FUNDAMENTAL ISSUE #1

What are the key motives for holding money, and what variables do they indicate should influence the demand for money? There are three key motives for holding money. The transactions and

FIGURE 6–2   **THE DEMAND FOR REAL MONEY BALANCES**

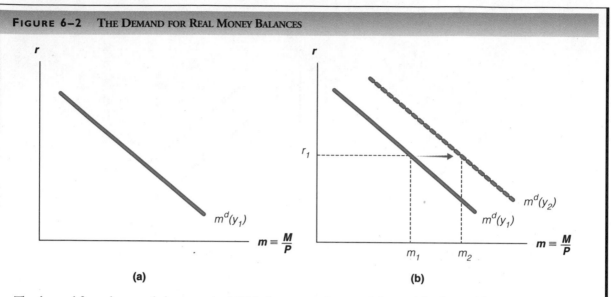

(a)

(b)

The demand for real money balances, $m = M/P$, is the total demand for real purchasing power. As shown in panel (a), the demand for real money balances slopes downward as a result of the portfolio motive for holding real money balances. The demand for real money balances shifts rightward when real income rises, as shown in panel (b), because of the transactions and precautionary motives for holding real money balances.

precautionary motives refer to the desire to hold money for use in planned and unplanned exchanges, respectively; both indicate that the demand for real money balances should depend positively on the level of real income. The portfolio motive refers to the allocation of a portion of financial wealth to money holdings as part of speculative strategies involving expectations about future interest-rate movements. This motive indicates that the demand for real money balances should depend negatively on the nominal interest rate.

THE MONEY SUPPLY AND THE EQUILIBRIUM NOMINAL INTEREST RATE

The nominal quantity of money, or the *money stock*, is the total amount of circulating exchange media. As already noted, in our modern world these media of exchange include coins and currency and checking deposits. Each week, the Federal Reserve sums the amounts of these components of the total quantity of money to get its basic overall measure of the money stock, which it calls M1. The Federal Reserve also tabulates broader measures of money, such as M2 and M3, which add other types of

ON THE WEB
*Obtain the Latest Data on
Monetary Aggregates at:*
http://www.stls.frb.org/fred

bank deposits to M1. Most other central banks around the world have adopted analogous measures of the money stocks of their respective nations.

The Supply of Money

Because central banks' measures of the money stock include various bank deposits, the nominal quantity of money in any nation responds in part to events that affect the nation's banking system. To influence a nation's nominal money stock, a central bank such as the Federal Reserve must institute policies that affect decisions made by the nation's banks and thereby alter the total amounts of deposits that they issue.

The Money Supply Schedule   Realistically, any central bank's ability to bring about desired changes in bank deposits is likely to be imperfect, and a central bank such as the Federal Reserve typically cannot precisely control the total amount of nominal money balances in circulation. Because banks likely will respond to interest-rate changes by altering the amount of deposits that they issue, the nominal quantity of money supplied in the economy usually will depend in part on interest rates.

Nevertheless, we shall simplify by assuming that a typical central bank can supply any desired quantity of nominal money balances in the form of non-interest-bearing cash and deposits. This assumption means that the quantity of money supplied will not, in our analysis, depend on the nominal interest rate. As a result, as shown in Figure 6–3, the nominal money supply function is *vertical,* and its position is determined by policies of the central bank. If the central bank institutes policies that increase the amount of currency in circulation or induce banks to issue more checkable deposits, then the money supply function will shift to the right, as shown in the figure.

FIGURE 6–3   THE NOMINAL MONEY SUPPLY SCHEDULE

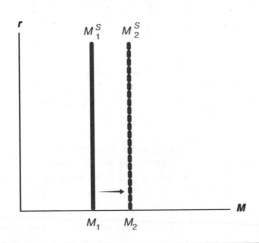

We assume that a nation's central bank can completely control the quantity of nominal money balances in the economy and that the quantity of money the central bank supplies is independent from the nominal interest rate. Under these assumptions, the nominal money supply schedule is vertical. It shifts rightward if the central bank increases the stock of money in circulation.

The Supply of Real Money Balances As we discussed earlier, the real purchasing power of money (M/P) is what really matters to all individuals in an economy. From the viewpoint of any central bank, therefore, it would be desirable to be able to control the quantity of real money balances directly. This is not possible, however. Central banks do not *set* prices, which are determined in markets for goods and services. As you will learn, all that a central bank can do is to conduct policies that influence the *equilibrium* price level. This means that the actual quantity of real money balances will depend on what the equilibrium price level turns out to be.

Figure 6–4 depicts diagrams of the supply of real money balances, denoted M^s/P. Panel (a) shows the effect on real money balances of a reduction in the nominal money stock, from M_1 to M_2, when the price level remains unchanged at P_1. The result is a decline in real money balances, from M_1/P_1 to M_2/P_1.

Panel (a) shows that if the price level were to remain constant, a central bank could, in principle, determine the quantity of real money balances. Realistically, however, the price level can change without a central bank implementing any policy actions. As panel (b) of the figure shows, a rise in the price level, from P_1 to P_2, shifts

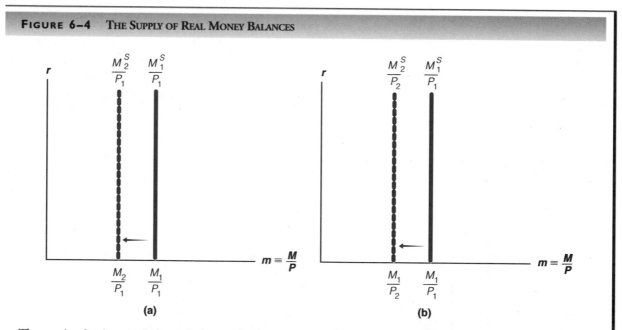

FIGURE 6–4 **THE SUPPLY OF REAL MONEY BALANCES**

(a)

(b)

The supply of real money balances is the purchasing power of the nominal quantity of money supplied by the central bank. As illustrated in this figure, two factors can cause a reduction in the supply of real money balances. One, illustrated in panel (a), is a reduction by the central bank in the nominal quantity of money in circulation at a given price level. The other, shown in panel (b), is a rise in the price level while the nominal money stock remains unchanged. In either instance, the supply of real money balances shifts leftward.

the real money supply schedule leftward even if the central bank leaves the nominal money stock unchanged, at an amount M_1. As a result, real money balances decline, from M_1/P_1 to M_1/P_2, without any action by the central bank.

We can conclude that the position of the supply schedule for real money balances depends on *both* the nominal money stock *and* the price level. A fall in the nominal money stock shifts this supply schedule leftward, while a rise in the nominal money stock shifts the schedule to the right. A rise in the price level shifts the supply schedule leftward, whereas a fall in the price level shifts the schedule to the right.

The Equilibrium Nominal Interest Rate

Both the supply and demand schedules for real money balances appear in Figure 6–5. The crossing point of the two schedules describes a situation in which all individuals in the economy are satisfied holding the nominal money stock supplied by the central bank, M_1, deflated by the current price level, P_1. Consequently, at this single point the quantity of real money balances demanded by the public is equal to the quantity of real money balances supplied by the central bank.

Attaining Equilibrium in the Market for Real Money Balances   The nominal interest rate adjusts to achieve this equilibrium point. Therefore, the nominal interest rate, r_1, is the *equilibrium* rate. To understand the adjustment process by which the equilibrium interest rate is determined, consider the situation in which the nominal interest rate is equal to r_2 in Figure 6–5. At this higher interest rate, there is an excess quantity of real money balances supplied. Individuals wish to hold fewer real money

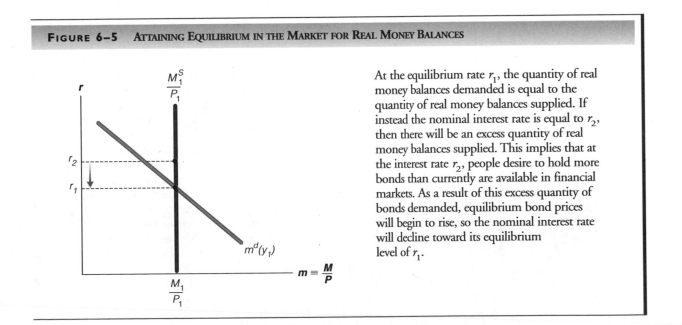

FIGURE 6–5   ATTAINING EQUILIBRIUM IN THE MARKET FOR REAL MONEY BALANCES

At the equilibrium rate r_1, the quantity of real money balances demanded is equal to the quantity of real money balances supplied. If instead the nominal interest rate is equal to r_2, then there will be an excess quantity of real money balances supplied. This implies that at the interest rate r_2, people desire to hold more bonds than currently are available in financial markets. As a result of this excess quantity of bonds demanded, equilibrium bond prices will begin to rise, so the nominal interest rate will decline toward its equilibrium level of r_1.

balances than the central bank has supplied. At the nominal interest rate r_2, people wish to hold more bonds than currently are available. Hence, there is an excess quantity of bonds demanded, which will cause bond prices to rise. Because there is an inverse relationship between the price of bonds and the nominal interest rate, the interest rate must fall toward the equilibrium level, r_1. At this equilibrium interest rate, both the bond market and the market for real money balances are in equilibrium.

The Liquidity Effect of Monetary Policy   Figure 6–6 shows the effect of an increase in the nominal quantity of money supplied by the central bank, from M_1 to M_2, assuming that the price level is fixed at an amount P_1. The rise in the nominal money supply causes the real money supply schedule to shift to the right. This results in an excess quantity of money supplied at the initial equilibrium interest rate, r_1. As in Figure 6–5, there now will be an excess quantity of bonds demanded, and bond prices will increase. This implies that the nominal interest rate must fall to a new equilibrium level, r_2.

    This fall in the interest rate caused by an increase in the nominal quantity of money without a change in the price level is the **liquidity effect** of monetary policy. It is called a liquidity effect because such an increase in the nominal quantity of money raises the overall liquidity in the economy. People will be satisfied with this higher liquidity level only if the equilibrium nominal interest rate declines. The resulting rise in bond prices discourages individuals from buying additional bonds, because of their concern that future bond price declines will yield capital losses. Thus,

LIQUIDITY EFFECT A fall in the equilibrium nominal interest rate resulting from a rise in the nominal quantity of money, holding the price level unchanged.

FIGURE 6–6   THE LIQUIDITY EFFECT OF MONETARY POLICY

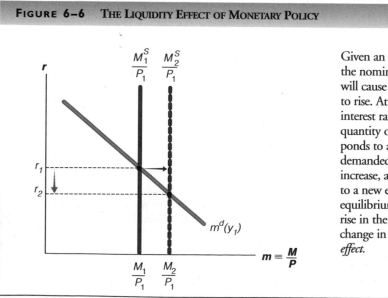

Given an unchanged price level, an increase in the nominal quantity of money in circulation will cause the supply of real money balances to rise. At an initial equilibrium nominal interest rate r_1, there then will be an excess quantity of money supplied, which corresponds to an excess quantity of bonds demanded. As a result, bond prices will increase, and the nominal interest rate will fall to a new equilibrium level, r_2. This fall in the equilibrium nominal interest rate caused by a rise in the nominal money stock without a change in the price level is called the *liquidity effect*.

as long as the interest rate declines and bond prices increase, people will be willing to hold the larger quantity of money in circulation.

The Real Balance Effect Figure 6–7 shows what will happen if the price level rises, from P_1 to P_2, while the nominal money stock is unchanged. The increase in the price level reduces the supply of real money balances. This means that the real purchasing power of the nominal money balances supplied by the central bank will decline. As a result, there will be an excess quantity of real money balances demanded at the initial equilibrium interest rate, r_1. At this initial equilibrium interest rate, people now desire more real purchasing power. To achieve this, they reduce their holdings of bonds at the interest rate r_1, and the result is an excess quantity of bonds supplied at that interest rate. Bond prices therefore begin to fall, and the nominal interest rate rises to a new equilibrium level, r_2.

This rise in the nominal interest rate caused by an increase in the price level with a constant nominal money stock is called the **real balance effect,** because it results from a change in the real purchasing power of the nominal money stock caused by a change in the price level.

REAL BALANCE EFFECT An increase in the nominal rate of interest that results from an increase in the price level, holding the nominal quantity of money unchanged.

FUNDAMENTAL ISSUE #2

How is the nominal interest rate determined in the traditional Keynesian model? The equilibrium nominal interest rate is the nominal rate of interest at which people are satisfied holding the

---

FIGURE 6–7   THE REAL BALANCE EFFECT

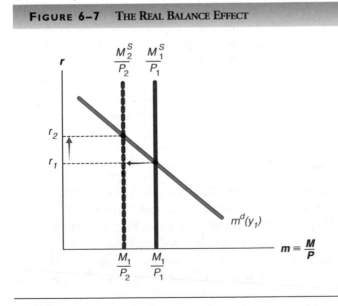

If the nominal quantity of money in circulation is unchanged, a rise in the price level will reduce the supply of real money balances. At an initial equilibrium interest rate r_1, therefore, there will be an excess quantity of money demanded, which corresponds to an excess quantity of bonds supplied. As a result, bond prices will decline, and the nominal interest rate will increase toward a new equilibrium value of r_2. This rise in the nominal interest rate caused by an increase in the price level is the *real balance effect*.

quantity of real money balances supplied through policies of the central bank. A rise in the supply of real money balances caused solely by an increase in the nominal money stock results in a liquidity effect, which causes a reduction in the equilibrium nominal interest rate. A reduction in the supply of real money balances caused solely by an increase in the price level results in a real balance effect, which causes an increase in the equilibrium nominal interest rate.

THE *LM* SCHEDULE

The liquidity effect and the real balance effect on the equilibrium nominal interest rate both stem from changes in the supply of real money balances. The equilibrium nominal interest rate also can be affected by changes in the demand for real money balances. As we discussed earlier in this chapter, a key factor affecting the position of the money demand schedule is the level of real income. Consequently, there must be a relationship between real income and the equilibrium nominal interest rate. As you will learn shortly, this relationship is summed up graphically by a schedule known as the *LM schedule*.

At the same time, as we showed in Chapter 5, a change in the real interest rate induces a change in desired real investment spending, which, in turn, causes a change in aggregate desired expenditures and in equilibrium real income. The real interest rate, in turn, is equal to the nominal interest rate minus the expected inflation rate. Therefore, there also is a relationship between equilibrium real income and the nominal interest rate, which can be captured on a diagram as a schedule called the *IS schedule*.

Because the equilibrium nominal interest rate depends on real income while, at the same time, equilibrium real income depends on the nominal interest rate, the equilibrium nominal interest rate and the equilibrium level of real income must be determined simultaneously. Our objective in the remainder of this chapter is to explain this process. Once we have done that, we shall be able to explore the traditional Keynesian theory of monetary policy.

Deriving the *LM* Schedule

LM SCHEDULE A set of combinations of real income and the nominal interest rate that maintains money market equilibrium.

The *LM* schedule is a set of all combinations of real income levels and nominal interest rates that maintain equilibrium in the market for real money balances. Figure 6–8 traces the derivation of the *LM* schedule. If real income rises from y_1 at point A to y_2 at point B, then due to the transactions and precautionary motives for holding money, the demand for real money balances will also increase. As a result, the demand schedule for real money balances shifts to the right, from $m^d(y_1)$ to $m^d(y_2)$, as shown in panel (a).

FIGURE 6–8   THE DERIVATION OF THE *LM* SCHEDULE

FIGURE 6–8   THE DERIVATION OF THE *LM* SCHEDULE

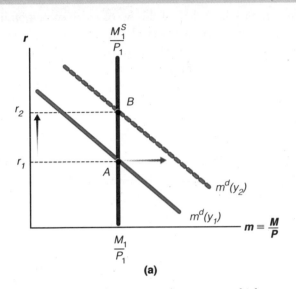

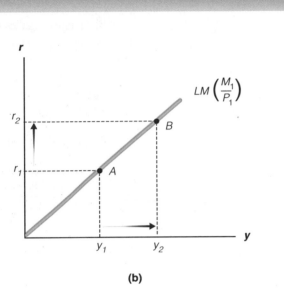

If real income rises from an initial amount to a higher level, y_2, then the demand for real money balances will increase, causing the equilibrium nominal interest rate to rise from r_1 at point A in panel (a) to r_2 at point B. Hence, as shown in panel (b), the real income–interest

rate combinations y_1 and r_1 at point A and y_2 and r_2 at point B will both maintain equilibrium in the market for real money balances given the current supply of real money balances. Hence, both points lie on the *LM* schedule.

Maintaining Money Market Equilibrium   Following the rise in real income, there will be an excess quantity of real money balances demanded at the initial equilibrium interest rate, r_1. Because people will desire to hold fewer bonds as they seek to increase their real money balances, the result will be an excess quantity of bonds supplied. Bond prices will decline, and the equilibrium nominal interest rate will rise, to r_2. As a result, the economy will move from a real income-nominal interest rate combination, y_1 and r_1 at point A, at which the market for real money balances initially was in equilibrium, to a new combination, y_2 and r_2 at point B, that continues to maintain money market equilibrium. These real income-nominal interest rate combinations are two representative points of money market equilibrium along the *LM* schedule displayed in panel (b).

The *LM* schedule's name stems from the notation used by an economist named John Hicks in 1937. He referred to the demand for money as desired liquidity, L. Money market equilibrium required setting desired liquidity equal to the quantity of money balances supplied by the Federal Reserve, M. Hence, in Hicks's original terminology, $L = M$ always held along the schedule for money market equilibrium.

A Constant Real Money Supply   It is important to recognize that our derivation of the *LM* schedule in Figure 6–8 depended on an unchanging supply of real money balances equal to M_1/P_1. To emphasize this fact, we have labeled the *LM* schedule in panel (b) as $LM(M_1/P_1)$.

This notation makes clear that we have derived this set of real income-nominal interest rate combinations *given* the nominal money stock M_1 and the price level P_1. If the supply schedule for real money balances had been in a different position, then we would have come up with a different set of combinations of real income and the nominal interest rate consistent with money market equilibrium. We would have derived a different *LM* schedule.

Determining the Elasticity of the *LM* Schedule

What determines the elasticity of the *LM* schedule? Answering this question will help us to understand the factors that determine the overall effectiveness of monetary policy in the traditional Keynesian framework.

The Interest Elasticity of the Demand for Real Money Balances   Figure 6–9 displays two demand schedules for real money balances. In both panels, we show how a rise in the nominal interest rate affects desired holdings of real money balances. We do this beginning with point *A*, which the two schedules share in common. At this point, the interest rate is r_1 and the quantity of real money balances demanded is m_1 in each panel. Any proportionate change in the interest rate, such as the proportion-

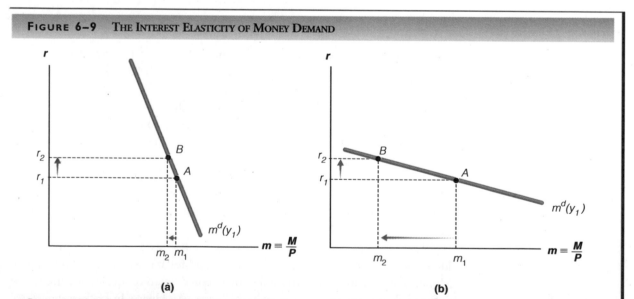

FIGURE 6–9   THE INTEREST ELASTICITY OF MONEY DEMAND

(a)

(b)

In panel (a), a given proportionate rise in the nominal interest rate from point *A* to point *B* causes a relatively small proportionate reduction in the quantity of real money balances demanded, so the demand for real money balances is relatively interest inelastic. In contrast, in panel

(b), the same proportionate interest-rate increase induces a relatively larger proportionate decline in the quantity of real money balances demanded. Thus, money demand is relatively more interest elastic in panel (b) than in panel (a).

ate interest-rate change entailed in a movement from point *A* to point *B* in each panel, will always yield a smaller proportionate rise in desired real money holdings for the demand schedule shown in panel (a), as compared with panel (b). Consequently, around point *A* the money demand schedule in panel (a) is *less elastic* as compared with the money demand schedule in panel (b).

The money demand schedule in panel (a) of Figure 6–9, therefore, illustrates a situation of relatively more **interest-inelastic money demand**, as compared with the money demand schedule in panel (b). This means that the interest sensitivity, or interest elasticity, of the demand for real money balances is lower in panel (a) than in panel (b) around point A. Alternatively, we can say that the money demand schedule in panel (b) shows a situation of relatively more **interest-elastic money demand**, as compared with the money demand schedule in panel (a). This means that the interest sensitivity, or interest elasticity, of the demand for real money balances is higher in panel (b) than in panel (a) around point A.

Interest Elasticity of Money Demand and the Elasticity of the *LM* Schedule
Figure 6–10 on page 194 shows how the interest elasticity of money demand affects the elasticity of the *LM* schedule. In panels (a) and (b), we again derive an *LM* schedule, but we assume that the demand for real money balances is relatively interest-inelastic. A rise in real income causes a rightward shift in the interest-inelastic money demand schedule in panel (a). Because individuals' money holdings are not very responsive to changes in the interest rate, they are satisfied holding the same quantity of real money balances at a significantly higher equilibrium nominal interest rate. As shown in panel (b), this means that the *LM* schedule, like the money demand schedule in panel (a), must be relatively inelastic.

In contrast, panels (c) and (d) of Figure 6–10 illustrate the derivation of the *LM* schedule when the demand for real money balances is relatively more interest-elastic and, therefore, comparatively more elastic (less inelastic) than in panel (a). Because people are much more sensitive to interest-rate changes when money demand is very interest-elastic, following a rise in real income they are satisfied holding the same quantity of real money balances only if the equilibrium interest rate rises by a relatively small amount. As a result, the *LM* schedule in panel (d) for the case of relatively interest-elastic money demand is more elastic than the *LM* schedule in panel (b) for the case of relatively interest-inelastic money demand.

Factors That Shift the *LM* Schedule

As we emphasized when we first derived the *LM* schedule in Figure 6–8, the position of the *LM* schedule depends upon the quantity of real money balances. This is so because we derive the *LM* schedule by increasing real income while keeping the quantity of real money balances unchanged.

A Change in the Nominal Money Stock   Now imagine a situation in which a central bank, such as the Federal Reserve, increases the nominal money stock while real income and the price level are unchanged. As shown in panel (a) of Figure 6–11

INTEREST-INELASTIC MONEY DEMAND Demand for money that is relatively insensitive to interest-rate variations.

INTEREST-ELASTIC MONEY DEMAND Demand for money that is relatively sensitive to interest-rate variations.

FIGURE 6–10 **THE INTEREST ELASTICITY OF MONEY DEMAND AND THE ELASTICITY OF THE *LM* SCHEDULE**

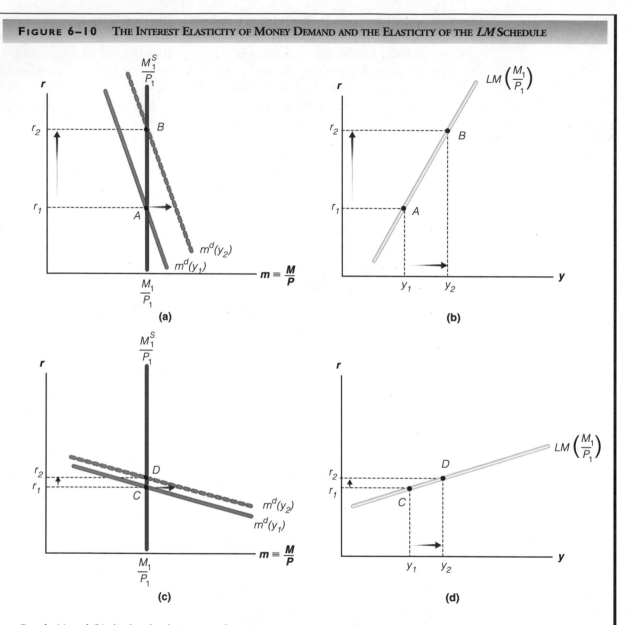

(a)　　　　　　　　　　　　　**(b)**

(c)　　　　　　　　　　　　　**(d)**

Panels (a) and (b) display the derivation of an *LM* schedule when the demand for money balances is relatively interest inelastic. A rise in money demand induced by a rise in real income causes a movement from point *A* to point *B* in the market for real money balances in panel (a). These points correspond to points *A* and *B* along the relatively inelastic *LM* schedule in panel (b). By

way of contrast, panels (c) and (d) show the derivation of an *LM* schedule when money demand is relatively interest elastic. In panel (c), an increase in the demand for real money balances induced by a rise in real income produces a movement from point *C* to point *D*. These points correspond to points *C* and *D* along the relatively elastic *LM* schedule that results, as shown in panel (d).

shows, this will cause a rise in the real quantity of money, from M_1/P_1 to M_2/P_1. Although real income will be unchanged at y_1, the equilibrium nominal interest rate will decline because of the liquidity effect, from r_1 to r_2.

Following the increase in the nominal money stock, there will now be a new real income-interest rate combination, y_1 and r_2 at point B, that will maintain equilibrium in the market for real money balances. Consequently, as shown in panel (b) of Figure 6–11, this combination will be on a new *LM* schedule, $LM(M_2/P_1)$, that lies below and to the right of the initial *LM* schedule, $LM(M_1/P_1)$. With the price level unchanged, therefore, a rise in the nominal money stock will increase the supply of real money balances and shift the *LM* schedule downward and to the right. In contrast, a decline in the money stock with an unchanged price level will shift the *LM* schedule upward and to the left.

A Change in the Price Level   Panels (c) and (d) of Figure 6–11 illustrate the effects of a rise in the price level with the nominal quantity of money and real income unchanged. In panel (c), an increase in the price level, from P_1 to P_2, will cause a fall in real money balances, from M_1/P_1 to M_1/P_2. Real income remains at the level y_1, but the real balance effect induces a rise in the equilibrium nominal interest rate, from r_1 to r_2.

After the rise in the price level, there will be a new real income-interest rate combination, y_1 and r_2 at point D, that will maintain equilibrium in the market for real money balances. Hence, as indicated in panel (d), this combination will be on a new *LM* schedule, $LM(M_1/P_2)$, above point C on the original *LM* schedule, $LM(M_1/P_1)$. With the nominal money stock unchanged, therefore, an increase in the price level will reduce the supply of real money balances and shift the *LM* schedule upward and to the left. In contrast, a decline in the price level with an unchanged nominal quantity of money will shift the *LM* schedule downward and to the right.

A Change in the Demand for Real Money Balances   The final factor that can affect the position of the *LM* schedule is a change in the demand for real money balances not caused by a variation in real income. For instance, suppose that there is a significant increase in the use of credit cards to make retail payments. As a result, people reduce their demand for real money balances at any given nominal interest rate. As panel (a) of Figure 6–12 shows (next page), the demand for real money balances will decline, from $m_1^d(y_1)$ to $m_2^d(y_1)$, with the quantity of real money balances supplied, M_1/P_1, and real income, y_1, unchanged. This causes the equilibrium interest rate to fall from r_1 to r_2.

As a result, as panel (b) of Figure 6–12 shows, equilibrium in the market for real money balances will be maintained at a new real income-interest rate combination at point B below point A on the original *LM* schedule. This means that the *LM* schedule will shift downward and to the right as a result of a fall in the demand for real money balances caused by the increased use of credit cards. Indeed, any decline in money demand not induced by a fall in real income would cause this to happen. In contrast, a rise in the demand for real money balances not caused by an increase in real income would shift the *LM* schedule upward and to the left.

FIGURE 6–11 **CHANGES IN THE REAL MONEY SUPPLY AND IN THE POSITION OF THE *LM* SCHEDULE**

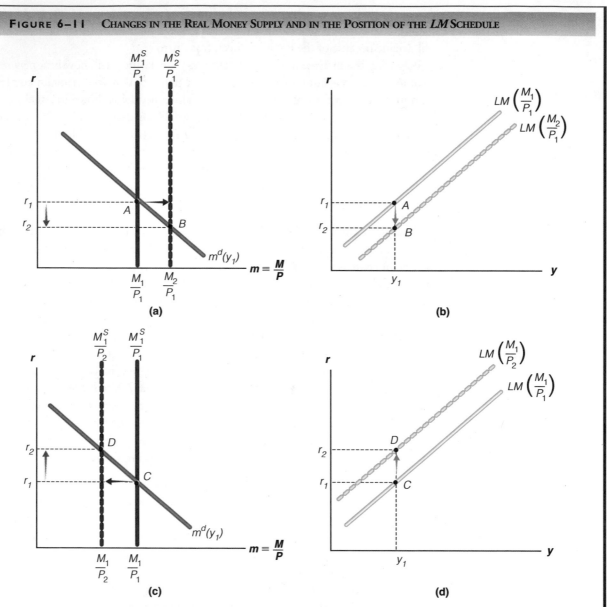

(a)

(b)

(c)

(d)

Panels (a) and (b) show the effects of an increase in the nominal money stock if the price level is unchanged. As shown in panel (a), the result is a rise in the supply of real money balances and a resulting movement from equilibrium point *A* to equilibrium point *B*. The new real income–interest rate combination y_1 and r_2 at point *B* in panel (b) lies directly below the original combination y_1 and r_1 at point *A*. Hence, the *LM* schedule will shift downward and to the right. Panels (c) and (d), in contrast, show that a rise in the price level with the nominal money stock unchanged results in a movement from equilibrium point *C* to equilibrium point *D*, as shown in panel (c). The new real income–interest rate combination y_1 and r_2 at point *D* in panel (d) lies directly above the original combination y_1 and r_1 at point *C*. Therefore, the *LM* schedule shifts upward and to the left.

FIGURE 6-12 THE EFFECT OF A FALL IN THE DEMAND FOR REAL MONEY BALANCES
ON THE POSITION OF THE *LM* SCHEDULE

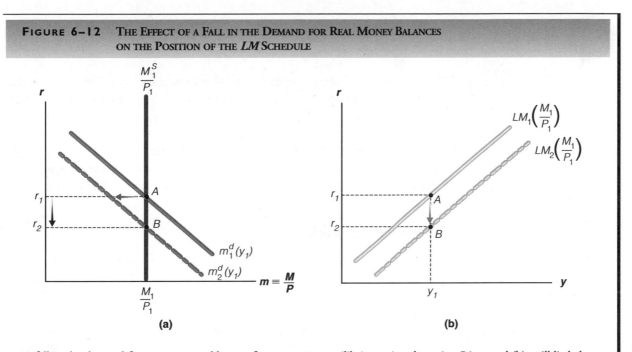

(a)

(b)

A fall in the demand for money caused by any factor other than a decline in real income will cause a decline in the equilibrium nominal interest rate, from r_1 at point A to r_2 at point B in panel (a). Because real income remains unchanged at y_1, the new real income–interest rate combination that will maintain money market

equilibrium, given by point B in panel (b), will lie below the initial real income–interest rate combination given by point A. Thus, a decline in the demand for real money balances not stemming from a fall in real income implies a downward and rightward shift in the *LM* schedule.

FUNDAMENTAL ISSUE #3

What is the *LM* schedule, and what factors determine its elasticity and position? The *LM* schedule is an upward-sloping set of all combinations of real income and the nominal interest rate that maintain equilibrium in the market for real money balances. The *LM* schedule is more inelastic if money demand is relatively interest-inelastic, and it is more elastic if money demand is relatively interest-elastic. The *LM* schedule shifts downward and to the right if there is an increase in the nominal money stock, a fall in the price level, or a decline in money demand not caused by a change in real income. A decrease in the money stock, a rise in the price level, or a rise in money demand causes the *LM* schedule to shift upward and to the left.

THE *IS* SCHEDULE

As you learned in Chapter 5, *equilibrium* real income must satisfy the condition that real income is equal to the sum of consumption spending, desired business investment spending, government expenditures, and export spending. You also know that desired investment spending is negatively related to the interest rate. This means that the interest rate must affect equilibrium real income. It follows that there must be combinations of real income and the nominal interest rate that maintain *equilibrium* real income. This set of real income-nominal interest rate combinations is the *IS* schedule.

Deriving the *IS* Schedule

Figure 6–13 shows the derivation of the *IS* schedule. Panel (a) shows the desired investment schedule. Recall from Chapter 5 that desired real investment spending is negatively related to the real interest rate, which is equal to the nominal interest rate less the expected inflation rate. If inflation expectations are unchanged, therefore, investment is inversely related to the *nominal* interest rate, as shown in the figure. As a result, a rise in the nominal interest rate, from r_1 to r_2, will cause desired real investment spending to fall from i_1 at point A to i_2 at point B.

As panel (b) indicates, this decline in desired investment spending caused by a rise in the nominal interest rate will cause the aggregate desired expenditures schedule to shift downward. As a result, equilibrium real income will decline, from y_1 to y_2. Hence, as shown in panel (c), the economy will move from the initial real income-nominal interest rate combination, y_1 and r_1 at point A, that is consistent with equilibrium real income to a new combination, y_2 and r_2 at point B.

IS SCHEDULE A set of possible combinations of real income and the nominal interest rate that are necessary to maintain an income-expenditure equilibrium, $y = c + i + g + x$.

These real income-nominal interest rate combinations A and B lie on an **IS schedule**, which is a set of combinations of levels of real income and nominal interest rates that maintain equilibrium real income. The *IS* schedule also was named in 1937 by John Hicks, who first derived the schedule by assuming a simple economy with no government sector or international trade and who used the leakages-injections approach to determining equilibrium real income. Because income is equal to desired expenditures all along the *IS* schedule, it is also true that, with no government or international trade, saving "leakages" from the income-expenditure flow will equal investment "reinjections." Thus, investment (i) will equal saving (s); hence, Hicks's term "*IS*."

Determining the Elasticity of the *IS* Schedule

Just as the elasticity of the *LM* schedule depends on the interest elasticity of real money balances, the elasticity of the *IS* schedule depends on the interest elasticity of desired investment. Figure 6–14 on page 200 illustrates this by considering a situa-

FIGURE 6-13   THE DERIVATION OF THE *IS* SCHEDULE

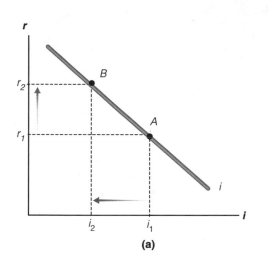

(a)

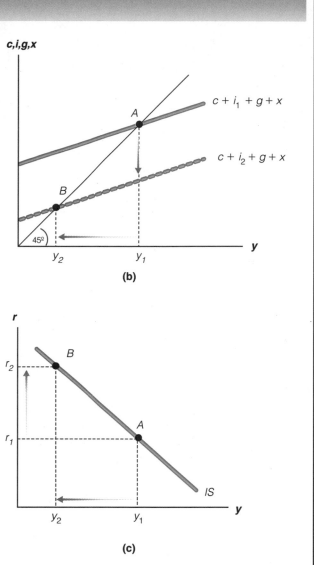

(b)

As shown in panel (a), an increase in the nominal interest rate will cause a movement from point *A* to point *B* along the investment schedule and result in a decline in desired investment expenditures. As panel (b) shows, this will reduce aggregate desired expenditures, causing a reduction in equilibrium real income, from y_1 at point *A* to y_2 at point *B*. As a result, the new combination of real income and the nominal interest rate, y_2 and r_2 at point *B* in panel (c), that is consistent with equilibrium real income and expenditures will lie above and to the left of the original combination y_1 and r_1 at point *A*. Hence, the *IS* schedule, which shows all combinations of real income and the nominal interest rate consistent with equilibrium real income and expenditures, slopes downward.

(c)

INTEREST-ELASTIC DESIRED INVESTMENT Desired investment spending that is relatively sensitive to interest-rate variations.

tion of relatively **interest-elastic desired investment** in panel (a), so that the investment schedule is very elastic. As a result, a relatively small increase in the nominal interest rate induces a relatively large decline in desired investment. This causes a relatively large downward shift in the aggregate expenditures schedule, resulting in a comparatively large reduction in equilibrium real income due to the multiplier effect. Thus, as shown in panel (c), when desired investment spending is relatively interest-elastic, the derived *IS* schedule is relatively elastic.

FIGURE 6–14   **THE INTEREST ELASTICITY OF DESIRED INVESTMENT AND THE ELASTICITY OF THE *IS* SCHEDULE**

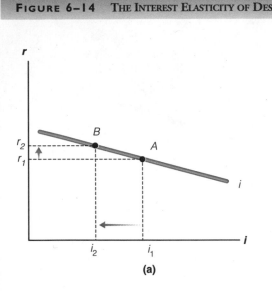

(a)

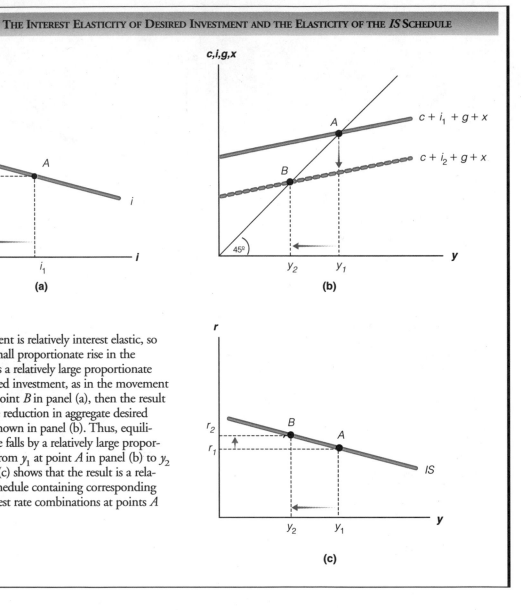

(b)

If desired investment is relatively interest elastic, so that a relatively small proportionate rise in the interest rate causes a relatively large proportionate reduction in desired investment, as in the movement from point *A* to point *B* in panel (a), then the result is a relatively large reduction in aggregate desired expenditures, as shown in panel (b). Thus, equilibrium real income falls by a relatively large proportionate amount, from y_1 at point *A* in panel (b) to y_2 at point *B*. Panel (c) shows that the result is a relatively elastic *IS* schedule containing corresponding real income–interest rate combinations at points *A* and *B*.

(c)

INTEREST-INELASTIC DESIRED INVESTMENT Desired investment that is relatively insensitive to interest-rate variations.

In contrast, in a situation of relatively **interest-inelastic desired investment**, relatively large changes in the interest rate cause comparatively small changes in desired investment, aggregate desired expenditures, and equilibrium real income. As a result, with relatively *interest-inelastic* desired investment the *IS* schedule is also be relatively *inelastic*.

Factors That Shift the *IS* Schedule

To derive the *IS* schedule in Figures 6–13 and 6–14, we considered only the effects of a rise in the nominal interest rate on desired investment spending, with all other factors that would affect autonomous desired expenditures unchanged. These factors include autonomous saving, autonomous imports, government expenditures, autonomous net taxes, and autonomous export spending. Reductions in autonomous saving, imports, or net taxes all will stimulate consumption spending and, at any given interest rate, induce a rise in aggregate desired expenditures, as shown in panel (b) of Figure 6–15. Likewise, an increase in government expenditures or autonomous export spending also induce an upward shift in the aggregated desired expenditures schedule.

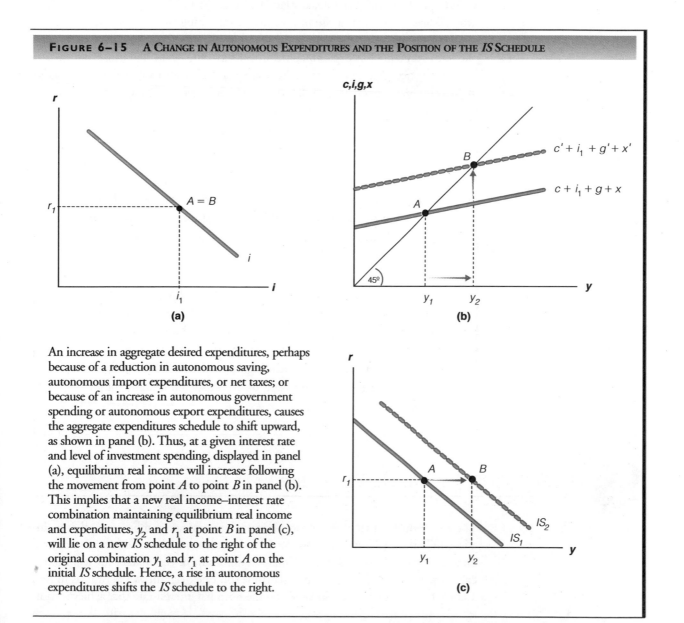

FIGURE 6–15   A CHANGE IN AUTONOMOUS EXPENDITURES AND THE POSITION OF THE *IS* SCHEDULE

An increase in aggregate desired expenditures, perhaps because of a reduction in autonomous saving, autonomous import expenditures, or net taxes; or because of an increase in autonomous government spending or autonomous export expenditures, causes the aggregate expenditures schedule to shift upward, as shown in panel (b). Thus, at a given interest rate and level of investment spending, displayed in panel (a), equilibrium real income will increase following the movement from point A to point B in panel (b). This implies that a new real income–interest rate combination maintaining equilibrium real income and expenditures, y_2 and r_1 at point B in panel (c), will lie on a new *IS* schedule to the right of the original combination y_1 and r_1 at point A on the initial *IS* schedule. Hence, a rise in autonomous expenditures shifts the *IS* schedule to the right.

The result is a rise in equilibrium real income, from y_1 at point A to y_2 at point B, even though desired investment spending has not changed in panel (a).

Any one of these possible sources of an increase in autonomous expenditures would induce a rise in equilibrium real income equal to the increase in aggregate autonomous expenditures times the autonomous spending multiplier. As panel (c) of Figure 6–15 indicates, the result would be a new real income-nominal interest rate combination, y_2 and r_1 at point B, that lies to the right of the original combination, y_1 and r_1 at point A. Therefore, any factor that causes an increase in aggregate desired expenditures, other than a rise in investment stemming from a fall in the nominal interest rate, shifts the *IS* schedule rightward by the amount of the resulting multiplier effect on equilibrium real income. In contrast, any factor that causes a *reduction* in aggregate desired expenditures, other than a fall in investment resulting from a rise in the nominal interest rate, shifts the *IS* schedule *leftward* by the amount of the resulting multiplier effect on equilibrium real income.

FUNDAMENTAL ISSUE #4

What is the *IS* schedule, and what factors determine its elasticity and position? The *IS* schedule is a downward-sloping set of all combinations of real income and the nominal interest rate for which aggregate desired expenditures equal real income. The *IS* schedule is more inelastic if desired investment is relatively interest-inelastic, and it is more elastic if desired investment is relatively interest-elastic. The *IS* schedule shifts to the right if there is an increase in autonomous desired expenditures stemming from a fall in autonomous saving, import spending, or taxes or from a rise in autonomous government spending, investment, or export spending. In contrast, a rise in autonomous saving, import spending, or taxes or a fall in autonomous government spending, investment, or export spending shifts the *IS* schedule to the left.

IS-LM EQUILIBRIUM AND DISEQUILIBRIUM

The *IS* schedule is a set of real income-nominal interest rate combinations that maintain equilibrium real income, and the *LM* schedule consists of real income-nominal interest rate combinations that maintain equilibrium in the market for real money balances. Thus, combining the two schedules on one diagram will permit us to find a single combination of real income and the nominal interest rate that achieves equilibrium real income while simultaneously achieving equilibrium in the market for real money balances.

Combining *IS* and *LM*

Figure 6–16 combines the *IS* and *LM* schedules. At point *E* in panel (a), the two schedules cross. Real income is equal to aggregate desired expenditures at the real income level y_1, because point *E* is on the *IS* schedule. At the same time, point *E* is also on the *LM* schedule. Consequently, the market for real money balances is in equilibrium at the interest rate r_1.

We call point *E* a point of **IS-LM equilibrium**. At any point such as *E*, the following is true:

IS-LM EQUILIBRIUM The point at which the *IS* and *LM* schedules cross, so that the economy simultaneously attains both an income-expenditure equilibrium and equilibrium in the market for real money balances.

> **A point of *IS-LM equilibrium* is a point that is common to both the *IS* schedule and the *LM* schedule, so that equilibrium real income is attained simultaneously with the nominal interest rate that attains equilibrium in the market for real money balances.**

FIGURE 6–16   *IS-LM* EQUILIBRIUM AND DISEQUILIBRIUM

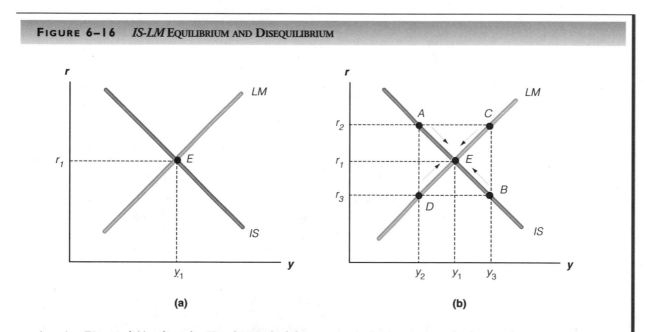

(a)

(b)

At point *E* in panel (a), where the *IS* and *LM* schedules cross, the market for real money balances is in equilibrium at the same time that real income equals aggregate desired expenditures. Points *A* and *B* in panel (b) are on the *IS* schedule but not the *LM* schedule, so at these points the market for real money balances is not in equilibrium. The interest rate must move back toward r_1 to reattain money market equilibrium. Points *C* and *D* are on the *LM* schedule but not the *IS* schedule, so at these points real income is not equal to aggregate desired expenditures. Real income must move back toward y_1 to reattain real income–expenditure equilibrium.

IS-LM Equilibrium and Disequilibrium

The reason that point E is an *equilibrium* point is explained in panel (b) of Figure 6–16. For instance, at point A, above the LM schedule at the interest rate r_2 and income level y_2, the nominal interest rate is too high to achieve equilibrium in the market for real money balances. As a result, there will be an excess quantity of money supplied at this interest rate. Consequently, the nominal interest rate will tend to fall toward r_1, and equilibrium real income will tend to rise along the IS schedule toward point E and the real income level y_1.

Now consider point B, below the LM schedule at the nominal interest rate r_3 and real income level y_3. At point B, the nominal interest rate is too low to maintain equilibrium in the market for real money balances. The result is an excess quantity of real money balances demanded, which causes the interest rate to rise toward r_1, inducing a movement up along the IS schedule toward point E and real income y_1.

Now think about point C in panel (b), which is to the right of the IS schedule at the nominal interest rate r_2 and real income level y_3. At point C, the level of real income is above its equilibrium level, which means that real income is greater than aggregate desired expenditures at the interest rate r_2. As we discussed in Chapter 5, in such a situation realized investment will be greater than desired investment, and firms will find themselves making undesired investment expenditures on inventories. Firms therefore reduce their real investment, which causes real income to fall toward its equilibrium level, y_1. As real income falls, the demand for real money balances will decline, causing a fall in the interest rate and a movement along the LM schedule from point C toward the equilibrium point E.

Finally, at point D, to the left of the IS schedule at the nominal interest rate r_3 and real income level y_2, the opposite situation would arise. At point D, the level of real income is below its equilibrium level, which means that real income is less than aggregate desired expenditures at the interest rate r_3. As a result, realized investment is less than desired investment. Firms will wish to increase their real investment spending, which will cause real income to rise toward its equilibrium level, y_1. As real income rises, the demand for real money balances will increase, inducing a rise in the interest rate and a movement along the LM schedule from point D toward the equilibrium point E.

FUNDAMENTAL ISSUE #5

What is an **IS-LM** *equilibrium?* An *IS-LM* equilibrium is a single point that the IS and LM schedules share in common. At this point, real income and the nominal interest rate both are consistent with an equilibrium flow of real income and an equilibrium in the market for real money balances.

MONETARY POLICY IN THE *IS-LM* FRAMEWORK

Monetary policy actions change the nominal money stock, thereby changing the real money supply (as long as the price level is unchanged) and altering the position of the *LM* schedule. Such actions must also change the location of an *IS-LM* equilibrium, thereby affecting *both* the equilibrium nominal interest rate *and* the equilibrium level of real income. This is why Keynes concluded that a linkage may exist among monetary policy, the nominal interest rate, and real economic activity.

INTERNET SOURCE

Learning about U.S. Monetary Policy Making

The Board of Governors of the Federal Reserve System
Internet URL: http://www.bog.frb.fed.us

Navigation: The above address is the Federal Reserve Board's homepage. To learn more about the Federal Reserve System and its functions, select from the homepage menu. You will also find menus for large numbers of Federal Reserve data sets.

The Effects of Monetary Policy Actions in the *IS-LM* Model

To understand the nature of the monetary policy linkage that Keynes proposed, let's use the *IS-LM* framework to explore the effects of an increase in the nominal money stock by a central bank such as the Federal Reserve. To keep things simple, for the time being let's assume that the price level remains unchanged. (We shall allow the price level to vary in response to monetary policy actions in Chapter 8.)

Figure 6–17 illustrates the effects of this central bank policy action. The first effect of an increase in the nominal money stock shown in panel (a), is a shift in the *LM* schedule downward and to the right, from $LM(M_1/P_1)$ to $LM(M_2/P_1)$ displayed in panel (b). This shift reflects the liquidity effect: Holding real income and the price level unchanged, an increase in the nominal quantity of money supplied by the central bank reduces the equilibrium interest rate in the market for real money balances. Now, however, we can take into account the response of real income.

As the nominal interest rate declines, from r_1 at point *E* in the direction of r_3 at point *F*, desired investment spending begins to increase. This causes a rise in aggregate desired expenditures, thereby inducing a movement down along the *IS* schedule from point *E* toward point *E'* in panel (b). Furthermore, as real income rises, so does the demand for real money balances in panel (a), which places upward pressure on the nominal interest rate. This keeps the nominal interest rate from declining all the way to r_3. Instead, the final equilibrium interest rate is r_2 at point *E'*. Likewise, the

---

FIGURE 6–17 **THE EFFECT OF AN INCREASE IN THE NOMINAL MONEY STOCK**

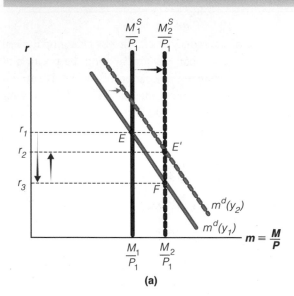

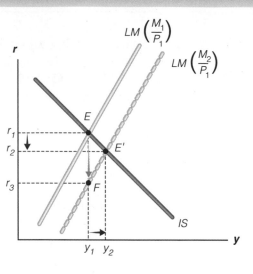

(a)

(b)

The result of an increase in the nominal money stock is a decline in the equilibrium interest rate in the market for real money balances from r_1 at point E to r_3 at point F in panel (a). This results in a downward shift in the LM schedule by the distance E–F in panel (b). The decline in the interest rate, however, induces a rise in desired investment and a consequent movement down along the IS schedule to a new IS-LM equilibrium at point E' at

the higher real income level y_2. As real income increases, the demand for real money balances rises in panel (a), causing the equilibrium interest rate to rise to r_2, which corresponds to an upward movement along the new LM schedule in panel (b), from point F to point E'. On net, therefore, the rise in the nominal money stock causes a reduction in the equilibrium nominal interest rate and an increase in equilibrium real income.

---

final equilibrium income level, y_2, is also at point E', where the IS schedule and the new LM schedule intersect in panel (b).

   We may conclude that the effects of an increase in the nominal money stock, holding the price level unchanged, are a decline in the equilibrium nominal interest rate and an increase in equilibrium real income. If instead the nominal money stock were reduced while the price level remained unchanged, the opposite results would follow: the equilibrium nominal interest rate would rise, and equilibrium real income would decline. (Predicting interest-rate movements is more difficult than this discussion may suggest; see the Policy Notebook: *Can Policymakers Predict Interest Rates?*)

The Keynesian Monetary Policy Transmission Mechanism

KEYNESIAN MONETARY POLICY TRANSMISSION MECHANISM A key implication of the traditional Keynesian theory in which a rise in the nominal quantity of money will, with an unchanged price level, reduce the nominal interest rate, thereby stimulating a rise in desired investment spending and aggregate desired expenditures, which, in turn causes equilibrium real income to rise.

The discussion in the preceding section illustrates the **Keynesian monetary policy transmission mechanism**, which is the fundamental Keynesian explanation for how a change in the nominal money stock is transmitted to real income. Our discussion

POLICY NOTEBOOK
Can Policymakers Predict Interest Rates?

Interest rates do more than equilibrate the market for real money balances. Changes in interest rates can affect the profitability of banks and other financial institutions. They can also determine whether an investment was a smart move or a foolish one. Much of monetary policy is based on predicted movements in "the" interest rate.

Not surprisingly, the business community and others often look to comments by economic forecasters and government officials for information about whether interest rates will be high or low in the future. Most such predictions are usually wrong. As one researcher put it, "predicting interest rates is like shooting a gun out the window of your house and hoping that a game bird will fly by." One study of interest-rate forecasts in the early 1990s found that forecasters missed all major interest-rate moves. Long-term studies demonstrate

that forecasters do no better than someone guessing interest-rate changes by flipping a coin.

A straightforward investment issue is also involved. Because the values of numerous assets ultimately depend on market interest rates, anyone capable of regularly predicting changes in interest rates will also be able to predict changes in many asset prices. Although this feat is not impossible, few, if any, forecasters have been able to do it consistently. Any forecaster who could predict an interest-rate change with certainty could make literally hundreds of millions of dollars in a very short time period.

FOR CRITICAL ANALYSIS:
What is the relationship between interest rates and financial asset prices?

indicates that there are two linkages by which this transmission takes place. First, an increase in the nominal money stock causes a liquidity effect that reduces the equilibrium nominal interest rate. Second, a fall in the interest rate causes desired investment and desired expenditures to rise. In the end, therefore, as summarized in Figure 6–18 on page 208, an increase in the nominal money stock causes a rise in equilibrium real income.

According to this proposed mechanism for monetary policy effects, the magnitude of the effect of a monetary policy action on real income depends on two factors. One is the size of the liquidity effect on the interest rate. If the liquidity effect is large, then the ultimate effect of a monetary policy action on real income is more likely to be sizable. If the liquidity effect is small, then the ultimate effect on real income is more likely to be negligible.

The size of the liquidity effect is determined by the elasticity of the *LM* schedule, which in turn depends on the interest elasticity of the demand for real money balances. If the demand schedule for real money balances is relatively interest-elastic, then the *LM* schedule is relatively elastic, and a change in the nominal money stock causes a relatively small change in the nominal interest rate. In contrast, if the demand schedule for real money balances is relatively interest-inelastic, then the *LM* schedule is relatively inelastic, and a change in the nominal money stock causes a relatively large

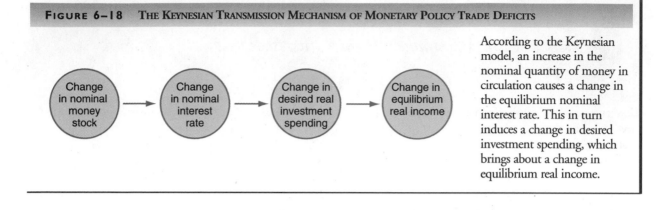

FIGURE 6–18 **THE KEYNESIAN TRANSMISSION MECHANISM OF MONETARY POLICY TRADE DEFICITS**

According to the Keynesian model, an increase in the nominal quantity of money in circulation causes a change in the equilibrium nominal interest rate. This in turn induces a change in desired investment spending, which brings about a change in equilibrium real income.

change in the nominal interest rate. Consequently, the lower the interest elasticity of the demand for real money balances—that is, the more inelastic the LM schedule is—the larger the liquidity effect resulting from a change in the quantity of money.

The other linkage, relating a given interest-rate change to the responsiveness of desired investment spending, depends on the interest elasticity of desired investment and the elasticity of the *IS* schedule. If desired investment is relatively interest inelastic, then the *IS* schedule also is relatively inelastic, and a given change in the interest rate will have a comparatively small effect on desired investment, aggregate desired expenditures, and real income. If desired investment is relatively interest-elastic, then the *IS* schedule is relatively elastic, and a given change in the interest rate will have a comparatively larger effect on desired investment, aggregate desired expenditures, and real income. Therefore, the more interest-elastic desired investment spending is—that is, the more elastic the *IS* schedule is—the stronger the second linkage in the monetary policy transmission mechanism will be.

We can conclude that, according to the Keynesian monetary policy transmission mechanism, a constant-price increase in the nominal money supply will cause the equilibrium nominal interest rate to fall and the equilibrium level of real income to rise. A constant-price decrease in the nominal money supply will cause the equilibrium nominal interest rate to rise and the equilibrium level of real income to fall. The size of the effect on real income will be larger when the demand for real money balances is relatively more interest inelastic, so that the *LM* schedule is more inelastic. When desired investment spending is relatively more interest-elastic, the *IS* schedule is more elastic, and the real income effect of monetary policy is enhanced.

FUNDAMENTAL ISSUE #6

What is the traditional Keynesian transmission mechanism for monetary policy? This is the set of linkages by which the Keynesian framework indicates that monetary policy actions should influence

> equilibrium real income. According to this proposed mechanism, an increase in the nominal money stock reduces the equilibrium nominal interest rate, thereby stimulating desired investment spending. This, in turn, raises aggregate desired expenditures, thereby increasing equilibrium real income.

THE BALANCE OF PAYMENTS AND THE *IS-LM* MODEL

According to the Keynesian monetary policy transmission mechanism, monetary policy actions can affect domestic income and interest rates. Accordingly, a central bank may decide to try to push the level of real income toward its long-run level as discussed in Chapter 4. By doing so, the central bank would be trying to help its nation's economy achieve **internal balance**, or the attainment of the level of real income consistent with the economy's long-run growth path.

INTERNAL BALANCE The attainment of the level of real income consistent with the domestic economy's long-run growth path.

EXTERNAL BALANCE The attainment of an objective for the composition of a nation's balance of payments.

A central bank may also care about how its actions influence the nation's international payment flows. That is, it may also want to achieve **external balance**, which would entail the attainment of some objective for private international flows of goods, services, income, and assets.

Maintaining Private Payments Balance

Achieving "external balance" is likely to mean different things to policymakers in different nations. In some nations, for instance, it may mean a goal of consistently running a trade surplus. In others, it might mean maintaining a surplus on the current account.

Recall from Chapter 2 that the balance of payments is the sum of the current account balance, the private capital account balance, and the official settlements balance. Let's suppose that a central bank would like the *private payments balance*—the sum of the balances on the current account and the capital account—to be equal to zero. That is, the central bank desires neither a surplus nor a deficit in the sum of the current account and the capital account. To aim for this objective, the central bank needs to understand how its policies will influence the size of the private payments balance.

Real Income and the Private Payments Balance   To understand the factors that determine the private payments balance in the balance of payments, let's first remember that the current account balance is equal to the balance of merchandise trade plus net service flows and net flows of cross-border income and transfers. The predominant component of the current account balance is the balance of merchandise trade. In addition, recall from Chapter 5 that the main determinant of the trade balance is

ON THE WEB
See the Census Bureau's Trade Data at: http://www.census.gov/foreign-trade/www/

domestic real income. A rise in domestic real income induces an increase in import spending, which pushes down the trade balance, while a fall in domestic real income depresses import spending, thereby improving the trade balance.

To see how this ultimately relates to monetary policy, consider Figure 6–19. Suppose that the private payments balance is equal to zero at point A, at a nominal interest rate equal to r_1 and a real income level equal to y_1. Now suppose that real income rises, to level y_2 at point C. In line with our reasoning above, at point C higher real income will stimulate a rise in import spending, which will reduce the trade balance, thereby pushing down the current account balance. Although higher real income at point C indicates that activity in the domestic economy has increased as compared with point A, it also implies higher imports and a worsened private payments balance. Consequently, under our assumption that the private payments balance is equal to zero at point A, it follows that at point C there is a *private payments deficit.*

The Nominal Interest Rate and the Private Payments Balance   If real income were to remain at y_2, then would the economy necessarily be "stuck" with a private payments deficit in its balance of payments? The answer is no. To see this, suppose that income remains equal to y_2 but that the nominal interest rate rises. This would produce a point such as point B in Figure 6–19, at a nominal interest rate of r_2.

An increase in the domestic nominal interest rate will make domestic financial assets, such as domestic bonds, more attractive to residents of other nations by increasing the returns they can earn on such assets. Consequently, foreign residents will increase their holdings of domestic financial assets. As you learned in Chapter 2,

---

FIGURE 6–19   THE *BP* SCHEDULE

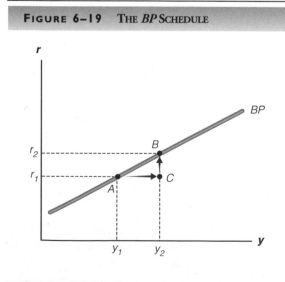

If real income rises from y_1 at point A, at which the private payments balance is equal to zero, to y_2 at point C, then the nation's import expenditures will increase, and its trade balance will decline. The result is a private payments deficit at point C. Reattaining private payments balance will require an increase in the nominal interest rate, which will induce foreign residents to hold more of the nation's financial assets, thereby improving its capital account balance. Hence, a point such as point B, which is above and to the right of point A, could represent another real income—interest rate combination consistent with a private payments balance. The set of all such combinations is the *BP* schedule.

such an increase in foreign holdings of domestic assets will increase the private capital account balance. This, in turn, will improve the private payments balance.

Let's assume that the interest-rate increase from r_1 to r_2 is sufficient to return the private payments balance to zero. If so, point B, like point A, represents a situation in which the nation's private payments balance is equal to zero. Indeed, points A and B both lie on a set of real income-nominal interest rate combinations that will maintain a zero private payments balance. This set of combinations slopes upward, because at higher real income levels the resulting increases in imports that will drive down the private payments balance will need to be offset by higher nominal interest rates to stimulate the purchases of domestic assets that will push the private payments balance back up to zero.

Traditionally, the set of real income–nominal interest rate combinations that maintains the private payments balance in the balance of payments accounts is referred to as the ***BP* schedule**, so we use this label in Figure 6–19. As we noted in Chapter 2, a common, albeit somewhat misleading, term for a private payments balance is "balance of payments equilibrium"; hence, the traditional notation "*BP*." In actuality, along the *BP* schedule, the sum of the current account balance and the capital account balance remains equal to zero at any given point.

> **BP SCHEDULE** A set of real income-nominal interest rate combinations that maintains a zero balance for private payments—sometimes called a "balance of payments equilibrium"—in the balance of payments accounts.

Balance of Payments Deficits and Surpluses in the *IS-LM* Framework

The implication of the *BP* schedule is that at a given time there is a limited set of combinations of real income and the nominal interest rate along which a nation can achieve a private payments balance of zero. As you have learned in this chapter, *equilibrium* values for real income and the nominal interest rate are determined by the intersection of the *IS* and *LM* schedules. This means that a private payments balance of zero can be achieved only if the *IS* and *LM* schedules happen to cross *on* the economy's *BP* schedule.

Achieving External Balance   Panel (a) of Figure 6–20 on page 212 shows a situation in which a nation has achieved external balance as we have defined this concept: The nation's *IS-LM* equilibrium occurs at a point on the country's *BP* schedule, at point *E*. This implies that the equilibrium nominal interest rate and the equilibrium real income level are consistent with a private payments balance of zero.

As you might imagine, a nation's central bank will face a challenge in determining the nominal interest rate and real income level consistent with its external balance objective. In fact, for a typical nation, achieving just the right real income-nominal interest rate combination to achieve external balance could be a difficult undertaking. Furthermore, achieving external balance *and* internal balance objectives *simultaneously* is likely to be a truly daunting task.

The Potential Trade-off between External and Internal Balance   Panel (b) of Figure 6–20 illustrates the nature of the difficulties that a central bank can face in trying to achieve both external and internal balance. Again, external balance is achieved at any point along the *BP* schedule. In addition, however, let's suppose that attaining

FIGURE 6–20 *IS-LM* EQUILIBRIUM AND THE *BP* SCHEDULE

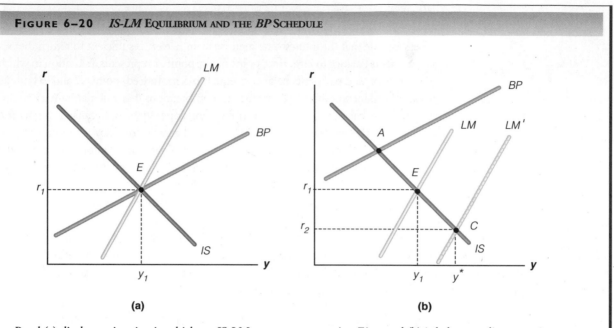

(a)

(b)

Panel (a) displays a situation in which an *IS-LM* equilibrium occurs at a point, denoted point *E*, on the *BP* schedule. At point *E*, therefore, the nation's economy attains a private payments balance. In contrast, the *IS-LM* equilibrium point *E* in panel (b) is below and to the right of the *BP* schedule, so there is a private payments deficit at that point. At the same time, equilibrium real income

at point *E* in panel (b) is below a policy target income level. Attaining *internal balance* via monetary policy would require increasing the quantity of money and thereby inducing the *LM* schedule to shift to the right, but this action would move the economy farther away from point *A*, at which *external balance* could be attained via achievement of a private payments balance.

internal balance requires reaching the real income level y^* at an *IS-LM* equilibrium such as the one at point *C*. At present, however, there is a private payments deficit at the *actual IS-LM* equilibrium point, at point *E*.

Keep in mind that the central bank can influence real income and the nominal interest rate solely by varying the nominal money stock to influence the position of the *LM* schedule. This means that the situation in panel (b) will be a "no-win scenario" for the central bank. The central bank could reduce the nominal money stock to attain point *A* along the *BP* schedule, thereby achieving its external balance goal, but this action would yield a real income level below the level consistent with the bank's internal balance objective. Suppose, instead, that the central bank increases the nominal money stock and shift the *LM* schedule to the position *LM'*, thereby attaining an *IS-LM* equilibrium at point *C* at the income level y^* that is consistent with internal balance. At point *C*, however, real income is too high for external balance, because import spending will increase and depress the nation's trade balance even further.

Hence, we usually would not expect that a central bank acting alone could achieve both internal and external balance objectives. Typically, the bank would need some assistance from a policymaker whose actions could influence the position of the *IS* schedule and/or the *BP* schedule. *Fiscal policies* that alter government spending and taxes can affect the position of the *IS* schedule, which means that monetary and fiscal policies together may achieve both internal and external balance. In addition, exchange-rate changes can influence the position of the *BP* schedule. We present a more detailed examination of fiscal policies and the potential role of exchange-rate adjustments in the next chapter.

FUNDAMENTAL ISSUE #7

How does monetary policy influence the composition of the balance of payments? A particular objective for the private payments balance may be achieved only along a set of real income-nominal interest rate combinations called the *BP* schedule. If an *IS-LM* equilibrium occurs at a point on the *BP* schedule, then the external balance objective can be attained. Variations in the nominal money stock that alter the equilibrium real income level and nominal interest rate can affect a nation's current account balance and its capital account balance, thereby influencing its private payments balance.

CHAPTER SUMMARY

1. **The Key Motives for Holding Money and the Variables That They Indicate Should Influence the Demand for Money:** Two key motives for holding money are the transactions and precautionary motives, which have to do with the need to hold money for use in planned and unplanned exchanges, respectively. Both motives indicate that the demand for real money balance should depend positively on the level of real income. The third key motive is the portfolio motive. This refers to the allocation of a portion of financial wealth to money holdings as part of speculative strategies based on anticipated future changes in interest rates and bond prices. The portfolio motive indicates that the demand for money should depend negatively on the nominal interest rate.

2. **The Determination of Nominal Interest Rates in the Traditional Keynesian Model:** At the equilibrium nominal interest rate, people are satisfied holding the quantity of real money balances supplied by the central bank. A liquidity effect on the nominal interest rate occurs when an increase in the nominal money stock alone causes a rise in the supply of real money balances that reduces the equilibrium nominal interest rate. A real balance effect on the nominal interest rate occurs when an increase in the price level causes a reduction in the supply of real money balances that raises the equilibrium nominal interest rate.

3. **The *LM* Schedule and the Factors That Determine Its Elasticity and Position**: The *LM* schedule is the set of all combinations of real income and the nominal interest rate that maintain equilibrium in the market for real money balances. It is more inelastic if money demand is relatively interest inelastic, and it is more elastic if money demand is relatively interest elastic. An increase in the nominal money stock, a fall in the price level, or a decline in money demand not caused by a change in real income shifts the *LM* schedule downward and to the right. A decrease in the money stock, a rise in the price level, or a rise in money demand shifts the *LM* schedule upward and to the left.

4. **The *IS* Schedule and the Factors That Determine Its Elasticity and Position**: The *IS* schedule is the set of all combinations of real income and the nominal interest rate for which aggregate desired expenditures equal real income. The *IS* schedule is more inelastic if desired investment is relatively interest inelastic, and it is more elastic if desired investment is relatively interest elastic. An increase in autonomous desired expenditures stemming from a fall in autonomous saving, import spending, or taxes or from a rise in autonomous government spending, investment, or export spending shifts the *IS* schedule upward and to the right. A rise in autonomous saving, import spending, or taxes or a fall in autonomous government spending, investment, or export spending shifts the *IS* schedule downward and to the left.

5. ***IS-LM* Equilibrium**: This occurs at the single point where the *IS* and *LM* schedules cross. At this point, real income and the nominal interest rate simultaneously achieve an equilibrium flow of real income and an equilibrium in the market for real money balances.

6. **The Traditional Keynesian Transmission Mechanism for Monetary Policy**: In the Keynesian macroeconomic model, this is the set of linkages through which monetary policy actions should affect equilibrium real income. According to the theory, a rise in the nominal money stock reduces the equilibrium nominal interest rate. This causes a rise in desired investment spending that increases aggregate desired expenditures and induces an increase in equilibrium real income.

7. **How Monetary Policy Influences the Composition of the Balance of Payments**: An objective for a nation's private payments balance can be achieved only along a set of real income-nominal interest rate combinations known as the *BP* schedule. Such an external balance objective may be attained only if an *IS-LM* equilibrium occurs at a point on the *BP* schedule. Changes in the nominal money stock alter the equilibrium real income level and nominal interest rate and thereby can influence a nation's current account balance and its capital account balance. This permits monetary policy to affect a nation's private payments balance.

QUESTIONS AND PROBLEMS

1. Explain in your own words why the *LM* schedule generally slopes upward. Would a change in real income cause a shift in the *LM* schedule or a movement along the schedule? Explain your reasoning.

2. Explain in your own words why the *IS* schedule generally slopes downward. Would a change in real income cause a shift in the *IS* schedule or a movement along the schedule? Explain your reasoning.

3. Explain in your own words what occurs at a point of *IS-LM* equilibrium.

4. If graphed on a diagram where the nominal interest rate is measured on the vertical axis and the quantity of real money balances is measured on the horizontal axis, what would the *classical* money demand schedule look like? Based on your answer, would you argue that the classical theory of the demand for money is more or less general than the Keynesian theory? Explain your reasoning.

5. Suppose that the GDP deflator is equal to 1 and that the nominal money stock is equal to $1.5 trillion. If the demand schedule for real money balances is given by the straight-line function (measured in trillions of dollars), $m^d = (0.9 \times y) - (80 \times r)$, what is the equation for the economy's *LM* schedule? Show your work, and solve for r on the left side of the equation that you derive.

6. Using the information from question 5, if y is equal to $7 trillion, what is the equilibrium nominal interest rate?

7. Suppose that desired investment spending is determined by the equation (measured in trillions of dollars), $i = 5.8 - (80 \times r)$. If government spending is equal to $2 trillion, real consumption spending is equal to a *fixed* value of $3 trillion, and export spending is equal to $1 trillion, what is the straight-line equation for the *IS* schedule? (Hint: set y equal to $c + i + g + x$ and solve the resulting expression with r on the left side of your solution.)

8. Using the information in question 7, if the nominal interest rate is 5 percent (that is, 0.05), what is the equilibrium level of real income?

9. Use your answers to questions 5 and 7 to calculate the single real income-nominal interest rate combination for an *IS-LM* equilibrium.

10. Explain in your own words why the *BP* schedule generally slopes upward.

11. Suppose that the *IS* and *LM* schedules happen to cross above and to the left of the *BP* schedule. Would the private payments balance be equal to zero, greater than zero, or less than zero? Explain your reasoning.

 CYBERTUTOR EXERCISES

1. How would the Federal Reserve go about reducing real income (y)?

2. One of the fundamental issues of Chapter 6 was the question "How does monetary policy influence the private payments balance?" Let's explore the answer to this question. Take France and create a scatter plot of the M2 money stock and the private payments balance. Does there seem to be any relationship? Next, create a time series plot of the M2 money stock and Real Exports of Goods and Services and Real Imports of Goods and Services. Do you see any relationship? Finally, create two scatter diagrams of the M2 money stock vs. imports and exports. Does this change your answer?

ON-LINE APPLICATION

As we discussed in this chapter, the Federal Reserve can influence market interest rates by changing the quantity of money in circulation. This application explores the Federal Reserve's role in determining interest rates.

Internet URL: http://www.finpipe.com/interest.htm

Title: Why Interest Rates Change

Navigation: Begin at the homepage of the Financial Pipeline (**http://www.finpipe.com**). Under "Subjects," select *Bonds.* In "Related Articles," click on *Why Interest Rates Change.*

Application: Read the article, and answer the following questions:

1. What does it mean for the Federal Reserve to "loosen monetary policy"? How does this affect market interest rates? Does this effect square with the discussion in this chapter?

2. If the Federal Reserve induces an increase in market interest rates, will the holder of a long-term bond be made better or worse off? Explain.

SELECTED REFERENCES AND FURTHER READING

Branson, William. *Macroeconomic Theory and Policy.* New York: Macmillan, 1978.

Hansen, Alvin. *A Guide to Keynes.* New York: Macmillan, 1953.

Harris, Laurence. *Monetary Theory.* New York: McGraw-Hill, 1981.

Hicks, John. "Mr. Keynes and the Classics: A Suggested Interpretation." *Econometrica* 5 (April 2, 1937): 147-159.

Keynes, John Maynard. *The General Theory of Employment, Interest, and Money.* New York: Harcourt Brace Jovanovich, 1964.

7

A Meaningful Role for Government—

FISCAL POLICY IN THE TRADITIONAL KEYNESIAN SYSTEM

FUNDAMENTAL ISSUES

1. How does government spending influence real income in the traditional Keynesian model?

2. How can the basic Keynesian model be adapted to account for income taxes?

3. Do cuts in income tax rates necessarily increase the government's budget deficit?

4. What is the Ricardian equivalence proposition?

5. How does traditional Keynesian theory indicate that government budget deficits and private payments deficits might simultaneously be reduced or even eliminated?

In 1797, Great Britain felt threatened. Not only were French troops helping Irish rebels against the British at Bantry Bay, but French armies had occupied the Netherlands, northern Italy, and Germany, upsetting the balance of power on the Continent. The British prime minister, William Pitt, was concerned that he would not have enough revenues to protect the British Crown. So he did the unthinkable—he imposed an income tax.

Since 1797 many countries have followed Pitt's example—income taxes have often been imposed and raised during periods of war. The United States imposed its first income tax in 1861 during the Civil War, although the tax did not become permanent until 1913. During World War I, Congress raised the maximum rate from 7 percent to 70 percent as the federal budget increased from $1 billion in 1916 to more than $19 billion in 1919. During World War II, federal spending rose from $9.6 billion in 1940 to more than $95 billion in 1945. At the same time, the highest marginal income tax rate was raised to 88 percent on incomes over $200,000, and the number of taxpayers rose from 14 million to 50 million.

Current federal income tax rates stem from many factors, war being only one of them. In addition, politicians, often on the advice of economic experts, have played with federal marginal income tax rates in order to engage in fiscal policy. In this chapter you will see how to integrate changes in taxes into a traditional Keynesian model that concerns the effects of fiscal policy.

The proper role of government in the U.S. economy emerged as perhaps the single biggest economic issue of the 1990s and the beginning of the twenty-first century. This broad issue has no easy solution, in part because it involves *two* separate questions. First, what place should government have in the various markets for such diverse goods and services as electrical power generation, drugs, health care, and banking? Second, what role, if any, should government play in trying to influence aggregate economic activity?

The first question is very important, but it is an issue for microeconomists, so we shall not consider it further in this text. In this chapter we shall contemplate the second question by examining the conduct of fiscal policy, or variations in government expenditures and taxes aimed at influencing real income. Because traditional Keynesian theory has had much to say about this topic, we shall use it as a basis for most of our discussion. Nevertheless, the classical model of Chapter 3 can also be brought to bear on fiscal issues, and from time to time we shall draw upon it as well. As you can imagine, the two approaches often lead to conflicting perspectives on the extent to which fiscal policy can perform a socially useful role.

GOVERNMENT SPENDING, TAXES, AND CROWDING OUT

As we discussed in Chapter 5, fiscal policy actions, such as changes in government spending or taxes, have multiplier effects on equilibrium real national income in the traditional Keynesian model. In addition, there is no guarantee in the traditional Keynesian model that real national income will always equal the natural level consistent with the economy's long-run growth path, as recessionary or inflationary gaps can exist from time to time. These potential problems provide a possible rationale for using fiscal policies to stabilize real national income.

In Chapter 6 we showed how real income and the nominal interest rate must adjust simultaneously to achieve an equilibrium flow of aggregate desired expenditures and equilibrium in the market for real money balances. Because total spending affects real income and, as a result, the demand for money, fiscal policy actions should influence the nominal interest rate. Changes in the interest rate should, in turn, feed back to affect total spending. We shall begin our discussion of fiscal policy by examining this interplay of economic forces touched off by any fiscal policy action. Then we shall turn our attention to issues relating to taxation policies and government deficits.

Fiscal Policy in the Basic *IS-LM* Model

To understand how fiscal policy influences interest rates and how the resulting interest-rate changes affect real income, let's return to the *IS-LM* model that we developed in Chapter 6. Furthermore, for now let's concentrate on the effects of changes in government expenditures.

Consider the effect of a rise in real government spending, from an amount equal to g_1 to a larger amount equal to g_2, holding everything else, including taxes, constant. In this situation, the government would have to finance the increase in its spending either by reducing an existing budget surplus or, more likely, by adding to an existing budget deficit.

INTERNET SOURCE

Tracking Federal Spending—The Latest Data

Federal Expenditures—The Census Bureau
Internet URL: **http://www.census.gov/ftp/pub/gov/fedfi/federal.txt**

Navigation: Go to *Subjects A–Z.* Go to *"E."* Click on *Federal Expenditures.*

Figure 7–1 on page 220 depicts the effects of this fiscal policy action in the *IS-LM* framework. The rise in government expenditures causes the *IS* schedule to shift rightward by the amount of the spending increase times the autonomous expenditures multiplier, $1/(1 - MPC)$. Consequently, at the initial equilibrium interest rate, r_1, real income will rise from y_1 to y_3, which is equal to the distance between the initial equilibrium at point E and point F. This rise in real income, however, will act through

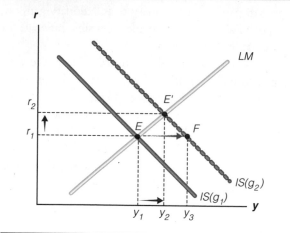

An increase in government spending shifts the *IS* schedule rightward. This causes equilibrium real income to rise, thereby inducing an increase in the demand for real money balances. As a result, the equilibrium nominal interest rate will increase, as shown by the movement upward along the *LM* schedule from point *E* to point *E'*. Holding inflation expectations unchanged, the real interest rate will increase, thereby causing a decline in desired investment expenditures and a movement back along the *IS* schedule from point *F* to point *E'*. Nevertheless, on the net the increase in government spending generally will cause a rise in the equilibrium nominal interest rate and an increase in equilibrium real income.

the transactions and precautionary motives to increase the demand for real money balances. This will cause an increase in the equilibrium nominal interest rate, from r_1 to r_2, that is shown by an upward movement along the *LM* schedule from point *E* to point *E'*. If inflation expectations are unchanged, the rise in the nominal interest rate will correspond to an increase in the real rate of interest.

Recall, however, that desired investment spending is inversely related to the real interest rate. Hence, the rise in the real interest rate owing to the upward movement in the nominal rate with unchanged inflation expectations will reduce investment expenditures and thus cause aggregate desired expenditures to decline once again. This causes real income to decline somewhat, to y_2. This decline in real income is shown by a movement back along the new *IS* schedule from point *F* to point *E'*. The amount of the fall in real income from y_3 back toward y_2 will equal the decline in investment spending times the autonomous expenditures multiplier, $1/(1 - MPC)$.

In the end, even though the rise in government spending initially causes real income to rise by a multiple amount, the induced rise in the interest rate will also cause investment expenditures to decline by a multiple amount. The *net* effect of the increase in real government expenditures on equilibrium real income typically is positive, as shown in Figure 7–1. Clearly, however, the fundamental nature of the Keynesian multiplier effect changes when we account for a change in the nominal interest rate that is induced by a rise in government spending. Equilibrium real income no longer rises by the full amount predicted by the basic multiplier framework developed in Chapter 5. In fact, the increase in equilibrium real income induced by fiscal policy could be much less than that model would indicate. How much less, it turns out, depends on the size of the *crowding-out effect*.

The Crowding-Out Effect

We encountered the crowding-out effect in Chapter 3. There we found that in the classical model there is *complete* crowding out: A deficit-financed increase in government expenditures crowds out an equal amount of private spending. In the classical model, complete crowding out also takes place because a rise in government spending causes private spending to decline by inducing an increase in the real interest rate, which could result from a rise in the nominal interest rate with unchanged inflation expectations.

Real income is predetermined in the classical model, however, by the position of the vertical aggregate supply schedule. In contrast, in the traditional Keynesian model, real income can vary in response to an alteration in government expenditures. Thus, generally complete crowding out does not occur.

What determines the relative size of the crowding-out effect? Suppose that we had drawn Figure 7–1 with a very inelastic *IS* schedule (so that desired investment was very interest-inelastic) and a very elastic *LM* schedule (so that the demand for real money balances was very interest elastic). With these elasticities, the amount of the final increase in equilibrium real income would have been very nearly the same as the amount of the rightward shift in the *IS* schedule. The crowding-out effect would have been very small.

In contrast, if we had drawn Figure 7–1 with a very elastic *IS* schedule (so that desired investment was relatively interest-elastic) and a very inelastic *LM* schedule (so that the demand for real money balances was relatively interest inelastic), then the final increase in equilibrium real income would have been very nearly equal to zero. Crowding out would have been very nearly complete. We may conclude that:

> **The crowding-out effect becomes larger as the interest elasticity of desired investment increases. The crowding-out effect also increases as the interest elasticity of the demand for real money balances declines.**

The extreme case of complete crowding out occurs with a perfectly elastic *IS* schedule (completely interest-elastic desired investment) and a perfectly inelastic *LM* schedule (completely interest-insensitive money demand). In this case, an increase in government expenditures shifts the *IS* schedule along itself, and no change takes place in the equilibrium real income level as a result. This outcome can occur only when desired investment spending falls by exactly the same amount as government expenditures rise. This special case is the *IS-LM* analogue to the classical model, in which there is complete crowding out. This is a sensible conclusion, because the classical model emphasizes the interest sensitivity of desired investment but assumes that money demand is completely interest insensitive. (For an example of the crowding-out effect, see on page 222 the Global Notebook: *French Policymakers Ignore Crowding-Out Effects.*)

ON THE WEB
For the Latest News from France, visit:
http://www.actufax.com/Reports/Englishr.htm

FUNDAMENTAL ISSUE #1

How does government spending influence real income in the traditional Keynesian model? The initial effect of a rise in government expenditures is an increase in real income equal to the increase in government spending times the autonomous expenditures multiplier. The rise in real income, however, causes an increase in the demand for money that pushes up the equilibrium nominal interest rate. Given current inflation expectations, this leads to a rise in the real interest rate and a reduction in desired real investment. As a result, some private spending is crowded out by the rise in government expenditures, so equilibrium real income rises by less than predicted by the basic multiplier analysis.

THE INCOME TAX SYSTEM IN THE KEYNESIAN FRAMEWORK

In the basic Keynesian model that we discussed in Chapter 5, the government assessed taxes as a lump-sum amount. Under this assumption, it is easy to figure out the effects of a tax cut in the *IS-LM* model. As in Figure 7–1, the *IS* schedule would shift to the right following a cut in lump-sum taxes. The amount of the shift in this event would be equal to the amount of the tax reduction multiplied by the tax multiplier, which you learned in Chapter 5 is equal to $-MPC/(1 - MPC)$. The rest of the explanation is identical to the effects that follow from a rise in government spending. Equilibrium real income would increase, but by less than the amount of the shift in the *IS* schedule. The reason is that as real income rose, so would the demand for real money balances and the equilibrium interest rate. As a result, real income would fall somewhat. On net, however, a lump-sum tax reduction would cause both the equilibrium nominal interest rate and the equilibrium real income level to rise, which would mirror the effects of a rise in government expenditures.

We doubt that many of you have ever paid taxes to the government in lump-sum amounts, however. In the United States, the federal and state governments typically assess *excise taxes*, *sales taxes*, *tariffs*, and *income taxes*. Excise taxes typically are assessed on consumer expenditures on specific goods and services. Sales taxes, which are imposed in many states, are a form of excise taxes that apply to consumer expenditures on *all*, or nearly all, goods and services in general. Tariffs, which are imposed by the federal government, are taxes on imported goods and services. Finally, income taxes are assessed on earnings of wages, interest, rents, and profits.

Trying to account for all of these various types of taxes in a single macroeconomic model would be complicated. Modifying the traditional Keynesian model to account for income taxes is a straightforward procedure, however. The income tax is the key source of tax revenues for the U.S. government, so we shall focus our attention on this form of taxation.

INTERNET ● SOURCE

U.S. Tax Laws

Newsgroup—Discussions of U.S. Taxes
Internet URL: ftp://rtfm.mit.edu/pub/usenet/news.answers/taxes-faq

Navigation: Access the Frequently Asked Questions (FAQ) file via anonymous FTP at the above address. You can subscribe to the **misc.taxes** newsgroup at the LISTSERV address, **LISTSERV@SHSU.EDU.** This is an unmoderated newsgroup for discussing current tax laws.

The Income Tax System

Figure 7–2 on page 224 shows the relative sizes of the various sources of tax revenues received by the U.S. government. The three basic types of income taxes—personal income taxes, corporate income taxes, and social insurance payroll taxes—together account for about 90 percent of the federal government's total tax revenues. The per-

FIGURE 7–2 THE SOURCES OF THE U.S. GOVERNMENT'S TAX RECEIPTS

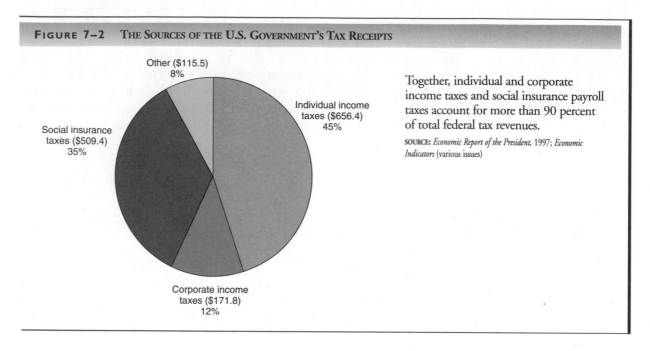

Other ($115.5)
8%

Individual income
taxes ($656.4)
45%

Social insurance
taxes ($509.4)
35%

Corporate income
taxes ($171.8)
12%

Together, individual and corporate income taxes and social insurance payroll taxes account for more than 90 percent of total federal tax revenues.

SOURCE: *Economic Report of the President,* 1997; *Economic Indicators* (various issues)

PROGRESSIVE TAX SYSTEM A system of taxation in which the amount of a tax that a person must pay increases as a percentage of the individual's income as the individual's income rises.

REGRESSIVE TAX SYSTEM A system of taxation in which the amount of a tax that a person must pay declines as a percentage of the individual's income as the individual's income rises.

PROPORTIONAL TAX SYSTEM A system of taxation in which the amount of a tax that a person must pay remains a constant percentage of the individual's income as the individual's income rises.

MARGINAL TAX RATE The rate at which tax payments rise when an individual's income increases; the change in taxes divided by the corresponding change in income, $\Delta t/\Delta y$.

AVERAGE TAX RATE The ratio of total net taxes to total income.

sonal income tax is a tax on all household income, and the corporate income tax is a tax on the accounting profits of corporations. Social insurance payroll taxes apply only to the wages and salaries of individuals.

Progressive versus Regressive Income Tax Systems   Any tax system is a **progressive tax system** if the amount of the tax assessed on an individual rises as a percentage of the individual's income as his income increases. In a **regressive tax system**, in contrast, the total tax paid by a person rises as a percentage of the person's income as her income declines.

Finally, in a **proportional tax system,** the total tax that a person pays remains a constant percentage of the individual's income as the individual's income rises. A proportional tax system is neither progressive nor regressive.

Marginal versus Average Tax Rates   In the United States, the income tax system is designed to be progressive. **Marginal tax rates**, or the rates at which taxes change as a person's income increases (the change in taxes divided by the corresponding change in income, $\Delta t/\Delta y$), rise as an individual's income increases. Some of the progressivity of the system is reduced by the ability to *deduct* various types of expenditures from taxable income, but on net the U.S. system is relatively progressive (see the Policy Notebook: *How Has Our Progressive Income Tax System Changed since 1913?*).

In contrast to the marginal tax rate, the **average tax rate** is simply the ratio of total tax payments to total income, or t/y. The marginal and average *income* tax rates that a person faces are identical in a proportional income tax system, because the individual always pays the same percentage of income taxes at any income level. In progres-

POLICY NOTEBOOK

How Has Our Progressive Income Tax System Changed Since 1913?

The first income tax was probably imposed in the 1200s and 1300s during times of war in the Italian city-states. Although the United States first enacted an income tax in 1861 to help pay for the Civil War, most Americans did not come to know the federal income tax until the Sixteenth Amendment was ratified in 1913, and even then very few had to pay it. Initially, the income tax was popular because it imposed only very low tax rates on only the highest incomes. The proponents of the Sixteenth Amendment viewed it as a way to force "robber barons" to pay taxes.

The left side of Table 7–1 shows the tax rates imposed in 1913, while the right side shows what these same tax rates would be in 1997 dollars. A 1 percent tax rate would

be in effect on incomes up to around $300,000. The highest tax rate, 7 percent, would take effect on incomes over $7.4 million.

Of course, current U.S. tax rates and brackets are quite different, as Table 7–2 shows. We should also note, though, that inflation-adjusted federal government expenditures increased more than 13,000 percent between 1913 and 1997.

FOR CRITICAL ANALYSIS:

How different would the U.S. economy be today if we had kept the 1913 personal income tax system?

TABLE 7–1   1913 U.S. INCOME TAX RATES AND TAX BRACKETS

1913 PERSONAL INCOME TAX SYSTEM		1913 PERSONAL INCOME TAX SYSTEM IN 1997 DOLLARS	
TAX RATE	INCOME LEVEL	TAX RATE	INCOME LEVEL
1%	Up to $20,000	1%	Up to $298,507
2%	$20,000–$50,000	2%	$298,507–$746,269
3%	$50,000–$75,000	3%	$746,269–$1,119,403
4%	$75,000–$100,000	4%	$1,119,403–$1,492,537
5%	$100,000–$250,000	5%	$1,492,537–$3,731,343
6%	$250,000–$500,000	6%	$3,731,343–$7,462,687
7%	Over $500,000	7%	Over $7,462,687

TABLE 7–2   CURRENT U.S. INCOME TAX RATES AND TAX BRACKETS

SINGLE PERSONS		MARRIED COUPLES	
MARGINAL TAX BRACKET	MARGINAL TAX RATE	MARGINAL TAX BRACKET	MARGINAL TAX RATE
$0–$24,000	15%	$0–$40,100	15%
$24,001–$58,150	28%	$40,101–$96,900	28%
$58,151–$121,300	31%	$96,901–$147,700	31%
$121,301–$263,750	36%	$147,701–$263,750	36%
$263,751 and up	39.6%	$263,751 and up	39.6%

SOURCE: U.S. Department of the Treasury.
Note: The system allowed a $3,000 exemption for single filers and $4,000 for a married couple.

Note: The system would allow a $44,776 exemption for single filers and $59,701 for a married couple.

sive or regressive income tax systems, however, the marginal and average income tax rates differ at various income levels. Suppose that a progressive system imposes a 10 percent income tax rate on the first $10,000 in income and a 20 percent tax rate on all income earnings above $10,000. In this system, an individual who earns $15,000 would pay $1,000 in income taxes on the first $10,000 in income and $1,000 on the additional $5,000 in income earnings. His total bill would be $2,000, and his average tax rate would be $2,000/$15,000, or 13⅓ percent. The 15,000th dollar earned would be taxed at a rate of 20 percent, however, so that would be the marginal tax rate faced at a level of income equal to $15,000.

Adapting the Keynesian Model to the Income Tax

A macroeconomic model with a progressive income system is very difficult to construct and analyze without using some sophisticated math. Nevertheless, we can illustrate all the essential ways that income taxes alter the Keynesian framework by examining a proportional income tax system. You should not confuse a proportional income tax with proposals for a *flat income tax system*, in which there is a constant marginal tax rate for all levels of taxable income. A flat tax system can be progressive if income earnings ranging from zero to some cutoff level are exempted from taxation. Under a proportional income tax, *all* income is taxed at the same marginal tax rate. Consequently, the marginal and average income tax rates faced by an individual are always equal under a proportional income tax, but these tax rates can differ under a flat tax that exempts low income levels from taxation.

The Tax Function We can capture the workings of a proportional income tax system in a macroeconomic model by using the following tax function:

$$t = t_0 + \tau y.$$

According to this tax function, the government's total real tax revenues are equal to an autonomous component plus a component that depends on real income. The autonomous component, t_0, includes tax revenues from other sources than the income tax, net of any transfer payments. The second component represents income tax revenues, which are directly proportional to real income. The marginal tax rate is τ (the Greek letter tau), which is a fraction.

Figure 7–3 shows the tax function on a diagram. The amount of net autonomous taxes, t_0, is the vertical intercept of the function, or governmental tax collections net of transfer payments if real income is equal to zero. The slope of the function, $\Delta t / \Delta y$, is the *overall* marginal tax rate, which is equal to τ. Note that even though the income tax is proportional, the overall marginal and average tax rates for the entire tax system are not equal, because the ratio of total net taxes to real income is equal to

$$t/y = (t_0 + \tau y)/y$$
$$= t_0/y + \tau.$$

Hence, the overall average tax rate, $t_0/y + \tau$, equals the marginal income tax rate, τ, only if net autonomous taxes are equal to zero. This typically will not be the case.

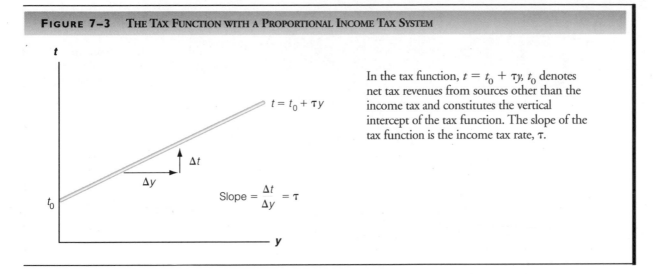

FIGURE 7–3   THE TAX FUNCTION WITH A PROPORTIONAL INCOME TAX SYSTEM

In the tax function, $t = t_0 + \tau y$, t_0 denotes net tax revenues from sources other than the income tax and constitutes the vertical intercept of the tax function. The slope of the tax function is the income tax rate, τ.

Consumption the and Income Tax Rate   To determine how accounting for an income tax system affects equilibrium real income in the traditional Keynesian model, we need to retrace the solution for an income-expenditure equilibrium using our new tax function. The first step in this process is to think about how an income tax affects household consumption. Recall from Chapter 5 that the consumption function is

$$c = (s_0 - im_0) + [(1 - b - d) \times y_d],$$

where s_0 denotes autonomous saving, im_0 denotes autonomous imports, b is the marginal propensity to save, d is the marginal propensity to import, and $y_d \equiv y - t$ is real disposable income. The factor $(1 - b - d)$, you will recall, is the marginal propensity to consume, or MPC.

If we substitute our new tax function into the consumption function, we get

$$
\begin{aligned}
c &= (s_0 - im_0) + [(1 - b - d) \times y_d] \\
&= (s_0 - im_0) + [(1 - b - d) \times (y - t)] \\
&= (s_0 - im_0) + [(1 - b - d) \times (y - t_0 - \tau y)] \\
&= (s_0 - im_0) - [(1 - b - d) \times t_0] + [(1 - \tau) \times (1 - b - d) \times y].
\end{aligned}
$$

The slope of the consumption function, $\Delta c / \Delta y$, therefore is equal to $(1 - \tau) \times (1 - b - d)$, or 1 minus the marginal tax rate times the MPC. This indicates that when a person receives an additional dollar of real income, the first thing that happens to that dollar is that it is taxed at the rate τ. Then only the portion $(1 - \tau)$ is available to allocate to additional consumption.

Figure 7–4 on page 228 displays the consumption function. Autonomous consumption is equal to $(s_0 - im_0) - [(1 - b - d) \times t_0]$, so this is the vertical intercept of the consumption function. The slope of the consumption function is equal to $(1 - \tau) \times (1 - b - d)$, or 1 minus the marginal tax rate times the MPC. This

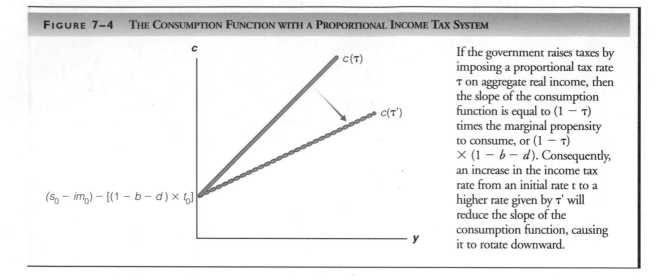

FIGURE 7–4   THE CONSUMPTION FUNCTION WITH A PROPORTIONAL INCOME TAX SYSTEM

If the government raises taxes by imposing a proportional tax rate τ on aggregate real income, then the slope of the consumption function is equal to $(1 - \tau)$ times the marginal propensity to consume, or $(1 - \tau) \times (1 - b - d)$. Consequently, an increase in the income tax rate from an initial rate t to a higher rate given by τ' will reduce the slope of the consumption function, causing it to rotate downward.

means that an increase in the tax rate, from a rate equal to τ to a higher rate equal to τ', will reduce the slope of the consumption function. Thus, an increase in the tax rate will *rotate* the consumption function downward, as shown in Figure 7–4.

The Income Tax Rate and Equilibrium Real Income   To determine equilibrium real income, we now follow the same steps that we used in Chapter 5. First, we impose the income-expenditure equality condition, $y = c + i + g + x$. For now, let's assume that desired investment spending is completely autonomous and equal to an amount i_0. If government spending and exports also are autonomous, then we can substitute our consumption function into our equilibrium expression to get

$$y = c + i + g + x$$

$$= (s_0 - im_0) - [(1 - b - d) \times t_0] + [(1 - \tau) \times (1 - b - d) \times y] + i_0 + g_0 + x_0.$$

Now, we can solve for y by subtracting $[(1 - \tau) \times (1 - b - d) \times y]$ from both sides to get

$$y - [(1 - \tau) \times (1 - b - d) \times y] = (s_0 - im_0) - [(1 - b - d) \times t_0] + i_0 + g_0 + x_0$$

or

$$\{1 - [(1 - \tau) \times (1 - b - d)]\} \times y = (s_0 - im_0) - [(1 - b - d) \times t_0] + i_0 + g_0 + x_0.$$

Now, if we divide both sides by $\{1 - [(1 - \tau) \times (1 - b - d)]\}$, we get our final solution for equilibrium real income with an income tax system:

$$y = \frac{1}{1 - [(1 - \tau) \times (1 - b - d)]}$$
$$\times \{(s_0 - im_0) - [(1 - b - d) \times t_0] + i_0 + g_0 + x_0\}.$$

As in Chapter 5, the equilibrium level of real income is equal to an autonomous expenditures multiplier times net autonomous expenditures.

With an income tax system, however, the size of the autonomous expenditures multiplier depends on the income tax rate τ. A reduction in the income tax rate reduces the denominator of the multiplier and therefore increases the size of the multiplier. Thus a cut in the income tax rate increases the size of the autonomous expenditures multiplier.

Figure 7–5 on page 230 explains why this is so. Panel (a) shows the effect of a decline in net autonomous expenditures, perhaps resulting from a fall in autonomous investment, when the tax rate is relatively low, so that the slope of the consumption function is relatively steep. Panel (b) displays the effect of an identical decline in net autonomous expenditures when the tax rate is relatively high, so that the consumption function's slope is relatively shallow.

As you can see, the multiplier effect is larger when the tax rate is lower. This phenomenon can be readily explained. A fall in, say, autonomous investment spending causes real income to decline. This causes a fall in consumption spending, which causes an additional fall in real income, and so on. At each step in this multiplier process, the fall in consumption spending is larger with a lower tax rate because the effect on disposable income is greater when the tax rate is lower. Consequently, the total size of the multiplier effect is larger with a lower income tax rate.

The Income Tax System as an Automatic Stabilizer

AUTOMATIC FISCAL STABILIZER A mechanism of government policy that automatically reduces volatility in real income caused by changes in autonomous expenditures.

The comparison in Figure 7–5 illustrates an important by-product of a government's use of an income tax system: the system functions as an **automatic fiscal stabilizer**, or a governmental policy mechanism that automatically mutes variations in real income arising from changes in autonomous expenditures.

To see this, imagine the result if the income tax rate were set equal to zero, which would imply elimination of the income tax. The consumption function would be as steep as possible, thereby steepening the aggregate desired expenditures schedule, $c + i + g + x$, as much as possible. Consequently, in the absence of the income tax system, equilibrium real income would respond as fully as possible to variations in autonomous aggregate expenditures, such as a fall in desired investment spending.

The income tax system is not the only type of automatic stabilizer constructed by governments. In the United States and many other nations, the government has linked transfer programs, such as unemployment benefits, Social Security, and welfare programs, to the incomes of recipients. Thus, when aggregate real income declines, more individuals' incomes fall below thresholds that qualify them for government benefits. Therefore total transfer payments increase as real income declines.

FIGURE 7–5   THE MULTIPLIER EFFECT WITH DIFFERENT INCOME TAX RATES

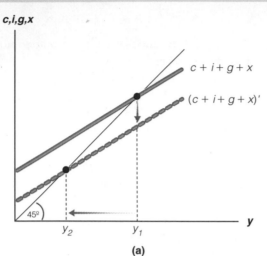

(a)

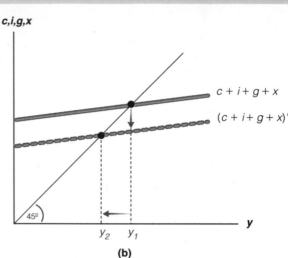

(b)

Both panels of this figure illustrate the effects of a decline in autonomous expenditures. The income tax rate in panel (a), however, is lower than the tax rate in panel (b). Consequently, the autonomous expenditures schedule is more steeply sloped in panel (a), and the result is a larger fall in equilibrium real income. This illustrates that the multiplier effect of a fall in autonomous expenditures on equilibrium real income is larger for lower income tax rates. Thus, an increase in the income tax rate tends to make equilibrium real income more stable in the face of variations in aggregate expenditures, as shown in panel (b).

In our model, we have assumed that transfer payments are a lump sum. If we were to link them to income, we would find that income-conditioned transfer payments, such as income taxes, function as an automatic fiscal stabilizer.

> **FUNDAMENTAL ISSUE #2**
>
> **How can the basic Keynesian model be adapted to account for income taxes?** This can be done by recognizing that the government's real net tax revenues must equal an autonomous component plus a component that is equal to the average income tax rate times the level of real income. As a result, the slope of the consumption function and the aggregate desired expenditures schedule depend on the income tax rate. A reduction in the tax rate steepens these schedules, which raises equilibrium real income while making equilibrium real income more sensitive to the effects of changes in autonomous aggregate expenditures.

TAXES, DEFICITS, AND REAL INCOME

The comparison in Figure 7–5 tells us that the stabilization benefit of the income tax system increases with higher income tax rates. Most of us, of course, do not like high income tax rates, because they leave us with lower disposable income to allocate to saving, import spending, and domestic consumption. Governments interested in the performances of their economies must recognize this as well. As you will see, when the government determines the income tax rate, it faces a trade-off between real income stability and the absolute size of income. A higher tax rate makes income more stable but also depresses real income. A lower tax rate stimulates real income but also makes income less stable in the face of a change in autonomous aggregate expenditures.

With an income tax system, the tax revenues of the government depend on both the tax rate and real income. Together with government expenditures, governmental tax collections also determine the size of the government's budget deficit. Hence, income tax rates, real income, and the deficit all must be related, as you will see shortly.

Tax Rate Changes and Equilibrium Real Income

Changes in the tax rate alter the slope of the consumption function by changing the portion of real income available for household consumption. Hence, tax rate changes must affect aggregate desired expenditures and, therefore, equilibrium real income.

Figure 7–6 on page 232 shows the effect of a tax rate reduction on equilibrium real income. A cut in the income tax rate steepens the consumption function and thereby steepens the aggregate desired expenditures schedule. This schedule rotates upward along the 45-degree line. Equilibrium real income increases.

A cut in the income tax rate increases the portion of each dollar of real income that may be allocated to saving, import expenditures, and consumption spending. Every individual thereby responds to a tax cut by allocating a greater share of total income earnings to consumption spending. This raises aggregate desired expenditures in proportion, thereby pushing up equilibrium real income.

Thus, a cut in the tax rate stimulates an increase in real income. As shown earlier, however, a tax rate reduction also tends to make equilibrium real income more susceptible to changes in autonomous expenditures. Any government faces this fundamental trade-off in determining the "best" overall income tax rate.

Do Cuts in Income Tax Rates Necessarily Increase Deficits?

Although the U.S. government's deficit has declined since the early 1990s, it still amounts to billions of dollars annually. Of course, inflation tends to push up the nominal value of the deficit each year, so current-dollar figures alone can be mislead-

FIGURE 7–6   THE EFFECT OF A CUT IN THE INCOME TAX RATE ON EQUILIBRIUM REAL INCOME

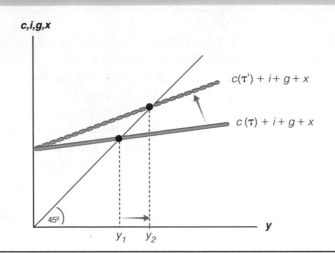

Because a cut in the income tax rate steepens the consumption function, the rate cut must also steepen the aggregate expenditures schedule. The result is an increase in equilibrium real income that arises from the stimulus to consumption spending owing to the cut in the tax rate.

ing indicators of the deficit's magnitude over time. Indeed, most economists argue that a more relevant measure of the government's deficit is its size relative to total economic activity. Figure 7–7 shows the federal government's deficit as a percentage of GDP since 1959. It also shows government expenditures and tax revenues as a percentage of GDP for the same period.

Government Spending, Taxes, and Deficits   As you learned in Chapter 3, the *primary deficit* is simply the difference between the government's expenditures and its tax revenues. The total government deficit includes interest payments on outstanding debt that the government issued to finance deficits in past years. The government cannot do much about the interest portion of each year's deficit after the fact, however. Indeed, if the government wants to contain current deficits and thereby reduce its accumulation of debts, all it can do is either reduce its spending or increase its tax revenues.

Nearly all political leaders say that the government should spend efficiently. In light of evidence of inefficiencies in various governmental programs, therefore, just about every candidate for political office is safe in saying that she or he favors less government spending.

Figure 7–7 indicates that, as a percentage of GDP, government expenditures increased considerably between 1959 and 1983. Since 1984 government spending has declined slightly relative to GDP, as has the federal deficit. Nevertheless, actual spending reductions have been too meager to eliminate the deficit without an increase in tax revenues.

Since 1993 the federal deficit as a percentage of GDP has declined somewhat. Although this is partly due to the slight decline in government spending, another reason is that U.S. government tax revenues have increased relative to GDP, as Figure

FIGURE 7–7   THE FEDERAL GOVERNMENT DEFICIT AS A PERCENTAGE OF U.S. GDP

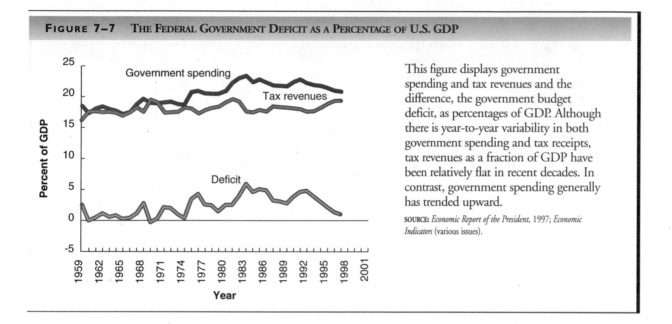

This figure displays government spending and tax revenues and the difference, the government budget deficit, as percentages of GDP. Although there is year-to-year variability in both government spending and tax receipts, tax revenues as a fraction of GDP have been relatively flat in recent decades. In contrast, government spending generally has trended upward.

SOURCE: *Economic Report of the President,* 1997; *Economic Indicators* (various issues).

7–7 indicates. Recall that the average tax rate is the ratio of total tax payments to total real income. Consequently, the plot of government tax receipts relative to GDP in Figure 7–7 is really a graph of the overall average tax rate in the United States since 1959. As you can see, the average tax rate it is not much higher today than it was in 1959, although it has varied over time.

The Static View of the Tax Rate and Tax Revenues   Because income taxes account for the bulk of the U.S. government's tax revenues, an issue of considerable concern is how income tax rates, real income, and the deficit are related. There are two perspectives on this issue: the static view and the dynamic view. The purely *static view* is based on the tax function we discussed earlier, which is given by

$$t = t_0 + \tau y.$$

Under this static view, we can visualize the relationship between the tax rate τ and tax revenues t by considering the diagram of the tax function in Figure 7–8. This is just a graph of the tax function, in which tax revenues are measured along the vertical axis and the tax rate is measured along the horizontal axis. In this diagram, therefore, t_0 is the horizontal intercept of the straight-line tax function, and real income, y, is the slope. This function tells us that as the tax rate declines, say from a value τ to a smaller value τ', the government's tax revenues fall, from t to t' Thus, according to this perspective, if Congress wishes to cut deficits, but prefers not to do so only by reducing government spending, it will need to increase the income tax rate. Certainly, the static view implies that Congress would not reduce tax rates if it wants to maintain or increase the government's tax revenues.

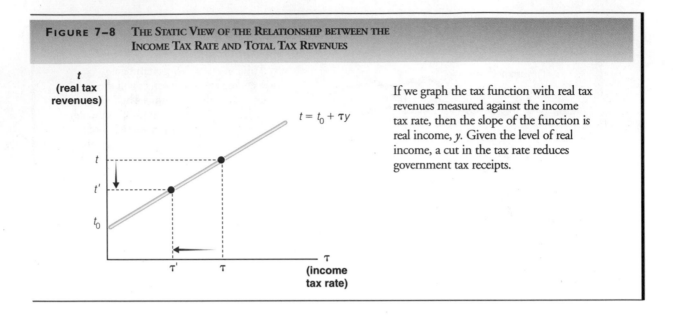

If we graph the tax function with real tax revenues measured against the income tax rate, then the slope of the function is real income, y. Given the level of real income, a cut in the tax rate reduces government tax receipts.

The Dynamic View of the Tax Rate and Tax Revenues   Careful consideration of Figure 7–8, however, indicates that there is a problem with the static view. An upper bound on the income tax rate is 100 percent, or $\tau = 1$. At this maximum possible tax rate, do you think it is likely that the government would collect any income tax revenues? After all, if the government is going to take all of people's income, they are likely to respond either by halting all work effort or, more likely, by finding ways to hide most or all of their income from the government. Indeed, nations with very high tax rates commonly also have the largest *underground economies*, or portions of their economies in which people conduct unrecorded transactions for the purpose of avoiding taxes (and, potentially, arrest for engaging in these and other illegal transactions).

Although the diagram in Figure 7–8 is mathematically correct, it really indicates that a reduction in the tax rate, τ, necessarily causes a fall in income tax revenues and hence total government tax receipts, *only if all other things, including* real income, *are equal.* The problem is that a change in the tax rate will alter real income, as we showed in Figure 7–5 on page 230. This change, in turn, will affect the slope of the tax schedule in Figure 7–8. The purely static view of the relationship between the tax rate and tax revenues ignores the fact that equilibrium real income changes when the tax rate is altered.

Figure 7–9 shows what happens when we take into account that tax rate cuts cause real income to rise. As we noted, at a tax rate of 100 percent, the government receives no income tax revenues. Hence, at point A the government's net tax receipts are autonomous taxes, t_0.

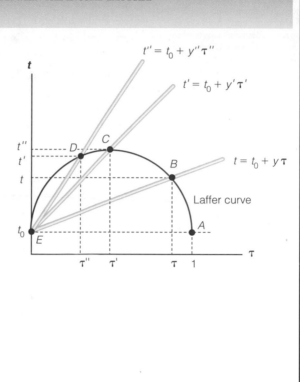

With a tax rate equal to 1 (100 percent) at point A, individuals would have no incentive to earn income, so government would collect no income tax revenues, and its only net tax receipts, t_0, would come from other sources. At point B, the tax rate is less than 100 percent, so the government collects some income tax revenues. A cut in the income tax rate reduces the portion of income that must be paid to the government as taxes, which tends to reduce the government's tax revenues and A raises equilibrium real income, causing the tax function to steepen. Consequently, a movement from point B to point C would result from a tax rate reduction, implying that a cut in the income tax rate could actually raise the government's total tax receipts. Of course, at a zero tax rate, at point E, the government could collect no income tax revenues. Therefore, continual tax rate cuts would ultimately reduce tax revenues, as indicated by a movement from point C to point D. The *Laffer curve* traced out by points A through E shows that at sufficiently high tax rates, cuts in income tax rates can yield increases in government tax receipts.

The figure also shows the tax function from Figure 7–8. Again, at a relatively high tax rate τ, real tax revenues would be equal to t at point B. A cut in the tax rate to τ' would cause equilibrium real income to rise, from y to a larger amount y', so the tax function would steepen. Indeed, real income could rise sufficiently that even though the tax rate applied to income would be lower, the net income tax revenues of the government would be equal to the higher level t' at point C. Under this dynamic view, therefore, *an income tax rate cut could actually cause tax revenues to rise.*

Nonetheless, at some point further cuts in the tax rate would reduce the government's tax revenues on net. For instance, reducing the tax rate once more, from τ' to τ'', would cause real income to rise from y' to a larger amount y'', which again would steepen the tax function. Yet tax revenues on net would decline as a result of this second tax rate reduction, from t' to t'' at point D.

Finally, if the tax rate were equal to zero, the government again would collect no income taxes, and its net tax receipts would equal only the autonomous amount of taxes, t_0, at point E.

LAFFER CURVE A relationship between income tax rates and income tax revenues, which shows that at sufficiently high tax rates, tax rate reductions can increase tax revenues, whereas at lower tax rates, tax rate reductions necessarily reduce tax revenues.

Points *A, B, C, D,* and *E* trace out a hill-shaped schedule known as the **Laffer curve**, after Arthur Laffer, the economist who popularized the dynamic view in the late 1970s and early 1980s. The Laffer curve indicates that if the income tax rate is sufficiently high, cutting the tax rate will raise income tax revenues. Only at lower rates will tax rate reductions necessarily reduce tax revenues. (For a medieval Islamic version of the Laffer curve, see the Global Notebook: *Islam and the Laffer Curve.*)

The difficult problem, naturally, is determining the location of the top point of the Laffer curve. The evidence on this issue is mixed. Shortly after significant reductions in average tax rates were enacted in the early 1980s, tax revenues declined, and the deficit increased sharply. At first glance, these events seem to support the static view. The difficulty with this off-the-cuff judgment, however, is that the U.S. economy went into a sharp recession in the early 1980s even as tax rates were cut, because autonomous investment and consumption declined sharply. Even though government spending also increased in the early 1980s (see Figure 7–7 on page 233), these declines in private spending led to a net reduction in equilibrium real income. Consequently, the true result of the 1980s experiment with the Laffer curve is difficult to judge.

FUNDAMENTAL ISSUE #3

Do cuts in income tax rates necessarily increase the government's budget deficit? A tax rate cut reduces the government's tax receipts and increases its deficit if government expenditures and real income do not change. A tax rate cut also causes a rise in equilibrium real income, which raises the government's revenues from the income tax system. Consequently, if the tax rate is sufficiently high, a cut in the tax rate can actually induce a rise in the government's total tax revenues.

 ## RICARDIAN EQUIVALENCE: CAN TAX POLICY MATTER?

During almost every electoral cycle in the United States, candidates for Congress or for president seem to debate the merits of a cut in income tax rates or "tax rebates" or some other type of short-term, autonomous tax reductions. To this point, our discussion indicates that these debates ought to center on the implications of such proposals for the volume and variability of economic activity and the size of the government's deficit.

In recent years, however, most debates about tax changes have focused on their implications for the *distribution* of income. Typically, one politician will propose a tax

GLOBAL NOTEBOOK
Islam and the Laffer Curve

The relationship between marginal tax rates and total tax revenues was not invented in the twentieth century by Arthur Laffer. Indeed, its history dates back to at least the fourteenth century. The greatest of the medieval Islamic historians, Abu Zayd Abd-Ar-Rahman Ibn Khaldun (1332–1406), included an Islamic view of the Laffer curve in his monumental book, *The Muqaddimah*.

Ibn Khaldun stated that "When tax assessments . . . upon the subjects are low, the latter have the energy and desire to do things. Cultural enterprises [businesses] grow and increase, . . . [therefore] the number of individual imposts [taxes] and assessments mounts." He went on to say that when taxes are increased both in size and rates, "the result is that the interest of subjects in cultural enterprises disappears,

because when they compare expenditures and taxes with their income and gain and see little profit they make, they lose all hope."

He concluded that "At the beginning of a dynasty, taxation yields a large revenue from small assessments. At the end of a dynasty, taxation yields a small revenue from large assessments."

FOR CRITICAL ANALYSIS:
Over time in the United States, the highest marginal tax rates have reached as high as 94 percent, yet the percentage of GDP accounted for by federal tax revenues has remained relatively constant. Apply Ibn Khaldun's economic theories to this fact pattern.

cut plan, and then another will respond that the plan would benefit high-income people disproportionately as compared with low-income people. The potential macroeconomic effects of tax cuts often get lost in the rhetoric of these discussions.

Some macroeconomists believe that the income distribution issue is an appropriate topic for debate. They contend that tax cuts cannot actually affect aggregate economic activity. In addition, they argue, tax changes cannot influence the variability of real income in response to changes in autonomous aggregate expenditures. All that changes in tax rates or autonomous taxes can do is affect the size of the government's deficit and, as many politicians emphasize, the distribution of income. In other words, according to this view, on the question of the effects of tax changes, the politicians have it right, and most economists have got it wrong.

Ricardian Equivalence

The basis for this argument is the *Ricardian equivalence proposition*. The elements of this proposition were outlined by a classical economist of eighteenth- and nineteenth-century Britain named David Ricardo (1772–1823). Ricardo advanced the idea that a cut in lump-sum taxes theoretically might have no effect on aggregate consumption. His reasoning was as follows. If a government maintains its current level of spending, then it must finance a tax cut today by issuing more bonds. In the future, the government must pay interest on these bonds. To pay this interest, which will be

**RICARDIAN EQUIVALENCE
PROPOSITION** The proposition
that if government spending will
be unchanged in the future,
people regard a current tax cut as
equivalent to a future tax increase
and therefore save the proceeds of
a tax cut rather than increasing
their consumption.

a flow of future expenditures by the government, taxes eventually will have to be increased. Foresighted taxpayers understand this and realize that a current tax cut implies a future tax increase. Consequently, rational, self-interested individuals will respond to a current tax cut by saving the increase in their disposable, after-tax income until the future time when the government increases taxes to pay interest on the debts arising from the current tax cut. Thus a current tax cut cannot raise current consumption, and therefore cannot stimulate real income.

In a nutshell, therefore, the **Ricardian equivalence proposition** is a simple idea. It states that a current tax cut implies a future tax increase to make interest payments on debt issued to finance the tax cut. Consequently, people allocate the current increase in their disposable income to saving, from which they can draw to pay the higher future taxes. That is, a tax cut today essentially is *equivalent* to a tax increase in the future. As a result, consumption and equilibrium real income are unaffected by a tax cut.

Note that the argument hinges on the maintenance of a constant level of government spending. A change in government spending, according to the Ricardian equivalence proposition, alters the flow of taxes that ultimately will be necessary to finance those government expenditures today and into the future. Hence, changes in government spending *do* affect equilibrium real income, because these changes affect lifetime flows of tax transfers to the government and thereby induce people to alter their private saving and consumption choices.

The Ricardian equivalence reasoning also works in the opposite direction for the case of a tax increase. If the government raises taxes today while keeping its spending level constant, then it will be able to pay off any existing debt more quickly and will be able to reduce taxes in the future. Consequently, people respond to a current tax increase by drawing from their stock of accumulated savings. They realize they will be able to replenish their savings when their future tax burden declines. As a result, they maintain their current level of consumption, and so equilibrium real income does not change.

Intergenerational Ricardian Equivalence   Until the early 1980s, modern economists had largely ignored or dismissed the Ricardian equivalence proposition. They argued, as we have throughout this text up to this point, that a current tax cut would increase present after-tax income and cause a rise in present consumption. Ricardo's reasoning, they suggested, relied on too much foresight by taxpayers. In addition, even if people realize that a tax cut today will require a future tax increase, such an increase might be so far in the future that today's generation will be dead and gone before the tax increase takes place. As a result, current autonomous changes in lump-sum taxes or changes in income tax rates should affect equilibrium real income for the current generation's economy.

Nevertheless, several modern economists, including Robert Barro of Harvard University, have contended that Ricardo may have had it right two centuries ago. Barro and others contend that self-interested individuals will indeed realize that a current tax cut is equivalent to a future tax increase. They also argue that individuals who care about the welfare of future generations, which will include their children, grandchildren, and other relatives, will also care about the tax burdens that those generations will face. Thus Barro and others propose that Ricardian equivalence applies not only to members of a current generation but to people *across* generations. Ricardian equivalence, they believe, is an *intergenerational* concept.

Consider the following example. Suppose that a political party adopts a platform proposing significant tax cuts without changes in prevailing levels of government expenditures. If a sufficient number of the party's candidates are elected and enact this plan, current taxes will decline, and the current government deficit will rise. Suppose also that this party becomes entrenched in power for a number of years and holds to its platform. Then taxes will be lower than before for a long interval, and the government's deficit will be higher.

Members of the current generation who are in their highest-income years (roughly ages forty to sixty) will be the primary beneficiaries of this long-lasting cut in taxes. Their disposable income will be larger than before and will remain at a higher level for several years. Nevertheless, these individuals will realize that the government's deficit has increased because of these tax cuts. They also will recognize that their children and grandchildren will ultimately face higher taxes to pay off the debt that will accumulate after a number of years of the low-tax policy. Because these members of the current, older generation care about their offspring, they will allocate the increase in their disposable income attributable to tax cuts to saving.

As members of the older generation age, their children and grandchildren will become taxpayers and will face higher tax burdens. These younger men and women will have a hard time paying their taxes while maintaining a standard of living as good as the older generation enjoyed. Out of concern for the welfare of their offspring, members of the older generation will pass along their accumulated savings to the younger generation, either in the form of gifts or in the form of **bequests**, or sums payable to their offspring after their deaths. In essence, then, *the older generation will effectively pay the taxes that have fallen on the young generation*. In this way, the tax increase that *apparently* benefited the older generation nevertheless ultimately will be paid by that generation.

Note that Ricardian equivalence still holds in this example because of **intergenerational transfers**, or transfers of disposable income via gifts or bequests from members of one generation to those of another. Ultimately, instead of changing their consumption levels, the older generation in our example save the proceeds of the tax cuts that they received and pass them on to their offspring. On net, then, the long-lasting tax cut for the older generation does not influence their consumption spending. In addition, the tax cut does not influence economic activity for *either* generation. The older generation saves the proceeds to give to the younger generation, who then pay higher taxes later from the proceeds of the gifts and bequests. Mem-

BEQUEST A sum payable to one's offspring at the time of death.

INTERGENERATIONAL TRANSFERS Transfers of disposable income, in the form of gifts or bequests, from one generation to another generation.

bers of the younger generation are able to spend the same amounts as before even though they, on paper at least, face a higher tax burden than the older generation faced.

Is the Logic of the Ricardian Equivalence Proposition Inescapable?   By the late 1980s, the group of macroeconomists supporting the Ricardian equivalence proposition and its implications for tax policy had grown to include many more than just Robert Barro and a few others. Indeed, among macroeconomists the notion of Ricardian equivalence transformed the topic of debate from how large the effects of tax cuts might be to whether tax cuts could have any effects at all.

One irony about the timing of this transformation of the economic debate was that it took place during the 1980s. As Figure 7–10 indicates, when U.S. government deficits were historically high relative to GDP, national saving rates were at historically low levels. This appears to contradict the Ricardian equivalence proposition, which indicates that saving rates should have *risen* as the federal deficit increased, as people saved to pay higher anticipated future taxes.

Nevertheless, studies of long-term periods indicate that there has been little historical relationship between government deficits and rates of saving and consumption, a finding that is consistent with the Ricardian equivalence proposition. Those who support the proposition argue that the recent turnaround in saving rates is indicative that the hypothesis ultimately will fit the 1980s. Members of the baby boom generation (people born between the end of World War II and 1960) are now

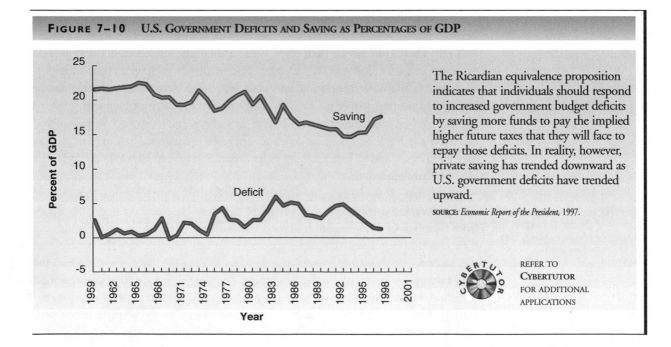

FIGURE 7–10   **U.S. GOVERNMENT DEFICITS AND SAVING AS PERCENTAGES OF GDP**

The Ricardian equivalence proposition indicates that individuals should respond to increased government budget deficits by saving more funds to pay the implied higher future taxes that they will face to repay those deficits. In reality, however, private saving has trended downward as U.S. government deficits have trended upward.

SOURCE: *Economic Report of the President,* 1997.

REFER TO
CYBERTUTOR
FOR ADDITIONAL
APPLICATIONS

in their prime income-earning years, they argue, and are increasing their saving so that they can transfer income to members of the next generation.

Other economists do not accept this explanation. In their view, a number of factors stand in the way of Ricardian equivalence:

- *Shortsightedness.* A number of economists contend that proponents of Ricardian equivalence give people too much credit for looking ahead. In fact, they argue, people are not nearly so sophisticated. Members of any given generation often struggle just to make their own ends meet, goes this counterargument, and cannot concern themselves with the tax burdens of their offspring until it is truly too late. As a result of this shortsightedness, members of a current generation *do* raise their consumption in response to a tax cut.

- *Liquidity constraints.* Even some economists who believe that people are rational and farsighted argue that the Ricardian equivalence logic is still flawed, in that it fails to take into account **liquidity constraints** that people face during their lives. These are constraints that people face on the availability of cash and credit to meet their spending needs at various points in their life spans. For instance, a couple in their thirties with several children may use the proceeds of a tax cut to purchase a larger house, simply because they are low on cash and cannot find lenders willing to extend them sufficient credit. Instead of saving the proceeds of the tax cut to pass onto their children, the couple facing a liquidity constraint will allocate the tax cut to higher consumption.

- *Tax rate changes.* The logic of Ricardian equivalence applies most directly to lump-sum tax changes. Changes in marginal tax rates, however, affect decisions about how much to work and thereby influence production of real goods and services. As a result, real incomes and consumption and saving choices could be affected by changes in marginal tax rates. Consequently, many opponents of Ricardian equivalence argue that the hypothesis fails to apply to changes in *tax rates*, though it might be relevant for tax rebates and other lump-sum tax changes.

- *Gift and bequest motives.* Other economists point out that people give gifts and bequests to their offspring for many reasons. One reason might be to help the offspring maintain their own living standards in the face of altered tax burdens. Another, however, might be to induce behavior that the parents desire from their offspring, such as caring for the parents when they reach old age. Such additional motives could explain many of the gifts and bequests parents give to their children, but the Ricardian equivalence reasoning ignores such factors.

- *Income uncertainty.* Martin Feldstein, who like Barro is an economist at Harvard University, has pointed out a potentially critical flaw in the fundamental Ricardian equivalence logic: Intergenerational Ricardian equivalence does not necessarily hold true when members of the older generation face *income uncertainty*. Even if they care about their offspring, at the time of a tax cut members of the older generation do not know what their future flows of income will turn out to be in later

LIQUIDITY CONSTRAINTS
Constraints on the availability of cash and credit that people face at points during their lives.

years—the situation that all of us arguably face. Therefore, to protect themselves against the risk that their incomes and consumption levels may turn out to be lower than they might otherwise wish, members of the older generation take advantage of a tax cut by increasing their consumption.

The debate about the Ricardian equivalence proposition is still in progress. At this point, most economists agree that Ricardian equivalence likely holds to at least a limited extent, thereby muting the effects of tax cuts on economic activity. David Ricardo developed many other theories, especially concerning labor market behavior and wages, but only his theory of tax policy continues, after two centuries, to be a significant source of controversy in macroeconomics. It appears that the Ricardian equivalence proposition was Ricardo's own bequest to the current generation of macroeconomists.

FUNDAMENTAL ISSUE #4

What is the Ricardian equivalence proposition? This proposition states that tax reductions will not affect total consumption or aggregate desired expenditures. The reasoning behind this proposition is that people recognize that a current tax reduction entails a rise in the government's debt that they will have to repay in the future. Therefore, they respond by saving the proceeds of a tax cut so that they or their offspring will be able to pay higher future taxes. Many economists concur with this proposition, although others point out that its relevance hinges on the degree to which people are shortsighted, the extent to which people face liquidity constraints, the applicability of the proposition to changes in tax rates, the motivations that people have for providing gifts and bequests to their offspring, and the degree of uncertainty that people have about their future incomes.

FISCAL POLICY, THE BALANCE OF PAYMENTS, AND THE EXCHANGE RATE

Why should we care about the size of the government deficit? One reason highlighted by the Ricardian equivalence debate is that a higher deficit today implies a greater tax burden for future generations. Another reason, which we now explore, is that larger government budget deficits can lead to a transfer of resources from home residents to citizens of other nations.

The Twin Deficit Problem Revisited

As you learned in Chapter 2, the U.S. merchandise trade balance has consistently been negative since the early 1980s. Partly because the trade deficit has been so large, the U.S. private payments balance—the sum of the current account balance and private capital balance for the United States—also has gone into a deficit position in recent years. During the 1980s and 1990s, the United States has run "balance of payments deficits": Private American households and firms have made more payments to foreigners than foreign households and firms have made to U.S. residents.

As we have seen, another deficit that grew during several of these same years was the U.S. government's budget deficit. Figure 7–11 shows the dollar values of both the private payments deficit and the U.S. government budget deficit since 1976. Until 1982, nominal the government budget deficit was not any larger than $75 billion. Since that year, however, it has ranged between somewhat less than $100 billion and $340 billion.

Figure 7–11 indicates that the United States began to run sizable private payments deficits at roughly the same time that the U.S. government's budget deficits ballooned. Since that time, the private payments deficit has tended to rise—aside from the 1991–1992 period when the United States received sizable payments relating to its military involvement in the Persian Gulf War—following increases in the federal government's deficit. As you learned in Chapter 5, economists refer to these simulta-

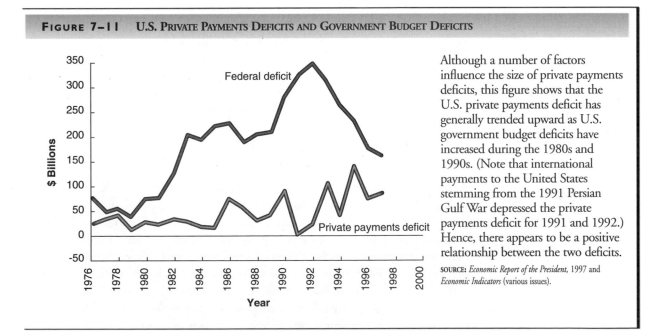

FIGURE 7–11   U.S. PRIVATE PAYMENTS DEFICITS AND GOVERNMENT BUDGET DEFICITS

Although a number of factors influence the size of private payments deficits, this figure shows that the U.S. private payments deficit has generally trended upward as U.S. government budget deficits have increased during the 1980s and 1990s. (Note that international payments to the United States stemming from the 1991 Persian Gulf War depressed the private payments deficit for 1991 and 1992.) Hence, there appears to be a positive relationship between the two deficits.

SOURCE: *Economic Report of the President*, 1997 and *Economic Indicators* (various issues).

neous private payments deficits and government budget deficits as *twin deficits*. To finance its large budget deficits, the U.S. government has borrowed significant amounts from foreigners. Foreigners must obtain dollars to buy the sizable quantities of U.S. government bonds issued to finance federal deficits. They obtain these dollars from Americans who purchase their products. By running large merchandise trade balances that account for most of the nation's private payments deficit, U.S. residents provide foreigners with the dollars that they use to purchase debt instruments issued by the U.S. Treasury.

ON THE WEB
Visit the U.S. Treasury at:
http://www.ustreas.gov

Fiscal Policy and the Private Payments Deficit

A number of factors, besides government budget deficits, influence the size of a nation's private payments balance. For instance, as you learned in Chapter 2, by definition the sum of the private payments deficit and the official reserves transactions account must equal zero. If governments of other countries alter their holdings of a nation's currency, then the nation's private payments deficit will necessarily be affected by those official reserve transactions.

Nevertheless, government budget deficits and private payments deficits in the balance of payments clearly appear to be related. Economists disagree, however, as to the appropriate mix of policies for reducing the twin deficits. To explore the nature of this disagreement, let's return to the framework that we developed in Chapter 6, in which we add the *BP* schedule to the *IS-LM* model so as to consider the international dimensions of policy actions.

CAPITAL MOBILITY The extent to which funds and financial assets may flow freely across a country's borders.

CAPITAL CONTROLS Legal restrictions on the holdings of foreign currencies or assets by the residents of a nation.

Capital Mobility and the Private Payments Deficit One of the sources of disagreement over how to respond to the twin deficit arises from the issue of **capital mobility**. This term refers to the degree to which financial assets and funds are free to flow across a nation's borders. A nation with high capital mobility permits such flows. A country with low capital mobility typically has legal impediments, known as **capital controls**, which typically include restrictions on the ability of the country's residents to hold and exchange assets denominated in the currencies of other nations. Capital controls thereby inhibit flows of funds and assets across the borders of a country. Capital mobility is often low in less developed nations that do not have advanced banking systems or financial markets.

The Case of Low Capital Mobility Recall from Chapter 6 that eliminating a private payments deficit entails attaining *external balance* by achieving an *IS-LM* equilibrium along the *BP* schedule, or the set of real income-nominal interest rate combinations consistent with a private payments balance of zero. Capital mobility plays an important role in the process of attaining external balance, because it affects the slope of the *BP* schedule. If capital mobility is very low because of capital controls and other impediments to flows of funds and assets, then the *BP* schedule is relatively steep. To understand why this is so, suppose that real income rises, thereby causing imports to rise and causing a current account deficit to occur. A capital inflow will then be needed to improve the nation's capital account balance sufficiently to maintain private payments balance. If capital mobility is low, however, foreigners will be reluctant to undertake the expense of overcoming capital controls and other barriers so as to hold financial assets issued in the country. Only a very large interest-rate increase that will provide a high interest return will induce foreigners to hold the country's financial assets.

Panel (a) of Figure 7–12 illustrates the situation that the government faces if it seeks both to balance its own budget and to attain private payments balance when capital mobility is low. Suppose that the current *IS-LM* equilibrium is at point *A*. This point is below and to the right of the *BP* schedule. Consequently, real income is high enough to stimulate imports that induce a trade deficit, and the interest rate is low enough that it will not attract sufficient capital into the country to improve the capital account balance and offset this trade deficit. In the absence of any monetary policy actions, attaining private payments balance will require a leftward shift of the *IS*

FIGURE 7–12   POLICY ACTIONS TO ELIMINATE PRIVATE PAYMENTS DEFICITS

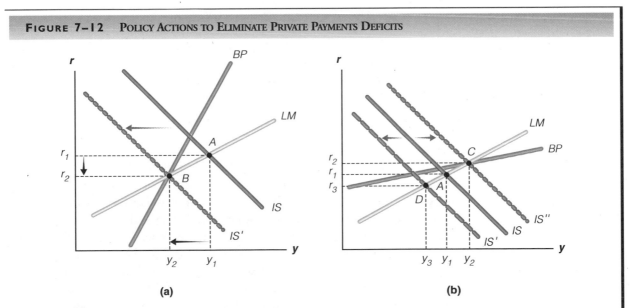

(a)   (b)

At point *A* to the right of the steeply sloped *BP* schedule in panel (a), there is a private payments deficit. If there is also a government budget deficit at point *A*, then a reduction in government spending will cause a movement to a new equilibrium point *B*, thereby reducing the budget deficit and reattaining private payments balance. Panel (b), in contrast, illustrates a situation of relatively high capital mobility. The *BP* schedule is much more shallowly sloped than in panel (a), although point *A* still

lies below and to the right of the *BP* schedule, indicating a private payments deficit. Even though the resulting movement from point *A* to point *D* will reduce the budget deficit, it will lead to a higher private payments deficit. Eliminating the private payments deficit would actually require an increase in government spending via a movement to point *C*. This action would raise the equilibrium interest rate and stimulate greater capital inflows from abroad.

schedule to point *B*. The government can accomplish this by increasing taxes, reducing government expenditures, or using a combination of both types of fiscal policy actions. Such policy actions will attack both deficits at the same time. The cost, of course, is the reduction in real income entailed by the movement from point *A* to point *B*.

The Case of High Capital Mobility   Many economists do not believe that panel (a) of Figure 7–12 is a good representation of the situation faced by the United States, which has relatively high capital mobility as compared with most other nations. They argue that panel (b) provides a better indication of the U.S. situation. Here, the *BP* schedule is very shallow. In this case, if an increase in real income causes imports to rise, thereby causing a trade deficit, then a small increase in the interest rate will attract enough flows of funds and assets from other nations to improve the capital account balance sufficiently to reattain a private payments balance along the *BP* schedule.

With high capital mobility, a private payments deficit again will arise if there is an *IS-LM* equilibrium below and to the right of the *BP* schedule, as at point *A* in panel (b). In this case, as shown in the diagram, reattaining external balance by eliminating the private payments deficit will require a *rightward* shift of the *IS* schedule, to the dashed schedule labeled *IS″*. To eliminate the private payments deficit that exists at point *A*, the government will need to *reduce* taxes or *increase* its spending or adopt some combination of these policies. This government action will raise the nominal interest rate. With high capital mobility, this interest-rate increase will attract sufficient volumes of funds and financial assets from foreigners to raise the nation's capital account balance by a large amount, thereby attaining private payments balance at point *C*.

Reducing taxes or increasing spending, however, will also worsen the government's budget deficit. Consequently, when an economy is at point *A* in panel (b), reducing the budget deficit will cause the *IS* schedule to shift in the *wrong direction*, to a position such as *IS′*. As a result, the interest rate will decline, and foreigners will remove their funds and assets, causing the nation's private payments deficit to worsen at point *D*. If the government is intent upon reducing its deficit, the only way out of this quandry is for the central bank to assist by conducting a contractionary monetary policy and shifting the *LM* schedule leftward. This could raise the nominal interest rate sufficiently to induce a net rise in the nation's capital account balance.

Exchange-Rate Adjustments to Twin Deficits   As we noted earlier, panel (a) of Figure 7–12 is not very applicable to the U.S. situation of the 1980s and 1990s because U.S. capital mobility is very high. Panel (b) does not fit the U.S. experience very well either, because it indicates that reducing the nation's private payments deficit will require actions that *increase* the government's budget deficit. Clearly, some important real-world factor must be missing from the examples in Figure 7–12.

The missing factor is the exchange rate. Since the early 1970s, both the Federal Reserve and the U.S. Treasury generally have permitted the exchange value of the dollar to move relatively freely in foreign exchange markets. Although both the Fed and the Treasury have tried to influence the exchange rate from time to time during the 1980s and 1990s, for the most part the dollar's value has adjusted to prevailing conditions.

Figure 7–13 takes this important fact into account. Consistent with the high capital mobility of the United States, it shows a very shallow *BP* schedule. The initial *IS-LM* equilibrium is at point *A*, at which there is a private payments deficit. Let's also assume that a twin deficit problem exists at point *A*, so that the government also experiences a budget deficit at this point.

If the exchange rate adjusts freely to the situation illustrated by point *A* in Figure 7–13, then the following sequence of events must take place. First, at point *A* the existence of a U.S. private payments deficit means, by definition, that Americans pay more dollars to foreigners than foreigners pay to Americans. To make the payments to foreigners, Americans must exchange their dollars for foreign currencies. This raises the demand for such currencies, so their values increase in terms of the dollar. In other words, foreign currencies **appreciate**, or gain value relative to the dollar, and the dollar **depreciates**, or drops in value relative to other currencies. Second, when the dollar loses value relative to other nations' currencies, the prices of goods imported to the United States from those countries become more expensive in terms of foreign currencies. This induces Americans to reduce their imports at any given level of real income and interest rate. The result is a *shift* of the *BP* schedule, such as that shown in Figure 7–13 by the movement to the new position *BP'*. In principle, therefore,

APPRECIATION A rise in the value of one nation's currency in terms of the currency of another nation.

DEPRECIATION A decline in the value of one nation's currency in terms of the currency of another nation.

FIGURE 7–13   FISCAL POLICY AND EXCHANGE-RATE ADJUSTMENTS THAT WOULD ELIMINATE THE TWIN DEFICITS

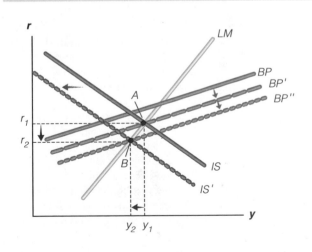

At point *A*, which is below and to the right of the initial *BP* schedule, there is a private payments deficit. Suppose that there is also a government budget deficit at point *A*, so that a twin deficit problem exists. With a floating exchange rate, the private payments deficit will tend to decline naturally, as the value of the nation's currency depreciates, causing a reduction in import spending and a rise in export expenditures that improve the nation's trade balance, thereby inducing the *BP* schedule to shift downward to the position denoted *BP'*. To reduce its budget deficit, however, the government needs to reduce its spending, which will cause the *IS* schedule to shift to the left, resulting in the new equilibrium point *B*. This point lies below and to the right of *BP'*, so again there is a private payments deficit. Further currency depreciation will ultimately eliminate this deficit by causing the *BP* schedule to shift once more, to *BP''*.

such an exchange-rate depreciation will automatically eliminate the U.S. private payments deficit without the need for any fiscal (or monetary) policy actions whatsoever.

If the government also wishes to reduce its budget deficit, however, it still will need to increase taxes or reduce its expenditures. This action causes the *IS* schedule to shift leftward, to *IS'*, thereby producing a new *IS-LM* equilibrium at point *B*, where once again there is a private payments deficit. With a flexible exchange rate, however, the exchange rate will depreciate further, and the *BP* schedule will again shift downward, toward the schedule labeled *BP"*. Ultimately, the government can balance its own budget as the exchange rate adjusts to reattain private payments balance at point *B*.

Does the story told by Figure 7–13 appear to match reality? Figure 7–14 provides some evidence on this issue. The figure shows the exchange value of the U.S. dollar in terms of the currencies of the United States' major trading partners since 1976. Notice how the value of the dollar changed following the large runup in the federal budget deficit and the trade deficit that occurred after 1982 (see Figure 7–11 on page 243). Clearly, the value of the dollar gradually declined after 1985, just as theory would have predicted.

The evidence regarding the response of the private payments deficit is not as clear, however. It continued to rise in the early 1990s, even as the dollar's value fell, and in the mid-1990s, even as the federal budget deficit gradually declined. Can we reconcile this pattern with the theory illustrated in Figure 7–13? The answer is that we can, if we recognize that the private payments balance needs *time* to adjust to changes in the exchange rate and in the federal deficit. If the theory's implications that a depre-

REFER TO
CYBERTUTOR
FOR ADDITIONAL
APPLICATIONS

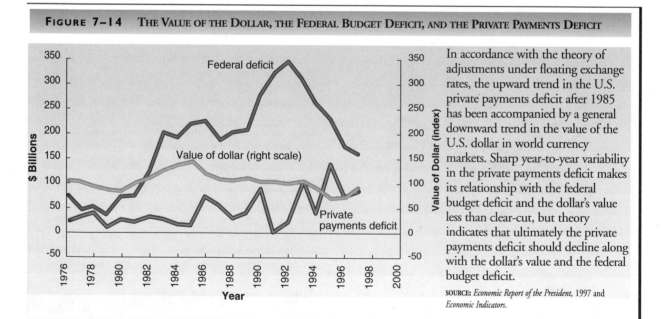

FIGURE 7–14   THE VALUE OF THE DOLLAR, THE FEDERAL BUDGET DEFICIT, AND THE PRIVATE PAYMENTS DEFICIT

In accordance with the theory of adjustments under floating exchange rates, the upward trend in the U.S. private payments deficit after 1985 has been accompanied by a general downward trend in the value of the U.S. dollar in world currency markets. Sharp year-to-year variability in the private payments deficit makes its relationship with the federal budget deficit and the dollar's value less than clear-cut, but theory indicates that ultimately the private payments deficit should decline along with the dollar's value and the federal budget deficit.

SOURCE: *Economic Report of the President*, 1997 and *Economic Indicators*.

ON THE WEB
*Visit the World Trade
Compass at:*
http://www.
tradecompass.com/

ciating dollar and a declining budget deficit should reduce the private payments deficit are correct, then in the coming years the latter deficit should begin to subside.

Of course, other factors besides the exchange rate may adjust to changes in government spending and taxation policies or to monetary policy actions. A key factor that we have pushed into the background in this chapter is the *price level*. We shall return our attention to this important macroeconomic variable in the following chapter.

FUNDAMENTAL ISSUE #5

How does traditional Keynesian theory indicate that government budget deficits and private payments deficits might simultaneously be reduced or even eliminated? Holding other factors constant, increases in the budget deficit must be financed by selling government bonds, many of which are purchased by foreign residents using dollars that they obtain by selling their goods to Americans. Under high capital mobility and with a flexible exchange rate, the traditional Keynesian theory indicates that both government budget deficits and private payments deficits may be reduced, with other factors unchanged, if the dollar's value in terms of other currencies declines sufficiently.

CHAPTER SUMMARY

1. **How Government Spending Affects Real Income in the Traditional Keynesian Model**: The direct effect of an increase in government spending is a rise in real income equal to the increase in government spending times the autonomous expenditures multiplier. When real income increases, the demand for real money balances rises, which causes an increase in the equilibrium nominal interest rate. Given current expected inflation, this implies a rise in the real rate of interest. The result is a crowding-out effect, as desired real investment declines. Consequently, equilibrium real income rises by less than predicted by the simplest Keynesian multiplier model.

2. **How the Basic Keynesian Model Can Be Adapted to Account for Income Taxes**: This can be accomplished by recognizing that the government's net tax receipts are comprised of autonomous net taxes plus income taxes, which equal the average income tax rate times income. Consequently, the slope of the consumption function and the aggregate desired expenditures schedule vary with changes in the income tax rate. A reduction in the tax rate steepens these schedules, thereby causing a rise in equilibrium real income. At the same time, however, a tax rate cut makes equilibrium real income more sensitive to the effects of changes in autonomous aggregate expenditures.

3. **How Cuts in Income Tax Rates Affect the Government's Budget Deficit:** Holding government spending and real income unchanged, a reduction in the average income tax rate reduces the government's tax revenues and increases its deficit. Nevertheless, a cut in the income tax rate also causes equilibrium real income to increase. This, in turn, raises the government's income tax receipts. Therefore, at a sufficiently high tax rate, a reduction in the tax rate can actually cause the government's total tax revenues to increase.

4. **The Ricardian Equivalence Proposition:** According to this proposition, tax cuts cannot affect total consumption or aggregate desired expenditures. The logic leading to this proposition is that a current tax reduction causes the government's debt to increase, so that people will realize that this higher deficit implies higher future taxes. Consequently, they save the proceeds of a tax cut so that they or their offspring will be able to pay these higher future taxes. Although a number of economists are swayed by the logic of this position, others contend that it is weakened by shortsightedness, liquidity constraints, the fact that tax changes typically are made via changes in tax rates, other factors that motivate gifts and bequests, and income uncertainty.

5. **How Traditional Keynesian Theory Indicates That Government Budget Deficits and Private Payments Deficits Might Simultaneously Be Reduced or Even Eliminated:** Other things unchanged, increases in the budget deficit must be financed by selling government bonds, a number of which foreigners buy using dollars that they obtain by selling their goods to Americans. The traditional Keynesian model implies that under high capital mobility and with a flexible exchange rate, both deficits can be cut, holding other factors equal, if the dollar's value declines sufficiently relative to the values of other nations' currencies.

 # QUESTIONS AND PROBLEMS

1. Explain in your own words the distinction between the marginal income tax rate and the average income tax rate.

2. Provide a verbal description of the process by which an increase in government spending can crowd out private investment spending. Explain why the interest elasticities of money demand and of desired investment influence the extent of crowding out.

3. Suppose that the marginal propensity to save is equal to 0.20, the marginal propensity to import is equal to 0.05, and the income tax rate is equal to zero. How much would equilibrium real income rise following a $1 billion increase in government spending if desired investment is completely interest-inelastic? How much would equilibrium real income rise if desired investment is completely interest-elastic? Explain briefly.

4. Suppose that the marginal propensity to save is equal to 0.20 and the marginal propensity to import is equal to 0.05. Calculate the autonomous expenditures multiplier for each of the following values of the income tax rate, assuming that the income tax system is proportional (round to the nearest hundredth): (a) $\tau = 0.10$; (b) $\tau = 0.20$; (c) $\tau = 0.50$. For which tax rate would equilibrium real income be most stable in the face of a change in autonomous aggregate expenditures? Explain your answer.

5. Explain in your own words how the income tax system performs the role of "automatic stabilizer."

6. Why does a lump-sum tax cut *shift* the aggregate expenditures schedule, whereas a cut in the income tax rate *rotates* the aggregate expenditures schedule? Explain your answer.

7. Suppose that the peak of the Laffer curve is at an income tax rate of 18 percent and that the current income tax rate is 22 percent. If the government maintains its current spending level, then would a cut in the income tax rate to 19 percent increase or reduce the government's deficit? Explain.

8. Assuming that the Ricardian equivalence proposition is correct, would the structure of an income tax system be completely irrelevant? Take a stand, and support your answer.

9. Why do some economists view the fact that saving and government deficits were generally inversely related during the high-deficit period of the late 1980s and early 1990s as evidence against the applicability of Ricardian equivalence? Explain your reasoning.

10. Explain in your own words why capital mobility and exchange-rate flexibility matter for evaluating the response of the private payments balance to a reduction in government spending.

CYBERTUTOR EXERCISES

1. What is the effect of a fiscal expansion on the equilibrium domestic nominal interest rate, equilibrium domestic real income, and the equilibrium exchange rate?

2. What is the effect of a fiscal expansion on the equilibrium domestic nominal interest rate, equilibrium domestic real income, and exchange rate?

3. Figure 7–10 in the text seems to contradict the Ricardian equivalence proposition, which states that savings rates should rise as the federal deficit increases. Create a scatter plot of the savings rate and federal deficit. Does the Ricardian equivalence proposition still fail to hold? If so, what is the relationship between the savings rate and the federal deficit?

4. Figure 7–14 in the text shows the relationship between the value of the dollar, the federal budget deficit and the private payments deficit from 1976–1997. Plot this data for the period leading up to 1972. Is this experience similar to that which prevails after 1976? How can you explain this?

ON-LINE APPLICATION

A quick way to keep up with the federal government's spending and taxation is by examining federal budget data at the White House internet address.

Internet URL: http://www.whitehouse.gov/

Title: Federal Budget Data

Navigation: Begin at the White House homepage. Select *Interactive Citizen's Handbook*, and click on *White House Offices and Agencies*. Select *Office of Management and Budget*, and click on *The Budget of the United States Government, Fiscal Year 1998*. Select *Search* *documents, on-line and download individual sections of documents.* In search box, key in "Summary of Receipts."

Application: Read the article and answer the questions that follow:

1. Scan down to "Table 1.2—Summary of Receipts, Outlays, and Surpluses or Deficits, 1789–2002," and click on the "Txt" icon. In what year did the U.S. government first report separate "Off-Budget" and "On-Budget" items? By how much would the "total" deficit for 1998 increase if off-budget items were excluded?

2. In what year did the federal government last operate with a budget surplus? When does the Office of Management and Budget project that the government will experience an overall budget surplus?

SELECTED REFERENCES AND FURTHER READING

Blejer, Mario, and Adrienne Cheasty. "The Measurement of Fiscal Deficits: Analytical and Methodological Issues." *Journal of Economic Literature* 39 (December 4, 1991): 1644–1678.

Federal Reserve Bank of Kansas City. *Budget Deficits and Debt: Issues and Options.* 1995.

Hakkio, Craig. "The Effects of Budget Deficit Reduction on the Exchange Rate." Federal Reserve Bank of Kansas City *Economic Review*, Third Quarter 1996, pp. 21–38.

Schultze, Charles. "Is There a Bias toward Excess in U.S. Government Budgets or Deficits?" *Journal of Economic Perspectives* 6 (Spring 1992): 25–43.

Sill, D. Keith. "Managing the Public Debt." Federal Reserve Bank of Philadelphia *Business Review*, July–August 1994, pp. 3–13.

Thornton, Daniel. "Do Government Deficits Matter?" Federal Reserve Bank of St. Louis *Review*, September–October 1990, pp. 25–39.

8

Is There a Trade-off between Unemployment and Inflation?—

THE KEYNESIAN AND MONETARIST VIEWS ON PRICE AND OUTPUT DETERMINATION

FUNDAMENTAL ISSUES

1. What factors determine aggregate demand in the traditional Keynesian model?

2. What factors determine the shape and position of the Keynesian aggregate supply schedule?

3. According to traditional Keynesian theory, what are the price and output effects of expansionary fiscal and monetary policies?

4. What is the Phillips curve?

5. How does monetarism differ from the traditional Keynesian theory?

6. How do the political business cycle model and supply shocks together potentially explain both cyclical inflation and episodes of stagflation?

A standard topic in the financial press is whether the Federal Reserve is going to "tighten the screws" or loosen them. Reporters constantly ask economists and financial experts to predict what the Fed will do with interest rates. Will the Fed raise rates because the economy is heating up too much? Will it lower them because the economy is potentially going into a recession? Clearly, some experts strongly believe that there is a relationship between changes in monetary policy and the nation's employment, unemployment, and output.

These discussions rarely address a side issue, however, in that they fail to distinguish between real *and* nominal *interest rates. Historically, a high interest rate has been evidence that a country's central bank has followed* loose *monetary policy in the past rather than that it is following tight monetary policy now. In the long run, consistent increases in the rate of growth of the money supply lead to higher rates of inflation. A higher rate of inflation normally leads to expectations of inflation and therefore to higher* nominal *interest rates. In the long run, most evidence seems to show that the monetary authorities have little effect on an economy's real rate of interest.*

Whatever view one takes of the relationship between monetary policy, including what the Fed does with nominal interest rates, and the relationship between unemployment, inflation, output, and the like, these are important macroeconomic issues that must be addressed. We do so in this chapter.

Chapters 5–7 have developed the key features of the traditional Keynesian theory of short-run business cycles and of the potential roles that monetary and fiscal policy may play in helping to smooth these cycles. Absent from our discussion to this point, however, has been a consideration of the determination of the price level and inflation in the Keynesian framework. This chapter considers this issue, which most sharply divides traditional Keynesian theory from the classical framework of Chapter 3 and from the modern renditions of the classical perspective that we shall take up in Chapters 9 and 11. The basic Keynesian theory of price and inflation determination also provides a foundation for more modern Keynesian approaches to explaining business cycles, which we shall discuss in Chapters 10 and 11.

As you will learn in this chapter, the fundamental differences between Keynesian macroeconomics and the classical model or other alternative theories concern whether there is a short- or long-run relationship between output and inflation. According to the classical theory, output is determined independently from inflation. In contrast, the Keynesian theory indicates that increased output can be achieved by incurring higher inflation, which also implies that lower unemployment will be associated with higher inflation rates. The reason for this conclusion, it turns out, is that the traditional Keynesian theory of price and inflation determination is significantly different from the one proposed by proponents of the classical framework.

AGGREGATE DEMAND IN THE KEYNESIAN FRAMEWORK

According to the classical theory discussed in Chapter 3, aggregate demand depends primarily on the quantity of money supplied by a central bank such as the Federal Reserve. Consequently, the quantity of money is the main determinant of the position of the aggregate demand schedule, which in the classical model is the set of real output–price level combinations for which people are satisfied holding the quantity of money supplied.

The traditional Keynesian model also implies a theory of aggregate demand. This theory is richer than the classical theory, however. Although this does not mean that the Keynesian model is necessarily the correct approach to understanding aggregate demand, it does mean, as you will see, that the Keynesian approach to aggregate demand is more "general." The classical aggregate demand schedule, it turns out, is a "special case" of the Keynesian aggregate demand schedule.

The Keynesian Aggregate Demand Schedule

As you learned in Chapter 6, in the Keynesian *IS-LM* diagram, the point at which the *IS* schedule and the *LM* schedule cross represents a combination of the nominal interest rate and real income for which aggregate desired expenditures equal income at the same time that the market for real money balances is in equilibrium. In addition, however, the Keynesian framework also includes a *real balance effect* on the nominal interest rate stemming from changes in the price level. A rise in the price level reduces the supply of real money balances, thereby causing the nominal interest rate to rise at any given level of real income. This causes the *LM* schedule to shift upward and to the left.

Panel (a) of Figure 8–1 on page 256 shows the real balance effect in a full *IS-LM* equilibrium. The initial equilibrium point in panel (a) is point A. An increase in the price level, from P_1 to P_2, causes a real balance effect on the nominal interest rate. This shifts the *LM* schedule upward, from $LM(M_1/P_1)$ to $LM(M_1/P_2)$. As the nominal interest rate rises, however, desired investment spending declines. As a result, aggregate desired expenditures decline, inducing a fall in equilibrium real income. This decline in equilibrium real income from y_1 to y_2 causes a leftward movement along the *IS* schedule to point B. The fall in real income reduces the demand for real money balances, which places a somewhat offsetting downward pressure on the nominal interest rate, which on net thereby increases from r_1 to r_2.

Panel (b) of the figure illustrates that the fall in real income resulting from the real balance effect means that both real income–price level combinations, y_1 and P_1 at

FIGURE 8–1   DERIVING THE KEYNESIAN AGGREGATE DEMAND SCHEDULE

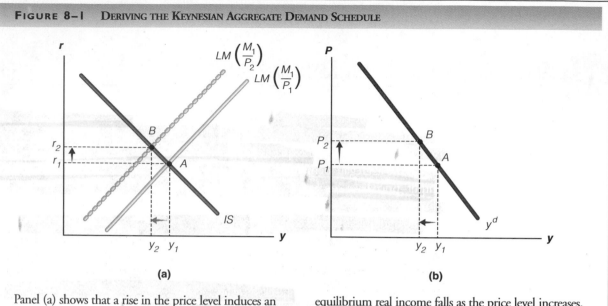

(a)   (b)

Panel (a) shows that a rise in the price level induces an increase in the equilibrium nominal interest rate through the real balance effect, as the *LM* schedule shifts back along the *IS* schedule from point *A* to point *B*. Because

equilibrium real income falls as the price level increases, the aggregate demand schedule containing the real income–price level combinations *A* and *B* slopes downward in panel (b).

point *A* and y_2 and P_2 at point *B*, are consistent with *IS-LM* equilibrium. Consequently, both of these real income–price level combinations maintain equilibrium real income and equilibrium in the market for real money balances. They are two possible combinations of real income and the price level that lie on a set of points that will maintain *IS-LM* equilibrium as the price level changes. This set of real income–price level combinations consistent with *IS-LM* equilibrium is the Keynesian aggregate demand schedule, denoted y^d. Thus:

> **The Keynesian theory of aggregate demand stems directly from the
> *IS-LM* model. At all price levels and real income levels along the
> Keynesian aggregate demand schedule, *IS-LM* equilibrium is attained.**

Monetary Policy and Aggregate Demand

In Figure 8–1, we derived the aggregate demand schedule by considering only the real balance effect arising from an increase in the price level. All other factors, including the nominal money stock, M_1, were unchanged. Hence, a change in other factors affecting the positions of the *IS* or *LM* schedules will alter the position of the aggregate demand schedule.

For instance, suppose that actions of the central bank increase the nominal quantity of money supplied from M_1 to a larger amount, M_2. Panel (a) of Figure 8–2 shows that at an initial real income–price level combination y_1 and P_1 at point A, the rise in the nominal money stock will induce a downward and rightward shift of the LM schedule. There is a new IS-LM equilibrium at point B. The liquidity effect arising from the increase in the nominal money stock will reduce the nominal interest rate from r_1 to r_2, and equilibrium real income will rise, from y_1 to y_2.

The real income–price level combination y_2 and P_2 lies to the right of the original aggregate demand schedule, denoted $y^d(M_1)$ in panel (b). Nevertheless, this new point B in panel (b) is consistent with the IS-LM equilibrium at point B in panel (a). Because the Keynesian aggregate demand schedule is a set of real income–price level combinations that maintain IS-LM equilibrium, point B in panel (b) is on a *new* aggregate demand schedule. Consequently, a rise in the nominal quantity of money will shift the aggregate demand schedule to the right. That is, a rise in the nominal money stock will *increase aggregate demand.*

In contrast, a reduction in the nominal money stock will shift the LM schedule to the left, causing equilibrium real income to fall at any given price level. The aggregate

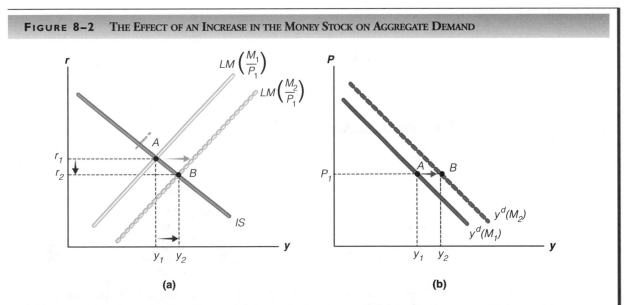

FIGURE 8–2 THE EFFECT OF AN INCREASE IN THE MONEY STOCK ON AGGREGATE DEMAND

With an unchanged price level, an increase in the nominal quantity of money in circulation causes an increase in the amount of real money balances and shifts the LM schedule downward and to the right along the IS schedule from point A to point B in panel (a). Because the resulting real income level at point B in panel (b) corresponds to the same price level, this new equilibrium real income–price level combination lies on a new aggregate demand schedule to the right of the real income–price level combination at point A on the original aggregate demand schedule. Thus, an increase in the nominal money stock will cause an increase in aggregate demand to $y^d(M_2)$.

demand schedule will shift leftward as a result of the fall in the nominal quantity of money supplied. Thus, a decline in the nominal money stock will reduce aggregate demand.

It is important to recognize that the amount aggregate demand shifts as a result of a change in the money stock depends on the size of the liquidity effect that the change in the money stock exerts. The size of the liquidity effect, in turn, depends on the relative elasticities of *IS* and *LM*. As discussed in Chapter 6, these relative elasticities depend on the interest elasticity of desired investment to spending and on the interest elasticity of money demand, respectively. In other words, the size of the effect of a change in the money stock on aggregate demand depends on the linkages of the Keynesian monetary policy transmission mechanism. As you learned in Chapter 6, the linkages in this mechanism strengthen as the *LM* schedule becomes more inelastic (as the demand for real money balances becomes more interest inelastic) and as the *IS* schedule becomes more elastic (as desired investment spending becomes more interest elastic).

It follows that the effects of monetary policy actions on aggregate demand become larger as the *LM* schedule becomes more inelastic. In the extreme case in which the *LM* schedule is perfectly inelastic, so that money demand is completely interest inelastic, monetary policy actions have the largest possible effects on aggregate demand. This case corresponds to the situation in the classical model of Chapter 3. Changes in the nominal interest rate had no effect on desired money holdings, which were determined by the Cambridge equation of money demand, so the classical version of the *LM* schedule is perfectly inelastic. In this sense, therefore, the classical model's aggregate demand schedule is a "special case" of the Keynesian aggregate demand schedule.

Fiscal Policy and Aggregate Demand

In Chapter 3, we showed that in the classical model, deficit-financed government spending completely crowds out an equal-sized amount of private spending. The classical model thereby indicates that fiscal policy actions have no effect on aggregate demand, but simply redistribute existing goods and services between the government and the private sector. As discussed in the last chapter, however, the traditional Keynesian framework proposes that the fiscal crowding-out effect is incomplete. As a result, fiscal policy should be able to influence aggregate demand in traditional Keynesian theory.

Figure 8–3 demonstrates that this reasoning is correct. Panel (a) displays the *IS-LM* effects of a rise in real government expenditures, from g_1 to g_2, with the price level unchanged at P_1. The immediate result is a rightward shift in the *IS* schedule by the amount of the increase in government spending times the autonomous spending multiplier, $1/(1 - MPC)$. The rise in real income causes the demand for real money balances to rise, which, in turn, leads to a rise in the equilibrium nominal interest rate that will cause desired real investment spending to decline. Crowding out

---

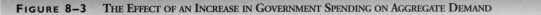

FIGURE 8–3   THE EFFECT OF AN INCREASE IN GOVERNMENT SPENDING ON AGGREGATE DEMAND

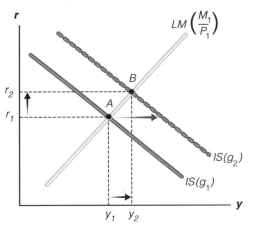

(a)

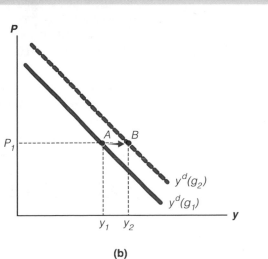

(b)

With an unchanged price level, an increase in government spending will shift the *IS* schedule rightward along the *LM* schedule from point *A* to point *B* in panel (a). The resulting real income level at point *B* in panel (b) corresponds to the same price level. This new equilibrium real income–price level combination will be located on a new aggregate demand schedule to the right of the real income–price level combination at point *A* on the original aggregate demand schedule. Consequently, an increase in government spending will cause an increase in aggregate demand to $y^d(g_2)$.

---

is not complete, however, so equilibrium real income will rise, from y_1 at point *A* to y_2 at point *B*.

Point *B* in panel (a) is a new *IS-LM* equilibrium, so the real income–price level combination y_2 and P_1 must lie on a new aggregate demand schedule at point *B* in panel (b). That is, the rise in government spending shifts the aggregate demand schedule outward and to the right, which means that the rise in real government expenditures will raise aggregate demand.

It is important to recognize that changes in private spending have an analogous effect on aggregate demand. For instance, an autonomous increase in consumption spending or net export spending also will shift the *IS* schedule rightward, thereby causing an increase in aggregate demand.

Note that a tax cut will have the same basic effects as a rise in government spending. In the case of a lump-sum tax reduction, the only difference is that the *IS* schedule will shift rightward by the amount of the tax cut times the tax multiplier, $-MPC/(1 - MPC)$. In the more realistic case of a cut in the income tax rate, the *IS* schedule will shift by a different amount, but again aggregate demand will rise.

The extent to which fiscal policy actions can influence aggregate demand depends on how much crowding out occurs. As you learned in Chapter 7, the extent of the crowding out effect increases as the *LM* schedule becomes more inelastic (as the demand for real money balances becomes more interest inelastic) and as the *IS* schedule becomes more elastic (as desired investment spending becomes more interest elastic). In the extreme case when the *LM* schedule is perfectly inelastic and the *IS* schedule is perfectly elastic, crowding out is complete, and fiscal policy has no influence on aggregate demand in the economy. Hence, if money demand is completely interest inelastic and desired investment is completely interest elastic, the traditional Keynesian model mimics the classical theory's prediction that fiscal policy cannot affect aggregate demand. More generally, however, the Keynesian model proposes a potential role for fiscal policy in influencing aggregate demand, prices, and real output. To understand how both fiscal and monetary policy may exert short-run effects on prices and real output, however, we must develop the Keynesian theory of how these macroeconomic variables are determined.

FUNDAMENTAL ISSUE #1

What factors determine aggregate demand in the traditional Keynesian model? Two key factors influence the position of the Keynesian aggregate demand schedule. One is the set of elements that together compose autonomous aggregate expenditures, such as government spending and taxation and autonomous consumption, investment, and net exports. The other is the nominal money stock. As a result, both fiscal and monetary policy actions can influence the position of the Keynesian aggregate demand schedule.

KEYNESIAN AGGREGATE SUPPLY: STICKY NOMINAL WAGES

Recall from Chapter 3 that the classical economists made three important assumptions when they examined the market for labor and derived the classical aggregate supply schedule:

1. Workers, consumers, and entrepreneurs are motivated by rational self-interest.
2. People do not experience money illusion.
3. Pure competition prevails in the markets for goods and services and for factors of production.

Proponents of the Keynesian approach to aggregate supply typically have no trouble accepting the first classical proposition. They doubt the generality of the latter two assumptions, however. The Keynesians argue that because information is imperfect, in the short run people have no choice but to exhibit money illusion, even if they are rationally motivated by self-interest. In addition, they contend that self interest can induce workers and firms to set up institutional arrangements that inhibit pure competition, thereby making wages and prices less than fully flexible. We begin our discussion of the Keynesian approach to aggregate supply by considering the effects of wage stickiness (we postpone the slightly more complicated issue of potential price inflexibilities until Chapter 11). Then we discuss the implications of imperfect information for the theory of aggregate supply.

Explaining Wage Inflexibility

Why might nominal wages be inflexible, or "sticky"? One possible explanation is the existence of minimum-wage laws that place artificial floors on wages that firms can pay. Other factors that could artificially boost workers' effective nominal compensation, such as legal impediments to nominal wage cuts, also might make nominal wages sticky, at least in a downward direction.

ON THE WEB
Visit the AFL-CIO at:
http://www.aflcio.org

Another potential reason for wage inflexibility is the widespread unionization of a nation's work force. Organized groups of workers may seek to keep their nominal wages at levels that they feel are appropriate relative to other occupations. In a highly unionized economy, **explicit contracts**—legally binding contracts laying out the terms for workers' compensation, benefits, and so on—establish wages for specified periods, such as one, two, or three years. Union contracts typically allow wages to rise above specified levels but do not permit wages to fall below those levels, even though some workers are laid off as a result. Consequently, widespread unionization could also account for downward inflexibility of the nominal wage.

EXPLICIT CONTRACTS Contractual arrangements in which the terms of relationships between workers and firms, especially about wages, are in writing and legally binding upon both parties.

Of course, wage contracts are not limited to unionized industries. Many white-collar workers, for instance, have explicit contracts with their employers. In addition, a number of labor economists contend that workers and firms adopt **implicit contracts**. These are tacit agreements that firms will not reduce workers' wages when economic activity ebbs in exchange for the right not to raise wages as much as the market wage would indicate when business conditions improve. In effect, such a contract is an insurance scheme: Workers pay an insurance premium in the form of lower-than-market wages in good times in exchange for insurance coverage in the form of higher-than-market wages in bad times. Widespread use of implicit contracts could result in relatively rigid nominal wages across upturns and downturns of business cycles.

IMPLICIT CONTRACTS Unwritten agreements between workers and firms, concerning terms of employment such as wages; the agreements may or may not be legally binding.

Proponents of the view that nominal wages are inflexible typically offer one or more of these rationales for their position. We shall discuss the real-world evidence on the importance of contracts in the U.S. economy in greater detail in Chapter 10. For now, let's try to evaluate how widespread nominal wage inflexibility will affect the theory of aggregate supply.

Wage Stickiness and the Aggregate Supply Schedule

Recall from Chapter 3 that the aggregate supply schedule for an economy is the set of real output–price level combinations that maintain labor-market equilibrium. To see how nominal wage inflexibility affects the nature of the aggregate supply schedule, consider Figure 8–4. Panel (a) is a diagram of the labor market with the nominal wage measured on the vertical axis. Panel (b) shows the aggregate production function. Panel (c) is a diagram of real output–price level combinations.

FIGURE 8–4 THE KEYNESIAN AGGREGATE SUPPLY SCHEDULE WITH WAGE INFLEXIBILITY

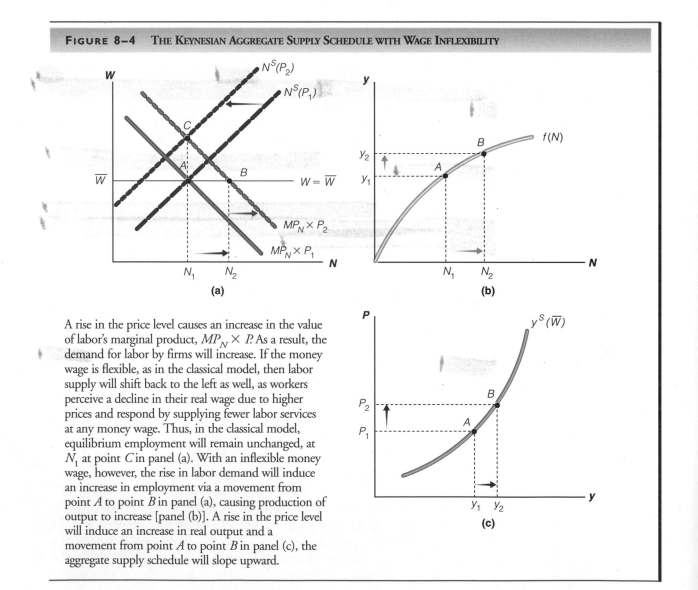

A rise in the price level causes an increase in the value of labor's marginal product, $MP_N \times P$. As a result, the demand for labor by firms will increase. If the money wage is flexible, as in the classical model, then labor supply will shift back to the left as well, as workers perceive a decline in their real wage due to higher prices and respond by supplying fewer labor services at any money wage. Thus, in the classical model, equilibrium employment will remain unchanged, at N_1 at point C in panel (a). With an inflexible money wage, however, the rise in labor demand will induce an increase in employment via a movement from point A to point B in panel (a), causing production of output to increase [panel (b)]. A rise in the price level will induce an increase in real output and a movement from point A to point B in panel (c), the aggregate supply schedule will slope upward.

In the classical model, the labor supply schedule slopes upward, as shown by the dashed schedule $N^s(P_1)$ in panel (a). If the general level of nominal wages is determined by legal requirements and explicit and implicit contracts, however, the aggregate wage rate in the economy may be regarded as fixed in the short run, at $W = \overline{W}$. This means that workers supply whatever amount of labor that firms demand at this nominal wage. Recall from Chapter 3 that if the price level is P_1, then the value-of-marginal-product schedule, $MP_N \times P_1$, represents the labor demand schedule. Consequently, at the fixed nominal wage $W = \overline{W}$, the amount of labor demanded is equal to N_1 at point A in panel (a). Referring to the aggregate production function in panel (b), this yields the level of real output y_1. Consequently, at the price level P_1, the real output level consistent with equilibrium employment with a fixed nominal wage $\overline{W}$ is y_1. This is one point, labeled point A in panel (c), on the economy's aggregate supply schedule.

Now consider the effect of a rise in the price level, from P_1 to P_2. This causes the value of labor's marginal product to rise to $MP_N \times P_2$. Hence, the demand for labor in panel (a) will increase. In the classical model, the labor supply will then decline, from $N^s(P_1)$ to $N^s(P_2)$, as workers recognize that the rise in the price level reduces the real wage that they earn. Thus, in the classical theory the resulting labor-market equilibrium is at point C, with no change in employment. If nominal wages are fixed through laws and contracts, however, then the classical labor supply schedule no longer plays any role, and point C is not attained. Instead, the rise in labor demand leads to an increase in employment to N_2, at point B in panel (a). As a result, real output rises to y_2 in panel (b). The result is a new real output–price level combination y_2 and P_2 at point B in panel (c).

Points A and B are both consistent with fixed-wage equilibrium outcomes in the labor market. Therefore, both of these points lie on an upward-sloping *Keynesian aggregate supply schedule*. Because we have derived this aggregate supply schedule under the assumption that the nominal wage is fixed at $W = \overline{W}$, we label it $y^s(\overline{W})$. Note also that the aggregate supply schedule is convex, or bowed upward. It has this shape because the production function is concave, or bowed downward (due to the law of diminishing marginal returns). Therefore, successive increases in the price level stimulate increases in labor demand and employment that induce successively smaller gains in real output production.

Finally, because we derive the aggregate supply schedule for a *given* fixed wage, a change in the fixed nominal wage rate will require us to derive a new aggregate supply schedule. At a higher nominal wage, employment levels and, hence, corresponding output levels will always be lower. As a result, if the fixed nominal wage increases, the amounts of real output corresponding to various price levels will be lower, and the aggregate supply schedule will lie to the left of its original position. A rise in the nominal wage, perhaps as a result of union demands for wage increases or from an increase in the legal minimum wage, will shift the aggregate supply schedule upward and to the left. The higher value for the fixed nominal wage will reduce aggregate supply.

KEYNESIAN AGGREGATE SUPPLY: IMPERFECT INFORMATION

As we noted earlier, proponents of the Keynesian approach also disagree with the classical assumption that people never exhibit money illusion. Economists typically believe that well-informed people always care about their real wages. Therefore, if people did possess complete information, the classical and Keynesian theorists would not disagree on this issue. If people live in a world of uncertainty, however, then information about the actual price level may not always be available. Furthermore, people are never fully informed about *future* events. These observations form the basis for an alternative Keynesian theory of aggregate supply.

The Sources of Uncertainty

Let's consider a worker's decision to supply labor services today. He may have a reasonably good idea about some specific prices of goods and services today, because he has made recent trips to retail stores. Nevertheless, he will not have up-to-date information about prices at all stores. Nor will he have full information about how prices may have changed at stores that he recently visited. Certainly, he can consult newspaper ads, and he could even subscribe to government and Federal Reserve publications that report recent price indexes. Nevertheless, ads constitute small samples, and reliable price index numbers are available only on a monthly basis, after the fact. The worker's information about the overall price level will always be somewhat uncertain.

This means that when our worker tries to decide how much labor to supply, he must base his decision on his *perception* of what the current real wage is and on his *anticipation* of what it will be during the period when he agrees to work at that wage. In other words, he must form an *expectation* of the value of the real wage that he will earn if he works at any given nominal wage that a firm offers him. To do this, he must form an expectation of the price level, which we shall denote P^e.

Imperfect Information and Aggregate Supply

To see how imperfect information motivates a Keynesian theory of aggregate supply, consider Figure 8–5. Here, we assume that nominal wages are flexible (we shall consider wage contracts in the presence of imperfect information in Chapter 10). Consequently, as in the classical model, the equilibrium nominal wage is determined by the intersection of the labor demand and labor supply schedules in panel (a). As in the classical theory, we assume that if the current price level is equal to P_1, then the labor demand schedule is the value of labor's marginal product, $MP_N \times P_1$. If workers base their labor supply decisions on their anticipation of the overall price level, however, the position of the labor supply schedule depends on their price expectation. Let's suppose that the specific value of this price expectation is $P^e = P_1$, so that workers anticipate that the price level during their period of employment will be

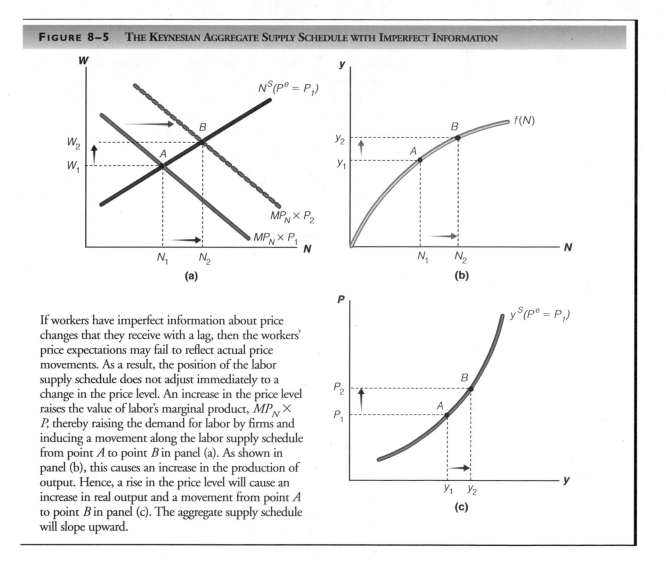

FIGURE 8–5   **THE KEYNESIAN AGGREGATE SUPPLY SCHEDULE WITH IMPERFECT INFORMATION**

If workers have imperfect information about price changes that they receive with a lag, then the workers' price expectations may fail to reflect actual price movements. As a result, the position of the labor supply schedule does not adjust immediately to a change in the price level. An increase in the price level raises the value of labor's marginal product, $MP_N \times P$, thereby raising the demand for labor by firms and inducing a movement along the labor supply schedule from point A to point B in panel (a). As shown in panel (b), this causes an increase in the production of output. Hence, a rise in the price level will cause an increase in real output and a movement from point A to point B in panel (c). The aggregate supply schedule will slope upward.

equal to P_1, and the position of the labor supply schedule is given by $N^s(P^e = P_1)$. Consequently, at point A in each panel of Figure 8–5, workers correctly anticipate the *actual* price level. Given this correct expectation, the equilibrium nominal wage in panel (a) is equal to W_1, and equilibrium employment is equal to N_1. The amount of real output produced is equal to y_1 in panel (b), and the resulting real output–price level combination is P_1 and y_1 in panel (c).

Suppose however, that the price level rises to P_2, above the value P_1 that workers expected. Because information about this change is not readily available, workers do not immediately recognize that this price change has taken place. Thus, they maintain their price expectation at $P^e = P_1$, and the position of the labor supply schedule in panel (a) does not change. Firms, however, observe the rise in the prices of the goods and services that they sell and the resulting increase in the value of labor's marginal product, to $MP_N \times P_2$. As a result, labor demand rises, and the equilibrium nominal wage increases to W_2 at point B in panel (a).

Because workers do not have sufficient information to realize that the nominal wage has risen because of an increase in the price level, they perceive the increase in the nominal wage as an increase in the real wage. Workers therefore supply more labor services, as shown by the movement upward along the labor supply schedule to the new equilibrium employment level N_2 at point B. As panel (b) shows, this rise in employment then induces an increase in real output, from y_1 to y_2. As a result, there is a new real output–price level combination, y_2 and P_2 at point B in panel (c), that lies above and to the right of the original combination at point A. The schedule containing both point A and point B is the aggregate supply schedule. We label this schedule $y^s(P^e = P_1)$, because we have derived it given this specific value for workers' expected price level.

Now consider what would happen if workers were to raise their price expectation. This would shift the labor supply schedule back to the left somewhat. Then we could derive another aggregate supply schedule like the one in Figure 8–5, except that for any given price level we would plot lower employment and output levels. Consequently, the aggregate supply schedule that we would derive would lie to the left of the one in Figure 8–5. We can conclude that a rise in the expected price level will shift the aggregate supply schedule leftward. In other words, higher price expectations will reduce aggregate supply.

This Keynesian aggregate supply schedule, like the one we derived for the case of inflexible nominal wages, slopes upward and has a convex, or bowed, shape. In this case, however, the rationale for the slope and shape of the aggregate supply schedule is imperfect information. As you can see, removing *either* the classical assumption of pure, unhindered determination of market wages *or* the classical presumption that no basis exists for worker money illusion is sufficient to produce an upward-sloping aggregate supply schedule. We may conclude that in the Keynesian model there is a positive relationship between the price level and the amount of real output produced by firms.

FUNDAMENTAL ISSUE #2

What factors determine the shape and position of the Keynesian aggregate supply schedule? There are two Keynesian theories of aggregate supply, and both imply that the aggregate supply schedule slopes upward and is convex. One proposes that nominal wages are inflexible. According to this theory, a rise in nominal wages following union demands for higher wages or increases in a legal wage minimum will shift the aggregate supply schedule upward and to the left. The

> other theory follows from the assumption that workers have imperfect information about the price level. This theory indicates that a rise in the expected price level will shift the aggregate supply schedule upward and to the left.

THE KEYNESIAN MARKET FOR REAL OUTPUT

Let's summarize the traditional Keynesian theories of aggregate demand and aggregate supply. The Keynesian aggregate demand schedule is the set of all combinations of real income (output) that maintain *IS-LM* equilibrium or, in other words, in which aggregate desired expenditures equal real income and the quantity of real money balances demanded equals the quantity of real money balances supplied. The aggregate demand schedule slopes downward, and its position depends on the nominal money stock and on factors that influence aggregate autonomous expenditures, including fiscal policy instruments such as government spending and taxation.

The Keynesian aggregate supply schedule slopes upward, either because nominal wages are inflexible or because workers have imperfect information concerning the price level. For the remainder of this chapter, we shall simply draw the aggregate supply schedule as upward sloping (and convex) and offer a specific rationale for the upward slope only when doing so is required for the purposes of the specific issue under consideration.

Combining Aggregate Demand and Aggregate Supply

Figure 8–6 on page 268 combines the two schedules on a single diagram of the market for real output. They intersect at point *E*, where the equilibrium price level, labeled P_1, is determined. Several conditions hold simultaneously at point *E*:

1. Because point *E* is on the aggregate demand schedule, the economy is operating on its *IS* schedule, and aggregate desired expenditures are equal to the level of real income y_1.
2. Because point *E* is on the aggregate demand schedule, the economy is operating on its *LM* schedule, and the quantity of real money balances demanded at this real income level y_1 is equal to the real value of the quantity of money balances supplied, evaluated at the price level P_1.
3. Because point *E* is on the aggregate supply schedule, workers and firms are willing and able to produce the level of real output y_1 at the price level P_1.

Point *E* satisfies all of these conditions *given* the factors that determine the positions of the aggregate demand and aggregate supply schedules. Changes in aggregate desired expenditures or in the nominal money stock, which may be induced by fis-

FIGURE 8–6 **EQUILIBRIUM IN THE KEYNESIAN MARKET FOR REAL OUTPUT**

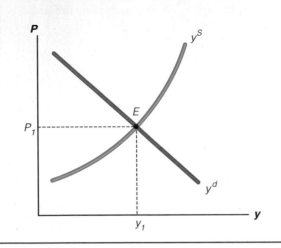

In the Keynesian model, the equilibrium price level and the equilibrium level of real output arise at the intersection of the aggregate demand and aggregate supply schedules. This point, denoted *E,* is on the aggregate demand schedule and corresponds to a point of *IS-LM* equilibrium. Therefore, the market for real money balances is in equilibrium, and real income is equal to aggregate desired expenditures. At the same time, this point is on the aggregate supply schedule so at the price level P_1 corresponding to point *E,* workers and firms are willing and able to produce the equilibrium real output level.

cal and monetary policy actions, can change the positions of the schedules and thereby alter the location of point *E.*

Fiscal Policy, Prices, and Real Output

Recall that in the classical model of Chapter 3, fiscal policy actions leave both real output and the price level unaffected. The reason is that changes in government spending or taxes only cause redistributions of existing output. Hence, they are unable to affect the position of the classical aggregate demand schedule.

In contrast, fiscal policy actions typically influence equilibrium real output and prices in the traditional Keynesian model. To see why, consider Figure 8–7. In panel (b), the economy begins at point *E* at an equilibrium price level equal to P_1 and an equilibrium real output level y_1. Because point *E* in panel (b) is on the aggregate demand schedule, there is a corresponding *IS-LM* equilibrium at point *E* in panel (a). Suppose that government expenditures increase from an initial amount g_1 to g_2. This fiscal policy action will shift the *IS* schedule rightward from $IS(g_1)$ to $IS(g_2)$ in panel (a), causing real income to rise toward y_3 at point *F.* The aggregate demand schedule will shift rightward by the amount of this increase in real income on the *IS-LM* diagram, or the distance from point *E* to point *F,* in panel (b).

Following the rise in aggregate demand from $y^d(g_1)$ to $y^d(g_2)$, however, workers and firms will not produce all the output demanded by households, firms, and the government at the price level P_1. Workers and firms will be willing to increase production of real output only if the price level rises toward a new equilibrium value equal to P_2. Hence, there will be a movement upward along the aggregate supply schedule in panel (b), from point *F* to point *E'.* The rise in the price level will cause

FIGURE 8–7   THE PRICE AND OUTPUT EFFECTS OF A RISE IN GOVERNMENT EXPENDITURES

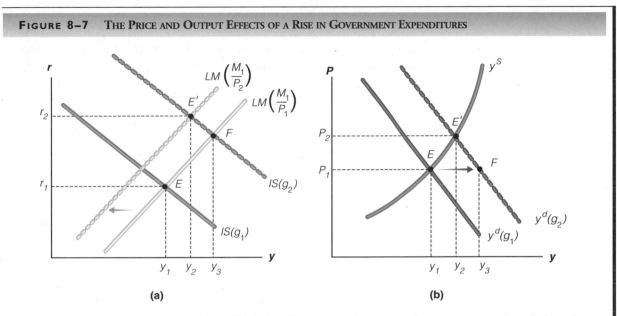

(a)   (b)

An increase in real government spending will shift the *IS* schedule rightward along the *LM* schedule, causing a movement from point *E* to point *F* in panel (a) and inducing a rightward shift of the aggregate demand schedule by the distance *E–F* in panel (b). Workers and firms will be willing to produce more real output, however, only if the price level increases as shown by the

upward movement from point *E* to point *E'* along the aggregate supply schedule in panel (b). This increase in the price level will reduce the quantity of real money balances, thereby shifting the *LM* schedule leftward in panel (a). On net, the increase in real government expenditures leads to a rise in the equilibrium price level and an increase in the equilibrium level of real output.

real money balances to decline, which will result in a leftward shift of the *LM* schedule in panel (a). This shift implies a movement upward along the new aggregate demand schedule in panel (b), from point *F* to point *E'*, to the final equilibrium real output level, y_2.

The net effect, therefore, of an increase in real government expenditures is a rise in both the equilibrium real output and the equilibrium price level. Note that a tax reduction will induce analogous effects. Indeed, any rise in net autonomous aggregate expenditures, such as a rise in autonomous investment, consumption, or exports will induce a rise in equilibrium output and prices.

Monetary Policy, Prices, and Real Output

In the classical model discussed in Chapter 3, monetary policy actions are able to influence aggregate demand, but because the aggregate supply schedule is vertical, money stock changes have no effect on equilibrium real output. As a result, in the classical macroeconomic model, money is said to be neutral.

Money is nonneutral in the traditional Keynesian macroeconomic framework. To understand why this is so, consider Figure 8–8. At an initial output-market equilibrium at point E in panel (b), with the nominal stock M_1, the aggregate demand schedule is given by $y^d(M_1)$, and the equilibrium price level and quantity of real output are equal to P_1 and y_1, respectively. This output-market equilibrium point must correspond to point E on the *IS-LM* diagram in panel (a). Suppose now that the central bank raises the nominal money stock from M_1 to M_2. This action will cause the *LM* schedule to shift to the right in panel (a), from $LM(M_1/P_1)$ to $LM(M_2/P_1)$, resulting in a new *IS-LM* equilibrium at point F, at the higher real income level y_3. The aggregate demand schedule in panel (b) will shift rightward by the same amount, the distance from point E to point F.

After the rightward shift in aggregate demand from $y^d(M_1)$ to $y^d(M_2)$, workers and firms continue to produce only the real output level y_1 at the price level P_1 in panel (b). Firms will increase their production only if the price level increases to the

---

FIGURE 8–8   THE PRICE AND OUTPUT EFFECTS OF A RISE IN THE MONEY STOCK

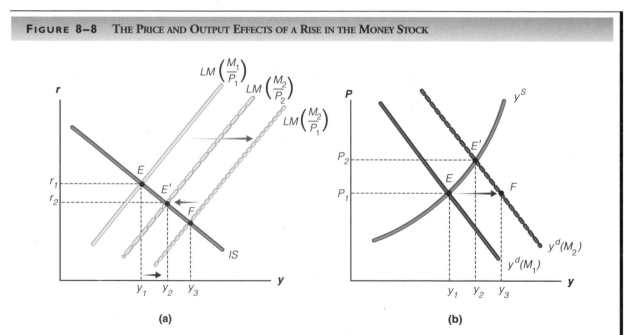

(a)

(b)

An increase in the nominal quantity of money in circulation will shift the *LM* schedule downward and to the right, thereby causing a movement from point E to point F in panel (a) and inducing a rightward shift of the aggregate demand schedule by the distance $E–F$ in panel (b). Nevertheless, workers and firms will be willing to produce more real output only if the price level increases, as shown by the upward movement from point E to point

E' along the aggregate supply schedule in panel (b). This increase in the price level will reduce the quantity of real money balances, thereby shifting the *LM* schedule back up and to the left in panel (a). On net, the increase in the money stock lead to a rise in the equilibrium price level and an increase in the equilibrium level of real output.

new equilibrium level, P_2. This increase will induce a movement upward along the aggregate supply schedule in panel (b), from point F to point E'. The rise in the price level will cause a decline in the amount of real money balances, so the LM schedule will shift back to the left, from $LM(M_2/P_1)$ to $LM(M_2/P_2)$ in panel (a). This will cause a movement back along the new aggregate demand schedule in panel (b), from point F to point E', and a fall in the quantity of real output demanded, to y_2.

On net, therefore, a central bank expansion of the nominal money stock increases both the equilibrium price level *and* equilibrium real output. Because monetary policy is nonneutral in the traditional Keynesian model, proponents of this model typically prescribe expansionary or contractionary monetary policy actions to stabilize real economic activity. The notion that the Federal Reserve and other central banks can stabilize real output—and, by implication, employment—contrasts sharply with the classical position, which contends that price-level stabilization is all that monetary policy can accomplish.

FUNDAMENTAL ISSUE #3

According to traditional Keynesian theory, what are the price and output effects of expansionary fiscal and monetary policies? In the Keynesian aggregate demand-aggregate supply model, a rise in government expenditures, a tax cut, or an increase in the nominal money stock will cause an increase in aggregate demand. The result will be a rise in the equilibrium price level and an increase in equilibrium real output.

THE PHILLIPS CURVE

Speculation about Federal Reserve actions to "spur employment" or "slow the pace of economic growth" appears every week or two in such financial news publications as the *Wall Street Journal.* Many media commentators also discuss the pros and cons of using monetary and fiscal policy actions to reduce the unemployment rate. Periodically, politicians debate the merits of policy proposals aimed at such goals.

The prevalence of these discussions indicates how widely the Keynesian model has influenced thinking about macroeconomic policy. These discussions are consistent with traditional Keynesian theory, which predicts an inverse relationship between the inflation rate, which Federal Reserve policies can influence, and the unemployment rate. This proposed inverse relationship is widely known as the *Phillips curve*, and it has been a controversial topic in modern macroeconomics.

The Origins of the Phillips Curve

The Phillips curve is named for its discoverer, A. W. Phillips, who conducted a study of British data. He found strong evidence for an inverse relationship between nominal wages and unemployment rates. Other economists then noticed that nominal wages typically moved in the same direction as the inflation rate. This led to the idea of plotting the inflation rate and the unemployment rate on the same diagram. The result was the modern **Phillips curve**, which is a plot of the relationship between unemployment and inflation rates for a given period.

Figure 8–9 displays unemployment rate–inflation rate combinations for the United States from 1961 to 1969. As you can see, during that interval there was a strikingly smooth, inverse relationship between the two macroeconomic variables. Higher inflation rates were associated with lower rates of unemployment. (See, however, the Global Notebook: *Can European Policymakers Exploit the Phillips Curve?*)

The Keynesian Model and the Phillips Curve

The discovery of the Phillips curve appeared to support the Keynesian theory of aggregate supply. To see why this is so, consider Figure 8–11. Panel (a) displays a Keynesian aggregate supply schedule together with four possible positions of the aggregate demand schedule and, hence, four possible points of aggregate output-market equilibrium. Panel (b) shows the aggregate production function. Panel (c) depicts a

PHILLIPS CURVE A curve that shows an inverse relationship between inflation and unemployment rates.

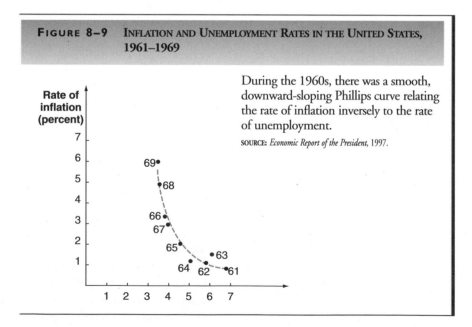

FIGURE 8–9 **INFLATION AND UNEMPLOYMENT RATES IN THE UNITED STATES, 1961–1969**

During the 1960s, there was a smooth, downward-sloping Phillips curve relating the rate of inflation inversely to the rate of unemployment.

SOURCE: *Economic Report of the President*, 1997.

GLOBAL NOTEBOOK:

Can European Policymakers Exploit the Phillips Curve?

The data for the United States in Figure 8–9 show an inverse relationship between the rate of inflation and the rate of unemployment between 1961 and 1969. Should we conclude that this relationship is a universal phenomenon? Figure 8–10 suggests that we should not. As Figure 8–10 shows, the unemployment rate in Europe remained almost constant from 1967 to 1974 in spite of an increasing inflation rate.

Even if one believes in the Phillips curve analysis, the possibility that European policymakers can reduce their double-digit unemployment rates (the average for the European Union is above 11 percent) by creating higher rates of inflation seems remote. According to Figure 8–10, the relation-ship between European unemployment and inflation from the 1960s through the 1990s has never been consistent enough to be utilized by policymakers.

Additionally, two British economists, David Blansch Clower and Andrew Oswald, conducted more complete research. They looked at additional data across twelve European countries and concluded that there has never been a consistent relationship between unemployment and inflation in those countries.

FOR CRITICAL ANALYSIS:

Does Figure 8–10 "prove" that there is not an inverse relationship between unemployment and inflation?

ON THE WEB
Visit the European Union at:
http://www.europa.eu.int

FIGURE 8–10   INFLATION AND UNEMPLOYMENT RATES IN EUROPE, 1967–1995

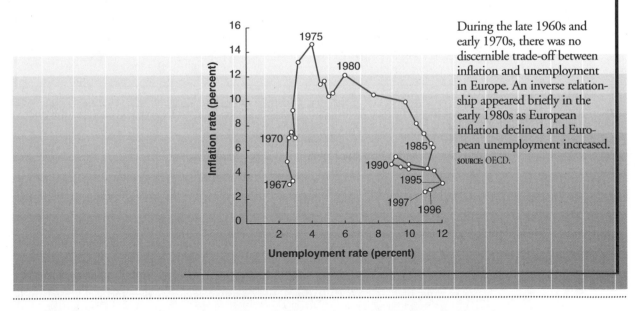

During the late 1960s and early 1970s, there was no discernible trade-off between inflation and unemployment in Europe. An inverse relationship appeared briefly in the early 1980s as European inflation declined and European unemployment increased. SOURCE: OECD.

FIGURE 8–11 THE THEORETICAL BASIS FOR THE PHILLIPS CURVE

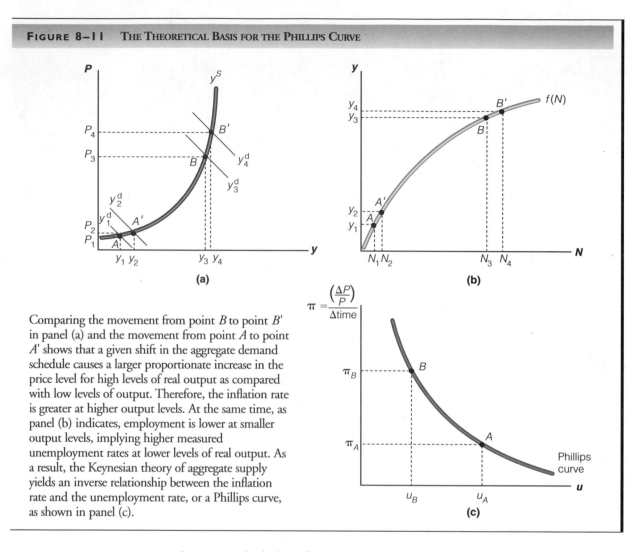

Comparing the movement from point *B* to point *B'* in panel (a) and the movement from point *A* to point *A'* shows that a given shift in the aggregate demand schedule causes a larger proportionate increase in the price level for high levels of real output as compared with low levels of output. Therefore, the inflation rate is greater at higher output levels. At the same time, as panel (b) indicates, employment is lower at smaller output levels, implying higher measured unemployment rates at lower levels of real output. As a result, the Keynesian theory of aggregate supply yields an inverse relationship between the inflation rate and the unemployment rate, or a Phillips curve, as shown in panel (c).

diagram in which the inflation rate, π, is measured on the vertical axis and the unemployment rate, u, is measured on the horizontal axis.

Deriving the Phillips Curve Now consider two extreme cases: a sharp, aggregate demand–induced recession versus a significant aggregate demand–induced economic expansion. Let's contemplate the recession first. This situation results from relatively low levels of aggregate demand, as illustrated by the positions y_1^d and y_2^d on the aggregate demand schedule in panel (a), which lead to relatively low equilibrium output levels y_1 and y_2, respectively, at points *A* and *A'*. Note that a movement from point *A* to point *A'* causes a relatively small increase in the price level, from P_1 to P_2. Because the rate of inflation is the proportionate change in the level of prices per unit of time, or $\pi = (\Delta P/P)/(\Delta \text{time})$, such a rise in aggregate demand yields a relatively low inflation rate, denoted π_A in panel (c). In addition, in panel (b) output levels at points A and A' are low relative to the scale on the horizontal axis. As panel (b) indicates, at these low levels of output, employment is also low. This, in turn, implies that the average of the unemployment rates at points A and A', denoted u_A, is high. The result of this comparison of points A and A' in panels (a) and (b), therefore, is the unemployment rate–inflation rate combination u_A and π_A at point A in panel (c).

Now let's consider the second situation in which real output is in an expansion phase of the business cycle. Then positions such as y_3^d and y_4^d on the aggregate demand schedule are applicable, and equilibrium real output levels at points B and B' are high relative to the scale on the horizontal axis in panel (a). An increase in aggregate demand illustrated by these two aggregate demand schedules leads to a larger proportionate increase in the price level as a result of the absolute rise in the price level, from P_3 to P_4. Hence, there is a relatively high inflation rate, denoted π_B, entailed in the movement from point B to point B'. The reason is that at high levels of aggregate demand, equilibrium occurs along the steepest portion of the aggregate supply schedule, where the law of diminishing returns yields the smallest effects on the quantity of real output following a rise in the price level. As shown in panel (b), at points B and B', workers and firms are producing output along the shallower portion of the aggregate production function. Along this portion of the production function, employment is high. Therefore, the average of the unemployment rates at point B and B', denoted u_B, is low. This new unemployment rate-inflation rate combination that we have deduced is point B in panel (c).

Points A and B in panel (c) of Figure 8–11 are two points along a Phillips curve. This Phillips curve is convex, or bowed inward, because of the law of diminishing marginal returns. Theoretically, a given increase in the inflation rate tends to push unemployment down by a larger amount when unemployment is high than when unemployment is low. In addition, our derivation of the Phillips curve has intentionally been simplified, in that we have looked only at one-time changes in the price level instead of more realistically considering continuous variations. Nevertheless, the important point that stems from Figure 8–11 is that the Phillips curve slopes downward. The Keynesian theory of aggregate supply yields the trade-off between the inflation rate and the unemployment rate that U.S. data from the 1960s fit so well. Even though we have varied the positions of the aggregate demand schedule to trace out the Phillips curve in Figure 8–11, the key point is that it is the upward-sloping, convex aggregate supply schedule that implies the Phillips curve relationship. Thus, we may conclude that:

> **An essential implication of the Keynesian theory of aggregate supply is the existence of a trade-off between the inflation rate and the unemployment rate. The Keynesian model predicts that a rise in the rate of inflation should lead to a decline in the rate of unemployment.**

The Phillips Curve and the Benefits and Costs of Inflation   As we noted earlier, the Phillips curve has been a controversial idea in macroeconomics. It has engendered debate for two reasons. One reason, as we will see in the next section, is that many economists have doubts about the validity of the concept. The other reason involves the effects that would follow from the application of the concept, assuming that it is valid. Assuming for this discussion that the Phillips curve concept is correct, then we could reduce unemployment by creating inflation and being willing to live with any costs due to the inflation. Indeed, people who particularly abhor unemployment regard the Phillips curve trade-off as beneficial: Sufficiently high inflation could, in principle, nearly eradicate unemployment.

Those who strongly dislike unemployment would be more willing to accept inflation-related costs than those who would bear them most heavily, however. Table 8–1 summarizes the costs of inflation and inflation variability. As the table indicates, all members of society bear these costs to some extent, but some are hurt more than others. Those who are hurt most include owners of businesses that lose out on profit opportunities and must incur costs of changing prices, savers and financial institutions that are creditors, and those who pay taxes that are not indexed to inflation. U.S. income tax brackets have been indexed to inflation since the 1980s, but in many countries individuals can be subject to higher tax rates simply because inflation has pushed their nominal incomes into income ranges subject to higher rates.

Consequently, if the Phillips curve idea is "true," then it creates scope for sharp divisions in society. Some groups will be more likely to prefer inflationary policies, while others will be more likely to oppose such policies. Indeed, as we shall discuss shortly, the Phillips curve provides a potential basis for a political theory of business cycles.

FUNDAMENTAL ISSUE #4

What is the Phillips curve? The Phillips curve is an inverse relationship between the unemployment rate and the inflation rate predicted by the Keynesian theory of aggregate supply. The existence of such a trade-off between unemployment and inflation would imply that society must make a choice between low inflation and low unemployment.

THE LONG-RUN PHILLIPS CURVE AND POLITICAL BUSINESS CYCLES

As we noted, the other reason that the Phillips curve has proved to be so controversial is that a number of economists believe that it is, at best, a very tenuous relation-

TABLE 8-1   THE COSTS OF INFLATION AND INFLATION VARIABILITY

TYPE OF COST	CAUSE
Resources expended to economize on money holdings (more trips to banks, etc.)	Rising prices associated with inflation
Costs of changing price lists and printing menus and catalogues	Individual product/service price increases associated with inflation
Redistribution of real incomes from individuals to the government	Inflation that pushes people into higher, nonindexed nominal tax brackets
Reductions in investment, capital accumulation, and economic growth	Inflation variability that complicates business planning
Slowed pace of introduction of new and better products	Volatile price changes that reduce the efficiency of private markets
Redistribution of resources from creditors to debtors	Unexpected inflation that reduces the real values of debts

ship. While not discounting its existence during the 1960s, they have pointed to evidence of its breakdown in years afterward, and they have questioned its usefulness over any long-run period. This challenge to the long-term relevance of the Phillips curve has been led by a group of economists known as *monetarists*.

The Monetarist Challenge to the Unemployment-Inflation Trade-off

MONETARISTS Economists who believe that the main factor influencing aggregate demand is the nominal money stock and that there is not a long-run trade-off between inflation and unemployment.

The **monetarists** are so-named because their original contribution to macroeconomics was their focus on the role of money as the primary determinant of aggregate demand. This group of economists, which was led by Milton Friedman, the late Karl Brunner, and Allan Meltzer, reemphasized the classical view that monetary stability was the key to price stability.

The monetarists' overarching contribution, however, has been on the subject of the Phillips curve. Beginning in the late 1960s, they challenged the then-prevailing view that the Phillips curve was a stable relationship that policymakers could exploit to reduce unemployment at the cost of higher inflation. In the long run, the monetarists contended, such policies would succeed only in raising inflation, while having little measurable impact on the unemployment rate.

During the 1960s, few economists were receptive to this argument. After all, as Figure 8–9 indicates, Keynesian theory seemed to explain the data very well. Beginning in the 1970s, however, more economists began to pay attention to the monetarists. In 1969, Milton Friedman predicted that the smooth unemployment-inflation trade-off summarized in Figure 8–9 on page 272 could not last very long.

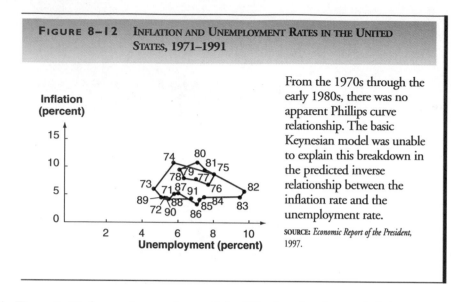

FIGURE 8–12 INFLATION AND UNEMPLOYMENT RATES IN THE UNITED STATES, 1971–1991

From the 1970s through the early 1980s, there was no apparent Phillips curve relationship. The basic Keynesian model was unable to explain this breakdown in the predicted inverse relationship between the inflation rate and the unemployment rate.

SOURCE: *Economic Report of the President,* 1997.

As Figure 8–12 shows, the experience of the following decades verified this prediction: There was no smooth Phillips curve from the 1970s through the early 1990s.

The Long Run and the Natural Rate of Unemployment   What reasoning led the monetarists to forecast that the Phillips curve trade-off will break down? Their argument has its roots in the Keynesian imperfect-information theory of the upward-sloping aggregate supply schedule. According to the monetarists, this theory applies only to the **short run**, or a period short enough that information is imperfect and expectations of inflation do not necessarily match actual inflation. In the long run, they contend, the aggregate supply schedule is vertical, as in the classical model.

The key to the monetarists' argument is their definition of the *long run.* Monetarists define the **long run** as a period sufficiently lengthy that workers can compile enough information about developments in the economy that their inflation expectations correctly match true inflation rates. In the long run, therefore, workers are fully informed, as the classical model assumes. Unlike the classical theorists, however, the monetarists do not contend that the economy is always in this long-run position. Instead, they argue that it naturally tends *toward* that state over the passage of several years.

This reasoning leads to the logical conclusion that in the long run, when full information is available, expected inflation equals actual inflation, and the classical presumption of a vertical aggregate supply schedule will actually hold. Price-level changes then will not affect real output, because they will not influence equilibrium employment. As a result, changes in the inflation rate will not affect the unemployment rate. Therefore, as discussed in Chapter 5, in the long run the economy will tend toward a *natural rate of unemployment,* or the rate of unemployment that arises under full information when the economy is on its long-run growth path (see Chapter 4's discussion of economic growth). The natural unemployment rate stems from

SHORT RUN According to the monetarists, an interval short enough that workers do not have complete information about aggregate prices and inflation; therefore expected prices and inflation may differ from actual prices and inflation.

LONG RUN According to the monetarists, an interval long enough that workers can compile full information about aggregate prices and inflation; therefore expected prices and inflation are equal to actual prices and inflation.

structural and frictional unemployment, as discussed in Chapter 5. (See on page 280 Policy Notebook: *Is There a Relationship between the Natural Rate of Unemployment and Inflation?*)

Getting from the Short Run to the Long Run   This is not to say that the monetarists entirely rule out the existence of a trade-off between unemployment and inflation. Monetarists agree with Keynesian theorists that cyclical variations in the unemployment rate do occur. They also do not argue with the evidence that during some short-run periods these cyclical components of unemployment may be inversely related to the inflation rate.

Indeed, the monetarists have no quarrel with the traditional Keynesian theory's assumption that workers can have incomplete information about prices and inflation. Their point is that incomplete information is a short-run phenomenon. In the long run, people are more nearly fully informed, and so the Keynesian theory of aggregate supply is not as useful over the long term.

Figure 8–13 summarizes the monetarist perspective. Panel (a) is an aggregate demand–aggregate supply diagram relating the price level and real output, while panel (b) is a Phillips curve diagram relating the inflation rate and the unemployment

FIGURE 8-13   AGGREGATE SUPPLY AND THE PHILLIPS CURVE IN THE SHORT RUN AND THE LONG RUN

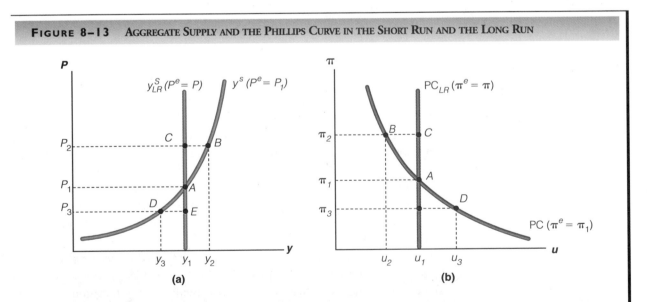

(a)   **(b)**

In the short run, which is a period sufficiently short that price and inflation expectations do not adjust in the face of actual inflation, the level of real output can vary as the actual price level changes, as shown by movements along the aggregate supply schedule between points B and D in panel (a). Likewise, variations in the actual inflation rate can result in changes in the unemployment rate, as shown by movements between points B and D in panel (b). In the long run, however, price and inflation expectations can fully adjust, so as the price level varies between points C and E in panel (a) there are no changes in real output, and the long-run aggregate supply schedule is vertical, and the long-run Phillips curve in panel (b) also is vertical.

POLICY NOTEBOOK:

Is There a Relationship between the Natural Rate of Unemployment and Inflation?

Some economists have embodied the relationship between the rate of inflation and the natural rate of unemployment in what they call NAIRU, or the non-accelerating-inflation rate of unemployment. In effect, the NAIRU approach relates the rate of unemployment to the *rate of change* of inflation. The idea is that only one rate of unemployment is consistent with a constant rate of inflation, whether that rate is at 3 percent or 10 percent per year. According to the NAIRU theory, if unemployment is below this critical rate, workers will demand and receive bigger pay increases, and the rate of inflation will rise. If the unemployment rate is above this critical rate, pay increases will be modest or nonexistent, and the rate of inflation will be stable or even decline.

The evidence is mixed as to whether there is a specific natural rate of unemployment that is consistent with a constant inflation rate. Until the mid-1990s, some evidence suggested

that when the rate of unemployment fell below 6 percent, the rate of inflation would increase. Since the mid-1990s, however, the unemployment rate in the United States was less than 6 percent, and the rate of inflation stayed constant or fell during that time period.

More specifically, economists Douglas Staiger, James Stock, and Mark Watson examined the NAIRU over recent decades and discovered that it ranged from 4.6 percent to 6.9 percent. The authors concluded that "The NAIRU is known with substantially less precision than is implicitly assumed in the current debate."

FOR CRITICAL ANALYSIS:
Why does it matter that the range of the estimated NAIRU is so wide?

rate. Panel (a) depicts two aggregate supply schedules. One, which corresponds to the Keynesian aggregate supply schedule, is the *short-run aggregate supply schedule* implied by the monetarists' reasoning. Along this short-run aggregate supply schedule, workers have imperfect information, so they form an expectation of the price level, such as $P^e = P_1$, that varies in the face of actual price changes that are unknown to the workers in the short run. As a result, if the actual price level rises from P_1 to P_2 in the short run, real output will increase from y_1 toward y_2 at point B. Alternatively, if the actual price level declines from P_1 to P_3 in the short run, real output will fall from y_1 toward y_3 at point D.

In the long run, however, workers become fully informed, so their expectation of the price level is always equal to the actual price level, and the *long-run aggregate supply schedule* is the vertical schedule of the classical model. In the long run, therefore, changes in the price level leave real output unaffected. A rise in the price level ultimately will cause a movement from point A to point C in the long run. A fall in the price level eventually will cause a movement from point A to point E in the long run.

Likewise, panel (b) displays two Phillips curves. One, the downward-sloping Phillips curve, is derived from the upward-sloping short-run aggregate supply curve (see Figure 8-10 on page 273). A price-level increase will raise the inflation rate, causing a short-run decline in the unemployment rate along the downward-sloping *short-run Phillips curve* (*PC*), from point *A* to point *B*. Because workers' price expectations cannot adjust in the short run, they have a temporarily fixed *inflation expectation*, denoted $\pi^e = \pi_1$. As a result, in the short run a rise in the inflation rate, from π_1 to π_2 in panel (b), can induce workers to supply more labor to firms, and the unemployment rate will fall. In contrast, a decline in the inflation rate from π_1 to π_3 can cause workers to reduce the quantity of labor services that they supply, and the unemployment rate can rise in response, as shown by the movement from point *A* to point *D*.

The *long-run Phillips curve* (PC_{LR}), however, is vertical, because the long-run aggregate supply schedule is vertical. In the long run, workers are fully informed, so their inflation expectation π^e is equal to actual inflation. Hence, a rise in the inflation rate ultimately leaves the unemployment rate unaffected, as shown by the movement along the long-run Phillips curve from point *A* to point *C*. Furthermore, a fall in the inflation rate ultimately has no long-term impact on the unemployment rate, as shown by the movement from point *A* to point *E*. The unemployment rate u_1 therefore will be the economy's natural rate of unemployment.

FUNDAMENTAL ISSUE #5

How does monetarism differ from the traditional Keynesian theory? The monetarists have argued that the nominal money stock is the main determinant of aggregate demand. Furthermore, they have proposed a blend of the Keynesian and classical theories of aggregate supply, in which the short-run imperfection of information makes the aggregate supply schedule slope upward in the short run but the availability of full information in the long run produces a vertical aggregate supply schedule. According to the monetarist view, the Phillips curve slopes downward in the short run. In the long run, however, it is vertical at the natural rate of unemployment.

Political Business Cycles and Alternative Theories of Stagflation

The monetarists essentially proposed a link between the traditional Keynesian theory's short-run emphasis and the classical model's long-run aspects. The link is based on price and inflation expectations, which are ill-informed in the short run but based on full information in the long run. This combination of the two theoretical approaches to macroeconomics provides the foundation for what is known as the theory of *political business cycles*. It also forms the basis for alternative theories of *stagflation*, or the simultaneous occurrence of high inflation and unemployment rates.

The Political Business Cycle   How might political factors influence the business cycle? It is a short step from Figure 8–13 to an answer to this question. To see why, consider Figure 8–14. Suppose that, as shown in panel (a), the natural rate of unemployment is equal to u_N, which gives the position for the vertical, long-run Phillips curve. In addition, suppose that the current inflation rate is equal to π_1. Finally, suppose that this is also the inflation rate that people anticipate, so that the short-run Phillips curve crosses point A, which illustrates the current unemployment rate–inflation rate combination.

Imagine now that a political party campaigns on the platform of reducing unemployment to a target unemployment rate, u_T, that is below the natural rate of unemployment. After winning sufficient offices, the party embarks on monetary and fiscal policies that expand aggregate demand and push up the price level. The result is a rise in the inflation rate. In the short run, this can achieve the unemployment rate target u_T by moving the economy back along the short-run Phillips curve *toward* point B. The decline in the unemployment rate occurs because workers temporarily fail to rec-

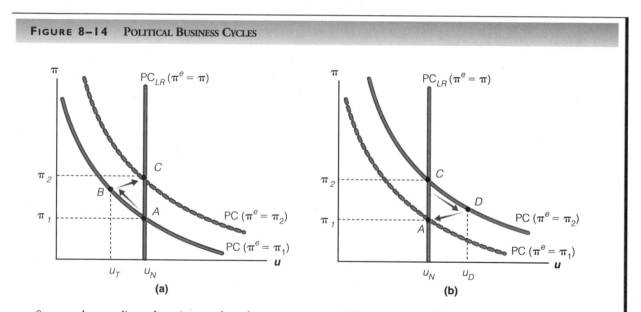

FIGURE 8–14   POLITICAL BUSINESS CYCLES

(a)

(b)

Suppose that a policymaker tries to reduce the unemployment rate toward a target level, u_T, in an effort to pursue short-term political gains by taking advantage of a short-run trade-off between inflation and unemployment. Panel (a) shows that increasing the inflation rate toward point B along the short-run Phillips curve might reduce the unemployment rate somewhat in the short run, but in the long run a rightward shift in the

Phillips curve caused by increased inflation expectations would lead to an increase in the unemployment rate back toward the natural rate at point C. Then, as panel (b) indicates, reducing the inflation rate would require a short-run rise in the unemployment rate at point D, until a decline in inflation expectations would induce a leftward shift of the Phillips curve and a fall in the unemployment rate toward point A.

ognize the rise in inflation that erodes the real value of their wages. As a result, they supply more labor services to firms, and unemployment declines.

According to the monetarist theory, however, workers eventually will begin to recognize that the inflation rate has increased. As their inflation expectations rise, the short-run Phillips curve *shifts* upward and to the right. After sufficient time has passed for workers to become fully informed, the short-run and long-run Phillips curves cross at a new point, at point *C*. As the short-run Phillips curve shifts, the unemployment rate begins to rise once again. Ultimately, the economy reaches point *C* at the natural rate of unemployment u_N, but at a higher inflation rate π_2 that is fully anticipated by workers.

At this point, another political party argues that inflation is the economy's number-one problem and promises that, if elected, it will enact a program to cut the inflation rate. After winning the next election, this new party in power embarks on *its* program. The effects that the political business cycle theory predicts are illustrated in panel (b) of Figure 8–14. Now that the economy is at the unemployment rate–inflation rate combination at point *C*, the new party in power must engage in monetary and fiscal policies that reduce aggregate demand and depress price increases. These policies reduce the inflation rate from π_2 to, say, π_1 once again. In the near term, however, this will require a movement downward and to the right along the short-run Phillips curve, to point *D*. As a result, the unemployment rate will rise above the natural rate of unemployment, *toward* u_D. The unemployment rate will fall back toward the natural rate only after sufficient time has passed for workers to recognize the lower inflation in the economy. As their inflation expectations decline from $\pi^e = \pi_2$ to $\pi^e = \pi_1$, the short-run Phillips curve will shift back down and to the left, and the unemployment rate once again will return to its natural level, at point *A*.

A prediction of the political business cycle theory, therefore, is that a democratic society can easily fall into a cyclical pattern of seeking lower unemployment in the short run, only to find that the cost is higher inflation. Efforts to reduce inflation will follow, but at the short-run cost of higher unemployment rates. The inflation and unemployment experience of the United States between 1971 and 1991 in Figure 8–12 on page 278 appears to fit the theory's prediction. After two decades of higher inflation accompanied by short-run declines, increases, and then declines in the unemployment rate, the United States in 1991 was not too far from the point from which it might have embarked on a quest for lower unemployment in 1971.

INTERNET ● SOURCE

Keeping Up with the Potential Sources of Political Business Cycles —U.S. Political Parties on the Internet

Democratic Party Economic Views
Internet URL Listing:

1. The Democratic Leadership Committees: http://www.senate.gov/~dpc/Dem-Policy/general/dpc.html

2. Compuserve's Democratic Forum: Go: CIS:DEMOCR

Republican Party Economic Views
Internet URL Listing:

1. The Republican Liberty Caucus: http://w3.ag.uiuc.edu/liberty/rlc/index.html

2. America Online's Heritage Foundation/Policy Review Forum on AOl (Keyword: "Heritage Foundation")

Other Political Parties' Economic Policy Perspectives

1. Libertarian Party: http://www.lp.org

2. Socialist Party: http://www.socialist.org

3. Green Parties: http://www.greenparties.org

STAGFLATION The simultaneous observation of rising inflation rates and declining real output and rising unemployment rates.

Explaining Stagflation   Embedded in the political business cycle theory is one possible explanation for **stagflation**, a rather awkward but nevertheless descriptive term for the occurrence of high inflation at the same time that real output is declining and the unemployment rate is rising. As panel (a) of Figure 8–14 shows, the theory indicates that stagflation typically will occur as inflation expectations increase following a politically motivated attempt by policymakers to reduce the unemployment rate below its natural rate.

Stagflation can also occur for another reason that does not rely so much on cynical views about the motives of politicians. If you look at the unemployment rate–inflation rate combinations that occurred in the 1970s and 1980s in Figure 8–12 on page 278, you will notice that one can trace out three distinct periods: the first three years of the 1970s, the period 1974–1978, and the period 1979–1983. In each interval the short-run Phillips curve apparently shifted to the right. If the monetarist-based political business cycle theory were the only explanation available to us, we would have to conclude that inflation expectations appear to have increased three times in succession after the 1960s to yield these three separate short-run Phillips curves.

SUPPLY SHOCKS Changes in the position of the aggregate supply schedule caused by significant changes in the costs of factors of production or in technological capabilities.

In fact, however, other events transpired during the 1970s. These were **supply shocks**, which are changes in the position of the aggregate supply schedule caused by significant changes in the costs of factors of production or in technological capabilities. The supply shocks of the 1970s largely stemmed from large increases in oil prices brought about first by an Arab oil embargo and then by the coordinated actions of the broader group of OPEC nations in the later 1970s. Both of these supply shocks undoubtedly account for the multiple shifts of the Phillips curve that took place in the 1970s. To the extent that the political business cycle theory may account for the U.S. experience in the 1970s and 1980s, therefore, higher inflation expectations and supply shocks *together* will have accounted for the periods of stagflation that took place during these years.

The 1990s: The Return of the Phillips Curve?   As the United States begins a new century, it has returned to an environment of relatively low inflation and unemployment. Figure 8–15 plots inflation and unemployment rate combinations that have occurred since 1985. Although these points constitute a "cluster" rather than a smooth curve, they appear to indicate the return of a generally downward-sloping relationship between inflation rates and unemployment rates. This might be taken as evidence that reductions in unemployment can be achieved at the cost of slight increases in inflation. Indeed, one can still find media reports about major political figures arguing that the U.S. government should embark on new policies to take advantage of the apparent Phillips curve trade-off.

If the monetarists and political business cycle theorists are correct, however, such policies might lead the United States into yet another round of lower unemployment and renewed inflation, followed by efforts to wring out inflation at the short-run cost of even higher unemployment. It remains to be seen if political leaders and voters have learned the lessons of the recent past.

As we shall discuss in the following chapters, not all economists agree with the monetarist and political business cycle interpretation of the data. Nevertheless, this interpretation has become the starting point for most modern theories. All such theories now include *expectations* as a key element. Where theories now diverge is in the mechanisms that they envision for expectations and for the relative roles of supply- and demand-side factors in determining the paths that business cycles follow.

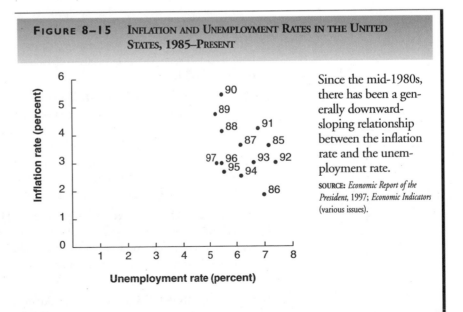

FIGURE 8–15   INFLATION AND UNEMPLOYMENT RATES IN THE UNITED STATES, 1985–PRESENT

Since the mid-1980s, there has been a generally downward-sloping relationship between the inflation rate and the unemployment rate.

SOURCE: *Economic Report of the President,* 1997; *Economic Indicators* (various issues).

FUNDAMENTAL ISSUE #6

How do the political business cycle model and supply shocks together potentially explain both cyclical inflation and episodes of stagflation? The political business cycle model builds on the monetarist theory of the short- and long-run Phillips curves to show how political pressures to reduce unemployment can lead to increased inflation and to higher inflation expectations, resulting in lower unemployment initially but higher unemployment later on. It also provides a potential explanation for why efforts to reduce inflation can lead to higher unemployment initially but lower unemployment afterward. Higher inflation expectations and supply shocks together cause the short-run Phillips curve to shift upward, so that both higher inflation and higher unemployment—known as stagflation—can result.

CHAPTER SUMMARY

1. **The Factors That Determine Aggregate Demand in the Traditional Keynesian Model**: Two key factors affect the position of the Keynesian aggregate demand schedule. One is the set of elements that comprise autonomous aggregate expenditures. These include government spending and taxation and autonomous consumption, investment, and net exports. The other key factor is the nominal quantity of money. Consequently, both fiscal and monetary policy actions can affect the position of the Keynesian aggregate demand schedule.

2. **The Factors That Determine the Shape and Position of the Keynesian Aggregate Supply Schedule**: According to the sticky-wage and imperfect-information theories of aggregate supply, the aggregate supply schedule is upward sloping and has a convex shape. Under the sticky-wage theory, a rise in nominal wages, perhaps as a result of union demands for higher wages or an increase in a legal wage minimum, will shift the aggregate supply schedule upward and to the left. Under the imperfect-information theory, a rise in the expected price level will also shift the aggregate supply schedule upward and to the left.

3. **The Price and Output Effects of Expansionary Fiscal and Monetary Policies in the Traditional Keynesian Model**: According to this theory, an increase in government expenditures, a tax cut, or a rise in the nominal quantity of money will raise aggregate demand. This will cause an increase in both the equilibrium price level and equilibrium real output.

4. **The Phillips Curve**: This is a downward-sloping schedule that traces a proposed inverse relationship between the unemployment rate and the inflation rate. Such a relationship,

which is an implication of the Keynesian theory of aggregate supply, will indicate that society must trade off higher inflation for lower unemployment, and vice versa.

5. **How Monetarism Differs from the Traditional Keynesian Theory**: The monetarists have argued that the nominal quantity of money is the primary factor influencing aggregate demand. In addition, the monetarists have developed a theory that combines elements of the Keynesian imperfect-information theory of aggregate supply and the classical full-information theory of aggregate supply. According to this mixed theory, imperfect information makes the short-run aggregate supply schedule slope upward and the short-run Phillips curve slope downward. The availability of full information in the long run, however, makes both the aggregate supply schedule and the Phillips curve vertical.

6. **How the Political Business Cycle Model and Supply Shocks Together Potentially Can Explain Both Cyclical Inflation and Episodes of Stagflation:** Using the monetarist theory of the short- and long-run Phillips curves as a foundation, the political business cycle theory provides a potential explanation for how politically motivated efforts to reduce unemployment can lead to higher inflation and inflation expectations, resulting at first in lower unemployment but eventually causing higher unemployment. It also provides a possible reason for why efforts to reduce inflation can push unemployment up initially but lead to lower unemployment later on. Increased inflation expectations and supply shocks together can shift the short-run Phillips curve upward, thereby causing stagflation, or simultaneous high inflation and unemployment rates.

QUESTIONS AND PROBLEMS

1. In the classical model, fiscal policy actions do not influence aggregate demand, but in the Keynesian theory, they do. Why is this so?

2. List the various factors that can cause inflation in the classical model. Then construct a similar list for the Keynesian theory. Which list is longer? Explain why this is so.

3. Consider the following equations for a fictitious economy, which has no government:

   LM schedule: $r = 160 - [2 \times (M/P)] + (8 \times y)$

   IS schedule: $r = 160 - (8 \times y)$

a. Suppose that the nominal money stock is equal to 160 and the price level is equal to 2. What is the equilibrium level of real income?

b. Suppose that the nominal money stock remains equal to 160 but the price level falls to 1. What is the new equilibrium real income level? What does this imply about the slope of the aggregate demand schedule?

4. Explain verbally, and with diagrams to the extent that they assist, why a sudden decline in price expectations shifts the short-run aggregate supply schedule downward and to the right.

5. Explain in your own words why money is nonneutral in the traditional Keynesian model.

6. In 1996, a few senators delayed for several months the full Senate's approval of Alan Greenspan's nomination to a third term as chair of the Federal Reserve Board. One of this group was quoted as saying in the floor debate, "Every time growth starts to go up, they [the Federal Reserve] push on the brakes [reduce money growth], robbing working families and businesses of the benefits of faster growth." (Interpretations are in brackets.) Were this senator's views more likely swayed by classical, Keynesian, or monetarist theory?

7. Explain verbally, and with diagrams to the extent that they assist, why a sudden decline in price-level and inflation expectations shifts the short-run Phillips curve downward and to the left. (Hint: You should find that your answer to question 4 will be helpful in answering this question.)

8. Explain why the long-run Phillips curve is vertical.

9. Economists have not reached agreement on how lengthy the time horizon for the "long run" is in the context of the long-run Phillips curve. Would you anticipate that this period is likely to have been shortened or extended by the advent of more sophisticated computer and communications technology? Explain your reasoning.

10. Evaluate the ability of the political business cycle theory alone to explain the behavior of inflation and unemployment rates since the 1960s. Explain your reasoning.

CyberTutor Exercises

1. An increase in transfers reduces net autonomous taxes. What effect will an increase in government transfers have on the *IS* and *LM* schedules and the aggregate demand schedule?

2. What effect will an increase in the price level have on the *IS* and *LM* schedules and the aggregate demand schedule?

3. What will happen to the nominal and real wages and aggregate supply if the capital stock increases, assuming that labor and capital are complements in production?

4. What effect does a rise in the price level have on aggregate supply?

5. There is a contentious debate whether unemployment rises as inflation falls. Plot the inflation rate and unemployment rate against time. Looking at this time series plot, do you see any periods when there was a downward-sloping Phillips curve? If so, create a scatter plot of the inflation rate against the unemployment rate during this time period. Was your suspicion correct? Can you suggest why the Phillips curve seems to hold during certain time periods and not others?

6. Consider France and determine whether it exhibits a downward sloping Phillips curve. Also examine a few different time periods (for example the 1980s and 1990s) to see if the Phillips curve slopes downward during these time periods.

ON-LINE APPLICATION

According to Keynesian theory, the unemployment rate should be relatively sensitive to changes in the inflation rate. This application allows you to take a direct look at unemployment and inflation data to judge for yourself whether or not the two variables appear to be related.

Internet URL: http://stats.bls.gov:80/eag/table/html (or ...eag/table.html)

Title: Bureau of Labor Statistics: Economy at a Glance

Navigation: Begin at the homepage of the Bureau of Labor Statistics (http://stats.bls.gov).

Application: Perform the indicated operations, and answer the following questions:

1. Click on "Economy at a Glance." Then scan down to "Prices," and click on the graph box next to "Consumer Price Index." Take a look at the solid line showing inflation in the graph box. How much has the inflation rate varied since 1992? Compare this pattern with previous years.

2. Back up to "Economy at a Glance," and now click on the graph box next to "Unemployment Rate." Take a look at the graph box. During which recent years was the unemployment rate approaching and at its peak value? Do you note any appearance of an inverse relationship between the unemployment rate and the inflation rate (part 1 above)?

SELECTED REFERENCES AND FURTHER READING

Cross, Rod. *The Natural Rate of Unemployment: Reflections on 25 Years of the Hypothesis.* Cambridge: Cambridge University Press, 1995.

Fuhrer, Jeffrey. "The Phillips Curve Is Alive and Well." Federal Reserve Bank of Boston *Economic Review*, March/April 1995, pp. 41–56.

Laidler, David. "The Legacy of the Monetarist Controversy." Federal Reserve Bank of St. Louis *Review*, March/April 1990, pp. 49–64.

Mayer, Thomas, ed. *The Political Economy of American Monetary Policy.* Cambridge: Cambridge University Press, 1990.

Mayer, Thomas, ed. *The Structure of Monetarism.* New York: Norton, 1978.

Roberts, John. "New Keynesian Economics and the Phillips Curve." *Journal of Money, Credit, and Banking* 27 (November 1995): 975–984.

Tootell, Geoffrey. "Restructuring, the NAIRU, and the Phillips Curve." Federal Reserve Bank of Boston *New England Economic Review*, September/October 1994, pp. 31–44.

Unit III

Rational Expectations and Modern Macroeconomic Theory

9

The Pursuit of Self-Interest—

RATIONAL EXPECTATIONS, NEW CLASSICAL MACROECONOMICS, AND EFFICIENT MARKETS

FUNDAMENTAL ISSUES

1. What is the distinction between adaptive and rational expectations?

2. What are the key assumptions underlying new classical macroeconomics?

3. How do policy anticipations determine the actual effects of policy actions in the new classical model?

4. What is the policy ineffectiveness proposition, and what is its implication for the conduct of policies intended to have real effects?

5. What is the efficient markets theory, and what is its main implication?

6. How are exchange rates determined, and what is foreign exchange market efficiency?

Not too long ago, the same page of the International Herald Tribune *featured two articles, one entitled "Rate Watch Resumes, Weakening Blue Chips," and the other entitled "Awaiting a Stream of U.S. Economic Data, the Dollar Slides." According to the first article, U.S. stock prices had fallen for the first time in three days because of market concerns that rising interest rates would curb corporate profit growth. Securities dealers indicated that investors were reluctant to take big chances before the release of the Labor Department's employment cost index for the second quarter. Apparently, investors felt that if wages were rising too quickly, the Federal Reserve might react by increasing interest rates. The increase in interest rates would presumably be aimed at slowing down the economy and at the same time would reduce bond prices. So-called Fed watchers were being consulted on a regular basis for their views on what the Fed might do.*

According to the second article, dealers in the foreign exchange market also said investors were waiting for economic data from the Labor and Commerce Departments. Would there be market-shifting news? What would the government report indicate about payroll costs and consumer confidence? Any increase in interest rates by the Fed would probably lead to a higher dollar price in the foreign exchange markets. The reasoning is straightforward: If interest rates rise in the United States relative to the rest of the world, more foreigners will invest in U.S. assets and therefore will demand more dollars. The foreign exchange price of the dollar will be pushed up as a result.

Whether the subject is Fed watching or foreign exchange predictions, the rule of thumb today is that many individuals who make decisions in this economy do so rationally with as much information as they can. Accordingly, the subject of this chapter is how people form rational expectations and how we can use this concept to understand the theory of efficient markets.

THE RATIONAL EXPECTATIONS HYPOTHESIS

The monetarists blended aspects of the classical and traditional Keynesian approaches in their effort to explain how macroeconomic policies affect real output, employment, and the rate of inflation in the short run and in the long run. In the short run, the monetarist approach looks much like the traditional Keynesian theory, whereas in the long run the monetarist model essentially duplicates the classical theory.

Binding together the classical and Keynesian approaches was no mean feat for the monetarists. As you have seen, the hybrid model that the monetarists and others have pieced together provides the basis for the idea of political business cycles and for simple theories of stagflation. The monetarist model also identifies the important role that inflation expectations can perform in determining the pace of economic activity, the unemployment rate, and the rate of inflation.

Missing from the basic monetarist theoretical framework, however, was a clear explanation for how people form inflation expectations. As macroeconomists sought to apply the monetarist ideas to develop a more complete understanding of factors that might influence business cycles, they began to recognize that how people forecast inflation is a key determinant of business cycle peaks, troughs, and durations. Hence, economists needed to carefully consider the assumptions about expectation formation in their theories.

Expectations and Macroeconomics

In Chapter 8 you learned that the monetarist model indicates that adjustment to the long-run, classical equilibrium takes place when workers have information about true changes in the rate of inflation. In the long run, therefore, workers experience no money illusion, and the unemployment rate is equal to the natural rate of unemployment.

Before this long-run, classical equilibrium is reached, however, the monetarist framework implies that workers essentially are handicapped by a lack of full information. Because of information imperfections in the short run, workers must forecast the price level and the inflation rate so that they can decide how much labor to supply at prevailing nominal wages. If the actual price level and inflation rate differ from the expectations, workers' perceptions of their real wage earnings will turn out to be incorrect. The short-run results are a deviation in the unemployment rate from the natural rate of unemployment, variations in real output from the long-run, classical level of output, and fluctuations in the price level and inflation rate. In other words, business cycles occur.

At what point does the short-run period of the traditional Keynesian theory end? In other words, how does the economy make the transition to the long-run state described by the classical theory? The basic monetarist model tells us only that the long run is an interval whose length is determined by the availability of information. As long as expectations are based on imperfect information, the short-run Keynesian theory is applicable, and real output and the unemployment rate can vary with changes in the price level and the inflation rate.

Exactly what information is really available to people in the short run? How do they use this information to forecast the price level and the inflation rate? Clearly, the choices that people make depend on such factors, yet the macroeconomic theories that we have considered to this point are silent on these issues.

One element that separates *modern* macroeconomics—the study of the aggregate economy during the latter portion of the twentieth century—from the macroeconomics of the past is a greater effort to clarify the role that the *expectations formation process* plays in macroeconomic models. Modern macroeconomists have developed clear-cut hypotheses for how people forecast the price level and inflation rate, and they incorporate these hypotheses into their theories of the determination of real output, employment, the price level, and the inflation rate.

Macroeconomists have adopted two basic types of hypotheses about how people form expectations. One is the hypothesis of *adaptive expectations*. The other is the *rational expectations hypothesis*, which has dominated modern macroeconomic thinking. Our first task in this chapter is to explain why this is so.

Adaptive Expectations

Many of the choices that we make each day depend on our anticipations of future events. Should you register for a course this term when the instructor is a professor with an average-quality reputation, or should you wait until next term when the course will be taught by a better instructor, but the tuition rate may be higher? Should you buy a sweater at a department store today, or do you expect that it will be on sale in a couple of weeks? Should you take a job at the salary you have been offered for the coming year, or would you be better off searching for a position at a higher salary, given that you expect the price level to rise during the coming year?

Clearly, to make any decisions that have future consequences, you must act on forecasts that you make based on whatever information you currently possess. This information includes the prices of goods and services that you buy each day in your own town or city, prices of items that you see advertised in local and national media, and information that you can glean from reports on regional or national television news programs.

How do you use such information to infer the current aggregate inflation rate for the United States? How do you forecast future inflation? Most likely, you would have trouble providing a detailed, scientific answer to either of these questions. Certainly, it is unlikely that you engage in any formal statistical analysis or use a computer to make your forecast. You probably just make your "best guess" based on the information available to you.

What is a person's best guess of inflation? Simply saying that people do the best they can with limited information is not a very specific statement. As you have learned, macroeconomists need to make more specific assumptions when they construct theories of output and price-level determination. For this reason, in recent years they have developed precise conceptions about alternative processes by which people form expectations.

Adaptive Expectations Processes   One way to make an inference of the aggregate price level or to forecast the future inflation rate is to do so "adaptively." Let's consider an example. Imagine that someone asks you for your forecast of the U.S. inflation rate for next year. How would you come up with an answer?

One approach might be to collect data on inflation rates for the past twenty or twenty-five years. You then could plot this information on a chart and make a rough drawing of the "trend line" along the points and beyond. The next point on your trend line would be your forecast of next year's inflation rate.

If you have taken a statistics course, you might use a more sophisticated method. You could use statistical techniques to determine the specific equation for the trend line that best fits the inflation data that you have collected. With this equation, you could give a predicted value, or forecast, of the inflation rate for a given year, including next year.

Either method would require you to sacrifice time and effort to collect and analyze years of inflation data. If you do not wish to incur this opportunity cost to make a sophisticated forecast, you could choose a simpler method. For instance, you might just guess that next year's inflation rate will turn out to be an average of the inflation rates over the past three years. Even simpler, you might guess that next year's inflation rate will turn out to be similar to the inflation rate during the past year.

ADAPTIVE EXPECTATIONS
Expectations that are based only on information from the past up to the present.

Each of the above forecasting methods is an example of an **adaptive expectation** process, because each method uses only past information. Whether you draw a rough trend line, use statistical techniques to calculate an exact trend line, compute a three-year average, or just extrapolate from the current inflation rate, you are basing your inflation forecast solely on past data.

Implications of Adaptive Expectations   As you learned in Chapter 8, one way to derive an upward-sloping Keynesian aggregate supply schedule and a downward-sloping Phillips curve is to assume that workers make choices based on imperfectly informed forecasts of the price level and inflation rate. If the workers' forecasts turn out to be incorrect, then the results are movements along the aggregate supply schedule and the Phillips curve. Misperceptions caused by imperfect information lead to changes in real output and the unemployment rate.

The production of real output by more or fewer workers requires the passage of time, however. Consequently, short-run output and employment adjustments cannot occur until an interval passes and workers realize that their forecasts of the price level and inflation rate were wrong. During this interval, which corresponds to the monetarists' notion of the short run, workers can fail to realize that a rise in the nominal wage may stem solely from an increase in the price level. As a result, when the nominal wage rises, for a time workers can misperceive this rise in the nominal wage as a rise in their real wage, leading them to supply more labor services. This permits firms to produce more real output.

The hypothesis that workers use adaptive expectations processes is consistent with this traditional Keynesian theory of aggregate supply and the Phillips curve. If workers make their price-level and inflation forecasts adaptively, then they must always wait until new information about the price level and inflation rate appears before changing their expectations. Consequently, over some intervals workers will not be able to avoid experiencing money illusion concerning their wages, and policy actions that raise the price level will always cause workers to misperceive their true real wages, at least for a short time. Thus, such policies can have short-run effects on real output and the unemployment rate.

Drawbacks of Adaptive Expectations   Just because an expectations hypothesis happens to fit a theory does not mean that it is a reasonable hypothesis. Indeed, many economists reject the idea of adaptive expectations. For one thing, if people really were to use adaptive expectations processes, they often would make forecasts that they realize in advance should turn out to be wrong. Suppose, for instance, that your adaptive method for forecasting next year's inflation rate is to calculate an average of the inflation rates for the past three years. If this average is equal to 3 percent, then that will be your forecast of the inflation rate for next year. Now suppose that you read in the newspaper that a new majority on the Federal Reserve have decided to increase money growth significantly, as compared with previous years. Sticking with your three-year-averaging procedure for calculating the average inflation rate means that you must consciously ignore this new information, even though any reasonable person would recognize that higher money growth may push up next year's inflation rate. As a result, a macroeconomic model based on the hypothesis of adaptive expectations will yield forecasts of the rate of inflation that are consistently less than the actual inflation rate. Thus, any macroeconomic theory based on adaptive expectations will be internally inconsistent, because the people whose behavior the model attempts to mimic behave in a way inconsistent with new information.

Another troublesome aspect of the hypothesis is that there is no way to say, in advance, which adaptive expectations process is "best." For example, one individual might draw a chart of twenty-five years of past annual inflation rate data to plot a rough trend line to guide her forecasts, another person might use the same technique using data from the previous forty years, and yet another might use fifty years of data. Someone else might calculate a weighted average of inflation over the past five years. Indeed, the number of possible adaptive expectations schemes is infinite. Which one should we include in a macroeconomic model? There is no good way to answer this question.

Rational Expectations

In the 1970s, macroeconomists began to confront the quandary that adaptive expectations posed for evaluating the traditional Keynesian and monetarist efforts to allow for imperfect information in their theories. Motivating an upward-sloping aggregate supply function and a downward-sloping Phillips curve seemed to require adaptive expectations, yet incorporating specific schemes for adaptively formed price-level and inflation rate expectations in macroeconomic models seemed both arbitrary and inconsistent.

In 1969, an Indiana University economist named John Muth proposed an alternative way to think about how people form expectations. Then Robert Lucas of the University of Chicago and others, including Thomas Sargent of Stanford University, Neil Wallace of the University of Miami, and Robert Barro of Harvard University, followed up on Muth's idea to derive a possibly better way to think about how price-level and inflation rate expectations are formed.

The approach to expectations that Muth, Lucas, and others developed is called the **rational expectations hypothesis**. According to this hypothesis, an individual makes the best possible forecast of a macroeconomic variable such as the price level or inflation rate using all available past *and current* information *and* drawing on an understanding of what factors affect the macroeconomic variable. In contrast to an adaptive forecast, which only looks backward because it is based on past information, a rational forecast looks forward while taking past information into account as well.

> **RATIONAL EXPECTATIONS HYPOTHESIS** The idea that individuals form expectations based on all available past and current information and on a basic understanding of how the economy works.

Consider, for instance, our earlier example of someone who initially made an inflation forecast using an average of the past three years' inflation rates but then learned that the Fed intended to increase the money growth rate substantially. If your goal is to make the best prediction of inflation so as to make the best possible choices for the coming year, then sticking with your original, adaptive forecast clearly would not be in your own best interest. The *rational* way to respond to the new information is to use your own understanding of how a higher money growth rate will influence the price level and the inflation rate. Then you update your inflation rate forecast accordingly.

Hence, the difference between adaptive and rational expectations can be summarized in the following manner:

> An *adaptive* expectation is based only on past information. In contrast, a *rational* expectation takes into account both past and current information, plus an understanding of how the economy functions.

Advantages of the Rational Expectations Hypothesis   Because the rational expectations hypothesis does not impose artificial constraints on how people use information, it is a more general theory of expectations formation than the hypothesis of adaptive expectations. Whereas the adaptive expectations process is restricted to past information, the rational expectations hypothesis states that if an individual can improve upon an adaptive forecast, then that individual will do so.

Under some circumstances, a person's rationally formed expectation may look like an adaptive expectation. If a person has only past information and no special insight into how the economy functions, then an adaptive forecast may be the best that person can do. In this case, an adaptive expectation will be the individual's rational expectation.

Usually, however, people will use all available current information plus all their knowledge about the economy's workings when they try to infer the price level and forecast the inflation rate. Consequently, under most circumstances, a rationally formed expectation will differ from a purely adaptive expectation.

We must emphasize that even though rational expectations generally are better than adaptive expectations, forecasts based on all current information and an understanding of how the economy works still will not always be correct. For instance, the widespread adoption of Doppler radar by the National Weather Service has improved the ability of weather forecasters to predict where tornadoes may form. As a result, tornado forecasts are better than before, but they still are not always on the mark. Likewise, rationally formed forecasts are better, on average, than adaptive forecasts. Nevertheless, the actual price level and inflation rate can still turn out to be different than people rationally predicted.

Are There Limits on Rationality?   The rational expectations hypothesis presents a couple of conceptual problems of its own. One problem is that the hypothesis is very broad, so broad that incorporating it fully into a macroeconomic model can prove challenging. For instance, each individual in an economy has her or his own perspective on how the economy works. In addition, at any given instant each person is informed to a somewhat different extent about current economic developments. Should economists therefore try to model every individual's expectations formation procedure?

A related difficulty is that each individual in the economy should act on his or her rationally formed expectation of the price level and the inflation rate. This means that the actual price level and inflation rate will depend on how all form their expectations. If each person realizes that others' expectations affect the actual price level and inflation rate, does this mean that each person should attempt to forecast others' forecasts?

To get around these problems, macroeconomists often use two simplifying assumption when they construct theories that include rational expectations. Under the **representative agent assumption**, a macroeconomic model presumes that each person in the economy has access to the same information and has the same conception of how the economy works. This gets around the issue of different expectations across individuals in the economy. Furthermore, by assuming that all people make the same forecast, the representative agent assumption also avoids the problem of individuals worrying about others' forecasts.

The second common assumption used in macroeconomic models with rational expectations is that people in the economy understand how the economy functions. That is, a macroeconomist using the rational expectations hypothesis typically assumes that the people whose aggregate behavior their models try to describe behave *as if* they understand that the economy works according to the macroeconomists' own theory. This assumption boils down to presuming that the people in a macroeconomic model *know the model.*

REPRESENTATIVE AGENT ASSUMPTION The assumption that all people in an economy have access to the same information and have the same understanding of how the economy works.

As you will learn in Chapter 11, a number of macroeconomists today question the wisdom of assuming that people are all the same and understand exactly how the price level and inflation are determined. Nevertheless, both the representative agent assumption and the assumption that people understand the workings of the economy greatly simplify the inclusion of the rational expectations hypothesis in any macroeconomic model. For this reason, we shall also adopt these assumptions in this chapter and in Chapter 10.

INTERNET SOURCE

Making Sure Your Own Expectations Are Up to Date

STAT-USA—Recent Domestic and International Socioeconomic Data on the Internet
Internet URL: **http://www.stat-usa.gov**

Navigation: Start at STAT-USA homepage above. Scan down to *Daily Economic News* and click on. For other recent information, click on *Domestic Economic News and Statistical Series.*

FUNDAMENTAL ISSUE #1

What is the distinction between adaptive and rational expectations? An adaptive expectation is formed using only past information. In contrast, a rationally formed expectation is based on past and current information and on an understanding of how macroeconomic variables are determined.

NEW CLASSICAL HYPOTHESES

The first macroeconomists to incorporate the rational expectations hypothesis in their theories are known as *new classical economists*. Beginning in the 1970s, this group argued that expectations are so important that they should play a key role in any macroeconomic theory. The theory that the new classical economists promoted returned to themes of the classical theory that we surveyed in Chapter 3.

Because the new classical economists were the first to include the rational expectations hypothesis in their macroeconomic models, at one time many economists used the terms "new classical theory" and "rational expectations theory" interchangeably. As we shall discuss in Chapters 10 and 11, however, most other macroeconomists—including some whose theories are very nonclassical—now use the rational expectations hypothesis in their models as well. Thus, it is important to recognize that the rational expectations hypothesis does not necessarily lead to new classical conclusions. Instead, the rational expectations hypothesis is just a part of a broader theory now known as *new classical macroeconomics.*

The Basis of New Classical Theory: Wage and Price Flexibility

The key assumption of the new classical theory is that pure competition, with completely flexible wages and prices, prevails in the economy. This, you will recall from Chapter 3, is also a primary presumption of classical theory.

Adopting this assumption means ruling out stickiness of nominal wages that might result from explicit or implicit wage contracts or from minimum-wage laws. While not denying that such contracts exist in the real world, many new classical theorists conclude that the contracts play such a minor role in the larger scheme of things that they cannot keep wages from moving to levels consistent with equating the quantity of labor demanded with the quantity of labor supplied in the labor market. This, of course, is exactly what the original classical economists proposed. This assumption, of course, conflicts with traditional Keynesian theory. As you will learn in Chapter 10, it also conflicts with Keynesian approaches that incorporate the rational expectations hypothesis. (See the Policy Notebook on page 302: *Can We Assume That Prices Are Flexible?*)

In addition, the pure competition assumption rules out the possibility that prices of goods and services may adjust slowly to changes in economic conditions. As we shall discuss in Chapter 11, some modern Keynesian theorists argue that pure competition is so rare that prices of goods and services typically are not determined in purely competitive markets. The new classical economists, in contrast, contend that competitive markets are the rule, rather than the exception.

Self-Interest and Rational Forecasts

The new classical theory is based on two additional assumptions. The first is that people are motivated by rational self-interest. Most economists would say this assumption should underlie any economic model. Macroeconomic models typically assume that people pursue their own self-interest.

The other key assumption of new classical theory is that no one has complete information, but all individuals nevertheless form rational expectations. To do so, they use all available past and current information and their understanding of how the economy functions.

As you will now see, these assumptions lead to some striking implications about the effects—and the lack of effects—of macroeconomic policies intended to stabilize the economy. These implications have engendered considerable debate among macroeconomists. This ongoing debate is the subject of most of the remainder of this book.

POLICY NOTEBOOK

Can We Assume That Prices Are Flexible?

One of the mainstays of traditional Keynesian and some new Keynesian theories is that prices are "sticky." In contrast, one of the assumptions of the new classical model is that prices freely adjust to equilibrium levels and therefore are not "sticky" at non-market-clearing levels. Any notion of the speed of transmission of monetary and/or fiscal policy depends critically on the validity of this notion. If prices are indeed sticky, then adjustment takes time. If prices of goods and services increase immediately in the same proportion as, for example, an increase in the money supply, adjustment would occur instantaneously.

Recently, Mark A. Wynne, senior economist at the Federal Reserve Bank of Dallas, reviewed the studies that purported to examine the question of whether prices are sticky. Wynne was only able to find three studies that made what he considered a serious attempt to document price stickiness in the U.S. economy since World War II. Additionally, the studies that exist covered an extremely small part of gross domestic product. He points, for example, to an often-cited study by Stephen Cecchetti that dealt only with the newsstand prices of magazines. Magazines clearly constitute a triv-

ial part of our annual GDP. Also, because the three research studies did not want to deal with quality changes, they chose homogeneous products and thus were limited to low-tech products such as magazines, steel, lumber, shoes, and shirts.

Finally, Wynne points out that all of the studies examined only posted prices. It is not clear that posted prices really provide much evidence about actual transaction prices. If buyers and sellers can alter product characteristics to change the price per constant-quality unit, then the stickiness of posted prices really doesn't tell us much. To the extent that price may not be the sole mechanism that is used to allocate goods and services, any observation about whether prices remain rigid is of less interest to macroeconomists.

In conclusion, there is not much evidence one way or the other to support (or reject, for that matter) the assumption of sticky prices. Presumably, this could become an area of fruitful future research.

FOR CRITICAL ANALYSIS:
What are some of the ways that the price per constant-quality unit can adjust without the posted price changing?

ON THE WEB
Visit the Federal Reserve Bank of Dallas at:
www.dallasfed.org

FUNDAMENTAL ISSUE #2

What are the key assumptions underlying new classical macroeconomics? As in other macroeconomic theories, the new classical model assumes that people pursue their self-interest. Like the classical model, the new classical framework is based on the assumption that purely competitive behavior leads to the determination of flexibly adjusting wages and prices. Finally, like the Keynesian and monetarist theories of aggregate supply, the new classical model assumes that information is imperfect in the short run. People form price-level and inflation rate expectations rationally, however, in the new classical model.

THE ESSENTIAL FEATURES OF THE NEW CLASSICAL MODEL

You learned in Chapter 8 that the traditional Keynesian theory of aggregate supply relies on the assumption that workers decide how much labor to supply based on fixed expectations of the price level and the inflation rate. Consequently, a higher price level and inflation rate induced by increased aggregate demand cause workers to misperceive resulting nominal wage increases as higher real wages. Thus, workers supply more labor services, equilibrium employment rises, and firms produce more real output. Because the monetarist theory of short-run price-level and output determination shares this feature, it yields these same short-term implications.

The new classical theory challenges the idea of fixed expectations, because rigid expectations typically arise under the hypothesis of adaptive expectations. Under the rational expectations hypothesis, the traditional Keynesian predictions about workers' behavior indicate that they behave irrationally, unless one is willing to argue that workers cannot observe factors that will raise aggregate demand or fail to understand that rises in aggregate demand will increase the price level and the inflation rate. Typically, the new classical economists argue, workers are smarter than the traditional Keynesian and monetarist theories give them credit for being. They pay attention to factors that affect aggregate demand, and they update their forecasts based on a recognition that such factors ultimately will affect the price level and the inflation rate.

Making Rational Forecasts by Anticipating Policy Actions

Among the factors that affect aggregate demand are monetary policy actions and, at least according to traditional Keynesian theory, fiscal policy actions. According to the new classical theory, people understand this and therefore pay close attention to current and anticipated future policy actions by central bank or governmental officials. They follow current policy actions by keeping up with media reports, and from such reports they make inferences about likely future policy actions.

Policy Anticipations and Rational Forecasts   To capture the idea that people track current policies and try to forecast future policies, the new classical economists propose that workers' expectation of the price level, P^e, depends in part on their expectation of the money stock, M^e. In addition, to the extent that people believe that fiscal policies affect aggregate demand and the price level, P^e also depends on their expectation of government expenditures, g^e, and their expectation about the level of taxes, t^e.

It is important to recognize that M^e, g^e, and t^e all denote the settings of monetary and fiscal policy variables that people *anticipate*. The central bank, of course, determines the actual quantity of money, M. Likewise, the government determines its actual expenditures, g, and actual taxes, t. Actual policy choices by the central bank and the government may or may not correspond to what people anticipate. How closely actual events correspond to expectations depends on how well people are able to predict central bank and government policy choices.

Fed Watching   A real-world example of the sort of forecasting behavior that the new classical model proposes is known as **Fed watching**. A number of economists make a living by observing each nuance of Federal Reserve policymaking and selling forecasts of likely Fed policy actions during the coming weeks or months. Many of these professional "Fed watchers" work as independent consultants, but some are employed by banks, investment firms, and other financial services corporations.

In terms of the new classical model, Fed watchers help people keep their forecasts of monetary policy, M^e, as up-to-date as possible. You might wonder why people are willing to pay for Fed watchers' services instead of just watching the Fed themselves. The reason is that the Fed is a quasi-independent agency of the federal government that has been able to keep many aspects of its decision-making process secret. Consequently, forecasting the Fed's next move is more of a challenge than, say, anticipating how politicians, who typically make their views on spending or tax policies very public, are likely to vote on fiscal policy actions. People with some inside knowledge of the Fed, such as former Fed economists, often become Fed watchers. Although former Fed employees are "out of the loop" once they leave their Fed jobs, they still may have more insight into how the Fed is likely to act than people with no Fed experience. People lacking any Fed background then may be willing to pay for the expertise of the Fed watchers.

The Effects of Macroeconomic Policy Actions in the New Classical Model

Now let's consider the new classical theory of short-run output and price-level determination. The foundation of the new classical theory is the monetarist short-run model, which in turn corresponds to the traditional Keynesian theory. As shown in Figure 9–1, the aggregate demand schedule slopes downward, and its position depends on the actual values of the money stock, government expenditures, and taxes, denoted M_1, g_1, and t_1, respectively. As in the Keynesian imperfect-information theory of aggregate supply, the aggregate supply schedule slopes upward. Its position depends on people's expectation of the price level, P^e.

As discussed above, however, key determinants of the price-level expectation that people form are their specific anticipations of monetary and fiscal policy choices, denoted M_1^e, g_1^e, and t_1^e. Hence, we label the aggregate supply schedule as $y^s(P^e: M_1^e, g_1^e, t_1^e)$ to indicate that its position depends on the expectation of the price level, which in turn depends on anticipated values of policy variables.

Policy anticipations may not always be correct. Nevertheless, we shall assume that initially these anticipations *are* correct, so that $M_1^e = M_1$, $g_1^e = g_1$, and $t_1^e = t_1$. Consequently, $P^e = P_1$ at point E in Figure 9–1, so initially people expect the equilibrium current price level. The question now is what effects policy *changes* will have on the equilibrium price level and real output, depending on whether or not people correctly anticipate them.

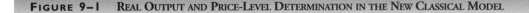

FIGURE 9–1 **REAL OUTPUT AND PRICE-LEVEL DETERMINATION IN THE NEW CLASSICAL MODEL**

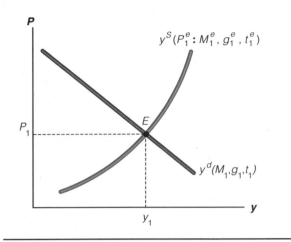

According to the new classical theory, individuals form their current expectation of the price level P_1^e, which influences the position of the aggregate supply function, based on their rational forecast of monetary and fiscal policy choices, M_1^e, g_1^e, and t_1^e. A nation's central bank determines the actual money stock, M_1, while its government sets the actual level of government spending, g_1, and net real taxes, t_1. These policy changes affect the position of the aggregate demand schedule. Together, aggregate demand and aggregate supply determine the equilibrium price level and the equilibrium amount of real output.

The Effects of Anticipated Policy Actions   Figure 9–2 on page 306 illustrates the effects of policy actions that are *correctly* anticipated. These actions are an increase in the money stock, from M_1 to M_2, a rise in government spending from g_1 to g_2, and a tax reduction from t_1 to t_2. These policy actions together shift the aggregate demand schedule rightward, as shown in the figure.

Suppose that people correctly anticipate these policy actions, meaning that they alter their expectations of the monetary and fiscal policy variables to $M_2^e = M_2$, $g_2^e = g_2$, and $t_2^e = t_2$. As a result, people anticipate the rise in the price level brought about by the policy-induced increase in aggregate demand. This rise in their price expectation implies an expectation that the real wage will fall. Workers cut back on their supply of labor to firms, and firms supply less real output at any given price level. As a result, the aggregate supply schedule, y^s, will shift leftward, as shown. At the new short-run equilibrium point, E', the equilibrium price level is higher, at P_2, but real output remains unchanged, at y_1. Correct anticipations of the monetary and fiscal policy actions effectively neutralize their effects on actual real output. Correctly anticipated monetary and fiscal policy actions thereby will have no real output effects, *even in the short run*. They will result only in a higher price level.

To understand why these effects occur, recall from Chapter 3 that the classical aggregate supply schedule is vertical, because in the classical model people have full information. As a result, any increase in the price level resulting from a rise in aggregate demand will be fully anticipated, so real output will not change. The example in Figure 9–2 differs from the classical model of Chapter 3 only in that information is not complete. Nevertheless, by correctly anticipating policy actions that will raise aggregate demand and the price level, the people in our example act as though they had complete information. Consequently, the outcome looks very "classical": Real output is not affected by a policy-induced rise in aggregate demand.

FIGURE 9–2   THE EFFECTS OF CORRECTLY ANTICIPATED POLICY ACTIONS

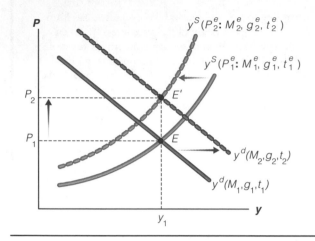

Expansionary monetary and fiscal policy actions, such as an increase in the money stock, an increase in real government expenditures, or a reduction in real net taxes, will cause a rightward shift in the aggregate demand schedule. In the new classical theory, if people correctly forecast these policy actions, then they will fully anticipate the increase in the price level that the actions will induce. Accordingly, individuals will raise their price expectation, causing a leftward shift in the aggregate supply schedule. On net, the equilibrium price level will rise, but the equilibrium amount of real output will remain unchanged.

The Effects of Unanticipated Policy Actions   Of course, people cannot always correctly predict macroeconomic policies. A majority of Congress might enact a spending increase, but the president might unexpectedly veto the spending bill. The Federal Reserve might announce that it plans a particular growth rate for the money stock but may not successfully induce that money growth rate. The Fed might even intentionally change the money growth rate relative to its announced intention because of changes in economic activity that it believes require a policy response. If the Fed fails to communicate its change in policy, people will not correctly anticipate its action.

Figure 9–3 displays the effects of monetary and fiscal policy actions that people completely fail to anticipate. Again, the policy actions are an increase in the money stock, from M_1 to M_2, a rise in government spending from g_1 to g_2, and a tax reduction from t_1 to t_2, which together shift the aggregate demand schedule rightward.

Because workers anticipated that the money stock, government spending, and taxes would remain equal to M_1, g_1, and t_1, respectively, in the short run they misperceive any rise in the nominal wage as indicating an increase in their real wage. The nominal wage increase occurs, because a rise in the price level caused by the unanticipated increase in aggregate demand increases the demand for labor. Workers increase the quantity of labor services that they supply, and firms produce more real output. In the short run, therefore, the equilibrium price level will rise, from P_1 to P_2, and equilibrium real output will increase, from y_1 to y_2, as the aggregate demand schedule shifts along the aggregate supply schedule from point E to point E'.

In the long run, according to the new classical model, people ultimately recognize that these monetary and fiscal policy actions have taken place. They eventually adjust their policy anticipations appropriately, and their price-level expectations increase. In

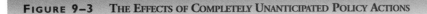

FIGURE 9–3   THE EFFECTS OF COMPLETELY UNANTICIPATED POLICY ACTIONS

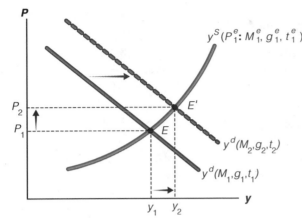

If the central bank increases the nominal quantity of money in circulation and if the government raises real government spending or reduces real net taxes, then the aggregate demand schedule will shift rightward. If these policy actions are completely unanticipated, then individuals will not have forecast the actions, and their price expectations will remain unchanged. Consequently, the aggregate supply schedule's position does not change, and the rise in aggregate demand induces an increase in both the equilibrium price level and the equilibrium level of real output.

the long run, therefore, the aggregate supply schedule will shift leftward as in Figure 9–2. As in the monetarist framework, an unanticipated policy-induced increase in aggregate demand will exert no effects on longer-run equilibrium real output. In the short run, however, real output will rise.

FUNDAMENTAL ISSUE #3

How do policy anticipations determine the actual effects of policy actions in the new classical model? On the one hand, if people are able to anticipate monetary or fiscal policy actions correctly, then they will adjust their price and inflation expectations accordingly. As a result, correctly anticipated policy actions have no real effects. On the other hand, policy actions that people are not able to anticipate have short-run effects on real output, employment, and the unemployment rate that mirror those predicted by Keynesian and monetarist theory.

THE POLICY INEFFECTIVENESS PROPOSITION

The examples in Figures 9–2 and 9–3 illustrate the key policy implications of the new classical theory. Only macroeconomic policy actions that are not fully anticipated can affect real output in the short run. Correctly anticipated policy actions can have no effects on real output. This means that correctly anticipated actions also cannot influence employment or the unemployment rate.

The Policy Ineffectiveness Proposition

POLICY INEFFECTIVENESS PROPOSITION The new classical conclusion that if policy actions are anticipated, they have no real effects in the short run; nor do policy actions have real effects in the long run even if the policy actions are unanticipated.

These conclusions form the basis for a key implication of the new classical theory—the **policy ineffectiveness proposition**. This proposition states that *systematic*, or predictable, macroeconomic policy actions should have no short-run effects on real variables, such as employment, the unemployment rate, or real GDP. Systematic policy actions that people can anticipate lead only to changes in the price level and the inflation rate.

The policy ineffectiveness proposition applies only to the effects of systematic policy actions that people can anticipate. *Unsystematic* policies, which people cannot always anticipate fully, can still have short-run real effects. Although these effects disappear in the long run, as in the monetarist model, in principle they could be sizable in the short run.

Hence, the new classical theory has the following key implications for macroeconomic policymaking:

> **According to new classical theory, macroeconomic policy actions that individuals and firms fully anticipate have no effects on real variables such as output and employment. Only unanticipated policy actions that people cannot predict in advance can influence real GDP and employment.**

A Rationale for Policy Subterfuge?

Although it has opened up somewhat in recent years, the Federal Reserve remains a secretive institution. Innocent-looking Fed documents and memoranda carry labels such as "confidential" or "highly confidential."

In 1975, a Georgetown University law student filed suit against the Federal Reserve under the 1966 Freedom of Information Act, which empowers any U.S. citizen to request any government document and places the burden of proving the need for secrecy on the government agency that possesses the document. The student requested immediate release of the instructions that Fed officials give to traders who conduct the Fed's open-market operations in the government securities markets. In 1976 a U.S. district court ruled in the student's favor. For the next three years, the Fed pursued an appeal to the United States Supreme Court. Ultimately, the Supreme Court remanded the case back to the district court, which then decided in the Fed's favor. Since that time, the Fed has continued its policy of secrecy. Government prosecutors have supported the courts' legal interpretations of the Fed's authority by prosecuting a Federal Reserve bank director in 1989 for leaking votes on discount rate changes and a former governor of the Federal Reserve Board in 1994 for allegedly divulging inside information about the policy inclinations of Federal Reserve bank presidents.

This defense of monetary policy secrecy fits neatly into the new classical framework. After all, the new classical model indicates that monetary policy actions can have real effects only if they are unanticipated. Thus, the only way that the Fed could exert short-run effects on real output would be if its actions were unpredictable. Hence, the new classical theory potentially could explain both the Fed's unwillingness to divulge its true policy intentions. To affect real output, Fed officials would have to engage in such lack of clarity, if not in outright subterfuge.

Of course, secrecy potentially could lead to *less* macroeconomic stability, especially if unexpected policy changes induce sharp reactions in the choices of consumers, workers, and firms. For this reason, most new classical theorists argue that secrecy actually may create more instability in economic activity. They prescribe the elimination of most policy secretiveness in favor of consistent, predictable policy actions that are less likely to be destabilizing. According to new classical theory, of course, such predictable actions will have no effects on real output, but most new classical theorists argue that society would be better off in this event. We shall revisit this particular issue in Chapter 13.

FUNDAMENTAL ISSUE #4

What is the policy ineffectiveness proposition, and what is its implication for the conduct of policies intended to have real effects? The policy ineffectiveness proposition of the new classical theory is that systematic, or predictable, monetary and fiscal policies can have no short-run or long-run effects on real output, employment, or unemployment. This means that if policymakers wish to induce changes in such real variables, they must undertake policy actions that are unsystematic, or unpredictable.

RATIONAL EXPECTATIONS AND EFFICIENT MARKETS

The new classical economists have applied the rational expectations hypothesis to the theory of the determination of the price level and real output. Another important application of the rational expectations hypothesis, however, is in the area of financial markets.

Efficient Markets Theory

You learned in Chapter 6 that bond prices are inversely related to interest rates. To demonstrate this inverse relationship, we considered perpetual bonds that pay an infinite stream of coupon returns. To calculate the price that someone would be willing to pay for such a bond, we summed up the discounted present value of the stream of coupon returns. To compute the discounted present value of each year's coupon return, we used the current market interest rate. What if the market interest rate might vary from year to year? Then the price of the bond would actually equal the *expected* discounted present value of the stream of coupon returns, based on people's *expectations* of future market interest rates.

Rational Expectations and Financial Asset Returns   Let's think about how we might apply the rational expectations hypothesis to this more realistic view of how bond prices are determined. Under the rational expectations hypothesis, an optimal forecast reflects all available past *and* current information as well as an understanding of how the relevant variable is determined. In the case of an interest return, therefore, the rational expectations hypothesis would indicate that the expected future market interest rates used in bond-price calculations would be the rational forecast of future interest returns by those who purchase and hold financial assets.

As a result, the price of a perpetual bond is equal to the rationally anticipated discounted present value of the sum of future coupon returns. The market price thereby incorporates rationally formed expectations.

EFFICIENT MARKETS THEORY A theory that stems from applying the rational expectations hypothesis to financial markets; it states that equilibrium bond prices should reflect all past and current information plus bond traders' understanding of how bond prices are determined.

Efficient Markets Theory   This reasoning forms the basis for the **efficient markets theory**. This theory states that prices of financial assets should reflect all available information, including bond traders' understanding of how financial markets determine asset prices. As applied to the perpetual bond we studied in Chapter 6, the theory of efficient markets indicates that the current price of a bond should be equal to the rational forecast of the discounted value of the sum of coupon returns yielded by the bond.

More generally, the efficient markets theory says that the price of *any* financial asset should reflect the rational forecast of the asset's returns. Consequently, any bond price should reflect a recognition of all available information by those who trade the bonds. If the market bond price failed to reflect all such information, then the implication would be that the market functions inefficiently, because traders could earn higher returns on bonds by considering the unused information.

Can People "Beat the Market"?

Recognition that failure to use all available information will lead to lower returns than bond traders otherwise could earn leads to the key implication of the efficient markets theory: In an efficient financial market, there should be no unexploited opportunities for traders to earn higher returns. If such opportunities existed, some traders would buy or sell more bonds. This would cause the market price of the bonds to change.

What direction would the bonds' price move? The answer is that it would adjust to its efficient-market price that would reflect the rational forecasts of traders. Rational expectations in the bond market would lead to trading that would yield this efficient-market price.

Does this mean that no trader can ever earn profits from trading bonds? The answer clearly must be no, otherwise people would not earn their livelihoods by speculating in bond markets. Nevertheless, the efficient markets theory does indicate that bond speculators should not be able to earn profits from taking advantage of unused information for very long. Any unexploited information will quickly be recognized by a sufficient number of bond traders that bond prices will adjust quickly. Profits from such trades may be significant, but they also will be fleeting. (See Policy Notebook on page 312: *Should Using Inside Information Be Illegal?*)

FUNDAMENTAL ISSUE #5

What is the efficient markets theory, and what is its main implication? The efficient markets theory states that the market price of a financial asset should take into account all available information in that market. This theory, which follows from the application of the rational expectations hypothesis to financial markets, indicates that unexploited opportunities to earn higher returns in a financial market should not exist at the equilibrium price of the financial asset traded in that market.

INTEREST PARITY AND FOREIGN EXCHANGE MARKET EFFICIENCY

The concept of market efficiency does not apply only to financial asset prices and interest rates that are determined in a nation's domestic financial markets. It may also be extended to markets for financial assets that are traded internationally, such as bonds and national currencies. Ultimately, then, currency exchange rates, national interest rates, and expectations all must be related.

Exchange-Rate Determination

How is the exchange rate, or the dollar's exchange value in terms of other currencies, determined? We touched on this issue in Chapter 3, but let's consider it in more detail now that you understand the importance of information and expectations.

Should Using Inside Information Be Illegal?

Learning to read the financial pages will not ensure that your money income will increase, but it will make it easier to make more money. All you have to do is throw darts. Let's see how.

In 1967 the editors of *Forbes* taped the financial pages of a major newspaper to a wall and threw darts at the stock prices. The editors hit the stocks of twenty-eight different companies and invested a hypothetical $1,000 in each. By 1984 the original $28,000 had grown in value to $132,000, excluding dividends paid—a gain of 370 percent. Over the same period, the value of the Dow Jones Industrial Average increased less than 40 percent. Perhaps even more impressive, the editors' random selection of stocks outperformed the recommended stock portfolios of most of the gurus of stock forecasting. How did the darts do it?

Public Information of Little Value

Suppose that you, and you alone, noticed that the price of a particular stock moved in a predictable manner. For concreteness, let's assume the price rose 5 percent on even-numbered days and fell 5 percent on odd-numbered days, resulting in (approximately) no average change over time. Knowing this fact, how do you make money? You simply buy shares of the stock just before it is due to rise and sell shares of the stock just before it is due to fall. If you started the year with, say, $1,000 and reinvested your profits, following this strategy would yield profits in excess of $500,000 by the end of the year. If you were able to continue this process for a second year, your wealth would approach $270 million!

Of course, as your wealth accumulated, your purchases and sales based on "buying low and selling high" would start to affect the price of the stock. In particular, your sales would drive high prices down. Ultimately, your buying and selling in response to predictable patterns would eliminate those patterns. There would be no profit potential left to exploit. This is *exactly* what happens in the stock market—except that it happens much faster than a single person could accomplish it alone.

At any point in time, tens of thousands, even millions of people are looking for any bit of information that will enable them to forecast the future prices of stocks. Responding to any information that seems useful, these people try to buy low and sell high. As a result, *all publicly available information that might be used to forecast stock prices is taken into account—leaving no forecastable profit opportunities.* Because so many people are involved, this process occurs quite swiftly. Indeed, evidence suggests that *all* information entering the market is fully incorporated into stock prices within less than a minute of its arrival. Hence, most public information you obtain will prove to have little value.

Inside Information May Have Great Value, Though

Clearly, then, public information is of little value. If you could obtain inside information, however, the situation would be different. Suppose that a close friend who works at, say, Microsoft tells you that Microsoft has just discovered a new way to use the Internet that is ten times better than before. In principle, you could profit handsomely by purchasing the stock of Microsoft before the information becomes public. If you do so, however, you are guilty of a crime.

Currently, the use of inside information is illegal. Some have argued that the law should be changed. After all, if inside information were legal, the price of the stock would attain its true value more rapidly. Presumably, according to critics of the current law, people who wanted employment positions from which they could profit from inside information would compete for those positions and drive down salaries so that their total expected income would be no greater than it currently is. In the meantime, the stock and bond markets would become more efficient.

FOR CRITICAL ANALYSIS:

Even if legalizing the use of inside information would make stock and bond markets more efficient, what are the arguments in favor of keeping it illegal?

FOREIGN EXCHANGE MARKETS
Markets in which currencies of different nations are exchanged.

The exchange rate is a price that is determined in markets for foreign exchange. Therefore, the value of the exchange rate is determined by the interactions between the forces of demand and supply in **foreign exchange markets**, which are the markets in which individuals, businesses, governments, and central banks exchange currencies of various nations.

Exchange Rates   Before we discuss foreign exchange markets, you need to understand how exchange rates are measured. Consider Figure 9–4 on page 314, which displays exchange rates for selected nations' currrencies as they appear each day in the *Wall Street Journal*.

For purposes of discussion, we shall confine our attention to the value of the dollar in terms of the German deutsche mark (DM). Figure 9–4 indicates that as of January 9, 1997, $1 could have purchased about 1.58 DM. This meant that the exchange rate at that time was 1.58 DM per dollar, which we can write as 1.58 DM/$. But it also meant that 1.58 DM could have purchased $1, or that 1 DM could have purchased $1/(1.58) = $0.63. Hence, the 1997 dollar–deutsche mark rate of exchange could also have been expressed as 0.63 dollars per DM, or 0.63 $/DM.

As you can see, because the exchange rate measures the value of one nation's currency in terms of the currency of another nation, it can always be expressed in two ways. Consequently, we must specify which measure we are using when we discuss changes in exchange rates. Just saying that the exchange rate "rose" or "fell" means little unless we know which of the two measures we have in mind. Throughout our discussion, we shall look at the dollar–deutsche mark exchange rate from a U.S. perspective: We shall express the exchange rate in terms of dollars that must be given up in exchange for deutsche marks, such as the 0.63 $/DM exchange rate that applied in June 1997. This is the dollar value of the deutsche mark. An increase in this exchange rate indicates an appreciation of the value of the deutsche mark relative to the dollar and, equivalently, a depreciation of the value of the dollar relative to the deutsche mark.

INTERNET SOURCE

On-Line Currency Conversions

Olsen and Associates—Currency Converter
Internet URL: **http://www.oanda.com**

Navigation: Start at the Olsen & Associates homepage (**http://www.oanda.com**). Click on *164 Currencies Converter.* Select the currencies you wish to compare, and enter the amount of one currency to convert to the other at the current exchange rate.

Imports and the Demand for Foreign Currency   The primary reason that U.S. residents might desire to obtain the currency of another country is that they wish to

FIGURE 9–4   EXCHANGE RATES

CURRENCY TRADING

Thursday, January 9, 1997

EXCHANGE RATES

The New York foreign exchange selling rates below apply to trading among banks in amounts of $1 million and more, as quoted at 4 p.m. Eastern time by Dow Jones Telerate Inc. and other sources. Retail transactions provide fewer units of foreign currency per dollar.

Country	U.S. $ equiv. Thu	Wed	Currency per U.S. $ Thu	Wed
Argentina (Peso)	1.0012	1.0012	.9988	.9988
Australia (Dollar)	.7812	.7805	1.2801	1.2812
Austria (Schilling)	.09025	.09043	11.080	11.058
Bahrain (Dinar)	2.6525	2.6525	.3770	.3770
Belgium (Franc)	.03074	.03080	32.535	32.470
Brazil (Real)	.9606	.9607	1.0410	1.0409
Britain (Pound)	1.6961	1.6880	.5896	.5924
30-Day Forward	1.6950	1.6869	.5900	.5928
90-Day Forward	1.6925	1.6843	.5908	.5937
180-Day Forward	1.6885	1.6802	.5923	.5952
Canada (Dollar)	.7398	.7399	1.3518	1.3516
30-Day Forward	.7412	.7414	1.3491	1.3488
90-Day Forward	.7440	.7442	1.3440	1.3437
180-Day Forward	.7478	.7479	1.3373	1.3370
Chile (Peso)	.002355	.002352	424.55	425.25
China (Renminbi)	.1201	.1201	8.3268	8.3272
Colombia (Peso)	.0009935	.0009985	1006.50	1001.50
Czech. Rep. (Koruna)				
Commercial rate	.03657	.03662	27.342	27.307
Denmark (Krone)	.1663	.1663	6.0134	6.0118
Ecuador (Sucre)				
Floating rate	.0002766	.0002766	3615.00	3615.00
Finland (Markka)	.2128	.2121	4.6995	4.7150
France (Franc)	.1879	.1879	5.3220	5.3220
30-Day Forward	.1882	.1882	5.3125	5.3126
90-Day Forward	.1889	.1889	5.2928	5.2935
180-Day Forward	.1901	.1901	5.2602	5.2617
Germany (Mark)	.6339	.6352	1.5776	1.5744
30-Day Forward	.6351	.6364	1.5745	1.5714
90-Day Forward	.6376	.6389	1.5685	1.5652
180-Day Forward	.6416	.6430	1.5586	1.5552
Greece (Drachma)	.004053	.004049	246.73	246.98
Hong Kong (Dollar)	.1293	.1292	7.7367	7.7390
Hungary (Forint)	.006112	.006139	163.61	162.89
India (Rupee)	.02789	.02787	35.855	35.875
Indonesia (Rupiah)	.0004232	.0004233	2362.75	2362.15
Ireland (Punt)	1.6628	1.6664	.6014	.6001
Israel (Shekel)	.3079	.3079	3.2477	3.2474
Italy (Lira)	.0006500	.0006483	1538.50	1542.50

Country	U.S. $ equiv. Thu	Wed	Currency per U.S. $ Thu	Wed
Japan (Yen)	.008591	.008639	116.40	115.75
30-Day Forward	.008628	.008676	115.91	115.26
90-Day Forward	.008700	.008750	114.95	114.28
180-Day Forward	.008814	.008865	113.45	112.80
Jordan (Dinar)	1.4075	1.4075	.7105	.7105
Kuwait (Dinar)	3.3322	3.3367	.3001	.2997
Lebanon (Pound)	.0006446	.0006445	1551.25	1551.50
Malaysia (Ringgit)	.4028	.4018	2.4825	2.4885
Malta (Lira)	2.7473	2.7624	.3640	.3620
Mexico (Peso)				
Floating rate	.1276	.1278	7.8390	7.8220
Netherland (Guilder)	.5649	.5655	1.7703	1.7685
New Zealand (Dollar)	.7078	.7072	1.4128	1.4140
Norway (Krone)	.1551	.1540	6.4492	6.4926
Pakistan (Rupee)	.02529	.02529	39.540	39.540
Peru (new Sol)	.3814	.3814	2.6218	2.6218
Philippines (Peso)	.03798	.03800	26.332	26.318
Poland (Zloty)	.3455	.3460	2.8945	2.8900
Portugal (Escudo)	.006345	.006307	157.61	158.55
Russia (Ruble) (a)	.0001788	.0001787	5594.00	5595.00
Saudi Arabia (Riyal)	.2666	.2666	3.7505	3.7503
Singapore (Dollar)	.7116	.7116	1.4053	1.4053
Slovak Rep. (Koruna)	.03259	.03259	30.688	30.688
South Africa (Rand)	.2141	.2141	4.6705	4.6705
South Korea (Won)	.001181	.001184	846.75	844.75
Spain (Peseta)	.007536	.007546	132.70	132.52
Sweden (Krona)	.1446	.1431	6.9155	6.9865
Switzerland (Franc)	.7302	.7334	1.3695	1.3635
30-Day Forward	.7325	.7357	1.3652	1.3593
90-Day Forward	.7369	.7401	1.3570	1.3511
180-Day Forward	.7438	.7470	1.3444	1.3386
Taiwan (Dollar)	.03637	.03638	27.492	27.489
Thailand (Baht)	.03902	.03902	25.630	25.625
Turkey (Lira)	.00000907	.00000911	110215.00	109755.00
United Arab (Dirham)	.2723	.2723	3.6720	3.6720
Uruguay (New Peso)				
Financial	.1145	.1145	8.7300	8.7300
Venezuela (Bolivar)	.002098	.002098	476.70	476.70
SDR	1.4292	1.4315	.6997	.6986
ECU	1.2327	1.2308	....	....

Special Drawing Rights (SDR) are based on exchange rates for the U.S., German, British, French, and Japanese currencies. Source: International Monetary Fund.

European Currency Unit (ECU) is based on a basket of community currencies.

a-fixing, Moscow Interbank Currency Exchange.

Each day the *Wall Street Journal* reports data on exchange rates for the currencies of more than fifty nations.

SOURCE: *Wall Street Journal*, 1997.

buy goods and services produced in that nation. To help envision the factors that influence the quantity of a foreign currency, such as the deutsche mark, that U.S. residents might wish to obtain, consider an example. Suppose that a U.S. consumer purchased a German-manufactured coffeemaker in August 1991. The German manufacturer sent the coffeemaker to the United States to be sold that year at a price of 43 DM. Thus, at the 1991 exchange rate of 0.58 $/DM, the dollar price of the coffeemaker was equal to 42.91 DM × 0.58 $/DM, or $24.94.

Now imagine that the same consumer considered buying the same coffeemaker model in July 1995. Suppose further that the deutsche mark price of the coffeemaker remained unchanged, at 43 DM, between 1991 and 1995. Nevertheless, the deutschemark strengthened relative to the dollar, so exchange rate increased to about 0.72 $/DM. As a result, the dollar price of the coffeemaker rose to 43 DM × 0.72 $/DM = $30.96. Hence, in dollar terms the price of the coffeemaker rose by $6.02, which amounted to a 24.1 percent price increase.

When faced with such a sizable increase in the dollar price of the German-manufactured coffeemaker, the U.S. consumer may have decided to buy a U.S.-made coffeemaker instead. Likewise, other U.S. residents likely tended to cut their purchases of goods manufactured in Germany, which will experience similar dollar price increases. Consequently, U.S. importers reduced their orders for German-made products, which these importers purchased from German firms using deutsche marks acquired in the foreign exchange market. Hence, the amount of deutsche marks demanded in the foreign exchange market fell as a result of the rise in the dollar–deutsche mark exchange rate from 0.58 $/DM to 0.72 $/DM. It follows that the *demand schedule* for deutsche marks slopes downward, as shown in Figure 9–5.

Exports and the Supply of Foreign Currency   We must also think about the effect of a rise in the dollar–deutsche mark exchange rate from the perspective of German residents. Suppose that a German importer buys U.S.-manufactured computer microchips for resale in Germany. For the sake of argument, suppose also that a typical lot of microchips has a dollar price of $500 and that this base price did not change between 1991 and 1995. At the 1991 exchange rate of 0.58 $/DM, the deutsche mark price of the lot of microchips during that year would have been $500/(0.58

FIGURE 9–5   THE MARKET FOR GERMAN DEUTSCHE MARKS

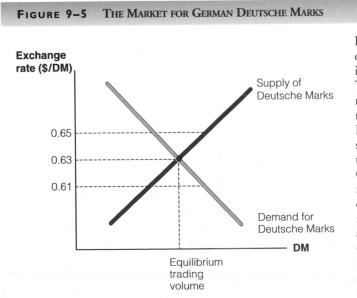

Holding other factors constant, as the dollar price of the deutsche mark declines, U.S. residents are inclined to purchase more German-made goods. Therefore they convert more dollars into deutsche marks, thereby increasing the quantity of deutsche marks demanded in the foreign exchange market. Hence, the demand schedule for deutsche marks slopes downward. At the same time, a decline in the dollar price of the deutsche mark induces German residents to cut their purchases of U.S.-made goods, thereby reducing the quantity of deutsche marks supplied in the foreign exchange market. Consequently, the deutsche mark supply schedule slopes upward. At the equilibrium exchange rate, or dollar price of the deutsche mark, the quantity of deutsche marks supplied is equal to the quantity of deutsche marks demanded.

$/DM), or 862 DM. In 1997, however, at the exchange rate of 0.72 $/DM, the same computer sold at a deutsche mark price of $500/(0.72 $/DM), or about 694 DM. Therefore, from the perspective of a German consumer, the U.S. price of the lot of microchips fell by 168 deutsche marks, or by about 19.5 percent.

This sizable fall in the deutsche mark price of the U.S.-manufactured microchips tends to induce a rise in German purchases of U.S. microchips. In like manner, declines in prices of other U.S. export goods caused German purchases of U.S. goods to rise. German importers increased their orders for U.S. export goods, which they bought with dollars that they obtained in the foreign exchange market. These German importers supplied more deutsche marks in exchange for dollars. Consequently, the rise in the dollar–deutsche mark exchange rate from 0.58 $/DM to 0.72 $/DM increased the quantity of deutsche marks supplied in the foreign exchange market. As Figure 9–5 shows, the *supply schedule* for deutsche marks generally was upward sloping.

The Equilibrium Foreign Exchange Rate   Figure 9–5 also depicts the determination of an *equilibrium exchange rate* between the deutsche mark and the dollar. This is the rate of exchange of dollars for deutsche marks at which the amount of deutsche marks demanded is equal to the amount of deutsche marks supplied in the foreign exchange market.

In Figure 9–5, we assume that the equilibrium exchange rate is 0.63 $/DM. If the exchange rate happened to be above this level, perhaps at the rate of 0.65 $/DM, then there would be fewer deutsche marks demanded than supplied. Some German residents who wished to supply deutsche marks for dollars would be unable to sell their deutsche marks at this exchange rate, so they would be obliged to offer the deutsche marks at a lower exchange rate. Consequently, the exchange rate would fall toward the equilibrium rate of 0.63 $/DM. In contrast, if the exchange rate fell below the equilibrium rate, say, to 0.61 $/DM, then there would be more deutsche marks demanded than supplied, and so the exchange rate would tend to rise back toward the equilibrium rate of 0.63 $/DM.

ON THE WEB
Obtain Currency Quotes from the GNN/Koblas Converter at:
http://bin.gnn.com/cgi-bin/gnn/currency

Covered and Uncovered Interest Parity

Although we have explained demand and supply in the foreign exchange market solely by referring to exports and imports of goods, U.S. residents also hold financial assets issued in Germany, and German residents hold financial assets issued in the United States. U.S. financial assets are denominated in dollars and pay dollar-denominated interest returns, while German financial assets are denominated in deutsche marks and pay deutsche mark–denominated interest returns. Because the exchange rate measures the relative values of the two currencies, the exchange rate must play a role in relating interest rates in the two countries.

Covered Interest Parity   If you take another look at Figure 9–4 on page 314, you will note that more than one exchange rate is listed for several major U.S. trading

SPOT EXCHANGE RATE The rate of exchange for currencies to be traded immediately

FORWARD EXCHANGE RATES The rate of exchange for currencies specified in forward currency contracts.

FORWARD CURRENCY CONTRACTS Agreements to deliver a unit of a nation's currency in exchange for another at a specified price on a given date.

partners. Along with the **spot exchange rate**, which is the rate of exchange for currencies to be traded immediately, or "on the spot," **forward exchange rates** are listed. These are the market exchange rates on **forward currency contracts**, which call for delivery of a unit of a nation's currency in exchange for another at a predetermined price on a specified date.

The existence of forward currency contracts plays a central role in relating national interest rates. To see why, suppose that a U.S. resident has two alternatives. One is to purchase a one-period, dollar-denominated bond that has a market interest yield of i_{US}. After one year, the U.S. resident will have accumulated $1 + i_{US}$ dollars for each dollar saved.

The other option is to use each dollar to buy German deutsche marks at the spot exchange rate of S dollars per deutsche mark, thereby obtaining $1/S$ deutsche marks with each dollar. The U.S. resident could use the $1/S$ deutsche marks to buy a one-year German bond that pays the rate i_G. After a year, he will have accumulated $(1/S)(1 + i_G)$ *deutsche marks*. When the U.S. resident buys the German bond, however, at the same time he sells this quantity of deutsche marks in the forward market at the forward exchange rate of F dollars per deutsche mark. This "covers" him against risk of exchange-rate changes by ensuring that the effective return on the German bond will be $(F/S)(1 + i_G)$.

The returns on the two bonds will be the same if $1 + i_{US} = (F/S)(1 + i_G)$. As you will demonstrate in a problem at the end of the chapter, this means that the U.S. resident will be willing to hold bonds only if i_{US} is approximately equal to i_G plus the quantity $(F - S)/S$:

$$i_{US} = i_G + (F - S)/S.$$

COVERED INTEREST PARITY A prediction that the interest rate on one nation's bond will approximately equal the interest rate on another nation's bond plus the forward discount, or the difference between the forward exchange rate and the spot exchange rate divided by the forward exchange rate.

This equation is called the **covered interest parity** condition. The quantity $(F - S)/S$ is called the *forward discount*, so the condition of covered interest parity says that the interest rate on a U.S. bond should approximately equal the interest rate on the foreign (German) bond plus the forward discount.

Note that if F were equal to 0.73 dollars per deutsche mark and S were equal to 0.72 dollars per deutsche mark, then $(F - S)/S$ would be equal to $(0.73 - 0.72)/0.72 = 0.014$, a positive number. This means that the dollar would have a lower value in terms of deutsche marks—it would take more dollars to buy deutsche marks—in the forward exchange market than in the spot exchange market. Thus, the dollar would trade at a *discount* in the forward market. Consequently, covered interest parity tells us that the interest rate on the U.S. dollar–denominated bond should be higher than the interest rate on the German deutsche mark–denominated bond.

In contrast, if F were equal to 0.57 dollars per deutsche mark and S were equal to 0.58 dollars per deutsche mark, then $(F - S)/S$ would be equal to $(0.57 - 0.58)/0.58 = -0.017$, a negative number. Thus, the dollar would trade at a "negative discount," also known as a *premium*, in the forward market. Then covered interest parity tells us that, as a consequence, the interest rate on the U.S. dollar–denominated bond should be lower than the interest rate on the German deutsche mark–denominated bond.

Uncovered Interest Parity   The covered interest parity condition is very useful for evaluating why nations' interest rates may differ. It does not tell us, however, why a forward discount or premium exists. This is where expectations come into the story.

Suppose that a U.S.-based mutual fund is considering holding either U.S. Treasury bonds or bonds issued by the German government. The bonds have the same maturity, and the mutual fund perceives that they are equally risky. Hence, the mutual fund views the bonds as perfect substitutes. Suppose that the current spot dollar–deutsche mark exchange rate is $S = 0.63$ \$/DM. Note that if S were to rise during an interval, say, to 0.67 \$/DM, more dollars would be required to obtain one deutsche mark. The dollar would *depreciate* relative to the deutsche mark.

Suppose that the dollar depreciates relative to the deutsche mark at a rate s over time. A positive value of s indicates a positive *rate of depreciation* of the dollar versus the deutsche mark. This implies that the value of the dollar falls relative to the deutsche mark. In fact, between 1991 and 1995, the dollar depreciated relative to the deutsche mark at an average rate of almost 6 percent per year, before recovering the lost ground during subsequent years.

Now consider the situation faced by the mutual fund. If it holds the dollar-denominated U.S. Treasury bond, then its total return is simply the interest return i_{US}. If it holds the German government bond, then it earns interest at the rate i_G. In addition, however, the mutual fund anticipates that the dollar value of the deutsche mark–denominated bond will rise at an expected rate of s^e.

This mutual fund—as well as others making a similar choice—will be willing to hold either U.S. or German government bonds only if the expected returns on the two bonds are the same. This will be the case when

$$i_{US} = i_G + s^e.$$

For the mutual fund to be willing to hold *both* the U.S. and German government bonds, the U.S. Treasury bond rate must equal the German government bond rate plus the rate at which the dollar is expected to depreciate relative to the deutsche mark.

This condition makes a lot of sense. It says that a dollar-denominated U.S. Treasury bond will yield a return comparable to the return on a German bond only if the U.S. bond's yield is higher to compensate for any expected depreciation in the dollar relative to the deutsche mark. Hence, the amount by which the U.S. Treasury bond yield will exceed the German government bond yield is equal to the rate at which the dollar is expected to depreciate relative to the deutsche mark, or s^e.

The name of the last equation is the **uncovered interest parity** condition. It applies to interest yields on bonds with identical risks and terms to maturity that are denominated in different national currencies. According to the uncovered interest parity condition, the yield on a bond denominated in a currency that is expected to

UNCOVERED INTEREST PARITY A prediction that the interest rate on a bond denominated in a currency that is expected to depreciate must exceed another nation's bond rate by the rate at which the currency is expected to depreciate plus a risk premium.

depreciate must exceed another nation's bond yield by the rate at which the currency is expected to depreciate.

We have simplified by assuming that the U.S. and German bonds are equally risky. Even though both U.S. and German bonds should be relatively free of the risk of default by the respective governments, people may still regard one government's bond as slightly more risky than the other government's bond. For instance, in the event of a financial crisis in the Western Hemisphere, such as the Mexican peso crisis of 1995, people might worry that the U.S. government's finances might become entangled in the crisis, affecting returns on U.S. government bonds. If the U.S. bond is relatively more risky than another, then the uncovered interest parity condition becomes

$$i_{US} = i_G + s^e + RP,$$

where RP denotes a risk premium, or an extra amount that must be built into the U.S. bond's interest rate to induce people to hold both U.S. and German bonds of equal maturities.

Foreign Exchange Market Efficiency

Note that the two interest parity conditions just discussed provide two reasons why the interest rates on a U.S. bond might be higher than the interest rate on an otherwise identical German bond. One reason, provided by the *covered* interest parity condition, is that the U.S. bond may trade at a discount in the forward market. In that case, the differential between the U.S. bond's rate and the German bond's rate would equal

$$i_{US} - i_G = (F - S)/S.$$

The other reason is implied by the *uncovered* interest parity condition, which says that the U.S. bond's interest rate should exceed the German bond's interest rate by an amount equal to the expected rate of depreciation of the dollar plus any risk premium:

$$i_{US} - i_G = s^e + RP.$$

The only way that both of these interest parity conditions are satisfied is if the right-hand terms in both are equal, or if

$$(F - S)/S = s^e + RP,$$

which states that the forward discount for the dollar relative to the deutsche mark is equal to the rate at which the dollar is expected to depreciate relative to the deutsche mark plus any risk premium. This last condition is known as the condition for **foreign exchange market efficiency**. It states that in an efficient foreign exchange market, spot and forward exchange rates should adjust to the point at which the forward discount reflects the expected rate of currency depreciation and any risk premium. Under the rational expectations hypothesis, the expected rate of currency

FOREIGN EXCHANGE MARKET EFFICIENCY A situation in which the equilibrium spot and forward exchange rates imply a forward discount that is equal to the expected rate of currency depreciation plus any risk premium.

depreciation should be the rational forecast of the depreciation rate, or the forecast of depreciation based on all available information and an understanding of how exchange rates are determined.

Another way of thinking about the foreign exchange market efficiency condition is to relate it to the efficient market theory. This theory broadly states that the price of a financial asset should reflect all available information. The foreign exchange market efficiency condition is analogous. It states that the spot and forward exchange rates, which are the spot and forward prices of a nation's currency, should take into account rational forecasts of the extent to which the nation's currency will depreciate. As a result, the forward discount relating the spot and forward exchange rates should reflect all available information.

Considerable evidence indicates that covered interest parity holds in foreign exchange markets. The evidence on uncovered interest parity and, consequently, of foreign exchange market efficiency is more mixed. If the rational expectations hypothesis is correct, then the expected rate of depreciation should reflect a rational forecast. Consequently, studies of foreign exchange market efficiency also entail trying to determine if exchange-rate expectations are formed rationally. Trying to determine statistically whether foreign exchange market efficiency and rational expectations both hold at the same time is a difficult proposition, and economists continue to investigate the efficiency of foreign exchange markets.

FUNDAMENTAL ISSUE #6

How are exchange rates determined, and what is foreign exchange market efficiency? Exchange rates are determined by the forces of demand and supply in foreign exchange markets. The spot exchange rate is the exchange rate for currency to be exchanged immediately, and the forward exchange rate is the rate of exchange on currency to be delivered at a later date. Foreign exchange market efficiency requires that the forward discount, or the difference between the forward and spot exchange rates divided by the spot exchange rate, equal the expected rate of currency depreciation plus a risk premium. This efficiency condition holds if both the covered and the uncovered interest parity conditions are satisfied.

 # CHAPTER SUMMARY

1. **The Distinction between Adaptive and Rational Expectations**: An expectation that is formed adaptively is based only on past information. A rational expectation is formed

using all available past and current information and relying on an understanding of how the economy works.

2. **The Key Assumptions Underlying New Classical Macroeconomics**: The new classical model assumes that people pursue their self-interest, and it also follows the classical model by assuming that flexible wages and prices are determined in purely competitive markets. In contrast to the classical theory, the new classical model is based on the assumption of imperfect information in the short run. In contrast to the traditional Keynesian and monetarist theories, however, in the new classical model people form rational price-level and inflation rate expectations.

3. **How Policy Anticipations Determine the Actual Effects of Policy Actions in the New Classical Model**: If people can fully anticipate monetary or fiscal policy actions, then they will adjust their price-level and inflation rate expectations, and the policy actions will have no real effects. Policy actions that are not fully anticipated, however, have short-run effects on real output, employment, and the unemployment rate that are the same as those predicted by traditional Keynesian and monetarist theory.

4. **The Policy Ineffectiveness Proposition and Its Implication for the Conduct of Policies Intended to Have Real Effects**: The new classical policy ineffectiveness proposition states that systematic, predictable macroeconomic policy actions cannot exert either short-run or long-run effects on real output, employment, or unemployment. Hence, if monetary or fiscal policymakers wish to change real output, employment, and unemployment, they must find ways to enact policies that are unsystematic, or unpredictable.

5. **The Efficient Markets Theory and Its Main Implication**: According to the efficient markets theory, which stems from applying the rational expectations hypothesis to the determination of bond prices, the market price of any financial asset should reflect information available in that market. As a result, opportunities to earn interest returns higher than the equilibrium market return should not exist.

6. **Exchange-Rate Determination and Foreign Exchange Market Efficiency**: Demand and supply in foreign exchange markets interact to determine the equilibrium exchange rate. The spot exchange rate applies to currencies traded immediately, and the forward exchange rate applies to currency delivered at a later date. The foreign exchange market efficiency condition states that the forward discount, which is the difference between the forward and spot exchange rates divided by the spot exchange rate, should be equal to the expected rate of currency depreciation plus a risk premium. This efficiency condition is met if both the covered and the uncovered interest parity conditions hold.

QUESTIONS AND PROBLEMS

1. In your own words, explain the distinction between an adaptive expectation and a rational expectation. Could the two ever be the same? Explain.

2. In your view, what are the two strongest arguments in favor of the rational expectations hypothesis? What are the two strongest arguments against the hypothesis? Support your answers.

3. Suppose that people are partly, but not fully, successful in anticipating a reduction in the money stock. Assuming that all other factors are the same, would real output decline in the short run, according to the new classical model? If so, would real output decline by as much as the traditional Keynesian and monetarist theories would predict? Explain your reasoning.

4. Evaluate the following statement: "In an important sense, the term *policy ineffectiveness proposition* is misleading." Justify your position.

5. Some new classical economists have argued that secrecy is necessary if monetary policy is to influence real GDP, but that the presence of monetary policy secrecy destabilizes GDP. Can you rationalize this perspective? Explain.

6. Which is more "general," in that it could still be correct even if the other were not—the rational expectations hypothesis or the efficient markets theory? Justify your position.

7. Would the efficient market theory be correct if illegal insider trading were widespread? Explain.

8. As discussed in this chapter, a U.S. resident who can cover risks of exchange-rate movements with a forward currency contract will be willing to hold both U.S. and German bonds if the return on each dollar held in the U.S. bond, $1 + i_{US}$, is equal to the return on the German bond, $(F/S)(1 + i_G)$. Note that F/S can be written as $[S + (F - S)]/S = 1 + (F - S)/S$, and use this fact to derive the covered interest parity condition. [Hint: Note that if $(F - S)/S$ is a small fraction and if i_{US} is a small fraction, then the product of i_G and $(F - S)/S$ is very close to zero.]

9. Explain, in your own words, the distinction between covered interest parity and uncovered interest parity.

10. Could the covered interest parity condition be met if the uncovered interest parity condition is not also satisfied? Why or why not?

 # ON-LINE APPLICATION

You can track exchange rates each day by clicking into the Federal Reserve Bank of New York's homepage (see Chapter 3 *Internet Source*).

Internet URL: http://www.ny.frb.org/pihome/mktrates/forex10.shtml

Title: The Federal Reserve Bank of New York—10 A.M. Midpoint Foreign Exchange Rates

Navigation: Start at the Federal Reserve Bank of New York's homepage (http://www.ny.frb.org). Select *Statistics* (http://www.ny.frb.org/pihome/mktrates). Click on *10 A.M. FX*

Application: For each day during a given week (or month), choose a currency from those listed and keep track of its value relative to the dollar.

1. Based on your tabulations, try to predict the value of the currency at the end of the next week *following* your data collections. Use any information you may have, or just do your best without any additional information. How close was your prediction?

2. According to the efficient markets theory, would you anticipate that daily access to additional information, over and above the information you used to make your own forecast, would lead to an improvement in your ability to forecast the value of your currency? Indeed, if you were to become an "expert" on foreign exchange markets, would the theory indicate that you should be able to earn higher profits on average, as compared with equally well-informed traders, by trading on your forecasts? Explain your reasoning.

SELECTED REFERENCES AND FURTHER READING

Lucas, Robert. *Studies in Business-Cycle Theory.* Cambridge, Mass.: MIT Press, 1981.

McCallum, Bennett. *Monetary Economics: Theory and Policy.* New York: Macmillan, 1989.

Melvin, Michael. *International Money and Finance* . 5th ed. Reading, Mass.: Addison-Wesley,1997.

Minford, Patrick, and David Peel. *Rational Expectations and the New Macroeconomics.* Oxford: Martin Robertson, 1983.

Sargent, Thomas, and Neil Wallace. "Rational Expectations and the Theory of Economic Policy." *Journal of Monetary Economics* 2 (April 1976): 169–183.

Stein, Jerome. *Monetarist, Keynesian, and New Classical Economics.* New York: New York University Press, 1982.

Taylor, Mark. "The Economics of Exchange Rates." *Journal of Economic Literature* 43 (March 1995).

10 *Rational Wage Stickiness—*
MODERN KEYNESIAN THEORY WITH RATIONAL EXPECTATIONS

FUNDAMENTAL ISSUES

 1. What are the essential elements of the modern Keynesian theory of wage stickiness?

2. In what respect is the modern Keynesian theory observationally equivalent to the new classical model?

3. How does the degree of wage indexation affect the elasticity of the aggregate supply schedule, and how does this play a role in determining the optimal degree of indexation?

4. What factors determine the duration of wage contracts, and what are the macroeconomic implications of overlapping contract intervals?

5. Are the wage contracting models proposed by the modern Keynesian theorists relevant in today's world?

Slowly but surely, the news leaked out. The findings of the federal government's blue-ribbon committee of top-notch economists would soon be released. For several years the economists had been studying the way the federal government measures changes in "the" price level. Specifically, they had been trying to deter-

mine whether the computation of the Consumer Price Index (CPI) involves any biases.

The experts concluded that the way the government has measured the rate of inflation over the last several decades has been flawed. According to them, the rate of inflation has probably been one-half to one percentage point less than the official number. These results were not unexpected. After all, for years even beginning economics textbooks have pointed out biases in the measurement of the CPI. For one thing, the CPI does not take improvements in quality into account very effectively. For another, the CPI has been measured with a fixed basket of goods and services that changes only rarely. Hence, the measurement of the CPI has ignored the fact that consumers have been substituting relatively more expensive goods in favor of relatively less expensive goods.

In any event, when the study was released, somewhat surprisingly it did not then arouse vehement protests even though a change in the computation of the CPI would affect all wage contracts with cost-of-living adjustments (COLAs). Because these contracts are fully indexed to the rate of inflation as measured by the change in the CPI, a lower CPI would result in smaller wage increases. To be sure, a few union economists argued that the CPI calculation was not flawed, but they did not get much press coverage.

How the CPI is measured certainly affects the way wages are indexed. To what extent are wages indexed in our economy? Why don't more workers have their wages indexed to the rate of inflation? If all workers had their wage contracts fully indexed, how might that change the effectiveness of monetary and fiscal policy? These are some of the questions that will be answered in this chapter.

THE RATIONALE FOR WAGE CONTRACTS

The new classical theory discussed in Chapter 9 brought about a revolution in macroeconomics. Its proponents were the first economists to include the rational expectations hypothesis in their models of the economy. The theory's predictions—that systematic (and, therefore, anticipated) macroeconomic policies should have no real effects and that only unanticipated policy actions should affect short-run real output and employment—changed the terms of the debate among macroeconomists. Before new classical theory, arguments had centered on whether monetary or fiscal policy had the greater effects and whether the effects of policy actions were long-lasting or short-lived. Following the new classical revolution, the main topic of discussion was under what circumstances macroeconomic demand management policies could matter at all.

Among proponents of traditional Keynesian and monetarist macroeconomics, there have been two reactions to this state of affairs. The initial response was a denial of the relevance of the rational expectations hypothesis. This, however, did not turn out to be a very fruitful course, given the greater generality of rational expectations as compared with adaptive expectations. The other reaction was to admit that prior theory had suffered from a poor treatment of expectations and to consider the implications of rational expectations for the traditional Keynesian and monetarist approaches.

Those who have followed the second course have sought to develop theories that include a role for rational expectations but, at the same time, accept that nominal wages may be sticky in the short run. As you learned in Chapter 8, nominal wage rigidity leads to an upward-sloping short-run aggregate supply schedule. Hence, even if people have rational expectations, wage stickiness might allow for gradual price adjustment to policy actions and for short-term employment and real output responses.

Long-term Contracts

The reason that wages and prices might be inflexible, according to these modern Keynesians, is that workers and firms in the real world often agree to contracts that set the terms, such as wages and benefits, over a given time period. The existence of such long-term contracts, argue modern Keynesians, can make the instantaneous adjustments of expectations to monetary policy actions moot even if such adjustments are possible. If workers agree to wage contracts with firms, for instance, they cannot adjust their behavior to changed expectations even if they might like to do so. As a result, as you will see, modern Keynesian theories conclude that monetary policy has real effects even following incorporation of the rational expectations hypothesis into macroeconomic theory.

This approach, which was spearheaded by Stanley Fischer of the Massachusetts Institute of Technology, Jo Anna Gray of the University of Oregon, and John Taylor of Stanford University, led to the development of what we shall call the *modern Keynesian model.* As you will learn in this chapter, the modern Keynesian model follows the new classical theory by relying on the rational expectations hypothesis. Its implications for macroeconomic policy turn out to be very different, however.

The assumption that workers and firms set wages using contracts has been a central feature of the modern Keynesian model. Let's begin by considering the features of wage contracts and possible explanations for their existence.

Explicit and Implicit Contracts

Recall that *explicit contracts* are formal, written agreements between workers and firms. Explicit one- to three-year contracts are common in unionized industries, but formal contracts are also used frequently in industries without unionized workers. For instance, firms hiring workers with undergraduate degrees typically extend formal position offers that state initial salaries and policies concerning the timing of future salary reviews.

Implicit contracts are unwritten, tacit agreements between firms and workers. Some modern Keynesian theorists argue that implicit contracts are more common than explicit contracts, but these claims are difficult to document because the contracts are not written. Nevertheless, the idea of implicit contracts is that workers and firms both try to follow certain unstated patterns of behavior in establishing standards for worker performance and remuneration.

Why Contract?

There is a general recognition among economists that labor contracts have been an important feature of many labor markets. What is less apparent to many economists is why workers and firms have been willing to bind themselves to contracts that set nominal wages over fixed intervals. On the one hand, firms surely would prefer to pay lower, market-determined nominal wages if consumers demand fewer of the goods and services that they produce. On the other hand, workers arguably would prefer to earn higher, market-determined nominal wages if the demand for their skills rises. Why, then, would either firms or workers be willing to enter into agreements that establish a nominal wage that may turn out to be inconsistent with demand and supply conditions in the market for labor?

There are three possible rationales for nominal wage contracts:

1. *Avoiding auction-market transaction costs.* One rationale for nominal wage contracts is that using the contracts saves firms and workers the trouble of "auctioning" workers' skills when labor demand and supply conditions go through temporary fluctuations. In the labor-market theory of the classical model that we discussed in Chapter 3, wages and employment adjust very quickly to changes in labor demand and supply conditions. This adjustment can occur, however, only if workers auction their skills continuously to firms making the highest bids for their talents. In many labor markets, it is difficult to visualize such instantaneous and continuous adjustments taking place.

   For example, consider the situation faced by an engineer whose specialty is nuclear power. If the market for nuclear engineers continuously auctioned their skills, then nuclear engineers would have to be willing to move themselves and their families to a different nuclear power plant at any time. These continual relocations would impose sizable costs upon the engineers. A continuous auction would also force the firms that operate nuclear power plants to conduct constant searches for replacement engineers, making it difficult for the firms to maintain a stable production process. Economists call such costs of maintaining an auction market for labor skills *labor-market transaction costs.* One explanation for the existence of wage contracts is that labor-market transaction costs could be large enough to induce nuclear engineers and other workers to negotiate contracts with their employers.

2. *Risk aversion.* Another possible reason for the existence of contracts is *risk aversion.* If market wages rise unexpectedly, workers will be better off while firms will not. If market wages fall unexpectedly, firms will be better off while workers will not. Consequently, to protect themselves from the risks that can arise when wages are market determined, workers and firms may agree to fix the wage in advance.

3. *Asymmetric information.* A final, related rationale for nominal wage contracts is **asymmetric information,** or information possessed by one party to an economic transaction but not by the other. Individual workers may not always be privy to information about their employer's revenues, costs, and profits, so they may perceive benefits from contractual agreements that bind the employer to providing guaranteed wage payments. From an employer's perspective, information about the productivity of various workers also is imperfect. By providing a guaranteed wage payment for a specified amount of work effort, the employer may give each worker an incentive to produce a minimum desirable amount of work effort. Consequently, both workers and firms might see a wage contract as a way to offset problems arising from asymmetric information.

ASYMMETRIC INFORMATION
Information that is possessed by one party to an economic transaction but is unavailable to the other party.

THE THEORY OF RATIONAL CONTRACTING

The modern Keynesian theory combines both wage stickiness and imperfect information from the traditional Keynesian model. In addition, it follows the new classical theory by adopting the rational expectations hypothesis. Consequently, the modern Keynesian model adopts the new classical assumption that people make rational forecasts of the price level and the inflation rate in the face of imperfect information, but it forgoes the new classical assumption that purely competitive markets determine flexible nominal wages.

The traditional Keynesian theory of wage stickiness that we discussed in Chapter 8 assumes that workers and firms fix nominal wages via contracts, but it provides no explanation of how workers and firms determine a particular contract wage. The modern Keynesian theory, in contrast, seeks to explain what nominal wage workers and firms will set via a contractual agreement. The theory proposes that both parties to a wage contract choose a contract wage based on their rational expectations of the conditions that will prevail in the labor market during the period in which the wage contract is in force. Consequently, the modern Keynesian model of wage contracts follows the new classical theory by imposing the requirement that workers and firms act on the basis of rational forecasts.

Expected Labor-Market Equilibrium

To develop their theory of rational wage contracts, the modern Keynesian economists begin by thinking about how labor markets would work if there were no wage contracts at all and if workers and firms had complete information. In these circumstances, the nominal wage would adjust to ensure that the quantity of labor supplied would equal the quantity of labor demanded. At this equilibrium nominal wage, denoted W^* in Figure 10–1, the equilibrium quantity of labor services supplied by workers and demanded by firms is equal to N^*. The equilibrium values of the nominal wage and employment in Figure 10–1 are the *full-information* values of the wage and employment, because they would arise if workers and firms have complete information about the price level, so that $P^e = P$.

Recall from Chapter 3 that Figure 10–1 displays the classical labor-market equilibrium. The desirable property of the classical equilibrium is that at the full-information nominal wage W^*, firms wish to purchase the same quantity of labor services that workers wish to supply. Thus, the desires of both producers and workers are satisfied at this nominal wage rate, and there is neither a shortage of labor nor a surplus (or unemployment) at this nominal wage.

As discussed above, however, there also are potential drawbacks associated with allowing market forces to determine the nominal wage. As noted above, these could include transaction costs that workers and firms must incur to continually auction labor services, the risk of significant wage volatility arising from shifts in labor demand and supply, and problems in dealing with asymmetric information. In light of these difficulties, workers and firms may choose to fix the nominal wage over a period of time. The lengths of contracts vary in the real world, and terms of contracts typically overlap. For the sake of simplicity, however, we shall assume that all contracts are for one year and that they all begin and end at the same time.

FIGURE 10–1   FULL-INFORMATION LABOR-MARKET EQUILIBRIUM

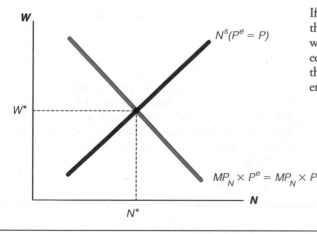

If workers and firms both possessed full information, then they would correctly anticipate the actual price level that would prevail. Hence, the expected price level, P^e, would equal the actual price level, P, and W^* and N^* would be the full-information values of the money wage and employment, respectively.

Nevertheless, we assume that workers and firms in an otherwise competitive labor market would like to preserve the desirable properties, such as the absence of unemployment, that a classical labor-market equilibrium could attain. Consequently, the shared goal of workers and firms when they negotiate a contract wage for a coming year is to try to achieve the same equilibrium wage and employment level that they *anticipate* would arise in the classical labor-market equilibrium.

The problem is that when workers and firms conduct their contract negotiations, they do not know the precise conditions that will prevail during the forthcoming contract year. What they *can* do, however, is to do the best that they can to set the same nominal wage that would hold, on average, in the absence of contracts. In other words, at the time that workers and firms negotiate a wage contract, they can try to achieve the full-information nominal wage rate that they *expect* the classical labor auction market otherwise would yield during the contract period. If this effort is successful, they will exactly replicate the classical labor-market equilibrium without having to incur transaction costs, face risks of wage volatility, or experience the full scope of problems arising from asymmetric information.

ON THE WEB
For Information about Innovative Employee Compensation, see:
http://www.fed.org/

The Wage Contract

Figure 10–2 illustrates how rational wage contracting would work according to the modern Keynesian theory. At the beginning of a contract interval, workers and firms agree to set the contract wage at the level that they expect the classical, full-information nominal wage will turn out to be, denoted W^{*e}. This is the nominal wage at which workers and firms expect the quantity of labor demanded will equal the quantity of labor supplied during the year in which the contract will be binding.

FIGURE 10–2   DETERMINING THE CONTRACT WAGE

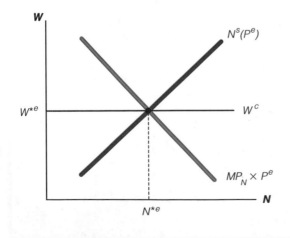

According to the modern Keynesian contract theory, workers and firms determine the contract wage based on their expectation of the price level that will prevail during the term of the contract. This price expectation implies anticipated positions for the labor demand and supply schedules and, consequently, an expectation of the full-information money wage and employment level, denoted W^{*e} and N^{*e}, respectively. In an effort to achieve the full-information employment level, workers and firms then set the contract wage, W^c, equal to the expected full-information wage.

Of course, at the beginning of the contract year, workers and firms do not know what the actual price level will be during that year. Hence, they have to make a rational forecast of the price level, labeled P^e. Figure 10–2 indicates, in light of their rational expectation of the price level, both workers and firms anticipate that during the coming year the labor supply schedule of workers will, on average, be in the position $N^s(P^e)$. In addition, they anticipate that the average position of the labor demand schedule will be the expected value of labor's marginal product, $MP_N \times P^e$. The expected wage consistent with classical labor-market equilibrium, W^{*e}, conceptually is determined by the intersection of these two schedules. To assure that they will achieve the expected equilibrium employment level, N^{*e}, at least on average, workers and firms set the contract wage, denoted W^c, equal to the anticipated market-clearing nominal wage, W^{*e}.

The Aggregate Supply Schedule

This rationally constructed nominal wage contract only assures that workers and firms will *anticipate* achieving the classical labor-market equilibrium. Once the contract wage is contractually set, however, the price level may or may not turn out to be equal to the price level that workers and firms anticipated when they conducted their contract negotiations.

Suppose that the actual price level, P_1, turns out to be the level workers and firms expected when they set the contract wage, P^e. Panel (a) of Figure 10–3 on page 332 shows, in this situation workers and firms correctly anticipate the value of labor's marginal product during the contract period, so that $MP_N \times P^e = MP_N \times P_1$. This determines the location of the labor demand schedule, and the equilibrium employment level, N_1, will be the quantity of labor demanded at the contract wage, $W^c = W^{*e}$, at point A. At this employment level, firms produce the real output level y_1, at point A in panel (b). Hence, at the price level P_1, the corresponding real output level is y_1, and this price level–real output combination is point A in panel (c).

Now consider the outcomes that result if the actual price level rises above $P^e = P_1$, to P_2. This price level is higher than workers and firms anticipated when they negotiated their contracts, so the value of labor's marginal product is also higher, at $MP_N \times P_2$. Consequently, firms demand more labor than they anticipated, and workers provide more labor services at the contract wage than they expected. Equilibrium employment is equal to N_2 at point B in panel (a). Given this quantity of labor, panel (b) indicates that firms will produce the real output level y_2, thereby yielding the price level–real output combination P_2 and y_2 at point B in panel (c).

In contrast, if the actual price level is below the value that workers and firms anticipated, at P_3, then the value of labor's marginal product during the contract period will be below its anticipated level, at $MP_N \times P_3$, and employment and real output will equal N_3 and y_3, respectively, at points C in panels (a) and (b). This will yield the price level–real output combination P_3 and y_3 given by point C in panel (c).

FIGURE 10–3   **DERIVING THE AGGREGATE SUPPLY SCHEDULE WITH RATIONAL WAGE CONTRACTS**

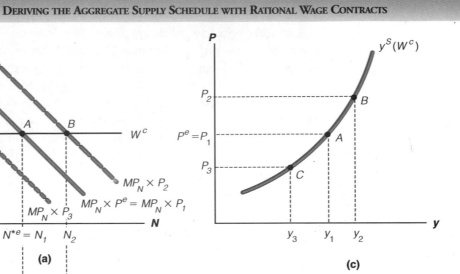

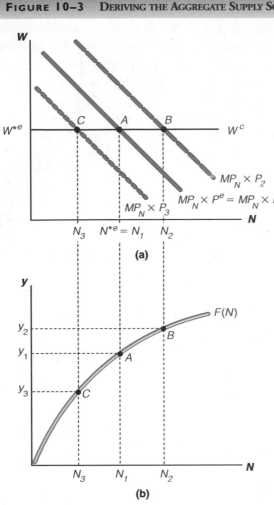

(a)

(b)

(c)

In the basic contract model, workers and firms set the contract wage, W^c, equal to the anticipated wage that would have prevailed in the absence of contracting, given by W^{*e} in panel (a). If workers and firms correctly anticipate the price level consistent with this outcome, so that $P^e = P_1$, then employment will equal N_1 at point A in panel (a), so that real output is y_1 at point A in panel (b). This yields the price level–real output combination P_1 and y_1 at point A in panel (c). If the price level is higher than workers and firms expected, however, then the result is a rise in employment at the contract wage, shown by the movement to point B in panel (a). Thus, real output will rise to point B in panel (b), yielding the price level–real output combination at point B in panel (c). Likewise, if the price level is lower than workers and firms expected, then employment will fall to point C in panel (a), causing a decline in real output to point C in panel (b). The result will be the price level–real output combination at point C in panel (c). Points A, B, and C thereby will lie on an upward-sloping aggregate supply schedule. The position of this schedule will depend on the contract wage, W^c.

The schedule containing points A, B, and C in panel (c) is the economy's aggregate supply schedule under rational wage contracting. Because we have derived this aggregate supply schedule given the specific contract wage W^c, we label it $y^s(W^c)$. As in the traditional Keynesian theory, the aggregate supply schedule slopes upward.

FUNDAMENTAL ISSUE #1

What are the essential elements of the modern Keynesian theory of wage stickiness? According to the modern Keynesian theory, workers and firms may wish to establish wage contracts to save on transaction costs, reduce the risk of wage variability, or address informational asymmetries that they face. To establish contract wages, workers and firms must rationally forecast the price level for the interval that the contract will be in force. Once the contract wage has been established, however, unexpected variations in the price level can cause employment and real output to change. As a result, the aggregate supply schedule slopes upward.

OBSERVATIONAL EQUIVALENCE

Like the new classical theory, the modern Keynesian contract-based theory is based on the rational expectations hypothesis. In contrast to the new classical theory, however, which assumes that pure competition ensures flexibility of all wages and prices, the modern Keynesian theory assumes that contracts cause stickiness in the nominal wage.

Another feature shared by both theories is the concept of a full-information employment level toward which the economy gravitates in the long run. This aspect of the monetarist elaboration of the traditional Keynesian model has become a common element of both modern approaches. We shall touch on this issue again when we consider the theory of macroeconomic policy in Chapters 12 and 13.

In what respects are the theories different? To answer this question, we begin by thinking about how policy actions can influence real output and prices in the modern Keynesian model. As you will see, in the basic version of this theory, the new classical and modern Keynesian approaches are not easy to distinguish individually.

Policy Effects in the Basic Modern Keynesian Framework

Figure 10–4 shows that in the one-period contracting framework that we have discussed, policy actions typically have short-run effects on real output and employment. The nominal wage is rigid during the contract interval, so an expansionary monetary or fiscal policy action will lead to a rise in aggregate demand that will induce increases in both the price level and real output, as shown by the movement from point E to point E'. To produce the higher output level, firms will hire more labor services, thereby raising employment and reducing the unemployment rate.

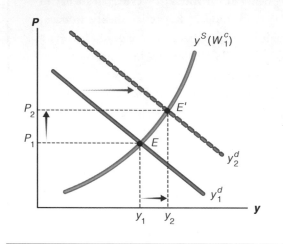

If workers and firms fail to anticipate a rise in aggregate demand during the term of wage contracts, an unexpected rise in the price level will result. The result would be a movement from point E to point E' and an increase in equilibrium real output. Hence, unanticipated policy actions that cause aggregate demand to change will induce variations in real output.

This does not mean, however, that macroeconomic policies will always have short-run effects on real GDP. Suppose that the central bank and the government follow systematic, predictable policies. If so, then workers and firms will be able to predict the policy actions that will occur during the contract period. Figure 10–5 shows the effects that the modern Keynesian contracting theory predicts will occur in this situation. If workers and firms do not expect policy actions that will expand aggregate demand, they will agree to the contract wage W_1^c, which is the nominal wage that they expect during the period of the contract. This yields the aggregate supply schedule $y^s(W_1^c)$, and the equilibrium price level and real output are P_1 and y_1 at point E in the figure.

Consider now what happens in the event of expansionary monetary and fiscal policies that workers and firms anticipate before reaching a contractual agreement. As the figure shows, these policies shift the aggregate demand schedule outward and to the right, to y_2^d, causing the price level to rise. Workers and firms anticipate this rise in the price level, however, so they also anticipate a rise in the market nominal wage during the contract interval. As a result, they agree to a higher contract wage, W_2^c, which shifts the aggregate supply schedule leftward. As a result, during the contract period there will be a higher price level at point E', but no change in equilibrium real output. The expansionary monetary and fiscal policies have no real effects.

Observationally Equivalent Theories

The examples illustrated in Figures 10–4 and 10–5 are very similar to those that we examined in our discussion of the new classical theory in Chapter 9. They imply that

FIGURE 10–5   THE EFFECTS OF POLICY ACTIONS THAT WORKERS AND FIRMS ANTICIPATE

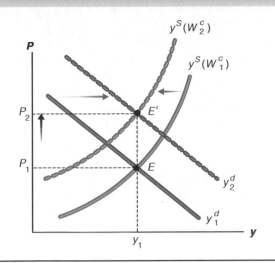

If workers and firms fully anticipate a rise in aggregate demand during the term of wage contracts, then they will expect a higher price level and will raise the contract wage. As a result, the aggregate supply schedule will shift leftward. The actual price level will rise from the initial equilibrium level P_1 at point E to a higher level P_2 at point E', but equilibrium real output will remain unchanged. Consequently, fully anticipated policy actions that induce changes in aggregate demand will have no real output effects.

OBSERVATIONAL EQUIVALENCE
The fact that the basic version of the modern Keynesian theory, which assumes sticky wages, makes some of the same fundamental policy predictions as the new classical model, which is based on pure competition with completely flexible wages.

policies that workers and firms cannot correctly anticipate before reaching contractual agreements will affect real output and employment during the term that the agreements are binding. In contrast, fully anticipated policy actions will induce workers and firms to adjust the contract wage accordingly, so the policy actions will have no influence on equilibrium real output or employment.

This similarity between the policy predictions of the basic new classical and modern Keynesian theories is known as **observational equivalence.** It poses something of a problem for macroeconomists because it complicates efforts to determine whether the new classical approach or the modern Keynesian theory better "fits" real-world data. Even though the two theories are based on very different assumptions—pure competition with completely flexible wages in the new classical theory versus contractual wage setting with fixed wages in the modern Keynesian model—in their most basic forms they offer very similar policy predictions. Both theories predict that real employment and output variations should occur only in the event of unanticipated changes in the price level, which macroeconomists often call price-level "misperceptions" or "surprises." As you learned in Chapter 9, in the new classical model price-level misperceptions can occur, for instance, when a central bank or government makes mistakes, is misunderstood, or is insincere in its policy announcements. In the modern Keynesian model, surprise changes in the price level can take place whenever the price level differs from the level that workers and firms anticipated when they negotiated their wage contracts. This price-level misperception can occur for the same reasons proposed in the new classical theory.

Hence, both theories provide the same fundamental message:

> **In both the new classical and the modern Keynesian models, actual real output should differ from full-information output whenever price-level misperceptions take place.**

Consequently, both theories are observationally equivalent in their predictions, making testing one theory against the other a tricky proposition. Although the modern Keynesian theory indicates that real output and employment responses to price level surprises might be longer lived than under the new classical theory, especially if long-term contracts are widespread in the economy, such subtle differences are hard to capture in real-world data.

For this reason, economists interested in determining which, if either, theory has greater relevance have pursued two lines of research. One has been to determine if real output and employment really do respond only to price-level misperceptions, as *both* theories predict. If not, this would indicate that *neither* theory fits the facts very well. In contrast, if the evidence indicates that real output and employment do vary directly with surprise movements in the price level, then at least one of the theories may fit the facts. The initial research on this issue, which was conducted in the 1980s, found little evidence that price-level surprises had real output effects. In the 1990s, however, Jo Anna Gray of the University of Oregon and David Spencer of Brigham Young University along with Magda Kandil of the University of Wisconsin—Milwaukee have used more advanced measures of full-information output and employment and have found more evidence supporting both theories.

The second line of research has been to identify aspects of the modern Keynesian theory of wage contracting that separate it more clearly from the new classical approach. The idea here is that wage contracting may have other features that will lead to further predictions that will distinguish the contracting theory. We turn next to some of these potential features of wage contracts that could have macroeconomic implications.

FUNDAMENTAL ISSUE #2

In what respect is the modern Keynesian theory observationally equivalent to the new classical model? Basic versions of both the modern Keynesian theory and the new classical approach make the same fundamental prediction: Unanticipated policy actions are more likely to have effects on employment and real output, whereas fully anticipated policy actions should have no real effects. Hence, the theories are observationally equivalent in that they have similar basic implications even though they stem from very different perspectives on how the labor market functions.

WAGE INDEXATION, CONTRACT LENGTH, AND OVERLAPPING CONTRACTS

COST-OF-LIVING ADJUSTMENT (COLA) A clause in a wage contract that calls for the nominal wage to be adjusted in response to changes in the price level.

The basic one-period contracting model that we have discussed ignores some important issues with considerable real-world relevance. One is the possibility that contracts could contain clauses calling for **cost-of-living-adjustment (COLA),** which automatically adjust nominal wages to changes in the price level. Another is the issue of contract length. As noted above, longer contracts extend the interval during which unexpected policy actions can affect real output and employment. Finally, in the real world contracts do not begin or end at the same time. Instead, they overlap. Let's consider how proponents of the modern Keynesian theory have sought to extend the basic contracting framework to incorporate each of these issues.

Nominal Wage Indexation

In the past (and to a lesser degree in the present, as discussed later in the chapter), workers and firms have frequently negotiated wage agreements that provide for the automatic adjustment of wages during the interval in which the contract is binding. Usually, these COLA contracts set a *base wage* that creates a floor on workers' earnings and then specify additional wage payments in the event of inflation. Under a standard COLA contract, if the price level rises, the wage paid to workers automatically increases, typically at set intervals of time, such as every quarter or every six months. The presence of COLA clauses in wage contracts is an explicit example of what economists call **wage indexation.** In this situation, contracted wages are

WAGE INDEXATION The automatic adjustment of contract wages to changes in the price level.

"indexed," or adjusted automatically to changes in the price level.

Another common way to index wages is to relate them to a firm's performance through payments of commissions, bonus plans, or other types of profit-sharing arrangements. Thus, when the firm's sales increase as a result of price increases, workers share in the higher revenues, and their wage effectively adjusts automatically.

Considering all types of wage indexation can be a difficult task. To keep things as simple as possible, let's consider a situation in which all wages in the economy are determined via contracts with COLA clauses requiring fully proportionate adjustment of the wage to changes in the price level. In other words, the contracts specify that every time the price level rises by one unit, the nominal wage must increase by one unit. Furthermore, let's suppose that the contracts call for continuous adjustment of the wage during the contract interval (though continuous adjustment is rare in practice). Finally, let's assume that the contracts permit full upward *or* downward movement of the nominal wage as the price level rises or falls, even though clauses calling for both types of adjustments also are rare.

Completely Indexed Wages   Under these assumptions, Figure 10–6 on page 338 shows what would happen during the contract term if the price level turned out to be higher than workers and firms anticipated when they set the base contract wage,

FIGURE 10–6 **THE AGGREGATE SUPPLY SCHEDULE WITH FULLY INDEXED NOMINAL WAGES**

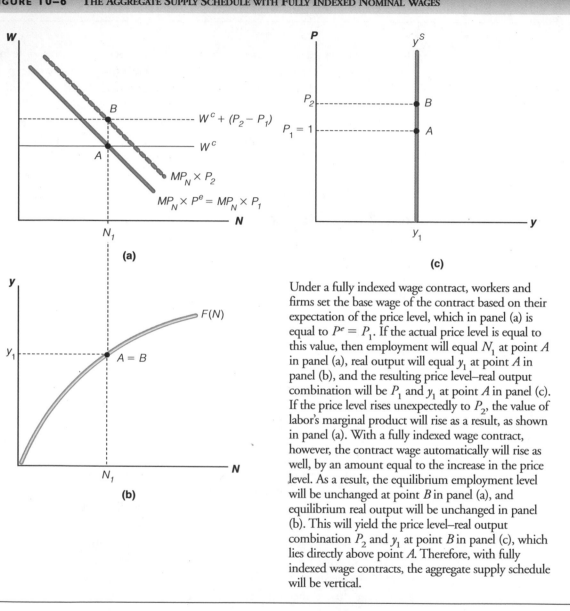

(a)

(b)

(c)

Under a fully indexed wage contract, workers and firms set the base wage of the contract based on their expectation of the price level, which in panel (a) is equal to $P^e = P_1$. If the actual price level is equal to this value, then employment will equal N_1 at point A in panel (a), real output will equal y_1 at point A in panel (b), and the resulting price level–real output combination will be P_1 and y_1 at point A in panel (c). If the price level rises unexpectedly to P_2, the value of labor's marginal product will rise as a result, as shown in panel (a). With a fully indexed wage contract, however, the contract wage automatically will rise as well, by an amount equal to the increase in the price level. As a result, the equilibrium employment level will be unchanged at point B in panel (a), and equilibrium real output will be unchanged in panel (b). This will yield the price level–real output combination P_2 and y_1 at point B in panel (c), which lies directly above point A. Therefore, with fully indexed wage contracts, the aggregate supply schedule will be vertical.

W^c. As in the basic contracting model that we discussed earlier, W^c is set equal to the nominal wage that workers and firms anticipate will arise in the absence of the contract. In the absence of any price-level changes, the points labeled A in panels (a), (b), and (c) show the determination of equilibrium employment and output at this base wage, where we have assumed that initially workers and firms correctly anticipate the actual price level, so that $P^e = P_1$. We simplify further by assuming that the initial value of the price level is equal to one, so that a variation in the price level is equivalent to a proportionate price-level change.

Fully indexed contracts require that the nominal wage rise in proportion to any price-level increase. Thus, if the price level rises from P_1 to P_2, then the actual wage received by workers will equal W^c plus an amount equal to the rise in the price level, or $W^c + (P_2 - P_1)$. The rise in the price level causes labor demand to increase as the value of labor's marginal product rises. At the same time, however, firms also have to pay a proportionately higher nominal wage. As shown in panel (a), this means that employment does not change. As a result, as panel (b) indicates, real output also is unaffected. Therefore, the new real output–price level combination y_1 and P_2 shown by point *B* in panel (c), lies directly above point *A*. The aggregate supply schedule with completely indexed wages is completely inelastic.

The shape of this aggregate supply schedule is, of course, the same as in the classical model of Chapter 3. Wages under a completely indexed wage contract adjust equiproportionately to changes in the price level. This mirrors the one-for-one adjustment of nominal wages to price changes that arises in the classical framework with full information and flexible wages and prices. Hence, the aggregate supply schedule under complete indexation also is vertical.

Partial Indexation and the Slope of the Aggregate Supply Schedule Many U.S. industries use wage contracts without COLA clauses. Indeed, as shown in Figure 10–7, the portion of U.S. employment contracts containing indexation clauses fell from 61 percent in the mid-1970s to just over 20 percent in the late 1990s (later on we shall consider some possible reasons for this sharp decline). Furthermore, in industries that use contracts with COLA clauses, indexation has rarely been as full or as flexible as we assumed in our example in Figure 10–6. Hence, most modern Keynesian theorists would argue that, in the aggregate, nominal wages have been only *partially* indexed to the inflation rate in the United States. Thus, according to the modern Keynesian contracting theory, the aggregate supply schedule has not been completely inelastic, but neither has it been as elastic as a fixed-wage theory would imply.

Note that the example in Figure 10–6 indicates that under complete wage indexation and a completely inelastic aggregate supply schedule, changes in the price level induced by variations in aggregate demand will have no effects on real output and employment. Consequently, full indexation of all wages in the economy would be optimal if the only sources of economic fluctuations were factors causing greater variability in aggregate demand, such as volatility in autonomous consumption, investment, or imports. In that case, by completely indexing wages to price changes workers and firms could ensure that they would always maintain the desired, full-information levels of employment and real output.

In light of this implication, why aren't all contracted wages completely indexed? One likely reason is that volatility of relative prices of key resources such as oil or sud-

FIGURE 10-7   **THE SHARE OF U.S. LABOR CONTRACTS CONTAINING INDEXATION CLAUSES, 1956–PRESENT**

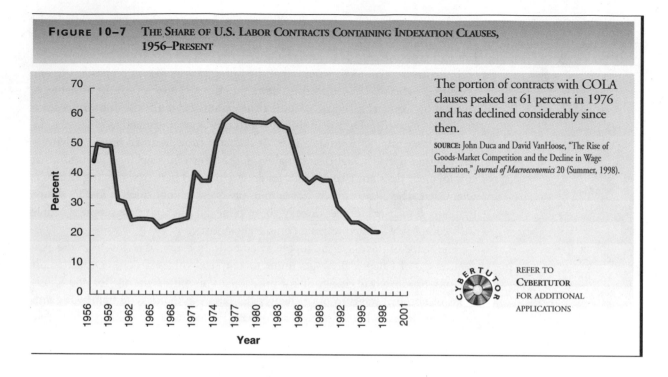

The portion of contracts with COLA clauses peaked at 61 percent in 1976 and has declined considerably since then.

SOURCE: John Duca and David VanHoose, "The Rise of Goods-Market Competition and the Decline in Wage Indexation," *Journal of Macroeconomics* 20 (Summer, 1998).

REFER TO **CYBERTUTOR** FOR ADDITIONAL APPLICATIONS

den technological changes can cause the position of the aggregate supply schedule to vary. Figure 10–8 shows that if both relatively elastic and completely inelastic aggregate supply schedules (around point E) shift leftward by the same amount, then for a given position for the aggregate demand schedule the effect on real output (and, hence, employment) is larger when the aggregate supply schedule is completely inelastic. As we noted earlier, complete indexation of nominal wages makes the aggregate supply schedule vertical, so full wage indexation is not always best for workers and firms.

This reasoning indicates that aggregate wage indexation should decline if variability in aggregate demand declines relative to variability in aggregate supply. To the extent that this may have occurred in the United States since the mid-1970s, it could represent one possible explanation for the decrease in the share of contracts with indexed contracts shown in Figure 10–7.

FUNDAMENTAL ISSUE #3

How does the degree of wage indexation affect the elasticity of the aggregate supply schedule, and what role does this elasticity play in determining the optimal degree of indexation? If contract wages are completely indexed to changes in the price level, then wages adjust equiproportionately with price-level variations as in the classical model, which yields a completely inelastic aggregate supply schedule. In contrast, with nonindexed wage contracts, the aggregate supply schedule is relatively elastic around a particular price level, because the nominal wage does not adjust at all in response to changes in the price level. Complete wage indexation insulates real output and employment from the effects of variability in aggregate demand, but magnifies the output and employment responses to variability in aggregate supply. Consequently, in the presence of both sources of macroeconomic fluctuations, neither completely indexed nor nonindexed wage contracts are best for limiting variability of employment and real output.

Optimal Contract Length

So far we have assumed that the length of a wage contract is a year. Some wage contracts have terms two to three times that long. Others have shorter durations. What factors determine the length of a contract that sets nominal wages?

Negotiation Costs As we noted earlier, one of the primary reasons why people might agree to fix wages via contracts is to avoid having to haggle over wages from week to week and month to month. Negotiating new contracts can be very time-

---

FIGURE 10-8 **THE EFFECTS OF A DECLINE IN AGGREGATE SUPPLY WITH NONINDEXED AND COMPLETELY INDEXED CONTRACT WAGES**

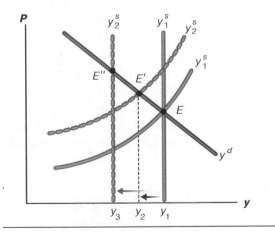

If aggregate supply schedules that arise under nonindexed and fully indexed wage contracts shift leftward by the same amount, then the effect on equilibrium real output is greater in the case of the fully indexed wage contracts. Higher variability of output under full wage indexation implies that employment will also be more variable. Consequently, full wage indexation is less desirable for workers and firms when aggregate supply is highly variable.

consuming. Consequently, a key component of the total *negotiation cost* for a contract is the opportunity cost that is entailed. Both workers and firm owners and managers could do other things with the time that they spend nailing down the terms of a contract.

In addition, contract negotiations entail potentially sizable direct costs. A union, for instance, may pay professional negotiators or consultants to help make a strong case for why the workers deserve higher base wages. A business may incur similar expenses to explain why it cannot raise base wages as much as workers desire.

The total negotiation cost of contracting is the sum of these opportunity costs and direct costs. Naturally, we would predict that as the cost of contract negotiation increases, the duration of a typical contract should also rise. By lengthening the term of a contract, workers and firms can postpone incurring contract negotiation costs.

The Optimal Contract Duration In light of these potentially high negotiation costs, why don't contracts last for several years? The answer is that as the term of a nonindexed contract lengthens, so does the period over which workers and firms must try to anticipate factors that could cause the price level to vary, thereby inducing variability in the full-information wage and employment level.

For example, suppose that a union is contemplating adopting either a one-year or a two-year contract. With the one-year contract, the union must try to rationally forecast the labor demand and supply conditions for the coming year. With the two-year contract, the union's horizon for trying to anticipate these conditions stretches out another year.

If factors that can affect labor demand over a two-year period, such as the price level, are expected to be relatively stable, then the union may feel comfortable going with the two-year contract and saving on the negotiation costs that two successive one-year contracts would entail. If the union anticipates a highly variable price level, however, resulting from significant variability in aggregate demand and aggregate supply, then it would tend to prefer one-year agreements. In that case, the union could negotiate a more appropriate base wage after a year has passed and uncertainty about labor-market conditions has been resolved.

As this reasoning indicates, the determination of the optimal length of a wage contract involves a trade-off between contract negotiation cost and the variability of aggregate demand and aggregate supply. As the cost of negotiating a contract increases, the optimal contract length tends to rise. As variability of aggregate demand or aggregate supply rises, the optimal contract length tends to decline. (The federal government sets some private contract wages, as discussed in the Policy Notebook: *Should the Link between Local Union-Scale Wages and Certain Construction Wages Be Broken?*)

Overlapping Contracts and Persistence

Because the duration of wage contracts in an industry or at an individual firm depends on the nature of the trade-off between industry- and firm-specific negotia-

Should the Link between Local Union-Scale Wages and Certain Construction Wages Be Broken?

For more than sixty-five years, federal legislation (the Davis-Bacon Act) has required contractors working on any federally subsidized construction site to pay what the Department of Labor determines to be the local union-scale wages. In effect, the secretary of labor is empowered to establish minimum "prevailing" wages. The secretary of labor has discretion in deciding what "prevailing" wages mean. In general, this agency has determined that the *highest* union wage rate earned within a large radius of the construction site is in fact the prevailing wage. Often, the Wage Determination Division of the Department of Labor sets "prevailing" rates on the basis of union wages in places that are not even contiguous to the counties where the government construction work is being done.

Sometimes prevailing wages have been based on wages paid to union workers in a city in another state. For example, union rates in Washington, D.C., have been used to set a schedule of minimum rates for a construction project in Virginia, which effectively made them more than $2 an hour higher than those actually prevailing in the city where the work was being done. Prevailing rates in St. Louis, Missouri, have been determined by looking at Chicago; rates in Indiana have been determined by looking at union wages in Illinois.

In some cases "prevailing" wages have been calculated using fictitious projects, ghost workers, and companies set up to pay artificially high wages. For example, the secretary of labor discovered that rates in Oklahoma were determined by rates paid on a project to build underground storage tanks. The problem is that no such project was ever built. Other examples of Davis-Bacon fraud have surfaced in Colorado, Idaho, Missouri, and Ohio.

The Effects on Union Wages

We can be sure that union management is fully aware that the Wage Determination Division determines prevailing wages by looking at union wages. In their bargaining sessions with employers, negotiators for construction unions have become more and more intent on increasing the negotiated rates. Because about 30 percent of all construction work in the United States involves some federal money, the Davis-Bacon Act (and the similar Walsh-Healey Act) affects a large number of wages.

Critics also claim that the need to pay "prevailing" wages on construction projects has had the effect of discriminating against minority construction workers, especially African Americans and Hispanics, in our nation's inner cities.

FOR CRITICAL ANALYSIS:

In addition to minority construction workers, which groups might suffer because of the Davis-Bacon Act?

tion costs and volatility in the price level induced by aggregate demand and supply variability, we would expect to see contract lengths differ across industries and firms. In addition, because workers and firms make their own decisions about the timing of contract negotiations, we would anticipate that the dates when contracts begin and end would be *staggered.* In other words, all one-year contracts would be unlikely to begin on January 1 of each year. Some might begin on that day, but many others might begin on any other day of a year.

As a result of different durations and contract staggering, contracts across the economy *overlap.* Figure 10–9 on page 444 shows how contracts might overlap in an

FIGURE 10–9 OVERLAPPING WAGE CONTRACTS

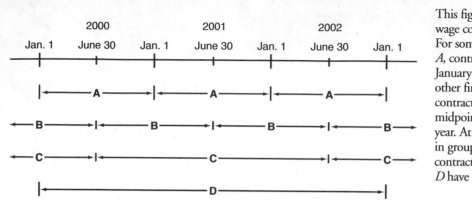

This figure illustrates how wage contracts can overlap. For some firms, denoted group *A*, contracts begin and end on January 1 of each year. For other firms, denoted group *B*, contracts begin and end at the midpoint of each calendar year. At the same time, firms in group *C* have two-year contracts, while firms in group *D* have three-year contracts.

economy. Some firms, denoted group *A*, have one-year contracts that begin and end on January 1 of each year, while the firms in group *B* have one-year contracts beginning and ending on June 30. At the same time, workers in some unionized industries (groups *C* and *D*, respectively) have two- and three-year contracts that overlap with the one-year contracts.

Policy Implications of Overlapping Contracts Does the overlapping nature of contracts make any difference for the effects of macroeconomic policies? Consider Figure 10–9. The groups of workers whose new contracts begin on January 1, 2000 (groups *A* and *D*) will negotiate contract wages with their employers based on the information they possess at that date. Workers whose contracts begin on June 30, 2000 (groups *B* and *C*) will set base wages using any additional information that became available between January 1, 2000 and June 30, 2000. Note that if the four groups, *A* through *D*, include all workers in the economy, then the aggregate wage for any period, such as the six-month interval between June 30, 2000, and January 1, 2001, will be just the weighted average of the contract wages established by the four groups of workers and firms.

Workers and firms in groups *B* and *C* will be able to take into account any policy changes that take place between January 1, 2000, and June 30, 2000, when they make rational forecasts of the price level for their contract intervals. Consequently, the aggregate wage during the June 30, 2000–January 1, 2001 interval will *partially* take into account any changes in macroeconomic policy. Firms and workers in groups *A* and *D*, however, cannot consider these policy changes when they negotiate wages. Thus, even some systematic changes in monetary policy will *not* be fully taken into account by these groups of workers and firms, who will be constrained by the contract decisions that they made earlier. Even if workers and firms in groups *A* and *D* made rational choices on January 1, 2000, they cannot respond to systematic policy changes until their next contract renewal dates.

The implication of this example is that in an economy with overlapping contracts, the modern Keynesian theory indicates that systematic macroeconomic policy actions potentially can have longer-lasting real effects. This can happen simply because a portion of all workers and firms set their wages via long-term contracts, which limit their ability to respond quickly to systematic policy changes. As a result, the modern Keynesian theory with overlapping contracts indicates that the effects of both anticipated and unanticipated policy actions on employment and real output should be much longer lasting than predicted by the new classical model. Hence:

> **A key prediction of modern Keynesian theory is greater persistence in policy-induced business cycle recessions or expansions.**

Should Wage Contracts Be Synchronized? The potential for more persistent recessions that is implied by staggered and overlapping contracts has led some macroeconomists to propose that employment and real output would be more stable if all wage contracts had the same term. Contracts that begin and end at the same times would be *synchronized*, or identically timed. Contract synchronization, these macroeconomists argue, would ensure that all workers and firms have the same information when they anticipate conditions during the coming contract period. A possible drawback of synchronization is that it would induce greater aggregate wage response to past and expected future policy actions each period when contracts are renegotiated, as compared with a world of overlapping contracts. An advantage is that persistence in business cycles in a contract-dominated economy would be limited to the common interval of all the synchronized contracts.

Many other macroeconomists, however, believe that staggered contracting has significant advantages that help to offset the persistence of the output change that it induces. As we noted earlier, one advantage is that staggered, overlapping contracts help to mute responses of the aggregate wage to changes in aggregate demand conditions, thereby limiting the size of wage changes and the effects that they ultimately may have on the price level. Consequently, even though staggered, overlapping contracts theoretically may lead to more persistent business cycles, such contracts also tend to limit the size of business cycle downturns.

FUNDAMENTAL ISSUE #4 ⬤

What factors determine the duration of wage contracts, and what are the macroeconomic implications of overlapping contract intervals? The optimal length of a wage contract declines as the cost of negotiating a contract decreases and as the variability in the price level caused by aggregate demand and supply fluctuations increases. Because negotiation costs typically vary across firms and industries, contracts typically have different durations and consequently are staggered. The modern Keynesian theory indicates that overlapping contracts lead to persistent long-term effects of aggregate demand fluctuations on employment and real output.

CAN WAGE CONTRACTING THEORIES EXPLAIN BUSINESS CYCLES?

The contract-based modern Keynesian theory represents the main response of Keynesian proponents to the new classical revolution. In key respects the theory's predictions mirror those of the new classical approach. Nevertheless, the modern Keynesian theory indicates that wages are unlikely to be nearly as flexible as the new classical theory presumes, unless wages are fully indexed to changes in the price level. In the presence of variability in aggregate supply, however, the theory predicts that complete wage indexation should be rare.

The modern Keynesian theory also implies that there is greater scope for aggregate demand fluctuations to have more persistent effects on real economic activity. Consequently, proponents of contract-based macroeconomic theories have argued that such theories can help to explain short-run business cycles. They also contend that the theories can be used to develop policies that stabilize aggregate demand and thereby limit the magnitude of business cycles.

As you will learn in Chapter 11, a number of macroeconomists disagree completely with this view. They doubt the ability of the modern Keynesian approach to explain key macroeconomic regularities, and they question the usefulness of the approach as a guide for macroeconomic policy.

Key Predictions and Evidence on Wage Contracting Theories

The first line of attack on modern Keynesian theory focuses on some basic predictions that stem from contract-based theories. Critics of these theories contend that they simply do not do a good job of fitting the facts.

Real Wages: Counter- or Pro-Cyclical? According to the modern Keynesian theory, nominal wages typically will be nonindexed or at most partially indexed. Consequently, a rise in the price level should not lead to an equiproportionate rise in the nominal wage. This has an important implication: If the contract-based theories are correct, then rises in the price level induced by increases in aggregate demand should cause real wages to decline. In other words, real wages should move *countercyclically*. During expansions caused by rising aggregate demand, average real wages should decline. During recessions induced by declining aggregate demand, average real wages should rise.

In fact, however, many studies of the overall behavior of real wages in the United States have found that real wages tend to rise during business cycle expansions and fall during business cycle contractions. This apparent *procyclical* behavior of the average U.S. real wage, argue critics, casts serious doubt on the applicability of the modern Keynesian theory, at least to the U.S. economy.

Proponents of contract-based theories have responded that studies of the cyclical behavior of the aggregate real wage are very sensitive to how wages are averaged and to the frequency of the data that one analyzes (that is, whether the researcher looks at monthly, quarterly, or annual wage and price-level data). In addition, David Card of Princeton University has pointed out that contract wages theoretically are countercyclical only if all other things are held constant. In the real world, however, other factors that influence contract wages do change over time. As a result, looking at the behavior of the aggregate real wage over time without taking into account other factors that affect wage negotiations could lead to misleading conclusions. After controlling for various factors that might affect negotiated wages, such as issues specific to individual firms and industries, Card has concluded that observed patterns in real wages are consistent with the predictions of modern Keynesian contract theory.

Wage Indexation: Do the Facts Fit the Theory?   The modern Keynesian theory also indicates that significant variability in aggregate demand relative to variability in aggregate supply should induce workers and firms to increase the extent of wage indexation. In contrast, reduced relative aggregate demand volatility should lead to decreased use of COLA contracts.

Nevertheless, average U.S. wages have shown a fairly low level of indexation to price-level changes during periods of high aggregate demand variability. Indeed, indexation has been used so infrequently that Robert Gordon of Northwestern University has called the low overall degree of wage indexation the "indexation puzzle." Studies conducted during the late 1980s found that even among industries with explicit contracts, the use of COLA clauses did not always appear to increase during periods of highly volatile aggregate demand or of low variability in aggregate supply, as the basic theory of indexation would predict. To critics, this apparent failure of the modern Keynesian theory's key prediction provided further evidence of its inapplicability to the U.S. economy.

Proponents of the contract-based approach have responded in two ways. One has been to conduct more refined studies. Some of these studies have indicated that the apparent failures of the modern Keynesian theory may have stemmed from measurement problems and imperfectly constructed tests of the theory's implications. Others, such as a study by Donald Dutkowsky of Syracuse University and H. Sonmez Atesoglu of Clarkson University, have tried to test the broad implications of contracting theories. Indeed, Dutkowsky and Atesoglu have found evidence favoring a one-year contracting model as a good approximation for the U.S. economy.

Another response has been to try to make the basic contracting theory somewhat more realistic. For instance, COLA contracts typically call for wages to rise when inflation increases but hold wages unchanged in the face of unexpected declines in inflation. Recasting the basic contract model to account for asymmetric indexation potentially can help explain why indexation is less frequently utilized than the basic contracting model predicts.

In addition, the basic contracting model drops the classical assumption that the nominal wage adjusts to equate the quantity of labor demanded with the quantity of labor supplied, but it nevertheless maintains the classical presumption that firms are purely competitive. A reformulation of the contracting model that allows for imperfect competition among firms indicates that greater competition among firms makes employment and real output at each firm less sensitive to aggregate demand variability. Consequently, increased competition would lead to less indexation. Figure 10–10 indicates that greater competition could help explain the decline in the use of COLA contracts since the mid-1970s. The same period has seen a steady increase in competition in U.S. product markets, arising both from greater competition among U.S. firms and from increased competition from foreign sources.

The Decline of Wage Contracts: Are Contract-Based Theories Relevant in Today's World?

Although proponents of the modern Keynesian theory have provided a number of responses to critics of their contract-based theories, even some of the proponents themselves have reason to question their theories' ability to explain business cycles and to predict the effects of policies. The reason is that the world has become a much more competitive place. In addition, technological change, increased information flows, and greater labor-force mobility have undermined key rationales for wage contracts.

The Decline of Unionization   The bulk of long-term wage contracts in the United States typically have been union contracts. As Figure 10–11 shows, however, unionization of the workforce has been in steady decline since the middle of the twentieth century. A similar trend is occurring in other countries. (See on page 350 the Global Notebook: *Union Membership Worldwide*.)

This decline has occurred for a number of reasons. For one thing, workers traditionally formed unions and negotiated with employers over many other terms of employment besides wages. Job safety, pension arrangements, health-care coverage, and other fringe benefits have often been key items for negotiation. During the past fifty years, however, federal and state governments increasingly have taken on the tasks of regulating safety in the workplace, supervising pension funds, and guaranteeing availability of essential health-care services. This increased government role surely has undercut the perceived need for unions in the minds of many workers.

FIGURE 10–10   THE SHARE OF U.S. LABOR CONTRACTS WITH INDEXATION CLAUSES AND A MEASURE OF OVERALL COMPETITION AMONG U.S. FIRMS

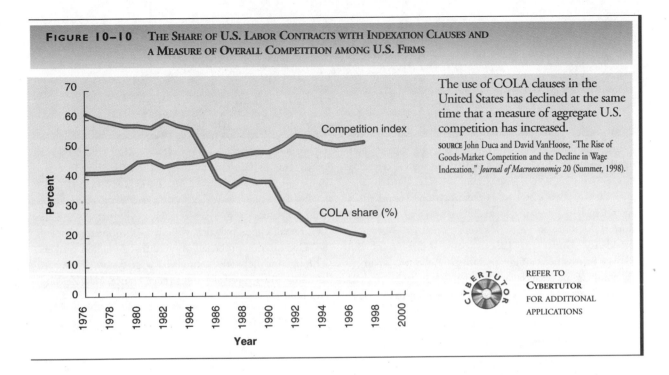

The use of COLA clauses in the United States has declined at the same time that a measure of aggregate U.S. competition has increased.

SOURCE John Duca and David VanHoose, "The Rise of Goods-Market Competition and the Decline in Wage Indexation," *Journal of Macroeconomics* 20 (Summer, 1998).

REFER TO
CYBERTUTOR
FOR ADDITIONAL
APPLICATIONS

FIGURE 10–11   UNIONS' SHARE OF U.S. PRIVATE-SECTOR EMPLOYMENT AND A MEASURE OF OVERALL COMPETITION AMONG U.S. FIRMS

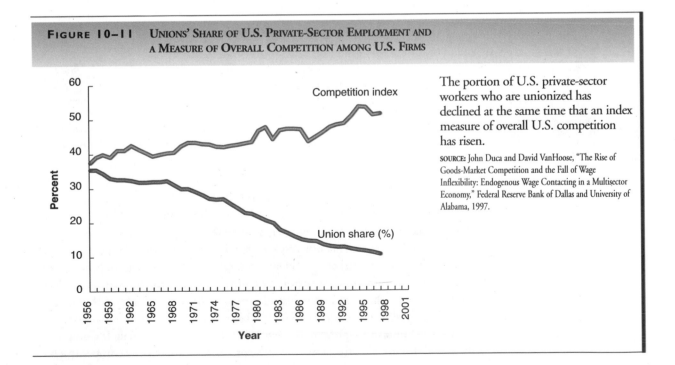

The portion of U.S. private-sector workers who are unionized has declined at the same time that an index measure of overall U.S. competition has risen.

SOURCE: John Duca and David VanHoose, "The Rise of Goods-Market Competition and the Fall of Wage Inflexibility: Endogenous Wage Contacting in a Multisector Economy," Federal Reserve Bank of Dallas and University of Alabama, 1997.

GLOBAL NOTEBOOK
Union Membership Worldwide

Private-sector union membership has been falling in the United States for years. The same trend is occurring in many other countries. Even in countries that might seem to be favorably disposed to unions, union membership has fallen over the last two decades. For example, in France union membership fell steadily from 22.3 percent to 9.7 percent during the fourteen years of socialist François Mitterrand's presidency. Under the Labour party leadership of Bob Hawke in Australia, union membership also fell. Japan has shown the same pattern since the 1970s.

A number of researchers have examined why union membership continues to fall, even in politically receptive environments. According to Jonus Pontusson of Cornell University, the percentage of the work force that belongs to a union correlates closely with plant size. Apparently, it is easier and less expensive per worker to organize a single 1,000-worker plant than one hundred 10-worker plants. Throughout much of the world, plant size has declined and therefore, according to Pontusson, so has union coverage.

Another factor is that throughout most of the developing world, the service sector is growing in importance. Service workers are more difficult to organize than industrial workers. According to Harvard's labor economist, Richard Freeman, "Unions are strong among coal miners. [They] are in a dangerous situation together and that builds solidarity."

Finally, unions have been most successful in countries with centralized wage systems, such as Germany where the I.G. Metall Union bargains with the Gesamtmetall Employers' Organization on behalf of more that 3 million workers. Throughout the world, centralized wage systems have been breaking down, especially in Australia, France, New Zealand, and Italy.

FOR CRITICAL ANALYSIS:

In the United States, virtually all government employees are involved in the service sector. Nevertheless, the percentage of government workers who belong to unions has held steady at about 38 percent for more than two decades. Why has it been easier to organize government employees than private-sector employees in the service sector?

ON THE WEB
Visit the Australian Government's Homepage at:
http://gov.info.au/

Second, greater competition among U.S. firms and industries has undermined the economic feasibility of the union movement. Figure 10–11 also shows a measure of the overall extent of competition in U.S. markets for goods and services. The decline in the extent of unionization clearly has coincided with a rise in overall competition in U.S. product markets. One reason for this inverse relationship between unionization and competition is that one rationale for forming a union is to attain sufficient labor-market power to bargain for wages above the competitive level, which is more feasible in industries that are not very competitive. For instance, in years past a number of industries consisted of only a few very large firms, so the firms may have earned excess profits that unions could extract from the firms' owners and managers. Greater competition in these industries would reduce the availability of higher-than-competitive profits for firms, thereby eliminating one reason to form a union.

Another reason that greater competition undercuts the rationale for union contracting is that it makes the demand for the products of imperfectly competitive firms more sensitive to price changes by increasing the range of available substitute products and, as a result, raising the elasticity of demand for the goods and services produced by each business. This ultimately makes labor demand more sensitive to fluctuations in aggregate demand and supply. As a result, long-term union contracts become less attractive to both workers and firms, because the contracts lead to greater variability in employment and real output.

INTERNET SOURCE

Learning about Unions

AFL/CIO—The American Federation of Labor/Congress of Industrial Organizations
Internet URL: http://www.aflcio.org/

Navigation: Start at the AFL-CIO's homepage (http://www.aflcio.org). To obtain information about individual unions, scan down the homepage and click on *Union Organizations and Other Sites on the Web.* Then click on *Unions and Union Organizations on the Web* to obtain a list of individual union web sites that you can browse through to learn more about individual unions.

The Reemergence of the Classical Labor Market?   The decline in U.S. unionization is indicative of a broader pattern of change in U.S. labor markets, which casts at least some doubt on the ability of modern Keynesian contract-based theories to explain business cycles or to provide prescriptions for monetary and fiscal policy-making. The advent of computer technology has reduced the scope for informational asymmetries by making more information available to both workers and their employers. Consequently, the incentive to adopt contracts intended to protect against such problems has been reduced.

Indeed, a recent trend has been for individuals to form consulting businesses, selling their labor services to a variety of firms instead of working for a single company for a long period. Although traditional worker-firm relationships of the past remain the predominant form of labor-market interactions, the growth of consulting arrangements represents a movement toward a more nearly classical, auction-market structure in a number of U.S. labor markets. This trend is another reason why the contract-based approach of the modern Keynesian theory has arguably become somewhat less relevant as a complete macroeconomic model.

Multisector Models: A Call for Help?   Many proponents of modern Keynesian theory recognize that the effects of recent trends have been undermining the ability of wage contracting models to explain all the features of the economy. Some modern Keynesians have therefore embedded contracting theories in broader macroeconomic models that admit the existence of a variety of individuals, markets, and industries.

MULTISECTOR MODELS
Macroeconomic models in which the structures of various sectors of the economy correspond to different theories.

Such **multisector models,** they argue, might help to explain why no single macroeconomic theory generally fits all the available evidence.

For example, a multisector framework would predict that real wages would be countercyclical in sectors of the economy where wage contracts are important, but procyclical in other sectors. This could help to explain why the behavior of *aggregate* real wages and price levels for the economy as a whole seems to be both partially consistent and partially inconsistent with predictions of both theories.

Those who work with multisector models also propose that they can help to explain some of the difficult trade-offs that macroeconomic policymakers face. In a multisector macroeconomic model in which some sectors fit the modern Keynesian contracting theory while others do not, policymakers would have difficulty identifying policy actions that would stabilize all parts of the economy simultaneously. For instance, a contracting sector might benefit from a particular monetary policy action, while a classical sector might not gain or might even lose from the same action. A research study of 450 U.S. manufacturing industries by Vivek Ghosal of Miami University and Prakash Loungani of the Federal Reserve has found evidence favoring the applicability of such a multisector approach.

Modern Keynesian theorists are not the only macroeconomists who have begun to explore the possibility that *disaggregated* theories may be an improvement over purely aggregate macroeconomic models. Macroeconomists of both Keynesian and classical persuasions have developed multiple-sector models. Nevertheless, in most respects the differences separating the two groups have, if anything, widened in recent years, as you will learn in the next chapter.

FUNDAMENTAL ISSUE #5

Are the wage contracting models proposed by the modern Keynesian theorists relevant in today's world? Critics of the modern Keynesian theory of wage stickiness have questioned the theory's ability to explain the actual behavior of macroeconomic variables. Proponents of the modern Keynesian approach have responded to these criticisms by offering evidence supporting the predictions of their models and by refining their theories. Nevertheless, widespread changes in U.S. labor markets have made it increasingly difficult to apply the theory broadly to the U.S. economy. This has led some proponents of the modern Keynesian approach to consider multisector models in which some portions of the economy fit the classical theory while others adopt wage contracts.

CHAPTER SUMMARY

1. **The Essential Elements of the Modern Keynesian Theory of Wage Stickiness:** The modern Keynesian theory hypothesizes that workers and firms may desire to use wage contracts to avoid the transaction costs entailed in continual wage bargaining, to reduce risks associated with wage variability, or to deal with problems arising from asymmetric information. The theory predicts that workers and firms must make rational forecasts of the price level to set the appropriate wage for the interval that the contract will be in force. During the contract term, unanticipated fluctuations in the price level can induce changes in employment and real output. Consequently, the aggregate supply schedule is upward sloping.

2. **How the Modern Keynesian Theory Is Observationally Equivalent to the New Classical Model:** The essential predictions of basic versions of both theories are the same. Both approaches indicate that unexpected policy actions are more likely to have effects on employment and real output, whereas completely anticipated policy actions should have no real effects. Therefore, the two theories are observationally equivalent in their fundamental implications even though they are based on very different views about the functioning of the labor market.

3. **How the Degree of Wage Indexation Affects the Elasticity of the Aggregate Supply Schedule, and How That Matters for the Optimal Degree of Indexation:** Under full wage indexation, the contract wage is adjusted equiproportionately to changes in the price level. Hence, as in the classical model, the aggregate supply schedule is completely inelastic. Under a nonindexed wage contract, however, the nominal wage does not adjust at all to price-level variations, so the aggregate supply schedule is relatively elastic around a particular price level. Full wage indexation protects real output and employment from the effects of aggregate demand volatility, but enlarges the effects on output and employment caused by fluctuations in aggregate supply. Therefore, neither fully indexed nor nonindexed wage contracts are necessarily better for minimizing variability of employment and real output when there is variability in both aggregate demand and aggregate supply.

4. **The Factors That Determine the Duration of Wage Contracts and the Macroeconomic Implications of Overlapping Contract Intervals:** The optimal duration of a wage contract falls as the contract negotiation costs decline and as the volatility in the price level resulting from aggregate demand and supply variability rises. Contract negotiation costs differ across firms and industries, so contract beginning and ending dates are staggered. The modern Keynesian theory predicts that the resulting overlapping of contracts causes aggregate demand fluctuations to have persistent effects on employment and real output.

5. **The Relevance of Wage Contracting Models Proposed by the Modern Keynesian Theorists in Today's World:** Recent changes in the structure of U.S. labor markets have caused some to question the modern Keynesian theory's ability to explain the actual behavior of macroeconomic variables. Proponents of this approach have responded by offering evidence supporting the predictions of their models, by refining their theories, and by

proposing multisector models in which some portions of the economy fit the classical theory while others adopt wage contracts.

QUESTIONS AND PROBLEMS

1. Explain, in your own words, why modern Keynesian economists theorize that fixed-wage contracts may be "rational."

2. Suppose that the price level during a contract interval turns out to be lower than what workers and firms anticipated when they negotiated the contract. Would workers end up working more or fewer hours than they had expected to work? Explain your reasoning.

3. Suppose that labor-force participation by teenage workers suddenly increases during a period in which wage contracts are in force for all firms and workers in an economy. According to the modern Keynesian model, what would be the effects, if any, on employment, unemployment, and real output? Explain your reasoning.

4. Explain, in your own words, the concept of observational equivalence as it applies to the basic one-period modern Keynesian contracting model and the new classical theory.

5. Would significant contract staggering and overlap in the general Keynesian wage contracting model make the implications of contracting theory observationally *in*equivalent to the new classical theory? Support your answer.

6. Should governments require all wage contracts to be negotiated on the same dates each year? Justify your stand on this issue.

7. Suppose that all workers and firms agreed to cost-of-living-adjustment clauses in wage contracts that called for complete indexation of nominal wages to changes in the price level. In such a setting, could unanticipated increases in the nominal money stock affect employment and real output? Explain.

8. If real GDP variability and employment volatility over business cycles became significantly less pronounced, this would tend to indicate that aggregate demand and supply variability had declined. What would be the likely effect on the average duration of wage contracts among the portions of the labor market that typically use such contracts? Explain your reasoning.

9. Use diagrams of the market for real output and of the labor market with fixed-money-wage contracts to explain how the *real* wage should respond to a decline in aggregate demand in the basic Keynesian one-period contracting model. In light of the model's prediction, explain why evidence indicating procyclical real wage variations might cast doubt on the validity of the model.

10. Suppose that the economy is composed of two sectors. Sector 1 is made up of workers and firms whose behavior is best described by the classical theory, while sector 2 is composed of workers and firms who use nonindexed wage contracts that are staggered and overlapping. Would the real wage be counter- or pro-cyclical in sector 1? In sector 2? If sector 1 is significantly larger than sector 2, would the aggregate real wage for the economy as a whole be significantly counter- or pro-cyclical? Explain.

CyberTutor Exercises

1. What is the effect of a rise in the price level on the equilibrium nominal wage, the equilibrium real wage, and the aggregate supply schedule?

2. Suppose that a management guru discovers a new management technique that increases worker productivity throughout the economy. What effect will this have on the equilibrium nominal wage, the equilibrium real wage, equilibrium employment and the aggregate supply schedule?

3. Consider Figure 10–7 in the text. Wage indexation may be especially important in times of rapid inflation so that workers' real wages will remain stable. This would suggest that the share of U.S. labor contracts containing indexation clauses would be highest in periods of high inflation. Create a scatter plot of the U.S. unemployment rate vs. the share of U.S. labor contracts containing indexation clauses. What is the relationship between wage indexation the inflation rate? Why do you think this relationship holds?

4. Consider Figure 10–11 in the text. Among some economic pundits there is a feeling that as unionization increases, employment will fall. Let's see if they are right. Graph the unions' share of U.S. private sector employment against unemployment. Do the data support this simple relationship?

On-Line Application

As discussed in this chapter, some economists in recent years have advocated a multisector approach to macroeconomics. Although this approach typically emphasizes differences across structures of the industrial goods market and the labor market, it also could allow for differences in macroeconomic structures across geographical regions of an economy. This application permits you to evaluate whether such an approach might have any merit.

Internet URL: http://www.dol.gov

Title: Department of Labor

Navigation: Begin at the homepage of the Labor Department, which is the above address. Then click on *Labor Related Data*. Next, click on *Bureau of Labor Statistics*.

Application: Perform the indicated operations, and answer the following questions:

1. Choose "Most Requested Series." Then scan down "BLS Regional Offices' Most Requested Series." From this list, you can click on any regional office of your choice. Do so, and select *Unemployment Rate U.S.* Scan the data for the past two or three years. Does the unemployment rate fluctuate?

2. Now take a look at the unemployment rates for two or three individual cities and regions by clicking on data sources of your choice from various regions of the nation.

Compare the data for the cities or regions that you have chosen with the overall U.S. unemployment rate data. Are there significant differences, either in the magnitudes of the unemployment rates or in the extent to which they vary over time?

SELECTED REFERENCES AND FURTHER READING

Card, David. "Unexpected Inflation, Real Wages, and Employment Determination in Union Contracts." *American Economic Review* 80 (September 1990): 669–688.

Duca, John, and David VanHoose. "The Rise of Goods-Market Competition and the Decline in Wage Indexation," *Journal of Macroeconomics* 20 (Summer, 1998).

Duca, John, and David VanHoose. "Optimal Wage Indexation in a Multisector Economy." *International Economic Review* 32 (November 1991): 859–867.

Dutkowsky, Donald, and H. Sonmez Atesoglu. "Wage Contracting in the Macroeconomy." *Journal of Money, Credit, and Banking* 25 (February 1993): 62–78.

Fischer, Stanley. *Indexing, Inflation, and Economic Policy.* Cambridge, Mass.: MIT Press, 1986.

Fischer, Stanley, ed. *Rational Expectations and Economic Policy.* Chicago: University of Chicago Press, 1980.

Ghosal, Vivek, and Prakash Loungani. "Evidence on Nominal Wage Rigidity from a Panel of U.S. Manufacturing Industries." *Journal of Money, Credit, and Banking* 28 (November 1996): 650–668.

Gray, Jo Anna. "Wage Indexation: A Macroeconomic Approach." *Journal of Monetary Economics* 2 (April 1976): 221–235.

Gray, Jo Anna, and David Spencer. "Price Prediction Errors and Real Activity: A Reassessment." *Economic Inquiry* 28 (October 1990), 658–681.

Gray, Jo Anna, Magda Kandil, and David Spencer. "Does Contractual Wage Rigidity Play a Role in Determining Real Activity?" *Southern Economic Journal* 58 (1992): 1042–1057.

Taylor, John. "Aggregate Dynamics and Staggered Contracts." *Journal of Political Economy* 88 (February 1980): 1–23.

VanHoose, David, and Christopher J. Waller, "Discretion, Wage Indexation, and Inflation," *Southern Economic Journal* 58 (October 1991), 356–367.

11

Market Failures versus Perfect Markets—

NEW KEYNESIANS VERSUS REAL-BUSINESS-CYCLE THEORISTS

FUNDAMENTAL ISSUES

1. What has motivated macroeconomists to propose additional theories of how the economy functions?

2. What are the key features of new Keynesian theories?

3. What are coordination failures, and why do new Keynesians believe that they may be important?

4. How do real-business-cycle theorists explain short-term fluctuations in real output?

5. What is quantitative theory, and why is it so controversial?

Policymakers in Washington, D.C., may think they have control over the key variables that determine what happens in the U.S. economy. In reality, the policymakers are not always in control. For example, they certainly were not capable of stopping the run-up in oil prices in the 1970s. Nor have economic policymakers ever been able to stop the country from going to war—Vietnam is just one case in point.

Now consider a positive event in our history. The computer revolution has had a major impact on not only the U.S. economy but the global economy. Nev-

ertheless, policymakers were nowhere to be seen a few years ago when, for example, the retail price of a 16-megabyte memory chip dropped from around $400 to $99.

Some macrotheorists argue that real events such as these can drive the U.S. economy in ways that will create business cycles. Hence, business cycles can be thought of as sudden variations in the technological capabilities of firms. Such a theory may be capable of explaining some of the ups and downs in overall national economic activity.

In this chapter you will read about real-business-cycle theorists, who believe that technological changes, among other things, matter. You will also discover that other theorists believe that market failures may offer an explanation for changes in overall business activity.

WHY ARE THERE NEW THEORIES?

In many respects, the widespread adoption of the rational expectations hypothesis by modern Keynesian and new classical theorists alike has revolutionized macroeconomics. At the same time, however, the gulf separating the Keynesian- and classical-oriented approaches to macroeconomic theory and policy analysis widened during the 1990s. On the one hand, incorporating the rational expectations hypothesis into fully articulated theories of the economy has led a number of today's proponents of the Keynesian approach to develop business cycle models with considerable stickiness of wages and prices. These new theories constitute *new Keynesian macroeconomics*. On the other hand, many proponents of the new classical approach have reached the conclusion that business cycles arise naturally in an economy with fully flexible wages and prices. The macroeconomic models that they have developed comprise the *real-business-cycle* approach to macroeconomics. Our goal in this chapter is to help you to understand why there is such a gap between these two schools of thought, so that you will be able to judge for yourself in the coming years which approach has the greater practical relevance.

You might wonder why macroeconomists have developed yet more theories. Aren't the classical, traditional Keynesian, monetarist, new classical, and modern Keynesian theories enough? The answer is that even though the rational expectations hypothesis helped to resolve long-standing issues about how to include information and expectations in macroeconomic models, by itself it did not provide macroeconomists with a better explanation of the actual performances of real-world economies. Indeed, incorporating rational expectations into previously existing models, which essentially is what the modern Keynesian and new classical theorists have done, opened a Pandora's box of new problems for macroeconomists. Even though the rational expectations hypothesis is intuitively appealing and makes macroeconomic models internally consistent, the modern Keynesian and new classical theories that resulted have had trouble explaining observed *persistence* in employment and real output movements.

The Great Puzzle Posed by the Great Depression

The extreme example of this failure is the Great Depression that gripped the United Kingdom, the United States, and many other nations during the 1930s. A common explanation for the Great Depression, originally proposed by Milton Friedman and other monetarists, is that the Great Depression was set off by a large decline in the nominal money stock between 1929 and 1933. In fact, the quantity of money in the United States fell by over one-third during that interval, inducing a sizable decline in aggregate demand.

Other competing explanations for the onset of the Great Depression have been offered, but like this monetarist explanation, they focus on the decline in aggregate demand. Both new classical and modern Keynesian theories face a problem, though, in explaining why the Great Depression lasted for such a long time. After all, the policy actions that permitted a continual fall in the money stock and induced the decline in aggregate demand were repeated until they became systematic and, thus, predictable. As you learned in Chapter 9, the new classical theory's central tenet is that predictable policy actions should have no effects on employment and real output. Nonetheless, the Great Depression persisted until the outbreak of World War II in Europe in 1939.

As we discussed in Chapter 10, the modern Keynesian theory with staggered and overlapping contracts might help to explain why the large fall in aggregate demand of the early 1930s had such persistent effects. Nevertheless, this contract-based theory also falters when confronted with both the extreme severity and the significant persistence of the Great Depression. Unions and explicit wage contracts existed in the 1930s, but they actually became more prevalent as the Great Depression progressed. During the early years of the depression, they were not widespread in U.S. labor markets. Even if they had been, it would be difficult for the modern Keynesian theory to explain the persistent declines in real output that occurred in the 1930s. Like the new classical theory, the contract-based model predicts that systematic declines in the quantity of money and the price level will be anticipated, so that within a few years employment and real output will tend to return to their long-run, "natural" levels. The modern Keynesian theory has trouble explaining why this failed to happen over the course of an entire decade.

Modern GDP Persistence

The Great Depression is an extreme example of persistence in employment and real output movements. In the 1980s macroeconomists developed new techniques for

TIME SERIES Observed values of macroeconomic variables over successive time intervals.

examining **time series,** or data recorded over successive periods of time. They discovered that temporary changes in economic conditions often have long-lasting effects on real GDP. Nevertheless, macroeconomic theories, such as those we have discussed up to this point, indicated that such temporary changes should simply result in "blips," or short-term GDP fluctuations that ultimately would peter out. In fact, however, many variations in economic conditions seem to have long-lasting effects on GDP.

To a large extent, the development of the new Keynesian and real-business-cycle theories stems from efforts by macroeconomists to understand what could cause temporary changes in economic conditions to persist for months and years afterward. Although these theories are offshoots of the modern Keynesian and new classical approaches that we discussed in the previous two chapters, their emphasis on the persistence issue is what classifies them, at least for the present, as "new" macroeconomic theories.

New theories can be useful, but they also can turn out to be dead ends. You should keep this in mind as you read this chapter. A decade or two from now, some of the approaches discussed in this chapter will have been debunked. Others, however, likely will provide the basis for policy analysis by the coming generation of economists and policymakers. This is why it is important for you to study these new theoretical approaches: In the not-so-distant future, at least one of these theories may guide macroeconomic forecasting and policymaking.

FUNDAMENTAL ISSUE #1

What has motivated macroeconomists to propose additional theories of how the economy functions? Earlier theories have not been successful in explaining why real GDP seems to exhibit persistent responses to otherwise short-lived changes in economic activity. Hence, macroeconomists have developed new theories that potentially can explain this phenomenon.

STICKY-PRICE THEORIES: NEW KEYNESIAN MACROECONOMICS

In the classical and new classical theories, the key to rapid adjustments of real output to the level consistent with an economy's long-run growth potential is flexibility of wages and prices. Inflexible wages and prices are one possible reason why real output might vary from its long-run level. As we discussed in Chapter 10, the modern Keynesian theory has focused its attention on wage inflexibilities. New Keynesian theories, however, concentrate on possible *sources* of stickiness in the price level. Inflexible prices of goods and services could help to explain why real output might be variable in the short run. Price stickiness also might be part of a rationale for persistence in output changes in response to temporary changes in economic conditions. Together with wage stickiness, price stickiness can also lead to real wage rigidities that could help to explain unemployment.

Why Would Prices Be Sticky, and Why Does It Matter if They Are?

Until the early 1970s, traditional Keynesian theorists often worked with models in which the price level was fixed. Just as we assumed in Chapters 5 through 7 that the price level was "given," macroeconomists used to envision a world with inflexible prices, so that real output adjusted to changes in desired autonomous spending. Thus, autonomous changes in household consumption spending, investment spending by firms, exports, or imports could account for business cycles.

Clearly though, prices change every week and every month. Indeed, since the end of World War II the United States has consistently experienced inflation. By definition, therefore, the price level has risen over time. How then can new Keynesian theorists feel comfortable developing models in which prices are sticky? Let's consider this question before we explore the new Keynesian theories any further.

Is There Inertia in the Price Level?   New Keynesians argue that persistent inflation does not necessarily mean that the prices of goods and services adjust quickly and fully to changes in current market conditions. For instance, a short-run average inflation rate of 3 percent might mask the fact that if prices adjusted as flexibly as possible to changes in demand or in firms' production costs, the short-run inflation rate would have been much higher.

For reasons that we shall discuss later in the chapter, sluggishness in price adjustments, or **price inertia,** is a central feature of most new Keynesian theories. Figure 11–1 on page 362 displays estimates of an index measure of price inertia for five industrialized nations spanning the period from the end of the 1950s through the late 1980s. The higher the value of this index, the more inertia there is in prices of goods and services in a nation. As you can see, according to this measure the United States experienced the greatest sluggishness in price adjustment, as compared with Germany, France, the United Kingdom, and Japan.

Trying to Explain Price Rigidity: New Keynesian Macroeconomics   In light of Figure 11–1 and other evidence of price stickiness, the new Keynesian theorists believe that the assumption of complete price-level flexibility in the United States and other nations is unwarranted. In their view, any complete macroeconomic theory should account for the existence of such rigidities and for their potential to explain key features of business cycles, including output persistence.

Although the new Keynesian approach began to attract many adherents during the 1980s, it actually began in the 1960s and early 1970s. During this earlier period,

PRICE INERTIA A tendency for the price level to resist change over time.

ON THE WEB
Visit the Homepage of the United Kingdom at:
http://www.cm.cf.ac.uk/Places/uk.html

FIGURE 11–1 **MEASURES OF PRICE INERTIA FOR FIVE INDUSTRIALIZED NATIONS**

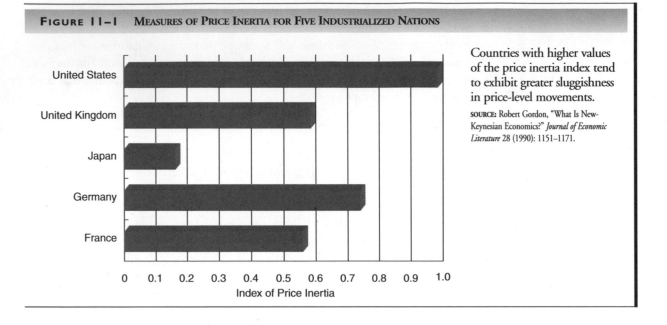

Countries with higher values of the price inertia index tend to exhibit greater sluggishness in price-level movements.

SOURCE: Robert Gordon, "What Is New-Keynesian Economics?" *Journal of Economic Literature* 28 (1990): 1151–1171.

a number of macroeconomists tried to construct more sophisticated Keynesian models. As in the earlier model that we summarized in Chapters 5 through 7, these models had fixed prices. In contrast to the basic Keynesian framework, however, these models had "microeconomic foundations." In the macroeconomic frameworks that emerged from this approach, real output was *demand determined,* rather than supply determined as in the classical model. As a result, real output adjusted to market conditions. Short-term business cycles therefore could be explained by variations in aggregate demand.

This approach largely was abandoned by the late 1970s, however. The theory lacked an explanation for price rigidity, and the development of the rational expectations hypothesis seemed to explain why short-run and long-run price-level and output adjustments might differ. Moreover, experience with the Arab oil embargo in 1973 and the sharp effects on real GDP after the run-up in oil prices in the mid-1970s indicated that supply-side factors clearly were important determinants of real output, so a purely demand-based macroeconomic theory made little sense.

Later on, proponents of the new Keynesian approach brought the theories of price rigidities back to life by developing sticky-price models in which the reasons for price rigidities are fully explained and prices respond at least partially to changes in supply-side factors. This is where the idea of price inertia comes in. Theories that predict price inertia indicate that prices can still change with variations in factors affecting business production costs. Nevertheless, sluggishness in price adjustments can lead to considerable short-term variability of real output as a result of variations in aggregate demand, as in the earlier fixed-price theories.

Imperfect Competition and Market Failures   During the past twenty years, new Keynesian theorists have proposed a number of explanations for price inertia and its implications for business cycles. Although these theories differ in many respects, they typically share two features. First, most new Keynesian theories depart from the classical assumption of purely competitive markets for goods and services or for factors of production. Recall that in purely competitive markets, there are many buyers and sellers, there is free entry into and exit from markets, and products that firms produce and the services of factors of production are indistinguishable. New Keynesian theories, in contrast, are based on the assumption of **imperfect competition.** This refers to market environments in which the number of buyers or sellers may be limited, there may be barriers to market entry or exit, or firm products or factor services may be differentiated.

The other feature common to many new Keynesian models is **market failure,** or the failure of a private market to reach an equilibrium that reflects all the costs and benefits entailed in producing a good or providing a factor service. An example of a market failure is an **externality,** or a situation in which a private cost or benefit differs from a social cost or benefit because of spillover effects stemming from the production or consumption of a good or service. Consider, for instance, noise pollution in the form of classical, country & western, rap, or rock music that booms from car stereos on city streets. Such pollution is made possible by the production and sale of car speakers capable of amplifying sound. The firms that produce car speakers receive private benefits from their sale, and enthusiasts of classical, country & western, rap, and rock music benefit from the ability to listen to the music at high-decibel levels. Meanwhile other people incur costs because they must listen to music when they would prefer peace and quiet. These spillover costs that nonenthusiasts incur are not reflected in the equilibrium price and quantity in the market for car stereo speakers.

The noise pollution produced by booming car speakers is a *microeconomic* externality, or an externality that arises in a single market. New Keynesian proponents contend that there also are **macroeconomic externalities.** In these situations, equilibrium in all, or at least many, markets fails to account for spillovers across markets, so that equilibrium aggregate real output, employment, and the price level all differ from their long-run, natural levels.

The nature of proposed new Keynesian macroeconomic externalities varies across the diverse range of new Keynesian theories. Nonetheless, as we shall discuss in more detail shortly, the proposed macroeconomic externalities arise from the inability of individuals and firms to coordinate their actions. The alleged existence of such *coordination failures* is the cornerstone of the new Keynesian approach to macroeconomics. Before we try to understand the nature of coordination failures, however, let's first survey the main new Keynesian theories.

Small-Menu-Cost Models

What might account for price inertia? After all, profit-maximizing firms adjust their output to the point at which marginal revenue is equal to marginal cost. Further-

---

IMPERFECT COMPETITION A market environment that may have a limited number of buyers or sellers, barriers to market entry or exit, or differentiated firm products or factor services.

MARKET FAILURE The potential failure of a private market equilibrium to reflect all costs and benefits relating to production of a good or service.

EXTERNALITY A spillover effect that arises when market exchanges affect the well-being of an individual or firm that is not a party to the exchanges.

MACROECONOMIC EXTERNALITIES Situations in which aggregate equilibrium in all, or at least many, markets fails to account for spillovers across markets, so that equilibrium aggregate real output, employment, and the price level all differ from their long-run, natural levels.

more, as firms adjust their output to profit-maximizing levels, market prices should adjust as well.

If prices somehow are relatively rigid even as market conditions change, then profit-maximizing firms must have a *reason* not to vary prices. This is an example of how imperfect competition and market failures might play a role. According to one new Keynesian approach, known as the *small-menu-cost theory,* the absence of pure competition and macroeconomic externalities together could help to account for price inertia and ultimately could help to explain business cycles and the persistent response of real output to temporary changes in economic conditions.

The Administered Pricing Hypothesis   The idea that imperfect competition could help to explain price rigidities was first suggested in the 1930s by an economist named Gardiner Means. His theory, which became known as the **administered pricing hypothesis,** proposed that firms that are not purely competitive are able to *set* prices and to maintain relatively *inflexible* pricing policies over lengthy intervals.

Initially, a number of economists were attracted to Means's hypothesis, because they thought that it could assist in explaining the observed stickiness of prices in several U.S. industries during the Great Depression. For instance, as Table 11–1 shows, product prices of agricultural implements and motor vehicles fell by only 6 percent and 16 percent, respectively, while output declined significantly—by 80 percent—in both industries. In other industries, however, such as petroleum and agricultural products, price declines were much more pronounced. Thus, proportionate output reductions were much smaller in these industries. Ultimately, however, the administered pricing hypothesis was abandoned, because it was difficult to understand why even imperfectly competitive firms would fail to change their prices in response to variations in the demand for their products or in the face of changes in their costs of production.

Resurrecting an Old Idea   The small-menu-cost theory, which was first proposed by N. Gregory Mankiw of Harvard University and subsequently was refined in the

ADMINISTERED PRICING HYPOTHESIS The view that imperfectly competitive firms set prices of their products at relatively unchanging levels for lengthy intervals.

TABLE 11–1   DECLINES IN PRICES AND PRODUCTION FOR SELECTED U.S. INDUSTRIES, 1929–1933

INDUSTRY	PERCENTAGE DECLINE IN PRICE	PERCENTAGE DECLINE IN PRODUCTION
Agricultural implements	6	80
Motor vehicles	16	80
Textile products	45	30
Petroleum	56	20
Agricultural products	63	6

SOURCE: Robert Gordon, "What Is New-Keynesian Economics?" *Journal of Economic Literature* 28 (1990): 1151–1171.

SMALL MENU COSTS The costs firms incur when they make price changes, including both the costs of changing prices in menus or catalogues and the costs of renegotiating agreements with customers.

1980s and 1990s, has brought the administered pricing hypothesis back to life, albeit in a new form. As the theory's name indicates, the basis of the theory is the proposal that firms incur small but measurable costs, called **small menu costs,** when they change the prices that they charge their customers. These costs could take the form of expenses entailed in printing new price tags, menus, and catalogs. They also could include costs incurred in bringing together firm managers for meetings on price changes or in renegotiating business deals with customers.

Figure 11–2 illustrates the small-menu-cost theory as applied to an individual, imperfectly competitive firm whose product differs slightly from those of rival producers. Consequently, the firm faces a downward-sloping demand schedule, labeled D. We assume that the demand schedule is a straight line, which means that the marginal revenue schedule is also a straight line. In addition, we simplify by assuming that the firm's marginal cost (MC) is constant and equal to its average cost (AC), and we consider only a single production period to which these demand and cost schedules apply. When the demand schedule is in the position denoted by D_1, the marginal revenue schedule is located at the position labeled MR_1. If the firm faces this level of demand and marginal revenue, it maximizes its profit by producing output up to the point at which marginal revenue is equal to marginal cost. The profit-maximizing output level therefore is equal to y_1. The firm then charges a price, P_1, that its customers are willing to pay, which we can determine by reading off the demand schedule at the output level y_1. The profit earned by the firm then is equal to total revenue minus total cost, or $(P_1 \times y_1) - (AC \times y_1)$. This is equal to $(P_1 - AC) \times y_1$, which is the maximum profit at the level of demand given by D_1.

FIGURE 11–2   PROFIT GAINS AND LOSSES FROM A FIRM'S FAILURE TO CHANGE ITS PRICE WHEN DEMAND FOR ITS PRODUCT DECLINES

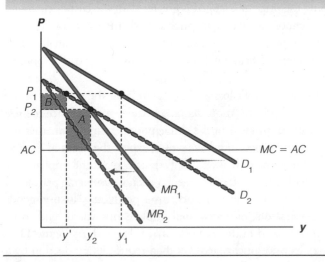

If the demand and marginal revenue schedules faced by an imperfectly competitive firm shift downward, and the firm fails to reduce its price, its profit gain is the area B. If the firm cuts its price to P_2, its profit gain is the area A. Consequently, a firm interested in maximizing its profit normally would reduce its price from P_1 to P_2, because $A - B$ is greater than zero, implying that a price cut will result in a net profit gain. If the cost of adjusting its price is greater than the amount $A - B$, however, the firm will leave its price unchanged at P_1.

Now think about what will happen if the demand schedule shifts inward, to D_2. Because the marginal revenue is derived from the demand schedule, the marginal revenue schedule will shift inward as well, to MR_2. You learned in your microeconomics principles course that the firm should then adjust its output level to the new point at which marginal revenue equals marginal cost, which is at the output level y_2. The firm will reduce the price of its product to P_2, and its new maximum profit will be equal to $(P_2 \times y_2) - (AC \times y_2)$, or $(P_2 - AC) \times y_2$.

Normally, we assume that a firm faces no costs in changing its price. Suppose that in the face of small menu costs such as those we discussed earlier, the firm contemplates leaving its price unchanged when demand declines from D_1 to D_2. If the firm follows this course by holding its product price steady at P_1, then at the reduced level of demand D_2 the firm will be able to sell only the level of output y', and its profit will be equal to $(P_1 \times y') - (AC \times y')$, or $(P_1 - AC) \times y'$. This profit level is lower than the profit the firm could have earned by reducing its price to P_2, which we just noted would equal $(P_2 - AC) \times y_2$. If the firm keeps its price unchanged, its profit loss is the difference between the two profit levels that the firm could earn.

We can calculate this difference by examining Figure 11–2. If the firm produces the output level y', and keeps its price at P_1 instead of cutting its price to P_2 when demand falls, the firm will obtain a profit increase equal to the area labeled B. At the profit-maximizing price P_2 at the lower level of demand, however, producing y' units of output instead of the actual profit-maximizing output level y_2 will yield a profit reduction equal to area A. Hence, the net profit reduction that the firm will experience by keeping its price fixed at P_1 when demand declines from D_1 to D_2 is equal to the amount $A - B$.

This means that the firm's decision on whether or not to change its price will depend on a simple comparison of the size of the profit reduction from keeping its price fixed, $A - B$, with the small menu cost it would incur if it changes its price. If the profit loss from keeping the price unchanged is greater than the cost of changing its price, then the firm will choose to change its price as basic microeconomics principles suggest it should. If the profit loss from leaving its price fixed is smaller than the cost of cutting its price, then the firm will leave its price unchanged. The price of its product will be "sticky."

It turns out that the size of the profit loss $A - B$ depends on the elasticity of the demand schedule at the original price. A more elastic schedule would reduce the size of the profit loss $A - B$. One determinant of the elasticity of demand is whether the good is regarded as a "luxury" or a "necessity." We would expect the demand for luxury goods, including big-ticket items such as automobiles or agricultural implements, to be more elastic than the demand for necessities such as energy-producing petroleum products or food-related agricultural products. Hence, firms producing "luxury" goods such as motor vehicles, new tractors, or agricultural implements would tend to be more likely to leave their prices fixed in the face of a fall in demand. As Figure 11–2 indicates, a firm that leaves its price unchanged will then reduce its production by a larger amount when demand declines, from y_1 to y', rather than from y_1 to y_2.

If you refer back to Table 11–1, you will see that this story appears to fit the facts that Gardiner Means documented in the 1930s. Essentially, the small-menu-cost model provides the basic theoretical explanation for the administered pricing hypothesis that was lacking at the time Means proposed the hypothesis.

INTERNET SOURCE

The Government's Efforts to Limit Administered Pricing

U.S. Department of Justice—The Antitrust Division
Internet URL: http://www.usdoj.gov/atr/atr.htm

Navigation: Start at the homepage of the U.S. Justice Department (http://www.usdoj.gov). Scan down the page and click on *Justice Department Organization,* then on *Alphabetically by Organization,* then on *Antitrust Division.*

From Menu Costs to Macroeconomic Externalities   Figure 11–2 depicts the behavior of a single firm. Firms throughout the economy face their own specific demand schedules and have their own marginal and average cost schedules. According to the theory, some firms will reduce their prices in the face of declining product demand. Others will leave their prices fixed.

Laurence Ball of Johns Hopkins University and David Romer of Harvard University have shown how this mix of responses by firms can have macroeconomic implications. The foundation of their argument is that the products of firms are substitutable in consumption, albeit imperfectly. When one set of firms chooses to cut their prices in the face of an overall decline in demand for goods throughout the economy, consumers allocate more of their spending to consumption of the output of those firms, although on net the firms' production levels still will fall. As a result, though, fewer consumer funds are available for spending on the goods produced by firms that keep their prices fixed. Demand at each of the fixed-price firms then declines further, thereby reinforcing the output declines at those firms. Consequently, the decisions by some firms to cut their prices have spillover effects onto firms that do not change their prices, and vice versa. As we shall discuss in more detail later, this could be a source of macroeconomic externalities that could cause business cycles to occur and to persist.

Problems with the Small-Menu-Cost Model   Critics of the small-menu-cost model point out that the theory assumes that firms attempt to maximize profits only for a single period. More realistically, however, firms earn flows of profits over time. To see why this poses a problem for the small-menu-cost analysis, look at Figure 11–2 once again, and consider the profit loss that a firm will experience if it leaves its price unchanged in the face of a long-lasting decline in demand as illustrated in the figure. The firm will incur the profit loss $A - B$ *every period* from now into the future.

Hence, from today's perspective, the firm's total profit loss actually will be the discounted sum of all future values of $A - B$, which is a significantly larger amount than the one-period loss equal to $A - B$. In contrast, the small menu cost that the firm will incur in changing its price is a once-and-for-all cost. Therefore, a firm that wishes to maximize the discounted value of current and future profits in the face of a long-lasting decline in demand will leave its price unchanged only if $A - B$ is *very* small or if the small menu costs are not *too* small.

Another difficulty that critics have with the theory is that it focuses only on the costs of price changes. Arguably, however, changing production levels of real output could also entail significant costs. If such output adjustment costs exist, then an imperfectly competitive firm would be less willing to keep its price the same, because doing so would require a greater change in its output.

New Keynesian Explanations for Unemployment

Firms that are not pure competitors in the markets for their output also behave differently in the market for labor. Recall from Chapter 3 that the value of labor's marginal product is equal to $P \times MP_N$, or the product price times the marginal product of labor. For a purely competitive firm, the value of labor's marginal product determines the firm's demand for labor. From the perspective of profit maximization, however, what a firm cares about most is the *marginal revenue product of labor,* which is equal to marginal revenue times labor's marginal product, or $MR \times MP_N$. As Figure 11–2 indicates, marginal revenue is less than the product price for an imperfectly competitive firm. Therefore, an imperfectly competitive firm's demand for labor is below the demand for labor by a purely competitive firm.

Efficiency Wage Theory   This is the starting point for a key new Keynesian theory of unemployment, which is known as **efficiency wage theory.** This hypothesis proposes that the productivity of workers depends on the real wage rate and that imperfectly competitive firms respond to this relationship by employing fewer workers.

EFFICIENCY WAGE THEORY An approach to explaining unemployment that is based on the hypothesis that the productivity of workers depends on the real wage rate.

The idea that workers' productivity may depend on the real wage rate developed from the observation that higher real wage payments in developing countries led to better nutrition and education for workers. As a result, workers' productivity improved. New Keynesian theorists have built on this idea by arguing that higher real wage payments by firms increase employees' morale and loyalty, thereby inducing them to work harder and more efficiently. Thus, in contrast to standard labor-market theory in which the marginal product of labor is unrelated to the real wage, higher real wages could raise the marginal product of labor.

When the Nobel Prize–winning economist Robert Solow of the Massachusetts Institute of Technology considered the implication of a positive relationship between the real wage and labor's marginal product, he found that it gives imperfectly competitive firms an incentive to hold the real wage fixed. The reason is that paying a real wage below the fixed value reduces a firm's wage costs but raises costs on net because of lost worker productivity caused by diminished morale and reduced loyalty to the firm. Paying a real wage above this value would yield efficiency gains that would be more than offset by the resulting rise in the firm's wage costs. Therefore, the imperfectly competitive firm maximizes its profits at a fixed *efficiency wage*.

If the real wage is fixed, then it cannot adjust to the point at which the quantity of labor demanded is equal to the quantity of labor supplied. Consequently, the amount of labor supplied at the efficiency wage paid by an imperfectly competitive firm could easily exceed the quantity of labor that the firm actually will employ at that real wage. The result would be an excess quantity of labor supplied, or unemployment.

Of course, one obvious problem with the efficiency wage theory is that it ignores the fact that firms compensate their employees in other ways besides direct wage payments. A firm can try to improve its workers' morale and increase their loyalty by rewarding them with special bonuses, quality pension plans, sales commissions, shares of the firm's profits, or perhaps even ownership shares. If these various additional forms of labor compensation are considered, the efficiency wage is no longer necessarily inflexible. This reduces the strength of the efficiency wage theory as a possible explanation for unemployment. (For a real-world example of a wage increase improving productivity, see on page 370 the Policy Notebook: *Do Efficiency Wages Make Economic Sense, or Could Henry Ford Have Been Right?*)

Insider-Outsider Models   The other new Keynesian theory that focuses on labor-market behavior is known as the **insider-outsider theory.** Proponents of this theory contend that a firm's current employees (insiders) may have an advantage in maintaining their jobs and wages, thereby imposing barriers on the firm's ability to hire others (outsiders) who otherwise would be willing to work at a lower real wage.

According to the insider-outsider theory, firms regard the training of their employees as a type of *capital investment*. Hiring new employees would force a firm to incur additional training expenses, so replacing existing employees would entail a cost that might not be offset by lower wage costs for new employees who are less fully trained. As a result, current employees are able to exercise some control over the terms under which the firm hires new employees.

Although this theory is most clearly applicable to settings with employee unions, some new Keynesian theorists contend that it applies to many nonunionized settings. Terminating a current employee often requires a firm to pay termination wages and perhaps offer retraining programs if it wishes to avoid a court fight with a disgruntled employee and his or her attorney. Hiring a new employee often entails incurring sizable advertising and search costs. Together, these costs, new Keynesians argue, could contribute to the development of insider-dominated labor markets that impose high barriers to entry by outsiders. Hence, these outsiders will be unemployed even though they are willing to work for lower real wages than firms pay current insiders.

INSIDER-OUTSIDER THEORY The notion that because a firm views its current, "insider" employees as an investment that would be costly to replace, the insiders are able to inhibit the hiring of unemployed "outsiders" at real wages below those earned by the insiders.

POLICY NOTEBOOK:

Do Efficiency Wages Make Economic Sense, or Could Henry Ford Have Been Right?

After earlier experiments with a horseless carriage, Henry Ford finished building his first car in 1896. After trying to get it into production without success for several years, in 1903 he started the Ford Motor Company. His most spectacular early success was with the Model T Ford that he introduced in 1908 and was producing on an assembly line by 1913. By 1914, standardized parts in the assembly-line procedure had greatly improved productivity, but monthly labor turnover was 40 to 60 percent in Ford's factory. Workers complained that assembly-line work was monotonous and that the production quotas assigned to them were constantly being increased.

Ford Increases Wages

In 1914, the standard daily wage in the automobile industry was about $2.50 (about $30 in today's dollars and with no benefits such as health insurance). Henry Ford ordered his managers to start paying workers $5 a day. Ford later argued that the increase in wages was a "cost-cutting" move. The evidence bears him out. Absenteeism dropped by over 70 percent. Moreover, labor turnover virtually disappeared. Consequently, Ford's managers had to spend less time training new workers. Ford Motor Company's profits increased by over 100 percent between 1914 and 1916 (on an annualized basis).

FOR CRITICAL ANALYSIS:

Besides efficiency wages, what alternatives do managers have to provide incentives to their workers to become more efficient?

An attractive feature of the insider-outsider theory is that it provides a potential explanation for both *involuntary* unemployment and *persistent* unemployment. The wage contracting models discussed in Chapter 10 predict that unemployment could arise if the price level during a contract interval turns out to be lower than workers and firms expected when they negotiated the contract wages. In a sense, however, this unemployment is voluntary, because it results from a voluntary contract agreement. In addition, unless price-level reductions unexpectedly persist, the contract-based modern Keynesian models can at best explain short-term unemployment. The insider-outsider theory also provides potential explanations for observed differences in wages and unemployment within and across industries and countries.

A key weakness of the theory, however, is that it often takes the existence of insiders for granted. It also fails to explain why entrepreneurial outsiders would remain unemployed when they could work together and establish a firm that competes with the firms that employ current insiders. Implicitly, the theory seems to rely on the existence of legal restrictions that inhibit such activities, rather than on behavioral relationships that make them a natural outcome. For this reason, some economists contend that the insider-outsider theory best applies to nations where rigid labor laws govern the interactions between workers and firms, such as France, Spain, and Germany (see the Global Notebook: *The Insider-Outsider Model Applied to Europe*).

GLOBAL NOTEBOOK

The Insider-Outsider Model Applied to Europe

The average family in France or Germany has a relatively high standard of living, compared to the period immediately after World War II or even to poorer European countries such as Portugal today. Nonetheless, not everyone in those countries or in the rest of Europe has a job. At the beginning of the 1970s, when the U.S. unemployment rate was a little less than 5 percent, the average rate for all of Europe was half that. Since then, unemployment rates in the United States have varied, falling to around 5 percent during the last half of the 1990s. Today, in the European Union (EU) the unemployment rate is over 11 percent—more than a fourfold increase since 1970. In France the unemployment rate exceeds 12.6 percent.

In any typical supply and demand model, competition for jobs should cause wages to fall and the quantity demanded of labor to rise, thereby eliminating at least part of the excess unemployment. That has not happened in Europe. This is a classic example of the insider-outsider model.

The Impossibility of Offering to Work for Less

In many European countries, the outsiders—those who are unemployed—are legally prevented from offering to work for less than the stated minimum wage. Furthermore, the minimum wage is not all that an employer has to pay. In many European countries, additional "social charges" cause the effective minimum wage to be twice what the worker actually receives. Additionally, European employers are often discouraged from hiring new workers because they are required to offer hefty severance pay if they decide to fire a

recently hired employee. Even during economic expansions, the number of new hires is relatively small in Europe. Additionally, workers cannot offer to take less than the legally legislated number of weeks of paid vacation. This ranges from a minimum of five weeks to as high as six and seven weeks in some EU countries, plus other paid legal holidays.

At present, the insiders have a great retirement plan, overseen and normally paid for by the government. In France, for example, train drivers can retire at age 50, automobile and other blue-collar workers at age 55, and most civil servants and white-collar workers at 60. White-collar workers receive pension payments for life of up to 80 percent of the final salary, and blue-collar workers receive up to 70 percent of the final salary.

The Incentive to Remain an Outsider (Unemployed)

Many European countries offer incentives to workers to remain unemployed—outside the labor market—if they are laid off or fired. The amount of unemployment payments and other benefits can sometimes equal a worker's former after-tax income. Not surprisingly, people tend to remain unemployed for a long time. More than half of Europe's unemployed have been out of work for a year or more, compared with less than 10 percent in the United States.

FOR CRITICAL ANALYSIS:
What might be some illegal ways European workers can offer to work at wages below the legal minimum?

FUNDAMENTAL ISSUE #2

What are the key features of new Keynesian theories? New Keynesian theories share two key features. One is the view that imperfect competition is widespread. The other is the view that market failures are commonplace and lead to macroeconomic externalities.

Small-menu-cost models combine these features to explain why prices might be sticky and real output might fluctuate. In addition, efficiency wage theory and insider-outsider models use these features as a basis for explaining involuntary unemployment.

COORDINATION FAILURE

The small-menu-cost, efficiency wage, and insider-outsider theories are the three dominant new Keynesian frameworks. Together, these models potentially explain sticky prices and variable output as well as rigid real wages and unemployment.

As noted above, the rigidity in real wages predicted by the efficiency wage theory potentially could help to explain persistent unemployment, as could institutional rigidities that implicitly lie behind the insider-outsider framework. Nevertheless, the key new Keynesian explanation for persistent responses of real output to temporary changes in economic conditions lies in the idea of **coordination failure.** This refers to the inability of workers and firms to plan and implement labor supply, production, and pricing decisions because of macroeconomic externalities that affect workers and firms in different ways. New Keynesians argue that the failure of workers and firms to share information and to make decisions jointly makes them particularly susceptible to such externalities and can lead to levels of real output that persistently differ from the economy's natural, long-run level.

COORDINATION FAILURES
Spillover effects between workers and firms that arise from movements in macroeconomic variables that hinder efforts by individual households and firms to plan and implement their consumption, production, and pricing decisions.

Coordination Problems with Heterogeneous Workers and Firms

The key to the potential for coordination failures is *heterogeneity.* Workers and firms will only be interested in coordinating their actions if they otherwise might respond differently to events such as variations in the quantity of money, fiscal policy actions, or changes in autonomous exports.

Sources of Heterogeneity   Several types of heterogeneity could exist:

1. **Differences in Relative Size.** The most obvious source of heterogeneity is *size.* Firms vary in size from small businesses to regional firms, national companies, and multinational corporations. Many workers bargain individually with their employers, others participate in professional associations that establish certification standards for their members, and still others belong to unions that engage in collective bargaining on behalf of their members.
2. **Cost differences.** One reason that firms vary in size is that there are cost differences across firms. Even businesses of similar size can have heterogeneous costs, however, because they adopt slightly different technologies. Consequently *cost differences* across firms are another potential source of heterogeneity.

3. **Product differentiation.** As noted earlier, a key justification for imperfect competition is that firms may produce differentiated products. Because new Keynesian theorists typically rely on imperfect competition as a motivation for their theories, *product differentiation* is a natural type of heterogeneity for them to consider in their models.

4. **Differing tastes and preferences.** Workers and consumers can also have *varying tastes and preferences*. Differences in workers could lead to heterogeneities in worker training and abilities and to different degrees of responsiveness of the labor supply when real wages change. Because consumers' tastes vary, their responses to changes in tax policy, for instance, are likely to differ.

5. **Differing information.** Finally, workers, consumers, and firms may be *differentially informed* about the economy. For example, they may have different views about how the economy functions. Even if they agree on this issue, some may have a better idea of the actual state of the economy than others. Consequently, they are likely to respond differently to actual changes in economic conditions.

Macroeconomic Externalities and Coordination Problems   Heterogeneity among workers, consumers, and firms is the key rationale for macroeconomic externalities that new Keynesians argue are central to understanding business cycles and real output persistence. If various groups of workers, consumers, or firms respond differently to changing economic conditions, then spillover effects across groups can take place.

For example, the onset of a recession reduces the real incomes of nearly all households, including those that had planned to save by purchasing stocks and bonds of growing firms planning to expand their operations. This decline in real income reduces the sales revenues of all firms, including the expansion-oriented firms that had planned to use a portion of their revenues to finance sizable capital investments in the near future. Hence, a recession forces growing firms to issue more stocks and bonds at exactly the time that households have less real income available to purchase additional financial assets. Cutbacks in planned investment by these firms then further reduce the sales revenues of established firms and small businesses, leading them to reduce their employment of members of households that allocate most of their income to consumption spending. Such spending cuts may hit small businesses particularly hard, contributing further to the general business downturn.

This example is similar to the traditional Keynesian multiplier analysis, but it adds to the story by including heterogeneous households and firms. It also emphasizes the potential for spillover effects across different groups of households and firms. In the aggregate, such spillover effects constitute macroeconomic externalities.

Coordination Failures and Persistence in Business Cycles

What can household and firm heterogeneity contribute aside from an elaboration of the standard multiplier analysis? New Keynesian proponents argue that it potentially can explain why seemingly temporary changes in economic conditions can cause the aggregate economy to get "stuck" in a recession. It might also explain why a temporary policy action might be able to get the economy back onto a longer-term expansion path.

Strategic Interactions and More Than One Macroeconomic Equilibrium   An important by-product of the presence of heterogeneous groups in an economy is the potential for **strategic interactions,** or the *inter*dependence of economic choices that people make either as individuals or together with others. Economists use *game theory,* or the theory of how people make decisions in light of strategic interactions, to analyze the equilibrium choices that emerge in such settings.

In general, game theory allows for groups to interact strategically in a number of ways. There are two primary forms of interaction, however. One is **noncooperative behavior.** As the term implies, this refers to an environment in which each household or firm looks out for its own interests irrespective of the interests of other households or firms. The other behavioral mode is **cooperative behavior.** This describes a setting in which households and firms work together to achieve their common good.

It turns out that noncooperative behavior often leads to more than one possible equilibrium. Biologists observe this in the behavior of insect populations. For example, consider fire ants, which began to spread through the southern tier of the United States some years ago. These ants construct mounds in clay or sandy soil and swarm against any invaders. Each colony of fire ants tends to look out for its own interests. This noncooperative behavior typically leads to two types of outcomes. One, sometimes called a *high-level equilibrium,* occurs when the fire ant colonies spread relatively uniformly over an area, and the individual colonies achieve success in the form of sufficient nourishment for each generation of ants. The result is relatively stable ant populations. Another outcome of the noncooperative behavior, however, can be "turf wars," in which the fire ant colonies fight over space and food following external events such as droughts. The result in this case is sharp variations in fire ant populations in locales affected by such events. This sometimes is called a *low-level equilibrium.*

Explaining Recessions and Expansions: High-Level versus Low-Level Equilibria
Although we like to think that human beings are considerably more advanced than fire ants and other insects, like fire ants we are social animals who seek to interact with others of our species. At the same time, we all also value our individual independence from others, which naturally can engender noncooperative behavior.

New Keynesian proponents contend that when combined with heterogeneities that naturally exist across households and firms, noncooperative behavior in human societies can lead to multiple outcomes for human *economies* that are not unlike those experienced by fire ant populations. When economic conditions are relatively stable and predictable, new Keynesians argue, noncooperative behavior can yield a high-level equilibrium of relatively stable employment, real output, and prices. When some

STRATEGIC INTERACTIONS The interdependence of economic decisions that people make individually or as part of groups.

NONCOOPERATIVE BEHAVIOR An economic setting in which people look out for their own well-being without regard for the well-being of others.

COOPERATIVE BEHAVIOR An economic setting in which people work together to maximize their joint well-being.

kind of outside "shock" occurs, however, such as a change in government or central bank policy or a fall in autonomous spending, noncooperative behavior can push the economy into a low-level equilibrium that can persist until another external shock pushes the economy back into the high-level state.

Noncooperative behavior among heterogeneous households and firms could therefore help to explain persistent recessions or steady economic expansions. In the new Keynesian theory, such variations in economic activity, which we call business cycles, stem from the human propensity to behave noncooperatively. Failure to coordinate thereby can cause busts and booms for human economies just as it can lead to busts and booms in fire ant populations.

Coordination Failure as a Justification for Activist Policies   Imagine what would happen if fire ants could coordinate their activities. If queen fire ants centralized their egg production and various colonies of fire ants worked together, fire ant populations would remain as stable as the environment would permit, and fire ants could spread even more rapidly. Indeed, biologists have found some evidence that natural selection may have begun to favor fire ants that behave this way: Giant, cooperative fire ant colonies have been found in some locations in the South (not good news for those allergic to fire ant stings!).

Although new Keynesian arguments are not typically based on biological analogies, they point to the same basic implication for human economies. Given the potential for noncooperative behavior and the resulting failures to coordinate to produce alternating high- and low-level outcomes, perhaps government can perform the role of "economic coordinator." Taken to an extreme, this could be perceived as an argument for central planning of the type that the old Soviet Union abandoned and that even China has relaxed in recent years.

More generally, however, new Keynesians view the potential for economies to get stuck in low-level noncooperative states as a key rationale for active monetary and fiscal policy responses to sudden changes in economic conditions. In this sense, the new Keynesian theory can be regarded as a more "high-tech" version of the traditional Keynesian argument favoring an activist role for governmental policies.

FUNDAMENTAL ISSUE #3

What are coordination failures, and why do new Keynesians believe that they may be important? Coordination failures are situations in which individual households and firms are unable to follow through on intended spending and production plans because of macroeconomic externalities. New Keynesians argue that noncooperative decision making by heterogeneous households and firms leads to more than one possible equilibrium state for the economy. If the economy sinks into a low-level equilibrium a persistent recession could result, then requiring activist macroeconomic policy responses to push the economy into a higher-level equilibrium.

THE REAL-BUSINESS-CYCLE CHALLENGE

Even as new Keynesian theorists have emphasized the potential importance of household and firm heterogeneities and provided rationales for activist monetary and fiscal policies, another group of macroeconomists has followed a sharply different course. These macroeconomists have developed models that generally are based on the assumption of *homogeneous,* or identical, households and firms. Such models typically indicate that little, if any, stabilizing role exists for policymakers in modern economies.

REAL-BUSINESS-CYCLE THEORY An approach to macroeconomic theory in which variations in technology and productivity are the key factors accounting for cyclical fluctuations in real output.

This alternative approach is called **real-business-cycle theory.** As its name implies, this approach to macroeconomics hinges on the idea that *real* factors, such as technological or productivity changes, induce cyclical fluctuations in economic activity. Real-business-cycle theorists believe that the key to identifying the determinants of employment, real output, and inflation is to develop a more complete understanding of the processes that govern labor supply and firms' output production and capital investment. According to these theorists, these are the factors that ultimately matter in determining employment and real output.

The Essential Features of Real-Business-Cycle Models

Real-business-cycle models share two key elements. First, as in the new classical model from which they have been developed, they are *equilibrium* models. Wages always adjust to equate the quantity of labor demanded with the quantity of labor supplied, and prices always move to equilibrate the desired purchases of goods and services with the amount of goods and services supplied.

DYNAMIC MODELS Economic models intended to explain how variables such as real output, employment, and the price level vary over time.

Second, real-business-cycle models are **dynamic models,** meaning that they are intended to describe how macroeconomic variables such as real output, employment, and the price level move over time. Although adherents of other macroeconomic schools of thought have also developed dynamic versions of their basic theoretical frameworks, the basic elements of the frameworks could always be captured on two-dimensional diagrams relating one macroeconomic variable to another. Real-business-cycle theorists cannot do this, because one axis on a diagram must always measure time.

Technology Shocks and Real GDP   Following the classical theory that we discussed in Chapter 3, real-business-cycle theorists argue that real output ultimately is determined by supply-side factors such as the productive capabilities of firms, population and labor force participation, and the willingness of workers in the labor force to supply their skills. For this reason, real-business-cycle models focus on such real factors as the key sources of macroeconomic fluctuations.

Figure 11–3 illustrates one key source of macroeconomic fluctuations in the real-business-cycle model: technology shocks, or sudden variations in the technological capabilities of firms. Such sudden changes in technology cause a change in the shape and position of the aggregate production function, $F(N, K)$. For instance, a spurt of new techniques for producing high-speed computer processing chips, as occurred in the 1990s, will cause a jump in the productive capacity of firms that make computers and will improve the efficiency of the computers that they build. This will raise the productivity both of computer manufacturers and of all companies that use computers. For the economy as a whole, this improved productivity will yield an increase in the marginal product of labor, which translates into an increase in the slope of the aggregate production function, as shown in Figure 11–3. The production function will rotate upward, so for any given capital stock, such as K_1, real output will rise, from y_1 to a higher level y_2. Real output will increase, and an economic expansion will ensue.

Some technological innovations turn out to be disappointments, however. Implementation of a more inefficient technology will, for a time, make existing capital less productive than it was in the past. For example, some computer makers switch to a new just-in-time inventory system that ultimately fails to speed deliveries and, for a time, actually slows them down. This will reduce aggregate productivity, causing the production function to rotate downward. Real output then will fall from y_2 to a lower level y_3, as shown in Figure 11–3

FIGURE 11–3   TECHNOLOGY SHOCKS AND REAL OUTPUT VARIATIONS

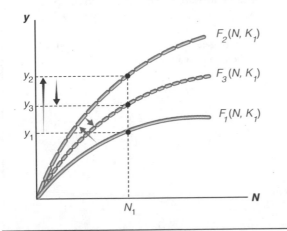

In real-business-cycle models, variations in real output stem primarily from technology shocks, or factors that cause the aggregate production function to rotate. At any given quantity of labor, such as N_1, such rotations in the production function will lead to variations in real output over time.

Real Business Cycles   The technological shocks illustrated in Figure 11–3 will end up producing cyclical behavior in real GDP. If we interpret the subscripts 1, 2, and 3 in Figure 11–3 as referring to points in time, then we can plot the behavior of real GDP over time in Figure 11–4. To do this, we assume that the intervals between the two shocks that we have envisioned are of equal length.

Figure 11–4 displays a sample real business cycle that corresponds to our example. It has a short-run expansion followed by a short-run downturn. As we discussed in Chapter 4, such upward and downward movements in real GDP typically characterize real-world business cycles.

Policy Implications of Real-Business-Cycle Models   In many respects, the real-business-cycle models have the same basic policy implications as the classical model of Chapter 3. Tax rate changes can influence the amount of real output produced, although Ricardian equivalence (see Chapter 7) tempers that conclusion. Lump-sum tax changes and variations in government spending typically act only to redistribute real output between the private sector and the government, because real output is supply-side determined.

Real business-cycle theory differs from the classical model in its treatment of money and the effects of monetary policy. Recall from Chapter 3 that the classical model assumes that the nominal money stock is fully controlled by a central bank. In contrast, in the real-business-cycle theory the nominal quantity of money supply is determined largely by interactions between the depository financial institutions and the public. Real-business-cycle proponents contend that when people's real income

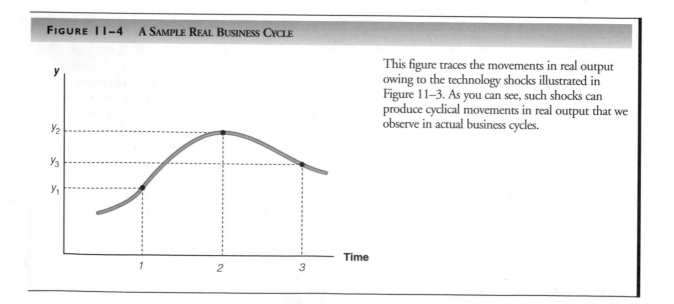

FIGURE 11–4   A SAMPLE REAL BUSINESS CYCLE

This figure traces the movements in real output owing to the technology shocks illustrated in Figure 11–3. As you can see, such shocks can produce cyclical movements in real output that we observe in actual business cycles.

rises, so does their demand for transactions services from banks (as in the Keynesian transactions motive for holding money). Banks respond by increasing their production of transactions services and, hence, deposits that are included in the nominal money stock. The total amount of bank deposit money, called **inside money** because its quantity depends on conditions within the banking system, depends on real income and is outside the control of a central bank. Indeed, the quantity of inside money adjusts automatically to changing economic conditions and performs no separate causal role with respect to any macroeconomic variables.

INSIDE MONEY Bank deposit money.

Consequently, in the real-business-cycle model inside money does not affect the price level. Only **outside money** can do that. Outside money is composed of currency and bank reserves, which a central bank *can* control because they are determined by the central bank's policies. The amount of outside money determines the level of aggregate demand. Because the real-business-cycle theory's aggregate supply schedule is vertical, the amount of outside money effectively *determines* the price level.

OUTSIDE MONEY Money in the form of currency and bank reserves.

A number of economists have found the real-business-cycle theory attractive, largely because it is so clearly based on microeconomic principles. Following the classical model, all households and firms pursue their self-interest, and pure competition prevails with complete price and wage flexibility. In addition, households and firms put any new information to its best possible use. Many economists find these assumptions much more palatable than assumptions of fixed prices, contracted nominal wages, or rigid real wages.

FUNDAMENTAL ISSUE #4

How do real-business-cycle theorists explain short-term fluctuations in real output? According to real-business-cycle theory, short-term output variations stem almost solely from temporary changes in technology and productivity. Furthermore, such output variations take place in equilibrium without need for price or wage rigidities.

Induction versus Deduction: Calibration or Hypothesis Testing?

One of the most controversial aspects of real-business-cycle theory has been the approach that many of its advocates have used in evaluating the theory's relevance. This approach has led to considerable philosophical debate among economists concerning the merits of inductive versus deductive approaches to macroeconomics.

Induction versus Deduction   Economists have prided themselves on their use of the *scientific method.* This refers to a manner in which scientists try to formulate and evaluate their theories. To develop a theory, scientists look at the world around them and attempt to classify their observations based on regularities in the data that they collect. Then they look for relationships in the data and develop theories of causation that could potentially account for these relationships. Traditionally, scientists have then used statistical methods to determine whether the observed data support their theories.

INDUCTION The process of drawing conclusions about real-world behavior from observation of real-world data.

DEDUCTION The process of making testable predictions about real-world behavior based on a theoretical framework.

The scientific method entails both *induction* and *deduction*. **Induction** refers to the process of drawing a general conclusion from reference to observed data, whereas **deduction** refers to the act of making a prediction about real-world outcomes based on a theoretical model. Major advances in the science of astronomy, for instance, have resulted from both induction and deduction. For example, the sixteenth-century Danish observational astronomer Tycho Brahe accumulated large volumes of data of planetary observations. Based upon these observations, the German astronomer and mathematician Johannes Kepler was able to infer certain regularities in planetary motion that he realized could be explained if planets followed elliptical orbits. This inductive process led Kepler to develop an initial theory of planetary motion. Later in the seventeenth century, the English physicist Isaac Newton used Kepler's theory to develop a deductive theory for accurately predicting the positions of planets, moons, stars, and other astronomical objects.

The inductive and deductive approaches have produced notable failures in astronomy as well. The 2nd-century astronomer Claudius Ptolemy, for instance, used inductive principles to develop a purely geometrical representation of planetary motions. He envisioned the planets moving along a great system of circles with the earth at the center. Ptolemy's system worked, but it did not describe the universe that we inhabit. More recently, observations of changing brightness in a revolving neutron star led astronomers to propose a complicated deductive theory for what could cause an otherwise inexplicable phenomenon. It later turned out that the observatory where data had been collected had been built on sandy soil and that the observed wobble in the neutron star stemmed from a wobble in the telescope itself.

These examples from astronomy illustrate the potential gains and pitfalls from the use of induction and deduction in macroeconomics. Just as the economy experiences cycles, so does the study of the economy. At times macroeconomists favor deductive techniques, and at other times they seem to become enamored of more purely inductive approaches. In macroeconomics today, part of the struggle between competing groups stems from philosophical differences about the merits of induction versus deduction.

Deduction and Hypothesis Testing in Macroeconomics   Until the advent of real-business-cycle theory, the deductive approach dominated the study of macroeconomics. Economists would develop theories and then assess their relevance by applying statistical techniques to real-world data. If the data appeared to "fit" the theory, then the theory would be judged to have received sufficient support to be retained and improved.

To implement this approach, economists traditionally develop *testable hypotheses,* or predictions that stem from their theories. Then they try to evaluate how well their theories fit real-world observations. Before the advent of real-business-cycle theory, macroeconomists of various schools of thought commonly used actual time-series observations of macroeconomic variables in statistical models to test hypotheses implied by their deductively formulated theories.

Induction, Calibration, and Quantitative Theory   Real-business-cycle theorists, however, have developed an alternative technique for evaluating their models. This approach, which is called **calibration,** involves several steps. First, real-business-cycle theorists use estimates of elasticities developed in statistical studies *in their own theoretical models.* They also utilize real-world data for variables such as employment or real output from some point in time. Second, they use computers to calculate how these variables would change over time in the models that they construct. As discussed above, real-business-cycle models typically yield equilibrium outcomes that are cyclical. Finally, the researchers compare the cyclical properties of their *artificially created data*—measures of business cycle duration and variation—with the properties of real-world data. If their artificially generated data exhibit cycles that nearly match those in actual economies, then real-business-cycle theorists judge their models to be successful. If not, they modify the models in an effort to achieve a better fit with real-world data.

CALIBRATION The use of estimated elasticities and real-world data to create artificial data with theoretical models for the purpose of evaluating the extent to which one's theory appears to match real-world observations.

Real-business-cycle theorists call their approach **quantitative theory,** or the use of numerical calculations to develop theoretical models that fit observed business cycle facts. Some critics of real-business-cycle theory argue that quantitative theory really amounts to inductive "curve-fitting," a process that mathematicians developed long ago to approximate the actual shape of complicated curves by splicing together equations of many different curved functions. Indeed, some critics liken the quantitative theory approach to Ptolemy's earth-centered system of planetary motion. Just as Ptolemy's system could predict, yet turned out to be dead wrong, such critics argue, quantitative theory could lead to the development of elaborate mathematical models of the economy that predict well for a short while but ultimately will prove to be far off the mark.

QUANTITATIVE THEORY An approach to macroeconomic theorizing in which a model is evaluated by comparing the movements in artificial data generated by the model itself with the behavior of real-world macroeconomic data.

Proponents of quantitative theory counter that as a social science, economics does not have the luxury of looking for physical laws such as those that planets must follow. According to Martin Eichenbaum of Northwestern University, for instance, every macroeconomic model is likely to make incorrect predictions along at least one dimension, so there is no *true* model of the aggregate economy. The goal of quantitative theory, he contends, is to identify the dimensions along which various theories fail to fit the facts, thereby helping researchers to improve their models so that they ultimately can come very *close* to describing the true behavior of workers and firms in the economy.

FUNDAMENTAL ISSUE #5

What is quantitative theory, and why is it so controversial?
Quantitative theory is the use of calibration techniques to evaluate theoretical models. Calibration entails incorporating estimates of elasticities and initial values from real-world data in theoretical models and then using the models to calculate artificial data. Comparisons of the artificially produced data with real-world data then permit the researcher to evaluate how well the theory fits the facts. This approach to evaluating macroeconomic theories is controversial because it relies heavily on inductive reasoning instead of the deductive reasoning that has guided macroeconomics in the past.

WHAT HAVE THE NEW THEORIES TAUGHT US?

As we indicated at the beginning of this chapter, only time will tell if either new Keynesian theories or real-business-cycle models will help us better predict the macroeconomy. A generation from now, one or both attempts to better understand the economy may be a fading memory. Nevertheless, both approaches have important messages that macroeconomists have been exploring in ongoing research.

Key Messages of the New Keynesian Theory

Real-business-cycle theorists and many other macroeconomists who think of themselves as monetarists or as traditional or modern Keynesians have not been entirely willing to accept all aspects of new Keynesian models. Some disagree with the view that imperfect competition could be so widespread, especially in a U.S. economy that has witnessed two decades of significant deregulation of a number of industries. Others have trouble accepting the idea that price or wage rigidities are so widespread that they could fully explain business cycles and their persistence.

Heterogeneity May Be Important   Nonetheless, the new Keynesians have shown that household and firm heterogeneities could prove helpful in understanding features of business cycles. To the extent that such heterogeneities induce spillover effects that create macroeconomic externalities, they could cause real output to deviate from the natural level it would attain in the absence of such effects.

Game Theory May Provide Some Answers   Another key message of new Keynesian theory is that macroeconomists may be able to gain insights from applying game theory in their models. As we discussed earlier in this chapter, new Keynesian theory proposes that noncooperative behavior can lead to more than one equilibrium for the economy, which then potentially could alternate between equilibrium states from time to time. To the new Keynesians, this provides a justification for using governmental or central bank policy actions to "bump" the economy into a better equilibrium whenever it slips into a less desirable equilibrium.

Although real-business-cycle theorists and others generally are not persuaded by this argument, macroeconomists of all stripes have recognized that theories of strategic interactions among individuals and firms—the subjects of game theory—could prove useful in understanding important issues. As you will learn in Chapter 13, this has been particularly true in the area of macroeconomic policy. Considerable research has been devoted to the analysis of games between policymakers and the public, and the findings have caused both economists and government officials to rethink the structures of policymaking institutions.

Key Messages of the Real-Business-Cycle Theory

Despite the considerable research that real-business-cycle theorists have conducted during the past two decades, many macroeconomists have doubts about the ultimate usefulness of most of these models for macroeconomic forecasting and policymaking. Even so, most macroeconomists have been persuaded that real-business-cycle theorists have made some very important points.

Supply-Side Factors Are Important   In the 1960s, traditional Keynesians and monetarists argued about whether monetary or fiscal policy had the greater effect on aggregate demand and real output. Then, in the 1970s, new classical and modern Keynesian proponents debated whether monetary or fiscal policy could have *any* systematic impacts on real output via their effects on aggregate demand. In the midst of their arguments about the aggregate demand channel for monetary and fiscal policies, many macroeconomists lost sight of the importance of productivity and technology as determinants of real output.

The real-business-cycle theory's renewed emphasis on these factors has altered the landscape in macroeconomics. Real-business-cycle proponents have proved that technology and productivity can influence the course of business cycles, even if they have not convinced all macroeconomists that these are the *only* factors that cause real output to deviate from its long-run growth path.

Business Cycles May Be Fundamentally Related to Economic Growth   Another message of the real-business-cycle theory is that it may be misleading to study business cycles and economic growth as separate topics. As we noted in Chapter 4, the ultimate determinants of economic growth are real factors such as technological progress and growth in population and labor-force participation rates. Short-term variations in these factors can cause cyclical fluctuations in real output that in turn may feed back to affect the economy's longer-term growth rate.

In this respect, real-business-cycle models and the new growth theory that we discussed in Chapter 4 share considerable common ground. Indeed, one reason that both approaches have attracted so many adherents is that developments in the real-business-cycle models have related so closely to new approaches to the theory of economic growth. Some observers of the real-business-cycle theory have concluded that its ultimate achievement could be a merging of the theory of short-run business cycles with a broader theory of an economy's long-term growth.

Future Prospects

The deep philosophical divisions over the quantitative theory approach of real-business-cycle proponents are likely to continue until either the new Keynesian theory or the real-business-cycle approach does a much better job of making predictions that businesspersons and policymakers can rely on to guide their decisions. At present, both approaches show some promise of bearing fruit. On the one hand, new Keynesian macroeconomics potentially can explain price stickiness, unemployment, and persistent states of recession or expansion. On the other hand, real-business-cycle theorists can provide quantitative theories that mimic real-world business cycles and offer hope of combining business cycle theory with the theory of economic growth.

In their current forms, however, both approaches cannot simultaneously be correct, because they are based on fundamentally different views of the economy. Whereas the new Keynesian theory relies on imperfect competition, heterogeneities, macroeconomic externalities, and coordination failures, the real-business-cycle approach depends on pure competition, homogeneity, perfect markets, and rational, self-interested individuals and firms. Ultimately, some combination of the two approaches may be the wave of the future in macroeconomics. Already some new Keynesian theorists have begun to use techniques borrowed from real-business-cycle enthusiasts. At the same time, some proponents of real-business-cycle theory have begun to experiment with models that include sticky wages and prices. It remains to be seen if the two approaches will ever find a common ground.

CHAPTER SUMMARY

1. **The Motivation for New Macroeconomic Theories:** Most existing theories have difficulty explaining why real GDP shows persistent reactions to relatively short-term changes in economic conditions. The development of new macroeconomic theories represents an effort to deal with this failure of the existing theories.

2. **The Key Features of New Keynesian Theories:** The two main features of new Keynesian theories are the assumption of imperfect competition and the perception that widespread market failures cause macroeconomic externalities. These features are used in small-menu-cost models to propose explanations for why prices might be relatively inflexible and for why real output can vary considerably in the short run. Efficiency wage theory and insider-outsider models use the two features as a foundation for proposing models to explain involuntary unemployment.

3. **Coordination Failures and New Keynesians' Contentions That They May Be Important:** Coordination failures occur when households and firms cannot implement planned expenditures and production as a result of macroeconomic externalities. New Keynesians contend that noncooperative interactions among heterogeneous households and firms can cause more than one equilibrium state to exist for the economy. In a low-level equilibrium, a persistent recession could result. In that case, macroeconomic policy actions might be required to move the economy to a higher-level equilibrium.

4. **How Real-Business-Cycle Theorists Explain Short-Term Fluctuations in Real Output:** Real-business-cycle models indicate that short-run output variability arises because of temporary variations in technology and productivity. These macroeconomic models predict that short-term business cycles take place in the absence of any stickiness in wages or prices.

5. **Quantitative Theory and Why It Is Controversial:** Quantitative theory involves the use of calibration, which is a technique for using estimated elasticities and some real-world data to calculate artificial data using theoretical models. Real-business-cycle theorists compare such artificially produced data with real-world observations to evaluate the extent to which their models fit real-world facts. This approach is controversial because it relies on inductive reasoning, rather than on deductive reasoning, which macroeconomists have generally used in the past.

QUESTIONS AND PROBLEMS

1. Use an aggregate demand–aggregate supply diagram to explain why the existence of widespread price stickiness would be extremely important in judging the potential effectiveness of monetary and fiscal policies.

2. In question 1, you used an aggregate demand–aggregate supply diagram to evaluate the essential policy implications of price stickiness. According to the new Keynesian small-menu-cost theory, is there really an aggregate supply schedule for the economy as a whole? Why or why not? (Hint: Note that in microeconomics, there is no industry supply schedule in the theories of monopoly, oligopoly, or monopolistic competition.)

3. Suppose that the marginal product of labor depends positively upon the real wage that workers earn. What happens to the production function if the real wage rises? Explain.

4. Government regulation of labor-market function is more prevalent in a number of European nations than in the United States. Discuss how this difference might be related to many economists' belief that the insider-outsider model explains European unemployment better than it explains U.S. unemployment.

5. In your own words, explain why some new Keynesian theorists believe that coordination failures may be important for understanding business cycles.

6. Suppose that a new firm devises a strategy for significant long-term growth, but a major economy-wide recession makes it impossible for the firm to implement the plan. In response, the firm cuts back on its expansion plan and lays off some of its employees,

who are unable to find other jobs. As a result, these unemployed workers must cut back on their spending. Is this a coordination failure? Support your answer.

7. Explain how real-business-cycle theory is more closely related to the new classical theory of Chapter 9 than it is to the modern Keynesian theory of Chapter 10.

8. Some economists have extended the analogy of real-business-cycle calibration modeling to Ptolemaic astronomy (see the discussion on pages 380–381). They argue that like Ptolemaic astronomy, which allowed early astronomers to predict the locations of planets in the heavens but could not have assisted modern scientists, who rely on Newton's laws, to send rocket-propelled probes to the planets, real-business-cycle calibration models will never assist in real-world policymaking. Do you agree with this analogy? Take a stand, and justify your answer.

9. Do you find inductive theorizing more or less convincing than deductive theorizing? Or do you believe that both should play a role in macroeconomic theory? Justify your answer.

10. As far as you can tell from your reading of this chapter, do the new Keynesian and real-business-cycle theories share any common ground? Or are the two approaches so distinct that they could never converge? Explain your position on this issue.

CYBERTUTOR EXERCISES

1. Suppose that demand for the monopoly firm's product declines. What effect will this have on the amount of output produced by the profit-maximizing monopoly firm and on the price that it charges for its product? Furthermore, suppose, in the face of this decline in demand, the monopoly does not change its price level. What effect would this have on equilibrium quantity and profits?

2. In CyberTutor, there is a graph of real GDP growth rate. Identify at least four recessions from this graph. How do new Keynesian and real business cycle theorists explain these cycles? In your opinion, which view is more reasonable? Why?

ON-LINE APPLICATION

In general, labor unions exist to bargain for wages and benefits on behalf of their member workers, to protect their members from unsafe working conditions, and to lobby for laws that the unions feel are consistent with their members' interests. Many economists also regard unions as a potentially good application of the insider-outsider theory of unemployment.

Internet URL: http://www.aflcio.org/welcome.html

Title: American Federation of Labor–Congress of Industrial Organizations

Navigation: Start at the AFL-CIO's homepage (**http://www.aflcio.org**).

Application: Perform the indicated operations, and answer the following questions:

1. Click on *Welcome to LaborWeb.* Then click on *78 Labor Unions* to obtain a list of unions that compose the AFL-CIO. Do these unions appear to represent the interests of all workers or just workers in specific firms or industries?

2. Is your answer to question 1 consistent with the insider-outsider theory? Why or why not?

SELECTED REFERENCES AND FURTHER READING

Ball, Laurence, and David Romer. "Sticky Prices as Coordination Failures," *American Economic Review* 81 (1991): 539–552.

Duca, John, and David VanHoose, "Has Greater Competition Restrained Inflation?" Working Paper, Federal Reserve Bank of Dallas and University of Alabama, 1997.

Eichenbaum, Martin. "Some Comments on the Role of Econometrics in Economic Theory." Federal Reserve Bank of Chicago *Economic Perspectives,* January/February 1996, 22–31.

Gordon, Robert. "What Is New-Keynesian Economics?" *Journal of Economic Literature* 28 (1990): 1151–1171.

Hoover, Keven. "Facts and Artifacts: Calibration and the Empirical Assessment of Real-Business-Cycle Models." *Oxford Economic Papers* 47 (1992): 24–44.

King, Robert. "Quantitative Theory and Econometrics." Federal Reserve Bank of Richmond *Economic Review,* Summer 1995, 53–105.

Mankiw, N. Gregory, and David Romer, eds. *New Keynesian Economics.* Cambridge, Mass.: MIT Press, 1991, vols. 1 and 2.

Stadler, George. "Real Business Cycles." *Journal of Economic Literature* 32 (1994): 1750–1783.

Unit IV
MACROECONOMIC POLICY

12

What Should Policymakers Do?— OBJECTIVES AND TARGETS OF MACROECONOMIC POLICY

FUNDAMENTAL ISSUES

1. What are the ultimate goals of macroeconomic policy?

2. Why might a central bank use an intermediate monetary policy target?

3. What are the pros and cons of alternative intermediate monetary policy targets?

4. Why might a government desire to reduce its budget deficit, and how might it accomplish this goal?

5. What is the assignment problem faced by monetary and fiscal policymakers of a nation that seeks to attain both domestic and international policy goals?

It is late at night, but the finance committee at Intel Corporation, the world's largest and most successful semiconductor maker (revenues approaching $20 billion a year), is hard at work. The company's chief executive, Andrew Grove, is thinking of starting a new company that will produce three-dimensional software systems for the Internet. The project will cost only $100 million—not very *much for a company as large as Intel, but not pocket change either. The finance committee has decided to issue corporate bonds worth $75 million and to pay for the rest out of cash reserves. Now the members are finishing the legal work before the bond sale, which is scheduled for next week. The phone rings. Intel's investment bankers in New York are calling. Word on the street is that the Fed is going to raise interest rates tomorrow in an attempt to cool off what is perceived as an overheated economy. The head of the finance committee calls Andy Grove at home. When Grove hears the news, he decides that the project is not worth the higher interest rate Intel will have to pay to borrow funds from the public. He cancels the project.*

Although this scenario is completely hypothetical, it does illustrate how changes in interest rates might affect a business's desire to invest. Thus, monetary policy and its implications can be important for an individual company's decision making. In this chapter, you will learn how the Fed might try to target interest rates. You will also learn about other possible targets of macroeconomic policy as well as the problems policymakers face when they try to attain both domestic and international policy goals simultaneously.

THE GOALS OF MACROECONOMIC POLICY

Up to now, we have examined several broad theories of how macroeconomic policy actions may influence real output, employment, and prices. We have shown that each of these theoretical approaches—classical, traditional Keynesian, monetarist, new classical, modern Keynesian, new Keynesian, real-business-cycle—has its own special implications for fiscal and monetary policies.

We have not yet asked some very tough questions, however. What should fiscal and monetary policymakers do? What goals should they try to achieve? How should they go about pursuing those goals? In this chapter, you will learn that even when there is widespread agreement on the appropriate *objectives* of macroeconomic policy, the best way to *implement* that policy still may not be apparent.

In this chapter, we shall begin by examining the factors that determine the **ultimate goals,** or final macroeconomic objectives, of fiscal and monetary policymakers. Then we shall devote the bulk of the remainder of the chapter to contemplating how policymakers might go about trying to pursue these goals.

ULTIMATE GOALS The final objectives of macroeconomic policies.

Potential Ultimate Macroeconomic Goals

Most macroeconomists focus on three sets of goals that monetary and fiscal policymakers might pursue.

Inflation Goals   As we noted in Chapter 8, a number of costs stem from high and variable inflation (see Table 8–1 on page 277). In light of these inflation costs, policymakers have justification for trying to maintain low inflation. In addition, they have a strong rationale for limiting year-to-year variability in inflation rates.

Output Goals   According to the classical, new classical, and real-business-cycle theories, monetary and fiscal policymakers can do little to affect real output over any time horizon, and the monetarist and modern Keynesian theories generally indicate that there is little scope for long-run output effects of monetary and fiscal policies. Nonetheless, several theories indicate that unexpected changes in the growth rate of the money stock can affect real output over short-run intervals. Therefore, another potential ultimate goal of macroeconomic policy might be to prevent sharp swings in real GDP relative to its natural, full-information level. According to some of the macroeconomic theories we have discussed, pursuing this policy goal could mitigate business cycles.

Employment Goals   Labor is a key factor of production, and in a democratic society workers also account for the bulk of voters. Consequently, both fiscal and monetary policymakers are likely to feel pressures to pursue policies that aim to prevent significant variability in worker unemployment rates and that might spur greater growth in real output and employment.

Legislated Ultimate Goals

Can macroeconomic policymakers pursue inflation, output, and employment goals simultaneously? Certainly, stabilizing output around its long-run natural level often will be consistent with stable employment and a low unemployment rate. Nevertheless, as you learned in Chapter 8, the possible existence of a short-run Phillips curve trade-off indicates that there may be conflicts among macroeconomic objectives.

For this reason, societies sometimes choose to make macroeconomic goals explicit. In the United States, two laws lay out a course for macroeconomic policymakers. The *Employment Act of 1946* legally commits all agencies of the federal government to the objectives of "maximum employment, production, and purchasing power." Thus, this act officially seeks the highest possible employment and real output levels as well as low inflation. The law is silent, however, as to exactly how the U.S. government should address potential trade-offs among the goals.

In 1978, Congress established more concrete objectives when it passed the *Full Employment and Balanced Growth Act,* more commonly known as the *Humphrey-Hawkins Act.* This law set two goals: an unemployment rate of 3 percent and an inflation rate of 0 percent. As it turned out, the actual unemployment rate in 1983 exceeded 9 percent, and actual inflation was about 5 percent, illustrating the problems with trying to legislate explicit objectives. By the late 1990s, however, the unemployment rate had fallen to below 5 percent, and the inflation rate hovered between 3 and 4 percent, which were closer to the 1978 targets. Nevertheless, most macroeconomists are doubtful that the natural rate of unemployment in the United States is as low as 3 percent.

In the face of potentially conflicting ultimate goals and generally vague guidance from legislators, how should central bank and government officials conduct monetary and fiscal policies? What near-term goals should they pursue in an effort to achieve broader, ultimate macroeconomic policy objectives? These are the issues that we shall address in the remainder of this chapter and in the chapters that follow.

FUNDAMENTAL ISSUE #1

What are the ultimate goals of macroeconomic policy? The ultimate goals of a government fiscal authority or central bank are the final objectives of its policy strategies and actions. Under the terms of 1946 and 1978 legislation, the formal goals of the U.S. government and the Federal Reserve System include low and stable inflation rates, high and stable output growth, and a high and stable employment level.

 # FINDING AN INTERMEDIATE TARGET FOR MONETARY POLICY

As you have learned in previous chapters, nearly every approach to macroeconomics—with the exception of the real-business-cycle model—indicates that monetary policy actions can potentially have short-term or even longer-term effects on real output and employment. All macroeconomic theories imply that monetary policy actions influence the price level.

Hence, central banks clearly perform important tasks. Indeed, some observers have called the chair of the board that directs the operations of the Federal Reserve System, the U.S. version of a central bank, the second-most-important person in the United States, after the president. Before considering the theory of Federal Reserve policymaking in light of its output, employment, and inflation objectives, let's begin with an overview of exactly how the Federal Reserve System works and how the Fed implements monetary policy.

Monetary Policymaking in the United States: The Federal Reserve System

The U.S. Congress established the Federal Reserve System in 1913. Congress created a partly private, partly public institution that it intentionally did not call a "central bank." Private U.S. banks could become members of the Federal Reserve System by purchasing shares in the system. By doing so, they placed themselves under Fed regulation while gaining potential access to Fed loans. These banks had only a minority vote in choosing Fed officials, however. Congress also established a Federal Reserve Board to oversee and coordinate the activities of twelve Federal Reserve district banks around the nation, and it empowered the president to appoint members to this board, subject to Senate approval. One automatic member was the secretary of the Treasury.

One of Congress's key objectives in establishing the Fed was to prevent banking panics, such as those the nation had experienced in 1893 and 1907. After the Fed failed to halt widespread banking panics following the stock market crash of 1929, Congress decided in 1935 to restructure the institution. Congress renamed the top board the "Board of Governors of the Federal Reserve System," and it removed the Treasury secretary from this board. Congress centralized power over the Federal Reserve System, which previously had been shared with the Federal Reserve banks, within this board. These changes ultimately transformed the Fed into a true central banking institution.

DISCOUNT RATE The rate of interest that the Federal Reserve charges to lend to a banking institution.

RESERVE REQUIREMENTS Federal Reserve rules mandating that banks maintain reserve holdings that are proportional to the dollar amounts of transactions accounts.

The seven members of the Fed's Board of Governors have a number of duties. They authorize any change in the Fed's **discount rate,** which is the interest rate that the twelve Federal Reserve banks charge on loans that they extend to U.S. banking institutions. Under terms of the Depository Institutions Deregulation and Monetary Control Act of 1980, they also have the authority to determine **reserve requirements,** or rules that require banks to set aside a fraction of each dollar of checking deposits in a cash reserve, either in the banks' vaults or in the form of deposits at Federal Reserve banks. In addition, the Board of Governors has oversight authority over the Fed's district banks.

FEDERAL OPEN MARKET COMMITTEE (FOMC) A group composed of the seven governors and five of the twelve presidents of the Federal Reserve banks that determines how to conduct the Fed's open-market operations.

OPEN-MARKET OPERATIONS The Federal Reserve's purchases or sales of U.S. government securities.

The Federal Open Market Committee   All seven Board governors serve on the Federal Reserve's twelve-member **Federal Open Market Committee (FOMC).** The remaining five voting members of the FOMC are presidents of the Federal Reserve banks. The president of the Federal Reserve Bank of New York is always a voting member of the FOMC, and the remaining eleven Federal Reserve bank presidents rotate into the other four voting positions on the committee on a regular basis.

The FOMC is the Fed's key policymaking body, because it determines policy for the Fed's **open-market operations,** which are the Fed's purchases and sales of U.S. government securities. The Fed conducts daily trading in government securities markets through a department of the Federal Reserve Bank of New York. This department, commonly known as the *Trading Desk,* determines the amount of securities to buy or sell based on instructions from the FOMC.

Because the seven members of the Fed's Board of Governors have numerical superiority relative to the other FOMC members, the governors have considerable authority over the day-to-day conduct of monetary policy. Furthermore, the chair of the Board of Governors automatically serves as chair of the FOMC. Finally, the FOMC oversees Fed foreign exchange market operations, so the governors also have considerable influence over the Fed's international policymaking.

The FOMC meets eight to ten times each year. At these meetings, the voting members of the FOMC determine the wording of the formal instructions for open-market operations and foreign exchange trading at the Federal Reserve Bank of New York. The chief supervisor of this bank's Trading Desk serves as the FOMC's account manager and communicates daily with designated subcommittees of FOMC members.

INTERNET ● SOURCE

The Fed on the Net

Federal Reserve System—Internet Addresses

A wealth of information about the Fed is available on the Internet, courtesy of the Fed itself. The following are Internet homepage addresses for the Fed's Board of Governors and all twelve Federal Reserve Banks:

Federal Reserve Source	*Internet URL: http:// . . . . . .*
Board of Governors	www.bog.frb.fed.us
Federal Reserve Bank of Atlanta	www.frbatlanta.org
Federal Reserve Bank of Boston	www.std.com/frbbos/
Federal Reserve Bank of Chicago	www.frbchi.org
Federal Reserve Bank of Cleveland	www.clev.frb.org
Federal Reserve Bank of Dallas	www.dallasfed.org
Federal Reserve Bank of Kansas City	www.kc.frb.org
Federal Reserve Bank of Minneapolis	woodrow.mlps.frb.fed.us
Federal Reserve Bank of New York	www.ny.frb.org
Federal Reserve Bank of Philadelphia	www.libertynet.org/~fedresrv/fedpage.html
Federal Reserve Bank of Richmond	www.rich.frb.org
Federal Reserve Bank of San Francisco	www.frbsf.org
Federal Reserve Bank of St. Louis	www.stls.frb.org

How the Fed Influences the Quantity of Money in Circulation   The FOMC is the Fed's key policymaking body because open-market operations are the main mechanism by which the Fed affects the amount of money in circulation in the United States. When the Federal Reserve Bank of New York's Trading Desk executes a purchase of U.S. government securities, it wires funds to the account of the private bank from which it purchases the securities. In this manner, the Fed begins the process of creating new money.

It is only the start of the process, however. For instance, suppose the Trading Desk purchases $1 million in government securities from a securities dealer who has the Fed wire the funds to its checking deposit account in a private bank based in Chicago. The Fed will respond by applying a $1 million credit to that bank's reserve account at the Federal Reserve Bank of Chicago. The private bank then will earmark these funds for the dealer's checking deposit account. The Fed imposes a 10 percent reserve requirement on most of U.S. checking deposits, so the private Chicago bank will be able to lend $900,000 of the funds that it receives via the security dealer's deposit. Suppose further that Chicago bank makes a loan of $900,000 to a construction company based in Louisville, Kentucky, and that this company places the funds in its checking account at a Louisville bank. Now the Louisville bank has $900,000 in new cash reserves. Of these, it could lend as much as 90 percent of these funds, or $810,000. Ultimately, these funds will expand deposits at yet another bank, either in Louisville or elsewhere.

As we discuss in more detail later in the chapter, checking account deposits are part of today's measures of the amount of money in circulation. Consequently, the Fed's $1 million security purchase in our example causes the total quantity of money in circulation to increase by an amount much greater than $1 million. The Chicago security dealer's checking deposits will increase by $1 million, the Louisville construction company's checking deposits rise by $900,000, and some other loan recipient's checking deposits will rise by $810,000. This process continues until the Fed's security purchase has had an ultimate *multiplier effect* on the total quantity of checking deposits included in the nation's money stock.

Computing the Deposit Multiplier   To determine the size of the multiplier effect in our example, let's denote the amount of checking deposits at private banks as D, and let's call the total amount of cash reserves of these banks R. Finally, let's denote the Fed's ratio for determining required reserve holdings as q. Hence, if banks hold no more cash reserves than the Fed requires them to hold, total reserves in the banking system will be $R = q \times D$, and any change in reserves owing to a change in checking deposits at banks will be equal to $\Delta R = q \times \Delta D$. By rearranging this relationship, we can find the change in checking deposits owing to a change in reserves induced by a Fed purchase of securities. To do so, we simply solve for ΔD by dividing both sides by q, which yields:

$$\Delta D = (1/q) \times \Delta R.$$

Inserting the numbers from our example of a Fed security purchase that causes an initial bank reserve expansion of $1 million with a required reserve ratio of 10 percent, ΔR equals $1 million, and $1/q$ equals $1/(0.1) = 10$. Therefore, ΔD equals $1 million $\times$ 10, or $10 million, so the Fed's $1 million security purchase ultimately will cause the quantity of money in circulation to rise by a multiple amount of $10 million. The ratio $1/q = 10$ is the "money multiplier."

Realistically, the final multiplier effect of a Fed security purchase is smaller than this amount. A key reason is that people hold some money in the form of currency. Suppose that the Chicago securities dealer and the Louisville construction company in our example had chosen to convert some of the funds they received into currency rather than depositing all of the funds into checking accounts at their banks. Then their banks will have had fewer funds available to lend. This would have reduced the extent of the deposit multiplier process. Another factor that typically depresses the size of the deposit multiplier effect is bank holdings of reserves over and above those that are required. To the extent that banks hold such *excess reserves,* they have fewer reserves available to lend at each stage of the multiplier process.

The Fed's Policy Instruments, the Quantity of Money, and Intermediate Targets Although the Fed cannot control the total quantity of deposits in the banking system directly, it clearly can influence this amount by conducting open-market operations—buying or selling securities. In addition, by varying reserve requirements the Fed can affect the size of the money multiplier linking a change in reserves caused by its open-market operations to the total amount of money in circulation. Finally, the Fed can influence the total amount of reserves held by private banks by changing the discount rate that it charges these institutions, thereby inducing them to increase or reduce the amounts of reserves that they borrow from the Federal Reserve banks.

As you can see, the Federal Reserve and other central banks of the world cannot directly "control" the quantity of money in circulation. In theory, central banks could use their policy instruments, such as the Fed's open-market operations, discount rate, and reserve requirements, to try to vary the quantity of money in a precise effort to achieve their inflation, output, and employment objectives. Typically, however, most central banks have sought to achieve **intermediate targets** of monetary policy. An intermediate target is a macroeconomic variable whose value a central bank tries to control because it believes that doing so is consistent with its ultimate objectives. Intermediate targets are distinguishable from the central bank's ultimate policy goals but are sufficiently closely related that they can serve as stand-ins or proxies for the ultimate objectives, as indicated in Figure 12–1 on page 398.

The Rationales for Intermediate Targeting

There are two rationales for using an intermediate target in monetary policy. One is the difficulty that central bank officials have understanding and reaching agreement about the ways in which monetary policy affects inflation, real output, and employment in the short and long run. The other rationale is that even if central bank policymakers could unanimously agree on how their policy actions influence economic activity, they typically possess limited information about the economy.

Problems with Directly Pursuing Ultimate Policy Goals As you have learned by now, there is no shortage of theories about how monetary policy actions affect inflation, real output, and employment. Different central bank officials often subscribe to distinctly different theoretical views. These disagreements can complicate the efforts of central bank policymakers to reach a consensus on the best way to attain ultimate policy objectives.

Consequently, seeking to achieve an intermediate monetary policy target might be viewed as a *compromise* approach in the absence of complete agreement among

INTERMEDIATE TARGET A macroeconomic variable whose value a central bank seeks to control because it believes that doing so is consistent with its ultimate objectives.

FIGURE 12–1 **THE INTERMEDIATE TARGETING STRATEGY FOR MONETARY POLICY**

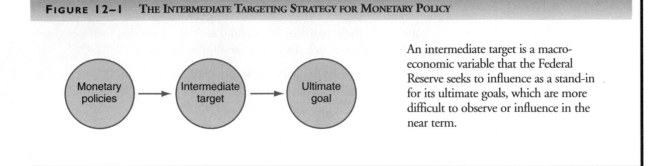

An intermediate target is a macroeconomic variable that the Federal Reserve seeks to influence as a stand-in for its ultimate goals, which are more difficult to observe or influence in the near term.

---

central bank officials about the best way to aim directly at ultimate goals. For example, as we shall discuss in more detail shortly, an intermediate target variable that several central banks have used in the past is the nominal money stock. Not all economic theories agree that changes in the money stock affect real output and employment, but all theories indicate that a given change in some specific measure of the nominal quantity of money should cause the price level to move in the same direction, if not in exactly the same proportion. If they cannot agree on any other aspect of monetary policy, central bank officials might decide to try to achieve a money stock growth rate objective, because that is the only policy approach on which a consensus exists.

Conducting Monetary Policy with Limited Information   Although an intermediate target is sometimes adopted as a compromise, there also is a strong economic justification for using an intermediate target even when all policymakers agree on what is the "true" macroeconomic theory. The reason is that central bank officials must conduct monetary policy in the absence of perfect information. Some macroeconomic variables, such as interest rates or the quantity of money or credit, can be measured from day to day or week to week. Other variables, such as nominal income, may be estimated on a weekly basis but generally are known only on a monthly basis. Still others, particularly the price level, real GDP, and employment, can be tracked only from month to month. Even then, central bank and government statisticians often revise their calculations of these variables in the weeks following their initial release.

Consequently, current information about the central bank's ultimate policy goals—inflation, real output, and employment—typically is less readily available. In contrast, interest rates, money, and credit data are more likely to be available for observation and use at any given moment. Nominal income data are not as quickly forthcoming as these financial data, but nominal income estimates generally are available more frequently than information about ultimate policy goal variables.

The notion of using a macroeconomic variable as an intermediate target follows naturally from the fact that information about other variables are more readily available, as compared with information about ultimate objectives. By aiming to achieve an intermediate target, a central bank can more directly infer whether or not it may be on the way to achieving the basic intent of its policies. Otherwise, monetary policymakers might have to wait much longer to make this assessment.

Choosing an Intermediate Target Variable

A central bank that decides to use an intermediate-targeting approach to conducting monetary policy must choose the appropriate macroeconomic variable to serve as its intermediate policy objective. In choosing among a number of possible target variables, the central bank considers several criteria.

Characteristics of Intermediate Targets   To be useful, an intermediate target variable should exhibit four key attributes:

1. *Frequently observable.* Because having up-to-date information is a fundamental rationale for using an intermediate targeting approach, an intermediate target variable should be observable more frequently than ultimate goal variables. As we noted, the price level, real GDP, and employment usually are observable at monthly intervals. Consequently, a central bank will likely choose an intermediate target variable that can be observed from week to week or, even better, from day to day.

2. *Consistency with ultimate goals.* The target value for an intermediate variable should be consistent with the central bank's ultimate objectives. It will be counterproductive for a central bank to hit its chosen intermediate target successfully, only to discover that it had widely missed its goals for inflation, output, and employment.

3. *Definable and measurable.* Defining and measuring an intermediate target variable should be a straightforward task. If a potential intermediate target variable is susceptible to redefinition because of intermittent regulatory or technological changes, a central bank will have trouble measuring the target variable consistently. Inconsistent measurements would make it more difficult to evaluate the variable's relationship to ultimate policy goals.

4. *Controllable.* An intermediate target variable should be a macroeconomic variable whose value the central bank can readily influence. Otherwise, attaining its intermediate target and achieving its ultimate policy objectives will be difficult even if the intermediate target variable and the ultimate goals are closely related.

The Menu of Potential Intermediate Target Variables   Central banks around the globe have adopted a number of different intermediate targeting procedures over the years. Several alternative categories of macroeconomic variables might qualify as intermediate monetary policy targets.

MONETARY AGGREGATES Measures of the quantity of money in circulation.

1. *Monetary or Credit Aggregates.* Many nations, including Germany, the United Kingdom, and Japan, have experimented with procedures that use **monetary**

aggregates, or alternative measures of the nominal money stock, as intermediate target variables. In the United States, the Federal Reserve in the past has targeted the monetary aggregates that it calls M1 and M2. M1 is defined as currency (Federal Reserve notes and coins) plus transactions deposits (funds in interest-bearing and non-interest-bearing checking accounts). M2 consists of M1 plus various savings deposits, highly liquid overnight financial instruments, and various money market mutual fund balances.

The basic rationale for targeting a monetary aggregate has been that various macroeconomic theories indicate that the quantity of money should help determine aggregate demand, thereby influencing the price level and, possibly, real output and employment. Thus, central banks have believed that there should be a relationship between monetary aggregates and their inflation, output, and employment objectives. In addition, central banks clearly have the ability to influence monetary aggregates, and their values typically are known weekly.

Nevertheless, central banks have had some difficulties using monetary aggregates as intermediate targets. One problem has been that regulatory and technological changes have blurred the lines among various financial assets that function as money. In the United States, for instance, the Federal Reserve has redefined M1 or M2 every few years as new forms of money-like assets have emerged. The existence of more than one monetary aggregate is itself indicative of the problems defining "money" entails. In the 1980s and early 1990s, a breakdown in the previously consistent relationship between the basic M1 and M2 aggregates and GDP presented another, particularly bothersome problem.

ON THE WEB
*Learn More About Russia's
Economy at:*
http://www.online.ru

Another quantitative financial target, which central banks in China and Russia have emphasized, is a *credit aggregate* target, which is a measure of the volume of lending. One type of credit aggregate is *total credit,* or the total amount of all lending in an economy. A narrower credit aggregate is *bank credit,* or total lending by banks. Through their monetary policy instruments, central banks can affect such measures of credit. For instance, as we noted earlier, expansion of bank lending accompanies the multiple expansion of bank deposit money. Hence, Fed policy instruments can affect total credit as well as the total quantity of money in circulation. Additionally, credit aggregates usually are straightforward to define and to measure, and credit data usually are observable weekly.

Credit aggregates, however, suffer from problems similar to those associated with monetary aggregates. In particular, relationships between credit measures and ultimate goals generally have been *at least* as tenuous as relationships between monetary aggregates and ultimate goals (see the Policy Notebook: *Does the Credit View of Monetary Policy Make Sense?*).

2. *Interest Rates.* An alternative credit-market variable that can serve as an intermediate monetary policy target is the *price of credit,* or the nominal interest rate. Central banks can observe interest rates daily and often by the minute. In addition, central banks' policy actions can have clear-cut effects on nominal interest rates.

POLICY NOTEBOOK
Does the Credit View of Monetary Policy Make Sense?

Many studies have purported to show that monetary policy affects the economy through credit channels. This notion has been called the credit view of monetary policy. If this view is correct, monetary policy actions should be examined in terms of their effects on credit, and not just on interest rates. The question is whether this link between monetary policy and credit actually exists.

Daniel L. Thornton of the Federal Reserve Bank of St. Louis has carried out numerous tests to determine the validity of the credit view. In particular, he tried to see whether monetary policy actions had a direct effect on bank lending. He found a very small positive and statistically significant relationship between Federal Reserve actions and both bank loans and bank deposits, but this relationship existed only prior to the early 1980s. Since then, no statistical relationship appears to be in operation.

Thornton points out that financial innovations in the last decades have dramatically reduced the special nature of bank credit. Financial innovations and deregulation have expanded the financing options available to small and medium-sized firms and reduced their dependence on banks. Consequently, the portion of credit provided by banks is declining. Banks now account for only 45 percent of total credit, a decline of 25 percentage points since the 1970s.

FOR CRITICAL ANALYSIS:
What are alternative sources of loans for businesses?

Interest rates and economic activity are not always closely related, however. While lower interest rates can spur capital investment and economic activity, increased income raises the demand for credit and pushes nominal interest rates upward. Hence, the relationship between nominal interest rates and real income is not always predictable. In addition, many interest rates, including interest rates on financial instruments with short and long maturities, could be potential targets.

3. *Nominal GDP.* In recent years many economists have proposed using *nominal gross domestic product (GDP)* as an intermediate target. Even though nominal GDP data are not available more frequently than observations of real GDP and the price level, the essential argument favoring targeting nominal GDP hinges on the fact that nominal GDP by definition is equal to real GDP times the GDP price deflator. There are a number of competing theories about how the money stock relates to the price level and real output and prices, but this definitional relationship indicates that if a central bank wishes to stabilize real output and prices, then minimizing variations in nominal GDP output will help contain volatility in either of these ultimate goal variables. We shall illustrate this argument shortly.

FUNDAMENTAL ISSUE #2

Why might a central bank use an intermediate monetary policy target? Central banks such as the Federal Reserve sometimes adopt an intermediate target because of limitations on the availability of data on ultimate objectives and different views about how monetary policy actions influence ultimate policy goals. An intermediate target variable should be observable with greater frequency than ultimate goal variables, easy to measure, subject to influence through monetary policy actions, and closely related to ultimate policy objectives. Possible intermediate target variables include money and credit aggregates, interest rates, and nominal GDP.

Choosing An Intermediate Target

No single potential intermediate target variable stands out as the clear best choice. Hence, in choosing the target, a central bank will likely consider various macroeconomic factors. By applying concepts you have already learned, we can examine these factors.

Targeting the Nominal Interest Rate   Figure 12–2 explains the way a central bank can choose and maintain a nominal interest rate target. In panel (b), we assume that the ultimate target for real GDP is equal to y^*. Given the location of the *IS* schedule, attaining and maintaining this real income target will require achieving the nominal interest rate target r^*. This will require assuring that the *LM* schedule crosses the *IS* schedule at point A in panel (b). To achieve its nominal interest rate target, the central bank will have to make sure that the supply of real money balances, M_1^s/P_1, crosses the demand schedule for real money balances, $m_1^d(y^*)$, at point A in panel (a).

Suppose, however, that there are variations in the demand for real money balances that arise, say, from changes in the technology by which people make payments, and not from any change in real income. An increase in the demand for real money balances, to $m_2^d(y^*)$, will cause the equilibrium nominal interest rate to start to rise from r^* toward r_2, at point B in panel (a). As a result, the *LM* schedule in panel (b) will shift upward by the vertical distance between point A and point B. If the central bank does nothing to offset this change, the rise in the interest rate will ultimately lead to a decline in real investment and, consequently, a fall in real income to level y_2 at point C in panel (b), which is below the central bank's target income level y^*. To keep this sequence of events from occurring, the central bank could raise the quantity of money from M_1 to M_2. This will shift the supply schedule for real money balances rightward and return the equilibrium interest rate to r^* at point A' in panel (a) and

FIGURE 12–2 TARGETING THE NOMINAL INTEREST RATE IN THE FACE OF MONEY DEMAND VARIATIONS

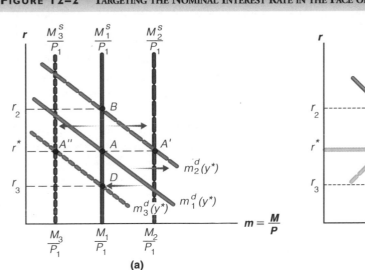

(a)

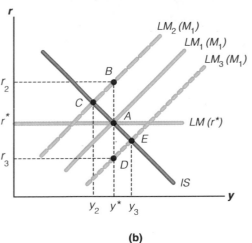

(b)

If the initial equilibrium quantity of real money balances and real income arises at points *A* in panels (a) and (b), respectively, then the displayed variations in the demand for real money balances will cause movements between points *B* and *D* in panel (a) that will induce the upward and downward shifts of the *LM* schedule between points *B* and *D* in panel (b). As a result, equilibrium real income will vary between points *C* and *E* in panel (b). To prevent

such variability in real income at the current price level, the central bank could expand the nominal money stock as money demand rises [point *A'* in panel (a)] and contract the money stock in the face of a decline in money demand [point *A"* in panel (a)]. This policy effectively would make the *LM* schedule horizontal at the targeted interest rate in panel (b), thereby maintaining an *IS-LM* equilibrium at point *A.*

reattain the initial *IS-LM* equilibrium at point *A* in panel (b). This will keep the nominal interest rate at the targeted level and thereby achieve the ultimate real output objective y^*.

If instead money demand falls, from $m_1^d(y^*)$ to $m_3^d(y^*)$, then maintaining the target nominal interest rate r^* will require a reduction in the money stock, from M_1 to M_3. This will keep the equilibrium nominal interest rate from declining toward r_3 at point *D* in panel (a). Instead, the equilibrium point *A"* will be attained, and a downward vertical shift in the *LM* schedule by the distance from point *A* to point *D* in panel (b) will be prohibited. This policy action thus will prevent real income from ultimately moving above the target level y^* to y_3 at point *E* in panel (b).

Note that by targeting the nominal interest rate, the central bank does not allow the *LM* schedule to shift. It always reacts to changes in the demand for real money balances by raising or reducing the nominal money stock as required to keep the nominal interest rate at its target level. Under this targeting procedure, the central bank effectively makes the *LM* schedule *horizontal.* As real income varies, the nominal interest rate remains unchanged at an equilibrium that the central bank targets. Hence, $LM(r^*)$ in panel (b) is the *effective LM schedule* if the central bank targets the nominal interest rate.

Clearly, adopting the nominal interest rate as an intermediate target is the best monetary policy procedure in the face of variations in money demand. Unfortunately for a central bank, however, other factors in the economy also can change unexpectedly. Figure 12–3 illustrates the effects of variations in autonomous expenditures. Recall from Chapter 6 that a decline in autonomous consumption, investment, government spending, or exports or a rise in net taxes or autonomous import spending will cause a multiple reduction in equilibrium real income. This translates into a leftward shift of the *IS* schedule that is equal to the total decline in real income, shown by the movement from point *A* to point *B* in the figure, as the *IS* schedule shifts from IS_1 to IS_2. Because the effective *LM* schedule is horizontal if the central bank targets the nominal interest rate, equilibrium real income will decline by the full distance of the shift in the *IS* schedule, from y^* to y_2. In contrast, if the central bank instead allows the equilibrium nominal interest rate to vary normally with changing money market conditions and thus to fall to r_2, then the resulting *IS-LM* equilibrium will be point *C*, and equilibrium real income will only decline to y'_2. *Not* targeting the nominal interest rate actually will allow the central bank to come closer to achieving its real income target y^* in the face of a variation in autonomous expenditures that reduces real income.

Likewise, *not* targeting the interest rate will result in a smaller increase in equilibrium real income if autonomous consumption, investment, government spend-

---

FIGURE 12–3   TARGETING THE NOMINAL INTEREST RATE IN THE FACE OF VARIATIONS IN AUTONOMOUS EXPENDITURES

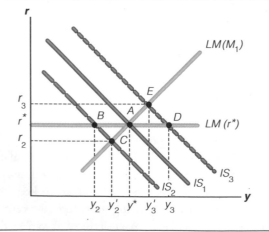

Changes in autonomous saving, imports, net taxes, exports, or government spending will cause fluctuations in the position of the *IS* schedule, causing movements along a typical, upward-sloping *LM* schedule from point *A* to point *C* or from point *A* to point *E*. If the central bank targets the nominal interest rate, however, the result will be an effectively horizontal *LM* schedule. Changes in autonomous expenditures will then cause even greater variability in equilibrium real income, between points *B* and *D*. Consequently, targeting the nominal interest rate is a less desirable policy in the presence of variations in autonomous expenditures.

ing, or exports rise or if net taxes or autonomous imports decline. Any one of these changes in autonomous spending will shift the *IS* schedule to the right, from IS_1 to IS_3 in Figure 12–3. If the central bank targets the nominal interest rate, the result will be the largest possible rise in equilibrium real income, from the target level y^* at point *A* to the level y_3 at point *D*. In contrast, if the central bank foregoes targeting the interest rate, then the new *IS-LM* equilibrium will be point *E*, at the interest rate r_3 and the real income level y'_3. Again, *not* targeting the nominal interest rate is the more desirable policy in the presence of autonomous spending variations that cause a change in the location of the *IS* schedule. (For other questions about the desirability of targeting interest rates, see on page 407 the Policy Notebook: *Can the Fed Really Target Interest Rates?*)

Targeting a Monetary Aggregate   What should a central bank do if variations in autonomous expenditures are significant, making the nominal interest rate less attractive as an intermediate monetary policy target? Figure 12–4 on page 406 gives one possible answer, which is to target the nominal quantity of money instead. Under this intermediate targeting procedure, the central bank selects a target quantity of money, M^*. By choosing this target, the central bank places the *LM* schedule, $LM(M^*)$, in the location that it anticipates will lead to its ultimate real income objective y^* , given the expected location of the *IS* schedule, shown by IS_1. As in Figure 12–3, variations in autonomous expenditures could cause the *IS* schedule to be at IS_2 or at IS_3, below or above the position that the central bank anticipated. Then equilibrium real income will fall somewhat below or rise somewhat above the real income target level, as the resulting *IS-LM* equilibrium points will lie between points *B* and *C*, causing equilibrium real income to vary between y_2 and y_3. Although equilibrium real income will deviate somewhat from the target level y^*, using the money stock as an intermediate target is preferable to targeting the nominal interest rate, which will permit much wider variations in real income between y'_2 at point *D* and y'_3 at point *E*.

Note that the amount of variability in real income with a money stock target depends on the elasticity of the *LM* schedule around the intersection with the *IS* schedule. If the *LM* schedule in Figure 12–4 were to become less elastic, then the extent of the variability in real income caused by unexpected changes in the position of the *IS* schedule would decline. Recall from Chapter 6 that the main determinant of the elasticity of the *LM* schedule is the interest elasticity of the demand for real money balances. A reduction in the interest elasticity of money demand will cause the *LM* schedule to become less elastic. Consequently, we can conclude that targeting a monetary aggregate is likely to be a better approach than targeting the nominal interest rate in the face of variability in autonomous expenditures if the demand for real money balances is very interest-inelastic.

As Figure 12–5 shows, however, targeting the nominal quantity of money is less desirable than targeting the nominal interest rate when the demand for real money balances itself is variable. Panel (a) illustrates the effects of an autonomous change in

FIGURE 12–4   TARGETING THE MONEY STOCK IN THE FACE OF VARIATIONS IN AUTONOMOUS EXPENDITURES

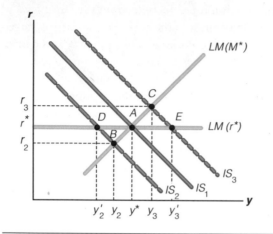

If a central bank establishes a target for the quantity of money in circulation, the *LM* schedule will slope upward. Thus, changes in autonomous saving, imports, net taxes, exports, or government spending that cause shifts in the *IS* schedule will result in movements along the *LM* schedule between points *B* and *C*. Volatility in real income will be less than the variations between points *D* and *E* that would take place if the central bank targeted the nominal interest rate instead.

FIGURE 12–5   TARGETING THE MONEY STOCK IN THE FACE OF MONEY DEMAND VARIATIONS

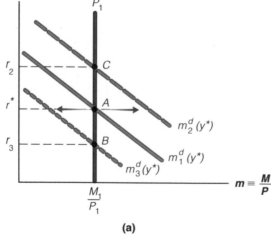

(a)

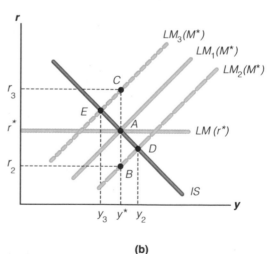

(b)

When a central bank targets the quantity of money in circulation, changes in the demand for real money balances will cause the equilibrium nominal interest rate to vary between points *B* and *C* in panel (a), thereby causing the position of the *LM* schedule to vary between points *B* and *C* in panel (b). As a result, equilibrium real income will vary along the schedule, between points *E* and *D*.

POLICY NOTEBOOK

Can the Fed Really Target Interest Rates?

When the Fed targets "the" interest rate, it is referring to the *nominal* interest rate. Recall that the nominal interest rate is equal to the real interest rate plus the expected inflation rate. Businesses undertake investment decisions based on real, rather than nominal, interest rates, however. In general, real interest rates are relatively high when economic growth prospects are buoyant and investment demand is concomitantly strong. During periods of high growth and robust investment, real interest rates are typically around 3 percent. The average since 1960 has been around 2 percent. According to Harvard economist Robert J. Barro, the Fed does not have much influence over expected real interest rates, even in the short run. He argues that such rates are determined by the world demand and supply of credit, which is a function of the worldwide willingness to save compared to the desire to invest. Barro maintains that the Fed is in fact a "passive observer with respect to movements in real interest rates."

Monetarist economist Milton Friedman is even more direct on this issue than Robert Barro. Friedman states: "I believe that the idea that a central bank can target interest rates is utterly false. Interest rates are partly a real magnitude, partly a nominal magnitude. The Federal Reserve cannot target real interest rates and has done great damage by trying to do so."

The analysis of interest rates in the press often (if not always) fails to distinguish between real and nominal interest rates. A high nominal interest rate is evidence that a country's central bank has been pursuing *loose* monetary policy in the past, rather than tight monetary policy. The reason is that in the long run, consistent increases in the rate of growth of the money supply lead to higher rates of inflation. A higher inflation rate normally leads to expectations of inflation and therefore to higher nominal interest rates. Thus, although many people associate contractionary monetary policy with high interest rates, the converse may often be true.

FOR CRITICAL ANALYSIS:
If the Fed cannot control real interest rates, what can it control?

---

the demand for money that causes variations in money market equilibrium between points *B* and *C*, respectively. When the central bank keeps the quantity of money at its target level M^*, these variations in the demand for money will cause the equilibrium nominal interest rate to vary between r_2 and r_3. Because variations in the demand for money that are not caused by changes in real income cause the *LM* schedule's position to change, the position of the *LM* schedule will vary between $LM_2(M^*)$ and $LM_3(M^*)$, as shown in panel (b). Therefore, equilibrium real income could ultimately vary between y_2 at point *D* and y_3 at point *E* in panel (b) under a money stock target. In contrast, using a nominal interest rate target instead would have kept the nominal interest rate unchanged and maintained the target level of real income y^* at point *A*.

The fundamental point that the examples in Figures 12–2 through 12–5 illustrate was first made by William Poole of Brown University more than twenty-five years ago:

> **If a central bank must choose between targeting the nominal interest rate or targeting a monetary aggregate, then the key criterion the bank should consider is the main source of variability that it faces.**

If the main source of variability is money demand and, hence, the position of the *LM* schedule, then the nominal interest rate is the preferable intermediate target. In contrast, if the main source of variability is changes in autonomous expenditures and, hence, the position of the *IS* schedule, then targeting a monetary aggregate is a more desirable approach.

Nominal GDP Targeting   Both interest rate targeting and monetary targeting involve a disadvantage that has been hidden thus far in our discussion by our implicit assumption that the price level is unchanging. Interest rate targeting or monetary targeting to stabilize real income at a target level in the presence of a fixed price level often amounts to stabilizing aggregate demand. Real-business-cycle theorists, however, have documented that in the real world, at least some real income variability arises as a result of variability in the aggregate supply schedule.

To see this, consider Figure 12–6. If a central bank selects the nominal interest rate or the money stock as its intermediate target, then the *best* it can do is to stabilize aggregate demand by ensuring that, for a given level of prices, the economy stays at the same *IS-LM* equilibrium at its real income target, y^*, at point *A*. If there is no variability in the aggregate supply schedule, there will be no inflation, and the central bank will attain both its real output and its inflation goals. If there is considerable vari-

---

FIGURE 12–6   THE PROBLEM OF AGGREGATE SUPPLY VARIABILITY

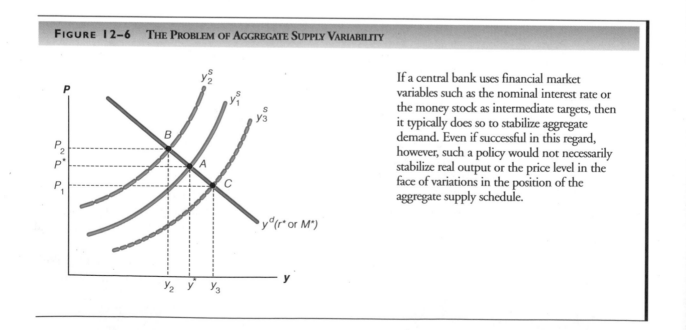

If a central bank uses financial market variables such as the nominal interest rate or the money stock as intermediate targets, then it typically does so to stabilize aggregate demand. Even if successful in this regard, however, such a policy would not necessarily stabilize real output or the price level in the face of variations in the position of the aggregate supply schedule.

ation in the position of the aggregate supply schedule, however, as shown by the variation between y_2^s and y_3^s, then the equilibrium level of real income will vary between y_2 at point B and y_3 at point C. In addition, the price level will vary between P_2 and P_3. Thus, the central bank will fail to attain a zero-inflation goal even though it might succeed in perfectly stabilizing aggregate demand.

Hence, nominal interest rate targeting and money stock targeting both fail to account for the output and inflation effects of aggregate supply variability. The position of the economy's aggregate supply schedule does vary from time to time. Consequently, a number of economists have proposed nominal GDP as an alternative intermediate target.

Figure 12–7 is based on a graphical approach to understanding nominal GDP targeting first proposed by Michael Bradley of George Washington University and Dennis Jansen of Texas A&M University. The figure shows how nominal GDP targeting will work in the face of factors causing a decline in aggregate demand. If a central bank targets nominal GDP, it will treat nominal income, $Y = P \times y$, as its intermediate target. Thus, the central bank will vary the quantity of money as needed to ensure that $P \times y = Y^*$ always holds, where Y^* denotes the central bank's nominal GDP target. In Figure 12–7, we assume that the target level of real GDP is $8,000 billion, or $8 trillion. Obviously, this target can be achieved by many price level–real income combinations, such as $P_1 = 4, y_1 = 2,000; P_2 = 5, y_2 = 1,600;$ and $P_3 = 8, y_3 = 1,000$. These and all other price level–real income combinations consistent with the nominal GDP target lie along the bowed schedule (called a rectangular hyperbola) labeled $Y^* = 8,000$.

FIGURE 12–7   TARGETING NOMINAL GDP IN THE FACE OF A DECLINE IN AGGREGATE DEMAND

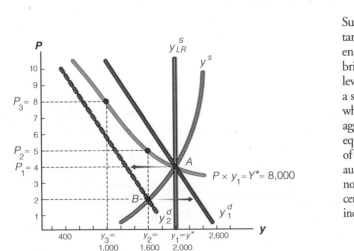

Suppose the central bank adopts an intermediate target of $8,000 billion ($8 trillion). Then it will enact monetary policies that achieve an equilibrium price level and equilibrium real output level at a point such as point A, which lies along a set of price level–real output combinations for which $P \times y = Y^* = 8,000$. If there is a fall in aggregate demand that results in a decline in the equilibrium price level and the equilibrium level of output, nominal income will decline. By automatically raising aggregate demand to push nominal income back toward the target level, the central bank will automatically stabilize both real income and the price level.

At point *A* in Figure 12–7, the aggregate demand and aggregate supply schedules intersect at the equilibrium price level $P_1 = 4$ and the equilibrium real output level $y_1 = 2,000$. In addition, the natural, full-information level of output in the figure is equal to $y^* = 2,000$. This is the real output level at which workers and firms have complete information, so the long-run aggregate supply schedule, denoted y_{LR}^s, is vertical. Hence, at point *A* the market for real output is in equilibrium at the natural output level, and so the central bank's nominal income target achieves this level of real output. In addition, if the central bank can keep the market for real output at point *A*, it will prevent any rise in the price level, thereby curtailing inflation.

Now consider how the central bank will respond to a decline in aggregate demand from y_1^d to y_2^d in Figure 12–7. The fall in aggregate demand will cause real income and the price level to begin to decline toward levels consistent with point *B*, so nominal income will also begin to fall. The central bank will respond by increasing the quantity of money to raise nominal GDP back to its target level. Therefore, by conducting monetary policy to maintain nominal income at the intermediate target level of $Y^* = 8,000$ nominal units, the central bank automatically will stabilize aggregate demand and achieve both its real output and its inflation goals.

Consequences of Aggregate Supply Variability   As we noted, stabilizing aggregate demand often is all that nominal interest rate targeting or money stock targeting can achieve. The advantage of nominal GDP targeting is that it potentially can reduce the inflationary consequences of aggregate supply variability, as shown in Figure 12–8. Suppose there is a fall in aggregate supply that is caused by an event such as a worldwide increase in oil prices, a war, or an agricultural famine. As a result, the econ-

---

FIGURE 12–8   TARGETING NOMINAL GDP IN THE FACE OF A DECLINE IN AGGREGATE SUPPLY

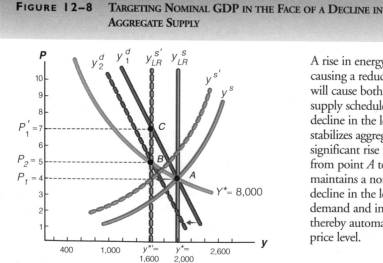

A rise in energy prices, a war, a famine, or another factor causing a reduction in the economy's long-run output level will cause both the long-run and the short-run aggregate supply schedules to shift leftward by the amount of the decline in the long-run output level. If the central bank stabilizes aggregate demand, the long-run result will be a significant rise in the price level shown by a movement from point *A* to point *C*. If instead the central bank maintains a nominal GDP target, it will respond to the decline in the long-run output level by reducing aggregate demand and inducing a final equilibrium at point *B*, thereby automatically limiting the rise in the equilibrium price level.

omy's short-run aggregate supply schedule will shift leftward from y^s to $y^{s'}$ by an amount equal to the unavoidable decline in the natural, full-information output level, from $y^* = 2,000$ to $y^{*'} = 1,600$. Thus, the long-run aggregate supply schedule will also shift to the left by this same amount, from y_{LR}^s to $y_{LR}^{s'}$. In the absence of any response from the central bank, the equilibrium price level will rise from $P_1 = 4$ toward $P' = 7$ at point C, and so nominal income will begin to rise toward $Y^{*'} = P' \times y^{*'} = 7 \times 1,600 = 11,200$. With either an interest rate or a money stock targeting procedure that will stabilize aggregate demand, these would be the new, much higher values for the price level and nominal GDP. With a nominal GDP target of $Y^* = 8,000$ nominal units, however, the central bank will need to reduce the money stock, thereby lowering aggregate demand. This will yield an actual equilibrium price level equal to $P_2 = 5$ at point B, thereby containing the inflationary effects of the reduction in aggregate supply. Consequently, we can reach the following conclusions:

> **A key advantage of nominal GDP targeting is that it restrains the inflationary consequences of aggregate supply variations. In this respect, nominal GDP targeting is preferable to policy procedures that target monetary aggregates or interest rates.**

Of course, one problem with using nominal GDP as an intermediate target is that nominal income data are not available much more frequently than observations of ultimate goal variables such as the price level and real GDP. Nevertheless, a growing number of economists who otherwise are proponents of competing theoretical approaches have begun to agree that nominal GDP targeting might be a worthwhile approach to conducting monetary policy.

FUNDAMENTAL ISSUE #3

What are the pros and cons of alternative intermediate monetary policy targets? Using a nominal interest rate as an intermediate target helps to stabilize aggregate demand if money demand is highly volatile while aggregate desired expenditures are relatively stable. In contrast, adopting a money stock target makes aggregate demand more stable if aggregate desired expenditures are variable while money demand is relatively stable. A potential advantage of nominal GDP targeting over targeting either a nominal interest rate or a monetary aggregate is that aiming for a nominal GDP target automatically stabilizes aggregate demand and also minimizes the inflationary effects of variations in aggregate supply. A disadvantage, however, is that accurate nominal GDP data are not available as frequently as data on interest rates and monetary aggregates.

DEFICITS, DEBT, AND FISCAL POLICY: HOW TO BALANCE THE BUDGET

The last time that the U.S. government spent fewer revenues than it collected was in
1969. In every year since 1969, the federal government has experienced budget
deficits. Does federal deficit spending make it easier or more difficult to attain ultimate macroeconomic goals? Can the federal government fully control the size of its
deficits? Before we tackle these important public policy questions, let's begin by considering some facts about federal deficits and the government debt.

The Government Debt

As we noted in Chapter 3, a government budget deficit occurs whenever the government spends more than it receives in tax revenues (and user fees). To finance
deficits, the U.S. government must borrow by issuing Treasury bills, notes, and
bonds. By so doing, the government accumulates an indebtedness to those who purchase its securities.

The National Debt   At any given time, the accumulated amount of all outstanding amounts owed to private holders of government-issued securities is the net
national debt. Therefore, any year that the government runs a deficit, it contributes
to the national debt.

NATIONAL DEBT The total
accumulation of amounts that the
government currently owes to
private holders of its debt.

The absolute dollar amount of the national debt by itself does not give us much
information about its relative importance in the U.S. economy. Figure 12–9
shows how the net national debt has varied relative to gross domestic product during the past few decades. After reaching a peak during World War II, the net
national debt as a percentage of GDP declined to about 25 percent in 1974. Since
that year, however, this ratio, apart from a decline in the late 1980s, risen steadily
to about 50 percent.

Is there anything inherently "bad" about a high ratio of net national debt to GDP?
After all, one might reason, running deficits and accumulating debt might allow the

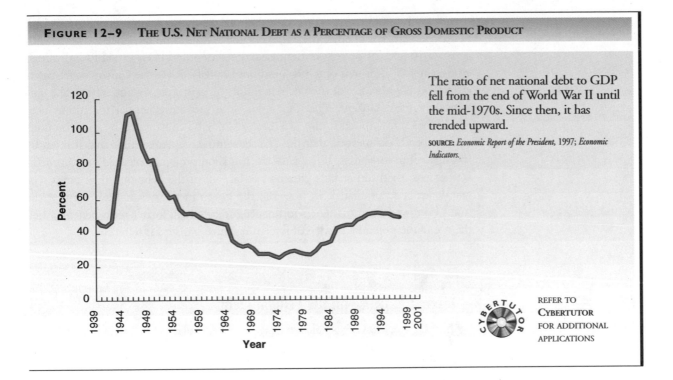

FIGURE 12–9   THE U.S. NET NATIONAL DEBT AS A PERCENTAGE OF GROSS DOMESTIC PRODUCT

The ratio of net national debt to GDP fell from the end of World War II until the mid-1970s. Since then, it has trended upward.

SOURCE: *Economic Report of the President, 1997; Economic Indicators.*

REFER TO **CYBERTUTOR** FOR ADDITIONAL APPLICATIONS

government to spend funds on programs intended to assist those in need or to maintain a broad police and military network for internal national security and defense from external threats. Certainly, it is possible that benefits could flow from debt accumulation. Nevertheless, accumulating greater debt in pursuit of such benefits is not costless. Large national debt-to-GDP ratios impose burdens on society, because the debts ultimately must be repaid.

Two important social burdens can stem from accumulating a sizable national debt. One is that debts accumulated in current years must be repaid in the future. As we noted in our discussion of the Ricardian equivalence proposition in Chapter 7, deficit spending that adds to today's national debt ultimately must be repaid by future generations. Hence, if we add to the national debt this year to reap the benefits that greater government spending can provide, future generations will have to sacrifice a flow of benefits that they otherwise could receive if they did not have to face the prospect of repaying the higher debt that will result from this year's budgetary decisions.

Not all benefits from government spending are short-term, of course. As noted in Chapter 11, government expenditures on infrastructure investments—highways, waterways, airports, and the like—constitute longer-term investment that can have payoffs for future generations by increasing their real incomes. To the extent that such future payoffs arise, the social burden of the national debt is reduced.

A second social burden is that some national debt repayments entail flows of U.S. resources to citizens of other nations. As Figure 12–10 indicates, since the mid-1970s between 10 and 20 percent of the net national debt has been issued to individuals who are not U.S. citizens or to organizations located outside the United States. Interest payments to holders of such debt amount to transfers of resources from U.S. citizens to foreign citizens. This can reduce the income potential for future U.S. generations. How much future U.S. citizens may be constrained by these transfers again depends on the way that the U.S. government spends funds that it raises by issuing debt to foreigners. If it spends the funds on projects that yield only immediate benefits, then future U.S. citizens will face all of the debt that their parents or grandparents accumulated. If, however, the government uses at least some of the funds borrowed from foreigners to finance projects with longer-term benefits, then the size of the potential burden of foreign resource transfers is reduced.

INTERNET ● SOURCE

Interest Expense on the Federal Debt

The U.S. Treasury Office—Interest Expense on the Public Debt Outstanding
Internet URL: **http://www.publicdebt.treas.gov/opd/**

Navigation: Begin at the U.S. Treasury Office homepage (**http://www.ustreas.gov**). Select *Treasury Offices* and then select *Bureau of the Public Debt.* Then click on *The Public Debt* (**http://www.publicdebt.ustreas.gov/opda.htm**). Finally, click on *Interest Expense on the Public Debt Outstanding.*

Do Government Budget Deficits Matter?

Our discussion indicates that deficits can matter if they add to a government debt that truly is burdensome to society. In addition, there are two other reasons why any generation might be concerned with high deficits.

The Crowding-Out Problem   Recall from Chapters 3 and 7 that high government budget deficits can *crowd out* private spending. By inducing a rise in the interest rate, deficit spending by the government reduces private investment. If saving also increases with a rise in the interest rate, then private consumption may decline as well. To some extent, the crowding-out effect is simply a resource transfer from the private sector to the government. Nevertheless, if private investment entails greater capital accumulation as compared with government expenditures, then longer-term economic growth can be slowed by deficit spending.

The Twin Deficit Problem   In Chapters 5 and 7, you learned about the *twin deficit problem,* which is the direct relationship between the government budget

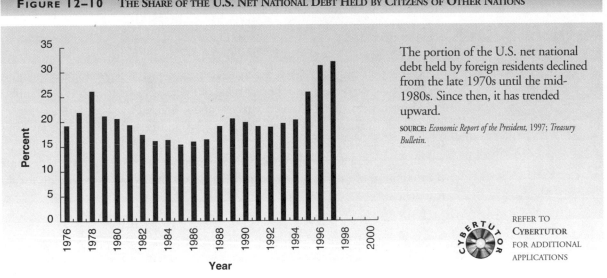

FIGURE 12–10 THE SHARE OF THE U.S. NET NATIONAL DEBT HELD BY CITIZENS OF OTHER NATIONS

The portion of the U.S. net national debt held by foreign residents declined from the late 1970s until the mid-1980s. Since then, it has trended upward.

SOURCE: *Economic Report of the President*, 1997; *Treasury Bulletin*.

REFER TO
CYBERTUTOR
FOR ADDITIONAL
APPLICATIONS

deficit and the merchandise trade deficit. As we have noted, a significant portion of government debt is issued to foreign citizens, who purchase government bonds using dollars that they obtain by selling goods to Americans. If the government consistently runs budget deficits, then Americans must consistently be net purchasers of foreign-produced goods and services if they wish to continue borrowing from foreigners to finance the government's deficit spending. This implies that if Americans desire lower merchandise trade deficits, they must either reduce their reliance on foreign purchases of U.S. government debt or find a way to reduce the government's deficit.

Can the Government Budget Deficit Be Reduced?

ON THE WEB
Visit the Congressional Budget Office at:
http://gopher.cbo.gov:7100/

From a purely arithmetic standpoint, the problem of reducing the government budget deficit has a simple solution a third grader can figure out: Reduce spending, raise taxes, or both. From a political standpoint, however, the task is not nearly so simple. Reaching agreement on *which* form of spending to cut, or on *which* taxes to increase, is a complicated process.

As we discussed in Chapter 7, it is possible that deficits induced by cuts in tax rates may be *self-correcting* if the reductions in marginal tax rates spur growth in real income that raises the government's tax revenues on net. Many economists have concluded, however, that over the long run government deficits ultimately stem from *excess spending* relative to tax collections. As we shall demonstrate, this perspective indicates that governments cannot postpone tough choices forever if they really desire to bring their budgets into balance.

What It Would Take to Maintain a Balanced Budget To consider the various factors that influence a government's deficit and the prospects for eliminating a deficit, let's begin by defining the real value of the deficit to be

$$d \equiv g + (I/P) - t.$$

This definition says that the real deficit, d, is equal to total real government spending on goods and services, g, plus the real value of interest payments on the outstanding government debt (nominal interest payments, I, divided by the GDP deflator, P) minus real net tax revenues (taxes net of transfers), t. Recall that the simple tax function that we considered in Chapter 7 is $t = t_0 + (\tau \times y)$, where τ is the income tax rate and t_0 is net autonomous taxes. Consequently, we substitute the tax function into the definition of the real government deficit to get the following expression for the real deficit:

$$d = g + (I/P) - t_0 - (\tau \times y).$$

Note that this equation tells us that the real deficit rises, naturally, if government spending increases or if the government must make higher interest and principal payments on outstanding debt. The deficit declines if autonomous taxes increase or if income tax revenues rise, either because the tax rate rises while real income stays unchanged or because real income increases with a constant tax rate. In addition, the deficit declines as the price level rises, because a rise in the price level reduces the real value of interest and principal payments that the government must make to holders of its debt.

To think about the conditions required to achieve a balanced budget, let's note that under a balanced budget, there will be a zero deficit. If $d = 0$, we can substitute this into our deficit equation to find the condition that must hold for the government's budget to be balanced:

$$0 = g + (I/P) - t_0 - (\tau \times y).$$

If we add $\tau \times y$ to both sides of this equation, we get

$$(\tau \times y) = g + (I/P) - t_0.$$

Then, if we divide by τ, we find the value that real income would have to attain to yield a balanced budget with all the other factors affecting the deficit held constant:

$$y = (1/\tau) \times [g + (I/P) - t_0].$$

Figure 12–11 shows a diagram of this expression. By reducing the real value of interest and principal payments on government debt, I/P, higher values of the price level reduce the level of real income required to raise sufficient income taxes to maintain a balanced budget. As the price level approaches an infinite value, in fact, the real value of these payments approaches zero, and so the required real income level approaches its lowest possible value of $y = (1/\tau) \times (g - t_0)$. In contrast, as the price level declines toward a value of zero, the real value of interest and principal payments

FIGURE 12–11 THE *BB* SCHEDULE

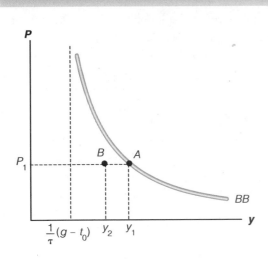

Along the *BB* schedule, the real government budget is balanced. Hence, the real deficit, which is equal to government spending plus the real value of interest payments on the national debt less net autonomous taxes and net income taxes, or $d = g + (B/P) - t_0 - (\tau \times y)$, is equal to zero. It follows that combinations of real income and the price level consistent with a balanced budget lie along a schedule, illustrated in this figure, whose equation is given by $y = (1/\tau) \times [g + (B/P) - t_0]$. At a point such as *A* on the *BB* schedule, the price level and real income level permit the government to maintain a balanced budget, given its current expenditures, interest payments on its debt, net autonomous taxes, and income tax rate. At a point to the left of the *BB* schedule, however, the price level and real income are too low to permit attainment of a balanced budget, and so the government operates with a budget deficit.

BB SCHEDULE All combinations of real income and the price level at which the government's budget is balanced at a given income tax rate, level of government expenditures, and amount of net autonomous taxes.

climbs, so higher real income is needed to provide sufficient income tax revenues to make those payments. We call the resulting schedule the **BB schedule,** because it is a set of combinations of the price level and real income that maintain a balanced budget for a given income tax rate, level of government spending, and level of net autonomous taxes. Point *A*'s combination of P_1 and y_1, for example, is one such combination.

At point *B* to the left of the *BB* schedule, the real income level y_2 is too low to generate sufficient real income tax receipts for the government to maintain a balanced budget, holding all other factors constant. Hence, at any point to the *left* of the *BB* schedule, the government runs a budget *deficit*.

Note that a tax rate reduction, an increase in government spending, or a reduction in autonomous net taxes will *shift* the *BB* schedule rightward. The reason is that all these changes will cause a deficit and thereby will require *higher real income* to raise income tax revenues and reattain a balanced budget, *holding the price level unchanged.* Thus, following a tax rate reduction, an increase in government spending, or a reduction in autonomous net taxes, new real income–price level combinations that will maintain a balance budget will lie to the right of the original set of combinations consistent with this objective.

Can Deficits Be Self-Correcting? Money Financing versus Bond Financing

Combining the *BB* schedule with aggregate demand and supply schedules can help us to determine how deficits might be eliminated. Of course, we know from earlier chapters that various theories have their own views on the shapes of the aggregate demand and aggregate supply schedules. Nevertheless, the traditional and modern

Keynesian theories, the monetarist theory, and the new classical theory all indicate that in the short run at least, the aggregate demand schedule slopes downward and that its position may depend to some extent on fiscal policy actions. These theories also agree that the short-run aggregate supply schedule slopes upward. Hence, the schedules are drawn under these assumptions in panel (a) of Figure 12–12. We assume that initially these schedules cross at point A along the BB schedule, so that the government's budget is balanced. Now let's consider what will happen if the government increases its expenditures from g_1 to a larger amount, g_2. This causes the BB schedule to shift rightward, from $BB(g_1)$ to $BB(g_2)$.

MONEY-FINANCED DEFICIT A government budget deficit that the government finances by selling its bonds to the central bank, which creates new money balances to purchase the bonds.

In Figure 12–12, we consider what happens in the case of a **money-financed deficit.** In this situation, a government finances its deficit by inducing the nation's central bank to purchase the bonds that the government issues to finance its deficit spending. The central bank must create additional money to buy the bonds, thereby causing a rise in the total quantity of money, from an initial value M_1 to a larger value M_2. Together with the rise in government spending (at least, according to most theories), the increase in the quantity of money will cause a short-run rise in aggregate demand and will result in a new equilibrium point B (in the new classical and modern Keynesian theories, point B will result if the policy action was unanticipated). Although the price level and real income will increase, point B lies to the left of the $BB(g_2)$ schedule in panel (a), so the government will run a budget deficit for a time, as shown in panel (b).

In the long run, however, people will raise their price and inflation expectations as they recognize the inflationary effects of the expansionary fiscal and monetary policy actions (see Chapter 8). This will cause the aggregate supply schedule to shift leftward, leading to a long-run equilibrium at point C, where real income is unchanged but the price level is higher, at P_3. We have also assumed that point C is on the new BB schedule, hence the government's budget is balanced again. Therefore, after some more time passes the real deficit ultimately returns to zero once again in panel (b). This need not occur, but our point is that the increase in the price level, from P_1 to P_2 in the short run and then from P_2 to P_3 in the long run, will tend to push the government's budget back toward balance without any need for the government to reduce its spending or raise autonomous taxes or the income tax rate.

From a government's perspective, therefore, money-financed deficits have the "virtue" of "inflating away" the real value of nominal interest and principal payments on any existing government debt. Inflation is only a virtue in this very limited sense, of course. Nevertheless, the example in Figure 12–12 helps to explain why so many governments fall into the trap of relying on money-financed deficits—and then must live with the inflationary consequences. Countries around the world, including Germany in the 1920s, Hungary in the 1940s, Israel in the 1970s, most South American countries during the 1970s and 1980s, Russia in the 1990s, and even the U.S. colonies in their first years of independence in the 1770s, have fallen into this trap of substituting one problem for another.

FIGURE 12–12 **BALANCING THE BUDGET WHEN DEFICITS ARE MONEY FINANCED**

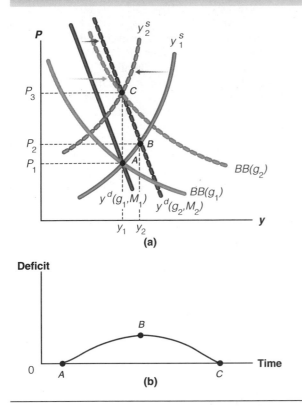

(a)

(b)

At point A in panel (a), the market for real output is in equilibrium on the BB schedule, so the government's budget is balanced, given its current expenditures, interest payments on its debt, net autonomous taxes, and income tax rate. Hence, panel (b) indicates a zero deficit at point A. A rise in government spending financed by an expansion in the quantity of money induces a short-run rise in the equilibrium price level and in equilibrium real output in panel (a). At the same time, however, the increase in government spending shifts the BB schedule rightward in panel (a), so the government will experience a budget deficit at point B, as shown in panel (b). Ultimately, higher price expectations cause the aggregate supply schedule to shift leftward, returning output to y_1, at point C in panel (a). This point could, in principle, lie along the new BB schedule, yielding a balanced budget at point C in panel (b).

BOND-FINANCED DEFICIT A government budget deficit that the government finances by issuing new bonds to private individuals and organizations.

Figure 12–13 on page 420 considers an alternative example, in which new spending by the government creates a **bond-financed deficit.** In this case, the deficit is financed solely by issuing new bonds to private individuals and organizations, so the central bank is not obliged to increase the quantity of money. As shown in panel (a), a rise in government spending again will cause the BB schedule to shift rightward, to $BB(g_2, B_1)$, where B_1 denotes the initial amount of bonds issued by the government. The rise in government spending will also cause an increase in aggregate demand, from $y^d(g_1)$ to $y^d(g_2)$, although by less than in the case of money-financed deficit spending because the money stock remains unchanged with a bond-financed deficit. Consequently, at short-run equilibrium at point B the government will experience a larger deficit in panel (b) of Figure 12–13, than in the case of the money-financed deficit that we show in panel (b) of Figure 12–12.

Once again, in the long run price expectations will rise, and the aggregate supply schedule will shift leftward, from y_1^s to y_2^s, yielding a final long-run equilibrium at point C in panel (a). In the absence of a rise in the money stock, however, the price level will rise by a smaller amount with bond-financed deficit spending. Conse-

FIGURE 12–13   BOND-FINANCED DEFICIT SPENDING

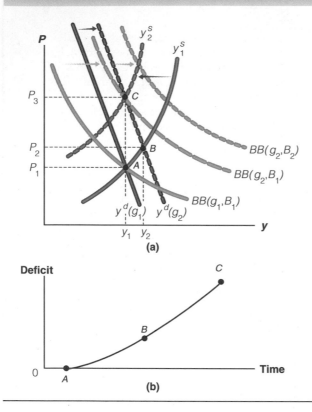

At point A in panel (a), the market for real output is in equilibrium on the BB schedule, so the government's budget is balanced. Therefore, panel (b) shows a zero deficit at point A. An increase in government spending financed by issuing bonds to private individuals causes a short-run rise in the equilibrium price level and in equilibrium real output in panel (a). The increase in government spending also shifts the BB schedule rightward to $BB(g_2, B_1)$ in panel (a), so the government will experience a budget deficit at point B, as shown in panel (b). Ultimately, higher price expectations will cause the aggregate supply schedule to shift leftward, returning output to y_1, at point C in panel (a). At the same time, however, the rise in interest payments on the newly issued government debt will cause a further rightward shift of the BB schedule, to $BB(g_2, B_2)$. Thus, the government deficit could be higher at point C, as shown in panel (b).

quently, point C is more likely to continue to lie to the left of $BB(g_2, B_1)$, so that a deficit will continue. Furthermore, because the government has relied solely on issuing bonds to private individuals and organizations, in the long run the nominal value of interest and principal payments will rise from an initial amount B_1 to a larger amount B_2. This will shift the BB schedule to $BB(g_2, B_2)$, which, can lead to an even higher deficit at point C than at point B, as panel (b) shows.

This example shows that relying primarily on bond-financed deficits makes it more likely that deficits will perpetuate over time. Ultimately, bond financing of deficits pressures governments to reduce spending or to raise taxes if they really desire to return to a balanced-budget environment. Most governments around the world in the past have financed deficits both by issuing bonds and by creating money. As we shall discuss in Chapter 13, however, there has been a recent trend toward granting central banks greater independence from governments. If this trend continues, we should anticipate that in the future governments will rely increasingly on bond-financed deficit spending. If so, governments that really wish to reduce their deficits will probably be more likely to make the politically difficult choices about spending cuts or tax increases more readily than they might have in the past. If they do not, they will have to rely upon real growth in their economies to spur sufficient additional tax revenues to close their deficit gaps.

FUNDAMENTAL ISSUE #4

Why might a government desire to reduce its budget deficit, and how might it accomplish this goal? Persistent government budget deficits add to the national debt, which can be a burden for future generations. In addition, government budget deficits can crowd out private spending and contribute to trade and private payments deficits in a nation's balance of payments. Although a nation's deficits in principle can be self-correcting if they are financed by the nation's central bank, the required creation of new money can have inflationary consequences. Bond financing of deficits via sales of government debt to private individuals and organizations ultimately forces governments to reduce their spending if they truly desire to reduce their budget deficits.

AIMING MONETARY AND FISCAL POLICIES AT THE DOMESTIC AND INTERNATIONAL OBJECTIVES: THE ASSIGNMENT PROBLEM

If a nation has an open economy and engages in significant trade with other nations, international considerations may affect its ability to achieve its ultimate inflation, output, and employment goals. In addition, many citizens may perceive that international variables themselves—such as the nation's merchandise trade balance or its private payments balance—should be ultimate policy goals. Consequently, monetary and fiscal policymakers in open economies typically face pressures to take international objectives into account as they contemplate the appropriate policy strategies to pursue.

Do International Factors Matter for Domestic Well-Being?

Why would individuals and firms in open economies want policymakers to pursue international objectives? One reason is that international factors may play a role in determining domestic goals. Another is that a number of workers and businesses may have a direct stake in the international sector of the economy.

International Objectives and Domestic Goals   Recall from Chapter 5 that two determinants of a nation's aggregate desired expenditures are export spending on the nation's output of goods and services by residents of foreign countries and import expenditures on foreign-produced goods and services by the nation's own citizens. A rise in export spending increases aggregate desired expenditures. In contrast, a rise in import spending reduces the portion of disposable income available for domestic consumption. Hence, both of these international factors influence the position of the nation's *IS* schedule, thereby affecting aggregate demand, the equilibrium price level and, potentially, short-run equilibrium real output and employment.

As a result, macroeconomic policymakers in an open economy must take exports and imports into consideration in their policymaking. If nothing else, policymakers must recognize that trade-related expenditures are likely to have an influence on aggregate demand that is separate from purely domestic influences. More broadly, however, policymakers may conclude that attaining their ultimate domestic objectives may require a "balancing" of international factors. For instance, the policymakers may seek to achieve balanced merchandise trade or a private payments balance equal to zero as a means of achieving their domestic inflation, output, and employment goals.

International Objectives as Ultimate Goals   In some nations, however, international objectives may be regarded as ultimate goals in and of themselves. For example, workers and firms in industries that rely on foreign purchases of the goods and services they produce may pressure their governments to pursue policies that promote exports. In addition, workers and firms in industries that depend on domestic purchases of their output may push central banks and government officials to enact policies that restrain imports. Such efforts by both types of interest groups could lead a nation's policymakers to seek merchandise trade and private payments *surpluses* as ultimate policy objectives.

Throughout history, nations have aimed for surpluses in their balance of payments accounts. In the seventeenth and eighteenth centuries, for instance, many British citizens advocated a policy of **mercantilism,** which is the idea that a key source of a nation's wealth is international trade and commerce. Key policy goals of the British mercantilists were to promote exports and to hinder exports. Of course, a fundamental problem with mercantilism is that if all nations seek trade and payments surpluses by limiting imports, international trade ultimately may come to a halt. Recognition of this fact led to the decline of mercantilism in the nineteenth century and greater emphasis on free trade among nations. Nevertheless, mercantilist arguments support the goals of various special interest groups, so they often emerge as political party planks or even as features of public policy. At a minimum, groups with international interests commonly exert pressures on policymakers to maintain trade and payments balances, if not surpluses.

MERCANTILISM The idea that a primary determinant of a nation's wealth is international trade and commerce, so that a nation can gain by enacting policies that spur exports while limiting imports.

Finding the Best Policy Mix for Internal and External Balance

Perhaps because they recognize that international factors influence domestic goals or because they face political pressures from mercantilist advocates, monetary and fiscal policymakers commonly express interest in attaining international objectives. Once they commit themselves to achieving international goals, however, policymakers confront a fundamental problem: Domestic and international objectives sometimes conflict. For instance, a cut in the tax rate may be an appropriate fiscal policy action to spur growth in a nation's real income, yet this tax cut could spur import spending and raise the merchandise trade deficit. Reducing money growth may be the best policy for a central bank to pursue to restrain inflation, but the interest-rate reduction that results may cause capital to flow out of the country, thereby causing a private payments deficit.

In principle, the solution to this potential conflict seems straightforward. After all, there are two policymakers: a central bank and a governmental fiscal authority. Similarly, there are two basic types of goals that they might pursue: international objectives and domestic objectives. Why not just assign one set of goals to the central bank and the other set to the fiscal policymaker?

Indeed, this division of goals is a possible solution to conflicts that can emerge between international and domestic goals. Nevertheless, a problem remains: Which policymaker should take responsibility for achieving which objectives? Should the central bank concentrate on the nation's real output goals while the government focuses on the private payments balance, or should the assignments be reversed? This question is known as the **assignment problem** in policymaking. Let's consider how the problem might be addressed in various circumstances that a nation with an open economy might face.

ASSIGNMENT PROBLEM The problem of determining whether monetary or fiscal policymakers should assume responsibility for achieving external balance or internal balance objectives.

The Policy Assignment Problem with Low Capital Mobility   As we discussed in Chapter 7, a key factor influencing how fiscal policies affect a nation's private payments balance is the extent to which capital is mobile. Recall that when barriers such as capital controls inhibit flows of financial resources across a nation's borders, the balance of payments, *BP*, schedule of real income–interest rate combinations that maintain a private payments balance of zero is relatively less elastic in the relevant range as compared with the *LM* schedule, as shown in panels (a) and (b) of Figure 12–14 on page 424. Each panel also displays the same initial *IS-LM* equilibrium point, denoted point *A*, which is below and to the right of the *BP* schedule, so that the nation experiences a private payments deficit. At point *A* in both panels, the interest rate is too low, at r_1, to induce capital inflows sufficient to overcome the sizable barriers to such flows, and real income is sufficiently high, at y_1, that import spending exceeds exports and generates a trade deficit.

Let's suppose that the country's exchange rate is fixed, at least in the near term, so that the *BP* schedule is stationary. In addition, let's consider a situation in which the

FIGURE 12–14 ACHIEVING INTERNAL AND EXTERNAL BALANCE WITH LOW CAPITAL MOBILITY

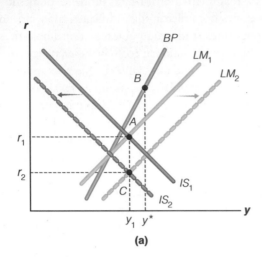 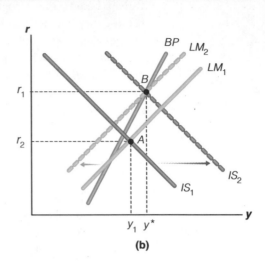

(a)   (b)

If capital is relatively immobile, then the *BP* schedule giving real income–interest rate combinations consistent with a private payments balance of zero is relatively steeply sloped. Both panels (a) and (b) illustrate the same initial equilibrium at point *A*, which lies below and to the right of the *BP* schedule, implying a private payments deficit. In panel (a), the central bank tries to attain internal balance by aiming to achieve a target level of real income, y^*, which requires a rightward shift of the *LM* schedule. At the same time, the government's fiscal authority aims to achieve external balance along the *BP* schedule, which requires a leftward shift of the *IS* schedule. The net result

illustrated in this figure is a new equilibrium at point *C* even farther below and to the right of the *BP* schedule, implying a greater private payments deficit. Hence, there is a mismatched assignment of internal and external balance objectives in panel (a). Panel (b) illustrates the result of a correct policy assignment: the central bank aims to achieve external balance at point *A* by shifting the *LM* schedule leftward at the same time, the government's fiscal authority shifts the *IS* schedule rightward. This assignment achieves point *B*. Here, the policymakers achieve both their internal and external balance objectives.

nation's policymakers have two goals. One is to achieve a zero private payments balance, which will require attaining an *IS-LM* equilibrium point on the *BP* schedule. This goal is the nation's international, or *external balance,* objective. The other goal is to achieve a target real income level, denoted y^*. This is the nation's domestic, or *internal balance,* objective. The issue that the country's policymakers face at point *A* is how to achieve both these objectives simultaneously. Doing so will entail attaining a new *IS-LM* equilibrium at point *B* in each panel.

To see why the assignment of domestic and international objectives to the appropriate policymaker is so important, consider the contrasting assignments illustrated in panels (a) and (b). In panel (a), the central bank aims to achieve internal balance by varying the quantity of money as needed to attain the real income objective, while the government conducts fiscal policies that are necessary to pursue the external balance objective of a zero private payments balance. With this policy assignment, the appropriate monetary policy action to aim for the real income target y^* is an increase in the nominal money stock. This action shifts the *LM* schedule rightward, to LM_2. At the same time, however, the appropriate fiscal policy action at point *A* is to reduce government expenditures or raise taxes, thereby causing the *IS* schedule to shift leftward to IS_2. This action reduces equilibrium real income, thereby restraining imports. The resulting *IS-LM* equilibrium is a real income–interest rate combination such as y_1 and r_2 at point *C* in panel (a). Yet point *C* could be even farther below the *BP* schedule than point *A* with no net increase in real income. Thus, the nation's private payments deficit problem will *worsen* even as it experiences no progress in moving toward attaining its internal balance objective.

Clearly, panel (a) illustrates a situation in which the monetary and fiscal policymakers have been assigned the *wrong goals*. As a result, their efforts to pursue their individual objectives push the economy *away* from those goals. Panel (b) shows what happens if the assignment of objectives is reversed, so that the central bank strives to achieve external balance while the government's fiscal authority seeks to attain internal balance. To aim for external balance, the central bank needs to reduce the money stock and shift the *LM* schedule leftward. The fiscal authority needs to increase its spending or cut taxes, thereby shifting the *IS* schedule rightward and raising equilibrium real income toward the target level. This combination of policy objectives and actions enables the policymakers to attain *both* internal balance *and* external balance at point *B* in panel (b).

The Policy Assignment Problem with Highly Mobile Capital   It will be tempting to conclude from the previous example that there is a single solution to the assignment problem, namely, that the government should aim its fiscal policies at an internal balance objective while the central bank strives to achieve external balance. Unfortunately, this assignment is likely to be correct only in the situation we considered in Figure 12–14, in which the exchange rate is fixed and there is low capital mobility. If we alter either of these background conditions, the nature of the assignment problem will change.

To see this, consider Figure 12–15. In both panel (a) and panel (b), the *BP* schedule is much more elastic in the relevant range than it was in Figure 12–14, indicating that capital is highly mobile across the nation's borders. Again, point *A* in both panels depicts an initial situation in which there is a private payments deficit and real income is below its target level. Panel (a) shows a possible result of assigning the external balance objective to the central bank and the internal balance objective to the government when capital is highly mobile. The central bank reduces the money stock, which raises the equilibrium interest rate and induces capital inflows that improve the private payments balance. Then the government increases its spending or cuts taxes in an effort to raise equilibrium real income. The resulting *IS-LM* equilibrium will depend on the shapes of the *IS* and *LM* schedules and on the extent to which the policy actions shift those schedules, but a *possible* result is point *C* in panel (a). At this

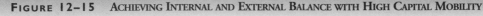

FIGURE 12–15 ACHIEVING INTERNAL AND EXTERNAL BALANCE WITH HIGH CAPITAL MOBILITY

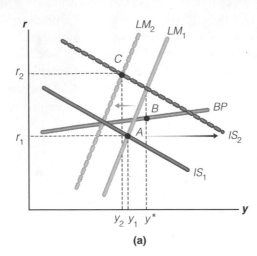

(a)

(b)

Both panels (a) and (b) illustrate the same initial equilibrium at point *A,* which lies below and to the right of the *BP* schedule, implying a private payments deficit. In panel (a), the central bank tries to attain external balance, which requires a leftward shift of the *LM* schedule toward the *BP* schedule. At the same time, the government's fiscal authority tries to achieve internal balance by aiming at a target level of real income, y^*. This requires a rightward shift of the *IS* schedule. The net result illustrated in this figure is a new equilibrium at the same real output level but at point *C* above and to the left

of the *BP* schedule, yielding a private payments surplus. Hence, there is a mismatched assignment of internal and external balance objectives in panel (a). Panel (b) illustrates the result of a correct policy assignment. Here, the central bank aims to achieve internal balance by shifting the *LM* schedule rightward toward y^* while the government's fiscal authority shifts the *IS* schedule rightward in pursuit of external balance along the *BP* schedule. This assignment achieves point *B,* at which the policymakers achieve both their internal and external balance objectives.

possible equilibrium point, the nation experiences a private payments surplus, and real income is lower than before. The policymakers did not achieve their objectives. Thus, the correct policy assignment when capital mobility is low could turn out to be the incorrect assignment when capital mobility is high.

Panel (b) shows what could happen if the policy assignments are reversed, so that the central bank seeks to attain internal balance while the government strives to achieve external balance when there is high capital mobility. To raise equilibrium real income, the central bank increases the money stock and shifts the *LM* schedule rightward. At the same time, the government increases its spending or cuts taxes. This shifts the *IS* schedule rightward, raising the equilibrium interest rate and stimulating more capital inflows that will improve the private payments balance. Thus, after this reassignment of policy goals, the nation's internal and external balance objectives could be attained at point *B.*

The assignment of policy objectives is not a trivial issue, as the examples in Figures 12–14 and 12–15 indicate. These examples illustrate that the degree of capital mobility is an important consideration in assigning goals to policymakers. Nevertheless, in both examples we assumed a fixed exchange rate. As you can imagine, allowing for the possibility of a floating exchange rate would further complicate the policy assignment problem. This is why disagreements are not uncommon between a central bank, such as the Federal Reserve, and a government fiscal agency, such as the U.S. Treasury (under the direction of the president and Congress), over which policymaker should be focusing on which objectives. Changing macroeconomic circumstances can necessitate changes in the appropriate assignment of policy objectives, and both policymakers may take time to recognize this and agree to an alteration of the goals upon which they should focus their attention.

FUNDAMENTAL ISSUE #5

What is the assignment problem faced by monetary and fiscal policymakers of a nation that seeks to attain both domestic and international policy goals? The assignment problem refers to the difficulty of ascertaining whether a monetary or fiscal policymaker should pursue an internal balance objective such as a real income target or an external balance objective such as a zero private payments balance. An incorrect assignment of these objectives between a central bank and a government fiscal authority can lead to greater departures from external and internal balance goals. To obtain a correct assignment of objectives that can permit both policymakers to achieve these goals simultaneously, the policymakers must take into account the extent to which capital is mobile and whether the exchange rate is fixed or flexible. Consequently, solving the assignment problem is a potentially complicated undertaking.

CHAPTER SUMMARY

1. **The Ultimate Goals of Macroeconomic Policy:** These are the final aims of the policy strategies and actions conducted by the government fiscal authority or central bank. In the United States, the Employment Act of 1946 and the Humphrey-Hawkins Act of 1978 established low and stable inflation, high and stable output growth, and high and stable employment as formal ultimate objectives of macroeconomic policy.

2. **Why a Central Bank Might Use an Intermediate Monetary Policy Target:** A central bank such as the Federal Reserve typically adopts an intermediate target because it faces

limitations on the availability of data on its ultimate objectives and different views about how monetary policy actions influence these ultimate policy goals. Any intermediate target for monetary policy should be a macroeconomic variable that can be observed more frequently than ultimate goal variables. In addition, this variable should be easy to measure, controllable via monetary policy actions, and closely related to ultimate policy objectives. The menu of possible intermediate target variables includes money and credit aggregates, interest rates, and nominal GDP.

3. **The Pros and Cons of Alternative Intermediate Monetary Policy Targets:** On the one hand, adopting a nominal interest rate target makes aggregate demand more stable when money demand is highly volatile while aggregate desired expenditures are relatively stable. On the other hand, using a monetary aggregate as an intermediate target stabilizes aggregate demand when aggregate desired expenditures are variable while money demand is relatively stable. Nominal GDP targeting automatically stabilizes aggregate demand and also minimizes the inflationary effects of variations in aggregate supply. Nevertheless, accurate nominal GDP data are available less frequently than data on interest rates and monetary aggregates.

4. **Why a Government Might Desire to Reduce Its Budget Deficit, and How It Might Accomplish This Goal:** Continually running government budget deficits adds to the accumulated national debt. This can be a burden for future generations. Furthermore, government budget deficits can crowd out private investment and can also worsen international trade and private payments deficits. In theory, a government's deficit can be self-correcting if it is financed by a central bank. Nevertheless, the creation of new money to purchase government debt increases the inflation rate. In the long run, bond financing of deficits via sales of government debt to private individuals and organizations places pressure on a government to reduce its spending if it is serious about reducing its deficit.

5. **The Assignment Problem Faced by Monetary and Fiscal Policymakers of a Nation That Seeks to Attain Both Domestic and International Policy Goals:** The assignment problem is the question of whether a monetary or fiscal policymaker should concentrate on achieving an internal balance objective such as a real income target or an external balance objective such as a zero private payments balance. Incorrectly assigning these objectives between the central bank and the government fiscal authority can cause both policymakers to end up further away from both goals. Achieving a correct assignment of objectives requires that policymakers consider the extent to which capital is mobile and whether the exchange rate is fixed or flexible. As a result, solving the assignment problem is a potentially complex task.

 # QUESTIONS AND PROBLEMS

1 From a day-to-day perspective, what is the primary way that the Federal Reserve conducts monetary policy? Why is this the case? Explain.

2. Briefly discuss the rationales for a central bank's adoption of an intermediate target. Which do you think is more important? Explain your reasoning.

3. List the key criteria for choosing among alternative intermediate targets of monetary policy. Does any one of these seem to be more important than the others? Why?

4. Suppose that household consumption spending and investment expenditures by firms are highly volatile, as compared with past years. At the same time, financial market conditions and desired money holdings by households and firms have been relatively stable. If you were in charge at the Fed and wanted to choose between targeting an interest rate or a monetary aggregate, which will you choose? Why?

5. What are the key advantages of using nominal GDP as an intermediate target of monetary policy? What are the disadvantages? Explain.

6. How can the national debt be a burden on future generations? Is it *necessarily* a burden? Justify your answer.

7. A "stock" is an amount at a point in time, while a "flow" is an addition to a stock that takes place over time. Is the national debt a stock or a flow? What about the federal deficit?

8. What is the mechanism by which a deficit potentially can be self-correcting when it is money financed? Is there any drawback to this approach to financing deficits?

9. Assuming that a nation chooses not to "money finance" a deficit, what options does its government face in trying to eliminate an existing deficit? Explain.

10. In your own words, explain the basic issue associated with the assignment problem. Why is solving this problem important?

CYBERTUTOR EXERCISES

1. Suppose that the government knows that, due to a sudden fall in consumer confidence, there will be a shock to aggregate desired expenditures. In anticipation of this shock, should the central bank fix the money stock or the nominal interest rate?

2. Suppose, instead, that there are only money demand disturbances. What is the optimal monetary policy?

3. Figure 12–9 in the text shows the U.S. net national debt as a percentage of GDP. Construct comparable variables for Japan and France and add their time series to this graph. How do these countries' experiences differ from the American experience?

4. Consider figure 12–10 in the text. How has the share of U.S. national debt held by citizens of other nations been changing over time? In you view, are there any problems associated with this? If so, what are those problems?

ON-LINE APPLICATION

This chapter provided a brief overview of how the Federal Reserve conducts monetary policy. This application allows you to obtain more information about the Federal Reserve's policy tools and procedures.

Internet URL: http://www.frbsf.org/system/econinfo/inbrief/guides.html

Title: How the Fed Guides Monetary Policy

Navigation: Begin at the homepage of the Federal Reserve Bank of San Francisco (http://www.frbsf.org). If this does not directly route you to the FedWest GateWay page, click on that link. Then, click on *Central Banking.* Next, click on *The Federal Reserve System,* followed by *The Fed in Brief.* Then, click on *How the Fed Guides Monetary Policy.*

Application: Read the article, and answer the following questions:

1. What three tools can the Fed use to conduct monetary policy? Which of these is most important on a day-to-day basis?

2. What is the Federal Open Market Committee's (FOMC's) role in the determination of the Fed's monetary policy actions? How could the FOMC increase the quantity of money, holding reserve requirements and the discount rate unchanged?

SELECTED REFERENCES AND FURTHER READING

Blejer, Mario, and Adrienne Cheasty. "The Measurement of Fiscal Deficits: Analytical and Methodological Issues." *Journal of Economic Literature* 39 (December 1991):1644–1678.

Blinder, Alan, and Robert Solow, "Does Fiscal Policy Matter?" *Journal of Public Economics* 2 (1973): 319–337.

Bradley, Michael, and Dennis Jansen. "Understanding Nominal GNP Targeting." Federal Reserve Bank of St. Louis *Review,* November/December 1989, pp. 31–40.

Caves, Richard, Jeffrey Frankel, and Ronald Jones. *World Trade and Payments: An Introduction.* 7th ed. Reading, Mass.: Addison-Wesley, 1996.

Federal Reserve Bank of Kansas City. *Achieving Price Stability.* Kansas City, Mo.: 1996.

Federal Reserve Bank of Kansas City. *Budget Deficits and Debt: Issues and Options.* Kansas City, Mo.: 1995.

Federal Reserve Bank of New York. *Intermediate Targets and Indicators for Monetary Policy: A Critical Survey.* New York: 1990.

Fischer, Stanley. "Toward an Understanding of the Costs of Inflation: II." In Stanley Fischer, ed., *Indexing, Inflation, and Economic Policy,* pp. 35–69. Cambridge, Mass.: MIT Press, 1986.

Fischer, Stanley, and Franco Modigliani. "Toward an Understanding of the Real Effects and Costs of Inflation." In Stanley Fischer, ed. *Indexing, Inflation, and Economic Policy,* pp. 7–33. Cambridge, Mass.: MIT Press, 1986.

Friedman, Benjamin. "Targets, Instruments, and Indicators of Monetary Policy." *Journal of Monetary Economics* 1 (October 1975): 443–473.

Poole, William. "Optimal Choice of Monetary Policy Instruments in a Simple Stochastic Macro Model." *Quarterly Journal of Economics* 84 (May 1970): 197–216.

13

What Can Policymakers Accomplish?

RULES VERSUS DISCRETION IN MACROECONOMIC POLICY

FUNDAMENTAL ISSUES

1. What are policy time lags, and how might they cause well-meaning macroeconomic policymakers to destabilize the economy?

2. What are the main arguments favoring discretionary policymaking?

3. Why is policy credibility a crucial factor in maintaining low inflation?

4. How might monetary policy credibility be achieved?

5. How might fiscal policy credibility be achieved?

6. What approaches have some nations with fixed exchange rates followed to make their policies credible?

The room is large but not too large. Members of the Congressional Oversight Committee sit at a long table at the front of the room. Each member has a microphone. In front of the long table is a smaller one with only one microphone. The rest of the room is filled with spectators. Sitting at the small table is

Alan Greenspan, chair of the Fed. He doesn't like these public appearances, but he doesn't have a choice. As a matter of law, the chair of the Fed must appear before the committee to explain what the Fed's objectives have been and how well the Fed has fulfilled them.

The press follows Greenspan's every word. Many try to extract some indication of what the Fed will do in the future. Meanwhile, the members of the committee are probably still trying to figure out what happened during the past six months. Usually, they are unable to get a clear statement from Greenspan—he is, after all, the master of obfuscation.

Some people believe that this semiannual testimony before Congress should be abolished. Some critics believe that the Fed chair should not have to explain anything, because the Fed should not engage in any discretionary monetary policy. These critics favor a monetary rule, under which a computer could be used to set a steady state of growth in the money supply. Other critics believe that the Fed should be completely independent and should not have to answer to Congress at all. Under current law, however, these critics notwithstanding, the Fed does have to set objectives and targets for its monetary policy and present them to Congress.

In this chapter we shall examine the arguments in favor of discretionary policy, both monetary and fiscal, as well as the arguments in favor of monetary rules, under which there would be no discretionary policy. In addition, we shall look at how nations with fixed exchange rates can make their policies credible.

In Chapter 12, we surveyed the various ultimate and intermediate objectives that monetary and fiscal policymakers may seek to achieve. We also discussed how they might seek to achieve those goals. As we noted in our discussion of intermediate monetary targets, one important hindrance to successful attainment of ultimate policy goals is the existence of information lags. A related problem that we shall consider in this chapter is the time that policymakers themselves take to adjust their policies in response to changing circumstances. This lag forces policymakers to decide whether they should alter their policies each time a short-term macroeconomic event occurs or maintain the policy that they believe has the best chance of achieving their goals over a longer horizon.

This choice between reacting to short-term changes in circumstances or sticking with a longer-term policy commitment can have critical consequences. For this reason, we shall devote this chapter to evaluating the trade-offs that central banks and governments face when deciding which approach to pursue.

TIME LAGS IN POLICYMAKING AND THE CASE FOR RULES

POLICY TIME LAG The time interval between the need for a countercyclical monetary policy action and the ultimate effects of that action on an economic variable.

A fundamental problem faced by any policymaker, be it the president of the United States, the Congress, the Federal Reserve, a public utility, or a college's board of trustees, is the existence of **policy time lags.** A policy time lag is the interval between the need for a policy action and the ultimate effects of that action on an economic variable. Any policymaker faces three types of constraints on its ability to make the best policy choices that it can as quickly as these choices should be made:

1. At any given time, policymakers face limited information about current events, particularly in the presence of time lags.
2. Policymakers are fallible and face constraints on their abilities to recognize and respond appropriately to changing circumstances, particularly in light of lags in their recognition of varying circumstances.
3. Policymakers are constrained by their lack of certainty about the actual effects of the policies they may enact and the timing of those effects.

Together, these constraints can slow policymakers' responses even in situations when speedy reactions are needed to attain the policymakers' goals.

Time Lags in Macroeconomic Policy

Macroeconomic policymaking involves three types of time lags: the *recognition lag,* the *response lag,* and the *transmission lag.* Let's discuss each in turn before considering their broader consequences.

The Recognition Lag   A key problem that fiscal and monetary policymakers confront as they pursue their ultimate inflation, output, employment, and balance of payments objectives is limited current information. Although government statisticians can estimate nominal GDP data weekly, they can compile data on GDP, the unemployment rate, the price level, and international transactions only monthly. Even then, the statisticians often revise these monthly computations when they discover measurement or calculation errors. Although the statisticians try to make their data as reliable as possible, computations of annualized GDP growth rates for certain quarters have had to be revised by more than 50 percent! Hence, policymakers cannot always rely on the accuracy of initial values for these macroeconomic goal variables.

Near-term data uncertainties complicate the lives of policymakers. To see why, suppose that a nation's inflation rate increases substantially owing to an unexpected rise in aggregate demand. Other things unchanged, an appropriate central bank response would be to cut back on the growth rate of the money stock. This action would help to curtail the rise in aggregate demand and alleviate resulting upward price pressures. In light of data limitations, however, central bank officials might not realize that inflation had started to rise until a number of weeks had passed.

The time between the need for a macroeconomic policy action and policymakers' recognition of that need is called the **recognition lag.** Sometimes the recognition lag is only a matter of a few weeks, but it can be longer. For instance, suppose that central bank officials notice the rise in the inflation rate, but are uncertain of its causes. Some officials might speculate that recent but temporary upticks in wage costs of businesses might be responsible, indicating no need for the central bank to take action. Misleading signals such as this might delay central bank action to contain inflation for several additional weeks. Consequently, the recognition lag could easily increase from a few weeks to a few months. This is true for both fiscal and monetary policy.

The Response Lag   Even after policymakers reach the conclusion that altered macroeconomic circumstances require a policy change, they may not decide on the appropriate action to take for some time. The **response lag** is the time between the recognition of the need for a change in macroeconomic policy and the actual implementation of that change.

In the United States, the response lag for monetary policy should never be more than six to eight weeks, because this is the typical interlude between formal meetings of Federal Reserve policymakers. In fact, the response lag for U.S. monetary policy could be shorter than this, because Federal Reserve officials across the nation communicate daily. The monetary policy response lag could be longer, however, if central bank officials have difficulty reaching a consensus on the best policy to implement. Faced with an observed rise in the inflation rate, for instance, some officials might contend that a swift, significant response is needed. Other officials, in contrast, might argue for a more gradual, measured response. Such disagreements could lead to delays in central bank policy actions, which could lengthen the monetary policy response lag significantly.

The response lag is often even longer for fiscal policy. In the United States, for instance, the executive office of the president and a majority of the 535 representatives and senators in the legislative branch must reach agreement on changes in the federal budget intended to address a given situation. This can be a laborious task that can take many months. Indeed, political gridlock can inhibit fiscal policy actions for years. Consequently, the response lag is typically much longer for fiscal policy than for monetary policy.

The Transmission Lag   It takes time for a fiscal or monetary policy action to transmit its effects to overall economic activity. The time that passes before an implemented policy fully exerts its macroeconomic effects is the **transmission lag.** In earlier chapters, we have shifted schedules and envisioned the effects of a particular policy action on real income or the price level without regard to the time that it takes for such effects actually to occur. In fact, months or even years may pass before the

---

RECOGNITION LAG The interval between the need for a countercyclical policy action and the recognition of this need by a policymaker.

RESPONSE LAG The interval between the recognition of a need for a countercyclical policy action and the actual implementation of that action.

TRANSMISSION LAG The interval that elapses between the implementation of an intended countercyclical policy and its ultimate effects on an economic variable.

effects of policy actions are transmitted to ultimate policy goal variables. Current estimates indicate, for instance, that the average monetary policy transmission lag is just over twelve months. Thus, together the recognition, response, and transmission lags could cause well over a year to elapse between the initial need for a monetary policy action and that action's final effects on the economy. Given the longer response lags that are common in fiscal policy implementation—sometimes several years—time lags of fiscal policy could be even longer.

Time Lags and the Case for Policy Rules

Time lags can pose a real problem for macroeconomic policymakers. To see why, consider Figure 13–1. The curve labeled y^a in panel (a) shows the path that real income will follow in the *absence* of any policy actions. For simplicity, we assume that the

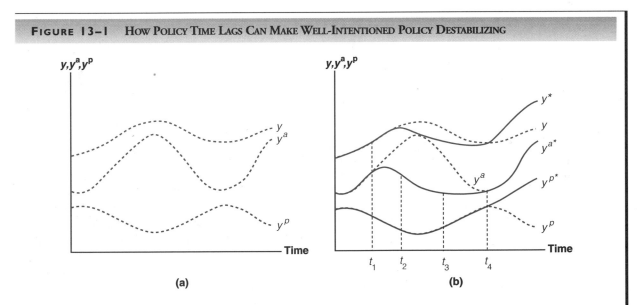

FIGURE 13–1   HOW POLICY TIME LAGS CAN MAKE WELL-INTENTIONED POLICY DESTABILIZING

(a)

(b)

Panel (a) illustrates a possible situation in which policy actions help to stabilize real income over time. The path labeled y^a illustrates a hypothetical anticipated path for real income in the absence of policy actions. The path labeled y^p shows a planned countercyclical path for contributions to real income based on macroeconomic policy, which causes the path of total real income, y, to be smoother than it would have been otherwise. Panel (b) shows the potential result of policy time lags. Here, the path of actual real income in the absence of policy, y^{a*},

falls below the path anticipated by the policymaker, y^a, beginning at time t_1. Because of the recognition lag, however, the policymaker fails to discover this has occurred until time t_2. The response lag slows the policymaker's response to this change until time t_3, and the transmission lag holds up the actual effects of the policy action until time t_4. By this time, the new policy contributions to real income are procyclical and destabilizing.

anticipated path of real income is a relatively smooth business cycle. The curve labeled y^p depicts the path of the policymaker's *planned* contributions to real income in light of its anticipation that real income in the absence of its policy actions will follow the path y^a.

Successful Countercyclical Policy   We assume that the policymaker's plan is to pursue a *countercyclical* policy strategy by adding to its contributions to real income when the policymaker anticipates that real income will decline. Conversely, the policymaker will reduce its contributions to real income when it expects real income to rise.

At any given time, the actual level of real income in the presence of policy actions, denoted y, will be the sum of y^a and y^p. Note that the figure assumes that macroeconomic policymaking can add permanently to total real income. As we have discussed in earlier chapters, not all economists agree that this can take place. Nevertheless, for purposes of illustration, we shall assume here and in other diagrams in this chapter that policy at least makes some permanent contributions. You should keep in mind, however, that according to the new classical and real-business-cycle theories, policy actions can at best cause short-term variations in real income.

If the policymaker successfully pursues its countercyclical policy strategy, the actual path of real income, y, will be smoother than the anticipated real income path in the absence of policy actions, y^a. In other words, the policymaker will successfully dampen the business cycle.

How Time Lags Can Worsen Business Cycles   The same curves shown in panel (a) of Figure 13–1 appear as dashed curves in panel (b). The solid curves, however, depict actual movements in real income that potentially could arise in the presence of policy time lags if the policymaker reacts to unexpected departures of real income from the path originally anticipated. In this example, we assume that the path of real income without any policy effects, labeled y^{a*}, drops below the level that the policymaker had anticipated beginning at a point in time denoted t_1. The path of y^{a*} then stays below its anticipated path until the time t_4, when it again returns to the anticipated path.

The time that passes between t_1 and t_2 is the time interval that elapses before the policymaker realizes that the actual path of real income has fallen below the anticipated path, or the *recognition lag*. At time t_2, the policymaker has no way of knowing that without policy actions real income ultimately will return to its anticipated path at time t_4. If the policymaker wishes to adjust its policy plan in an effort to maintain a countercyclical policy, then at time t_3 it may decide to implement a change in policy intended to contribute more to real income. The time that passes between t_2 and t_3 is the interval between recognition of the need for this policy change and its implementation, or the *response lag*.

Finally, a *transmission lag* occurs between t_3 and t_4 before the policy change begins to have an effect. By time t_4, the policy change finally begins to take effect, and the policy's contribution to real income increases. As a result, the actual path of policy contributions to real income, denoted y^{p*} turns upward, whereas the policymaker's *original* plan called for a reduction in policy contributions to real income beginning at time t_4. At t_4, however, real income in the absence of any policy contribution has already *returned* to its anticipated path. Consequently, the policymaker's well-meaning effort to stabilize actual real income ends up yielding a policy-influenced real income path denoted y^*, which is the sum of the y^{a*} and y^{p*} curves, that is *more variable* than it would have been if the policymaker had not reacted to the temporary fall in real income.

Thus, in this example, even though the policymaker has good intentions to conduct a countercyclical policy:

Time lags in recognition, response, and transmission can end up producing a *procyclical* policy.

The policymaker would have come closer to its original objective of smoothing the business cycle if it had stuck to its original planned policy path, y^p.

Almost fifty years ago, the Nobel Prize–winning economist Milton Friedman argued that situations such as the one illustrated in panel (b) of Figure 13–1 could be common occurrences. The essence of Friedman's argument was that monetary policymakers may have good intentions, but nevertheless their well-meaning attempts to stabilize real income may contribute to cyclical fluctuations in real income. This, Friedman argued, is a fundamental flaw arising from **discretionary policymaking,** or the process of undertaking macroeconomic policy responses on an *ad hoc* basis rather than staying the course with a fixed policy plan. In the presence of lengthy and variable policy time lags, Friedman contended, discretionary policymaking more often than not can end up destabilizing the economy.

This argument led Friedman to propose that a monetary or fiscal policymaker should adopt a **policy rule.** Under this approach, a central bank or government *binds* or *commits* itself to a strategy and follows it no matter what events take place. In Friedman's view, adhering to a clearly articulated policy rule should, on average, prevent unintentional destabilizing actions by policymakers. The simplest type of policy rule is for a policymaker to neither add nor subtract from its contributions to real income. For instance, the central bank could strive to maintain a constant growth rate for the nominal money stock. Another type of policy rule is a tax system that works as an *automatic* stabilizer, as we discussed in Chapter 7. Such a system somewhat offsets a decline or expansion in equilibrium real income by automatically reducing or raising tax collections respectively.

DISCRETIONARY POLICYMAKING The act of responding to economic events as they occur, rather than proceeding as it might previously have planned in the absence of those events.

POLICY RULE A commitment to a fixed strategy no matter what happens to other economic variables.

What are policy time lags, and how might they cause well-meaning macroeconomic policymakers to destabilize the economy? There are three types of policy time lags: (1) the recognition lag, or the time between the need for a macroeconomic policy action and a policymaker's realization of the need; (2) the response lag, or the interval between the recognition of the need for an action and the actual implementation of a policy change; and (3) the transmission lag, or the time from the implementation of a policy action and the action's ultimate effects on the economy. All told, these lags can sum to well over a year in duration. They can also lead a discretionary policymaker who responds to events as they apparently occur to enact a policy change that is procyclical, thereby destabilizing the economy. The existence of these lags is one argument in favor of policy rules, or fixed commitments to specific policy strategies.

POLICY FLEXIBILITY AND THE CASE FOR DISCRETION

Proponents of discretionary monetary and fiscal policies admit that policy time lags can pose serious problems for policymaking. Nevertheless, they contend that the potential social benefits of countercyclical policies are so great that macroeconomic policymakers should have the flexibility to attempt to smooth business cycles, rather than rigidly adhering to fixed rules. They also argue that central banks and governments are uniquely positioned to succeed in such endeavors more often than they fail.

Do Policymakers Have an Information Advantage?

One key argument favoring policy discretion is that situations can arise in which macroeconomic policymakers have more complete information about the economy than households and firms have. Policymakers may also be able to respond more fully to new information about changing market conditions.

As an illustration of the latter point, consider the modern Keynesian theory of wage contracting that we discussed in Chapter 10, in which workers and firms negotiate nominal wages in advance, based on the information that they have at that time. After the wages are set, the parties to the contract become better informed as economic events unfold. Unless wages are indexed to price changes, however, workers and firms cannot make any adjustments, aside from changes in employment that cause real output to fluctuate. Policymakers, in contrast, are not tied down to contracts and can vary their policy instruments in an effort to stabilize economic conditions and limit employment and output variations.

Proposed Information Advantages in Monetary Policy   The preceding example is specific to a particular theory, however. It is possible that policymakers have other inherent information advantages over the private sector that will make a difference under any theory of how the economy functions.

In the case of monetary policy, a commonly proposed information advantage of a central bank is its constant presence in financial markets. The Federal Reserve, for instance, trades government securities and bonds denominated in foreign currencies nearly every day. It also has considerable ability to influence the nation's nominal money stock. In addition, it regulates a large portion of U.S. banks. Furthermore, Federal Reserve economists tabulate large bodies of macroeconomic data.

The Federal Reserve's various activities give it the opportunity to keep tabs *simultaneously* on the pulse of financial markets, developments in the market for money, changing circumstances in the banking system, and economic fluctuations. As a result, the Federal Reserve arguably has the unique capability to integrate information about all aspects of the national economy, thereby giving it an information advantage over the private sector. Proponents of policy flexibility and discretion argue that this capability also makes the Federal Reserve uniquely qualified to attempt to conduct countercyclical monetary policy.

Proposed Information Advantages in Fiscal Policy   Some observers also argue that fiscal policymakers have advantages in compiling and processing information about the economy that give them the ability to conduct successful countercyclical policies. In the executive branch of the U.S. government, for instance, the Office of Management and Budget collects and collates large volumes of data related to the federal government's budget. In the legislative branch, the Congressional Budget Office performs a similar role. The president's Council of Economic Advisers analyzes these and other sources of information to make economic forecasts and advise the president and cabinet officers.

ON THE WEB
Visit the Council of Economic Advisors at:
http://www.whitehouse.gov/
WH/EOP/CEA/html/CEA.
html

Are the Proposed Information Advantages Real or Illusory?   Critics of discretionary policymaking counter that these supposed information advantages are, in fact, minimal or even nonexistent. They point to the sizable economic staffs of banks, other financial firms, and manufacturing corporations and to the elaborate economic consulting networks that give even small businesses access to significant volumes of information. Furthermore, the Internet has made considerable economic information available to anyone willing to invest some time and effort in locating it.

In the modern world, goes this counterargument, central bank or government policymakers are no more sophisticated than any well-trained, private individual. Consequently, there is no reason to believe that policymakers have any special ability to avoid the pitfalls of time lags and conduct countercyclical policies successfully.

As you will recall from Chapter 9, in the new classical theory policy actions can have real effects only if the actions are unanticipated by workers and firms. Otherwise, informed workers and firms will, on their own, alter their behavior in ways that lead to attainment of the economy's full-information, natural output level. New classical critics of discretionary policymaking therefore argue that, given the potential for policymakers to destabilize the economy in the presence of time lags and other impediments to their efforts, society would be better off if central banks and governments simply disseminated any information they have that households and firms do not possess. According to this view, any information advantage for policymakers is a two-edged sword, because it could lead to greater instability just as easily as it could permit policymakers to reduce cyclical fluctuations.

Do Policymakers Face Fewer Constraints?

As we noted in Chapters 9, 10, and 11, the rational expectations hypothesis revolutionized the way that macroeconomists think about the effects of monetary and fiscal policies. If households and firms form expectations rationally and take into account systematic policy actions, then policies cannot have real effects unless there are wage or price rigidities that keep market forces from nudging the economy toward its natural output level. Does this mean that policymakers have no ability to stabilize the economy in a world of rational expectations, even if they could minimize policy time lags and dodge other policy pitfalls?

The Altruistic Policymaker   Those who promote discretionary policies argue that even in a rational expectations world, policymakers have a key advantage over private individuals and firms: Policymakers do not feel obliged to profit from their actions. Suppose, for instance, that the stock market goes into a tailspin and bond prices plummet. Many financial institution managers and stockbrokers recognize that financial asset prices are falling below levels that are consistent with firms' profit potentials. Nevertheless, to protect depositors, clients, and their own institutions from further losses, the managers and brokers feel obliged to continue to sell—instead of starting to buy—shares of stock and bonds from their portfolios. As the values of the portfolios dwindle, all market participants experience a liquidity crunch. As the stock market sell-off becomes a rout, managers at many firms begin to worry that their access to bank loans during the coming weeks may be curtailed, forcing them to halt production and lay off workers. Then, the Federal Reserve announces that it stands ready to lend funds at a low nominal interest rate to any eligible institution. The stock and bond market tailspins suddenly halt as traders realize that liquidity will be easier to come by, requiring fewer sales from their stock and bond portfolios. Asset prices stabilize, and a crisis is averted.

This policy success story is not just a scenario. It actually happened in October 1987. Even though the immediate severity of the 1987 stock market crash paralleled the Great Crash of 1929, no economic depression followed. Indeed, the economy at most felt a tremor from the 1987 crash. The next recession did not occur until nearly four years later.

Proponents of discretionary policymaking see a deep message in this real-life story. The key to the Federal Reserve's 1987 success, they argue, was its willingness to lend funds, even though doing so would reduce the Federal Reserve System's income. After all, lending at low interest rates in the face of falling financial asset prices was not in the Fed's interest. Thus, lending at market rates would have raised the Federal Reserve's profits. Because it does not have a profit motive, the Federal Reserve can be *altruistic* and forgo its own interest in an effort to improve the well-being of the rest of society. The same argument can be offered in support of discretionary fiscal policymaking, because the government is not a profit-maximizing institution.

PUBLIC INTEREST THEORY A hypothesis that regards central banks and government policymakers as public servants that pursue the broad interests of society as a whole.

This argument lies at the heart of the **public interest theory** of policymaking. According to this perspective, central banks and government policymakers are in a unique position to pursue the broad interests of society as a whole. This position, in fact, gives them the capability to respond flexibly to changing circumstances in ways that private households and firms cannot.

PUBLIC CHOICE THEORY A hypothesis that views central banks and government policymakers as policymaking bodies composed of individuals who pursue their own self-interest.

Are There Limits to Altruism in Policymaking?   A more cynical perspective on policymaking is offered by the **public choice theory.** Adherents to this theory argue that we should assume that all individuals, including policymakers, act *as if* they are pursuing their own self-interest. Although central bank or government officials are not trying to maximize profits, according to this theory, they are attempting to maximize their own satisfaction in their chosen occupations. Certainly, for many this effort could entail a measure of altruism. Nevertheless, the pursuit of self-interest could also, at a minimum, induce policymakers to spend public funds unwisely on plush offices, larger staffs than are really needed, and bloated salaries for themselves and their employees. Even as observers have applauded the Federal Reserve's 1987 performance, they have questioned the 50 percent increase in its expenses that took place over the next few years.

The key macroeconomic issue raised by the public choice theory is whether policymakers' self-interests may stand in the way of the altruistic pursuit of broader economic goals. The president, for example, might justify increased spending on projects that benefit favored constituencies on the grounds that the spending is needed to counter a downturn in the business cycle. Likewise, members of Congress might justify tax cuts for industries that have donated to their campaigns as part of a fiscal policy action intended to stem a recession. Federal Reserve officials might promote interest-rate stability in part because such a policy will benefit banks that are key employers of former Federal Reserve policymakers and, consequently, may some day be *their* prospective employers (see on page 442 the Policy Notebook: *Why Does the Fed Engage in Churning?*).

Such concerns lead advocates of the public choice theory to argue that policy rules should be favored over policy discretion. Flexibility in policymaking, they contend,

POLICY NOTEBOOK
Why Does the Fed Engage in Churning?

Some critics take the public choice model to an extreme. They argue that the way the Fed conducts monetary policy directly benefits a handful of traders of U.S. government securities when there is no reason to do so.

Every business day, securities traders at the Federal Reserve Bank of New York engage in a frenzy of buying and selling U.S. government securities to implement monetary policy. Nevertheless, in a typical year, the net change in Fed holdings of government securities is a trivial part of total transactions. This process is aptly referred to as **churning.** Churning has generated a considerable amount of controversy. Some complain that the only beneficiaries of the trading are three dozen or so special securities dealers that earn enormous brokerage fees. (Note that when stockbrokers encourage excessive buying and selling of securities to increase their own profits, they are subject to prosecution.)

Federal Reserve officials claim that much of the supposed churning is really not churning at all. They contend that temporary transactions and those arranged on behalf of foreign central banks do not constitute churning. In particular, to provide reserves on a temporary basis, the Fed engages in repurchase agreements, or sales of securities under an agreement to repurchase them from dealers. When there is a "need" to drain reserves temporarily, the Fed arranges reverse repurchase agreements, or purchases of securities under an agreement to resell them to dealers.

FOR CRITICAL ANALYSIS:
Who benefits from Federal Reserve churning?

CHURNING Constant trading of U.S. government securities by the Federal Reserve Bank of New York; to achieve temporary changes in reserves, among other things; controversial because some critics charge that some of the trading is unnecessary.

can promote self-interested policy actions just as easily as it can permit altruistic efforts to improve social welfare.

INTERNET SOURCE
Open-Market Operations at the Trading Desk

The Federal Reserve Bank of New York—Open-Market Operations
Internet URL: **http://www.ny.frb.org/pihome/fedpoint/fed32.html**

Navigation: Start at the Federal Reserve Bank of New York's homepage (http://www.ny.frb.org). Select "Welcome," scan down the page, and click on *Open Market Operations.* Then read the description of the procedures that the Trading Desk uses.

FUNDAMENTAL ISSUE #2

What are the main arguments favoring discretionary policymaking? One justification for discretionary policies is that policymakers may have information advantages because they can

> tabulate and collate diverse sets of data on macroeconomic activity.
> Another is that policymakers are not profit-maximizing institutions.
> Therefore they may be able to act altruistically by pursuing broad
> social welfare goals.

DISCRETIONARY POLICY AND INFLATION

Another argument against discretionary policymaking hinges neither on policy time
lags nor on the pursuit of self-interest by policymakers. Indeed, this view is consistent
with policymakers having up-to-date information, responding quickly to that information, and influencing the economy immediately. It also allows for the possibility
that policymakers may behave altruistically. Nevertheless, its key implication is that
society will be worse off under discretionary policymaking than with a policy rule.

   This alternative approach was developed by Robert Barro of Harvard University
and David Gordon of Clemson University. Its focus is on the likely tendency of a discretionary macroeconomic policymaker to enact policies that are inflationary.

A Macroeconomic Policy Game and a Theory of Inflation

Recall from Chapter 11 that one of the few things that economists of different stripes
agree on is that *game theory*—the theory of strategic interactions among individuals
or institutions—can be a useful tool for addressing some macroeconomic issues.
Barro and Gordon have applied game theory to the problem of rules versus discretion in macroeconomic policymaking. You need not have studied game theory to
understand their essential argument, however. All you need are concepts that we have
discussed in earlier chapters.

Output-Market Equilibrium and Ultimate Policy Goals   Figure 13–2 on page
444 illustrates the setting that Barro and Gordon have considered, using the modern
Keynesian theory of wage contracting from Chapter 10 as a framework of analysis.
Because nominal wages are contracted at the level W_1^c, the short-run aggregate supply schedule, $y^s(W_1^c)$, slopes upward. In the long run, when workers and firms are
fully informed, nominal wages will adjust equiproportionately with price changes, so
the long-run aggregate supply schedule, y_{LR}^s, is vertical at the economy's current long-
run, full-information output level, denoted y_1. Finally, the aggregate demand schedule, y_1^d, slopes downward. A possible output-market equilibrium is point A, where all
three schedules cross at the equilibrium price level, P_1. Hence, point A depicts a situation in which the short-run and the long-run equilibrium coincide. Workers and
firms have negotiated a contract wage that happens to match the nominal wage that
would have arisen if the labor market had equilibrated the demand for labor with the
supply of labor, as in the classical model.

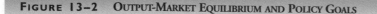

FIGURE 13–2 **OUTPUT-MARKET EQUILIBRIUM AND POLICY GOALS**

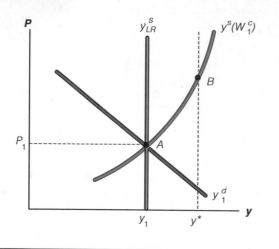

A full long-run equilibrium in the market for real output takes place at a point where the aggregate demand, short-run aggregate supply, and long-run aggregate supply schedules cross, such as point A. At this equilibrium point, the long-run, full-information output level is equal to y_1, and the equilibrium price level is equal to P_1. The output level y^* is the capacity level of output, which workers and firms could produce but currently do not because other factors, such as income taxes and costs of regulation, reduce the long-run, full-information output level below the capacity level. The basic theory of inflationary policy proposes that policymakers would like to raise the level of output toward the capacity level but also would prefer not to increase the price level.

CAPACITY OUTPUT The real output that the economy could produce if all resources were employed to their utmost.

In addition, Figure 13–2 includes an output level denoted y^*, which is the ultimate output objective of a macroeconomic policymaker. A key assumption is that this target output level is *greater* than the full-information, natural output level y_1. The reason is that y^* is the **capacity output** for the economy, or the real GDP that firms could produce if labor and other factors of production were employed to their utmost. One reason why the natural, full-information output level typically lies below the capacity output level is the existence of income taxes. By imposing a marginal tax rate on workers' incomes (see Chapter 7), the government induces workers to supply fewer labor services than they otherwise would have desired. As a result, firms produce less real output than they otherwise would have planned to produce in the absence of income taxes.

Another reason that the natural output level usually is below the capacity output level is the presence of government regulations. For instance, governments commonly restrict entry into various industries via licensing requirements, thereby restraining production of goods and services by those industries. Consequently, government regulations can reduce real output relative to what it would have been in the absence of regulations.

In addition to the capacity output goal y^*, the macroeconomic policymaker has one other ultimate objective—to minimize the inflation rate. Because the primary way to influence real output in the short run is through monetary or fiscal policy actions that change the position of the aggregate demand schedule, however, policymakers face a trade-off between their two goals. An increase in aggregate demand from point A in Figure 13–2 will cause a rightward movement along the short-run aggregate supply schedule, thereby raising real output toward the target y^* at point B. A rise in aggregate demand, however, will also cause the price level to rise, resulting in higher inflation. Therefore, remaining at the current equilibrium point *A* is more desirable from the standpoint of the policymaker's inflation objective. Consequently, a policymaker with both output and inflation goals typically will want aggregate demand to rise somewhat from point *A*, so as to increase real output. How much expansion of aggregate demand the policymaker will tolerate will depend on the relative weights that it places on its dual objectives of increasing output while keeping inflation as low as possible.

Policy Discretion and Inflation   Figure 13–2 depicted a setting with two sets of "players" in the macroeconomic policy game. On the one hand, to determine the contract wage, W^c, workers and firms must make their best rational forecast of the price level given their understanding of the policy goals of the macroeconomic policymaker and the trade-off it confronts. On the other hand, the macroeconomic policymaker must decide what action it should take to alter aggregate demand given its understanding of how workers and firms determine the contract wage.

Figure 13–3 depicts four *potential* outcomes that might arise from the interaction between workers and firm executives, who set the contract wage and thereby determine the position of the aggregate supply schedule, and the policymaker, which chooses a monetary or fiscal policy action that determines the position of the aggregate demand schedule. The four potential outcomes of this interaction are points *A*, *B*, *C*, and *D*. Let's consider each in turn.

FIGURE 13–3   POTENTIAL AND EQUILIBRIUM OUTCOMES OF A MACROECONOMIC POLICY GAME

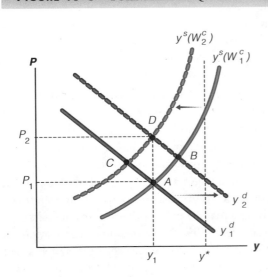

If the current equilibrium for the economy is point *A*, and if the policymaker's goals are to raise output toward the capacity output level y^* while keeping inflation low, then the policymaker's temptation will be to split the difference between these conflicting objectives by inducing a rise in aggregate demand, to point *B*. If workers realize that the policymaker has an incentive to permit prices to rise, however, they will bargain for higher contract wages, thereby shifting the aggregate supply schedule leftward. The result will be higher prices and lower real output at point *C*. To avoid this outcome, the policymaker will feel pressure to raise aggregate demand as workers expect. The final equilibrium is at point *D*, with unchanged real output but a higher price level. A noninflationary equilibrium in which the policymaker maintains a commitment to zero inflation at point *A* can result only if the policymaker's commitment is credible.

Point A is the same initial equilibrium point that we discussed in Figure 13–2. Because it is a long-run equilibrium point, the contract wage W_1^c reflects a correct expectation by workers and firms that the price level will be equal to P_1. Hence, at this initial point workers and firms produce the full-information output level.

Nevertheless, the macroeconomic policymaker wishes to raise real output above the full-information, natural level y_1 toward the capacity output level y^*. Consequently, the policymaker has an incentive to embark on a monetary or fiscal policy action that will raise aggregate demand from y_1^d to y_2^d in an effort to induce a short-run rise in real output, at point B. As noted earlier, a policymaker will not try to cause real output to rise all the way to the capacity level y^*, because this would entail greater inflation. Point B, therefore, represents a compromise outcome for the policymaker in light of the trade-off it faces: Real output will rise *toward* the capacity target at the cost of permitting *some* inflation.

We assume that workers and firms know the policymaker's goals, which implies that they will not let the point B outcome occur. At point B, the price level would be higher than workers and firms anticipated when they set the contract wage W_1^c. Hence, the real wage that workers would earn at point B is lower than they prefer, and real output would exceed the full-information, natural level that firms desire to produce. Therefore, point B cannot be an equilibrium point that could arise in the macroeconomic policy game. It would be inconsistent with the contracting strategy of workers and firms.

Instead, workers and firms will recognize that the policymaker has an incentive to shift the aggregate demand schedule from y_1^d to y_2^d, and they will respond by raising their price expectation and negotiating a higher contract wage, W_2^c. This will cause the aggregate supply schedule to shift leftward, from $y^s(W_1^c)$ to $y^s(W_2^c)$. The result will be point D, which is consistent with the contracting strategy of workers and firms. At this point, they will have chosen the contract wage optimally, taking into account the behavior they expect from the policymaker. In addition, point D is consistent with the policymaker's strategy, which is to raise aggregate demand in an attempt to increase output while keeping inflation low (even though, after the fact, the policymaker will not succeed in its effort). Consequently, unlike point B, point D *would* be a possible equilibrium in the monetary policy game.

Given that the policymaker will fail to expand real output toward the capacity goal, one might suppose that the policymaker would recognize its inability to raise output and commit itself to leaving the aggregate demand schedule at the position y_1^d. In other words, the policymaker would follow a policy *rule* instead of responding in a discretionary manner to incentives to try to raise real output in the short run. What if workers and firms do *not* believe that the policymaker will maintain its commitment to a policy rule? In that case, they will still raise their price expectation and negotiate an increase in the contract wage. This will cause the aggregate supply schedule to shift from $y^s(W_1^c)$ to $y^s(W_2^c)$. Then, if the policymaker follows through with its commitment to leave aggregate demand at y_1^d, point C will result. Point C, however, is inconsistent with the policymaker's strategy, because at this point inflation occurs and real output falls even *further* below the capacity objective. Therefore, point C could not be an equilibrium point in the macroeconomic policy game.

Under a special circumstance, one other equilibrium point—point A—could arise in the macroeconomic policy game. *If* the macroeconomic policymaker commits itself to maintaining the aggregate demand schedule at y_1^d, and *if* workers and firms believe that the policymaker will honor that commitment, then point A will be the final equilibrium point. There will be no inflation, the policymaker will accept its inability to raise real output toward the capacity level, and workers and firms will be satisfied at the long-run, full-information output level.

The Problem of Policy Credibility   Figure 13–4 is another version of Figure 13–3. It displays only the two possible equilibrium points of the macroeconomic policy game, points A and D, so that we can focus on these two potential outcomes. Point A results from commitment to a monetary policy rule, so it denotes a *commitment policy equilibrium.* Point D, in contrast, arises from the policymaker's inability or unwillingness to make such a commitment. In other words, point D is a point of *discretionary policy equilibrium.* Thus, these two points constitute the alternative outcomes that result from following a policy rule or pursuing discretionary policymaking.

POLICY CREDIBILITY The believability of a commitment by a central bank or governmental authority to follow specific policy rules.

The key determinant of which equilibrium point actually occurs is **policy credibility,** or the believability of the policymaker's willingness and ability to commit to a monetary rule. If workers and firms believe that the policymaker is willing and

---

FIGURE 13–4   THE INFLATION BIAS OF DISCRETIONARY POLICYMAKING

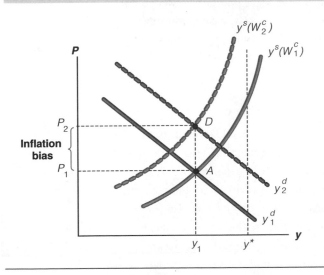

Point A represents a noninflationary equilibrium point of the macroeconomic policy game. It can arise only if the policymaker makes a credible commitment to zero inflation. In the absence of a credible anti-inflation commitment, point D will be the equilibrium point that arises from the macroeconomic policy game, as discussed in Figure 13–3. Hence, the increase in the price level entailed by the movement from point A to point D is an *inflation bias* resulting from discretionary policymaking.

able to follow through on its commitment, then the initial point *A* will remain the equilibrium of the macroeconomic policy game, and the economy will remain at its full-information output level without experiencing inflation. If workers and firms doubt the policymaker's willingness or ability to honor its commitment, however, this lack of policy credibility will lead to an equilibrium at point *D*.

TIME INCONSISTENCY PROBLEM A policy problem that can result if a policymaker has the ability, at a future time, to alter its strategy in a way that is inconsistent both with the desires and strategies of private individuals and with its own initially announced intentions.

Policy credibility is difficult to achieve in the setting that we have described because our example includes a **time inconsistency problem.** This problem arises because although commitment to a policy rule yields zero inflation, as at point *A,* this commitment will be inconsistent with the strategies of workers and firms if the policymaker is free to alter its policy strategy at a later time. Suppose that after workers and firms have committed themselves to a contract wage, the policymaker attempts to expand aggregate demand, which will help the policymaker achieve its output goal but will not benefit the workers and firms (point *B* in Figure 13–3). Hence, workers and firms protect themselves by raising the contracted wage before the policymaker acts, thereby forcing even a policymaker that might otherwise prefer to stick to a rule to expand aggregate demand to avoid a decline in real output (point *C* in Figure 13–3) . These interactions between workers and firms and the policymaker result in an equilibrium at point *D* in Figure 13–4.

INFLATION BIAS The tendency for the economy to experience continuing inflation as a result of discretionary monetary policy that takes place because of the time inconsistency problem of monetary policy.

The result of the time inconsistency problem and the lack of policy credibility in our example is a higher price level at point *D* as compared with point *A*. Economists call the difference between the new price level P_2 at point *D* and the initial price level P_1 at point *A* the **inflation bias** arising from discretionary macroeconomic policy. This bias toward inflation exists from the ability of a macroeconomic policymaker to determine its policies in a discretionary manner when there is a time inconsistency problem and a lack of policy credibility. The inflation bias of discretionary policy is a third reason—along with the potential for discretionary policy to be destabilizing in the presence of time lags and to serve policymakers' own narrow self-interests if the public choice perspective is correct—why many economists argue that society should find ways to dissuade policymakers from discretion by making policy rules credible. How society might accomplish this is our next topic.

FUNDAMENTAL ISSUE **#3**

Why is policy credibility a crucial factor in maintaining low inflation? If people establish nominal wage contracts, then a macroeconomic policymaker has an incentive to enact policies that will raise aggregate demand in an effort to expand real output toward its capacity level. Consequently, workers and firms negotiating wage contracts will be unlikely to believe a policymaker's stated intention to limit inflation, which would reduce the purchasing power of workers' wages. As a result, workers and firms will negotiate higher wages, thereby reducing aggregate supply and causing output to fall in the absence of higher aggregate demand. This pressures the policymaker into raising aggregate demand and thereby creating an inflationary bias. The only way a policymaker can avoid this inflation bias is to make a commitment to low inflation that is credible to workers and firms.

MAKING POLICY RULES CREDIBLE: MONETARY POLICY

It is one thing to argue that there are potential gains from sticking with a macroeconomic policy rule. It is another thing altogether, however, to establish a mechanism for attaining this outcome in the face of a time inconsistency problem.

Three types of macroeconomic policymaking are subject to time inconsistency problems: monetary policy, fiscal policy, and exchange rate policy. With each type of policymaking, the policymaker can gain from a short-run expansion of aggregate demand after workers and firms have tied themselves to nominal wage contracts. Despite this similarity, the practical approaches to making policy rules credible differ across these various forms of policymaking, so we shall discuss each area in turn, beginning with monetary policy.

As you have learned in earlier chapters, most macroeconomic theories indicate that money growth is a key determinant of the inflation rate. Consequently, this is the natural starting point for most discussions of how to reduce the inflation bias arising from discretionary policy. These discussions focus on finding a way to induce a central bank to follow a policy rule and to make such a rule credible.

Altering Monetary Policy Incentives via Wage Indexation

One approach to eliminating the inflation bias that can result from monetary policy discretion is to take away a central bank's incentive to create inflation. Recall from Chapter 10 that when workers and firms fully *index* nominal wages to unanticipated inflation, the economy's aggregate supply schedule becomes vertical. If wages are fully indexed to inflation, then a rise in the price level automatically causes the nominal wage to rise in equal proportion. As a result, the real wage remains unaltered when the price level changes, so the quantity of real output supplied stays constant at the natural, full-information level.

To see the implications of complete wage indexation for discretionary monetary policymaking, consider Figure 13–5 on page 450. Because wages are completely indexed, the aggregate supply schedule is vertical at the natural, full-information output level, y_1. As in Figures 13–3 and 13–4, however, the capacity output level, y^*, is greater than the full-information level of output. Assuming that the economy has initially achieved a

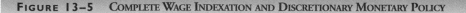

FIGURE 13–5   **COMPLETE WAGE INDEXATION AND DISCRETIONARY MONETARY POLICY**

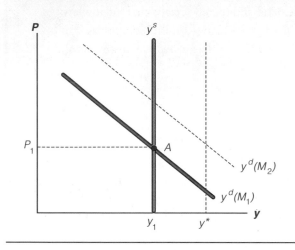

If workers and firms fully index money wages to unanticipated changes in the price level, then the economy's aggregate supply schedule will be vertical, as discussed in Chapter 10. In this case, even if the central bank acts in a discretionary manner, it will have no incentive to increase the quantity of money in circulation in an effort to expand aggregate demand. Even if it did so, the central bank would be unable to induce an increase in real output beyond its long-run, full-information level, y_1, in the direction of the capacity output level, y^*. Hence, the equilibrium point A will be maintained, and there will be no inflation bias.

short- and long-run output-market equilibrium at point A, then the central bank would, as in our earlier example of the time inconsistency problem, like to raise output toward its capacity output level while keeping inflation as low as possible.

Nevertheless, because full indexation makes the aggregate supply schedule vertical, the central bank cannot, even in the short run, induce a rise in equilibrium real output by increasing money growth and expanding aggregate demand. If the central bank attempts to raise the nominal money stock to shift the aggregate demand schedule from $y^d(M_1)$ to $y^d(M_2)$, the only result will be a higher price level and undesired inflation. Thus, the central bank has no incentive to expand aggregate demand. Point A will remain the equilibrium point, and there will be no discretionary inflation bias.

As we noted in Chapter 10, however, the overall extent of wage indexation in the United States actually has been low in recent years. If full wage indexation could solve the inflation bias problem, why don't more workers and firms index their wages? One reason is that wage indexation is not costless. Workers must negotiate indexed contracts with firms, and they may have to give up something, such as higher base wages, improved health-care coverage, or other nonwage benefits, in exchange for full wage indexation. If the costs of indexing contracts are sufficiently large, many contracts will not have indexation clauses.

Second, as we discussed in Chapter 10, full indexation stabilizes employment and output if fluctuations in aggregate demand are the main source of employment and output variability. If the aggregate supply schedule is variable, however, employment and output volatility is greater with fully indexed wage contracts.

Finally, the slope of the aggregate supply function is influenced by the *aggregate* degree of indexation of all wages. Hence, it is the combined decisions of all workers and firms in the economy that influence the slope of the aggregate supply schedule. To influence the central bank's incentives, all workers and firms would have to coordinate their contract negotiations on indexation. There is no easy way to do this, unless all workers were to join a few large, coordinating unions. To new Keynesians, this is an example of a coordination failure (see Chapter 11). Some new Keynesians, therefore, have advocated government policies requiring indexed contracts as a means of reducing the inflation bias of discretionary monetary policy.

Constitutional Limitations on Monetary Policy

Other economists, such as Milton Friedman of the Hoover Institution at Stanford University, have suggested that it might be better to try to constrain central banks directly, rather than forcing everyone else to determine wages differently than they otherwise would. This might be accomplished in the United States by amending the U.S. Constitution to require a constant annual growth rate for the quantity of money. This approach would seek to tie the hands of the Federal Reserve by legally *requiring* the Federal Reserve, or more broadly the U.S. government, to pursue a monetary policy rule. The legal requirement presumably would establish the credibility of the rule.

One problem with this idea is the difficulty of determining the appropriate numerical rule for money growth. After all, the U.S. economy's real output growth has varied from decade to decade. Whereas a 3 percent money growth rule might have been consistent with zero inflation in the 1960s, a 2 percent money growth rule might have been preferable for the 1990s.

Achieving Monetary Policy Credibility by Establishing a Reputation

In the absence of such radical institutional changes, how can a central bank make its commitments to low inflation more credible? One approach might be to establish and maintain a reputation as a "tough inflation fighter." To understand how this could enable a central bank to reduce the inflation bias, refer back to Figure 13–3 on page 445. Recall that if the central bank honors its commitment not to raise aggregate demand in pursuit of short-term output gains but is not believed by workers and firms, then the result will be higher inflation and reduced output, shown in the figure by a movement from point *A* to point *C*. If the central bank cares only about today's outcome, it will not want point *C* to occur. If the central bank wants to establish a reputation as an inflation fighter, however, then it might be willing to let the economy experience lower output at point *C*. In that event, henceforth, workers and firms might believe the central bank's promises not to increase aggregate demand.

A number of economists argue that this scenario occurred in 1979 after inflation had risen significantly during the preceding years, as shown in Figure 13–6 on page 452. According to these economists, in 1979 and 1980 the Federal Reserve held firm to a commitment to keep aggregate demand from increasing. At first workers and firms did not find this commitment to be credible. Then, in 1980 and 1981, the United States experienced a sharp recession, as a steady rise in nominal wages pushed up business costs and resulted in

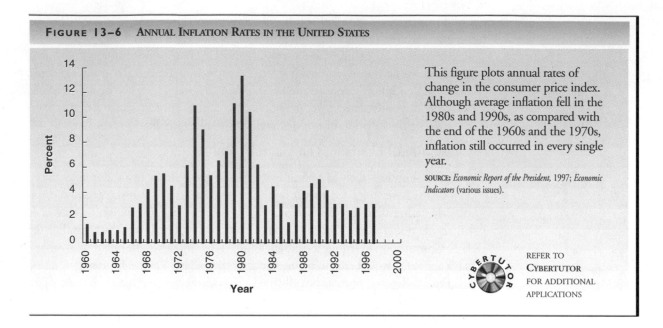

FIGURE 13-6 **ANNUAL INFLATION RATES IN THE UNITED STATES**

This figure plots annual rates of change in the consumer price index. Although average inflation fell in the 1980s and 1990s, as compared with the end of the 1960s and the 1970s, inflation still occurred in every single year.

SOURCE: *Economic Report of the President*, 1997; *Economic Indicators* (various issues).

REFER TO **CYBERTUTOR** FOR ADDITIONAL APPLICATIONS

a reduction in real output—just as the movement from point *A* to point *C* in Figure 13–3 indicates. As a result, in the years that followed, the Federal Reserve's commitment to lower inflation was credible, and actual inflation rates fell, as shown in Figure 13–6 (see the Policy Notebook: *Improving the Fed's Reputation by Using the Opportunistic Disinflation Approach to Monetary Policy.*)

Appointing a "Conservative" Central Banker

It is easier for a central bank official to make a credible commitment to low inflation if the official already has a reputation for being "tough" in the fight against inflation. Some observers of the Federal Reserve's fight against inflation in the 1980s have concluded that one reason the anti-inflation effort was so successful was President Jimmy Carter's 1979 appointment of Paul Volcker as the chair of the Federal Reserve's Board of Governors. Volcker was a Federal Reserve official who was well known as an opponent of inflation. The Federal Reserve's inflation-fighting reputation then was maintained, these observers argue, when President Ronald Reagan appointed Alan Greenspan, another known hawk on inflation, to that position.

The theory illustrated in Figure 13–4 on page 447 indicates that appointing anti-inflation central bank officials may indeed be a way to reduce the inflation bias of discretionary policymaking. A key factor influencing the size of the inflation bias is how much policymakers dislike inflation relative to how much they wish to try to raise real output toward its capacity level. Thus, appointing a **conservative central banker,** or an individual who dislikes inflation more than the average member of society, is one way to reduce the size of the inflation bias. Such central bankers will choose to ex-

CONSERVATIVE CENTRAL BANKER
A central bank official who dislikes inflation more than the average citizen in society and is therefore less willing to induce discretionary increases in the growth rate of the quantity of money in an effort to achieve short-run increases in real output.

POLICY NOTEBOOK

Improving the Fed's Reputation by Using the Opportunistic Disinflation Approach to Monetary Policy

Since Alan Greenspan became the chair of the Fed, the average rate of inflation has fallen dramatically. From 1976 to 1986, the inflation rate averaged 6.7 percent whereas from 1987 to today it has averaged 3.6 percent. Greenspan has taken a cautious, pragmatic approach to monetary policy. Two staff economists (Athanosios Orphanides and David Wilcox) who work for the Fed's Board of Governors have given a name to his approach—opportunistic disinflation.

Opportunistic disinflation follows the adage "if it ain't broke, don't fix it." According to this theory, when inflation is relatively low, policymakers are advised to wait for unforeseen recessions or favorable supply shocks, such as a significant reduction in the price of oil, to make further progress against inflation. Thus the Fed chair will continue to fight inflation, but will not do so on someone else's timetable. In particular, the Fed will not deliberately drive the economy into a recession to show its commitment to less inflation.

According to Fed insiders, in a closed-door policy session in 1989, Greenspan said that a recession would occur sometime during the next five years and that the Fed would move toward a zero rate of inflation at that time.

Not everyone agrees that the Fed should follow a policy of opportunistic disinflation. Those who are very much against inflation argue that the Fed should set a target and make steady progress to get rid of inflation completely.

FOR CRITICAL ANALYSIS:
Why would a policymaker such as Greenspan want to wait until a recession to further reduce the rate of inflation?

---

pand aggregate demand by a small amount, because a rise in aggregate demand is inflationary.

Central Banker Contracts

CENTRAL BANKER CONTRACT A legally binding agreement between a government and a central bank official that holds the official responsible for the nation's inflation performance.

In recent years several economists, including Carl Walsh of the University of California at Santa Cruz, have proposed establishing explicit **central banker contracts.** These are legally binding agreements between governments and central bank officials that call for the officials to be punished and/or rewarded based on the central bank's inflation performance. Research by Walsh and others indicates that such contracts could nearly eliminate the inflation bias of discretionary monetary policy.

As an example, New Zealand's Reserve Bank Act of 1989 established a central banker contract, which holds central bank officials directly responsible for any failure to maintain a stable price level in that nation. Under this law, if the top central bank official fails to meet clearly specified inflation targets, then under the terms of the contract, the official is subject to dismissal from the position.

In principle, a central banker contract also could reward officials for maintaining low and stable prices. For instance, central bank officials who eliminate inflation might be rewarded with higher salaries. Although some people argue that the officials would be receiving bonuses for doing the job that they were supposed to be doing in the first place, proponents of such central bank payment schemes argue that this might be a small cost for society to incur in exchange for reduced inflation.

An Independent Central Bank

The objective of central banker contracts is to make central bank officials more *accountable* for their performances. Using these contracts would not, however, rule out granting the officials considerable *independence* to conduct monetary policy as they see fit, while continuing to hold them responsible if inflation gets out of hand.

Indeed, many economists argue that central bank independence may be the key to maintaining low inflation rates. After all, conservative central bankers cannot establish a reputation as tough inflation fighters if they are hamstrung by legal requirements to try to achieve other objectives as well, such as a low unemployment rate or a high growth rate for real output. Furthermore, even if a central banker contract holds an official accountable for a nation's inflation performance, achieving the required performance may be difficult unless the official has sufficient independence to pursue this objective in the most efficient manner.

Central bank independence has two dimensions. One is *political independence,* or the ability to reach decisions without being influenced by the government and other outside individuals or groups. The other is *economic independence,* or the ability to control its own budget or to resist efforts by the government to induce the central bank to make loans to the government or to provide other forms of direct support to government policies. Hence, we can reach the following conclusion:

> **A truly independent central bank is both politically and economically independent. Political independence permits the central bank to conduct the policies that it believes to be best in the long run without being influenced by short-term political pressures. Economic independence gives the central bank the budgetary freedom to conduct these policies.**

Strong evidence that central bank independence is related to good inflation performance has been provided by the Harvard University economists Alberto Alesina and Lawrence Summers. This evidence is summarized in panels (a) and (b) of Figure 13–7. In each panel, an index of central bank independence is measured along the horizontal axis of the diagram. An increase in this index indicates that a nation's central bank is more politically and/or economically independent. In panel (a), average annual inflation rates between the middle 1950s and the late 1980s are measured along the vertical axis. The diagram shows an *inverse relationship* between central bank independence and average inflation, meaning that countries with more independent central banks tend to experience lower average inflation. Note that the two nations

FIGURE 13-7 CENTRAL BANK INDEPENDENCE, AVERAGE INFLATION, AND INFLATION VARIABILITY

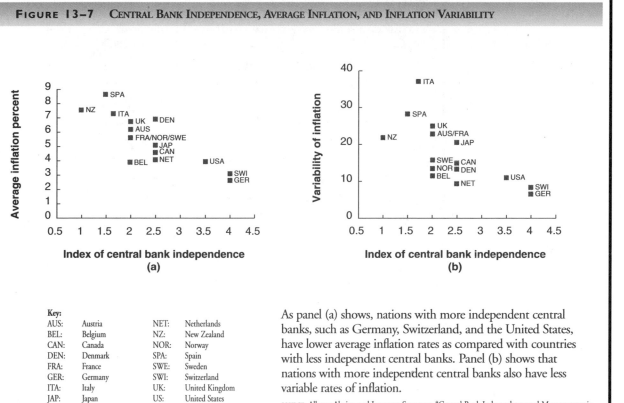

Key:

AUS:	Austria	NET:	Netherlands
BEL:	Belgium	NZ:	New Zealand
CAN:	Canada	NOR:	Norway
DEN:	Denmark	SPA:	Spain
FRA:	France	SWE:	Sweden
GER:	Germany	SWI:	Switzerland
ITA:	Italy	UK:	United Kingdom
JAP:	Japan	US:	United States

As panel (a) shows, nations with more independent central banks, such as Germany, Switzerland, and the United States, have lower average inflation rates as compared with countries with less independent central banks. Panel (b) shows that nations with more independent central banks also have less variable rates of inflation.

SOURCE: Alberto Alesina and Lawrence Summers, "Central Bank Independence and Macroeconomic Performance," *Journal of Money, Credit, and Banking*, (May 1993): 151–162.

with the most independent central banks, Germany and Switzerland, had average inflation rates of around 3 percent. The two nations with the least independent central banks, New Zealand (before its change in status) and Spain, experienced average inflation rates that were more than twice as high.

Panel (b) measures the variance of inflation along the vertical axis. Again we see an inverse relationship: Countries with more independent central banks tend to experience less inflation volatility. Thus, increased central bank independence tends to yield more price stability as well as lower average inflation.

The strong relationships displayed in Figure 13–7 have convinced a number of countries to grant more independence to their central banks. Recent examples include Japan, Mexico, France, England, and Pakistan. Western European nations considering the formation of a formal European Monetary Union with a single European central bank have also agreed that if and when such a central bank is established, it will have considerable independence from national governments.

FUNDAMENTAL ISSUE #4

How might monetary policy credibility be achieved? One possible approach is for workers and firms to index their wages completely. Total indexation would make the aggregate supply schedule vertical and eliminate a central bank's incentive to expand aggregate demand. A more direct approach is to make it illegal for central banks to allow inflation to exceed a specified rate. Alternatively, central bank officials could be signed to contracts that condition their employment or salaries on their inflation performance. To help ensure that central banks will be less likely to follow inflationary policies, governments can appoint conservative central bank officials who are known to have a distaste for inflation. Finally, central bankers can gain credibility by permitting output to fall in the near term as a way to convince workers of their commitment to low future inflation. To follow this strategy, the central bank must have sufficient independence.

MAKING POLICY RULES CREDIBLE: FISCAL POLICY

In democratic republics such as the United States, the government is designed to be relatively responsive to the desires of its citizenry. Achieving credible fiscal policies is complicated in a democratic nation, because citizens, either directly at the ballot box or indirectly via votes of their elected representatives, can repudiate fiscal commitments made at some earlier date. Ballooning deficits and national debts can result. Nevertheless, there are three ways in which fiscal policymakers can try to gain greater credibility and overcome the time inconsistency problem that they face.

Establishment of Legal Procedures in Government Budgeting

One way to gain greater fiscal credibility is to develop hard and fast rules for how a legislature can tax and spend. For instance, a legislature could require any representative proposing a tax or spending bill to explain how any necessary funding can be obtained while keeping the government's budget in balance.

The Gramm-Rudman-Hollings Act of 1985, and its amendment, was an example of this procedural approach to attaining greater fiscal credibility for the U.S. government. This law required automatic spending cuts if the U.S. government's deficit failed to stay on a predetermined path. (The law had little effect, though, and was in essence repealed by the Tax Act of 1990.)

The problem with the procedural approach to greater fiscal credibility, of course, is that a legislature can always vote to suspend its previously established rules. It can collectively "change its mind" about its commitment to greater budgetary discipline. Nevertheless, supporters of procedural constraints on fiscal policy argue that the constraints at least force a legislature to consider the credibility issue, even though they do not prevent all actions that lead to credibility losses.

Extralegislative Budget Balancing: Bipartisan Commissions

Although there are individual exceptions, politicians are notorious for having difficulty maintaining institutional credibility. Indeed, a number of politicians recognize this weakness and have experimented with *bipartisan commissions* as a possible solution. When faced with the necessity for a controversial spending or tax program, a legislature may establish a bipartisan commission and authorize it to examine the situation and make specific recommendations for fiscal actions.

In the 1980s and 1990s, for example, the U.S. Congress recognized that one way to reduce total federal spending and move closer to a balanced budget was to close a number of military bases across the country. The problem was that many local constituencies would lose from the closures. To distance itself from the difficult decisions of which bases to close and to improve the chances that the decisions would indeed be made, Congress established a base-closing commission. The commission was authorized to develop a list of military installations that were not crucial to the nation's defense and therefore should be closed. Congress precommitted itself to adopting or rejecting the entire slate of proposed closures. This move significantly enhanced the credibility of Congress's general commitment to cutting spending and moving toward a balanced budget.

A Balanced-Budget Amendment

To its advocates, the ultimate way to achieve greater U.S. fiscal credibility is a constitutional amendment requiring a balanced federal budget. Supporters of an amendment argue that it would force Congress to make the tough decisions required to balance constituents' demands for more federal spending with their conflicting demands for lower taxes. As a result, the credibility of fiscal policy would be enhanced considerably.

Critics point out that one flaw of a balanced-budget amendment is that it would take away the government's flexibility to run deficits during emergencies such as wars, and would thus impose considerable burdens on the citizens during such periods. They also suggest that Congress might use legal technicalities to evade the amendment, such as defining certain types of government expenditures as "off-budget" items, thereby achieving a "balanced budget" in name only.

Several times during the 1990s, however, Congress came extremely close to passing a balanced-budget amendment. It appears likely that such an amendment will be considered by future Congresses as well.

FUNDAMENTAL ISSUE #5

How might fiscal policy credibility be achieved? In democratic nations, gaining fiscal credibility often requires that legislatures adopt explicit rules to limit excessive spending. The U.S. Congress also has used bipartisan commissions to help deal with the political problems entailed in reducing government expenditures. A potential remedy to the fiscal credibility problem is a constitutional amendment requiring a balanced government budget.

MAKING POLICY RULES CREDIBLE: EXCHANGE-RATE POLICY

DEVALUATION A policy-induced reduction in the exchange value of a nation's currency relative to the currencies of other countries

In nations that are smaller than the United States and that traditionally have been more open to international trade, the exchange rate can be a very important instrument of macroeconomic policymaking. Exchange-rate **devaluations**—policy-induced reductions in the value of a nation's currency in terms of the currencies of other nations—make it less costly for foreigners to obtain a nation's currency and buy its goods. This can cause its exports to expand, thereby raising aggregate demand in that nation and causing a short-term rise in real output.

Hence, nations such as Mexico, Hong Kong (when it was a British Crown colony), Italy, and even the United Kingdom have periodically faced time inconsistency problems in their exchange-rate policies. A nation with an open economy always has an incentive to devalue its currency to push real output toward its capacity level, even though devaluations often are associated with upticks in the inflation rate. Hence, discretionary exchange-rate policy can lead to an inflationary bias.

A Fixed Exchange Rate as a Policy Rule

A nation's central bank or government can maintain a fixed exchange rate by standing ready to buy or sell the nation's currency at officially established rates of exchange for other currencies. As we shall discuss in more detail in Chapter 14, there are several justifications for a fixed exchange rate, the foremost being reduced risks of loss in the event of exchange-rate fluctuations.

Because of the potential for short-term output gains from currency devaluations, however, any nation that attempts to fix its exchange rate typically faces credibility problems. Indeed, a commitment to a fixed exchange rate is a type of rule. Attempting to make such a commitment entails a time inconsistency problem similar to those experienced in other forms of macroeconomic policymaking.

Nations have tried to establish their exchange-rate commitments in a variety of ways. In the nineteenth century, many nations established more credible linkages among their exchange rates by using a *gold standard,* in which the values of their currencies were tied to the value of gold. Since the early 1970s, however, very few nations have retained any kind of formal linkage to gold. Consequently, nations that try to fix their exchange rates now rely on alternative approaches to making their commitments to fixed exchange rates credible.

Maintaining Exchange-Rate Credibility

In today's fiat money system, all that "backs" the value of a nation's currency is the credibility of its monetary and exchange-rate policies. If a nation's policies are not credible, those who hold currencies, including *currency speculators* who make their living buying currencies when their values are low and selling them when their values rise, will not be willing to hold the nation's currency at the official exchange rate. Hence, if a nation with a fixed exchange rate is to maintain its commitment, it must persuade currency traders of two points. First, policymakers must convince currency traders that the official exchange rate is consistent with the underlying terms at which their nation trades goods with other countries. The terms of trade for goods exchanges are called the *real exchange rate,* or the rate of exchange for one nation's currency in terms of another currency adjusted for price differences across nations. If the quoted *nominal* rate of exchange unadjusted for price differences that a nation tries to peg in a fixed-exchange-rate system is inconsistent with the real exchange rate, then currency traders will not be willing to hold the nation's currency at the official exchange rate.

Second, policymakers must have sufficient reserves of other nations' currencies so that they can purchase their own nation's currency as necessary to maintain the fixed exchange rate. If foreign currency reserves fall too low to maintain the official exchange rate when changes in the foreign exchange market place downward pressure on the value of the nation's currency, then policymakers' commitment to the official rate will not be credible. They will be forced to abandon the commitment by devaluing.

The Great European Experiment In light of these factors, it can be very difficult for any nation to "go it alone" with a fixed exchange rate. If nations cooperate in maintaining fixed exchange rates, however, then pressures on their levels of foreign currency reserves can be reduced. In addition, in principle the nations would be able to coordinate and determine appropriate target exchange rates that are consistent with the real rates of exchange for the goods that they trade.

Most industrialized nations of the world participated in a cooperative arrangement from shortly after the end of World War II until 1971. This effort was called the *Bretton Woods system* in honor of the location where national governments agreed to cooperate in setting and maintaining a system of fixed exchange rates. Under this system, the value of the U.S. dollar was linked to the value of gold. Other nations then established fixed rates of exchange vis-à-vis the dollar, which automatically established fixed rates of exchange across all nations that participated in the system. The bulk of these nations were European countries.

The fiscal and monetary policy strains entailed in financing the Vietnam War ultimately destroyed the credibility of the U.S. commitment to the gold standard, however. In 1971, President Richard Nixon was forced to remove the dollar's link to gold, a move that left the Bretton Woods nations to fend for themselves. While some nations allowed their exchange rates to float freely in the foreign exchange markets, several nations that were members of the *European Community,* or *EC,* decided to coordinate their currencies in a system of fixed exchange rates. Following several failed attempts during the 1970s, in 1979 a group of EC nations formally established the *European Monetary System* (*EMS*) to maintain fixed exchange rates among their currencies. This system required central banks to intervene whenever their exchange rates varied more than specified percentages from the agreed rates of exchange. Although the central bank of the nation whose exchange rate was at variance with the official rate had primary responsibility for intervening, central banks of other EMS nations often assisted with their own interventions.

The key nation in the EMS was Germany, because its central bank had established the greatest credibility. Indeed, many observers have compared the EMS with the old Bretton Woods system, with the German mark performing the role for the EMS in the 1980s that the dollar had performed for much of the industrialized world between 1946 and 1971. As you can see in Figure 13–8, EMS nations succeeded in keeping their exchange rates in close proximity.

In 1992, however, the EMS experienced a major credibility breakdown. One problem was that the reunification of the eastern and western portions of Germany, which had been split after World War II, placed significant monetary and fiscal strains on that nation. Just as the Vietnam War made a U.S. commitment to Bretton Woods impracticable, the reunification stress called Germany's commitment to the EMS into question. At the same time, a recession hit other members of the EMS, including Italy, Denmark, France, and the United Kingdom. The real rates of exchange among these EC trading partners began to diverge from previous levels, and the system of fixed exchange rates became untenable by September 1992. At that time, Italy and the United Kingdom broke ranks and floated their currencies. France and other nations such as Denmark maintained the credibility of their commitments to the EMS, but at significant cost. They had to undertake expensive interventions in the foreign exchange markets and suffered higher unemployment stemming from the contractionary monetary policies that were required.

Despite this experience, EC nations, which now refer to themselves as members of the *European Union (EU)* formally remain committed to adopting a single currency by the beginning of the twenty-first century. Under the current timetable, the members will return to a fixed-exchange-rate system and then convert their currencies into a common currency unit called the "euro." It remains to be seen, however, whether credibility of fixed exchange rates can be reestablished in time to remain on this schedule (see the Global Notebook: *Will Europe Ever Have a Single Currency?*).

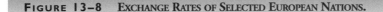

FIGURE 13-8   EXCHANGE RATES OF SELECTED EUROPEAN NATIONS.

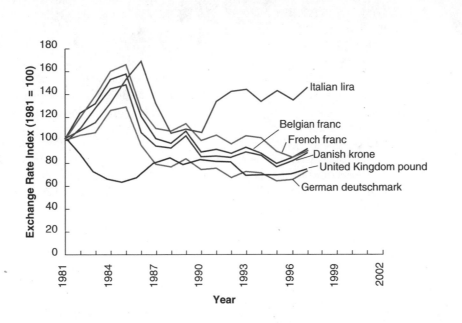

The dollar values of the Belgian franc, Danish krone, French franc, German deutschemark, and Italian lira moved together during the 1980s. By the early 1990s, the dollar value of the United Kingdom pound also moved in closer step with the dollar values of other European nations' currencies. For several years after 1992, however, the dollar exchange rates for the Italian lira and United Kingdom pound often moved in different directions relative to dollar exchange rates of neighboring countries.

INTERNET SOURCE

The European Union

The European Commission—Eurostat
Internet URL: http://www.europa.eu.int

Navigation: Start at the "Europa" homepage for the European Union at the above address. Click on *Welcome,* then *News,* then *Eurostat,* then *Press Releases,* then *Search By Key Words,* then *General Statistics.*

An Alternative Approach: Currency Boards   Nations outside Europe that wished to fix their exchange rates have largely been left to their own devices. Mexico is an example. Until December 1994, Mexico attempted to keep the value of its currency, the peso, within a fixed "trading band," or permitted range of exchange-rate variation, relative to the U.S. dollar. By linking the peso's value to the currency of its

GLOBAL NOTEBOOK

Will Europe Ever Have a Single Currency?

Currently, the European Union (EU) has fifteen members, each with its own currency. Current plans call for the EU to use a single currency, called the euro, by the end of this century. Many observers, however, doubt that Europe will ever have a single currency. They point out that a single currency is equivalent to a permanent fixed exchange rate system, similar to what we have in the United States. After all, the rate of exchange between dollars in California and dollars in New York is fixed at one to one. Thus, the euro used in Germany will have the same value as a euro used in France.

A single currency means that the fifteen separate countries cannot have fifteen separate monetary policies, just as the fifty U.S. states cannot have fifty separate monetary policies. There can be only one central bank in the EU. Under what circumstances will fifteen separate economies with fifteen separate political agendas agree to one central bank? Perhaps none.

Another serious problem will also have to be faced if a single currency is used throughout the EU. Currently, Belgium, Italy, and Sweden have public debts and government-provided pension plan liabilities that are many times one year's GDP. Hence, the risk of default on government debt in these countries is much higher than in, say, Germany. Nevertheless, residents of the weaker countries still buy their own governments' bonds because they are worried about exchange-rate risks if they invest money in other EU countries. Once exchange-rate risks are eliminated through a single currency, it is not clear how many residents of Europe's weaker countries will continue to purchase their own governments' bonds. At the same interest rate, they will prefer to purchase German government bonds. Consequently, interest rates in the weaker European countries may rise dramatically if a single currency comes into being.

FOR CRITICAL ANALYSIS:
Initially, each country will have to decide on an exchange-rate conversion from its own currency to the new single currency. Who will decide these fifteen separate exchange rates once and for all?

ON THE WEB
For an Economic Profile of Mexico see:
http://www.mexonline.com/business.htm

key trading partner, the United States, Mexico sought to keep its inflation rate in line with U.S. inflation and to lay a solid foundation for growing trade with the United States and other nations. On November 18, 1994, a headline in the *Wall Street Journal* indicated that the fixed-exchange-rate policy seemed to be successful: it read "Mexico Posts Surprisingly Solid Growth, as Turnaround in Economy Advances." An accompanying figure entitled "On the Move" showed annual Mexican GDP growth at nearly 5 percent.

Nevertheless, from February to December 1994 the peso's value fell by over 10 percent relative to the dollar, to the bottom of the Mexican government's official trading range. Then, in one day, December 21, the peso's exchange value suddenly plummeted by another 12.7 percent following an unexpected devaluation by the Mexican government. Within a week, the peso's value relative to the dollar dropped more than 35 percent in all. In January 1995, the Federal Reserve intervened in foreign exchange markets to boost the peso's value, and in February 1995 the U.S. Treasury made loan guarantees of up to $40 billion to the Mexican government.

The Mexican peso crisis of 1994–1995 occurred for a number of reasons, but the immediate cause was the loss of credibility of Mexico's commitment to its official peso-dollar exchange rate. The official rate was incompatible with the real rate of exchange between U.S. and Mexican goods. Therefore, to maintain the targeted exchange rate, the Mexican government had to buy pesos with dollars. Ultimately, it ran out of dollars and was forced to devalue the peso.

In light of the Mexican peso crisis, many observers have argued that a small nation cannot expect to succeed in pegging its exchange rate unless it adopts a **currency board** approach. A currency board is a rule-bound monetary policymaker that issues local currency that is backed 100 percent by the currency of another nation. The first currency boards were established by nations that were members of the British Commonwealth, such as Hong Kong, the Cayman Islands, the Falkland Islands, and Gibraltar, which issued currency based on reserves of the British currency, the pound sterling. Singapore also has a currency board system. More recently, Argentina in 1991 established a currency board arrangement in which Argentine pesos were backed 100 percent by U.S. dollars.

CURRENCY BOARD A monetary policymaker that is bound to a commitment to issue currency that is backed 100 percent by the currency of another country.

A currency board approach to a fixed exchange rate is more credible than the standard approach because the 100 percent backing constraint ensures that a government cannot issue more currency than the amount of foreign exchange reserves it has on hand. Furthermore, this constraint means that a fixed one-to-one exchange rate can be maintained as long as the currency board abides by the rules of the system. Many have credited the solid macroeconomic performances of (pre-July 1997) Hong Kong and Singapore to their currency board arrangements. Argentina has also had good macroeconomic performance, although the Mexican peso crisis caused many currency traders to question whether Argentina's commitment to its currency board might be as flimsy as Mexico's commitment to its official foreign exchange trading band.

Although a currency board is not a panacea for a nation's economic problems, many have proposed the adoption of currency boards in nations that have experienced significant inflation during the 1990s, such as Russia and the countries of eastern Europe. Advocates of currency boards argue that adopting currency boards would help these nations cut their inflation rates by giving them the credibility that they need to fix their exchange rates relative to relatively low-inflation nations.

FUNDAMENTAL ISSUE #6

What approaches have some nations with fixed exchange rates followed to make their policies credible? Committing to a fixed exchange rate is a credible policy only if the targeted rate at which a nation's currency trades for the currency of another country is consistent with the real rate of exchange of those nations' goods. In addition, a nation must have sufficient reserves of foreign currencies that it can use, when needed, to buy its own currency to support its value. It is very difficult for a single, small nation to meet both of these criteria. In recent years, some European nations have banded together in an effort to share the burden of maintaining credible commitments to fixed exchange rates. In addition, other nations have adopted currency boards that back their currencies with reserves of currencies from other, low-inflation countries.

CHAPTER SUMMARY

1. **Policy Time Lags and How They Might Cause Well-Meaning Macroeconomic Policymakers to Destabilize the Economy:** Policy time lags are the intervals between the need for a policy action and the action's eventual effects on the economy. The recognition lag is the time between the need for a Fed policy action and the Fed's realization of the need, and the response lag is the interval between the recognition of the need for an action and actual implementation of a policy change. Finally, the transmission lag is the time between the implementation of a policy action and the action's ultimate effects on the economy. Together, these three policy time lags can amount to an interval in excess of a year. They can also cause a discretionary policymaker that reacts to changing circumstances to undertake a policy action that is procyclical, despite the policymaker's intention to enact a countercyclical policy. This potential for policy to destabilize the economy is a key argument favoring the adoption of policy rules, or fixed commitments to specific policy strategies.

2. **The Main Arguments Favoring Discretionary Policymaking:** One rationale for conducting macroeconomic policymaking in a discretionary manner is that central banks and governments may have information advantages through their abilities to compile and analyze various sources of data on macroeconomic performance. Another justification is that central banks and governments do not seek to maximize their profits. Consequently, they may be able to focus their attention on the well-being of society as a whole.

3. **Why Policy Credibility Is a Crucial Factor in Maintaining Low Inflation:** When nominal wage contracts exist, a macroeconomic policymaker can push real output toward its capacity level by increasing aggregate demand. Thus, workers and firms that establish wage contracts will doubt the sincerity of the policymaker's commitment to restrain inflation, and they will negotiate higher wages. This will reduce aggregate supply and cause real output to decline in the absence of higher aggregate demand. To avoid this outcome, the policymaker must raise aggregate demand and create an inflation bias. To mitigate this inflation bias, the policymaker must find a way to make its commitment to low inflation credible.

4. **How Monetary Policy Credibility Might Be Achieved:** By indexing their wages fully to inflation, workers and firms will make the aggregate supply schedule vertical and eliminate a central bank's incentive to expand aggregate demand. A more direct approach is to

make it unlawful for central banks to permit inflation in excess of a certain rate. Another approach is to sign central bank officials to contracts that base their continued employment or their salaries on a nation's inflation outcomes. To reduce the likelihood that central banks will pursue inflationary policies, governments can appoint conservative central banking officials who are known to dislike inflation. Finally, central banks can gain credibility by permitting real output to decline in the short run in the face of people's doubts about the bank's commitments to policy rules. To demonstrate its commitment in this way, however, a central bank must be sufficiently independent from political influences.

5. **How Fiscal Policy Credibility Might Be Achieved:** Democratic legislatures typically enact explicit budgeting rules to help limit government spending. In the United States, Congress also has entrusted bipartisan commissions with proposing spending cuts so as to avoid political infighting that could limit needed cuts. One possible way to ensure fiscal policy credibility would be to enact a balanced-budget amendment to the U.S. Constitution.

6. **Approaches Some Nations with Fixed Exchange Rates Have Followed to Make Their Policies Credible:** Credible commitment to a policy of maintaining a fixed exchange rate requires selecting a target exchange rate consistent with the real rate of exchange between nations and possessing sufficient reserves of foreign currencies to use in supporting the target exchange rate via exchange-market interventions. Because small nations often struggle to satisfy both of these conditions alone, individual European nations have formed a cooperative group to coordinate their exchange-rate policies. Other countries have established currency boards, which issue home currencies backed 100 percent with reserves of the currency of another, low-inflation country.

 # QUESTIONS AND PROBLEMS

1. List and define the three types of policy time lags. Which do you think is likely to be *least* problematical for monetary policy? Which do you think is likely to be the *greatest* problem for monetary policy? Explain your reasoning.

2. Which type of policy time lag do you believe is likely to be *least* problematical for fiscal policy? Which do you think is likely to be the *most significant* problem for fiscal policy? Explain your reasoning.

3. Discuss why central banks and governments may be uniquely qualified to conduct discretionary macroeconomic policies. How does the public choice theory create doubts about this notion?

4. Why can the time inconsistency problem lead to an inflation bias in macroeconomic policymaking when workers and firms contract wages?

5. Explain, in your own words, why full wage indexation may not be a viable solution to the time inconsistency problem.

6. Evaluate the following statement: "A real strength of performance contracts for central bankers is that they give central bankers policy discretion while subjecting them to a societal rule."

7. Explain the distinction between political and economic independence of central banks. Are both necessary if a central bank is to be truly free to conduct anti-inflationary monetary policies?

8. The U.S. government lists a number of its expenditures on a separate budget from the official budget that it uses to calculate the official federal government deficit. In recent years some members of Congress have proposed moving additional budget items "off the budget." Why does this proposal cast doubt on the ability of a balanced-budget amendment to make U.S. fiscal policy credible?

9. Critics of currency boards argue that they are unlikely to enhance a nation's exchange-rate credibility significantly unless preprogrammed computers replace the people on the currency board. Can you think of a reason why critics might make this argument?

10. In 1997, leaders of Germany and France argued about whether the proposed European Central Bank should be overseen by a committee of political leaders. French leaders supported establishment of such a group to ensure that political leaders could steer the European Central Bank toward policies consistent with higher economic growth for Europe. German leaders opposed the idea and argued that it would lead to higher European inflation. In light of what you have learned in this chapter, which country's leaders do you think were correct? Explain your reasoning.

CYBERTUTOR EXERCISE

Consider Figure 13–6 in the text. One of the tools the Federal Reserve has to affect inflation is the stock of money. Let's see if there is a relationship between the growth rate of the money stock and the inflation rate. Construct a money growth rate variable and plot it against the inflation rate. What relationship seems to exist? Does this relationship vary over time? What does this plot suggest about the Federal Reserve's role in combating inflation?

ON-LINE APPLICATION

As discussed in this chapter, member nations of the European Union are struggling with issues involving rules versus discretion in macroeconomic policymaking. This application acquaints you with issues concerning monetary policy in the EU.

Internet URL: http://www.europa.eu.int

Title: The European Union: The European Monetary Institute

Navigation: Begin at the above address for the homepage of the European Union, and click on *Welcome*. Then scan down the page and click on *Institutions*. Next click on *European Monetary Institute*, and then click on *Homepage*, then *General Overview*.

Application: Perform the indicated operations, and answer the following questions:

1. Click on *Historical Background*. Read this article. What are some of the key issues faced by European nations interested in coordinating their monetary policies?

2. Back up to *General Overview* once again, and click on *Structure and Organization of the EMI*. Read this article. Then back up to *General Overview*, and click on *Objectives, Tasks, and Functions of the EMI*. Read this section as well. In your view, based on these readings, is the EMI a European central banking institution? Support your answer.

SELECTED REFERENCES AND FURTHER READING

Barro, Robert J. *Macroeconomic Policy*. Cambridge, Mass.: Harvard University Press, 1990.

Bryson, Jay, Henrik Jensen, and David VanHoose. "Rules, Discretion, and International Monetary and Fiscal Policy Coordination, *Open Economics Review* 4 (April 1993), 117–132.

Cukierman, Alex. *Central Bank Strategy, Credibility, and Independence*. Cambridge, Mass.: MIT Press, 1992.

Dwyer, Gerald, Jr. "Rules and Discretion in Monetary Policy." Federal Reserve Bank of St. Louis *Review*, May/June 1993, pp. 3–14.

Pollard, Patricia. "Central Bank Independence and Economic Performance." Federal Reserve Bank of St. Louis *Review*, July/August 1993, pp. 21–36.

Sheffrin, Steven. *The Making of Economic Policy: History, Theory, Politics*. Cambridge: Blackwell, 1991.

VanHoose, David. "Monetary Policy Centralization, Rules, Discretion, and Conservative Central Bankers in the European Monetary System," *Journal of Economics and Business* 44 (November 1992), 247–263.

Waller, Christopher. "Performance Contracts for Central Bankers." Federal Reserve Bank of St. Louis *Review*, September/October 1995, pp. 3–14.

Waller, Christopher, and David VanHoose. "Discretionary Monetary Policy and Socially Efficient Wage Indexation," *Quarterly Journal of Economics* 107 (November 1992), 451–460.

Walsh, Carl. "Optimal Contracts for Central Bankers." *American Economic Review* 85 (March 1995):150–167.

14

Policymaking in the World Economy—

INTERNATIONAL DIMENSIONS OF MACROECONOMIC POLICY

FUNDAMENTAL ISSUES

 1. What are the pros and cons of fixed versus floating exchange rates?

 2. How do monetary and fiscal policy actions affect a nation's real income under fixed exchange rates?

 3. How do monetary and fiscal policy actions affect a nation's real income under floating exchange rates?

 4. In what ways is the world economy becoming more integrated, and how does greater integration affect macroeconomic policymaking?

5. How do nations' policies influence their relative rates of growth in a more integrated world economy?

The news wasn't good. The dollar lost ground against the mark and the yen as the market shrugged off positive comments about the dollar from an official at the Bundesbank (Germany's central bank) and ignored Japanese industrial production data that were much lower than expected.

According to dealers, the foreign exchange market was quiet because investors were waiting for crucial U.S. economic reports. The health of the U.S. economy was at issue, but at the same time the dollar was being pressured by the mark as the German currency continued to strengthen against other European currencies because the German central bank refused to lower interest rates. Concurrently, U.S. Treasury officials offered reasons why the dollar was going to rally.

At about that time, members of an official U.S. Treasury team were getting ready to go to the next meeting of the so-called Group of Seven—Canada, France, Germany, Italy, Japan, the United Kingdom, and the United States. Members of this group meet periodically to try to get a handle on which currencies are over- or undervalued. Whether they are ever successful is another story.

Actions such as these occur over and over in foreign exchange markets and in the highest levels of government. Clearly, the value of the dollar relative to other currencies must be important. In this chapter you will learn about the policy options that are available when dealing with foreign exchange rates.

FIXED VERSUS FLOATING EXCHANGE RATES

As we noted in Chapter 13, many nations, including the United States, in years past have sought to maintain fixed exchange rates. More recently, a number of nations have permitted their exchange rates to float, or be market determined. At the same time, some European nations have attempted to fix exchange rates among their own currencies while allowing their exchange rates vis-à-vis non-European nations to float.

What factors should a country take into account when choosing between fixed and floating exchange rates? How is a nation's ability to use monetary and fiscal policies to achieve ultimate macroeconomic objectives affected by its choice? We begin our exploration of the international dimensions of macroeconomics by contemplating these important questions.

Floating Exchange Rates and Foreign Exchange Risks

As you will learn later in the chapter, there are good reasons for a nation to allow the value of its currency to float. Naturally, once this decision is made, variations in the demand or supply of foreign exchange can cause the exchange rate to fluctuate. Changes in the exchange rate can affect the market value of financial assets that are denominated in foreign currencies. This can increase the risks that a nation's residents face, thereby forcing them to incur costs to avoid these risks.

Foreign Exchange Risk   The possibility that variations in market values of assets can take place as a result of changes in the value of a nation's currency is called the **foreign exchange risk** that residents of a country face because their nation's currency value can vary. There are three basic types of foreign exchange risk.

FOREIGN EXCHANGE RISK The possibility that fluctuations in exchange rates can cause variations in the market values of assets.

1. *Accounting risk.* When exchange rates change, the market value of assets denominated in foreign currencies changes even though the underlying interest returns on those instruments are unaffected. The risk that a country's residents may experience such variations in the market value of their foreign assets is known as **accounting risk.**

   To understand how accounting risk can arise, consider a situation in which a German company has granted trade credit to a U.S. company by sending it German export goods in exchange for a promise to pay for the goods upon their receipt two weeks hence. The U.S. company has agreed to pay the German firm 100,000 DM (deutsche marks) at that time. When the agreement was reached, 1 DM was equal to $0.65, so the value of the payment that the U.S. firm would owe the German company was equal to $65,000. Further suppose that before the goods are received, the dollar's value falls in the foreign exchange market, so that 1 DM rises in value to $0.70. Now the dollar value of the U.S. firm's liability is equal to $70,000. Solely as a matter of accounting, the U.S. company's dollar liabilities have risen as a result of the change in the dollar–deutsche mark exchange rate.

ACCOUNTING RISK The possibility that the market value of assets denominated in foreign currencies may vary as a result of changes in exchange rates even when the underlying interest returns on those assets are unaffected.

2. *Transaction risk.* Another type of foreign exchange risk is **transaction risk.** This is the possibility that the value of a financial asset relating to the funding of a transaction denominated in a foreign currency could change due to an exchange-rate movement that affects the underlying value of the transaction.

   Suppose for instance, that a U.S. company in the import-export business purchases a large volume of Japanese goods for distribution in the United States and finances the shipment with a loan from a U.S. bank. The bank issues a loan that guarantees payment to the Japanese company selling the goods, and the U.S. company agrees to pay for the goods in yen, the Japanese currency, upon their receipt. The shipment takes several weeks, and in the meantime the dollar's value relative to the yen declines sharply, so the U.S. firm must come up with more dollars to make its yen payment. If the U.S. firm has made many such agreements with Japanese importers, it could end up defaulting on its obligations, leaving the U.S. bank as the responsible party in the transaction. In this manner, changes in exchange rates can increase the risk that banks take on when they issue loans to finance import-export firms.

TRANSACTION RISK The possibility that the value of a financial asset involved in funding an exchange denominated in a foreign currency could vary with exchange-rate movements, thereby affecting the underlying value of the transaction.

3. *Currency risk.* In Chapter 9, we saw that when bonds with identical maturities and risk characteristics are issued by two different nations, the difference between the

bonds' interest rates should be approximately equal to the expected rate of depreciation of the currency of one of the nations relative to the currency of the other. Because exchange-rate variations can cause expectations of currency depreciation to change, interest rates on bonds and other financial assets issued by different nations can vary relative to one another. Hence, the underlying rates of return on financial assets denominated in other currencies can fluctuate as a result of changes in exchange rates. The possibility of such variations in underlying asset returns due to exchange-rate variability is known as **currency risk.**

CURRENCY RISK The possibility that rates of return on financial assets denominated in other currencies can fluctuate as a result of changes in exchange rates that cause variations in the market values of those assets.

HEDGE The act of adopting strategies to reduce the overall risk resulting from fluctuations in market values of assets caused by such factors as exchange-rate volatility.

Hedging against Foreign Exchange Risk A country's residents are not defenseless in the face of foreign exchange risk. They can **hedge** against such risks, meaning that they can adopt strategies intended to offset the risk arising from exchange-rate variations.

For instance, as discussed in Chapter 9, individuals and firms can use *forward currency contracts* to ensure that they will receive the current market forward exchange rate on the future delivery of a sum of currency. Forward currency contracts thereby help to shield a firm or an individual from accounting risk and transaction risk. To hedge against currency risk, people can use other types of financial instruments, such as *interest-rate forward contracts*. These financial contracts entail the sale of a financial instrument at a certain interest rate on a specific future date, thereby guaranteeing a predetermined interest return. Companies also use *interest-rate swaps* as hedges. These are contractual agreements under which firms trade the interest returns that they earn on bonds and other assets denominated in different currencies.

A Rationale for Fixed Exchange Rates Hedging is not costless, however. For one thing, experts in the use of hedging strategies charge fees and commissions to companies and individuals that use them. In addition, hedging strategies themselves can entail taking positions that can be risky if market conditions change unexpectedly. Thus, efforts to hedge against foreign exchange risk sometimes can expose an individual or firm to other kinds of risks.

One common justification for fixed exchange rates is that they could reduce or even eliminate hedging costs. With fixed exchange rates, the potential for exchange-rate variability would be significantly diminished. This would save households and businesses from incurring the costs of hedging against foreign exchange risks.

The Exchange Rate as a Shock Absorber

The argument for fixing exchange rates implies that people worldwide might be better off if their governments agreed to a system of completely rigid exchange rates. Indeed, taken to its logical extreme, the argument indicates that everyone might be better off with a *single world currency.* After all, if we all used the same currency, not only would all foreign exchange risks be eliminated, but we would no longer have to incur the costs of converting one currency into another. For instance, today a U.S. tourist traveling from New York to London must pay a fee to convert dollars to pounds. Such fees would no longer exist if U.S. and British citizens used the same currency.

If a system of rigid exchange rates—or even common currency—is so advantageous, why are there so many separate currencies with floating exchange rates in the world today? The answer must be that there are potential drawbacks to fixing exchange rates or adopting a single currency. Nations must have good reasons for preferring their own currencies and often permitting their exchange rates to float.

The Benefit of Separate Currencies and a Floating Exchange Rate   The theory of *optimal currency areas,* which was developed by Robert Mundell of Columbia University, attempts to explain why different nations might wish to issue separate currencies. It also seeks to determine under what circumstances people in different geographic regions, such as Oregon and New Jersey, might gain from adopting a common currency unit.

A Two-Region Example   To understand the basic concept of an optimal currency area, let's consider a fictitious example. Suppose that there is a large island divided into two separate regions with nearly equal areas. In each region, wages and other prices of factors of production are sticky in the short run. Let's call one Region X and the other Region Y. Residents of each region specialize in producing different goods and services. Even though households and firms in the two regions trade goods and services across the border between the regions, there are barriers to movement of people and their possessions across the border. It could be that the residents of each region have political differences that have led them to erect such barriers, or it might be that they speak different languages or have different cultures or religions that have induced them to establish obstacles to mobility between the regions. Whatever the reason, these obstacles prevent people in the two regions from offering to exchange labor or other factor services. All they can do is to take their final goods and services to the border to trade.

Each region has its own government, which issues its own currency. Consequently, to trade their goods and services, people in each region must convert their currencies at the prevailing exchange rate between the two currencies.

Adjusting to Changes in the Relative Demands for Regional Products   Suppose further that residents of both regions reduce their demand for goods and services produced in Region Y, and increase their demand for those produced in Region X. Consequently, the firms in Region Y cut back on their demands for labor and other factors of production, and real income in Region Y begins to decline. Because wages are sticky, unemployment begins to increase in Region Y. At the same time, to induce firms in Region X to raise production in light of the increased demand for their goods, real income begins to rise in Region X.

If there were no barriers to movement between the regions, residents of Region Y could offer to move to, or commute into, Region X to work, which would help ease both the unemployment problem in Region Y and the inflation problem in Region X. Because obstacles prevent this type of adjustment, however, the burden of adjustment falls on the exchange rate. Because Region Y's residents desire more imports from Region X, the demand for Region X's currency rises. The result is an appreciation of Region X's currency and a depreciation of the currency of Region Y. Thus, Region Y's goods become relatively cheaper, and more of them will be consumed. As a result, firms in that region will begin to increase their production again. Region Y's unemployment rate will begin to fall, and the imbalance between the regions will begin to disappear.

These adjustments will not take place unless the exchange rate is flexible. Consequently, when barriers to movement of labor and other factors of production exist, as in our example, having separate currencies with a floating exchange rate is the right thing to do. If productive factors are immobile between different geographic regions, the exchange rate absorbs the burden of adjusting to changing relative demand and supply conditions. In our island example, therefore, Regions X and Y benefit from having separate currencies. The exchange rate performs the role of "shock absorber" when market conditions on the island change. Though residents of both regions must face currency conversion costs and foreign exchange risks by letting their exchange rate float, they gain from the relative price variations made possible by quick adjustments in the market exchange rate. Such adjustments help speed the relief from rising unemployment caused by changes in the relative demands for the regions' products.

Optimal Currency Areas   Regions X and Y benefit from having separate currencies because of the stickiness of wages and other input prices and the presence of obstacles to movement of labor and other factors of production. To see this, suppose that residents of the two regions eliminate all barriers to island mobility. Now when demand for goods and services produced in Region Y declines, residents of that region can simply move to, or commute into, Region X to supply their labor and other factor services. An exchange rate is not needed to absorb the burden of adjustment to the altered circumstances. The people themselves can adjust by changing the location of their employment.

In this case, the entire island is an **optimal currency area,** or a geographic region in which fixed exchange rates can be maintained without hindering international adjustment. Indeed, Regions X and Y might want to contemplate adopting a single currency, because without any barriers to mobility of goods, services, and productive factors, the entire island, for all intents and purposes, constitutes a single, integrated economy.

OPTIMAL CURRENCY AREA A region in which fixed exchange rates can be maintained without inhibiting prompt internal adjustments of employment and output to changes in international market conditions.

Problems with Fixed-Exchange-Rate or Single-Currency Systems   The theory of optimal currency areas explains why nations might wish to use different currencies and to let their exchange rates float. If nations use immigration restrictions, capital controls, and the like to restrain the flow of people and other productive factors *across* their borders, then it makes sense to use their own currencies *within* their borders. Allowing the exchange rate to adjust to variations in international demand and supply conditions then permits speedier price, output, and employment adjustments to these variations. This explains why Brazil and Argentina, nations with somewhat different languages and cultures and relatively limited mobility of people and productive factors across their borders, prefer to have separate currencies and to let their exchange rate vary.

The theory also helps to explain why residents of Oregon and New Jersey both use dollars, even though they are separated by more than two thousand miles. Because there is such easy mobility of labor and capital in the United States, little social cost is associated with fixing a one-for-one exchange rate and adopting a common currency in these two states, as well as in the other forty-eight. By using a common currency, residents of these states also save the costs of avoiding foreign exchange risks. In addition, when an Oregon resident visits relatives in Newark or when a New Jersey resident buys goods listed in the catalogue of a Portland-based company, neither has to worry about costs of converting currencies.

Finally, the theory helps to explain why nations in some regions of the world, such as parts of East Asia and western Europe, have contemplated or even experimented with rigid exchange rates or common currencies. Nations in these regions have significantly reduced (but not eliminated) obstacles to flows of people and productive factors, and their economies are closely linked by trade in goods, services, and financial assets. Nevertheless, cultural and language barriers still exist in both parts of the world. It remains to be seen if either region will adopt a common currency during the twenty-first century.

FUNDAMENTAL ISSUE #1

What are the pros and cons of fixed versus floating exchange rates?
A key drawback of floating exchange rates is the resulting potential for foreign exchange risks stemming from exchange-rate variability. Fixing the exchange rate reduces the extent of foreign exchange risks. A key problem with a fixed exchange rate is that this policy approach eliminates the exchange rate's ability to serve as a shock absorber in the event of changing international market conditions. This is particularly true for nations with barriers to mobility of labor and other real productive factors. Such nations can benefit from adopting their own currencies and permitting their exchange rate to vary with changing market forces.

MACROECONOMIC POLICY WITH FIXED EXCHANGE RATES

Even though nations continue to use their own currencies, many still choose to fix their exchange rates. These nations judge that the costs of hedging against foreign exchange risks are greater than the costs arising from adjustments that may be required in the absence of shock-absorbing adjustments in the exchange rate.

How does the adoption of a fixed exchange rate influence the transmission of macroeconomic policies? What complications do policymakers face when they peg their exchange rate? Let's try to answer these questions using the analytical frameworks that we have developed in earlier chapters.

Monetary Policy under Fixed Exchange Rates

As we discussed in Chapter 13, a key problem of maintaining a fixed exchange rate is making a credible commitment to a particular exchange rate. Nevertheless, let's suppose that a country has established a credible fixed-exchange-rate commitment and examine how monetary policy actions would affect interest rates and real income in this setting.

In the examples that follow, we assume an unchanging price level following policy actions. You already know that the speed and extent of price-level adjustments depend on the position and elasticity of the aggregate supply schedule. Consequently, the following examples focus on how real income, and therefore the position of the aggregate demand schedule, would initially respond to a given policy action.

Initial Effects of an Expansionary Monetary Policy   Figure 14–1 on page 476 shows the immediate effects of a central bank action to increase the nominal money stock under a fixed exchange rate. In both panels, a monetary expansion, from M_1 to M_2, causes the *LM* schedule to shift rightward from an initial point *A*, at which, as we first discussed in Chapter 7, the country's private payments balance is equal to zero along the *BP* schedule. This results in a new *IS-LM* equilibrium point, point *B*, below and to the right of the *BP* schedule. Hence, a monetary expansion will result in a private payments deficit at point *B* in each panel.

In panel (a), capital mobility is low, so the *BP* schedule is relatively inelastic in the relevant range. Here, the main reason that a private payments deficit will occur is that the monetary expansion causes a rise in real income. This induces an increase in imports and a consequent trade deficit. Although the equilibrium interest rate will decline, the low capital mobility implies that little capital will flow out of the country. Thus, the main reason for the private payments deficit that arises at point *B* is the trade deficit caused by greater import expenditures at the higher income level y_2.

In contrast, in panel (b) capital mobility is high, so the *BP* schedule is relatively more elastic in the relevant range. In this case, a decline in the nation's equilibrium

FIGURE 14–1   THE INITIAL EFFECTS OF MONETARY POLICY WITH FIXED EXCHANGE RATES

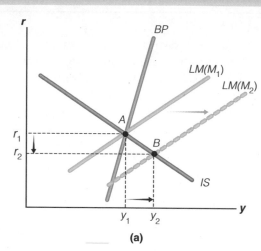

(a)

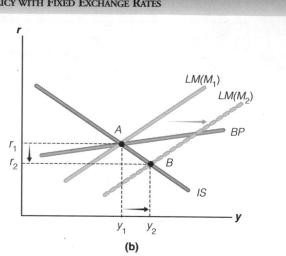

(b)

Both panels show how a monetary expansion initially affects the nominal interest rate and real income under a fixed exchange rate. In panel (a), the *BP* schedule is relatively inelastic, indicating a situation of low capital mobility. The decline in the equilibrium interest rate that occurs following a movement from point *A* to point *B* induces little capital outflow, but the rise in equilibrium

real income stimulates greater import spending. The result is a private payments deficit at point *B*. In panel (b), the *BP* schedule is much more elastic, implying a situation of high capital mobility. In this case, the decline in the equilibrium interest rate spurs a significant capital outflow that makes a key contribution to the resulting private payments deficit at point *B*.

interest rate to r_2 will cause a significant outflow of capital, so at point *B* the nation runs a sizable capital account deficit, which is a key contributor to the private payments deficit it will experience at this new equilibrium point. (For some perspective on the private payments deficit, see the Policy Notebook: *Should We Care Whether We Have a Private Payments Deficit?*)

Sterilized Monetary Policies   Following a period of monetary expansion that reduces the equilibrium interest rate and raises equilibrium real income, can a nation run private payments deficits indefinitely while maintaining a commitment to a fixed exchange rate? In principle, the answer is yes. A nation's ability to do this, however, depends on the amount of foreign exchange reserves held by its central bank and government. In addition, the ultimate effects of a monetary expansion depend on whether or not the nation's central bank conducts a policy of *sterilization*.

STERILIZATION A central bank action to prevent variations in its foreign exchange reserves from affecting the total amount of money in circulation.

Sterilization is a central bank action to prevent changes in its foreign exchange reserves from affecting its nation's money stock. The money that any central bank issues is a liability of the central bank that must be backed by its assets. In the United States, for instance, more than 90 percent of the liabilities of the Federal Reserve System are currency in circulation and dollar reserves held by U.S. banks with the Fed-

Should We Care Whether We Have a Private Payments Deficit?

The current account in the United States has been in deficit most years since the late 1970s. This is not a new phenomenon. During the 1880s, the United States often had current account deficits. They were matched by capital account surpluses, as the rest of the world sent capital to the United States to finance the building of the railroads and the development of the trans-Mississippi west. By the early 1900s, the United States had accumulated a long string of current account surpluses. By World War I, the United States had repaid all of its external debt and had become a net creditor. In 1980, in fact the United States was the world's largest creditor. By 1986, however, it was the world's largest debtor nation. Remember a very important identity, however: Whenever the United States has a deficit in its current account, its capital account and official settlements balance together must show a surplus.

Contrary to popular belief, the United States does not have a trade deficit because it is a weak economy that cannot compete in world markets. On the contrary, the United States appears to be a good place to invest capital because it offers strong prospects for growth and earnings opportunities. As long as foreigners wish to invest more in the United States than U.S. residents wish to invest abroad, the United States will have a deficit in its current account balance. U.S. residents are the beneficiaries of international capital flows. In other words, the current account deficit will exist as long as foreigners want to invest (on net) more in the United States.

FOR CRITICAL ANALYSIS:
Why are politicians, nevertheless, so worried about the international trade deficit?

---

eral Reserve. The Federal Reserve backs these money liabilities with holdings of U.S. government bonds and other assets, *including* assets denominated in foreign currencies, or the Federal Reserve's foreign exchange reserves. Only a small fraction of the U.S. money stock is backed by foreign exchange reserves of the Federal Reserve. In many other nations, foreign exchange reserves account for a much greater portion of central bank assets.

At point *B* in either panel of Figure 14–1, the fact that a nation runs a private payments deficit means that there will be market pressures for the nation's exchange rate to change. With low capital mobility, as in panel (a), the rise in real income at point *B* will induce the nation's residents to seek to acquire other nations' currencies so that they can purchase more imports, thereby raising their demand for foreign exchange and placing downward pressure on the value of their own nation's currency. At point *B* in panel (b), in contrast, a decline in the equilibrium interest rate will cause residents to wish to acquire more foreign capital. This also will entail purchasing more foreign currencies with their own nation's currency, which will tend to depress the value of their nation's currency in the foreign exchange markets.

To prevent the exchange value of its currency from declining at point *B* in either panel of Figure 14–1, the nation's central bank will have to sell some of its assets that are denominated in foreign currencies. This action will offset the rise in the demand for foreign currencies by its own citizens by increasing the supply of foreign currencies in the foreign exchange markets. Thus, this policy response will be required at point *B* if the central bank wishes to maintain the nation's fixed exchange rate. If the central bank sells some of its foreign currency reserves, however, its total assets will decline. This would require a decline in the bank's liabilities, including some of its money liabilities in circulation. To keep this situation from occurring, the central bank will have to add sufficient *domestic* assets, such as domestic government bonds, to prevent its total assets from falling. This is the process of sterilization.

The Monetary Approach to the Balance of Payments   What will happen if the central bank chooses not to sterilize after a monetary expansion that induces a private payments deficit and a decline in its foreign exchange reserves? Figure 14–2 illustrates the implications of such a decision. As in Figure 14–1, panels (a) and (b) of the Figure 14–2 show the immediate effects of a monetary expansion with low capital mobility and high capital mobility, respectively. In both cases, at a new equilibrium point *B,*

FIGURE 14–2   **THE FINAL EFFECTS OF A MONETARY POLICY EXPANSION WITHOUT STERILIZATION**

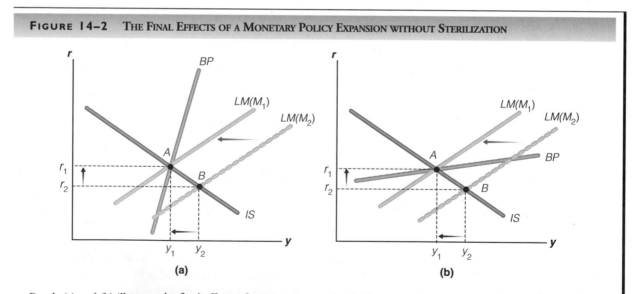

(a)   **(b)**

Panels (a) and (b) illustrate the final effects of an increase in the nominal quantity of money that first causes a movement from point *A* to point *B* and results in a private payments deficit, as shown in Figure 14–1. In panel (a), capital mobility is relatively low, so the resulting private payments deficit stems mainly from higher import expenditures. In panel (b), there is significant capital mobility, so the private payments deficit at point *B* results mainly from capital outflows. In either case, the private payments deficit implies an increased demand for foreign currencies by the nation's residents. To keep the exchange rate from changing, the nation's central bank will have to sell foreign exchange reserves. If the central bank does not sterilize this action, it will cause a reduction in the quantity of money in circulation and an ultimate movement back to point *A.*

the nation experiences a private payments deficit. This tends to depress the value of the nation's currency in foreign exchange markets, so the nation's central bank must sell some of its foreign exchange reserves to keep the exchange rate fixed.

If the central bank does not sterilize these outflows of foreign exchange reserves, its assets will decline, necessitating a decrease in the money liabilities that it issues. The nation's nominal money stock will start to fall. As shown in both panels of Figure 14–2, failure to sterilize ultimately will cause the nation's quantity of money to decline from M_2, the level to which the central bank originally had expanded the nation's money stock, back to M_1, the original quantity of money before the monetary expansion. The central bank's efforts to keep the exchange rate fixed by selling foreign exchange reserves ultimately will cause the nation's money stock to contract once more. As a result, the *LM* schedule will shift back to its original location, and the initial *IS-LM* equilibrium point *A* will be reattained.

> A *nonsterilized* monetary expansion with a fixed exchange rate ultimately leads to a contraction of the money stock and a return to the economy's initial equilibrium real income level and interest rate.

As a result of the fall in real income, in panel (a) imports decline and the trade deficit falls. In panel (b), a rise in the nominal interest rate leads to the return of capital and a decrease in the nation's capital account deficit. In both panels, the private payments balance ultimately returns to zero at point *A*.

Figure 14–2 illustrates a concept known as the **monetary approach to the balance of payments.** Under this view, a commitment to a fixed exchange rate causes a nation's money stock to vary with changes in foreign exchange reserves that are necessary to keep the exchange rate fixed. Without central bank sterilization, the result is an automatic adjustment toward a private payments balance.

Note that if a central bank tries to sterilize indefinitely, so as to keep real income at y_2 at point *B*, it must attempt to maintain a continuing private payments deficit that would place perpetual downward pressures on the nation's currency value. To keep the exchange rate fixed, therefore, the nation's central bank would have to continually sell foreign exchange reserves in the foreign exchange markets. No central bank has sufficient reserves of foreign-currency-denominated assets to mount such an effort for very long. Indeed, even sporadic efforts by the Federal Reserve and U.S. Treasury to maintain the dollar's value have led to significant losses of foreign currency reserves since the early 1980s. Since the United States began running significant private payments deficits in the early 1980s, these efforts have resulted in a cumulative loss of more than half of the foreign exchange reserves held by these two policymaking institutions. Smaller countries such as Mexico and Bolivia rarely have sufficient foreign exchange reserves available to fix exchange rates for a lengthy period via sterilized monetary expansions. Ultimately, nations such as these that attempt to expand real income via

MONETARY APPROACH TO THE BALANCE OF PAYMENTS A theory of unsterilized monetary policy under fixed exchange rates; changes in foreign exchange reserves required to maintain a fixed exchange rate cause a nation's money stock to adjust automatically in a direction that leads to attainment of a private payments balance of zero.

expansionary monetary policies must either permit their money stocks to contract or devalue their currencies by altering their exchange-rate targets.

Fiscal Policy under Fixed Exchange Rates

As you learned in the discussion of the twin deficit problem in Chapter 7, the degree of capital mobility influences the macroeconomic effects of fiscal policy actions. We will begin by reviewing this issue and then will contemplate how maintaining a fixed exchange rate automatically produces an interaction between fiscal and monetary policy decisions.

Fiscal Policy Effects with Different Degrees of Capital Mobility   Both panels in Figure 14–3 depict the effects of a bond-financed rise in government spending. In panel (a), capital mobility is low, so the *BP* schedule is relatively inelastic in the relevant range. In panel (b), capital is highly mobile, so the *BP* schedule is more elastic in the relevant range. In each panel we consider an initial point *A* at which there is an *IS-LM* equilibrium along the *BP* schedule, which implies that the private pay-

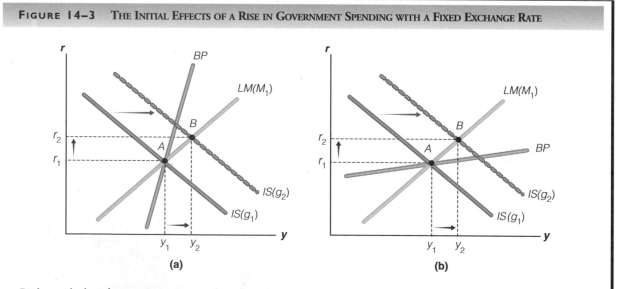

FIGURE 14–3   THE INITIAL EFFECTS OF A RISE IN GOVERNMENT SPENDING WITH A FIXED EXCHANGE RATE

Both panels show how an increase in real government expenditures initially induces an increase in the equilibrium nominal interest rate and a rise in equilibrium real income. In panel (a) the *BP* schedule is relatively inelastic, which implies a situation of low capital mobility. The increase in the equilibrium interest rate that occurs following a movement from point *A* to point *B* induces little capital inflow, but the rise in equilibrium real income stimulates greater import spending. The net result is a private payments deficit at point *B*. In panel (b) the *BP* schedule is much more elastic, which indicates a situation of high capital mobility. In this case, the rise in the equilibrium interest rate spurs a significant capital inflow that more than offsets the higher imports owing to the increase in equilibrium real income. This results in a private payments surplus at point *B* in panel (b).

ments balance initially is equal to zero. In addition, a rise in government spending causes a rightward shift in the *IS* schedule, from $IS(g_1)$ to $IS(g_2)$, that yields a new equilibrium point *B* in each panel, with a higher nominal interest rate r_2 and a higher level of real income y_2.

In panel (a), the increase in real income causes a rise in imports that leads to a trade deficit. Although the rise in the equilibrium interest rate induces some capital to flow into the nation, with low capital mobility this effect will be small. Consequently, on net there will be a private payments deficit, indicated by point *B*'s position below and to the right of the *BP* schedule. In panel (b), capital is much more mobile, so a significant capital inflow will occur as a result of the higher equilibrium interest rate. The resulting capital account surplus will more than counterbalance the trade deficit resulting from higher income and imports. Thus, panel (b) shows that with very high capital mobility, an increase in government spending results in a private payments surplus, because point *B* is above and to the left of the *BP* schedule.

A Fixed Exchange Rate as a Source of Fiscal Pressure on Monetary Policy   At point *B* in both panels of Figure 14–3, a nation will experience a private payments imbalance that will place market pressures on the exchange rate, thereby forcing the central bank to trade foreign exchange reserves to support the fixed exchange rate. When the central bank sterilizes by trading domestic bonds to keep the money stock from changing, the nation can remain at equilibrium point *B* in panel (a) only as long as the central bank's foreign exchange reserves held out. Running a continuous private payments deficit will place downward pressure on the nation's currency value, however, so the central bank will have to keep selling its foreign-currency-denominated assets. Eventually, it may run out of these assets and have to let the nation's currency value fall, but in the meantime the economy will remain at point *B*.

In panel (b), where there is a private payments surplus at point *B*, there will be *upward* pressure on the value of the nation's currency. As a result, to maintain a fixed exchange rate the central bank will have to *purchase* foreign-currency-denominated assets. Thus, the central bank will begin to accumulate more foreign exchange reserves. Sterilizing the effect that this accumulation otherwise would have on the money stock will require the central bank to sell domestic bonds. Then the economy can remain at point *B* in panel (b) as long as the central bank's holdings of domestic bonds remain undepleted.

Figure 14–4 on page 482 shows what will happen if the central bank is unable or unwilling to conduct sterilization operations following a rise in government spending. Again both panels show movements from an initial point *A* with a private payments balance of zero to point *B* where there is a private payments imbalance. In the case of low capital mobility depicted in panel (a), a failure to sterilize will result in a decline in the nation's quantity of money in circulation as the central bank sells foreign exchange reserves to maintain the nation's fixed exchange rate in the face of a private payments deficit at point *B*. This will cause the *LM* schedule to shift leftward as

Figure 14–4 **The Final Effects of an Increase in Government Spending without Sterilization**

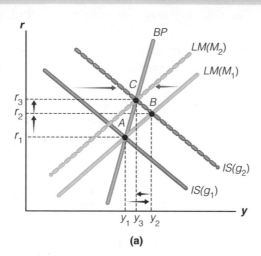

(a)

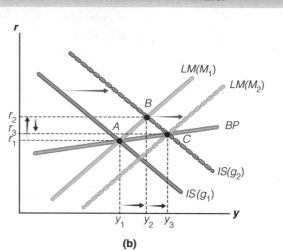

(b)

The panels of this figure illustrate the final effects of an increase in real government expenditures that initially causes a rightward shift in the *IS* schedule and a movement from point *A* to point *B,* as shown in Figure 14–3. In panel (a), capital mobility is relatively low, so a private payments deficit results from higher import expenditures that more than offset meager capital inflows. Hence, the nation's residents increase their demand for foreign currencies. To keep the exchange rate from changing, the nation's central bank will have to sell foreign exchange reserves, which without sterilization will cause a movement to point *C.* In contrast, in panel (b) there is significant capital mobility, so significant capital outflows more than offset increased imports, resulting in a private payments surplus at point *B.* As the nation's residents reduce their desired holdings of foreign currencies, the value of the nation's currency in foreign exchange markets will tend to rise. To keep the exchange rate from changing, the nation's central bank will purchase foreign exchange reserves, inducing a movement to point *C.*

the nation's money stock declines from M_1 to M_2, as predicted by the monetary approach to the balance of payments. This ultimately will lead to a new *IS-LM* equilibrium at point *C,* with a higher equilibrium interest rate r_3 and a somewhat lower equilibrium real income level y_3. The fall in real income will cause import spending to decline, thereby reducing the trade deficit and helping to produce a private payments balance equal to zero at point *C.* In this situation, the central bank no longer feels pressure to sell foreign exchange reserves to defend the fixed exchange rate.

In panel (b) of Figure 14–4, there is a private payments surplus at point *B* following a rise in government spending, because capital mobility is so high that the nation experiences a significant capital account surplus when its interest rate increases. As noted earlier, the central bank then will begin to accumulate foreign exchange reserves as it buys foreign-currency-denominated assets to maintain the fixed exchange rate. If the central bank does not sterilize, the nation's money stock will grow as the central bank's foreign exchange reserves increase. Thus, the *LM* schedule will shift to the right as the quantity of money in circulation increases from M_1 to M_2. As a result, the equilibrium interest rate will decline to r_3, causing a capital outflow that will return the private payments balance to zero at point *C* along the *BP* schedule.

Figures 14–3 and 14–4 illustrate an important implication of the monetary approach to the balance of payments under a fixed exchange rate: with a fixed exchange rate, fiscal policy actions place pressures on a nation's central bank. The central bank must respond to private payments imbalances induced by fiscal policy changes by depleting or accumulating foreign exchange reserves. In addition, it must decide whether or not to conduct sterilization operations by buying or selling domestic bonds to keep the nation's money stock from changing. As Figures 14–3 and 14–4 indicate, the effects of fiscal policy actions on a nation's real income depend on the choice that the central bank makes.

FUNDAMENTAL ISSUE #2

How do monetary and fiscal policy actions affect a nation's real income under fixed exchange rates? The effects of monetary policy actions with a fixed exchange rate depend in large measure upon the extent to which a nation's central bank sterilizes by preventing variations in its foreign exchange reserves from affecting the nation's nominal money stock. Under the monetary approach to the balance of payments, the immediate effects of unsterilized monetary policy actions on real income ultimately are reversed by offsetting changes in the quantity of money. Likewise, fiscal policy effects on a nation's real income also depend on a central bank's decision about sterilization. In general, however, an expansionary fiscal policy causes an unambiguous rise in real income, at least in the short run, when the exchange rate is fixed.

 ## MACROECONOMIC POLICY WITH FLOATING EXCHANGE RATES

As we have seen, with fixed exchange rates a nation's central bank must buy and sell foreign-currency-denominated assets to keep the exchange rate fixed, and it must decide whether or not to conduct sterilization operations as its foreign exchange reserves change. With floating exchange rates, a central bank is relieved of these responsibilities. As you will now learn, this tends to make the immediate real income and aggregate demand effects of monetary policy more potent, particularly in a world where capital is highly mobile. In contrast, fiscal policy under floating exchange rates may lose at least some of its ability to bring about initial real income and aggregate demand effects.

Monetary Policy under Floating Exchange Rates

Before we consider how monetary policy actions affect macroeconomic outcomes with floating exchange rates, let's begin by considering how changes in the exchange rate affect the positions of the *IS* and *BP* schedules.

The Effect of Changes in the Exchange Rate on the IS and BP Schedules
Figure 14–5 shows how a depreciation in the value of a nation's currency affects the *IS* and *BP* schedules. Panel (a) shows the effect of a currency depreciation on the *IS* schedule. A decline in the value of a nation's currency makes imports more expensive, so the nation's residents cut back on their import expenditures. At the same time, the nation's goods become less expensive for residents of other nations to purchase, so export expenditures rise. Both of these effects will lead to a rise in the nation's aggregate autonomous expenditures at any given interest rate, such as r_1 in panel (a). Hence, the level of real income consistent with an income-expenditure equilibrium will increase from y_1 at point A to y_2 at point B. Thus, the *IS* schedule will shift rightward, from IS_1 to IS_2, following a currency depreciation, as shown in panel (a).

FIGURE 14–5 THE EFFECTS OF A CURRENCY DEPRECIATION ON THE *IS* AND *BP* SCHEDULES

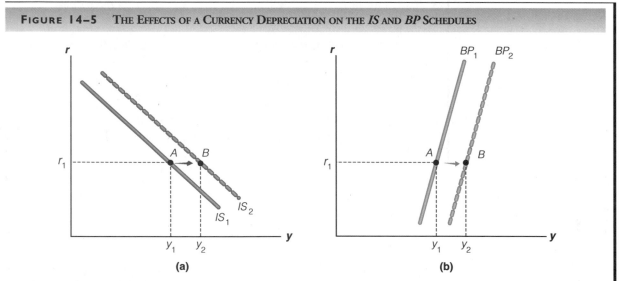

Depreciation of a nation's currency effectively makes the nation's goods less expensive for foreign residents and makes foreign goods more expensive for the nation's residents. Hence, export expenditures rise and import spending declines. The result is a rightward shift in the *IS* schedule from point A to point B in panel (a). At the same time, if point A in panel (a) corresponds to a situation in which the nation has a private payments

balance equal to zero, then point A will lie on the *BP* schedule, as shown in panel (b). The improvement in the merchandise trade balance and current account owing to the currency depreciation will then tend to induce a private payment surplus, so real income will have to increase to induce a rise in import spending. Hence, a currency depreciation will cause the *BP* schedule to shift rightward, as illustrated in panel (b).

A currency depreciation will also affect the position of the *BP* schedule. Recall that the *BP* schedule is the set of real income-interest rate combinations that maintains a private payments balance equal to zero, holding all other factors unchanged. As we just noted, however, a currency depreciation will cause a nation's exports to rise and its imports to fall at any given level of real income and at any given interest rate. Consequently, as shown in panel (b) of Figure 14–5, at a given real income–interest rate combination, such as y_1 and r_1 at point *A* on the *BP* schedule labeled BP_1, a currency depreciation will cause a trade balance improvement that will result in a private payments surplus at point *A*. To keep the private payments balance equal to zero, real income will have to increase to y_2, thereby stimulating increased import spending that will return the trade balance and, therefore, the private payments balance to zero. Thus, point *B* will be a point on a new *BP* schedule, denoted BP_2, that will result from a currency depreciation. A currency depreciation, we may conclude, will shift the *BP* schedule rightward, as shown in panel (b).

Expansionary Monetary Policy with a Floating Exchange Rate   Now we can examine the effect of an expansionary monetary policy action under floating exchange rates. We do this in panels (a) and (b) of Figure 14–6, where we begin with the same initial *IS-LM* equilibrium point *A* on an initial *BP* schedule labeled BP_1.

FIGURE 14–6   THE EFFECTS OF AN INCREASE IN THE MONEY STOCK WITH FLOATING EXCHANGE RATES

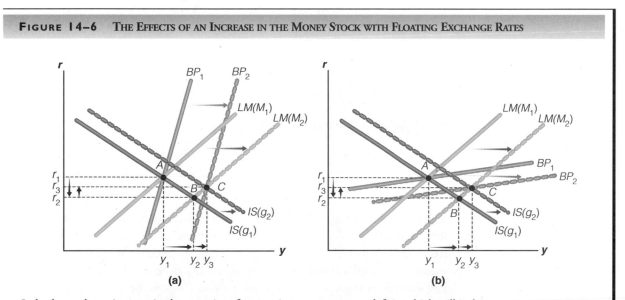

(a)   (b)

In both panels, an increase in the quantity of money in circulation causes a rightward shift in the *LM* schedule, thereby inducing a movement from point *A* to point *B*. In addition, in both panels the result is a private payments deficit at point *B*. In both panels, the result is a private payments deficit, which will induce a currency depreciation that will shift both the *IS* and the *BP* schedules rightward, leading to a final equilibrium with a zero private payments balance at point *C*.

Thus, initially the nation's private payments balance is equal to zero in both panels. In panel (a), the *BP* schedule is relatively inelastic in the relevant range, which indicates low capital mobility. In panel (b), capital mobility is much greater, so the *BP* schedule is relatively more elastic in the relevant range.

As usual, an increase in the money stock from M_1 to M_2 will cause the *LM* schedule to shift rightward. In both panels of Figure 14–6, therefore, there will be an initial movement from point *A* to point *B,* which lies below and to the right of the BP_1 schedule. Consequently, there is a private payments deficit at point *B.* With low capital mobility, in panel (a), the main reason for the private payments deficit is the rise in import spending spurred by an increase in real income from y_1 to y_2. With high capital mobility in panel (b), the key factor spurring the private payments deficit is the outflow of capital stemming from the decline in the interest rate from r_1 to r_2.

As a result of the private payments deficit that arises at point *B* in both panels of Figure 14–6, there will be a depreciation of the nation's currency in the foreign exchange markets, as the nation's residents increase their import spending and acquisition of foreign capital and as foreign citizens reduce their export spending and acquisition of the nation's capital. A currency depreciation, however, will make foreign goods more expensive to domestic residents and the nation's goods cheaper for foreign residents. Thus, the depreciation will cause export spending to rise and import spending to fall, and so the *IS* schedule will shift rightward, from IS_1 to IS_2. In addition, as we discussed earlier, the depreciation will cause the *BP* schedule to shift to the right, from BP_1 to BP_2. The eventual equilibrium point will be point *C,* at which the private payments balance will equal zero, so there is no further tendency for the nation's currency to depreciate. As Figure 14–6 shows, with both low and high capital mobility, a monetary expansion will cause a rise in real income, holding the price level and other factors unchanged.

Fiscal Policy under Floating Exchange Rates

Fiscal policy actions also induce changes in the value of a nation's currency when the nation's exchange rate floats. Capital mobility performs a key role in determining whether the currency's value rises or falls, however.

The Case of Low Capital Mobility   Panel (a) of Figure 14–7 on page 487 shows the effects of a bond-financed increase in government spending when a nation's capital mobility is low. With the exchange rate initially unchanged, a rise in government spending causes the *IS* schedule to shift rightward, from $IS_1(g_1)$ to $IS_1(g_2)$, resulting in a movement from point *A* to point *B.* Point *B* lies to the right of the BP_1 schedule, so the immediate effect of the rise in government spending will be a private payments deficit resulting from an increase in import spending stemming from a rise in real income. As a result of the private payments deficit, the nation's currency will depreciate, and net export spending will increase, thereby causing the *IS* schedule to shift rightward once more, to $IS_2(g_2)$. In addition, the depreciation will cause the *BP*

FIGURE 14-7 THE EFFECTS OF AN INCREASE IN GOVERNMENT SPENDING WITH A FLOATING EXCHANGE RATE

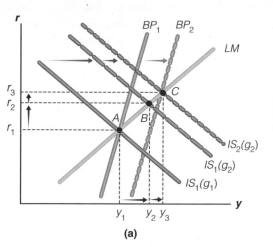

(a)

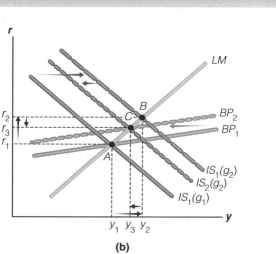

(b)

In both panels, an increase in government expenditures causes an initial rightward shift in the *IS* schedule, thereby inducing a movement from point *A* to point *B*, which leads to an increase in the equilibrium nominal interest rate and an increase in equilibrium real income. In panel (a), where the relatively low elasticity of the *BP* schedule implies low capital mobility, greater import spending will more than offset a small capital inflow and cause a private payments deficit to arise at point *B*. This will induce a currency depreciation that will shift both the *IS* and the

BP schedules to the right, leading to a final equilibrium with a zero private payments balance at point *C*. In panel (b), where the relatively high elasticity of the *BP* schedule implies high capital mobility, significant capital inflows will more than offset greater import expenditures and cause a private payments surplus to occur at point *B*. This will induce a currency appreciation that will shift both the *IS* and the *BP* schedules leftward, leading to a final equilibrium with a zero private payments balance at point *C*.

schedule to shift to the right, from BP_1 to BP_2. The final equilibrium point, with other factors such as the price level unchanged, will be point *C*, at which there once again is a zero private payments balance and, thus, no tendency for the nation's currency to depreciate further.

The Case of High Capital Mobility When capital is very mobile, as in panel (b) of Figure 14–7, the effects are different from those shown in panel (a). A bond-financed increase in government expenditures initially has an identical effect, as shown by the immediate movement from point *A* to point *B* in panel (b). With high capital mobility, however, the rise in the interest rate from r_1 to r_2 will cause significant capital inflows that will lead, on net, to a private payments *surplus* at point *B*, which lies above the BP_1 schedule. Consequently, foreign residents will seek to acquire more of the nation's currency to purchase domestic capital, so the value of the nation's currency will *appreciate*. This will make foreign goods cheaper to the nation's own residents but will make the nation's goods more expensive for foreign residents, spurring import spending and slowing export expenditures. As a result, the nation will experience a fall in autonomous expenditures, and the *IS* schedule will shift *leftward*, from $IS_1(g_2)$ to $IS_2(g_2)$. The currency appreciation will also cause the *BP* schedule to shift leftward, from BP_1 to BP_2. At the final equilibrium point *C*, real income on net will be higher, at y_3, than it was at the beginning level of y_1. Nevertheless, high capital mobility clearly alters the economy's adjustment to a bond-financed rise in government spending by muting the effects of the government spending increase on equilibrium real income.

FUNDAMENTAL ISSUE #3

How do monetary and fiscal policy actions affect a nation's real income under floating exchange rates? An expansionary monetary policy action results in a private payments deficit that leads to a depreciation of a nation's currency, thereby stimulating export expenditures while inhibiting import spending. Consequently, expansionary monetary policy actions cause a nation's real income to rise in the short run. The effects of fiscal policy actions on a nation's private payments balance and the value of its currency depend on the degree of capital mobility. Under most circumstances, an expansionary fiscal policy action causes at least a slight short-term increase in a nation's real income level. The extent of the rise in real income declines as the degree of capital mobility increases, however.

 MACROECONOMIC POLICY IN AN INTEGRATED WORLD ECONOMY

In many respects, the nations of the world have become more interconnected with each passing decade. Global news networks and the Internet now broadcast up-to-the second reports of activities in far-flung regions of the globe. The governments of many nations often work together to develop cooperative approaches to smoothing political tensions among pairs or groups of nations. Countries enter into coordinated military projects from time to time.

In the economic sphere, the process by which interrelationships develop among national markets for goods, services, factors of production, and financial assets is called **international economic integration.** In a fully integrated world economy, all national borders would be artificial demarcations indicating only political separations among countries. There would be no "British markets," "Chinese markets," or "Australian markets." Instead there would be a single world marketplace, and prod-

INTERNATIONAL ECONOMIC INTEGRATION The growth of interconnectedness among the world's markets for goods, services, factors of production, and financial assets.

ucts, resources, and funds would flow freely across borders in search of the highest returns available to owners, wherever they might reside.

Are National Economies Becoming More Integrated?

In an integrated world economy, people would have no difficulty buying goods, services, and resources in one nation, moving them across national borders, and reselling them to residents of other countries. Recall from Chapter 3 that *international arbitrage*, or the act of buying a good in one nation for profitable sale in another, is a key rationale for the *purchasing power parity* proposition. This proposition states that the price of a good in one nation should be the same as the exchange-rate-adjusted price of the same good in another nation. Thus, if P is the price of a good, service, or resource in one nation, P^* is the price of the same good, service, or resource in another nation, and E is the rate of exchange of the first nation's currency for the currency of the second nation, then purchasing power parity implies that $P = P^* \times E$.

Does Purchasing Power Parity Hold for Aggregate Prices?   The purchasing power parity proposition stems from the assumption that people can engage in international arbitrage. Furthermore, the ability to engage in international arbitrage requires the capability to trade goods across national borders. Thus, a key way for economists to gauge the extent of world market integration is to determine whether the purchasing power parity proposition is consistent with the actual behavior of prices around the globe.

Accordingly, economists have studied the purchasing power parity proposition's relevance to measures of aggregate prices, such as nations' GDP deflators or consumer price indexes. Under this approach, in the purchasing power parity relationship, $P = P^* \times E$, P and P^* are interpreted as aggregate price indexes in the two nations. If national markets are sufficiently integrated to permit international arbitrage to take place, then the aggregate price level in one nation should equal the exchange-rate-adjusted aggregate price level in another nation.

Economists have consistently found that this aggregate interpretation of purchasing power parity very rarely holds true over short intervals. Indeed, the purchasing power parity proposition fails dramatically over periods as long as a decade. Only over intervals spanning more than one decade do nations' price levels tend to show convergence to the purchasing power relationship. In a 1996 review of purchasing power parity studies, Kenneth Rogoff of Princeton University points out that it can take as long as two to five years for half of a deviation from purchasing power parity to be "made up" by price-level and exchange-rate adjustments. Other recent studies indicate that while purchasing power parity among aggregate prices may be satisfied over very long intervals spanning several decades, it is not satisfied in the short run. International arbitrage does not appear to take place very quickly. This conclusion weakens the argument that world markets are integrated, because it implies that nations' price levels tend to be determined largely by national factors alone.

There are good reasons, however, to expect that the purchasing power parity proposition might not hold for aggregate price measures even though it is satisfied for a large portion of goods, services, and resources around the globe. One key problem with applying the purchasing power parity proposition to aggregate price indexes is that different nations consume quite different sets of goods. For example, in one nation meat may comprise a large percentage of people's diets, while in another fruits and vegetables may be much more important. Likewise, travel and transportation expenses may be important daily costs for typical residents of one nation, while residents of another nation tend to work close to home. As a result of such differences in national consumption patterns, comparisons among aggregate price indexes likely will be invalid tests of the purchasing power parity proposition.

Most studies have tried to take this problem into account, yet they still find that the purchasing power parity proposition fails to hold over relatively lengthy horizons. Other factors unrelated to market integration might account for this conclusion, however. Transportation costs and tariffs (taxes on international trade) may allow relatively large price deviations to take place before international arbitrage becomes profitable. In addition, shifts in the real terms of trade among the goods that nations produce can require relatively long spans of time for prices to adjust. Likewise, all nations produce goods and services, known as *nontradables,* that are not suited to international trade. Baby-sitters, for example, typically do not cross national borders to provide short-term services. Some nations consume more nontradables than other nations do, making the evaluation of the purchasing power parity proposition using aggregate price indexes a problematic exercise.

Does Purchasing Power Parity Hold for Individual Goods? In light of these pitfalls, economists have tried another approach to evaluating world market integration by examining the extent to which purchasing power parity holds for individual goods that, in principle, should be tradable across national boundaries. Even this approach has problems, however. After all, a Japanese-manufactured automobile sold in the United States may be regarded as a "different good" than a U.S.-made automobile that otherwise might be part of the same auto classification.

The Economist magazine has proposed studying a single good, McDonald's Big Mac sandwich. McDonald's strives to ensure that the identical recipe is used for the Big Mac in the more than eighty nations that now have McDonald's fast-food restaurants. Table 14–1 displays local-currency prices of the Big Mac and the dollar-equivalent prices in terms of prevailing exchange rates for the United States (where the local currency is, of course, the dollar) and thirty-two other nations as of April 1997. For that month, the dollar price of the Big Mac ranged from a low of $1.16 in China to a high of $4.02 in Switzerland. The average Big Mac price in the United States was $2.42. If the purchasing power parity proposition applies to the Big Mac, which is a nearly identical good in every country where the sandwich is sold, then such wide deviations in its dollar-denominated price should not occur. According to *The Economist*'s "Big Mac Index," the purchasing power parity proposition fails.

TABLE 14–1: **THE "BIG MAC INDEX" OF CURRENCIES' PURCHASING POWER**

| | BIG MAC PRICES | | IMPLIED PPP* THE DOLLAR | ACTUAL DOLLAR EXCHANGE RATE 4/7/97 | LOCAL CURRENCY UNDER(−)/OVER(+) VALUATION† % |
	IN LOCAL CURRENCY	IN DOLLARS			
United States‡	**$2.42**	**2.42**	—	—	—
Argentina	Peso2.50	2.50	1.03	1.00	+3
Australia	A$2.50	1.94	1.03	1.29	−20
Austria	Sch34.00	2.82	14.0	12.0	+17
Belgium	BFr109	3.09	45.0	35.3	+28
Brazil	Real2.97	2.81	1.23	1.06	+16
Britain	£1.81	2.95	1.34††	1.63††	+22
Canada	C$2.88	2.07	1.19	1.39	−14
Chile	Peso1,200	2.88	496	417	+19
China	Yuan9.70	1.16	4.01	8.33	−52
Czech Republic	CKr53.0	1.81	21.9	29.3	−25
Denmark	DKr25.75	3.95	10.6	6.52	+63
France	FFr17.5	3.04	7.23	5.76	+26
Germany	DM4.90	2.86	2.02	1.71	+18
Hong Kong	HK$9.90	1.28	4.09	7.75	−47
Hungary	Forint271	1.52	112	178	−37
Israel	Shekel11.5	3.40	4.75	3.38	+40
Italy	Lire4,600	2.73	1,901	1,683	+13
Japan	¥2294	2.34	121	126	−3
Malaysia	M$3.87	1.55	1.60	2.50	−36
Mexico	Peso14.9	1.89	6.16	7.90	−22
Netherlands	Fl5.45	2.83	2.25	1.92	+17
New Zealand	NZ$3.25	2.24	1.34	1.45	−7
Poland	Zloty4.30	1.39	1.78	3.10	−43
Russia	Rouble11,000	1.92	4,545	4,739	−21
Singapore	S$3.00	2.08	1.24	1.44	−14
South Africa	Rand7.80	1.76	3.22	4.43-	−27
South Korea	Won2,300	2.57	950	894	+6
Spain	Pta375	2.60	155	144	+7
Sweden	SKr26.0	3.37	10.7	7.72	+39
Switzerland	SFr5.90	4.02	2.44	1.47	+66
Taiwan	NT$68.0	2.47	28.1	27.6	+2
Thailand	Baht46.7	1.79	19.3	26.1	−26

NOTES: *Purchasing-power parity; local price divided by price in the United States.
†Against the dollar.
‡Average of New York, Chicago, San Francisco and Atlanta.
††Dollars per pound.

SOURCE: "Big McCurrencies: Can hamburgers provide hot tips about exchange rates?" *The Economist*, April 12, 1997, p. 71.

Many economists have concluded from studies of both aggregate prices and prices of individual goods that there is little evidence that the world's markets for goods, services, and factors of production are strongly integrated. Others differ, arguing that there is considerable evidence of greater trade flows among nations, which indicates considerable scope for arbitrage. Short-term failures of the purchasing power parity proposition, they contend, stem largely from continued artificial barriers, such as tariffs, that limit the speed of arbitrage in an otherwise increasingly integrated world economy.

The Globalization of Financial Markets

Although people disagree about the extent to which world product and factor markets are integrated, most observers agree that there is considerable evidence of greater *financial market integration.* Satellite communications and computer technology together have made possible the nearly instantaneous transfer of billions of dollars, yen, deutsche marks, and other national currencies. As a result, national financial markets have become increasingly interconnected in a global financial system.

International Financial Arbitrage   Recall from Chapter 9 that individual rationality in the formation of expectations leads to the view that financial markets should be *efficient,* meaning that prices of bonds and other financial assets should reflect all available information and traders' understanding of how those prices are determined. The process by which market efficiency is achieved is *international financial arbitrage,* or the purchase and sale of financial assets, such as national currencies, bonds, and stocks, across national boundaries.

EUROCURRENCY MARKETS
Markets for financial assets that are denominated in currencies issued by nations other than the nation in which the financial assets are held.

A key mechanism linking nations' financial markets is the **Eurocurrency markets,** which are markets for funds denominated in currencies issued by nations other than the nation in which the funds actually are held. These markets are known as Eurocurrency markets because initially most of their trading involved funds held on deposit in European banks. Today, however, Eurocurrency trading takes place in Japan, Hong Kong, China, Australia, and other nations around the globe.

Banks and other financial institutions use the Eurocurrency markets to gather deposit funds and redirect them to activities in nations beyond the country of origin. As a result, the Eurocurrency markets are now the focus of global financial arbitrage. For example, suppose that interest yields on dollar-denominated assets held in the United States decline. Many individuals and corporations that hold such assets will respond by shifting their funds to Eurodollar deposits in London, Tokyo, and other locations outside the United States. In addition, many traders will convert their dollar-denominated assets to assets denominated in other nations' currencies. As a result, interest yields on assets denominated in currencies other than the dollar will change, and the international interest parity conditions that we discussed in Chapter 9—*covered interest parity* and *uncovered interest parity*—will more nearly be satisfied.

Are International Interest Parity Conditions Satisfied?   Recall from Chapter 9 that the covered interest parity condition states that the difference between interest yields on bonds with identical maturities and equivalent risks but different currency denominations should equal the forward discount, or the difference between the forward and spot exchange rates divided by the spot exchange rate. Mark Taylor of the International Monetary Fund, Jeffrey Frankel of the University of California at Berkeley, and others have provided considerable evidence that interest-rate differentials for most developed nations have satisfied the covered interest parity condition since the early 1980s.

The evidence for the uncovered interest parity proposition—that one nation's interest rate should exceed another's by an amount equal to the expected rate of currency depreciation plus a risk premium—is more mixed. Many economists have devoted considerable attention to this issue and have generally concluded that problems with determining the nature of the risk premium complicate using uncovered interest parity as an indicator of the extent of financial market integration.

The Broadened Scope for Financial Integration   As a result, researchers have looked for other possible measures of the scope of international financial integration, such as the extent to which international stock and bond prices move together or the degree to which asset portfolios of nations' savers include financial assets issued in nations other than their countries of residence. Again, the evidence is mixed. Country-specific factors can cause stock and bond prices to move in contrary directions. Legal restrictions can hinder people from holding financial assets issued in other nations even when obtaining those assets is otherwise relatively easy.

Nevertheless, most studies point to greater stock and bond market linkages across national borders. Although national financial markets do not yet behave as one, they increasingly react to the same events. A key reason is the proliferation of computer trading systems that span a number of nations. An example is a computer-assisted trading system called *Globex,* which is owned and operated by the Chicago Mercantile Exchange. A U.S. trader with a Globex account can use a personal computer software program to enter the Globex system and learn prevailing bid and offer prices and trading volumes for financial assets in any major financial market in the world. Thus, a trader can enter the Globex system at 10:00 P.M. eastern daylight time in the United States, when U.S. financial markets are closed but East Asian financial markets are open. If the trader sees an acceptable bid for a Singapore financial asset, then she or he can place an order to sell the asset. The Globex system automatically verifies that the order satisfies current Singapore exchange requirements and places the trader's order next in line for execution. Then the system automatically executes the trade. As a result, a trader based in the United States can react to changing market conditions in Singapore or nearly any other location in the world, at any time, day or night.

INTERNET • SOURCE

Keeping Up with the Changing World Economy

The Central Intelligence Agency—World Factbook
Internet URL: http://www.odci.gov/cia/publications/97fact/

Navigation: Start at the homepage for the Office of the Director of Central Intelligence (http://www.odci.gov). If you agree to the listed conditions, click on

Click here to continue. Then click on *Publications.* Next, click on "1998 World Factbook" (or the Factbook with the latest available date). To find a country, click on the first letter of its name, then scan to the country of interest and click. Then take a look at economic data for this country.

Macroeconomic Policies with Perfect Capital Mobility

Capital mobility plays a crucial role in determining the effects of monetary and fiscal policy actions. Many observers argue that greater financial market integration around the world is producing a situation in which markets for financial capital in the United States, western Europe, Japan, and other areas are interlinked. If the world reaches the point at which financial resources are as mobile *across* national borders as they are *within* nations, then we will experience **perfect capital mobility.**

Macroeconomic Policies with Perfect Capital Mobility and Fixed Exchange Rates Figure 14–8 illustrates the monetary and fiscal policy implications of perfect capital mobility under fixed exchange rates. In both panels, the *BP* schedule is *perfectly elastic,* because with perfect capital mobility, the smallest change in the nation's interest rate will cause very large movements of funds across its borders.

Panel (a) of Figure 14–8 shows the effects of a central bank's expansion of the money stock when capital is perfectly mobile and the central bank is committed to maintaining a fixed exchange rate. Such a monetary expansion, from M_1 to M_2, would shift the *LM* schedule to the right and cause a movement from an initial *IS-LM* equilibrium at point *A* on the *BP* schedule to a new *IS-LM* equilibrium at point *B* below the *BP* schedule.

The resulting decline in the equilibrium interest rate will cause the nation to experience significant capital outflows, so it will run a private payments deficit. To keep the value of the nation's currency from falling, the central bank will have to respond by selling foreign exchange reserves. If it sterilizes, then for at least some period of time the central bank can maintain equilibrium point *B*. In the absence of sterilization, however, the monetary approach to the balance of payments implies that the loss of foreign exchange reserves eventually will cause the nation's money stock to decline to its original level. Consequently, with perfect capital mobility and a fixed exchange rate, a nonsterilized monetary expansion ultimately will have no effect on real income. Monetary policy will be impotent in such a setting.

In contrast, fiscal policy's ability to affect real income under a fixed exchange rate will, if anything, be enhanced if capital is completely mobile, as shown in panel (b) of Figure 14–8. A bond-financed increase in government spending from g_1 to g_2 will cause the *IS* schedule to shift rightward, resulting in an equilibrium at point *B* above the *BP* schedule. The nation will experience a private payments surplus because the higher interest rate r_2 will induce capital inflows.

PERFECT CAPITAL MOBILITY A situation in which financial resources are as mobile across a nation's boundaries as they are within those boundaries.

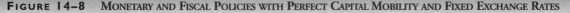

FIGURE 14–8 **MONETARY AND FISCAL POLICIES WITH PERFECT CAPITAL MOBILITY AND FIXED EXCHANGE RATES**

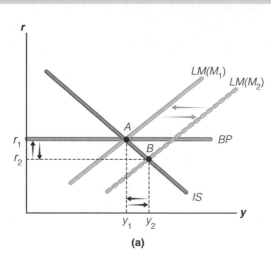

(a)

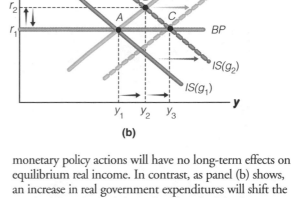

(b)

Panel (a) illustrates the effects of an unsterilized increase in the quantity of money when there is perfect capital mobility, so that the *BP* schedule is perfectly elastic. The expansion of the money stock causes a rightward shift of the *LM* schedule along the *IS* schedule, from point *A* to point *B*, which causes a private payments deficit. To keep the nation's currency from depreciating, the central bank will have to sell foreign exchange reserves, causing the *LM* schedule to shift back to point *A*. Hence, unsterilized

monetary policy actions will have no long-term effects on equilibrium real income. In contrast, as panel (b) shows, an increase in real government expenditures will shift the *IS* schedule rightward along the *LM* schedule, from point *A* to point *B*. To prevent an appreciation, the central bank will purchase foreign exchange reserves, which will cause the money stock to increase, thereby shifting the *LM* schedule rightward to a final equilibrium at point *C*.

At point *B*, the central bank will begin to accumulate foreign exchange reserves as it acquires foreign-currency-denominated assets in its efforts to maintain a fixed exchange rate. If the central bank sterilizes to keep the money stock from changing, then the economy will remain at point *B* indefinitely. In the absence of sterilization, however, the increase in foreign exchange reserves will lead to a rise in the nation's money stock, and the *LM* schedule will shift rightward until the private payments balance again equals zero at a new *IS-LM* equilibrium point *C* on the *BP* schedule. In this circumstance, fiscal policy will have its largest possible effect on equilibrium real income, at least in the short run in which we have abstracted from changes in the price level.

Macroeconomic Policies with Perfect Capital Mobility and Floating Exchange Rates What are the policy implications of *perfect* capital mobility under *floating* exchange rates? To answer this question, consider Figure 14–9, in which perfect capital mobility again is implied by the horizontal *BP* schedules in both panels. Panel (a) illustrates the effects of a monetary expansion with perfectly mobile capital. If the cen-

---

FIGURE 14–9   **MONETARY AND FISCAL POLICIES WITH PERFECT CAPITAL MOBILITY AND FLOATING EXCHANGE RATES**

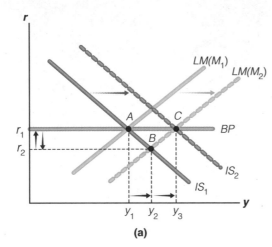

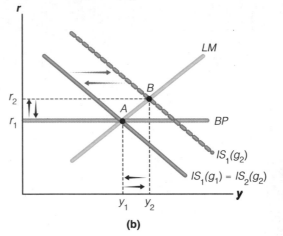

(a)

(b)

Panel (a) illustrates the effects of an increase in the amount of money in circulation when there is perfect capital mobility under a floating exchange rate. This expansion of the money stock causes a rightward shift of the *LM* schedule along the *IS* schedule, from point *A* to point *B*, which induces a private payments deficit, which in turn will cause the nation's currency to depreciate. This will stimulate increased export spending and induce a reduction in import expenditures, thereby causing the *IS*

schedule to shift rightward to point *C*. In contrast, as shown in panel (b), an increase in real government expenditures will shift the *IS* schedule rightward along the *LM* schedule, from point *A* to point *B*, which leads to a currency appreciation. This in turn will cause autonomous export spending to decline while stimulating a rise in autonomous import expenditures, thereby causing the *IS* schedule to return to its original position at point *A*.

---

tral bank increases the money stock from M_1 to M_2, the *LM* schedule will shift rightward. At point *B*, the induced decline in the equilibrium interest rate will spur considerable capital outflows, so the nation will operate for a time with a private payments deficit. With a floating exchange rate, however, this will result in a depreciation in the nation's currency, which will cause import spending to decline and export spending to rise. Consequently, the *IS* schedule will shift rightward, from IS_1 to IS_2. At the final equilibrium point *C*, the nation's private payments balance again will equal zero. In addition, there will be no further pressure on the value of its currency. Finally, real income will increase as fully as possible, from y_1 to y_3, or by the amount of the horizontal distance that the *LM* schedule shifted to the right. In contrast to the case of fixed exchange rates, monetary policy will have its most *potent* effect on aggregate demand with a floating exchange rate and perfect capital mobility.

Panel (b) illustrates the effects of a bond-financed increase in government spending, from g_1 to g_2. The immediate effect will be a rightward shift in the *IS* schedule, from $IS_1(g_1)$ to $IS_1(g_2)$. At the new equilibrium point *B*, the initial rise in the interest rate will induce significant capital inflows and a private payments surplus. The country's currency will appreciate, causing import spending to rise and export expenditures to fall. As a result, the *IS* schedule will shift back to the left, to $IS_2(g_2)$, which is the same as its original position. Thus, the final equilibrium will be point *A* once again, and real income will be unaffected, on net, by the rise in government spending. Essentially, with perfect capital mobility fiscal policy is subject to *complete crowding out*. A rise in government spending will crowd out an equal amount of net export spending by foreign residents because of the currency appreciation that the fiscal policy action causes. Hence, equilibrium real income will not be affected. In contrast to the fixed-exchange-rate case, with a floating exchange rate fiscal policy actions are *impotent* in affecting aggregate demand when capital is perfectly mobile.

Real-World Policy Implications of Perfect Capital Mobility   These contrasting conclusions about the effects of monetary and fiscal policies under fixed versus floating exchange rates have important implications for a world that may be close to achieving perfect capital mobility among many nations. Recall from Chapter 8 that we can derive the aggregate demand schedule from combinations of *IS-LM* equilibrium. Hence, our conclusion that with a fixed exchange rate, the real income effects of fiscal policy actions will be larger than the effects of monetary policy actions implies that:

> **Fiscal policy is a more important determinant of aggregate demand if the exchange rate is fixed and capital is perfectly mobile. With a flexible exchange rate, however, the reverse conclusion follows. Monetary policy has greater effects on aggregate demand if the exchange rate floats and there is perfect capital mobility.**

Since the early 1970s, many industrialized nations have permitted their exchange rates to float. Although central banks and governments have intervened from time to time to influence their nations' exchange rates, for the most part they have allowed market forces to determine currency values (see the Policy Notebook: *Can the U.S. Treasury Actually Control the Dollar's Value?*). At the same time, these nations have experienced more nearly perfect capital mobility as their financial markets have become more fully integrated. As a result, in these nations monetary policy has almost certainly become a more important determinant of aggregate demand than fiscal policy is.

INTERNET SOURCE

The Fed's International Operations

The Federal Reserve Bank of New York—Intervening in Foreign Exchange Markets
Internet URL: http://www.ny.frb.org/pihome/fedpoint/fed44.html

Navigation: Start at the homepage for the Federal Reserve Bank of New York (http://www.ny.frb.org). Then select "Welcome." Scan down the introduction, and click on *Intervening in Foreign Exchange Markets* to read about the Fed's procedures in conducting such interventions.

POLICY NOTEBOOK
Can the U.S. Treasury Actually Control the Dollar's Value?

On numerous occasions, the U.S. Treasury has entered foreign exchange markets to prevent the value of the dollar from changing according to shifts in the supply and demand for dollars. When the dollar fell relative to the yen a few years ago, for example, the Federal Reserve and the Treasury attempted to lift it by buying dollars in the foreign exchange market. The Secretary of the Treasury also tried "jawboning," or making such statements as "This administration believes a strong dollar is in the best interests of the United States, and we remain committed to strengthening the fundamentals." Similar pronouncements are issued at the Group of Seven meetings that occur on an *ad hoc* basis. The participants may state, for instance, that the yen is too weak or the deutsche mark is too strong. These government interventions and pronouncements give the impression that government officials can change the value of a currency in a floating exchange rate system.

The Extent of Foreign Exchange Intervention

Does the evidence support this impression? Michael Bordo of Rutgers University and Anna Schwartz of the National Bureau of Economic Research examined data on the foreign exchange interventions coordinated by the Fed and the U.S. Treasury over a typical five-year period and reached two conclusions: (1) the interventions were sporadic and variable, and (2) they were very small in size relative to the magnitude of total trading. For example, in one day total foreign exchange trading amounted to $129 billion, yet Fed purchases of marks and yen during the entire month amounted to only $100 million. Indeed, in a typical year Fed purchases of marks and yen amount to about $20 billion or less than 15 percent of an average day's trading. After all, more than a trillion dollars of foreign exchange now change hands on a daily basis.

Potential Drawbacks of Currency Interventions

Not only are the interventions so small as to make any long-term effects unlikely, but they may have other drawbacks as well. Our Treasury and central bank's attempts at manipulating exchange rates are sporadic and therefore often unexpected. The temporary effects they may have on exchange rates can cause individuals and firms to experience unintended wealth transfers.

Secondly, such attempts by the Treasury and the Fed to manipulate the value of the dollar expose our government to the risks of foreign exchange losses. In that event, the taxpayers will end up paying.

FOR CRITICAL ANALYSIS:
Why are the Treasury and the Fed so concerned about the value of the dollar anyway?

In Europe, however, efforts to fix exchange rates among the fifteen member nations of the European Union (EU), which includes such countries as Germany, France, and the United Kingdom, have highlighted the importance of fiscal policy. Beginning in 1993 the EU nations eliminated nearly all legal barriers to capital flows. Although they have not yet achieved perfect capital mobility, that is their goal. In addition, their ultimate aim, as formalized in the 1992 *Treaty on European Union,* or *Maastricht Treaty* (because it was negotiated in the city of Maastricht in the Netherlands), is to adopt a common European currency by the end of the twentieth century.

In advance of this single currency, these nations have agreed that they will try to fix their exchange rates. As you have learned, with perfect capital mobility and fixed exchange rates, fiscal policy actions will have significant effects on aggregate demand. Consequently, as the last row of Table 14–2 shows, the Maastricht Treaty places a number of restrictions on the fiscal policy flexibility of the nations that wish to join the common-currency arrangement. The purpose of these restrictions is to make the common-currency agreement more *credible*. Otherwise, once capital becomes perfectly mobile and exchange rates are fixed, the governments of the member nations will have strong incentives to stimulate their own economies via expansionary fiscal policy actions. Note that Table 14–2 on page 500 indicates that as the European Union approached the 1999 deadline for currency union, many nations were struggling to meet the Maastricht Treaty's fiscal policy requirements.

FUNDAMENTAL ISSUE #4

In what ways is the world economy becoming more integrated, and how does greater integration affect macroeconomic policymaking? International economic integration refers to increased mobility of goods, services, factors of production, and financial resources across national borders and markets. The continuing failure of purchasing power parity to hold over intervals shorter than several decades indicates that national markets for goods, services, and productive factors are not yet fully integrated. There is more concrete evidence of greater integration of national financial markets, which in the limit would lead to perfect capital mobility. Under perfect capital mobility and fixed exchange rates, fiscal policy actions have their largest possible short-run effects on real income, whereas monetary policy effects are muted. With perfect capital mobility and a floating exchange rate, monetary policy actions have their greatest short-run effects on real income while fiscal policy actions are impotent.

POLICIES TO PROMOTE ECONOMIC GROWTH IN AN INTEGRATED WORLD ECONOMY

Of course, variations in aggregate demand achieved via monetary or fiscal policy actions at best bring about short-term changes in real output. As you learned in Chapter 4, in the long run what really affects a nation's ability to sustain significant

TABLE 14–2: **THE MAASTRICHT TREATY'S FISCAL POLICY RESTRICTIONS AND THE STANDING OF EUROPEAN UNION NATIONS AT SELECTED DATES**

	1997			1998		
	INFLATION* **(%)**	**PUBLIC DEFICIT AS A % OF GDP****	**PUBLIC DEBT AS A % OF GDP****	**INFLATION †** **(%)**	**PUBLIC DEFICIT AS A % OF GDP****	**PUBLIC DEBT AS A % OF GDP****
Germany	2.0	3.2	61.9	2.2	2.4	61.9
France	2.0	3.5	58.1	1.9	2.9	59.2
Italy	3.0	3.3	122.3	2.7	3.0	119.4
United Kingdom	2.8	3.5	57.0	3.2	2.2	56.5
Belgium	1.5	2.9	127.0	2.1	2.5	123.9
Denmark	2.5	0.3	67.8	2.7	0.3	65.5
Greece	7.5	6.5	109.3	5.9*	5.3	107.2
Ireland	3.0	0.9	70.0	2.4*	0.5	65.4
Luxembourg	1.9	0.5	7.8	2.0*	0.9	9.2
Netherlands	2.3	2.5	76.8	2.6	2.0	75.1
Portugal	2.8	2.9	69.0	2.7*	2.9	67.8
Spain	3.0	3.0	67.1	2.8	2.8	65.8
Austria	2.2	3.0	72.2	2.3	2.9	72.2
Finland	1.4	2.2	61.5	1.6*	1.4	61.7
Sweden	2.4	2.9	77.6	1.7	1.0	74.9
Maastricht target	**3.1**	**3.0**	**60.0**	**3.1**	**3.0**	**60.0**

NOTES: *International Monetary Fund forecasts
**European Monetary Institute projections.

real output levels are the factors that affect *economic growth*. These include population and labor-force participation, innovation and technology, and investment and capital accumulation.

What policies might the nations of the world adopt to enhance their long-term prospects? We close this chapter by considering this important issue.

Is There a Trade-off between Development and Growth?

Panel (a) of Figure 14–10 shows annual growth rates of world output, which is the annual percentage change in a weighted average of real GDP for all nations of the world, as calculated by the International Monetary Fund. In addition, panel (a) displays annual output growth rates for the United States, the European Union, and Japan, which are the more industrialized nations of the world. Panel (b) again displays world output growth rates, along with the annual growth rates for the less industrialized nations of Africa, Asia, the Middle East and Europe, and the Western Hemisphere.

As we discussed in Chapter 4, we must be cautious in making too much of year-to-year variations in growth rates. In addition, the annual growth rates in both panels show considerable variation from one year to the next as a result of business cycle fluctuations. Nevertheless, one clear message of Figure 14–10 is that since 1991 the

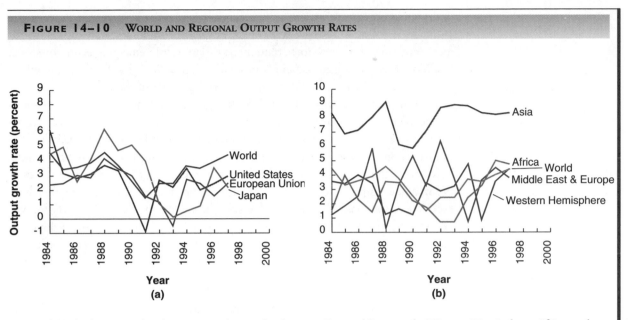

FIGURE 14–10 WORLD AND REGIONAL OUTPUT GROWTH RATES

Panel (a) displays annual real GDP growth rates for the European Union, Japan, the United States, and the world as a whole. In recent years, the output growth rates for the world as a whole have exceeded those of these industrialized regions. Panel (b) shows annual rates of real GDP growth for developing nations of Asia, the Middle East and Europe, the Western Hemisphere, Africa, and, again, the world as a whole. Output growth rates in developing Asian nations have outstripped those of other developing nations.

SOURCE: International Monetary Fund, *World Economic Outlook,* May 1997.

more developed regions of the world—the United States, the European Union, and Japan—have experienced output growth rates *below* the growth rates for the world as a whole. By way of contrast, the other, less economically developed regions have maintained rates of growth in the vicinity of or, in the case of less developed nations in Asia, well above the weighted-average rates of growth for world output.

Does Development Ultimately Reduce Growth?   One possible, albeit tentative, conclusion one might reach after examining Figure 14–10 is that highly developed nations cannot sustain high rates of growth. Indeed, many economists argue that strong forces depress the growth rates of more industrialized nations, as compared with the rates of growth experienced by less industrialized countries.

One key factor is that in a world with significant capital mobility, financial resources flow across national borders in pursuit of the highest possible rates of return. In many instances the locales that offer the highest returns are developing nations. These countries often have the greatest unexploited potential for growth and, consequently, for significant returns on saving and investment. In contrast, relatively fewer unexploited opportunities exist in highly industrialized nations. As a result, since the 1980s financial resources for development of greater technology, new capital investment, and improved work-force training have flowed into emerging economies such as China, Mexico, Argentina, and South Africa. These flows have spurred growth in these nations relative to the more industrialized countries of the world.

Another factor that may influence relative growth rates across the world's regions is that the most developed nations also have been democratic the longest. As we discussed in Chapter 4, recent research indicates that greater democracy initially leads to more economic freedom, which spurs increased economic growth. At the same time, however, to the extent that democracy promotes interest-group fights over shares of the national output, the country's growth may be stymied. The nations that have experienced the most significant output growth rates during the 1990s have also witnessed recent expansions of economic freedom for their citizens. This development may help to account for their relatively higher growth rates as compared with the more developed nations whose citizens have possessed such freedoms for some time.

Do National Policies Matter for Growth?   A number of economists argue that governmental policies also play a large part in determining relative differences in economic growth around the world. Many developing nations in Asia, for instance, have sharply reduced their restrictions on the flows of financial resources. As we noted earlier, this policy has fueled growth in these nations.

In contrast, until recently nearly every African nation maintained legal barriers limiting such flows. Efforts to relax many of these barriers in several African nations have undoubtedly helped to account for improved output growth on that continent during the 1990s.

Other governmental policies can also help to determine relative growth rates of nations. Among these are alternative mixes of fiscal policies and, in particular, different stances on taxation of labor and capital.

Fiscal Policy: The Growth Issue of the New Century?

Why might fiscal policy be an important factor influencing economic growth? Let's begin by thinking about some real-world fiscal issues that have arisen in Europe and the United States during the 1990s.

Deficits, Taxes, and Growth in the European Union   As we noted earlier in this chapter, nations of the European Union have sought to harmonize and constrain their fiscal policies. They have done this out of a recognition that increased capital mobility, combined with nearly fixed exchange rates among the EU's members, will make fiscal policy actions more important determinants of aggregate demand.

As Table 14–2 on page 500 indicates, all EU member nations must try to achieve government budget deficits that are no larger than 3 percent of their GDP. At the same time, however, the ability to reduce deficits via inflationary money creation is ruled out by inflation constraints that each EU member must strive to satisfy. Thus, every EU nation must decide whether to reduce its government deficit via spending reductions or tax increases. So far, most have opted for higher taxes. Indeed, in 1992 EU nations agreed to harmonize their *value-added tax systems* by establishing a *minimum* value-added tax rate of 15 percent in each nation (in a value-added system, tax rates are applied to the production and sale of goods at every stage of the goods' production). In the pursuit of higher tax revenues, most EU governments have since raised their value-added tax rates and applied them to an expanded set of goods and services.

As we discussed in Chapters 4 and 7, higher tax rates can depress real output growth by curtailing incentives for workers to offer more hours of labor each week and for firms to produce additional units of output each month. A number of observers conclude that the EU nations' governments have, thus far, chosen to maintain high levels of government expenditures—many of which finance a broad array of social services and transfer programs—rather than to reduce the size of the governments' shares of national output through lower tax rates that would spur increased economic growth.

Deficits, Taxes, and Growth in the United States   Many of these same observers contend that the United States faced a similar choice during the 1990s. Government spending to finance Social Security, Medicare, Medicaid, and other social programs increased dramatically since the early 1980s. Like the EU nations, in 1993 the U.S. government chose to raise taxes rather than cut spending, as Congress adopted President Clinton's plan to raise federal tax rates on income and on a variety of goods and services subject to federal excise taxes. Since 1993, as panel (a) of Figure 14–10 indicates, real output growth in the United States has fallen further below the weighted-average output growth of the world. To critics of the 1993 tax increases, the implication is clear: The choice of higher taxes held U.S. economic growth below a higher growth rate that the nation could have attained otherwise.

National Tax Policies Confront World Capital Mobility   Increasingly, governments of the world's nations are finding that fiscal policy changes can have rapid effects on economic growth. In the United States, for instance, capital mobility is extremely high. Consequently, a state that sharply reduces its tax rates on the property, output, and wages of businesses quickly attracts both new businesses and relocations of business operations from other states.

As the degree of capital mobility across *national* borders increases, governments of the world's *nation-states* increasingly will face similar situations. Just as individual states in the United States have discovered that special tax incentives can attract business start-ups and relocations, national governments are finding that in a world with greater capital mobility, tax and other policy changes can lead to quick rises or declines in relative growth rates.

The Great Growth Debate   At the close of the twentieth century, the debates about taxes and growth that have occupied the attention of European and U.S. leaders and citizens are spreading to encompass all nations of the world. As we discussed in Chapter 4, economic growth has negative spillovers in the form of increased pollution, destruction of forests, and higher urban congestion and associated social ills.

These negative spillovers from economic growth constitute externalities that many observers contend require increased governmental programs to address. Such programs, however, ultimately must be funded by tax revenues, raised by assessing taxes on property, on firm revenues and profits, and on personal incomes. In a world where higher taxes spur speedy capital outflows, nations that raise taxes to address the negative spillovers from growth may then face depressed relative rates of growth in per capita living standards.

Achieving a balance between the desire for government expenditures to address social ills and the desire for lower taxes to maintain economic growth promises to be *the* key economic issue of the early twenty-first century. The effort to achieve this balance may lead to great divisions among nations, or it may be a catalyst for a greater convergence of national living standards and sustained rates of economic growth. Which outcome results depends on the collective choices of the world's citizens during the initial decades of the new century.

FUNDAMENTAL ISSUE #5

How do nations' policies influence their relative rates of growth in a more integrated world economy? Tax policies can affect a nation's output growth. In a world where capital is becoming increasingly mobile, differences in tax rates on property, income, and profits can induce large and speedy shifts in financial resources from high-tax countries to nations with lower tax rates. The result will be changes in relative rates of economic growth.

CHAPTER SUMMARY

1. **The Pros and Cons of Fixed versus Floating Exchange Rates:** The main argument against floating exchange rates is that exchange-rate volatility caused by changing market forces can increase foreign exchange risks. Adopting a fixed exchange rate reduces the potential for such risks to arise, thereby saving people from having to incur costs to hedge against those risks. An important argument against fixed exchange rates is that in nations where workers and other factors of production are relatively immobile, pegging the exchange rate removes a key source of immediate flexibility in relative prices. Thus, a fixed exchange rate eliminates a key means by which the nations' employment and output levels can automatically adjust to changes in international market conditions.

2. **How Monetary and Fiscal Policy Actions Affect a Nation's Real Income under Fixed Exchange Rates:** If a nation's central bank sterilizes by preventing variations in its foreign exchange reserves from affecting the nation's nominal money stock, then a rise in the money stock can induce at least a short-term increase in real income as long as the central bank has sufficient reserves to keep the exchange rate fixed in the face of private payments deficits. The effects of unsterilized monetary policy actions on real income, however, eventually dissipate as changes in foreign exchange reserves cause the quantity of money to return to its initial level. The effects of fiscal policy actions also are influenced by a central bank's decision about sterilization, but with a fixed exchange rate an expansionary fiscal policy action typically causes real income to increase in the short run.

3. **How Monetary and Fiscal Policy Actions Affect a Nation's Real Income under Floating Exchange Rates:** A central bank action that increases the quantity of money in circulation causes a private payments deficit, which induces a currency depreciation that spurs export spending and reduces import spending. Thus, expansionary monetary policy actions cause short-run increases in a nation's real income level. Expansionary fiscal policy actions can result in private payments deficits or surpluses and currency depreciations or appreciations, depending on the degree of capital mobility. The size of the effect of a fiscal policy action on real income declines as capital mobility increases.

4. **How the World Economy Is Becoming More Integrated, and How Greater Integration Affects Macroeconomic Policymaking:** Studies of purchasing power parity indicate that the condition holds only over intervals spanning decades. This evidence implies that national markets for goods, services, and productive factors are not fully integrated worldwide. There is stronger evidence of increased financial market integration. Complete integration of the world's financial markets would permit perfect capital mobility. With perfect capital mobility and a fixed exchange rate, fiscal policy actions have their greatest short-run effects on real income, whereas monetary policy effects on aggregate demand are rendered impotent. Under perfect capital mobility and floating exchange rates, monetary policy actions have their largest possible real income effects, whereas fiscal policy actions have no effects whatsoever.

5. **How Nations' Policies Affect Their Relative Rates of Growth in a More Integrated World Economy:** When financial resources are highly mobile across national borders,

differences in national tax rates on property, income, and profits can cause sizable and swift movements of financial resources from high-tax countries to nations with lower tax rates. As a result, high-tax nations can experience lower rates of economic growth, while nations that reduce their tax rates can grow much faster.

QUESTIONS AND PROBLEMS

1. Consider a nation whose language is known by few people outside the nation's borders. In addition, legal and natural barriers prevent movements of other factors of production across the nation's borders. The nation's central bank maintains a fixed exchange rate. Recently, demand for the nation's primary products has declined worldwide. Could this nation gain from letting its exchange rate float? Explain your reasoning.

2. Why would Europe be better equipped to adopt a single currency if nearly all of its residents could speak at least one common language? Explain.

3. If a central bank maintains a fixed exchange rate but conducts unsterilized monetary policies, how will a contractionary monetary policy action ultimately affect the nation's private payments balance and its real income level, assuming that the price level is unchanged? Support your answer.

4. If a nation's central bank maintains a fixed exchange rate and conducts unsterilized monetary policies, how can a contractionary fiscal policy induce a change in the quantity of money in circulation? If capital mobility is low, will the nation's money stock expand or contract as a result? Explain.

5. Explain in your own words how a contractionary monetary policy action will affect a nation's private payments balance and the value of its currency under a floating exchange rate.

6. Explain in your own words how a contractionary fiscal policy action will affect a nation's private payments balance and the value of its currency under a floating exchange rate and low capital mobility.

7. Suppose that a nation has perfect capital mobility and a floating exchange rate. Currently, the economy is in a state of recession. Assuming that policy actions leave the price level unchanged, should the nation's fiscal authority or its central bank take the lead in trying to raise real income? Explain your reasoning.

8. In your view, are fixed or flexible exchange rates preferable in a world of increasing financial integration? Take a stand, and justify your position.

9. In a system of fixed exchange rates, does a nation's central bank gain or lose power to induce short-run changes in real income as world financial markets become more fully integrated? Explain.

10. In a system of floating exchange rates, does a nation's fiscal authority gain or lose power to induce short-run changes in real income as world financial markets become more fully integrated? Explain.

CyberTutor Exercises

1. What is the effect of an increase in the money stock on the equilibrium domestic nominal interest rate, equilibrium domestic real income, and the equilibrium exchange rate?

2. What is the effect of fiscal expansion on the equilibrium domestic nominal interest rate, equilibrium domestic real income, and the equilibrium exchange rate in a fixed exchange rate regime with perfect capital mobility?

3. What is the effect of an increase in the money stock on the equilibrium domestic nominal interest rate, equilibrium domestic real income, and exchange rate in a flexible exchange rate regime with imperfect capital mobility??

4. What is the effect of an increase in the money stock on the equilibrium interest rate, equilibrium domestic real income and the equilibrium exchange rate in a flexible exchange rate regime with perfect capital mobility?

5. What is the effect of an increase in government spending on the equilibrium domestic nominal interest rate, equilibrium domestic real income and the equilibrium exchange rate in a flexible exchange rate regime with perfect capital mobility?

On-Line Application

The World Bank publishes a number of reports about developing regions of the world. This application focuses on Africa.

Internet URL: http://www.worldbank.org/html/extpb/annrep97/wbar08.htm

Title: The World Bank Annual Report—Africa

Navigation: Start at the World Bank's homepage (http://www.worldbank.org). Scan to the bottom of the page, and click on *Countries and Regions.* Then click on *Africa.* Finally, click on *1997 Regional Perspectives* (or the most recently available report).

Application: Read the article and answer the following questions:

1. What are the broad trends in the economic performance of nations on the African continent? Are there variations in performance across African nations? What appears to account for these variations?

2. What role does the World Bank indicate that it is performing in helping African nations to achieve higher rates of economic growth? In light of what you have learned, do you forecast success for these efforts?

SELECTED REFERENCES AND FURTHER READING

Argy, Victor. *International Macroeconomics: Theory and Policy.* London: Routledge, 1994.

Bonser-Neal, Catherine. "Does Central Bank Intervention Stabilize Exchange Rates?" Federal Reserve Bank of Kansas City *Economic Review,* First Quarter, 1996, pp. 43–57.

Canzoneri, Matthew, Vittorio Grilli, and Paul Masson, eds. *Establishing a Central Bank: Issues in Europe and Lessons from the U.S.* Cambridge: Cambridge University Press, 1992.

Frenkel, Jacob, and Assaf Razin. *Fiscal Policies and the World Economy.* 3d ed. Cambridge, Mass.: MIT Press, 1997.

Giovannini, Alberto, and Colin Mayer, eds. *European Financial Integration.* Cambridge: Cambridge University Press, 1991.

Pakko, Michael, and Patricia Pollard. "For Here or to Go? Purchasing Power Parity and the Big Mac." Federal Reserve Bank of St. Louis *Review,* January/February 1996, pp. 3–21.

Rogoff, Kenneth. "The Purchasing Power Parity Puzzle." *Journal of Economic Literature* 34 (1996): 647–668.

Treaty on European Union. Maastricht, The Netherlands, 1992.

THE MACROECONOMICS CyberTutor™

The Interactive Study Environment Created Specifically For This Textbook

CyberTutor™ follows the organization of the chapters in the book and navigates much like a site on the World Wide Web. Direct links to the Web embedded within the program provide quick access to the textbook's Web site, which in turn features a plethora of Internet resources and links. Each chapter includes a Chapter Summary & Key Terms and Theoretical & Empirical Interactive Exercises.

Anyone who has taught or studied economics knows how helpful a good summary and terms list are. The **Chapter Summary & Key Terms** feature allows the student to review the main issues developed in the textbook chapter. It also includes an index of terms and a special section allowing the user to review the chapter's key terms and concepts. Initially, the student sees the terms without their definitions, which allows for self-testing. A mouse-click on any term results in a "pop-up" window with the full definition.

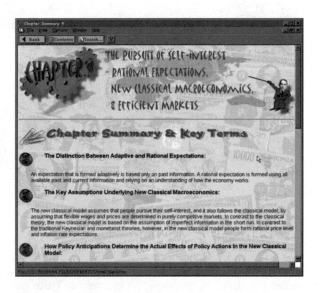

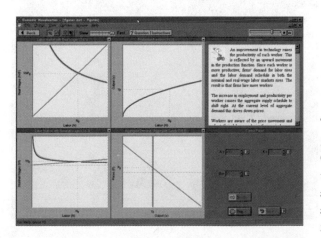

Theoretical Exercises help the student explore macroeconomic theory through an interactive system of graphs. Consider, for example, the following question: What are the effects of an increase in the capital stock on nominal and real wages? In the appropriate environment (see image at left), the student can adjust the capital stock and see the model animate from its initial to a new equilibrium. The

509

interactivity of the environment allows the student to experiment with other causes and effects relating to these graphs, going beyond those addressed in the question.

Empirical Exercises provide the student with a user-friendly environment in which to test macroeconomic theories. Here are two example exercises:

1. Some macro economists believe that there is an inflation-unemployment tradeoff such that at low levels of inflation there is a high rate of unemployment and vice-versa. The graph on the right looks at the 1960's experience and seems to confirm these economists' beliefs. Has this relationship continued to hold through the 1970's, 1980's and 1990's?

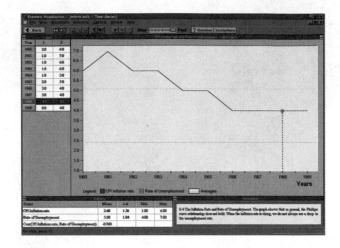

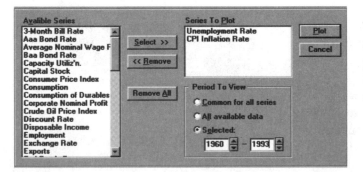

Time-series plotting is easy. In this example the student needs to change the time period of the plot that is already given with the exercise from 1960–1969 to 1960–1993. Now all that the student has to do is click on the PLOT Button.

The operation is simple, yet the implications are powerful. Once the student sees the new plot a fundamental implication of empirical analysis becomes apparent: Relationships that hold in one period do not necessarily hold in others — this scientific "truth" is time-sensitive! Furthermore, this simple plot has allowed the student, a "beginner economist," to cast doubt on a widely held theory. This is truly hands-on economics: The student directly participates in the process of falsification — the principal force behind modern deductive science!

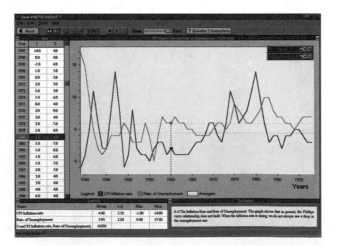

Scatter plots with a fitted OLS regression line are just as easy to create. Here is the second example exercise:

2. There is an economic theory that states that as real GDP rises imports should increase by more than exports so that the real trade balance will fall. Does the data confirm the theory?

A quick look in the variable list tells us that we do not have data for the Real trade balance on the CD; all we can find is the Nominal trade balance. Before we can run the regression (jargon is also something the student must learn) we must first derive a new variable. Sound complicated? Perhaps, but it's quite simple with the tool shown on the right. A few mouse clicks results in the knowledge that a Real variable actually means the Nominal variable divided by the CPI inflation rate. Voilà: Real Trade Balance. Even complex derivations are simple with this little "Derivator."

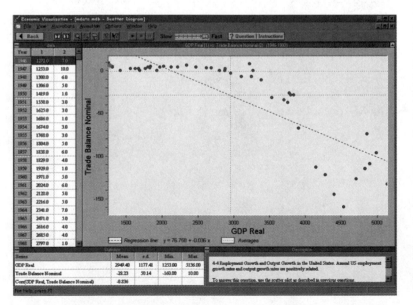

Finally, the student selects the two variables from a list (the one we just created can, of course, be saved for future use) and PLOT. This time the student's confidence in economic theory is reinforced! The data seems to confirm this theory rather well. In view of the previous exercise the student may also note that the relationship holds over a large period of time (1940's-1990's).

"Hmm . . . ," the student wonders, "could I select a period for which this relationship fails to hold? Perhaps specific historical events effected such a relationship?" With a click of the mouse each point's year and values can be identified in the table or, alternatively, each year and its associated values can be located on the plot.

CYBERTUTOR™ ALLOWS THE STUDENT TO:

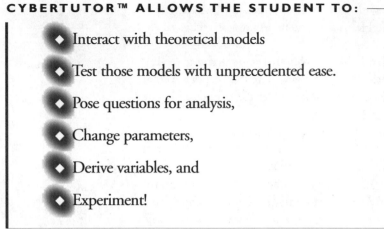

- Interact with theoretical models
- Test those models with unprecedented ease.
- Pose questions for analysis,
- Change parameters,
- Derive variables, and
- Experiment!

And . . .

- The exercises guide but do not limit your experiences within these environments.

- CyberTutor™ comes in a visually rich and dynamic package with animations & audio explanations.

- The More You Play the More You Learn!™

GLOSSARY

ACCOUNTING RISK The possibility that the market value of assets denominated in foreign currencies may vary as a result of changes in exchange rates even when the underlying interest returns on those assets are unaffected.

ADAPTIVE EXPECTATIONS Expectations that are based only on information from the past up to the present.

ADMINISTERED PRICING HYPOTHESIS The view that imperfectly competitive firms set prices of their products at relatively unchanging levels for lengthy intervals.

AGGREGATE DEMAND SCHEDULE (y^d) Combinations of various price levels and levels of real output for which individuals are satisfied with their consumption of output and their holdings of money.

AGGREGATE EXPENDITURES SCHEDULE A schedule that represents total desired expenditures by all the relevant sectors of the economy at any given level of real national income.

AGGREGATE NET AUTONOMOUS EXPENDITURES The sum of autonomous consumption, autonomous investment, autonomous government spending, and autonomous export spending, all of which are independent of the level of national income in the basic Keynesian model.

AGGREGATE SUPPLY SCHEDULE (y^s) Combinations of various price levels and levels of real output that maintain equilibrium in the market for labor services.

AGGREGATION The act of summing up the individual parts of the economy to obtain total measures of economy-wide performance.

APPRECIATION A rise in the value of one nation's currency in terms of the currency of another nation.

ASSIGNMENT PROBLEM The problem of determining whether monetary or fiscal policymakers should assume responsibility for achieving external balance or internal balance objectives.

ASYMMETRIC INFORMATION Information that is possessed by one party to an economic transaction but is unavailable to the other party.

AUTOMATIC FISCAL STABILIZER A mechanism of government policy that automatically reduces volatility in real income caused by changes in autonomous expenditures.

AUTONOMOUS CONSUMPTION Household consumption spending on domestically produced goods and services that is independent of the level of real income.

AUTONOMOUS EXPENDITURES MULTIPLIER A measure of the size of the multiplier effect on equilibrium real income caused by a change in aggregate net autonomous expenditures; in the simple Keynesian model, the multiplier is equal to $1/(MPS + MPIM) = 1/(1 - MPC)$.

AVERAGE PROPENSITY TO CONSUME (APC) Real household consumption of domestically produced goods and services divided by real disposable income; the portion of disposable income allocated to consumption spending.

AVERAGE PROPENSITY TO IMPORT $(APIM)$ Real household spending on imports divided by real disposable income; the portion of disposable income allocated to spending on imported goods and services.

AVERAGE PROPENSITY TO SAVE (APS) Real household saving divided by real disposable income; the portion of disposable income allocated to saving.

AVERAGE TAX RATE The ratio of total net taxes to total income.

BALANCE OF PAYMENTS ACCOUNTS A tabulation of all transactions between the residents of a nation and the residents of all other nations in the world.

BARTER The direct exchange of goods and services.

BASE YEAR A reference year for price-level comparisons, which is a year in which nominal GDP is equal to real GDP, so that the GDP deflator's value is equal to one.

BB SCHEDULE All combinations of real income and the price level at which the government's budget is balanced at a given income tax rate, level of government expenditures, and amount of net autonomous taxes.

BEQUEST A sum payable to one's offspring at the time of death.

BOND-FINANCED DEFICIT A government budget deficit that the government finances by issuing new bonds to private individuals and organizations.

BP SCHEDULE A set of real income–nominal interest rate combinations that maintains a zero balance for private payments—sometimes called a "balance of payments equilibrium"—in the balance of payments accounts.

BUSINESS CYCLE Fluctuations in aggregate real income above or below its long-run growth path.

CALIBRATION The use of estimated elasticities and real-world data to create artificial data with theoretical models for the purpose of evaluating the extent to which one's theory appears to match real-world observations.

CAMBRIDGE EQUATION An equation developed by economists at Cambridge University, England, which indicates that individuals desire to hold money in proportion to their nominal income.

CAPACITY OUTPUT The real output that the economy could produce if all resources were employed to their utmost.

CAPITAL Goods that people can use to

produce other goods and services in the future.

CAPITAL ACCOUNT The balance of payments account that records all nongovernmental international asset transactions.

CAPITAL CONTROLS Legal restrictions on the holdings of foreign currencies or assets by the residents of a nation.

CAPITAL GOOD A good that may be used in the production of other goods and services in the future.

CAPITAL MOBILITY The extent to which funds and financial assets may flow freely across a country's borders.

CENTRAL BANKER CONTRACT A legally binding agreement between a government and a central bank official that holds the official responsible for the nation's inflation performance.

CHAIN-WEIGHT REAL GDP A method of calculating real GDP for a given year that uses prices for both the year in question and the preceding year as weights.

CHURNING Constant trading of U.S. government securities by the Federal Reserve Bank of New York; to achieve temporary changes in reserves, among other things; controversial because some critics charge that some of the trading is unnecessary.

CIRCULAR FLOW DIAGRAM A chart that depicts the economy's flows of income and product.

CLOSED ECONOMY An economy that operates in isolation from the rest of the world.

COMPLEMENTS IN PRODUCTION The term for the situation in which an increased use of capital goods leads to greater use of labor in the production of goods and services.

COMPOUNDED GROWTH Accumulated growth in per capita real GDP over a given interval.

COMPOUND GROWTH RATE The annual rate at which per capita real GDP accumulates over a given interval.

CONSERVATIVE CENTRAL BANKER A central bank official who dislikes inflation more than the average citizen in society and is therefore less willing to induce discretionary increases in the growth rate of the quantity

of money in an effort to achieve short-run increases in real output.

CONSUMER PRICE INDEX (CPI) A weighted average of the prices of a large group of goods and services that the government determines a representative U.S. consumer buys each year.

CONSUMPTION SPENDING Total purchases of goods and services by households.

COOPERATIVE BEHAVIOR An economic setting in which people work together to maximize their joint well-being.

COORDINATION FAILURES Spillover effects between workers and firms that arise from movements in macroeconomic variables that hinder efforts by individual households and firms to plan and implement their consumption, production, and pricing decisions.

COST-OF-LIVING ADJUSTMENT (COLA) A clause in a wage contract that calls for the nominal wage to be adjusted in response to changes in the price level.

COUNTERCYCLICAL FISCAL POLICY A process for managing government spending and taxation so as to smooth out business cycles; the government runs deficits during times of recessions and surpluses during inflationary periods.

COVERED INTEREST PARITY A prediction that the interest rate on one nation's bond will approximately equal the interest rate on another nation's bond plus the forward discount, or the difference between the forward exchange rate and the spot exchange rate divided by the forward exchange rate.

CROWDING-OUT EFFECT The situation when private spending is reduced due to a rise in the real interest rate induced by an increase in the government's deficit.

CURRENCY BOARD A monetary policymaker that is bound to a commitment to issue currency that is backed 100 percent by the currency of another country.

CURRENCY RISK The possibility that rates of return on financial assets denominated in other currencies can fluctuate as a result of changes in exchange rates that cause variations in the market values of those assets.

CURRENT ACCOUNT The balance of

payments account that tabulates international trade and transfers of goods and services and flows of income.

CYCLICAL UNEMPLOYMENT The portion of total unemployment resulting from business cycle fluctuations.

DEDUCTION The process of making testable predictions about real-world behavior based on a theoretical framework.

DEPRECIATION (Currency) A decline in the value of one nation's currency in terms of the currency of another nation.

DEPRECIATION (Capital) The total market value of capital goods that are expended during the process of production.

DEPRESSION An especially severe recession.

DEVALUATION A policy-induced reduction in the exchange value of a nation's currency relative to the currencies of other countries.

DISCOUNT RATE The rate of interest that the Federal Reserve charges to lend to a banking institution.

DISCOUNTED PRESENT VALUE The value from today's perspective of funds to be received at a future date.

DISCRETIONARY POLICYMAKING The act of responding to economic events as they occur, rather than proceeding as it might previously have planned in the absence of those events.

DOMESTIC VARIABLES Macroeconomic variables that provide information about a nation's economic activity in isolation from the rest of the world.

DYNAMIC MODELS Economic models intended to explain how variables such as real output, employment, and the price level vary over time.

ECONOMIC GROWTH The annual rate of change in per capita real GDP.

ECONOMIES OF SCALE The realization of reduced average production costs via an increase in the size of a firm's operations through acquisition of new capital.

EFFICIENCY WAGE THEORY An approach to explaining unemployment that is based on the hypothesis that the productivity of workers depends on the real wage rate.

EFFICIENT MARKETS THEORY A theory that stems from applying the rational expectations hypothesis to financial markets; it states that equilibrium bond prices should reflect all past and current information plus bond traders' understanding of how bond prices are determined.

EQUATION OF EXCHANGE An accounting identity that states that the nominal value of all monetary transactions for final goods and services is equal to the nominal value of the output of goods and services purchased.

EQUILIBRIUM REAL INCOME The real income level at which aggregate desired expenditures are equal to the real value of domestic output.

EUROCURRENCY MARKETS Markets for financial assets that are denominated in currencies issued by nations other than the nation in which the financial assets are held.

EXCHANGE RATE The value of a nation's currency measured in terms of the currency of another nation.

EXPANSION The period during a business cycle when actual GDP begins to rise, perhaps even above its natural, long-run level.

EXPLICIT CONTRACTS Contractual arrangements in which the terms of relationships between workers and firms, especially about wages, are in writing and legally binding upon both parties.

EXTERNAL BALANCE The attainment of an objective for the composition of a nation's balance of payments.

EXTERNALITY A spillover effect that arises when market exchanges affect the well-being of an individual or firm that is not a party to the exchanges.

FEDERAL OPEN MARKET COMMITTEE (FOMC) A group composed of the seven Federal Reserve Board governors and five of the twelve presidents of the Federal Reserve banks that determines how to conduct the Fed's open-market operations.

FED WATCHING An occupation that involves developing and selling forecasts of Federal Reserve monetary policy actions based on careful examination of the process by which the Fed appears to make its policy decisions.

FISCAL POLICY Actions by the government to vary its spending or taxes.

FIXED-WEIGHT PRICE INDEX An overall measure of the price level that is computed using a weighted average of the prices of a fixed set of goods and services.

FLEXIBLE-WEIGHT PRICE INDEX An overall measure of the price level that automatically gives variable weights to the output of goods and services across time.

FOREIGN EXCHANGE MARKET EFFICIENCY A situation in which the equilibrium spot and forward exchange rates imply a forward discount that is equal to the expected rate of currency depreciation plus any risk premium.

FOREIGN EXCHANGE MARKETS Markets where currencies of different nations are exchanged.

FOREIGN EXCHANGE RISK The possibility that fluctuations in exchange rates can cause variations in the market values of assets.

45-DEGREE LINE A line that cuts in half the 90-degree angle of the coordinate axes on a diagram relating real income to aggregate desired expenditures; every point on the 45-degree line could, in principle, be a point of equilibrium at which real income equals aggregate desired expenditures.

FORWARD CURRENCY CONTRACTS Agreements to deliver a unit of a nation's currency in exchange for another at a specified price on a given date.

FORWARD EXCHANGE RATES The rate of exchange for currencies specified in forward currency contracts.

FRICTIONAL UNEMPLOYMENT The portion of total unemployment arising from the fact that a number of workers are between jobs at any given time.

GDP PRICE DEFLATOR A flexible-weight measure of the overall price level; equal to nominal GDP divided by real GDP.

GENERAL EQUILIBRIUM ANALYSIS An approach to analyzing the economy by examining the multiple interactions of all individual consumers, workers, and firms.

GOVERNMENT SPENDING Total state, local, and federal government expenditures on goods and services.

GROSS DOMESTIC PRODUCT (GDP) The value of all final goods and services produced during a given period; tabulated using market prices. GDP includes foreign residents' earnings from home production but excludes home residents' earnings abroad.

GROSS INVESTMENT Total spending on capital goods during a year, including depreciation expenditures.

GROSS NATIONAL PRODUCT A measure of a nation's total production that includes home residents' earnings abroad but excludes foreign residents' earnings from home production.

HEDGE The act of adopting strategies to reduce the overall risk resulting from fluctuations in market values of assets caused by exchange-rate volatility.

HUMAN CAPITAL The knowledge and skills possessed by people in a nation's labor force.

IMPERFECT COMPETITION A market environment that may have a limited number of buyers or sellers, barriers to market entry or exit, or differentiated firm products or factor services.

IMPLICIT CONTRACTS Unwritten agreements between workers and firms, concerning terms of employment such as wages; the agreements may or may not be legally binding.

INCOME IDENTITY An identity that states that real national income equals the sum of real household consumption, real household saving, real net taxes, and real imports.

INCOME VELOCITY OF MONEY The average number of times that each unit of money is used to purchase final goods and services in a given interval.

INDUCTION The process of drawing conclusions about real-world behavior from observation of real-world data.

INFLATION BIAS The tendency for the economy to experience continuing inflation as a result of discretionary monetary policy that takes place because of the time inconsistency problem of monetary policy.

INFLATIONARY GAP The amount by which aggregate desired expenditures exceed the level that would cause equilibrium real income to equal its long-run, natural level.

INSIDE MONEY Bank deposit money.

INSIDER-OUTSIDER THEORY The notion that because a firm views its current, "insider" employees as an investment that would be costly to replace, the insiders are able to inhibit the hiring of unemployed "outsiders" at real wages below those earned by the insiders.

INTEREST-ELASTIC DESIRED INVESTMENT Desired investment spending that is relatively sensitive to interest-rate variations.

INTEREST-ELASTIC MONEY DEMAND Demand for money that is relatively sensitive to interest-rate variations.

INTEREST-INELASTIC DESIRED INVESTMENT Desired investment that is relatively insensitive to interest-rate variations.

INTEREST-INELASTIC MONEY DEMAND Demand for money that is relatively insensitive to interest-rate variations.

INTERGENERATIONAL EXTERNALITIES Spillover effects of economic growth that take years to influence human welfare and therefore have different effects across generations.

INTERGENERATIONAL TRANSFERS Transfers of disposable income, in the form of gifts or bequests, from one generation to another generation.

INTERMEDIATE TARGET A macroeconomic variable whose value a central bank seeks to control because it believes that doing so is consistent with its ultimate objectives.

INTERNAL BALANCE The attainment of the level of real income consistent with the domestic economy's long-run growth path.

INTERNATIONAL ARBITRAGE The act of buying a good in one nation and selling it in another.

INTERNATIONAL ECONOMIC INTEGRATION The growth of interconnectedness among the world's markets for goods, services, factors of production, and financial assets.

INVESTMENT SPENDING The sum of purchases of new capital goods, spending on new residential construction, and inventory investment.

IS SCHEDULE A set of possible combinations of real income and the nominal interest rate that are necessary to maintain an income-expenditure equilibrium, $y = c + i + g + x$.

IS-LM EQUILIBRIUM The point at which the *IS* and *LM* schedules cross, so that the economy simultaneously attains both an income-expenditure equilibrium and equilibrium in the market for real money balances.

KEYNESIAN MONETARY POLICY TRANSMISSION MECHANISM A key implication of the traditional Keynesian theory in which a rise in the nominal quantity of money will, with an unchanged price level, reduce the nominal interest rate, thereby stimulating a rise in desired investment spending and aggregate desired expenditures, which in turn causes equilibrium real income to rise.

LAFFER CURVE A relationship between income tax rates and income tax revenues, which shows that at sufficiently high tax rates, tax rate reductions can increase tax revenues, whereas at lower tax rates, tax rate reductions necessarily reduce tax revenues.

LAW OF DIMINISHING MARGINAL RETURNS The law that states that each successive addition of a unit of a factor of production, such as labor, eventually produces a smaller gain in real output produced, holding other factors constant.

LIQUIDITY CONSTRAINTS Constraints on the availability of cash and credit that people face at points during their lives.

LIQUIDITY EFFECT A fall in the equilibrium nominal interest rate resulting from a rise in the nominal quantity of money, holding the price level unchanged.

LM SCHEDULE A set of combinations of real income and the nominal interest rate that maintain money market equilibrium.

LOANABLE FUNDS The term used by classical economists to refer to the amount of real income that households save, representing claims on real output.

LONG RUN According to the monetarists, an interval long enough that workers can compile full information about aggregate prices and inflation; thus expected prices and inflation are equal to actual prices and inflation.

MACROECONOMIC EXTERNALITIES Situations in which aggregate equilibrium in all, or at least many, markets fails to account for spillovers across markets, so that equilibrium aggregate real output, employment, and the price level all differ from their long-run, natural levels.

MACROECONOMIC VARIABLES Aggregate measures of total economic activity.

MACROECONOMICS The branch of economics that focuses on the study of the total economic activity of a nation.

MARGINAL PRODUCT OF CAPITAL (MP_K) The additional output that can be produced following the addition of another unit of capital.

MARGINAL PRODUCT OF LABOR (MP_N) The change in total output resulting from a one-unit increase in the quantity of labor employed in production.

MARGINAL PROPENSITY TO CONSUME (MPC) The additional consumption caused by an increase in disposable income; the change in consumption spending divided by the corresponding change in disposable income; the slope of the consumption function.

MARGINAL PROPENSITY TO IMPORT ($MPIM$) The additional import expenditures stimulated by an increase in disposable income; the change in import spending divided by the corresponding change in disposable income; the slope of the import function.

MARGINAL PROPENSITY TO SAVE (MPS) The additional saving caused by an increase in disposable income; the change in saving divided by the corresponding change in disposable income; the slope of the saving function.

MARGINAL TAX RATE The rate at which tax payments rise when an individual's income increases; the change in taxes divided by the corresponding change in income, $\Delta t / \Delta y$.

MARKET FAILURE The potential failure of a private market equilibrium to reflect all costs and benefits relating to production of a good or service.

MEDIUM OF EXCHANGE Money's role as a means of payment for goods and services.

MERCANTILISM The idea that a primary determinant of a nation's wealth is international trade and commerce, so that a nation can gain by enacting policies that spur exports while limiting imports.

MERCHANDISE BALANCE OF TRADE
Merchandise exports minus merchandise imports.

MERCHANDISE EXPORTS Domestic firms' sales of physical goods to residents of other nations.

MERCHANDISE IMPORTS Domestic residents' purchases of physical goods manufactured and sold by business firms located abroad.

MICROECONOMIC FOUNDATIONS A basic understanding of the behavior of individual components of the economy that underlies many macroeconomic theories.

MICROECONOMICS The branch of economics that focuses on the study of the allocation of resources and the determination of prices and quantities in individual markets.

MONETARISTS Economists who believe that the main factor influencing aggregate demand is the nominal money stock and that there is not a long-run trade-off between inflation and unemployment.

MONETARY AGGREGATES Measures of the quantity of money in circulation.

MONETARY APPROACH TO THE BALANCE OF PAYMENTS A theory of unsterilized monetary policy under fixed exchange rates; changes in foreign exchange reserves required to maintain a fixed exchange rate cause a nation's money stock to adjust automatically in a direction that leads to attainment of a private payments balance of zero.

MONEY An item that people are willing to accept in exchange for goods and services.

MONEY ILLUSION A situation that exists when economic agents change their behavior in response to changes in nominal values, even though real (adjusted for the price level) values have not changed.

MONEY-FINANCED DEFICIT A government budget deficit that the government finances by selling its bonds to the central bank, which creates new money balances to purchase the bonds.

MULTIPLIER EFFECT The ratio of a change in equilibrium real income to an increase in autonomous net aggregate expenditures. When the aggregate expenditure schedule shifts vertically, the equilibrium level of national income changes by a multiple of the amount of the shift.

MULTISECTOR MODELS Macroeconomic models in which the structures of various sectors of the economy correspond to different theories.

NATIONAL DEBT The total accumulation of amounts that the government currently owes to private holders of its debt.

NATIONAL INCOME ACCOUNTS Tabulations of the values of a nation's flows of income and product.

NATIONAL INCOME The sum of all factor earnings, or net domestic product minus indirect business taxes.

NATURAL GDP The level of real GDP that is consistent with the economy's natural rate of growth.

NATURAL RATE OF UNEMPLOYMENT The portion of the unemployment rate that is accounted for by frictional and structural unemployment.

NET EXPORT SPENDING The difference between spending on domestically produced goods and services by residents of other countries and spending on foreign-produced goods and services by residents of the home country.

NET INVESTMENT Gross investment minus depreciation; the result is equal to total expenditures on new capital goods.

NET NATIONAL PRODUCT GNP minus depreciation, or national income plus indirect business taxes.

NEUTRALITY OF MONEY A key classical conclusion that states that variations in money growth can influence only the price level and year-to-year inflation rates but have no effects on labor employment or the level of real output of goods and services.

NEW GROWTH THEORY A theory of economic growth that focuses on productivity growth as a key determinant of technological progress and the rate of growth of an economy.

NOMINAL GROSS DOMESTIC PRODUCT (NOMINAL GDP) The value of final production of goods and services calculated in current dollars with no adjustment for the effects of price changes.

NONCOOPERATIVE BEHAVIOR An economic setting in which people look out for their own well-being without regard for the well-being of others.

OBSERVATIONAL EQUIVALENCE The fact that the basic version of the modern Keynesian theory, which assumes sticky wages, makes some of the same fundamental policy predictions as the new classical model, which is based on pure competition with completely flexible wages.

OFFICIAL SETTLEMENTS BALANCE A balance of payments account that records international asset transactions involving agencies of home and foreign governments.

OPEN ECONOMY An economy that is linked by trade with other economies of the world.

OPEN-MARKET OPERATIONS The Federal Reserve's purchases or sales of U.S. government securities.

OPTIMAL CURRENCY AREA A region in which fixed exchange rates can be maintained without inhibiting prompt internal adjustments of employment and output to changes in international market conditions.

OUTSIDE MONEY Money in the form of currency and bank reserves.

PEAK The point along a business cycle at which real GDP is at its highest level relative to its long-run, natural level.

PERFECT CAPITAL MOBILITY A situation in which financial resources are as mobile across a nation's boundaries as they are within those boundaries.

PERPETUITY Nonmaturing bond that pays an infinite stream of coupon returns.

PHILLIPS CURVE A curve that shows an inverse relationship between inflation and unemployment rates.

POLICY CREDIBILITY The believability of a commitment by a central bank or governmental authority to follow specific policy rules.

POLICY INEFFECTIVENESS PROPOSITION The new classical conclusion that if policy actions are anticipated, they have no real effects in the short run.

POLICY RULE A commitment to a fixed strategy no matter what happens to other economic variables.

POLICY TIME LAG The time interval between the need for a countercyclical monetary policy action and the ultimate effects of that action on an economic variable.

PORTFOLIO MOTIVE The modern term for Keynes's basic idea of a speculative motive for holding money, in which people hold both money and bonds and adjust their holdings of both types of financial assets based on their speculations about interest-rate movements.

PRECAUTIONARY MOTIVE The motive to hold money for use in unplanned exchanges.

PRICE INERTIA A tendency for the price level to resist change over time.

PRIVATE PAYMENTS BALANCE The sum of the current account balance and the private capital account balance, or the net total of all private exchanges between U.S. individuals and businesses and the rest of the world.

PRODUCER PRICE INDEX (PPI) A weighted average of the prices of goods that the government determines a representative business buys from other businesses.

PRODUCT IDENTITY An identity that states that real domestic product is the sum of real household consumption, real realized investment, real government spending, and real export spending.

PRODUCTION FUNCTION A relationship between possible quantities of factors of production, such as labor services, and the amount of output of goods and services that firms can produce with current technology.

PROGRESSIVE TAX SYSTEM A system of taxation in which the amount of a tax that a person must pay increases as a percentage of the individual's income as the individual's income rises.

PROPORTIONAL TAX SYSTEM A system of taxation in which the amount of a tax that a person must pay remains a constant percentage of the individual's income as the individual's income rises.

PROTECTIONISM The adoption of policies that impose legal and economic barriers to international trade.

PUBLIC CHOICE THEORY A hypothesis that views central banks and government policymakers as policymaking bodies composed of individuals who pursue their own self-interest.

PUBLIC INTEREST THEORY A hypothesis that regards central banks and government policymakers as public servants that pursue the broad interests of society as a whole.

PURCHASING POWER PARITY A condition that states that if international arbitrage is possible, then the price of a good in one nation should be the same as the price of the same good in another nation, adjusted for the exchange rate.

PURE COMPETITION A situation in which there are large numbers of buyers and sellers in a market for a good, service, or factor of production and in which no single buyer or seller can affect the market price.

QUANTITATIVE THEORY An approach to macroeconomic theorizing in which a model is evaluated by comparing the movements in artificial data generated by the model itself with the behavior of real-world macroeconomic data.

QUANTITY THEORY OF MONEY The theory that people hold money for transactions purposes.

QUOTAS Quantity limitations on international trade of goods and services.

RATIONAL EXPECTATIONS HYPOTHESIS The idea that individuals form expectations based on all available past and current information and on a basic understanding of how the economy works.

REAL BALANCE EFFECT An increase in the nominal rate of interest that results from an increase in the price level, holding the nominal quantity of money unchanged.

REAL CONSUMPTION The real amount of spending by households on domestically produced goods and services.

REAL DISPOSABLE INCOME A household's real after-tax income.

REAL EXPORTS Real value of goods and services produced by domestic firms and exported to other countries.

REAL GROSS DOMESTIC PRODUCT (REAL GDP) A price-adjusted measure of aggregate output, or nominal GDP divided by the GDP price deflator.

REAL IMPORTS The real flow of spending by households on goods and services produced by firms in other countries.

REAL INTEREST RATE The nominal interest rate minus the expected rate of inflation.

REAL MONEY BALANCES The value of the nominal quantity of money adjusted for the price level; defined as the nominal money stock divided by the price level.

REAL NET TAXES The amount of real taxes paid to the government by households, net of transfer payments.

REAL REALIZED INVESTMENT SPENDING Actual real expenditures by firms in the product markets.

REAL SAVING The amount of real income that households save through financial markets.

REAL-BUSINESS-CYCLE THEORY An approach to macroeconomic theory in which variations in technology and productivity are the key factors accounting for cyclical fluctuations in real output.

RECESSION A decline in real GDP lasting at least two consecutive quarters, which can cause real GDP to fall below its long-run, natural level.

RECESSIONARY GAP The amount by which aggregate desired expenditures lie below the level that would cause equilibrium real income to equal its long-run, natural level.

RECOGNITION LAG The interval between the need for a countercyclical policy action and the recognition of this need by a policymaker.

REGRESSIVE TAX SYSTEM A system of taxation in which the amount of a tax that a person must pay declines as a percentage of the individual's income as the individual's income rises.

REPRESENTATIVE AGENT ASSUMPTION The assumption that all people in an economy have access to the same information and have the same understanding of how the economy works.

RESERVE REQUIREMENTS Federal Reserve rules mandating that banks maintain reserve holdings that are proportional to the dollar amounts of transactions accounts.

RESPONSE LAG The interval between the recognition of a need for a countercyclical policy action and the actual implementation of that action.

RICARDIAN EQUIVALENCE PROPOSITION The proposition that if government spending will be unchanged in the future, people regard a current tax cut as equivalent to a future tax increase and therefore save the proceeds of a tax cut rather than increasing their consumption.

SHORT RUN According to the monetarists, an interval short enough that workers do not have complete information about aggregate prices and inflation; therefore expected prices and inflation may differ from actual prices and inflation.

SMALL MENU COSTS The costs firms incur when they make price changes, including both the costs of changing prices in menus or catalogues and the costs of renegotiating agreements with customers.

SPOT EXCHANGE RATE The rate of exchange for currencies to be traded immediately.

STAGFLATION The simultaneous observation of rising inflation rates and declining real output and rising unemployment rates.

STANDARD OF DEFERRED PAYMENT Money's role as a means of valuing future receipts in loan contracts.

STANDARD OF LIVING The capability of an average resident of a nation to consume goods and services.

STERILIZATION A central bank action to prevent variations in its foreign exchange reserves from affecting the total amount of money in circulation.

STORE OF VALUE A function of money in which it is held for future use without loss of value.

STRATEGIC INTERACTIONS The interdependence of economic decisions that people make individually or as part of groups.

STRUCTURAL UNEMPLOYMENT The portion of total unemployment resulting from a poor match of workers' abilities and skills with current needs of employers.

SUBSTITUTES IN PRODUCTION The term for the situation in which increased use of capital leads to reduced use of labor in the production of real output.

SUPPLY SHOCKS Changes in the position of the aggregate supply schedule caused by significant changes in the costs of factors of production or in technological capabilities.

SUPPLY-SIDE ECONOMICS A school of economic thought that promotes government policies intended to influence real GDP by affecting the position of the economy's aggregate supply schedule.

TARIFFS Taxes imposed on the values of goods and services that are traded internationally.

TIME INCONSISTENCY PROBLEM A policy problem that can result if a policymaker has the ability, at a future time, to alter its strategy in a way that is inconsistent both with the desires and strategies of private individuals and with its own initially announced intentions.

TIME SERIES Observed values of macroeconomic variables over successive time intervals.

TRANSACTION RISK The possibility that the value of a financial asset involved in funding an exchange denominated in a foreign currency could vary with exchange-rate movements, thereby affecting the underlying value of the transaction.

TRANSACTIONS MOTIVE The motive to hold money for use in planned exchanges.

TRANSFER PAYMENTS Governmentally managed income redistributions.

TRANSMISSION LAG The interval that elapses between the implementation of an intended countercyclical policy and its ultimate effects on an economic variable.

TROUGH The point along a business cycle at which real GDP is at its lowest level relative to the long-run natural GDP level.

ULTIMATE GOALS The final objectives of macroeconomic policies.

UNCOVERED INTEREST PARITY A prediction that the interest rate on a bond denominated in a currency that is expected to depreciate must exceed another nation's bond rate by the rate at which the currency is expected to depreciate plus a risk premium.

UNEMPLOYMENT The number of people who are interested in finding a job but currently do not have one.

UNEMPLOYMENT RATE The percentage of the civilian labor force that is unemployed.

UNIT OF ACCOUNT A function of money in which it is used as a measure of the value of goods, services, and financial assets.

VALUE OF THE MARGINAL PRODUCT OF LABOR The marginal product of labor times the price of output.

WAGE INDEXATION The automatic adjustment of contract wages to changes in the price level.

INDEX